KU-795-175

Morocco

a Lonely Planet travel survival kit

Damien Simonis
Geoff Crowther

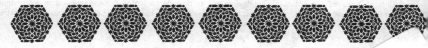

Morocco

3rd edition

Published by
Lonely Planet Publications
Head Office: PO Box 617, Hawthorn, Vic 3122, Australia
Branches: 155 Filbert St, Suite 251, Oakland, CA 94607, USA
10 Barley Mow Passage, Chiswick, London W4 4PH, UK
71 bis rue du Cardinal Lemoine, 75005 Paris, France

Printed by
Colorcraft Ltd, Hong Kong

Photographs by
Glenn Beanland (GB), Adrienne Costanzo (AC), Geoff Crowther (GC),
Hugh Finlay (HF), Jacqui Saunders (JS), Damien Simonis (DS)

Front cover: Carpet bazaar, R Everts (Horizon Photo Library)

First Published
July 1989

This Edition
April 1995

National Library of Australia Cataloguing in Publication Data

Simonis, Damien.
Morocco : a travel survival kit.

3rd ed.
Includes index.
ISBN 0 86442 249 0.

1. Morocco – Guidebooks. I. Crowther, Geoff, 1944- .
Morocco, Algeria & Tunisia. II. Title. III. Title:
Morocco, Algeria & Tunisia. (Series : Lonely Planet
travel sruvival kit).

916.4045

Damien Simonis

Damien Simonis is an Australian freelance journalist based in London. Since taking a degree in modern languages and working as a reporter and subeditor on *The Australian* in Sydney and *The Age* in Melbourne , he has worked, studied and travelled extensively in Europe and the Arab world. In addition to this guide, he has updated Lonely Planet's guides to *Jordan & Syria* and *Egypt & the Sudan*, as well as contributing to shoestring guides such *The Middle East*, *Africa* and *Mediterranean Europe*.

Damien has also worked for *The Guardian*, *The Independent* and *The Sunday Times* in London and written for publications in Australia, the UK and North America.

Geoff Crowther

Born in Yorkshire, England, Geoff took to his heels early on in search of the miraculous, taking a break from a degree in biochemistry. The lure of the unknown took him to Kabul, Kathmandu and Lamu in the days before the overland bus companies began digging up the dirt along the tracks of Africa.

In 1977, he wrote his first guide for Lonely Planet – *Africa on the cheap*. He has also written *South America on a shoestring*, guides to *Korea & Taiwan*, *Korea* and *East Africa* and has co-authored guides to *India*, *Kenya*, *Malaysia, Singapore & Brunei* and *Morocco, Algeria & Tunisia*.

He still spends at least six months overseas each year, these days often accompanied by his Korean wife, Hyung Poon, and his son, Ashley Choson. The trio live in a Korean temple-style house in northern New South Wales, Australia.

When not travelling or sweating over a hot computer, Geoff devotes his time to landscaping, playing guitar, dreaming up impossible schemes, arguing with everyone in sight, pursuing noxious weeds and brewing Davidson's plum wine. To his credit, he remains generally *compos mentis*.

From Damien

A project like this would be unthinkable without the help of many people and organisations in Morocco and outside it. To *MEED* and *The Guardian* in London, as always, thanks for access to their resources. Mohammed ben Madani, also in London, was helpful in the hunt for research material and insights into Moroccan life. Thanks also to the staff at Le Tiers Mythe bookshop in Paris for their indulgence while I rummaged through their wares.

The assistance of Abdelhamid Boumediene, secretary-general of the ONMT in Rabat, was indispensable.

In Tangier, Mohammed Abdel Aoui kindly showed me around some of the nooks and crannies of the kasbah. Thanks also to Mme Alawi Harrauni Aziza and Safi Abd ar-Razak in Meknès for making themselves available to me. James Turner and Elizabeth Renshaw (UK) helped me out, shared a laugh and provided some invaluable tips on tea. I am grateful to Lichir El Houcine in Taroudannt for letting me photograph his merchandise, and likewise to Mahna Mohammed in Tiznit. Thanks also to Ouhammou Mohammed of Tafraoute for his time and help. Brahim Toudaoui, of Imlil, gave me a hand during my all too brief stay in the High Atlas. Stuart & Gill (AUS) – it was an interesting trip back to Algeciras.

I am especially indebted to Michael Sklovsky of Ishka Handcrafts for his expertise on Moroccan arts & crafts.

Many thanks to Michèle Nayman in London for holding my fort for me while I was on the road.

Above all, I owe an immeasurable debt of thanks to my wife, Lucrezia, for her help and support, and for making a lot of things possible that would otherwise have been well beyond my reach. This book is for Ariana.

This Book

This first edition of Morocco is based on chapters of *Morocco, Tunisia & Algeria*, written by Geoff Crowther & Hugh Finlay. It was expanded and thoroughly revised by Damien Simonis.

From the Publisher

This edition of Morocco was edited at Lonely Planet's Melbourne office by Adrienne Costanzo, with the help of Janet Austin and Alison White. Thanks to Diana Saad, Janet Austin, Jane Fitzpatrick, Tom Smallman and Sarah Parkes for helping with the proofreading. Diana Saad also lent her expertise on the language section. Special thanks to Michael Sklovsky, who provided extra information for the Arts & Crafts colour section and generously allowed Lonely Planet staff to photograph items from his Ishka Handcrafts stores in Melbourne.

Jacqui Saunders handled the mapping, design and layout. Jane Hart, Maliza Kruh and Andrew Smith helped with the mapping. Maliza Kruh drew the illustrations and Valerie Tellini designed the cover. Glenn Beanland took several of the photos that appear in the Arts & Crafts colour section and was responsible for the section's design and layout. Ann Jeffree took care of the index.

Finally, thanks to all those travellers who took the time and effort to write to us with suggestions and comments; they are listed at the end of the book.

Warning & Request

Things change – prices go up, schedules change, good places go bad and bad places go bankrupt – nothing stays the same. So if you find things better or worse, recently opened or long since closed, please write and tell us and help make the next edition better.

Your letters will be used to help update future editions and, where possible, important changes will also be included in a Stop Press section in reprints.

We greatly appreciate all information that is sent to us by travellers. Back at Lonely Planet we employ a hard-working readers' letters team to sort through the many letters we receive. The best ones will be rewarded with a free copy of the next edition or another Lonely Planet guide if you prefer. We give away lots of books, but, unfortunately, not every letter/postcard receives one.

Contents

Map Legend

BOUNDARIES

················· International Boundary

——— – ——— – ——— – ········ Suburb Boundary

ROUTES

········· Freeway

········· Highway

········· Major Road

– – – – – – ········· Unsealed Road or Track

········· City Road

········· City Street

+++++++++++ ········· Railway

········· Underground Railway

········· Tropics

– – – – – ········· Walking Track

•••••••••••••••••• ········· Walking Tour

– – – – – – ········· Ferry Route

+H+H+H+H+H+H+H+H+ ········· Cable Car or Chairlift

AREA FEATURES

········· Park, Gardens

········· National Park

········· Built-Up Area

········· Pedestrian Mall

········· Market

+ + + + + ········· Cemetery

x x x x x ········· Non-Christian Cemetery

········· Beach or Desert

········· Rocks

HYDROGRAPHIC FEATURES

········· Coastline

········· River, Creek

– – – – ········· Intermittent River or Creek

········· Lake, Intermittent Lake

········· Canal

········· Swamp

SYMBOLS

✪ CAPITAL		········· National Capital
◉ Capital		········· Provincial Capital
🌑 CITY		········· Major City
● City		········· City
● Town		········· Town
● Village		········· Village
■		········· Place to Stay
▼		········· Place to Eat
▼		········· Pub, Bar
✉	☎	········· Post Office, Telephone
❶	❸	········· Tourist Information, Bank
◔	🅿	········· Transport, Parking
🏛	⛺	········· Museum, Youth Hostel
⚏	⚠	········· Caravan Park, Camping Ground
†	⬛†	········· Church, Cathedral
☪	✡	········· Mosque, Synagogue
⚊	⚌	········· Buddhist Temple, Hindu Temple

✚	★	········· Hospital, Police Station
✈	✈	········· Airport, Airfield
▭	✿	········· Swimming Pool, Gardens
❖	🐘	········· Shopping Centre, Zoo
☕	⛽	········· Cafe, Petrol Station
←	A25	One Way Street, Route Number
	⛏	········· Archaeological Site or Ruins
🏛	⚑	········· Stately Home, Monument
⛩	⛳	········· Castle, Golf Course
⌂	⛪	········· Cave, Hut or Chalet
▲	✳	········· Mountain or Hill, Lookout
🗼	⚓	········· Lighthouse, Shipwreck
)(	⚭	········· Pass, Spring
		········· Ancient or City Wall
		········· Rapids, Waterfalls
		········· Cliff or Escarpment, Tunnel
+++++		········· Railway Station

Note: not all symbols displayed above appear in this book

Introduction

Known to the Arabs as *al-Maghreb al-Aqsa*, loosely translated as 'the farthest land of the setting sun' or, more prosaically, the 'far West', Morocco stands at the western extremity of the Arab and Muslim world. From here was launched Islam's most successful penetration of western Europe – the occupation of Spain. And it was back into this land that the Muslims of Spain, or Al-Andalus, returned in the face of the Reconquista (Christian-led campaigns in Spain and Portugal to regain the territory taken by Moors in the 8th century). Separated from Europe by only the 15 km of the Strait of Gibraltar, Morocco is at once a crossroads and a frontier state – a gateway for Europeans south into Africa and for Africans and Arabs north into Europe.

For many, its greatest charm lies in the labyrinths of the imperial cities – Marrakesh, Fès, Meknès and Rabat – but there is much more. From Marrakesh the snowcapped High Atlas Mountains are clearly visible, and attract a growing number of trekkers, as indeed do the Middle Atlas and Anti-Atlas ranges. For others, the main drawcard is the eery solitude of the desert. Its lonely expanses drop off the back of the Atlas and sweep into the vast Saharan emptiness of Algeria.

In contrast to the desert are the beaches along the Atlantic and Mediterranean coasts. Some are burgeoning resorts filled with the same sun-seekers you'd expect to find in Ibiza or Benidorm, while others are comparatively unspoilt by the waves of tourists who regularly descend on Morocco from Europe.

Morocco is in a sense a hybrid. The Phoenicians and Romans once held sway here; before and since then the local Berber tribes have, in the mountains especially, retained a separate identity. Spain (which still maintains two enclaves in northern Morocco) and France have left their mark, but none so deep as that of the Arabs and Islam.

A land of rich variety, natural contrast and an extraordinarily mixed cultural heritage, much of Morocco was virtually unknown to outsiders until 1930s. It makes for a rich and unique travel experience.

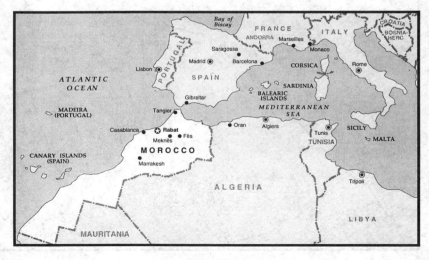

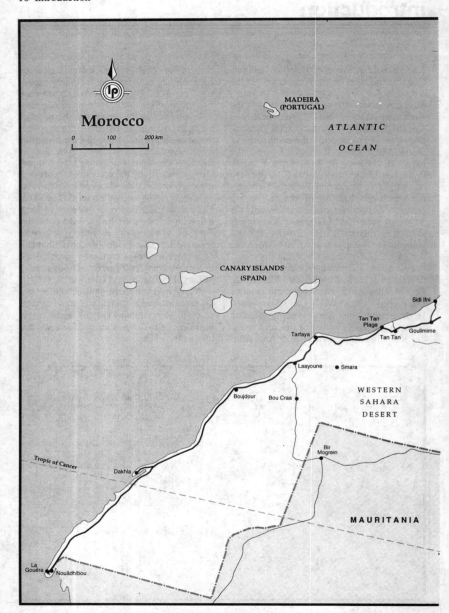

Morocco

0   100   200 km

MADEIRA
(PORTUGAL)

ATLANTIC

OCEAN

CANARY ISLANDS
(SPAIN)

Sidi Ifni

Tan Tan
Plage

Tarfaya   Tan Tan   Goulimime

Laayoune   • Smara

WESTERN
SAHARA
DESERT

Boujdour   Bou Craa

Bir
Mogrein

Tropic of Cancer

Dakhla

MAURITANIA

La
Gouéra Nouâdhibou

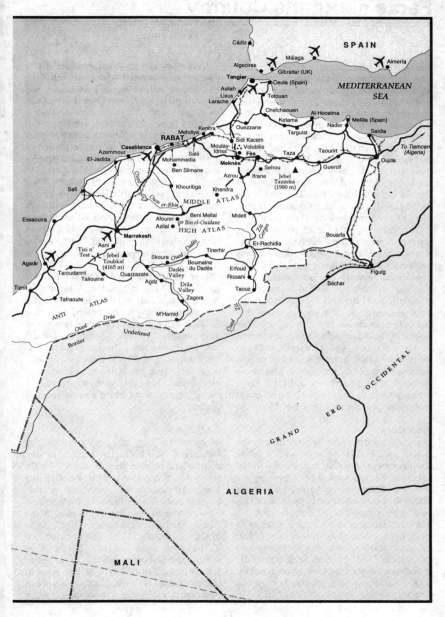

Facts about the Country

HISTORY

The early history of the area now known as Morocco is largely shrouded in mystery, with only limited shreds of evidence shedding any light on the society or societies that inhabited this territory at the limits of the known world in ancient times. Even after the arrival of the Phoenicians in North Africa, and later of the Romans, Vandals, Byzantines and Arabs, much of what historians know of the original inhabitants is based on limited and often ill-informed contemporary writings and broad assumptions drawn from them by modern scholars.

This goes not only for Morocco, but for the rest of what is known collectively to the Arabs as the Maghreb, which simply means 'sunset' or 'west' – Algeria and Tunisia. The invaders rarely made any great inroads from the coast or the cities, and in Morocco this was particularly the case. The Berbers, as the local peoples came to be known, were often compelled to recoil into the rugged fastnesses of the Sahara and Atlas, out of reach of the outsiders, and this split between Berber and urban invader has more or less remained a constant throughout Morocco's history. Central rulers, even of Berber tribes themselves, have rarely managed to exercise real power over the entire reach of Morocco.

Prehistory

The early history of Morocco is, if only for lack of sources offering more specific information, bound up with that of the rest of the Maghreb. Archaeological finds proving the presence of *Homo erectus* date back as far as 200,000 years ago, and some scholars believe they may date back further still. At this time, much of the Sahara is thought to have been covered in forest, scrub and savanna grasses, and was teeming with animal life. The last decent, regular rainfalls in the area are thought to have occurred by 6000 BC, after which grasslands began to give way to arid desert.

Evidence suggests the appearance of two different races in North Africa between about 15,000 and 10,000 BC – Oranian and then Capsian man (the former named after Oran in Algeria and the latter after Qafsah – ancient Capsa – in Tunisia). The origins of both are virtually unknown although they have been the cause of much speculation. It appears they fused with indigenous peoples and the long-term result was a spread of Neolithic (New Stone Age) culture. Rock paintings, particularly in the Hoggar in modern Algeria, are the greatest source of knowledge about this period, although there have been several archaeological finds in Morocco too. Many of their results are on view in the Archaeological Museum in Rabat.

It is from these peoples that the Berbers are thought to be descended. Allowing for regional variations and the paucity of clues, they appear to have been predominantly pastoralists, although they continued to hunt and also engaged in some agriculture. By the time the Phoenicians – the first of the outside civilisations from the east – made an appearance, the local inhabitants were already well established, although with what kind of social organisations and divisions remains unclear.

Carthage

Morocco was only marginally touched by the arrival of Phoenician traders on the scene. Coming from their capital in Tyre (in modern-day Lebanon), they patrolled the North African coast in search of suitable staging posts for the lucrative trade in raw metals from Spain. The foundation of the first of these places has been positively dated to the 8th century BC. Carthage, in modern Tunisia, became the main base, but the Phoenicians also had posts in Sicily, the Balearic Islands and along the North African coast to the Atlantic. In Morocco, they were ensconced in Tamuda (near present-day

Tetouan), Tingis (Tangier), Lixus and Mogador (Essaouira), which marked their farthest advance along the Atlantic. By the end of the 3rd century BC they had lost these possessions. By the 4th century BC, as Tyre faded and Carthage became arguably the richest city in the Mediterranean, it had attracted the attention of the Greeks and later the Romans, with both of whom Carthage clashed.

In the 5th century BC, as Carthage approached the apogee of its power, some of the city's more illustrious sons set out on voyages of discovery. Hanno headed off down the Atlantic coast of Morocco, leaving accounts of a fabled gold route. The area was much later confirmed to be a source of gold and slaves, but some historians think Hanno may just have been looking for good sources of fish.

By the 3rd century, after repeated clashes with Greek settlements in Sicily, Carthage came into direct conflict with the expanding power of Rome. Several wars ensued, culminating in the defeat of Carthage in the Second Punic War (218-201 BC), in which Han-

Punic Stele

nibal's forces came close to destroying Rome.

One fact that will not have served the Carthaginians well was the conscript and mercenary make-up of most of its armies. In Africa, where the indigenous people were treated particularly harshly, Carthage exacted not only a wartime tribute on produce of 50%, but drafted locals into the army, often without pay. The majority of them, known as Libyans (a vague designation for the people living to the south and east of Carthage), were heartily sick of Carthaginian control over large tracts of what is today Tunisia. Rump Carthage was constantly harassed not only by Libyan forces from beyond the Carthaginians' frontiers, but also by the Numidians to the west, whose most illustrious king was Massinissa. Finally, in 146 BC, after a three-year siege of Carthage in the Third Punic War, Rome decided that the city should be utterly destroyed, a task that they carried out with characteristic efficiency.

It is difficult to gauge what sort of legacy Carthage left behind with the Libyans, Numidians and, in the far west, the Mauri (Mauretanians or Moors), all of whom were more or less considered 'Berbers' by outside observers by the time the Arabs appeared on the scene some eight centuries later. Those who remained in Carthaginian-controlled territory were heavily exploited farmers, but it is said they learned more advanced agricultural methods from their oppressors. Some modern historians are beginning to have doubts about the extent of this supposed beneficial side-effect of the empire. A more concrete result seems to have been the forcing of others into the hinterland, principally into the Sahara desert and the Atlas Mountains, where many reverted to their seminomadic lifestyles. From there they were able launch attacks upon whatever outside power controlled the coast.

Rome

The sack of Carthage in 146 BC meant that Rome had come to Africa to stay, but for a century it remained content to do no more than maintain garrisons and a watchful eye over the scene. Towards the end of the pre-Christian era, however, Rome took a growing interest in North Africa, sending colonists, cranking up agricultural production for exportation to Italy and increasing direct control.

The Mauretanian kingdom that included what is now Morocco and much of northern Algeria had remained largely untouched by Carthage's influence, notwithstanding the existence of several small coastal trading enclaves, and direct interference by Rome was also minimal. Bocchus II of Mauretania died in 33 BC, bequeathing his kingdom to Rome, but the Romans were not interested, preferring to foster local rule. The kingdom was split into two provinces in about 40 AD – Mauretania Caesariensis, with its capital in Caesarea (in modern Algeria), and Mauretania Tingitana, with its capital at Tingis (Tangier). The Romans also established colonies at Lixus, succeeding the Phoenicians, and at Volubilis. This last became a minor centre of Graeco-Roman culture. Morocco, however, remained virtually cut off from the rest of Roman North Africa, thanks to the Rif and Atlas mountain ranges, and access was easiest by sea to ports like Tingis. The tribes of the Rif especially retained their independence and occasionally undertook small campaigns against the imperial power.

In the first three centuries AD, Roman North Africa, which had become a breadbasket for the empire, was comparatively stable and well off, providing 60% of the empire's grain needs and other commodities such as olive oil throughout Roman domains. Wealthy landed North Africans gradually entered Roman administration and eventually provided an emperor, the Libyan Septimius Severus, who took power in 193 AD.

The latter half of the 3rd century brought strife to the empire, and Rome's African possessions did not remain immune. Mauretania Tingitana was abandoned to local tribes as Rome rationalised its position, hanging on to an area comprising modern-day Tunisia, northern Algeria and parts of Libya and Egypt. The exception was the city of Tingis, which remained a Romanised enclave protecting the strategic crossing between Spain and North Africa.

The 4th century in what was left of Romanised Africa was marked above all by the increasingly rapid spread of Christianity (particularly after Constantine's conversion in 313 AD) and the resulting schism launched by Donatus, leader of the Donatists. The Donatists promoted a version of Christianity rooted in North African traditions, but some historians view it equally as a rejection of Roman society. The issue is almost academic, for greater forces were at work, attacking the core of an empire on its last legs.

Vandals & Byzantium

In 429 AD, King Gaeseric (or Genseric), who had been busy marauding in southern Spain, decided to take the entire Vandal people (about 80,000 men, women and children) across to Africa, bypassing Tingis, and within a few years he had defeated the Romans and wrung hefty concessions from them. By the middle of the century his ships were in control of much of the western Mediterranean and Rome was all but a spent force.

Vandal control over the former Roman provinces was hardly cast iron, and their indelicate exploitation of the local economy only served to accelerate its decline. In addition, tribes from surrounding areas, including the Atlas Mountains, harassed the newcomers. In the end the former masters of North Africa put an end to Vandal rule. Emperor Justinian, ruler of the eastern half of what had been the Roman empire, and keen to restore it to its former glory, sent an army to retake the core of North Africa in 533. The dream of a renewed Roman empire did not come off, and the eastern half, with its capital in Constantinople (modern Istanbul) came to be known as Byzantium. Little is known about subsequent Byzantine rule in North Africa, which appears to have been ineffectual at best, but it scarcely had any impact on the unfettered tribes of Morocco. A new force from a quite unexpected quarter was, however, about to unleash itself on the world.

The Coming of Islam

No-one in Morocco could have guessed that the tribal clashes and emergence of an obscure new religion in the distant peninsula of Arabia in the early 7th century would soon change the destiny of this untamed region. Islam's green banner was flying over the cities of Egypt by 640, but it was some time before the Arab armies ventured farther westwards.

When they did, it was a tentative effort. The first campaign west of Egypt took them to modern Tunisia, and they occupied several coastal Libyan towns on the way. By 649, although the Byzantines had been defeated in the field, the Arabs, with too few men, were unable to capitalise on their successes. They tried again in the 660s but, preoccupied with internal conflicts over who should be caliph (successor of the Prophet and effectively secular and spiritual leader of the Muslim world), they were defeated.

It was not until Uqba bin Nafi al-Fihri began his campaign of conquest that the full military force of Islam was brought to bear on North Africa. For three years from 669 he swept across the top of the continent, establishing Islam's first great city in the Maghreb, Kairouan (Qayrawan) in modern Tunisia. With an army of Arab cavalry and Islamised Berber infantry from Libya, he marched into the Atlas and is said to have reached the Atlantic.

A lull ensued, but Uqba went campaigning again, mostly in Morocco, in 681. It started well but finished disastrously. In 683 he was defeated by a Berber chieftain, Qusayla, and the Arabs were booted out of the Maghreb as far east as Libya. Qusayla occupied Kairouan, and the Byzantine cities sat tight, careful not to provoke any trouble.

Their days, however, were numbered and by 698 the Arabs had succeeded in evicting the Byzantines from North Africa. Various Berber tribes continued to resist, including those led by the legendary princess Al-Kahina.

Now Musa bin Nusayr took command of the conquering armies. It was he who finally pushed decisively into Morocco, and sensibly enough made allies rather than enemies of Berber tribes converted to the new religion, which, perhaps since it emerged in a tough desert and tribal environment, appealed to Berber sensibilities. By 710 Musa considered his work in Morocco done, and turned his attention to Spain. He and his lieutenant Tariq (the name 'Gibraltar' is a bastardisation of Jebel Tariq – 'Tariq's Mountain') set about conquering Spain. By 732 they had made their deepest advance, reaching Poitiers in France.

Moroccan Dynasties

Islam had come to stay in Morocco, but the Arabs soon made themselves unwelcome. Giving every sign of treating Berbers, including converts, as second-class citizens, the Arab governors were tossed out in a wave of religious fervour inspired by the Kharijite heresy, which had begun in the East but was taken up with great enthusiasm by the Berbers. By 740, the Arab rulers had been expelled from the entire Maghreb, nevertheless leaving behind a substantial Arab population. Although Tunisia and Algeria would again fall under the control of the Arabs, and then the Ottoman Empire in the 15th century, Morocco was never to come under the direct sway of the eastern Arab dynasties again.

Idriss, an Arab who had fled Abbassid (the ruling Baghdad dynasty) persecution, arrived in Morocco in the 780s and soon won the respect of enough Berber tribes to establish a dominant dynasty in northern Morocco, which is generally considered the first Moroccan state. He is credited with the founding of Fès, and his rise to power was sufficiently impressive for the caliph in Baghdad, Harun ar-Rashid, to send a mission to kill him. Idriss died of poisoning in 791. His son, only just born when Idriss died, did not take over in any sense until 803 (when he was 11!). By the time he died in 829, a stable state was in place dominating northern Morocco.

This state of affairs did not last long. By the middle of the following century, the Idrissids had been reduced to one of a number of bit players on a wider stage. The Umayyad Muslims of Al-Andalus (Spain) had become increasingly meddlesome in northern Morocco, largely as a result of their quarrels with the Fatimid dynasty that had installed itself in Tunisia (and in 969 in Cairo). The latter also managed to occupy Fès for a time.

Into the general chaos, which included the so-called invasion of the Maghreb by the Beni Hillal (Arab tribes encouraged west by the Fatimids), came a new force from the Moroccan Sahara. Inspired by a Qur'anic teacher, Abdallah bin Yasin, the Sanhaja confederation of various Berber tribes began to wage wars throughout southern and central Morocco. They were known as 'the veiled ones' (al-mulathamin) because of their dress, and later as the 'people of the monastery' (al-murabitin) – the Almoravids. In 1062 their leader, Youssef bin Tachfin, founded Marrakesh as his capital and led troops on a march of conquest that, at its height, saw a unified empire stretching from Senegal in Africa to Saragossa in northern Spain.

This brilliant flash was just that, for as quickly as they had risen, the Almoravids crumbled in the face of another Moroccan movement: strictly conservative Muslims known as 'those who proclaim the unity of God' (al-muwahhidin) – the Almohads. Inspired by the teachings of Mohammed ibn Tumart against the growing religious laxness of the Almoravids, his successor Abd al-Mu'min began a successful campaign against them. In the 30 years to 1160, the Almohads conquered all of Almoravid Morocco as well as what are now Algeria, Tunisia and parts of Libya. In the following years, Muslim Spain also fell. The greatest of his successors, Yacoub al-Mansour ('the Victorious'), continued the fight against dissidents in the Maghreb and the Reconquista

in Spain, so that by his death in 1199 in Marrakesh, Morocco's greatest dynasty was at the height of its power. The empire's main cities flourished in this golden age of Moroc-'can cultural development, but trouble was never far away.

The Almohads tended to treat most of their territories as conquered enemies, and drained them of wealth for the enrichment of Marrakesh and other selected power bases. Having expanded too quickly, the empire now began to crumble under its own weight. As it caved in, the Maghreb divided into three parts: Ifriqiyya (Tunisia) came under the Hafsids; Algeria under the Banu Abd al-Wad; and Morocco under the Merenids. Although borders have changed and imperial rulers have come and gone, this division has remained more or less intact until today.

The Merenids ruled until 1465 (although a rival family, the Wattasids, held effective power from as early as 1420). The mid-14th century marked the pinnacle of Merenid rule, to which are owed many of the monuments – especially religious schools (medersas) – that survive today. The Merenids also built Fès el-Jdid (New Fès) as their capital.

As the dynasty declined, Morocco slid into chaos. Seeing an opportunity, the adventurous maritime power of Portugal took Ceuta (Sebta) in 1415, only a few years after a Spanish force had debarked in northern Morocco to sack Tetouan in reprisal for piracy.

The Wattasids became the ruling dynasty, but by the early 16th century, Morocco was effectively divided into two shaky kingdoms: that of the Wattasids in Fès and the Saadians in Marrakesh.

Growing European interference caused Morocco to turn in on itself. Portugal's seizure of Sebta was just the beginning, and by 1515 Lisbon had a string of bases along the Moroccan coast. Spain took Melilla in 1497.

The rise of the Saadians, originally from Arabia, was largely due to the popularity of their energetic drive to turf out the Portuguese. After winning back some of the coastal bases from Lisbon, they began expanding north. Marrakesh was their capital from 1524, and Fès fell to them in 1554.

Ottoman & European Threats

Trouble was never far away, as the expanding Ottoman Empire, which eventually came to control all of the Maghreb up to Tlemcen (modern west Algeria), threatened Moroccan independence. War and empire-building create strange bedfellows, and Mohammed ash-Sheikh, the Saadian sultan, entered into an alliance with Spain to check the Turkish advance. It proved an uneasy arrangement, but probably helped to keep Morocco out of Turkish hands.

No sooner did the Turkish threat recede than a Portuguese army headed by King Dom Sebastian arrived in northern Morocco to help Mohammed al-Mutawwakil, who had been deposed by his Saadian uncle (helped to power by brief Turkish intervention), regain his throne. The ensuing Battle of the Three Kings in 1578 put an end to Portuguese pretensions in Morocco (they had by now lost many of their coastal footholds anyway), but the fact that European armies could land in force in Morocco underlined the country's tendency to act defensively in its relations with Europe.

Not long after the Battle of the Three Kings, the Saadian sultan Ahmed al-Mansour undertook a foreign campaign of his own, 'conquering' Timbuktu and taking home a rich booty in gold and slaves.

At the turn of the century, waves of Muslims who had stayed behind after the completion of the Christian reconquest of the peninsula began to arrive en masse from Spain, as the Catholic monarchy pursued a violent policy of national and religious unity. A whole community set up shop in Salé and Rabat, and soon acquired de facto autonomy as a base for the highly successful corsairs, or pirates, roaming not only the Mediterranean and Atlantic coasts, but daring to operate as far away as the Irish Sea and even off the coast of the Americas.

The Saadian sultanate could do little about this, and got precious little return from the corsairs' activities. Like the dynasties before it, the Saadians collapsed in a heap and were succeeded by the dynasty that has been in charge, often only nominally, until today – the Alawites (or Alaouites). Like the Saadians before them, they are of Arab origin and claim descent from the Prophet and therefore the right to be considered *sherifs*.

Alawite Rule

From early on in the 17th century, central rule in Morocco was virtually a figment of the imagination. The Saadians found themselves preoccupied with putting down local rebellions and into the growing vacuum stepped the Alawites. It was some 30 years from their first expansionist moves until Moulay ar-Rashid was able to secure the sultanate in the early 1660s. His successor, Moulay Ismail, made his capital in Meknès, which he set about turning into a Moroccan Versailles – mostly, it is said, with Christian prison labour. His reign lasted from 1672 to 1727, much of which was spent pacifying tribes inside Morocco with apparently boundless cruelty. As a result of his military efforts, Portugal was left with only one base in Morocco, Mazagan (modern El-Jadida), and Spain with four small bases on the north coast.

At the time of Ismail's death, Morocco was relatively stable and independent, but his passing saw a return to the usual pandemonium. Morocco's leaders over the following century presided over a stagnant country, periodically rocked by internal strife.

European Interference (to 1912)

Moulays Abd ar-Rahman and Mohammed bin Abd ar-Rahman, still grappling with internal problems, also had to face the unpleasant fact that increasingly powerful European powers were taking a growing interest in all of North Africa. France's occupation of neighbouring Algeria in 1830 was the most obvious manifestation of this development, and the sultan's powerlessness to do anything about it was further cause for worry.

As Europe's big players moved to secure advantages over each other, the competition for influence in Morocco grew. In 1856, Great Britain extracted a treaty guaranteeing free trade. French and Spanish influence also grew, although it waned again temporarily after 1870. Moulay al-Hassan (1873-94) began some economic, administrative and military reforms and managed to keep Europe at arm's length, but could not prevent attempts by Spain and Britain to get a foothold along the coast (Río de Oro, Ifni and Cap Juby). Europeans stepped up trade and set up industries in Morocco, but the benefit to Moroccans was minimal.

Al-Hassan's successor, Moulay Abd al-Aziz, came to the throne ill-prepared to cope with the problems in store for him. An attempt at tax reform and repeated French military intervention caused uproar. France virtually bought off Italy (offering it a free hand in Libya), Spain (with the promise of a northern sphere of interest in Morocco), and Great Britain (allowing it free reign in Egypt and the Sudan), and so in 1905 hoped to pull off the establishment of a protectorate with a so-called 'plan of reforms'.

Germany, which had been left out of the international wheeling and dealing, put paid to this and called for an international conference, achieving little more than to delay the inevitable. Moulay Abd al-Hafiz became sultan in 1909, but the situation had already slipped beyond the Moroccans' control. Germany was pacified by the other European powers in 1911 with concessions in the Congo (after sending a gunboat to Agadir and so pushing Germany and France to the brink of war), leaving the way free for France to move in. Spain had already sent troops to the northern zone allocated to it by agreement in 1904.

The French Protectorate (1912-1956)

The treaty of Fès, by which Morocco became a French protectorate, was signed on 30 March 1912, and although the sultan was to maintain the appearance of power, effective control rested with the governor, or resident-general, General (later Marshal) Lyautey and his successors. Spain controlled the northern tranche of the country and Tangier was made an international zone in 1923.

Moroccans were none too pleased. This was particularly true of those living in the mountains, who remained beyond colonial control. After WW I, Abd el-Krim led a revolt in the Rif and Middle Atlas Mountains, and for five years had the Spaniards and French on the run. Spain came close to a massive and embarrassing defeat and France only ended all effective Berber resistance in 1934.

The process of colonisation in the French zone was rapid. From a few thousand before 1912, the number of foreigners living in Morocco rose to more than 100,000 by 1929, when the Great Depression put a dampener on growth. The French built roads and railways, developed the port of Casablanca out of virtually nothing and moved the political capital to Rabat. In the French zone, *villes nouvelles* (new towns) were built next to the old medinas. This was largely a result of an enlightened policy on Lyautey's part – in Algeria he had witnessed the wholesale destruction of many old cities by his countrymen. The Spaniards followed suit in their zone, but on a much more modest scale.

WW II brought a new wave of Europeans into Morocco, virtually doubling their numbers, but it also brought hardship as prices rose and industry came to a standstill. After Franco came to power in Spain in 1939 and Hitler overran France in 1940, Spanish Morocco became a seat of Nazi propaganda, tending oddly enough to foment nationalist aspirations in the rest of the country. Various opposition groups were formed, but the French administration ignored pleas for reform. The Allied landings in North Africa in 1943 further muddied the waters, but the Free French Forces, in spite of US President Roosevelt's sympathy to the nationalists' cause, were adamant that nothing in Morocco should change. In January 1944 the Istiqlal (Independence) party led by Allal al-Fasi, one of Morocco's most intractable nationalists, demanded full independence.

When the war ended, nationalist feeling

grew, and the French became increasingly inflexible. Moroccans boycotted French goods and terrorist acts against the administration multiplied. The sultan, Mohammed V, sympathised with the nationalists, so much so that the French authorities in Rabat had him deposed in 1953 – an act that served only to make him a hero in the people's eyes and turn up the heat. In 1955, Paris allowed his return and talks began on handing power to the Moroccans.

Madrid's administration of the Spanish zone after the war was considerably less heavy-handed than that of the French, and in fact it became something of a haven for Moroccan nationalists. Spain had not been consulted on the expulsion of the sultan, and continued to recognise him. By this time there was virtually no cooperation at all between the two zones.

King Hassan II

Independence
Mohammed V returned to Morocco in November 1955 to a tumultuous welcome. Within five months he was able to appoint Morocco's first independent government as the French protectorate formally came to an end. Shortly afterwards, Spain pulled out of its zone in the north, but hung on to the enclaves of Ceuta, Melilla and Ifni. It abandoned the latter in 1970, but Madrid has shown no desire to give up the other two.

The sultan resumed virtually autocratic rule and, when the Istiqlal Party split into two groups in 1959 (Istiqlal and the more left-wing Union Nationale des Forces Populaires), he posed as mediator, above the mucky business of party politics. He did not have to fulfil this role for long, as he died in 1961. He was succeeded by his son, Hassan II.

The new king introduced a constitution in 1972 after a coup attempt in 1971 had delayed it, but another coup attempt that same year led him to suspend much of it. When elections were finally held in 1977, supporters of the king won a big majority. Both halves of the Istiqlal had by now gone into the opposition.

Western Sahara
Hassan II owes some of his popularity to his apparent *baraka* (good grace) in surviving two attempts to get rid of him, but more to the Green March by 350,000 unarmed Moroccans into the former Spanish Sahara, which he orchestrated in November 1975. After various about-faces, Madrid had decided to abandon the phosphate-rich territory in 1974, and pulled the last of its troops out shortly after the Moroccans walked in. Mauritania dropped its claims to any of the territory in 1979 in exchange for Rabat's renouncing any plans to absorb Mauritania, to which it had claimed historical rights.

In the late 1960s it had become clear that the 100,000 or so inhabitants of the territory wanted independence. The Popular Front for the Liberation of Saguia al-Hamra and Río de Oro (Polisario), set up to harass the Spaniards, did not take kindly to Moroccan intervention, and embarked on a long guerilla war against Rabat.

Backed by Libya and Algeria, Polisario scored occasional successes against the far superior Moroccan forces, but as the latter completed a ragged defensive wall inside the territory's Mauritanian and Algerian frontiers, Polisario's room to move became extremely limited. In 1984, Morocco and Libya proclaimed a 'union' in Oujda that came to nothing but resulted in the latter withdrawing its support for Polisario. As Algeria's internal problems grew in the late 1980s and early '90s, it too abandoned its Saharan protégés.

In 1991, the United Nations brokered a ceasefire that has more or less held since, on the understanding that a referendum on the territory's future would be held. Nothing has yet come of this, as the two sides cannot agree upon who should vote. Polisario wants only those registered as citizens prior to the Green March to participate, while Rabat naturally wants to include many of those who have since moved into Western Sahara, claiming many of them are originally from the territory. At the time of writing it looked as though Hassan II would eventually get his way. The UN, preoccupied with other problems, seems little disposed to devoting too much time to what it appears to regard as a backwater. There were signs too that European governments were losing interest in the issue and coming around to Rabat's point of view that the territory was historically a part of Morocco. Algeria, Polisario's main backers, has its own problems, and in a sign of rapprochement with Rabat signed an accord with Morocco in 1993 defining the border between the two countries. The nitty-gritty of this agreement has still to be implemented. A proposed referendum which was to take place in February 1995 has been indefinitely postponed.

Relations with Israel

Morocco has maintained a unique position in the Arab-Israeli conflict. Although at the time of writing the two nations still did not have diplomatic relations, Morocco had hosted Israeli guests, often in secret, long before Egypt's President Anwar Sadat went to Israel in 1977. Various Israeli senior politicians have travelled to Rabat incognito, and Shimon Peres, the present foreign minister, made several open visits, including one to

Ifrane in 1987. After signing a peace accord with the PLO in Washington in September 1993, Yitzak Rabin, the Israeli prime minister, stopped at Rabat on his way home to thank Hassan II for his behind-the-scenes work as intermediary.

There could be several reasons for Morocco's rather independent stance on Israel. After the Jewish state was established in 1948, the bulk of Morocco's Jewish population decided to move. The Israeli intelligence organisation, Mossad, organised the transfer with the connivance of Franco's Spain, while Rabat turned a blind eye to an operation it could have blocked. More than 80,000 of Morocco's Jews left via Ceuta and Melilla, heading on to France through Spain, and then to Israel. Mossad officials have since claimed that without Franco's help it could never have been done, and that Spain had asked nothing in return. This is now seen as a gesture of reconciliation after the horrors inflicted upon the Jews in WW II by the fascist states with which Franco's Spain had been closely identified. Morocco's motivation for cooperating seems less clear, but Moroccan Jews have long been allowed to holiday in Morocco and, officially at least, there is little bad blood between Jews and the rest of the Moroccan population.

The Present

The 1980s in Morocco were marked above all by economic stagnation and hardship. The situation deteriorated, and in 1984 there were scenes of open rioting over bread price rises in Fès in 1984, in which at least 100 people died.

Hassan II has friends in useful places, however, and the rulers of Saudi Arabia and the Gulf States are among them. Accorded most favoured nation trading status, these countries sometimes reciprocate when things are particularly bad: in 1985, US$250 million turned up in the central bank at a time when Morocco was practically bereft of foreign exchange reserves. Hassan's pro-allied position during the Gulf War in 1990-91 has done him no harm either. Although popular sentiment tended to side with Iraq's Saddam Hussein, Hassan managed to keep in with the West and the Gulf States in a low-profile fashion that aroused little rancour among his subjects.

Although things have improved in some sectors recently, unrest has bubbled below the surface, and occasionally bursts through. Strikes and riots over low wages and poor social conditions saw unions clashing with the authorities in the early 1990s. In one such event, at least 33 people died and hundreds were jailed. In early 1994, the trade unions were heading for renewed clashes with the authorities over pay and social policy, calling for mass protests and strikes.

In spite of constitutional reforms and more open recent elections (see Government), Hassan is still an absolute ruler. On the economic front, pressures of a rapidly expanding population, top-heavy public sector and disappointing progress in most industries remain considerable obstacles, but the news is not all black, particularly if Morocco secures a free trade deal with the European Union (EU; see Economy).

Despite the wave of fundamentalist trouble crashing over neighbouring Algeria and the very real problems confronting Hassan II and his people, it appears his baraka will hold for a while yet.

GEOGRAPHY

Morocco presents by far the most variegated geological smorgasbord in all North Africa, and some of the most beautiful countryside throughout the continent. With its long Atlantic and Mediterranean coasts it has remained to some degree shielded from the rest of the continent by the Atlas Mountain ranges to the east and the Sahara desert to the south.

Including the Western Sahara, occupied by Morocco since the Green March of 1975, the kingdom covers 710,850 sq km, more than a third of it in the disputed territory.

There are four distinct mountain ranges or massifs in Morocco, considered geologically unstable and leaving Morocco subject to earthquakes, such as the one that devastated Agadir in 1960. In the north, the Rif (some-times confusingly known as the Rif Atlas) forms an arc of largely impenetrable limestone and sandstone mountain territory, shooting steeply back from the Mediterranean to heights of about 2200 metres and populated largely by Berbers, many of whom are engaged in the cultivation of kif (the local name for marijuana).

Running north-east to south-west from the Rif is the Middle Atlas range (Moyen Atlas), which rises to a maximum altitude of 3290 metres. It is separated from the Rif by the only real access route linking Atlantic Morocco with the rest of North Africa, the Taza Gap.

The low hills east of Agadir rise to form the highest of the mountain ranges, the High Atlas, which more or less runs parallel to the south of the Middle Atlas. Its tallest peak, Jebel (Mt) Toubkal, is 4165 metres high and, like much of the surrounding heights, is covered in a mantle of snow through the winter and into spring. Farther south again, the lower slopes of the Anti-Atlas drop down into the arid wastes of the Sahara.

The rivers (known as *oued*, from the Arabic *wadi*) are mostly torrential and, depending on seasonal rainfall and melting snows, can flow quite strongly at certain times of the year. The Drâa, Ziz and the Dadès rivers, among others, drain off into the Sahara, although occasionally the Drâa completes its course all the way to the Atlantic coast north of Tan Tan. Among other rivers that drain into the Atlantic are the Sebou, which rises south of Fès and empties into the ocean at Mehdiya, about 40 km north of Rabat, and the Oum er-Rbia, which has its source in the Middle Atlas, north-east of Khenifra, and reaches the Atlantic at Azemmour, just north of El-Jadida.

Between each of the mountain ranges and the Atlantic lie the plains and plateaux, which are generally well watered and in places quite fertile.

South of the Anti-Atlas, the dry slopes, riven by gorges, trail off into the often stony desert of the Western Sahara, which is also the name the rebels of the former Spanish Sahara have given to the territory they want

CLIMATE

The geological variety of Morocco also gives it a wide range of climatic conditions.

Weather in the coastal regions is generally mild but it can become a little cool and wet, particularly in the north. Average temperatures in Tangier and Casablanca range from about 12°C (54°F) in winter to 25°C (77°F) in summer, although the daytime temperatures can easily go higher. Rainfall is greatest in the Rif and northern Middle Atlas, where only the summer months are almost dry.

While the interior of the country can become stiflingly hot in summer, particularly when the desert winds from the Sahara (known as the *sirocco* or *chergui*, from the Arabic *ash-sharqi*, meaning 'the easterly') are blowing, the Atlantic coast is kept comparatively agreeable by sea breezes. The southern Atlantic coast, however, is more arid. Rainfall here drops off and renders crop-growing less tenable.

The rainy season is from November to January, but can go on as late as April. From 1991 to late 1993, however, drought dried

to see independent of Morocco. This is a sparsely populated and unforgiving region bounded to the east and south by Algeria and Mauritania.

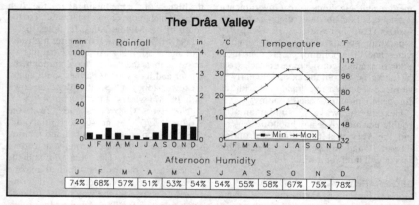

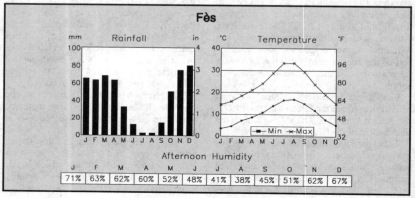

the country out and cut cereal production by around 60%. There was a sigh of relief when heavy rains struck in November 1993, replenishing reservoirs for drinking water, power stations and irrigation.

The lowlands can be quite hot during the day, even in winter, with the mercury hitting as high as 30°C, but temperatures drop quickly in the evening. In the mountains, it can get as cold as -20°C, and that is without taking the wind-chill factor into account. As snow can often block mountain passes, it is important to remember to have enough warm clothing to cope with an unwelcome night stuck in an unheated bus. In summer, the opposite is true during the day, particularly when the chergui is up, with temperatures easily exceeding 40°C. This goes for Marrakesh too.

In the desert, temperatures can swing wildly from day to night. This is due to the dryness of the atmosphere, which has almost no humidity.

The chergui, which is sometimes laden with dust, can occur at any time of the year, but is most common in spring.

FLORA & FAUNA

Until the first century or so of the Christian era, sweeping savanna and good pastures

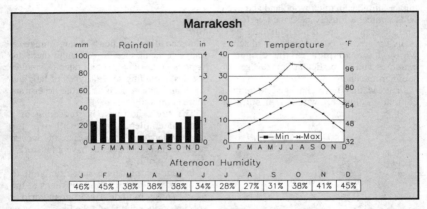

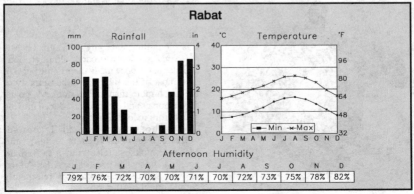

covered much of the Maghreb. But the process of desertification that had already been underway for thousands of years gradually forced the mainly Berber population to seek refuge in the mountains of the Atlas.

Nevertheless, the first-time visitor may be surprised at the amount of green encountered in a country more popularly associated with vast stretches of desert. Travellers arriving in northern Morocco after crossing the arid *meseta* (high plateau) of central and southern Spain are often struck by the comparative lushness they find across the Strait of Gibraltar.

Although many areas have suffered from deforestation, you can still find yourself at higher altitudes in thick woodland and even what could be loosely described as forest. The lower plains are, if not cultivated, generally covered by coarse grasses and scrub, which have adapted to the climate's extremes and in particular the ravages of summertime cherguis.

In areas that have managed to remain comparatively well wooded in spite of

human handiwork, cedar and various species of oak (including cork and evergreen) are among the more common native trees. Eucalyptus and the so-called Barbary fig are imports. In addition, you will see occasional stands of fir tree and junipers.

A tree peculiar to the south of the country is the *argan*, which bears a fruit not unlike the olive from which oil is extracted. You will come across date palms in various places, but they are only native to the desert fringes.

The best time to be walking in the mountains is during spring, when the slopes and even parts of near-desert areas are brightly decorated by a variety of wildflowers.

Birds

Morocco does not boast a huge range of native resident species. Although there are various kinds of eagles and falcons, smaller species, including several types of lark and finch and others peculiar to the desert, are more commonly found.

The stork, however, is something of a national emblem. They are all over the country, and there's barely a disused (or even used) minaret that doesn't have a fat stork's nest on top of it.

In addition, numerous species migrate to or through Morocco at various times of the year. These include flamingos, various species of duck, gulls and the like.

Animals

It is a long time since any of the great beasts of Africa roamed Morocco, although lions and elephants once made their home here. In fact, most of the time you'll be unlikely to see much more than mules, donkeys, goats, sheep, horses and camels, introduced into the area before recorded history.

Wild boar and foxes still abound. Gazelles, fennecs (desert foxes), and Macaque monkeys (also known as Barbary apes) can be seen in parts of the Atlas. A kind of wild sheep, the *mouflon*, is reasonably common in the Atlas too.

GOVERNMENT

For all the trappings of parliamentary democracy, Morocco remains essentially an absolute monarchy. In power since 1961, Hassan II is the latest in a long dynastic line, the Alawites, who have been at the helm, at least in name, since the 17th century. One of the titles the king takes for himself is Commander of the Faithful (amir al-mu'mineen), for his family claims descent from the Prophet Mohammed, through his grandson Al-Hassan bin Ali. As such, these monarchs have been considered sherifs of Morocco, much in the way that Mecca was traditionally ruled by a sherif. The religious significance of Hassan II's claim to legitimacy should not be underestimated, and goes part of the way to explaining how he has managed to stay in power for so long, when other traditional rulers in the Arab and wider Muslim world have tended to be toppled.

Constitution

Under a constitution established in 1972, political parties, trade unions and professional bodies were to take an active part in the country's administration. However, the king retained all real power and opposition parties have found themselves marginalised and continually complain of vote-rigging. The king reserved for himself the right to name his prime minister and ministers, control of the armed forces, the right to dissolve the Chamber of Representatives (*majlis an-nuwab* – parliament) and a raft of other powers.

In September 1992, a referendum was held on modifications to the constitution. To the dismay of many, the vote was an all-too resounding 'yes' – the usual 99%. Hassan II is playing a delicate game, trying to present an image of slow but definite democratisation to the West, and particularly to his European neighbours, with whom he wants closer economic links, while maintaining his power over the political life of the country. The opposition deemed the reform insufficient. Under it, the king renounces the right to appoint ministers, but not that of appointing the prime minister. As a sign of how

unsatisfactory the opposition parties found the changes, they used the 50th anniversary, on 11 January 1994, of the Istiqlal Party's demand for independence in 1944 to call for greater democracy in modern Morocco.

Elections & Political Parties

Elections to the 333-seat parliament are held in two stages. The first 222 seats are thrown open to a popular vote. The last of these took place in June 1993 (the first general polls since 1984), and were a considerable success for the four-party opposition Bloc Démocratique, which won 99 seats. However, the vote for the remaining 111 seats is carried out among trade unions and professional bodies, and traditionally favours loyalist groups. In September 1993, loyalists took 79 of these seats.

In the following months, the opposition refused to bend to the king's request that it join a government of national coalition. Nevertheless, the comparatively low (some would say realistic) turnout of voters – 63% – and the result will be a feather in his democratic cap abroad. Another pleasant surprise was the election of two women to seats in parliament – a first in Morocco.

The opposition parties forming the Bloc Démocratique are a ragbag of groups, including Istiqlal, the Union Socialiste des Forces Populaires, the former Communist Parti du Progrès du Socialisme and the smaller Organisation de l'Action Démocratique et Populaire. Ranged against them, particularly as they have refused to participate in the government formed in the wake of the 1993 elections, is a centre-right alliance of five promonarchy parties. The Mouvement Populaire, the biggest of them, attracts most of its support from the rural Berber population. Others include the liberal Union Constitutionelle and the Rassemblement National des Indépendants.

Tiers of Government

For administrative purposes, the country is divided into 40 provinces (*wilayat*), four of them making up the territory of the Western Sahara. The provinces are subdivided into *préfectures* (Casablanca is made up of five), which are further subdivided into *qaidates*, under the direction of *qaids*. Qaids (or *caids*) have similar powers to those of *pashas*, who are responsible for administering urban municipalities. Other local government officials go by the name of *moqadams*.

Outlook

In spite of several assassination attempts, and a relatively small Islamist movement operating in the country, the king's position as head of the government seems secure. Although Morocco is disturbed by the troubles plaguing Algeria next door, few believe the country will experience the same trouble. This does not make it an impossibility. Various radical Islamists are in jail, and Abdessalam Yassine, the leader of Al-Adl wal-Ihsan (Justice & Charity), the most important of such groups in Morocco, has long been under house arrest in Salé.

Amnesty International claims that, despite several releases of prisoners in recent years, more than 600 people remain incarcerated because of their political activities. Dissident Moroccans outside the country hope economic difficulties and Hassan's desire for greater integration into the Western economies will lead him to make concessions along the path to a more open government. The Morocco of today has often been compared to Franco's Spain of the 1950s and '60s. According to some, if Hassan II has a full innings, he might even be succeeded by a full parliamentary democracy.

ECONOMY

After years of mishaps and harsh austerity measures, there are signs that Morocco has turned a difficult corner. As the privatisation drive picks up steam and Morocco returns to international finance markets after 10 years of tough slimming measures imposed by the International Monetary Fund (IMF), analysts see hope of continued improvement. Along the way, maximum tariffs have come down from 400% to 35%, the dirham has moved close to full convertibility and Morocco has become a member of the General Agreement on Tariffs & Trade (GATT) – in fact Marrakesh was chosen as the site for signing the final accord ending the long-contested Uruguay Round in April 1994. As if to add to the cheer, heavy rains in November 1993 broke a two-year drought that had devastated agriculture, cutting cereal production alone by 58% in 1992.

Inflation has been brought down as low as 5% from highs above 12% in the mid-1980s, but unemployment remains at 20%, if not higher. Official estimates say the number of people living below the poverty line has dropped by a third to 13% of the populace since 1985. In that same period, it is claimed that per capita income has nearly doubled to US$1100 per annum.

If the news remains good, it will bring relief to a government anxiously watching the growing frustration of the country's underemployed young. (In 1994 the growing youth unemployment problem prompted the government to set up a special US$100,000 fund to promote job creation.)

Among the hopeful signals, however, are plenty of worrying indicators of an uneven economy. Foreign debt, at US$21.5 billion, remains a heavy burden, although Saudi Arabia's decision to forgive US$3 billion in loans in the wake of the Gulf War has eased the load. Morocco is still borrowing heavily. The World Bank says Morocco is the biggest recipient of its aid throughout North Africa and the Middle East.

Government figures put the number of poor by World Bank definitions at around four million, but the opposition claims the real figures are worse, and that the gap between wealthy and poor is widening. The average farm or factory worker's wage, for instance, does not rise above Dr 1000 a month, and is often less.

European Connection

King Hassan II pins great hopes upon anchoring Morocco as firmly as possible to the EU's orbit. To this end both sides are negotiating a deal to create a free trade zone between the EU and the kingdom by 1996. In 1987, Morocco applied for membership of the then EC, but was knocked back, and Mediterranean EU members fear a flood of cheap Moroccan agricultural produce will provide unwelcome competition. As it is, the trade balance between the EU and Morocco only moderately favours Europe. However, there are some quid pro quos to be made, and the EU is well aware of it.

The government has moved to stem illegal immigration to Europe and drug smuggling. In return, Western countries have promised US$1 billion to help persuade farmers in the Rif mountains to grow crops other than kif. European police chiefs fear Morocco could become a major route for South American hard drugs into Europe. The stakes are high, and the drugs issue gives Rabat some leverage when bargaining with the EU.

Resources

Agriculture still employs about 40% of the population, and although Morocco doesn't produce enough grain and cereals to meet its own needs, food exports (mainly fruits and vegetables) make up about 30% of the total exports. Occasional drought makes it impossible to predict what contribution the farm sector will make to the economy in any one year.

At the top of its mineral assets are phosphates, of which Morocco is said to have between two-thirds and three-quarters of the world's reserves (including those in the Western Sahara). It is the planet's third-biggest exporter of phosphates after the USA and the CIS. With world prices well down, it is not the money-spinner the government might have hoped for. Phosphate mining is controlled by the Office Cherifien des Phosphates, a state monopoly.

Other mineral exports include fluorite, barytes, manganese, iron ore, lead, zinc, cobalt, copper and antimony, but with phosphates accounting for 90% of mineral exports, these are relatively insignificant.

Although Morocco's search for oil has turned up nothing, there are two refineries for processing imported oil at Mohammedia and Sidi Kacem.

Remittances from the 1.6 million Moroccans living abroad (most of whom live in Europe and half in France) are the biggest source of foreign income. In 1992, they brought in Dr 19 million.

Tourism, hard hit by the effects of the Gulf War in 1990-91, is picking up again and is the second-largest hard-currency earner. About 3½ million visitors arrived in Morocco in 1992, a little over a third of them Europeans, and a big proportion of them

Harvesting Wheat

French. More were expected in 1993. Tourism is thought to provide jobs, both formal and 'informal', for half the working population of cities like Marrakesh. The informal (ie black) 'sector' of the economy is reckoned conservatively to make up 30% of GDP.

In addition to the ill-reputed US$2 billion hashish trade (Morocco is said to supply at least 30% of Europe's dope), there is a flourishing smuggling business in all sorts of consumer items via the Spanish enclaves in the north of the country.

A new link between Europe and the Maghreb is the gas pipeline under construction between Algeria and Spain. The Moroccan stretch will be 525 km long and cost US$1300 million. Spain, as the main beneficiary, is paying for the construction and gas is due to start flowing by 1996. This comes after a friendship treaty signed between Rabat and Madrid in June 1991. Since then, Spanish investment in Morocco has grown by leaps and bounds, while French investment has levelled off.

The ties to Europe have a down side, however. Morocco still exports too much to too few countries (France takes a third of the total), making it vulnerable to recession in Europe.

POPULATION

The population of Morocco is estimated at between 26 and 28 million. About half the total is under 20 years of age, and with a growth rate of 2.2%, the population threatens to become a destabilising factor in a country where a great rift separates the well-off minority and the growing legions of unemployed youth.

As the rural flight to the cities continues, the urban population continues to expand; more than two-thirds of the populace is estimated to live in the cities. By far the most populous city is the Atlantic port and commercial centre of Casablanca, with 2.9 million people. The capital, Rabat, numbers 1.23 million people if Salé is included. Marrakesh has about 1.4 million inhabitants, and

Fès is pushing close to a million. Meknès, Oujda and Agadir are not far behind.

PEOPLE
Arabs, Berbers & Moors

The bulk of the population is made up of Berbers or Arabs, although the distinction is not always easily made. The numbers of ethnic Arabs who came to Morocco with the first Islamic invasion of the 7th century, or 400 years later with the Beni Hillal, were comparatively small. Bigger contributions came from Spain as the Catholics evicted the Muslims in the course of the Reconquista. They have to a large degree mixed with Berbers, who in turn have in great measure been Arabised. When it is said that most of the inhabitants of the northern coastal areas and big cities are Arabic, what is usually meant is Arabic-speaking. Probably less than a quarter of the population is now monolingual in Berber, and bilingualism has increased thanks to modern communications and transport.

Little is known of the racial origins of the Berbers. The word 'Berber' comes from an Arabic word possibly borrowed from the Latin (and ultimately ancient Greek) *barbari*, signifying the non-Latin speaking peoples of the Maghreb. The antiquated name for this area of North Africa, Barbary, has the same origins.

The Berbers inhabit the mountain regions and parts of the desert, and are generally divided into three rough groups identified by dialect. Those speaking Riffian are, not surprisingly, found mainly in the Rif. The dominant group in the Middle Atlas speak Amazigh (also known as Tamazight or Braber), while in the High Atlas the predominant dialect is known as Chleuh. In truth, the tribal structure is much more fractured.

Europeans have long used the term 'Moors' as a generic description for the whole populace of the Maghreb, and even for the whole Muslim world. The name probably more justly refers to a group of people living in the south of Morocco, but also spread out across Mauritania, Algeria and Mali. 'Moor' was probably derived from the Greek word

'Mauros', which was used to describe these people. Only a small proportion of them, also known as the 'blue people' because of the colour of their attire and the fact that the dye lends a bluish hue to their skin, live on Moroccan soil. For simplicity's sake they can be roughly lumped together with the Tuaregs of southern Algeria. In spite of tourist hype, few if any actual Tuaregs live in Morocco.

Jews

Morocco once hosted as many as 160,000 Jews, roughly divided into those of obscure Berber origin and Arabic speakers who found themselves compelled to leave Andalusian Spain in the face of the Reconquista. By the end of the 1960s this population had dropped to 30,000, as most Jews opted to migrate to the state of Israel after 1948. The *mellah*, or Jewish quarter, of many Moroccan towns can still often be identified, but few Jews remain in the country.

Other Ethnic Groups

Growing commercial links with the interior of Africa over the centuries has attracted a population of Negroes from various parts of sub-Saharan Africa into the south of Morocco, particularly into the southern oases and desert settlements. Many originally came as slaves.

Morocco once played host to half a million foreigners, but since the end of the French protectorate in 1956, the number has dropped considerably. Among those who have been absorbed into the general populace are Iberians who came to Morocco when the Muslims were forced out of Spain. They were joined in later times by Spanish traders and workers, many of whom have also assimilated into the Moroccan populace.

EDUCATION

Morocco spends a lot on educating its young – as much as 27% of the state budget according to some claims – but still has a long way to go. In spite of enrolments of nearly four million children in schools and some 230,000 students in the country's 11 universities, UNESCO estimates that around half the adult male population is still illiterate. The figure among women is higher still – possibly as much as 70%.

The gulf between the urban and rural populations is also highlighted by literacy figures. As few as 23% of people living in the country can read, as opposed to 64% in the cities.

National service, which applies to males, lasts up to 18 months.

ARTS
Music

Invasion and cultural cross-fertilisation have bequeathed several musical traditions to Morocco. If you are seriously interested in buying recordings of various types of Moroccan music, try Le Comptoir Marocain de Distribution de Disques (☎ 269538) at 26 Ave Lalla Yacout, in Casablanca. They have a wide range of material on LP, cassette and CD. Popular cassettes can be had for a dollar or two at music stands throughout the country.

Arab-Andalusian Music In addition to the more 'standard' musical patrimony from Arab lands farther to the east, Morocco knows another classical tradition that developed in Muslim Spain under the guidance of a man called Ziryeb, a musician who settled in Granada in the 9th century.

He developed a suite system known as the *nawba*, which played on alternate use of rhythm and non-rhythm, and vocals and instrumental. In all, there are 24 *nawbat*; they are tightly structured, corresponding to the 24 harmonic modes of Andalusian music, and each is purportedly in tune with an hour of the day.

Another musical system that emerged under the guidance of the same man aligned music with the Ptolemaic system of viewing medicine and human health as determined by humours, the four chief fluids of the body (blood, phlegm, choler, melancholy).

As the Muslims were forced out of Spain by the end of the 15th century, the music moved and took root in Morocco. The palaces of Rabat and Oujda, among others, became havens for the preservation of the Andalusian tradition.

Of modern exponents of the art, Sheikh Salah was one of the best, and it is possible to pick up cassettes of his orchestra with little difficulty in Morocco, and even the odd CD in Europe.

Berber Music Long before the Arabs even knew of the existence of Morocco, the Berber tribes had been developing their own music, later enhanced by the arrival of various Arab instruments and styles.

Music is not just entertainment – it has also been the medium for storytelling and the passing on of oral culture from generation to generation. It can still be heard at *moussems* (pilgrimages), wedding ceremonies, public town or tribal gatherings and festivals, as well as at private celebrations. The music of any tribe is often a reflection of the musicality of the local dialect too. Instrumental pieces can be heard, but often the music is accompanied by songs and dancing. The latter can involve men *and* women, something that occasionally raises the hackles of some city (generally orthodox Arab) Muslims.

Storytelling is a big part of the musical repertoire of the Berbers. The *heddaoua* (wandering minstrels) move from one small town to another and recite poetry and the

---

Musical Instruments

Some of the instruments you may come across include the following:

amzhad: a single-chord violin, made of wood and a goatskin cover, and played with a horse-hair bow; it is a specifically Berber instrument

andir: a long, narrow trumpet, most often used for celebrations during Ramadan

bendir: other Berber names for this single-headed oriental drum are *tagnza* and *allun*

darbuka: a generic term for a form of drum typical throughout the Arab world; it is usually made of terracotta in the form of a jug, with a goatskin cover on one side

ghaita: a reed oboe, in wide use throughout Morocco

guedra: another kind of drum most commonly used by the so-called 'blue people' to accompany a dance performed solely by women; the dance is one you're less and less likely to see, except perhaps in a watered-down hotel floor show version

guimbri: a long lute with two or three strings

kanza: very loosely like a guitar, a three-stringed instrument with a rectangular base

kemenja: a typical Arab instrument, not unlike the Western viola

nira or **lira**: a generic Arabic term for various types of reed flute

qarqba (plural **qaraqib**): large, metal castanets

tbel or **tabala**: a cylindrical wooden drum hung around the neck, or held under the arm

zmar: an odd-looking double clarinette

like, often in a hazy allusive style usually attributable to the benefits of kif. They usually provide musical accompaniment, but dance is not necessarily part of the deal. They, like many manifestations of Berber and Arab traditional culture, are gradually giving way to the universal hypnotism of TV.

Contemporary Music

Various Moroccan musicians have experimented with moves to combine aspects of their heritage and Western influences. Hassan Erraji, a blind *oud* (Arab lute) player who moved to Belgium and studied European as well as Arab classical music, has put out several CDs, including ones entitled *Marhaba*, *La Dounia* and *Nikriz*. Although the Arab roots of his music prevail, he introduces other elements into some of his pieces that are well removed from the Oriental tradition, such as saxophone.

Aisha Kandisha goes several steps further, taking traditional sound and infusing what might seem to some an overwhelming stratum of modern Western music, hence perhaps the title of one CD, *Jarring Effects*.

Dance in El-Kelaâ M'Gouna to celebrate the end of harvesting

Raï Although identified more with Algeria, raï ('opinion') is fast gaining popularity in Morocco, and the voices of its leading exponents, such Cheb Khaled, can be heard in music stores as far east as Egypt and Jordan. Despite its distinctly Arabo-African rhythms, which owe much to Bedouin music, it is probably the most thoroughly Westernised music, using a variety of modern electrical instruments to create an often hypnotic effect. Morocco itself has given rise to several less well known raï performers.

Dance

Talk of dance in the Orient, and the first thing to pop into most Western minds is the belly dance, something you can see (for a price) at plenty of the more expensive tourist hotels (and occasionally in quite sleazy 'nightclubs' in the bigger cities, especially Casablanca), although it is not essentially a Moroccan art. You may also get a chance to see so-called folk dancing, which is usually a poor hotel imitation of the real thing out in the Berber backblocks.

A cross-section of some of the kinds of dance you may be lucky enough to encounter outside the hotels include the following:

ahidous
This is a complex circle dance seen in the Middle Atlas. Usually associated with harvest rites, it is an occasion for the whole community to join in. Alternating circles of men and women dance and sing antiphonally around musicians, usually playing bendirs only, but sometimes other instruments.

ahouach
This is linked to the ahidous of the Atlas Mountains, but is performed in the kasbahs of the south. The dancing this time is done by women alone, again in a circle around musicians.

guedra
See Musical Instruments on the previous page

gnaoua
This term refers mainly to Blacks (often descendants of slaves brought to Morocco from central and west Africa) who perform as musicians and acrobats in southern Morocco. They were once a not uncommon sight in the Djemaa el-Fna in Marrakesh, but have now become a rarity.

Architecture

Islamic Architecture

The jewels of medieval Moroccan urban architecture are to be found in the medinas of the Imperial Cities, especially in Fès and Marrakesh.

Initially at least, Moroccan architecture took its lead from eastern Islamic impulses. The earliest construction efforts undertaken by Muslims – more often than not mosques – inherited much from Christian and Graeco-Roman models. However, various styles soon developed and owed increasingly less to their architectural forbears. This is particularly so in Morocco and the Maghreb in general, where monumental prototypes left behind by other civilisations were scarcer than in Egypt, Syria and Iraq.

Indeed, a sweep from west to east across the Muslim world reveals a remarkable diversity in design obvious even to the untrained eye. The angular, austere Moroccan style, for example, contrasts with the opulent mosques of the Ottoman Turks, which are characterised by their great cupolas and pencil-thin minarets, as well as with the Persian-influenced, onion-shaped domes found in Iraq and countries farther east.

Mosques are generally built around an open courtyard, off which lie one or more covered halls (*liwans*). The liwan facing Mecca is the focal point of prayer. A vaulted niche in the wall called the *mihrab* indicates the direction of Mecca (the *qibla*), which Muslims must face when they pray.

Islam does not recognise priests as such, but the closest equivalent is the mosque's *sheikh*, a man schooled in Islam who often doubles as the *muezzin*, the one who calls the faithful to prayer.

At the main Friday prayers in particular, the sheikh gives a sermon (*khutba*) from the *minbar* – the pulpit raised above a narrow staircase, better examples of which are ornately decorated. As a rule, only the main community mosque (*jami'*) contains a minbar and is used for the main Friday prayers and sermon. Smaller local mosques (and this can mean just about any kind of place formally set aside for prayer) are known as *masajid*, the plural of *masjid*.

The mosque also serves as a kind of community centre, and often you'll find groups of children or adults getting lessons (usually in the Qur'an), people in quiet prayer and others simply sheltering in the tranquil peace of the mosque.

The minaret (from the word '*menara*', meaning lighthouse), most often consists of a square base leading to more slender cylindrical or hexagonal stages. Most have internal staircases for the muezzins to climb to the top; the advent of the microphone saves them that effort now.

In the Maghreb and Spain, however, the dominant style of minaret is square-based all the way to the top. This is the single most distinguishing characteristic of what is often referred to as Andalusian (from Al-Andalus) religious architecture. The comparison between such minarets and the belltowers of many Spanish churches is revealing. Only

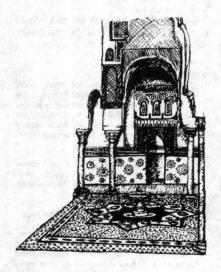

Mosque Interior

A: Ruins, Meknès (JS)
B: Medersa ben Youssef, Marrakesh (DS)
C: Fès el-Bali (JS)
D: Place el-Hedim, Meknès (DS)
E: Mausoleum of Moulay Ismail (DS)
F: Mausoleum of Moulay Ismail (DS)
G: Architecture, Fès (JS)
H: Kairaouine Mosque, Fès (DS)
I: Medersa ben Youssef, Marrakesh (DS)

A	B	C
D	E	F
G	H	I

A: Boy, Taroudannt (DS)
C: Water seller, Meknès (DS)
E: Guard, Mausoleum of Mohammed V, Rabat (DS)
G: Wedding procession, Taroudannt (DS)
I: Azrou Tuesday souq (DS)

B: Inside Bou Inania medersa, Fès (DS)
D: Busker, Taroudannt (DS)
F: Young locals (DS)
H: Camel shepherds (DS)

one rather small and comparatively modern minaret in the small sacred town of Moulay Idriss, near Meknès, departs from the standard – it's cylindrical.

The decoration of mosques (Moroccan and Andalusian religious buildings tend to be fairly austere on the outside) and many other public buildings is an exercise in geometric virtuosity. As Islam frowns on the artistic representation of living beings, the art of carving out complex arabesques of vines, palms and other flora in various deceptive designs merged with a growing tradition of intricate decorative calligraphy. Much of the decoration consists of more or less stylised verses from the Qur'an. The phrase *la illah illa Allah* (there is no god but Allah), appears in a seemingly unlimited variety of designs as an integral part of decoration, fusing religious precept and the very reference to God with the art that exalts Him.

In Morocco and Muslim Spain, this artform was taken to particular lengths in the delicate stucco and plaster carvings that are mostly found inside buildings. The carved woodwork ceilings in some liwans betray painstaking, graceful and, again, largely geometric decoration.

Although Spain's Muslim heritage has bequeathed more spectacular sites (such as the Alhambra in Granada), Morocco still offers a rich trove of monuments. The great Kairaouine (Qayrawin) mosque in Fès, with its elaborate interior decoration and vaulting that was developed over the centuries as an essential element of specifically Moroccan architecture, is the most impressive monument to Almoravid and Almohad power. It is a shame that non-Muslims are denied access to such treasures. The present ban on non-Muslims entering mosques and other functioning religious institutions is said to date back to an edict by France's first resident-general in Morocco, General Lyautey.

In compensation, there are many medersas open to view that reward a visit, the best of them built by the Merenjd dynasty. They, as with many other classic buildings throughout Moroccan cities, bear the hallmarks of Andalusian influence in

their green-tiled roofs (when you look out over a city like Fès, you can easily identify where the major monuments are by their roofs) and their intricate interior stucco and woodwork. Together with the *zellij* tiles that are used to decorate the lower strip of the inner walls, they left hardly a square centimetre free of artwork.

You will probably notice an important feature common to most buildings in Morocco, including mosques, medersas and private residences. The majority are built around an internal courtyard, with most windows overlooking the courtyard and far fewer facing on to the streets and the outside world. The reasoning combines practicality with custom, for such a structure maximises protection against the heat and maintains a premium on privacy.

Some of the greater city gates and towers (such as the Tour Hassan in Rabat) represent a sober but formidable reminder of the power of some of Morocco's past dynasties.

Berber Architecture Throughout the centuries, the Berbers of southern Morocco have adhered to an austere building style in their more important centres, unmoved by contact with other traditions, most notably those of Islam and the Arabs.

Three basic types of building are encountered: the agadir (Berber for granary); the kasbah, usually the abode of some local potentate around which would nestle the simple homes of his subjects; and the ksar (from the Arabic *qasr*, meaning castle or palace), a kind of fortified village that predominates in the Todra, Drâa and Ziz valleys. The kasbahs and *ksour* (plural of ksar), often look quite similar. The lower half of the defensive walls is earthen and the upper half is made of baked brick. The towers taper somewhat towards the top; there is little decoration in the top half and none in the lower half. Slit windows let light in and missiles out.

The most unfortunate thing about these ochre-coloured, starkly impressive constructions is their fragility. Within 50 years a magnificent new kasbah can be reduced by the elements to a ruinous pile of mud and rubble.

Western Influences By leaving the old indigenous cities intact and building new administrative zones alongside them, the French protectorate authorities saved much of Morocco's ancient patrimony and at the same time created a kind of time warp – the *villes nouvelles* built outside the old medinas are, to a greater or lesser extent, replicas of southern European cities of about the 1930s. For most people they are of little architectural interest, but Casablanca, which boomed as a modern port under the French, is home to a plethora of Art Deco buildings that can make a walk around the city centre and affluent areas like Anfa a pleasant excursion of discovery for European architecture buffs. Also of interest are some of the new-Mauresque outgrowths peculiar to Morocco.

Literature
Far from the heart of Muslim Arab civilisation and great seats of power and learning such as Cairo, Damascus, Baghdad and Jerusalem, Morocco has never really been at the forefront of Arab letters, although several greats spent time in Morocco.

They include Ibn Khaldun and Averroes (or Ibn Rushd). The former, who lived in the 14th century, is considered the foremost Arab historian. Born in Algeria, he spent some time in Fès, but his travels took him on to Spain, Cairo and Syria. Averroes, as he was known in the West, was equally known for his medical treatises and commentaries on Aristotle. Born in Cordova, in Muslim Spain, he spent his last years in Marrakesh.

Egypt, Lebanon and what was Palestine have produced a good share of modern literature, especially in Arabic, but to some extent also in French. Algeria has tended to dominate Maghreb literature, especially that in French, but this does not mean Moroccans have been inactive. The bulk of their literature is, however, not known beyond the Maghreb and France.

Among some of the better known writers are Tahar ben Jelloun, Abdel Krim Ghallab, Ahmed Sefrioui and Driss Chraïbi. For more details and a reading selection, turn to the Books entry in the Facts for the Visitor chapter.

Crafts
Morocco has a rich and variegated tradition of handicraft production, and the better souqs are crawling with items to keep the avid souvenir-hunter well occupied. See the Arts & Crafts colour section.

CULTURE
Traditional & Modern Lifestyle
For the first-time visitor to a Muslim country as much as for those who have already travelled through some, the curious mix of conservatism and Westernised 'liberalism' never ceases to confuse. In general, men take the leading public role in Moroccan society, whereas women are left very much in the background. Consequently, most travellers' contacts with Moroccans are with men. As a rule, a high degree of modesty is demanded of both sexes, in dress and behaviour. Even among the older or more traditionally minded, there are distinctions. While women of Arab descent are generally discouraged from, say, selling fruit and vegetables in shops and markets, Berber women have no trouble with this. Arab women are, theoretically, not supposed to dance, especially not in public. It is not, however, uncommon for Berber women to participate in communal dances with men.

None of the rules is adhered to uniformly, and in the bigger cities, especially Casablanca, the veil and *hijab* (head covering) are more the exception than the rule. Younger women walk around in stylish Western clothes and even the odd miniskirt can be seen. Possibly the most worrying fashion development in Morocco is the reappearance among the dress set of bell-bottomed jeans! In addition, women work in a wide range of jobs – most of the bus conductors on Rabat and Casablanca buses, for instance, are women, which is virtually unheard of in, say, Cairo or Damascus.

The strict segregation of the sexes in

public life that is characteristic in Muslim societies is far from uniform in Morocco, and predictably enough it is in the big cities where most mixing goes on. Most bars and cafés, however, remain largely a male preserve.

Taboos

Unfortunately, mosques in active use, including some of the most impressive, are off limits to non-Muslims. You may be able to get the odd glimpse through the doors, but don't push it if people make it known that your curiosity is not appreciated. The same applies to most other religious monuments still in use.

Avoiding Offence

Although dress codes vary quite widely from some of the chic parts of the cities to the conservative countryside, for the outsider it pays to err on the side of modesty. Women, in particular, are well advised to keep their shoulders and upper arms covered and to opt for long trousers or skirts. Stricter Muslims consider excessive display of flesh, whether male or female, offensive. Women who disregard such considerations risk arousing the ire of the genuinely offended and attracting unwanted interest in others. See Women Travellers in Facts for the Visitor. Obviously a little common sense goes a long way. You can get away with a lot more on the beaches of Agadir than in a Berber village in the Atlas Mountains.

Public display of affection is much frowned upon in most parts of the country.

Sport

Among the Western imports that have really stuck in Morocco, as indeed in many African

Morocco on Film

As far back as 1930, Hollywood's eyes turned to the Orient, when Marlene Dietrich starred in the not overly demanding Paramount picture, *Morocco*. Dietrich got an Academy Award nomination for her role as a cabaret singer finally trapped by true love – in the form of Gary Cooper. Not a second of what was Dietrich's American debut was filmed on location.

The same can be said of what is probably *the* Moroccan movie, *Casablanca*. Shot in 1942, the Humphrey Bogart classic had almost nothing to do with Casablanca, but was based on the activities of wartime Tangier, which maintained its international zone status during WW II. Rick's Café probably has more in common with that city's Dean's Bar, and visitors to Casablanca in search of traces of Ingrid Bergman and Claude Rains will be sorely disappointed by the paltry offerings – a few movie posters in the Hyatt Hotel's Bar Casablanca. In one of his more memorable exchanges, Bogart (Rick) says to Rains (Captain Louis Renault): 'I came to Casablanca for the waters.' 'What waters?' comes the reply. 'We're in the desert.' 'I was misinformed.' Nice line, but a little inaccurate. Believe it or not, Ronald Reagan was originally slated for the lead role.

Ten years later, a picture of a totally different calibre won the award for best film at the Cannes festival. Orson Welles' epic recreation of Shakespeare's *Othello* won little box office acclaim at the time, but has since gained a cult following. A restored copy of the film started doing the cinematic rounds again in 1994. Welles shot some of the scenes in Essaouira and the Citerne Portugaise of El-Jadida. A small square in Essaouira has been named in his honour.

Another cinema classic filmed in Morocco was *Lawrence of Arabia*, for which the kasbah of Aït Benhaddou, south of Marrakesh, was chosen as a set. Peter O'Toole was not the only one to leave his cinematic mark here. At least 20 films have been partly shot in the kasbah, including *Jesus of Nazareth*. The Sean Connery and Michael Caine classic, *The Man Who Would Be King*, was partly shot at another kasbah a few km from Aït Benhaddou, Tamdaght.

Another misplaced film is Bernardo Bertolucci's *The Sheltering Sky*. Although Paul Bowles had Oran (Algeria) in mind as the takeoff point for this very personal story, Bertolucci found Tangier a much better option. He chose various locations, including the Hôtel Continental in the medina, to set the American couple Port (John Malkovich) and Kit (Debra Winger) off on their bizarre and self-destructive adventure into the desert. Bowles, himself a longtime resident of what some know as Sodom-on-Sea, made a cameo appearance in the film. ■

countries, is football (soccer to some). Moroccans are avid fans, and it is not unusual to see crowds of men glued to TV sets to watch games between teams that have nothing to do with Morocco. The national team was good enough to qualify for the World Cup staged in the USA in 1994.

RELIGION
Islam
'Allahu akbar, Allahu akbar...Ashhadu an la Ilah ila Allah...Ashhadu an Mohammedan rasul Allah...Haya ala as-sala...Haya ala as-sala...'

Of all the sounds that assault the ears of the first-time visitor to Morocco, it is possibly that of the call to prayer that leaves the most indelible impression. Five times a day, Muslims are called, if not to enter a mosque to pray, at least to take the time to pray where they are. The midday prayers on Friday, when the sheikh of the mosque delivers his weekly sermon, or khutba, are considered the most important.

Islam shares its roots with the great monotheistic faiths that sprang from the harsh land of the Middle East – Judaism and Christianity – but is considerably younger than the former two. The holy book of Islam is the Qur'an. Its pages carry many references to the earlier prophets of both the older religions – Adam, Abraham (Ibrahim), Noah, Moses and others – but there the similarities begin to end. Jesus is seen merely as another in a long line of prophets that ends definitively with Mohammed. What makes Mohammed different from the rest is that the Qur'an, unlike either the Torah of the Jews or the Christian Gospels, is the word of God, directly communicated to Mohammed in a series of revelations. For Muslims, Islam can only be the apogee of the monotheistic faiths from which it derives so much. Muslims traditionally attribute a place of great respect to Christians and Jews as *ahl al-kitab*, the People of the Book. However, the more strident will claim Christianity was a new and improved version of the teachings of the Torah and Islam was the next logical step and therefore 'superior'. Do not be surprised if you occasionally run into someone wanting you to convert!

Mohammed, born into one of the trading families of the Arabian city of Mecca (in present-day Saudi Arabia) in 570 AD, began to receive revelations in 610 AD, and after a time started imparting the content of Allah's message to the Meccans. The essence of it was a call to submit to God's will (the word 'islam' means submission), but not all Meccans thought a great deal of it.

Mohammed gathered quite a following in his campaign against Meccan idolaters, but the powerful families of the city became so angry with him that he felt forced to flee to Medina (Islam's second most holy city after Mecca (in Saudi Arabia) in 622. Mohammed's flight from Mecca or *hijra* (migration) marks the beginning of the Muslim calendar. In Medina he continued to preach and increased his power base. Soon he and his supporters began to clash with the Meccans, led by powerful elements of the Quraysh tribe, possibly over trade routes.

By 632, Mohammed had been able to revisit Mecca and many of the tribes in the surrounding area had sworn allegiance to him and the new faith. Mecca became the symbolic centre of the faith, containing as it did the Ka'aba, which housed the black stone supposedly given to Abraham by the archangel Gabriel. Mohammed determined that Muslims should face Mecca when praying outside the city.

On his death in 632, the Arabs exploded into the Syrian desert, quickly conquering all of what makes up modern Syria, Iraq, Lebanon, Israel and Palestine. This was accomplished under the caliphs (successors), or Companions of Mohammed, of whom there were four. They in turn were succeeded by the Umayyad (661-750) dynasty in Damascus and then the Abbassid line (749-1258) in the newly built city of Baghdad.

Islam quickly spread west, first taking in Egypt and then fanning out across North Africa. By the end of the 7th century, the Muslims had reached the Atlantic and thought themselves sufficiently in control of the Gezirat al-Maghreb ('the Island of the West', or North Africa beyond Egypt) to consider marching on Spain in 710.

Islam is now the religion of about 99% of Moroccans. In order to live out a devout life, the Muslim is expected to carry out at least the Five Pillars of Islam:

shahada – This is the profession of faith, the basic tenet of the Muslim faith. 'There is no god but Allah, and Mohammed is His Prophet.' It is a phrase commonly heard as part of the call to prayer and at many other events, such as births and deaths. The first half of the sentence has virtually become an exclamation good for any time of life or situation. People can often be heard muttering it to themselves, as if seeking a little strength to get through the trials of the day.

sala – Sometimes written 'salat', this is the obligation of prayer, done ideally five times a day, when muezzins call the faithful to pray. Although Muslims can pray anywhere, it is considered more laudable to pray together in a mosque (masjid or jami'). The important midday prayers on Friday (the loose equivalent of Sunday Mass for Catholics), held in a special kind of mosque, the jami', are the high point of the week (the loose equivalent of Sunday mass for Catholics) are usually held in the jami', which is the main district mosque.

zakat – Alms-giving to the poor was from the start an essential part of the social teaching of Islam, and was later developed in some parts of the Muslim world into various forms of tax to redistribute funds to the needy. The moral obligation towards one's poorer neighbours continues to be emphasised at a personal level, and exhortations to give are often posted up outside mosques.

sawm – Ramadan, the ninth month of the Muslim calendar, commemorates the revelation of the Qur'an to Mohammed. In a demonstration of the Muslims' renewal of faith, they are asked to abstain from sex and from letting *anything* pass their lips from dawn to dusk every day of the month. This includes smoking. For more on the month of fasting *(Ramadan)*, see the Holidays entry in Facts for the Visitor.

hajj – The pinnacle of a devout Muslim's life is the pilgrimage to the holy sites in and around Mecca. Ideally, the pilgrim should go to Mecca in the last month of the year, Zuul-Hijja, and join Muslims from all over the world in the pilgrimage and the subsequent feast. The returned pilgrim can be addressed as *Hajj*, and in simpler villages at least, it is still quite common to see the word *Al-Hajj* and simple scenes painted on the walls of houses showing that its inhabitants have made the pilgrimage.

Sunnis & Shiites The power struggle between Ali, the last of the four caliphs of Mohammed and his son-in-law and the emerging Umayyad dynasty in Damascus caused a great schism at the heart of the new religion.

The succession to the caliphate had been marked by considerable intrigue and bloodshed. Ali, the father of Mohammed's sole male heirs, lost his struggle, and the Umayyad leader was recognised as the legitimate successor to the caliphate. Those who favoured the Umayyad caliph became known as the Sunnis. They are the majority of Muslims and are considered the orthodox mainstream of Islam. The Shiites, on the other hand, recognise only the successors of Ali. Most of the Shiites are known as Twelvers, because they believe in 12 imams (religious leaders), the last of whom has been lost from sight, but who will appear some day to create an empire of the true faith. The rest are called the Seveners because they believe that seven imams will succeed Ali.

The Sunnis have divided into four schools of religious thought, each lending more or less importance to various aspects of doctrine. In Morocco, where the population is virtually entirely Sunni, it is the Maliki school that predominates. The Malikis, along with the Hanafi school, are somewhat less rigid in their application and interpretation of the Qur'an than the other schools. An illustration of this emerged by the 15th century, when *qadis* (community judges) are recorded as having applied *shari'a* (Qur'anic law) in accordance with local custom rather than to the letter.

Saints & Mysticism Morocco is not alone in the Muslim world in hosting a strongly mystical offshoot of Islam, but is so perhaps in the weight this carries with a large part of the population.

From an early point in the life of Islam, certain practitioners sought to move closer to God through individual effort and spiritual devotion, rather than simply living by God's laws. These people came to be known as Sufis (from *suf*, meaning wool and referring to the simple woollen cord they tended to wear as a belt for their garments). Various orders of Sufis emerged throughout the lands where Islam held sway, and this was as true of Morocco as of anywhere else.

Orthodox Muslims regarded (and still regard) such groups with suspicion, particularly as the orders tend to gather in the name of a holy man (or *wali*, which has come to be loosely translated as 'saint', although saints in the Christian sense play no role in Islam). Public gatherings take many forms, from the dances of the 'whirling dervishes' to more ecstatic and extreme demonstrations of self-mutilation (where participants may, for instance, push skewers into their cheeks without feeling any pain). The orders generally gather at the mosque or tomb of their 'saint' and follow a particular *tariqa* (path), or way of worshipping. Various orders acquired permanence over the centuries – and 'membership' might run through generations of the same families, tracing their lineage back to the original saint or spiritual master and through him to the Prophet; the veracity of such links is of secondary importance.

This mystic tendency found particularly fertile ground in the traditions and superstitions of the Berbers. There is little doubt that the cults that prosper in Morocco do so mostly in rural Berber areas. The focal point of gatherings of such groups is generally a *zawiyya*, which could be a small meeting place or a big complex grouping mosque, school and hostels around the tomb of the saint, or marabout. Marabout, from the Arabic *muraabit*, is a word used more by French scholars than the locals, and has come to designate the saint *and* the tomb.

For orthodox Muslims, veneration of the saint is tantamount to worship of an idol, although Sufis would not see it that way. According to them, the wali is a 'friend' (the more literal meaning of wali) of God and so an intermediary, and marabouts are regarded in a similar fashion. The great moussems, to the tombs of such saints are as much a celebration of the triumph of the spirit as an act of worship of a particular saint.

Possibly the best known of these saints in Morocco is Moulay Idriss, whose tomb stands in the town of the same name outside Meknès. He died in 791, and is one of a number of equally venerated figures across the Muslim world, who include Ahmed al-Badawi in Tanta, Egypt, and Abdal Qadir in Baghdad.

In Morocco as elsewhere, such cults and their individualistic approach to Islam were considered by the mainly city-dwelling orthodox Muslims as deviant and by their leaders as politically dangerous.

And so, armed with imprecations against heresy, various attempts have been made to put an end to the phenomenon in Morocco, starting with the Almoravids. In more recent times, concerted efforts were made again in the 1930s, but there are two obstacles to such campaigns: the territory of the rural Berbers is difficult to control, and the people who follow the cults make up a big chunk of the total populace – you cannot simply get rid of them all!

Islamic Customs When a baby is born, the first words uttered to it are the call to prayer. A week later this is followed by a ceremony in which the baby's head is shaved and an animal is sacrificed.

The major event of a boy's childhood is circumcision, which normally takes place sometime between the ages of seven and 12.

Marriage ceremonies are colourful and noisy affairs which usually take place in summer. One of the customs is for all the males to get in their cars and drive around the streets in a convoy making as much noise as possible. The ceremony usually takes place in either the mosque or the home of the bride or groom. After that, the partying goes on until the early hours of the morning, often until sunrise.

The death ceremony is simple: a burial service is held at the mosque and the body is then buried with the feet facing Mecca.

When Muslims pray, they must follow certain rituals. First they must wash their hands, arms, feet, head and neck in running water before praying; all mosques have an area set aside for this purpose. If they are not in a mosque and there is no water available, clean sand suffices, and where there is no sand, they must just go through the motions of washing.

Then they must face Mecca – all mosques are oriented so that the *mihrab* (prayer niche) faces the right direction – and follow a set pattern of gestures and genuflections. Photos of rows of Muslims kneeling in the direction of Mecca with their heads touching the ground are legion. You regularly see Muslims praying by the side of the road or in the street as well as in mosques.

In everyday life, Muslims are prohibited from drinking alcohol and eating pork,

Islam & the West

Ignorance abounds in the West about the nature of Islam and Muslims, who are associated all too readily with a fearful image of unpredictable, gun-toting, unreasonable terrorists. Ever since the Crusades, this sort of image has tended to stick in the Western subconscious, and has been fuelled by the intractable conflict in the Middle East between Israel and its Arab neighbours and the determined campaign of demonisation of Arab leaders who are considered a menace to Western interests. Many Muslims point to conflicts in the heart of the West, such as the horrors perpetrated in Northern Ireland, and ask whether they make everyone living in Ireland and the UK bloodthirsty extremists.

It also has to be said that, although perhaps more familiar with Western ways than Westerners are with Arab ways, people in the Arab world, Muslims or otherwise, sometimes have a startlingly contorted picture of the West and what makes it tick. A combination of grudging respect for and envy of its wealth and technological advantages and occasionally a disdain for its perceived moral decadence colour the way many Muslims, including Moroccans, deal with Westerners. The soap operatic drivel of Western TV does little to help.

For all this, visitors to Morocco find that – hustlers, hasslers and touts aside – the reality could not be further from the truth. That a gulf separates East and West in terms of mentality and world view few would dispute, but the warmth accorded to outsiders by the average Moroccan belies any stereotypes of the typical Muslim. After all, Islam demands of its faithful a sense of community and hospitality to strangers.

Much is made of religious fundamentalism in Muslim countries, but it should be considered in the light of the role that religion plays in these countries. Islam is not just a religion that can be separated from daily life and government, as is now the case with the Christian churches in the West. Islam is, for want of a better word, more holistic in that it provides a framework for both secular and spiritual life. Calls for an Islamic state therefore do not sound as strange to Muslims as they do to Westerners. Having said that, it is probably fair to observe that the majority of ordinary Muslims do not favour such a development, and that the popular following of fundamentalist groups is not as great as some imagine. Much of the success they do have is less a result of religious fervour than a reflection of the frustrated hopes of many classes in countries grappling with severe economic difficulties. Morocco is not exempt from this, although neither the social stresses nor the fundamentalist movements are as great an issue as in, say, neighbouring Algeria. ∎

which is considered unclean, and must refrain from gambling, fraud, usury, and slander.

Jews

For details, see the preceding People section.

Christianity

There are precious few Moroccan Christians, and the existence of the odd modern church is due to the presence of Europeans over the centuries rather than local need. Nevertheless, there is evidence that Christianity made some inroads in North Africa during the period of Roman rule. How far it went beyond the Roman or Romanised population and upper classes is a matter of debate, although it appears that some Berber tribes turned, for a time at least, to the imported faith. For whatever reason, the departure of the Romans and later of the Byzantines was followed by the virtual disappearance of Christianity from North Africa.

LANGUAGE

The official language in Morocco is Arabic, although French, the legacy of the protectorate, is still widely used in the cities (much less so among rural Berbers) and remains surprisingly important in education, business and the press. Morocco's close ties to France also help to explain the continued importance of French.

There are three main Berber dialects in use, mainly in the Rif and Atlas Mountains. Modern means of communication have left only a minority of Berbers monolingual – most speak at least some Arabic.

To a lesser extent than French, Spanish has maintained some hold in northern parts of the country, where Spain exercised administrative control until 1956. You may also come across it in the territory of the former Spanish Sahara, over which Madrid relinquished control in 1975, and the former enclave of Sidi Ifni. In towns like Tetouan, for instance, Spanish is just as likely to be understood as French, if not more so, and a little knowledge of it can be a great asset.

In the main cities and towns you will find plenty of people, many of them touts you may not necessarily want to hang around with, who speak a variety of other languages, including English, German and Italian.

Arabic

Moroccan Arabic *(darija)* is a dialect of the standard language, but is so different in many respects as to be virtually like another tongue. It is everyday language that differs most from that of other Arabic-speaking peoples. More specialised or educated language tends to be much the same across the Arab world, although pronunciation varies considerably. An Arab from Jordan or Iraq will have little trouble discussing politics or literature with an educated Moroccan, but might have more trouble ordering lunch. The influence of French is seen in some of the words that Moroccan Arabic has taken on. An example is the use of the French word for 'coach' (intercity bus), *car*.

The spread of radio and TV has increased Moroccans' exposure to and understanding of what is commonly known as Modern Standard Arabic (MSA). MSA, which has grown from the classical language of the Qur'an and poetry, is the written and spoken lingua franca of the Arab world, and in fact not so far removed from the daily language of the Arab countries of the Levant. It is the language of radio and TV presenters and the press, and also of the great majority of modern Arabic literature.

Foreign students of the language constantly face the dilemma of whether first to learn MSA (which could mean waiting some time before being able to talk with shopkeepers) and then a chosen dialect, or simply to acquire spoken competence in the latter. Dialects supposedly have no written form (the argument goes it would be like writing in Cockney or Strine), although there is no reason why they could not avail themselves of the same script used for the standard language. If this leaves you with a headache, you will have some idea of why so few non-Arabs or non-Muslims embark on the study of this complex tongue.

If you do take the time to learn even a few

words and phrases, you will discover and experience much more while travelling through the country. Just making the attempt implies a respect for local culture that Moroccans all too infrequently sense in visitors to their country.

Pronunciation Pronunciation of Arabic can be tongue-tying for someone unfamiliar with the intonation and combination of sounds. Pronounce the transliterated words and phrases slowly and clearly.

The following guide should help, but it is not complete because the rules governing pronunciation and vowel use are too extensive to be covered here.

For a more comprehensive guide to the Arabic spoken in the Maghreb, get hold of Lonely Planet's *Moroccan Arabic Phrasebook*, by Dan Bacon with Abdennabi Benchehda & Bichr Andjar.

Vowels In spoken Moroccan Arabic, there are at least five basic vowel sounds that can be distinguished:

a like the 'a' in 'had' (sometimes very short)
e like the 'e' in 'bet' (sometimes very short)
i like the 'i' in 'hit'
o like the 'o' in 'hot'
u like the 'oo' in 'book'

The ‾ symbol over a vowel gives it a long sound.

ā like the 'a' in 'father'
ē like the 'e' in 'ten', but lengthened
ī like the 'e' in 'ear', only softer, often written as 'ee'
ō like the 'o' in 'for'
ū like the 'oo' in 'food'

Long vowels are also informally transliterated as double vowels, eg aa (ā), ee (ī), oo (ū).

Combinations Certain combinations of vowels with vowels or consonants form other vowel sounds (diphthongs):

aw like the 'ow' in 'how'
ai like the 'i' in 'high'
ei & ay like the 'a' in 'cake'

These last two are tricky, as one can slide into the other in certain words, depending on who is pronouncing them.

Consonants Most of the consonants used in this section are the same as in English. However, a few of the consonant sounds must be explained in greater detail.

Three of the most common are the glottal stop ('), the 'ayn' sound ('), and the 'rayn' (**gh**). These are two of the most difficult sounds in Arabic, so don't be discouraged if you aren't understood at first, just keep trying. Both can be produced by tightening your throat and sort of growling, but the ('gh') requires a slight 'r' sound at the beginning – it is like the French 'r'. When the (') comes before a vowel, the vowel is 'growled' from the back of the throat. If it is before a consonant or at the end of a word, it sounds like a glottal stop. The best way to learn these sounds is to listen to a native speaker pronounce their written equivalents.

The glottal stop is the sound you hear between the vowels in the expression 'oh oh!', or the Cockney pronunciation of 'water' (wa'er). It is caused by a closing of the glottis at the back of the throat so that the passage of air is momentarily halted. It can occur anywhere in the word – at the beginning, middle or end.

Other common consonant sounds include:

j more or less like the 'j' in 'John'
g for those who read some Arabic, it is worth noting that the Moroccans have added a letter for the hard 'g' (as in Agadir) – a kaf (letter'k') with three dots above it
H a strongly whispered 'h', almost like a sigh of relief

q a strong guttural 'k' sound. Often transcribed as 'k', although there is another letter in the Arabic alphabet which *is* the equivalent of 'k'

kh a slightly gurgling sound, like the 'ch' in Scottish 'loch'

r a rolled 'r', as in the Spanish 'para'

s pronounced as in English 'sit', never as in 'wisdom'

sh like the 'sh' in 'shelf'

ẑ like the 's' in pleasure

Double Consonants In Arabic, double consonants are both pronounced. For example the word *istanna*, which means 'wait', is pronounced 'istan-na'.

Transliteration What you read and hear will as often as not be two or three entirely different things. No really satisfactory system of transcribing the 'squiggles' of Arabic into Latin script has ever been devised, not for want of attempts.

Some semblance of standard 'rules' have been loosely agreed upon, but one big problem remains who has made the running. Where Anglo-Saxons have had the most influence, a transliteration system reflecting English phonemics has emerged, but where France held sway, and this means particularly in the Maghreb, Lebanon and Syria, quite another way of rendering Arabic emerged. In addition, the same word may be written in Latin script in all manner of ways, depending on, say, a sign-writer's own feelings about how the Arabic should appear in 'European'. The high rate of illiteracy among Moroccans does not help. Reliable standardisation is therefore an elusive goal. Names of hotels, restaurants and the like are spelled in this guide as they appear, however bizarre the variations.

Since most modern maps, books and the like dealing with Morocco tend to reflect French usage, this guide generally goes along with it.

There is only one word for 'the' in Arabic – *al* (before certain consonants, it modifies. In Arabic, Saladin's name is Salah ad-Din – 'righteousness of the faith'. Here, 'al' has been modified to 'ad' before the 'd' of Din), but in Morocco *el* is more commonly used. In Moroccan Arabic, the pronunciation is such that the initial 'a' or 'e' is hardly heard at all, and many language guides simply prefix words with 'l' to indicate this.

The letters 'q' and 'k' have long been a problem, and have been interchanged willy-nilly in transliteration. For a long time, Iraq (which in Arabic is spelled with what can only be described as its nearest equivalent to the English 'q') was written, even by scholars, 'Irak'. Another example of an Arabic 'q' receiving this kind of treatment is the word for market, 'souq' (often written as 'souk').

The word for castle or palace, *qasr*, is another example. In fact, the most common transliteration for it in Morocco is *ksar*, reflecting local pronunciation. The plural *qusour* is usually given as *ksour*.

It may be useful, especially to travellers who have been elsewhere in the Arab world and become accustomed to certain transliterations, to consult the following list of common sounds and words and their 'standardised' equivalents:

ou as in oued; it is the French equivalent of **w** in wadi (a usually dry, seasonal river bed). You may see references to the Alaouites (the dynasty of Hassan II) or, alternatively, to the Alawites. The name Daoud can also be written Dawud.

dj as in djebel; it is the French equivalent of simple **j** in jebel – mountain.

k often corresponds to the Arabic letter qaf, or the English **q**. Ksar versus qasr (castle) is an example.

e often appears where some would prefer to see an **a**. Vowels in Arabic are not as important as in other languages. Vowel and consonant order are sometimes at variance. The common word for school, hich also refers to older religious learning institutions, is madrassa, which most commonly appears as medersa.

Speaking Arabic When Arabic speakers meet, they often exchange more extensive and formalised greetings than Westerners are used to. How and when they are used varies from country to country, time to time and depends often on the social status of the people concerned. Even an attempt to use a couple of them (whether correctly or not) will not go astray. As in all the Arabic vocabulary in this section, some expressions tend to be more standard than Moroccan Arabic, but will be understood and often used. Occasionally both MSA and Moroccan versions are given. (The Moroccan version is followed by (M).)

When addressing a man or woman, the polite terms more or less equivalent to Mr and Mrs or Ms are *Si* or *Sidi* and *Lalla*, followed by the first name. You may be addressed as 'Mr John' or 'Mrs Anne'. A few basic greetings follow:

Greetings & Civilities

Hello (literally, 'peace upon you').	*as-salaam 'alaykum*
Hello (in response – 'and upon you be peace').	*wa 'alaykum as-salaam*
Goodbye ('go in safety').	*ma' as-salaama*
Good morning.	*sabaH al-khēr*
Good morning (in response).	*sabaH an-nūr*
Good evening.	*masa' al-khēr*
Good evening (in response).	*masa' an-nūr*
Please.	*'afak/'afik/'afakum* (to m/f/pl)
Thank you (very much).	*shukran (jazilan)*
You're welcome.	*la shukran 'ala wajib*
Yes.	*eeyeh/na'am*
Yes, OK.	*wakha* (M)
No.	*la*
No, thank you.	*la, shukran*
Excuse me.	*smeH leeya*
How are you?	*kayf Haalek? la bas?* (M)
Fine, thank you.	*la bas, barak Allah feek* (M)
Fine, thanks be to God.	*bikhēr, al-Hamdu lillah*

Essentials Here are some nuts and bolts to get you through the simple encounters:

I	*ana*
you	*inta/inti/intum* (m/f/pl)
he/she	*huwa/heeya*
we	*eHna*
they	*huma*
Why?	*laysh?*
now	*allaan/daba* (M)
Is there...?	*wash kayn...?* (M)
big/small	*kabeer/sagheer*
open	*meHlool*
Do you speak English?	*tatakallem ingleezee? wash kt'aref ngleezeeya?* (M)
Who is that?	*meen hadha? shkoon had?* (M)
I understand.	*fhemt*
I don't understand.	*ma fhemtesh*
Go ahead, move it, come on!	*zid!* (M)

Emergencies

Call the police!	*'eyyet al-bolis!*
Call a doctor!	*'eyyet at-tabeeb!*
Help me please!	*'awenee 'afak!*
Thief!	*sheffar!*
They robbed me!	*sheffaroonee!*

Small Talk

What's your name?	*asmeetak?*
My name is...	*ismee... smeetee...*(M)
How old are you?	*shaHak fi 'amrak?*
I'm 25.	*'aandee khamsa wa 'ashreen*
Where are you from?	*min een inta/inti/intum?* (m/f/pl)
I/We are from...	*ana/eHna min...*
America	*amreeka*
Australia	*ustralya*
Canada	*kanada*
England	*inglaterra*
France	*fransa*
Germany	*almanya*
Italy	*itaaliyya*

Japan	*al-yaban*	How many buses per day go to...?	
Netherlands	*holanda*	*fi/kayn kam kar kul yūm ila...?*	
Spain	*isbanya*	Please tell me when we arrive...	
Sweden	*as-sweed*	*qulnee emta nassil...*	
Switzerland	*sweesra*	Stop here, please.	
		qif hena, 'afak	

I am...	*ana...*	Please wait for me.	
American	*amreekanee* (m)	*intazarnee 'afak*	
	amreekaniyya (f)	May I/we sit here?	
Australian	*ustralee* (m)	*(wash) yimkin ajlis/najlis hena?*	
	ustraliyya (f)	Where can I rent a bicycle?	
British	*britaanee* (m)	*fein yimkin ana akra beshkleeta?*	
	britaaniyya (f)		
French	*fransee* (m)	address	*anwān*
	fransiyya (f)	air-conditioning	*kleemateezaseeyon*
Swedish	*sweedee* (m)	airport	*matār*
	sweediyya (f)	camel	*jamal*

Getting Around

I want to go to...		car	*tomobeel, sayara*
ureed/bgheet amshee ila...		crowded	*zHam*
What is the fare to...?		daily	*kull yūm*
bshaHal at-tazkara ila...?		donkey	*Humār*
When does the...leave/arrive?		horse	*Husān*
emta qiyam/wusuul...?		number	*raqm*
bus	*al-otobīs*	ticket	*werqa, tazkara*
	al-otobīsat (pl)	Wait!	*tsanna!*
intercity bus	*al-kar* (M)		
	al-keeran (pl)	**Directions**	
train	*al-qitar*	How far is...?	*kam kilo li...?*
	al-masheena (M)	left/right	*yasar/yameen*
boat	*as-safeena*		*leeser/leemen* (M)
	al-baboor (M)	here/there	*huna/hunak*
Where is (the)...?	*fein...?*	next to	*bi-janib*
bus station for...	*maHattat*	opposite	*muqabbal*
	al-otobīs li...	behind	*khalf/mor* (M)
train station	*maHattat*	Which?	*ash men?*
	al-masheena/	Where?	*fein?*
	al-qitar	north	*shamal*
ticket office	*maktab al-werqa/*	south	*janoob*
	at-tazkara	east	*sharq*
street	*az-zanqa*	west	*gharb*
city	*al-medīna*		
village	*al-qarya*	**Around Town**	
bus stop	*mawqif al-otobīs*	Where is (the)...?	*fein...?*
station	*al-maHatta*	bank	*al-banka*
		barber	*al-Hallaq*
Which bus goes to...?		beach	*ash-shaatta'*
ey kar yamshee ila...?			*al-plāẑ* (M)
Does this bus go to...?		embassy	*as-sifāra*
yamshee had al-kar ila...?		market	*as-sūq*
		mosque	*al-jāmi'*

Getting Around

Directions

Around Town

museum	*al-matHaf*
old city	*al-medīna*
palace	*al-qasr*
pharmacy	*farmasyan*
police station	*al-bolīs*
post office	*al-bōsta/maktab al-barīd*
restaurant	*al-mat'am*
university	*al-jami'a*
zoo	*Hadīqat al-Haywān*

I want to change...	*ureed/bgheet asrif...*
money	*fulūs*
US$	*dolār amreekānī*
UK	*jinay sterlīnī*
A$	*dolār ustrālī*
DM	*mārk almānī*
travellers' cheques	*shīkāt siyaHiyya*

Accommodation
Where is the hotel?
fein (kayn) al-otēl?
Can I see the room?
(wash) yimkin lee nshūf al-bayt?
How much is this room per night?
bshaHal al-bayt lilayl?
Do you have anycheaper rooms?
wash kayn bayt rakhees 'ala had?
That's too expensive.
ghaalee bazyaf
This is fine.
had mezyan

bed	*namooseeya*
blanket	*bataneeya*
camp site	*mukhaym*
full	*'amer*
hot water	*ma skhūn*
key	*saroot*
roof	*staah*
room	*bayt*
sheet	*eezar*
shower	*doosh*
toilet	*bayt al-ma, mirHad*
youth hostel	*oberẑ, dar shabbab*

Shopping
Where can I buy...?
fein yimkin ashteree...?

How much?	*bi-kam?*
	bish-hal? (M)
Too much.	*ghalee*
Do you have...?	*wash 'andkum...?*
stamps	*tawaaba*
	tanber (M)
newspaper	*al-jarida*

Time
When?	*emta?*
today	*al-yūm*
tomorrow	*ghaddan*
yesterday	*al-bareh*
morning	*fis-sabaH*
afternoon	*fish-sheeya*
evening	*masa'*
day/night	*nahar/layl*
week/month/year	*usbu'/shahr/'am*

What is the time?	*sa'a kam?*
	shahal fessa'a? (M)
At what time?	*fi sa'a kam?*
	fooqtash? (M)
after	*min ba'd*
on time	*fil-waqt*
early	*bakrī*
late	*mu'attal*
quickly	*dgheeya*
slowly	*bishwayya*

Days of the Week
Monday	*(nhar) al-itnēn*
Tuesday	*(nhar) at-talata*
Wednesday	*(nhar) al-arba'*
Thursday	*(nhar) al-khamīs*
Friday	*(nhar) al-juma'*
Saturday	*(nhar) as-sabt*
Sunday	*(nhar) al-ahad*

Months of the Year The Islamic year has 12 lunar months and is 11 days shorter than the Gregorian calendar, so important Muslim dates fall about 10 days earlier each (Western) year. It is impossible to predict exactly when they will fall, as this depends on when the new moon is sighted. The Islamic, or Hijra (referring to the year of Mohammed's flight from Mecca in 622 AD), calendar months are:

1st	*Moharram*
2nd	*Safar*
3rd	*Rabi' al-Awal*
4th	*Rabi' al-Akhir* or
	Rabi' at-Tani
5th	*Jumada al-Awal*
6th	*Jumada al-Akhir* or
	Jumada at-Taniyya
7th	*Rajab*
8th	*Sha'aban*
9th	*Ramadan*
10th	*Shawwal*
11th	*Zuul Qe'da*
12th	*Zuul Hijja*

In the Levant, in addition to the Hijra calendar, there is also another set of names for the Gregorian calendar. Luckily, in Morocco, the names of the months are virtually the same as their European counterparts and easily recognisable:

January	*yanāyir*
February	*fibrāyir*
March	*maaris*
April	*abrīl*
May	*māyu*
June	*yunyu*
July	*yulyu*
August	*aghustus/ghusht*
September	*sibtimbir/*
	shebtenber
October	*uktoobir*
November	*nufimbir/nu'enbir*
December	*disimbir/dijenbir*

Arabic Numbers Arabic numerals are simple enough to learn and, unlike the written language, run from left to right. Often you won't need to recognise the Arabic figures, as the European ones are commonly used in Morocco.

0	•	*sifr*
1	١	*wāHid*
2	٢	*itneen/jooj* (M)
3	٣	*talata*
4	٤	*arba'a*
5	٥	*khamsa*

6	٦	*sitta*
7	٧	*saba'a*
8	٨	*tamanya*
9	٩	*tissa'*
10	١٠	*'ashara*
11		*wāHidash*
12		*itna'ash*
13		*talattash*
14		*arba'atash*
15		*khamastash*
16		*sitt'ash*
17		*saba'atash*
18		*tamantash*
19		*tissa'atash*
20		*'ashreen*
21		*wāHid wa 'ashreen*
22		*itneen wa 'ashreen*
30		*talateen*
40		*arba'een*
50		*khamseen*
60		*sitteen*
70		*saba'een*
80		*tamaneen*
90		*tissa'een*
100		*miyya*
101		*miyya wa wāHid*
125		*miyya wa khamsa wa 'ashreen*
200		*miyyateen*
300		*talata mia*
400		*arba'a mia*
1000		*alf*
2000		*alfeen*
3000		*talat alāf*
4000		*arba'at alāf*

Ordinal Numbers

first	*'awwal*
second	*tānī*
third	*tālit*
fourth	*rābi'*
fifth	*khāmis*

French

The most commonly spoken European language in Morocco is French, so if the thought of getting your mind around Arabic is too much, it would be a good investment to learn some French. An inability on the part of Westerners to speak French is seen by some

French-speaking (and therefore at least bilingual) Moroccans as the height of ignorance.

The following words and phrases should help you communicate on a basic level in French:

Greetings & Civilities

Hello/Good morning/ Good day.	*Bonjour.*
Goodbye.	*Au revoir/Salut.*
Good evening.	*Bonsoir.*
(Have a) good evening.	*Bonne soirée.*
Good night.	*Bonne nuit.*
Please.	*S'il vous plaît.*
Thank you.	*Merci.*
You're welcome.	*De rien/Je vous en prie.*
Yes.	*Oui.*
No.	*Non.*
No, thank you.	*Non, merci.*
Excuse me.	*Excusez-moi/ Pardon.*
How are you?	*Comment allez-vous/Ça va?*
Well, thanks.	*Bien, merci.*

Essentials

I	*je*
you	*vous*
he/she	*il/elle*
we	*nous*
they	*ils/elles* (m/f)
Why?	*Pourquoi?*
now	*maintenant*
Is/Are there...?	*(Est-ce qu'.)il y a...?*
big/small	*grand/petit*
open/closed	*ouvert/fermé*
Do you speak English?	*Parlez-vous anglais?*
Who is that?	*C'est qui, celui-là/ celle-là?* (m/f)
I understand.	*Je comprends.*
I don't understand.	*Je ne comprends pas.*

Emergencies

Call the police!	*Appelez la police!*
Call a doctor!	*Appelez un médecin!*
Help me please!	*Au secours/Aidez-moi!*
Thief!	*(Au) voleur!*

Small Talk

What's your name?	*Comment vous appelez-vous?*
My name is...	*Je m'appelle...*
How old are you?	*Quel âge avez-vous?*
I'm 25.	*J'ai vingt-cinq ans.*
Where are you from?	*D'où êtes-vous?*
I/We are from...	*Je viens/Nous venons...*
America	*de l'Amérique*
Australia	*de l'Australie*
Canada	*du Canada*
England	*de l'Angleterre*
Germany	*de l'Allemagne*
Italy	*de l'Italie*
Japan	*du Japon*
Netherlands	*des Pays Bas*
Spain	*de l'Espagne*
Sweden	*du Suède*
Switzerland	*de la Suisse*
I am...	*Je suis...*
American	*américain/e* (m/f)
Australian	*australien/ne* (m/f)
British	*britannique* (m/f)
Swedish	*suédois/e* (m/f)

Getting Around

I want to go to...	*Je veux aller à...*
What is the fare to...?	*Combien coûte le billet pour...?*
When does the... leave/arrive?	*À quelle heure part/arrive...?*
bus	*l'autobus*
intercity bus/ coach	*le car*
train	*le train*
boat	*le bateau*
ferry	*le bac*
Where is the...?	*Où est...?*
bus station for...	*la gare routière pour...*

train station	*la gare*
ticket office	*la billeterie/le guichet*
street	*la rue*
city	*la ville*
village	*le village*
bus stop	*l'arrêt d'autobus*

Which bus goes to...?	*Quel autobus/car part pour...?*
Does this bus go to...?	*Ce car-là va-t-il à...?*
How many buses per day go to...?	*Il y a combien de cars chaque jour pour...?*
Please tell me when we arrive...	*Dîtes-moi s'il vous plaît à quelle heure on arrive...*
Stop here, please.	*Arrêtez ici, s'il vous plaît.*
Please wait for me.	*Attendez-moi ici, s'il vous plaît.*
May I sit here?	*Puis-je m'asseoir ici?*
Where can I rent a bicycle?	*Où est-ce que je peux louer une bicyclette?*

address	*adresse*
air-conditioning	*climatisation*
airport	*aéroport*
camel	*chameau*
car	*voiture*
crowded	*beaucoup de monde*
daily	*chaque jour*
donkey	*âne*
horse	*cheval*
number	*numéro*
ticket	*billet*
Wait!	*Attendez!*

Directions

How far is...?	*À combien de kilomètres est...?*
left/right	*gauche/droite*
here/there	*ici/là*
next to	*à côté de*
opposite	*en face*
behind	*derrière*
Which?	*Quel?*

Where?	*Où?*
north	*nord*
south	*sud*
east	*est*
west	*ouest*

Around Town

Where is the...?	*Où est...?*
bank	*la banque*
barber	*le coiffeur*
beach	*la plage*
embassy	*l'ambassade*
market	*le marché*
mosque	*la mosquée*
museum	*le musée*
old city	*le centre historique*
palace	*le palais*
pharmacy	*la pharmacie*
police station	*la police*
post office	*la poste*
restaurant	*le restaurant*
university	*l'université*
zoo	*le zoo*

I want to change...	*Je voudrais changer...*
money	*de l'argent*
US$	*des dollars américains*
UK	*des livres sterling*
A$	*des dollars australiens*
DM	*des marks allemands*
travellers' cheques	*des chèques de voyage*

Accommodation

Where is the hotel	*Où est l'hôtel?*
Can I see the room?	*Peux-je voir la chambre?*
How much is this room per night?	*Combien est cette chambre pour une nuit?*
Do you have any cheaper rooms?	*Avez-vous des chambres moins chères?*
That's too expensive.	*C'est trop cher.*
This is fine.	*Ça va bien.*

bed	*lit*
blanket	*couverture*
camp site	*camping*
full	*complet*
hot water	*eau chaude*
key	*clef or clé*
roof	*terrasse*
room	*chambre*
sheet	*drap*
shower	*douche*
toilet	*les toilettes*
washbasin	*lavabo*
youth hostel	*auberge de jeunesse*

Shopping

Where can I buy...?	*Où est-ce que je peux acheter...?*
How much?	*Combien?*
How much does it cost?	*Ça coûte combien?*
more/less	*plus/moins*
too much	*trop cher*
Do you have...?	*Avez-vous...?*
stamps	*des timbres*
newspaper	*un journal*

Time

When?	*Quand?*
today	*aujourd'hui*
tomorrow	*demain*
yesterday	*hier*
morning	*matin*
afternoon	*après-midi*
evening	*soir*
day/night	*jour/nuit*
week/month/year	*semaine/mois/an*

What is the time?	*Quelle heure est-il?*
At what time?	*À quelle heure?*
after	*après*
on time	*à l'heure*
early	*tôt*
late	*tard*
quickly	*vite*
slowly	*lentement*

Days of the Week

Monday	*lundi*
Tuesday	*mardi*
Wednesday	*mercredi*
Thursday	*jeudi*
Friday	*vendredi*
Saturday	*samedi*
Sunday	*dimanche*

Months of the Year

January	*janvier*
February	*février*
March	*mars*
April	*avril*
May	*mai*
June	*juin*
July	*juillet*
August	*août*
September	*septembre*
October	*octobre*
November	*novembre*
December	*décembre*

Numbers

0	*zéro*
1	*un*
2	*deux*
3	*trois*
4	*quatre*
5	*cinq*
6	*six*
7	*sept*
8	*huit*
9	*neuf*
10	*dix*
11	*onze*
12	*douze*
13	*treize*
14	*quatorze*
15	*quinze*
16	*seize*
17	*dix-sept*
18	*dix-huit*
19	*dix-neuf*
20	*vingt*
21	*vingt-et-un*
22	*vingt-deux*
30	*trente*
40	*quarante*
50	*cinquante*
60	*soixante*

70	*soixante-dix*
80	*quatre-vingts*
90	*quatre-vingt-dix*
100	*cent*
101	*cent un*
125	*cent vingt-cinq*
200	*deux cents*
300	*trois cents*
400	*quatre cents*
1000	*mille*
2000	*deux milles*
3000	*trois milles*
4000	*quatre milles*

Ordinal Numbers

first	*premier*
second	*deuxième*
third	*troisième*
fourth	*quatrième*
fifth	*cinquième*

Berber

There are three main dialects commonly delineated among the speakers of Berber, which in a certain sense also serve as loose lines of ethnic demarcation. In the north, centred on the Rif, the locals speak a dialect which has been called Riffian and is spoken as far south as Figuig on the Algerian frontier.

The dialect that predominates in the Middle and High Atlas and the valleys leading into the Sahara goes by various names, including Braber or Amazigh. More settled tribes of the High Atlas, Anti-Atlas, Souss Valley and south-western oases generally speak Chleuh, or Tashelhit.

Body Language

One of the most common sounds you will probably hear coming from the mouths of Moroccans will be a hiss. This is an all-purpose noise that can easily get on a newcomer's nerves. It is perhaps most commonly used by people riding bicycles or pushing carts to warn people to move out of the way; you will also often here the word *ba'alak!*, which means the same thing. A hiss can also simply be a means of getting your attention. Sometimes there is little doubt that it is the equivalent of the wolf whistle.

When well-acquainted people meet on the street, they will often shake hands and then fleetingly kiss the back of their fingers. It is not recommended you try this one out for yourself, as it requires a depth of acquaintance travellers are unlikely to build up with locals.

If someone draws a finger up and down their chin while trying to explain something to you, they are almost certainly telling you something about Berbers (nine times out of 10 it'll be some fellow telling you there is a Berber market on today, and that this is the only chance you'll have to see it – a tale not to be believed). ■

Facts for the Visitor

VISAS & EMBASSIES

Most visitors to Morocco require no visa and are granted leave to remain in Morocco for 90 days on entry. Exceptions to this rule include nationals of the Benelux countries (Holland, Belgium and Luxembourg) and South Africa, who can apply for a one-month single-entry visa (UK£4.20) or a three-month double-entry visa (UK£7).

Holders of British Visitors passports should note that the Moroccan authorities do *not* accept them.

The position of Israelis is, to say the least, anomalous. If the momentum towards a comprehensive peace between Israel and the Arab countries continues, all could soon change, and in late 1993 Israeli tour operators visited Morocco to look at the possibilities of doing business there. For the moment, the Moroccan consulate in M laga, southern Spain, seems to handle many of the visas requested by Israelis (about 5000 a year), generally of Moroccan origin. The process can be complicated, and the visa costs US$50. Despite the official position denying entry to those with Israeli stamps in their passports, the reality seems lax in this regard.

People requiring a visa who are contemplating travelling to and fro between Morocco and, say, Spain or Algeria, should consider getting a double-entry visa to avoid the hassle of applying for new visas. If you have to get a visa, you will need to fill in up to four forms and provide four photos. In Europe it generally takes one to two days to issue the visas.

In Spain, visas are available at consulates in Madrid, Barcelona, M laga and Las Palmas de Gran Canaria. A visa valid for one month in Morocco costs about 900 pta (Dr 60) and can be issued in 24 hours.

In Algeria, it is possible to get a Moroccan visa at Morocco's consulates in Algiers or Oran.

Children under the age of 12 must have their photo attached to their parents' passports if they do not carry their own.

Nationals of the following 10 European countries going on *organised* tours to Morocco only need their national identity cards to enter: Austria, Denmark, Finland, France, Germany, Iceland, Norway, Spain, Sweden and Switzerland.

Moroccan Embassies

Moroccan embassies and consulates can be found in the following countries:

Algeria
Embassy: 8 Rue des Cèdres, Parc de la Reine, Algiers (☎ 02-607737, 607408)
Consulates: 5 Ave de l'ANP, Sidi Bel Abbès, Algiers (☎ 02-243470)
26 Rue Cheikh Larbi Tebessi, Oran (☎ 06-333684)

Australia
Consulate: Suite 2, 11 West St, North Sydney, NSW 2060 (☎ 02-922 4999, 957 6717)

Canada
Embassy: 38 Range Rd, Ottawa KIN 8J4 Ontario (☎ 416-236 7391/2)
Consulate: 1010 Rue Sherbrooke West, Suite 1510, Montreal H3A 2R7 (☎ 514-288 8750, 288 6951)

Egypt
10 Sharia Salah ad-Din, Zamalek, Cairo (☎ 02-340 9677, 340 9849)

France
Embassy: 5 Rue Le Tasse, Paris 75016 (☎ 1-45.20.69.35)
Consulate: 19 Rue Sauliner, Paris 75009 (☎ 1-45.23.37.40)

Germany
Embassy: Goten Strasse 7-9, 5300 Bonn - Bad Godesberg (☎ 228-355044/5/6)
Consulate: Wiesenhuttenplatz 26, 6000 Frankfurt/Main (☎ 69-231737)

Japan
3-16-3, Sendagaya Shibuya-ku, Tokyo 151 (☎ 03-478 3271/2/3/4)

Libya
Embassy: Blvd Ben Achour, BP 908, Tripoli (☎ 021-600110, 021-601102)
Consulate: Madinat al-Hadaiq, Sharia Bashir Ibrahimi, Tripoli (☎ 021-34239, 021-41346)

Mauritania
    Tevragh Zeina 634, BP 621, Nouakchott (☎ 02-51411)
Netherlands
    Embassy: Oranjestraat 9, 2514 JB, The Hague (☎ 070-346 6917)
    Consulate: Oranje Nassaulan 1, 1075 AH Amsterdam (☎ 020-736215/6)
Portugal
    Rua Borges Carneiro 32, 1200 Lisbon (☎ 01-679193/4)
Spain
    Embassy: Calle Serrano 179, Madrid 2 (☎ 91-563 1090/150)
    Consulates: Calle Leizaran 31, 28002 Madrid (☎ 91-561-2145)
    Rambla de Cataluña 78, Barcelona 08008 (☎ 93-215 3470/4)
    Ave de Andalucia 15, M laga 29002 (☎ 95-329950/62)
    Ave Jose Mesa Y Lopez 8, Las Palmas de Gran Canaria (☎ 928-262859, 928-268850)
Tunisia
    Embassy: 39 Rue du 1er Juin, Mutuelleville, Tunis (☎ 01-782775)
    Consulate: 26 Rue Ibn Mandhour, Notre Dame, Mutuelleville, Tunis (☎ 01-283492)
UK
    Embassy: 49 Queen's Gate Gardens, London SW7 5NE (☎ 0171-581 5001)
    Consulate (visas): 97-99 Praed St Paddington, London SW2 (☎ 0171-724 0719)
USA
    Embassy: 1601 21st St NW, Washington DC 20009 (☎ 202-462 7979)
    Consulates: 767 Third Avenue, 30th floor, New York, NY 10017 (☎ 212-421 1580)
    437 Fifth Avenue, New York, NY 10016 (☎ 212-758 2625)

Visa Extensions

Should the 90 days most tourists are entitled to in Morocco be insufficient, it is possible to apply for an extension or even for residence, although the latter process is far from straightforward. It is probably easiest to leave the country and re-enter after a few days. Your chances improve if you enter by a different route the second time around.

People on visas, however, may prefer to try for the extension. Go to the Sûreté Nationale office in Rabat (off Ave Mohammed V) with your passport, a photo, a form (which you'll need to pick up beforehand at the same office) and a letter from your embassy requesting a visa extension on your

behalf. The entrance is round the back and you'll have to queue at a tiny booth just inside. With luck, it will take a maximum of three days to process.

Should this fail, or should you want to get residence, you will have to go to the Bureau des Étrangers of the police headquarters (Préfecture de Police) in the town you're in. You may well have to go to Rabat. The process is long and involves opening bank accounts, producing proof of your capacity to support yourself and reasons for staying – good luck.

Foreign Embassies in Morocco

Foreign embassies are concentrated in the capital, Rabat. In some cases the embassies do not deal with consular activities, or have separate consular offices elsewhere in the city. In addition, many countries have consulates and vice-consulates in other parts of the country (particularly Casablanca, and to a lesser extent in Tangier, Agadir, Oujda, Fès and Marrakesh). All are listed under the appropriate city or town entry. Visa information for various countries appears in the Rabat section (with the exception of Senegal, for which see Casablanca).

Visas for Ceuta & Melilla

These two enclaves are Spanish territory, so anyone requiring a visa to enter Spain will need one to get into the enclaves too. For more details on who needs visas and other requirements, see Foreign Embassies under the Information section of the Rabat chapter.

DOCUMENTS
Driving Licences

Although technically you need an International Driving Permit to drive in Morocco, most national licences are recognised. If bringing your own car, you will need all the appropriate documentation, including a Green Card (for details see the Getting There & Away chapter).

Hunting Licences

Morocco's hunting season lasts about nine months, but to engage in the sport you'll generally have to go with an organised group and you will require a local hunting licence.

Hostel & Student Cards
You can stay at most hostels without a membership card, usually for a couple of dirham extra. International student cards do not seem to open many magic doors (eg in museums and the like) in Morocco, although they may be useful for purchasing flight tickets out.

CUSTOMS
The importation or exportation of Moroccan currency is prohibited, but any amount of foreign currency, cash or cheques, may be brought into the country. Hang on to any exchange receipts as you will need them to re-exchange leftover dirhams on the way out of Morocco, which *is* possible (and with the receipts should be straightforward), in spite of what some Bank al-Maghrib employees may tell you (see Re-exchange).

Visitors are permitted to import up to 200 cigarettes and a litre of spirits. A *Customs Guide for Tourists* is supposedly, but not always, available from ONMT offices and consulates.

MONEY
A combination of cash, travellers' cheques and credit cards (particularly Visa and MasterCard) will give you several options and reduce the risk of being stranded should you lose one or the other.

Most hard currencies are readily accepted, but the Irish punt and Australian and New Zealand dollars are often refused. This goes for cash and cheques. Most banks do not charge a commission for changing cheques, but one that does is the Banque Marocaine du Commerce Extérieur (BMCE). They ask Dr 4.20 per cheque, which is deadly for small denomination cheques – try another bank.

Cash advances on credit cards and automatic teller machine (ATM) transactions generally carry a handling charge of about 1.5%, which is deducted from your account in addition to the amount you request.

You can also cash Eurocheques or international postal cheques in Morocco.

Currency
The Moroccan currency is the dirham (Dr), which is divided into 100 centimes. You will find notes in denominations of Dr 5, 10, 50 and 100 and coins of 1, 2, 5 (these are becoming a little on the rare side), 10, 20 and 50 centimes as well as Dr 1.

This sounds quite straightforward, but when dealing with shopkeepers you may come up against some local usages that could throw you. You will almost never hear the word 'centime', as more often than not prices are quoted in francs, an anachronism from the days of the French protectorate. A thousand francs is Dr 10 – so if you are told what sounds an outrageous amount for a bag of fruit, it might be an idea to ask if they mean francs, although often enough shopkeepers will 'convert' their price to dirhams for confused foreigners. Another unit sometimes used is the rial. It is especially common in the south, where 200 rials equals Dr 1. Elsewhere, a rial can refer to 20 or even 50 centimes.

Exchange Rates

AD100	=	Dr 21.08 (Algeria)
A$1	=	Dr 6.67
C$1	=	Dr 6.41
1FF	=	Dr 1.64
DM1	=	Dr 5.64
¥100	=	Dr 8.93
NZ$1	=	Dr 5.48
100 pta	=	Dr 6.78
UK£1	=	Dr 13.77
US$1	=	Dr 8.80

Changing Money
Banks You have a choice of banks where you can change money in Morocco, and generally it is a quick and efficient process. The currency, although not yet fully convertible, operates in a largely free market, virtually eliminating any black market. Rates vary little from bank to bank, but it

can't hurt to look around. Remember to have your passport, as you will need it to change travellers' cheques and get cash advances, and some banks will even want to see it when you change cash.

Probably the best of the banks is the BMCE. In the bigger cities, it usually has one branch with an out-of-office-hours change office where you can change cash or cheques or get a cash advance. In addition, the BMCE has the most widespread and reliable network of ATMs (guichets automatiques) allowing international transactions on Visa and MasterCard. The worst of the banks is the state Bank al-Maghrib (also known as Banque du Maroc), which appears to be stuck in the Stone Age and takes an eternity to process the simplest requests.

Other reasonable banks include the BMCI (Banque Marocaine pour le Commerce et l'Industrie), Banque Populaire (often the only bank to be found in southern towns), Uniban, Interbank. Exchanging cash and cheques is straightforward, and main branches of these banks can usually give cash advances on Visa and MasterCard. Computerisation ensures that this is a relatively quick operation.

Travellers' Cheques Travellers' cheques are not always accepted by banks advertising exchange facilities, though generally there is no problem. Apart from those already listed, banks that accept cheques include the Banque Marocaine pour l'Afrique et l'Orient, the Banque Crédit du Maroc and the Société Générale Marocaine de Banques. Some of these will ask you to show your travellers' cheque receipts, which of course you are supposed to keep separate from the cheques in case of loss. This argument seems lost on those bank employees who ask to see them, so go elsewhere if you strike this gratuitous irritation.

The best travellers' cheques to carry are American Express, if only because they have four branches in Morocco. They are represented by Voyages Schwartz SA at the following locations at:

87 Place du Marché Municipal (Mopatours office), Agadir (☎ 841082; fax 841066)
112 Ave Prince Moulay Abdallah, Casablanca (☎ 222946/7)
Immeuble Moutaouakil, 1 Rue Mauritania, Marrakesh (☎ 436600/3)
54 Blvd Pasteur, Tangier (☎ 933459/71)

Thomas Cook has just the one office in Morocco, care of KTI Voyages (☎ 398572/3/4; fax 398567), 4 Rue des Hirondelles, Casablanca.

Credit Cards As already noted, you can get cash advances on Visa and MasterCard, in various banks, especially the BMCE, which also has a wide network of ATMs. Most of the networks run by other banks are no good for foreign cards, but occasional exceptions to this rule are the BMCI's more modern branches.

Other banks where you can get cash advances on credit cards (although usually only at their main branches) include the Banque Populaire, Uniban and Interbank. As most of the banks are computerised, it usually takes little time to process cash advances. Any limits generally depend on the conditions attached to your particular card, although Dr 6000 seems to be the ceiling. The daily ATM limit on most cards is Dr 4000.

In addition to Visa and MasterCard, Access, Eurocard and a couple of others are accepted by many of the bigger hotels, restaurants and shops for payment of bills and purchases. Keep your eyes open, as some shopkeepers in particular like to whack on commissions of up to 5% which they claim are imposed on them by banks. Generally you're better off withdrawing money on a debit card or a credit card (that has been left in credit) and paying in cash.

Eurocheques Eurocheques up to a daily limit of Dr 2000 can be cashed at some banks. BMCE and Wafabank do this and take no commission.

Giros If you have a Giro or other postal account and can have international postal cheques issued on it, these can be changed in the main post offices. It seems few foreigners do so, so you may encounter some surprise if you ask.

Cash In more out-of-way places, particularly if you intend to spend a lot of time trekking in remote reaches of the Atlas Mountains, you should keep a reasonable supply of cash (local and your own) to cover you until you reach a decent-sized town again.

Changing Money on Arrival Nobody has anything good to say about changing money at airports. Even at the main Mohammed V gateway outside Casablanca, the two BMCE branches are notoriously slow and sometimes closed. They have ATMs too, but you can't always rely on them (this goes for ATMs all over the country).

Arriving from or heading for the enclaves of Ceuta and Melilla, the Moroccan banks on the border change *cash* only. The same goes for Algeria. It is difficult to obtain Moroccan currency in mainland Spain and not worth the effort. The banks in Melilla and Ceuta, however, deal in dirham at inferior rates (if you want to cash in dirham) to those in Morocco. Another option in the enclaves and on the borders is the black market (see below) – check the bank rates first, which are usually just as good.

Coming from Algeria, there is a bank in Figuig and plenty of banks and black marketeers in Oujda.

Re-Exchange

As importing and exporting Moroccan currency is illegal (though it's unlikely anyone will bother you if you take out a little as a souvenir), the best thing is to wind down to nothing as you approach the end of your trip.

Should you find yourself stuck with unseemly amounts of the stuff when you're about to leave, you can change it for hard currency at most Moroccan banks (including on the borders and at the airports) if you can present bank receipts proving exchange in Morocco – so hang on to these as you go.

Cash advance slips on credit cards should be sufficient, but you may have trouble with receipts issued by ATMs.

You can change dirhams for pesetas at banks in Ceuta and Melilla, but the rates are inferior to those in Morocco.

Black Market

The near convertibility of the dirham leaves little room for a black market, but you will find people in the streets asking if you want to exchange money, especially in Tangier and Casablanca. There is no monetary benefit to be had from such transactions, and unless you are desperate for cash when the banks are closed, it is wiser to avoid these characters.

There is also a frontier black market. You will find plenty of Moroccans dealing in dirhams and hard currencies on the Ceuta frontier and inside the Melilla enclave. In Ceuta itself and on the actual Melilla border there seems to be less activity.

Check bank rates before dealing with black marketeers. In Melilla, ignore the stories about disastrous bank rates and huge commissions – check the exact details with a bank first and then see what the street dealers have to say.

In Oujda and Figuig it is possible to buy and sell Algerian dinar for dirhams (in Oujda, you can also get hard currency). Discretion is the word, although the authorities seem to turn a blind eye to such transactions. When dealing in dinar, shop around before concluding an exchange. You can get dinar in Melilla too, though the rates are unlikely to be as good as in the two Moroccan frontier towns.

Costs

Although not the cheapest of all possible destinations, travellers coming to Morocco from, say, Spain will be pleasantly surprised. Those hoping to push their money furthest should, if they are willing to stick to the very bottom rung of hotels, a fairly monotonous diet and local transport, be able to get by on the equivalent of about US$15 to US$20 a day. For a few comforts, the odd taxi and a more varied diet, count on paying US$30 to US$40.

The following prices will give you some idea of what to expect. A bed in the cheapest pensions costs from about Dr 30 up. Fairly decent sandwiches and stall food can provide filling meals for as little as Dr 10, although a full sit-down meal in the lower-end restaurants will normally come to more like Dr 50. A kg of apples can cost anything from Dr 6 to Dr 13, and a kg of bananas about Dr 10.

A pot of tea in a normal *salon de thé* (tea shop or café) is worth Dr 2 to Dr 3. In similar places at the heart of tourist centres like the Djemaa el-Fna in Marrakesh, you're more likely to be looking at Dr 4 for a glass of mint tea so weak it's doubtful they put any tea in! Coffee tends to be a little more expensive. One litre of bottled water in the shops is about Dr 4. A 500 ml bottle of Coca Cola will set you back around Dr 5. Juice stands can be good value – a big freshly squeezed orange juice goes for as little as Dr 3.

Beer is not cheap. The two main local brands, Flag Spéciale and Stork, cost about Dr 12 and Dr 15 respectively in restaurants and bars. They are cheaper in liquor stores (about Dr 6 to Dr 8). Local wines, too, are much cheaper in liquor stores, where you'll pay from Dr 28 to Dr 35 for a decent drop that could easily cost you Dr 80 in a restaurant.

A packet of American contraband cigarettes will go for Dr 18 to Dr 22. You can, as many locals do, buy them one at a time for Dr 1. Local brands, such as Marquise, cost Dr 10 for 20.

Although you can buy many foreign newspapers and magazines in the bigger cities, they are not cheap; papers often start at more than Dr 20. The exception is the French press, which costs pretty much what it does in France and generally arrives on the same day. *Le Monde* costs Dr 8. Oddly, the Spanish press is usually days old and quite expensive, despite the country's proximity.

Practically all museums and monuments charge a standard Dr 10 entry charge. At about US$1, this is quite reasonable.

Tipping

Restaurant waiters generally expect a tip *(baksheesh)* – 10% is an unwritten rule in the swisher spots, although a dirham or two will do in smaller places such as cafés. If it's just a tea or coffee you've had, you're hardly going to cause a scandal if you leave nothing at all.

A whole range of other services, some of which you may not consider as such or even want, are also performed with the object of getting a tip. Hotel porters, museum guides and, of course, the hosts of hustlers hoping to guide you to shops, hotels, restaurants and bus stops also expect compensation.

You should not feel obliged to part with your change at the drop of a hat, but it is worth judging each situation on its merits. Bear in mind that this is how a lot of people make a living, and the exchange of small amounts of money to oil human affairs is a long-established tradition. On the other hand, aggressive hustling should not, if it can be helped, be rewarded. Parting with money left and right will probably ease your way, but it's this very attitude that has allowed the hustling scene to become such a phenomenon. For more on that subject, see Dangers & Annoyances.

Bargaining

Some people love it, others hate it, but whatever your view, bargaining is an integral part of Morocco's commercial culture. Those who have travelled elsewhere in the Arab world will be little enough surprised by this, and of course the sparring is at its toughest in the heavily touristed cities. This applies mainly to the souqs. With hotels, restaurants and transport fixed prices generally apply; taxis can be an exception to the rule.

Just about everyone has a personal modus operandi for dealing with merchants. The best advice is to enter into the spirit of the thing. By not bargaining where it is expected, you almost seem to rob the vendor of one of the pleasures of the trade (and yourself of cash).

When on the hunt for souvenirs and the

like, look around, indulge in the banter over prices and get a feel for what people are asking. You'll be invited for tea and countless samples of their wares will be laid out before you, along with countless reasons for buying them. Despite this or the sometimes overbearing tactics of some less scrupulous shopkeepers, there's never an obligation to buy. Let the salesperson give a price and then offer as little as one-tenth. Feign only mild interest in the item and be prepared to walk off as you haggle. If that fails, and you don't want to meet the vendor's offer, you'll probably find more of what you want around the corner. If, in the end, you decide not to buy, the final tactic invariably seems to be a long face or, very infrequently, anger. The guides will be as much a part of this game as the shopkeepers because the result is just as important to them. It can be a time-consuming process, but that is part of its charm – it's not a trip to your local department store.

Never embark on a discussion of prices if you are not really interested, as Moroccans attach a good deal of importance to your last word. If they accept one you name, they can get quite shirty if you turn around and say you're not interested.

Do not allow yourself to be intimidated into buying anything you don't want at a price you don't like. Whatever they tell you, no one can *make* you buy.

You may not have to part with any money at all. A lot of Western goods, such as decent jeans and printed T-shirts, can easily be traded against local products. It'll be up to you how much worth you attach to whatever you're trading and haggle accordingly.

Souq Survival

Bargaining in the souqs is essential, although when souvenir-hunting some Western visitors may sometimes get the impression it is a game reserved for them. Nothing could be further from the truth, as the following extract from *La Boîte à Merveilles*, by the Fès author Ahmed Sefrioui, demonstrates. Some of the merchant's lines may ring a bell, and the purchaser's replies are a neat introduction to basic souq survival tactics:

The shopkeeper asked: 'So you like this vest, Madame?'
'That depends entirely on how much it costs,' my mother replied.
'Ah well, in that case I'll start wrapping it up right away. I'm always happy to give serious customers a discount. Now this vest usually sells for five rials, but I'll let you have it for just four.'
'Let's cut out all the chitchat – I'll give you two rials.'
'You're offering less than what it cost me to buy it in the first place, I swear. I can't possibly let you have it for that price – I'd have to go begging in the streets tonight to feed my children.'
The shopkeeper had finished carefully folding up the vest and was looking for a sheet of paper to wrap it in.
'Listen,' said my mother, 'I've got kids and things to do at home; I haven't got time to hang around here bargaining with you. Would you let me have the vest for two and a quarter rials? I'm ready to make a sacrifice for my son, who would like so much to wear this on the day of Achoura.'
'I like the lad, so I'll make every effort for his sake – give me three and a half rials.' The shopkeeper held out his hand for the money, but my mother turned around, took me by the hand and started to walk off.
'Come on,' she said. 'There are plenty of vests in the Qissaria. We'll soon find a shopkeeper who talks sense.'
The shopkeeper cried out: 'Come back Madame! Do come back! Your son likes this vest ... take it ... pay me what you think is fair ...'
She pulled out two and a half rials, which she handed to the shopkeeper without a word. Not waiting long enough to hear his protests, she seized the package and dragged me off.

Translated from the French by Damien Simonis
Copyright Éditions du Seuil (1978)

Guides & Hustlers

More will be said about these chaps below, but on the subject of money, official guides will generally charge between Dr 30 and Dr 50 for a 'half-day'. It is as well to plan carefully where you want these people to take you and make sure they know their wage depends on their fulfilling their half of the bargain. The unofficial guides will often do the same for less, and can be OK. The same rules apply, and unfortunately sometimes you will get a bad one. A few dirhams will suffice if you want to be guided to a specific location (like a medina exit). Whatever you give, you'll sometimes get the you-can't-possibly-be-serious look. The best reply is the I've-just-paid-you-well-over-the-odds look.

Begging

Whatever advances Morocco may be making economically, great chunks of the population are still being left behind, and social security is an empty phrase here.

Although it is noticeable that well-heeled Moroccans are not always so willing to part with donations, it is hard to find a reason for not giving the elderly and infirm something. It is difficult to recommend giving children money; if they make a living out of begging now, they may have little incentive to stop later on.

WHEN TO GO

The most pleasant seasons to explore Morocco are spring (April to May) and autumn (September to October). Midsummer can be very pleasant on the coast but viciously hot in the interior. Likewise, winter can be idyllic in Marrakesh and farther south during the day, but you can be chilled to the bone at night. Do not underestimate the possible extremes of heat in the summer and cold in the winter, particularly in the High Atlas, of which some peaks are snow-capped up to six months of the year. Along the north coast and in the Rif Mountains, it can get cold and is frequently wet and cloudy in winter. If you want weather information, you can call ☎ 364242 in Casablanca.

WHAT TO BRING

Bring the minimum. There is nothing worse than having to lug loads of excess stuff around, so unless it's essential, leave it at home.

A backpack is far more practical than an overnight bag and more likely to stand up to the rigours of Moroccan travel. It is worth paying for a good one, as buckles and straps soon start falling off cheap backpacks. One of the best stockists in London is the YHA Adventure Centre, 14 Southampton St, London WC2.

For most of the year, a hat, sunglasses and sunscreen are useful to have, and in summer a must, particularly if you intend to spend any time in the desert. If you plan to hike in the Atlas Mountains, sturdy walking boots, a water bottle, and purification tablets or tincture of iodine are useful. You could well have to sleep out, so a sleeping bag and groundsheet are worth considering. It gets chilly in the mountains even in summer, so bring a warm jacket. In winter it can get particularly cold, and serious trekking above the snow level requires more specialised equipment. In winter it can get quite wet, so some kind of rainproof clothing is a good idea, and virtually essential if you're trekking in the mountains. You can also get waterproof covers to stick over your backpack.

For more detailed information, see the section on High Atlas Trekking.

Other handy items include a Swiss army knife, a universal sink plug (a tennis ball cut in half will often do the trick), a torch (flashlight), a few metres of nylon cord, earplugs (for successful sleeping in the noisier cheapies), a small sewing kit and a medical kit (see the Health section). Condoms, the pill and other contraceptives are available in the big cities. As a rule, however, you are better off bringing your own contraceptives – especially the pill, as you may well be unable to get hold of the appropriate dosage once in

Morocco. You should also bring any special medication.

SUGGESTED ITINERARIES

For those with limited time or resources, it is quite possible to map out itineraries taking in a selection of sights that are tailored to your interests. What follows are two suggested routes, but obviously there are plenty of possible combinations.

The Imperial Cities

For the history buff and urban creature, a tour of the Imperial Cities can be accomplished in pretty quick time if necessary, although you should set aside about two weeks to do them any justice. Equally, you could spend several weeks exploring the four great capitals of Morocco and some of the surrounding country.

If you arrive in Morocco by air, you could easily begin in **Marrakesh**. There are quite a few direct charter flights from European capitals; alternatively, the southernmost of the imperial cities is about four to five hours from Casablanca by bus or train. From here you can take a bus north to **Fès**, which is the longest stretch on such a circuit (up to 10 hours on the road). From Fès it is a short hop (less than an hour by train) to Morocco's 'Versailles' (a slightly hyperbolic description, but a common enough one): **Meknès**. While you're here, a recommended day trip would be to the best preserved site of Roman occupation in Morocco, **Volubilis**, which lies only about 33 km to the north.

To complete the circuit, and to wind down from some of the inevitable pressures of being in the main tourist honey pots, you can push on to **Rabat** (three to four hours by rail or road) and neighbouring **Salé**, where you can savour the pleasure of exploring a handful of monuments and modest medinas with virtually no hassle whatsoever. From Rabat you can go directly to the Mohammed V international airport south of Casablanca by shuttle bus or train, or head north to Tangier and across the Strait of Gibraltar to Spain.

For those coming down Spain, the obvious tack is to start with Meknès, and then loop around to Marrakesh via Fès, before making the trip back north via Rabat. The entire train journey time from Marrakesh to Tangier is 10 to 12 hours, so a couple of days in Rabat along the way would break it up nicely.

It is also common for travellers coming from Spain either to skip Rabat, or head there after Meknès and Fès, and pop into Casablanca for a brief visit before heading on to Marrakesh. If you have a little more time, this has the advantage of allowing you to then head south-west down the valleys towards the Sahara and finish up with a visit to Agadir or Essaouira to wind down on the Atlantic beaches.

Atlantic Coast & Southern Morocco

Starting in Tangier, those wanting to bypass the interior and keep close to the sea can quite easily make their way down the Atlantic coast, stopping in places that appeal and skipping those that don't. Although quite feasible with public transport, such a trip lends itself particularly well to those with their own vehicles. The trip as far as Agadir could be done in one week. If you want to head down to Dakhla or go inland from Agadir or Essaouira, you will need to allow two weeks.

First up from Tangier is the small town of **Asilah**, a pretty and comparatively prosperous spot featuring a small and largely Portuguese-built medina set on a broad sweep of ocean beach. Another 40 km south is **Larache**, a more derelict looking place, but with a tumbledown medina that invites exploration. The nearby attractions, about five km north, are the windswept and overgrown Roman bastion of **Lixus** and local beaches.

The next stop of interest would be **Rabat**, followed by **Casablanca**. The latter has some reasonable beaches in its southern suburbs. South-west of Casablanca is **El-Jadida** which, known as Mazagan, was the last of the Portuguese redoubts in Morocco.

A day trip from El-Jadida is another fortress town built by the Portuguese, the little visited **Azemmour**.

To proceed on to **Safi**, about 160 km farther south-west, you can either get there by public transport on the inland road, or if you have your own transport, follow the coastal road, which is a better route. The next main stop, **Essaouira** (another former Portuguese base), is one of the most popular Atlantic coast stops, with good beaches and surf, and a reasonably laid-back feel to it. From there it is another 170 km south to **Agadir**, which may be a little too much like Europe's Mediterranean resorts for some. There is nothing to stop you heading south away from the madding crowds to places like **Sidi Ifni**, **Tan Tan** and beyond into the wastes of what was known as the Spanish Sahara until 1975. The last big city on this route is Laayoune, after which it's a long and lonely 550 km south to **Dakhla**, which is great for fishing but not much else – you shouldn't have too much competition from other travellers this far down!

Alternatively, you could head inland from Essaouira or Agadir to **Taroudannt** and over the remarkable Tizi n'Test pass to Marrakesh. Although the second-largest city in Morocco may put some off with its swarms of hustlers and guides, few travellers will want to miss the chance to at least give the red city a glancing blow. From there, the obvious route would take you south-east down the Drâa Valley and to the edge of the **Sahara** via **Ouarzazate** and **Zagora**. From Ouarzazate you can also head east along the 'Route des Kasbahs', so called because of the sheer number of these fortified villages along the way. The **Dadès** and **Todra gorges** are highlights along the way to **Erfoud**. Heading north from Erfoud towards **Midelt** would complete the experience with a tour along the **Ziz Valley**.

To head out, you would then be best off making your way back to Marrakesh or even Fès and then on to your point of exit (unless of course Algeria is your next stop, in which case you'd be better off heading farther east to the pretty border post of **Figuig**).

TOURIST OFFICES
Local Tourist Offices
The Moroccans rely heavily on tourism as a source of national income, and the Office National Marocain du Tourisme (ONMT) has a network of offices throughout the country. These usually go by the name of Délégation Régionale du Tourisme. You will also occasionally find so-called *syndicats d'initiative* in some towns, although it appears these parallel offices are being wound down. The offices are sometimes quite helpful, but often simply stock standard colour brochures and little else. The addresses and telephone numbers of ONMT branches in Morocco have been listed under individual cities and towns.

Overseas Reps
The ONMT also maintains offices abroad. They generally stock glossy brochures, some tourist maps and lists of tour operators running trips to Morocco. If you get lucky, they might also have a free copy of *Maroc – Guide et Histoire*. Although hopelessly out of date, it is full of interesting bits and pieces. Copies in French and English are sporadically available in Moroccan bookshops for Dr 150 or more.

Australia
    c/-Moroccan Consulate, 11 West St, North Sydney, NSW 2060 (☎ 02-922 4999, 02-957 6717)
Canada
    2001 Rue Université, Suite 1460, Montreal H3A 2A6 (☎ 514-842 8111)
France
    161 Rue Saint Honoré, Place du Théâtre Français, 70075 Paris (☎ 1-42.60.63.50, 1-42.60.47.24)
Germany
    Graf Adolf Strasse 59, 4000 Düsseldorf 1 (☎ 211-370551/2)
Japan
    Owariya Building 4F-8, Banchi I Chome, Kandacho Chiyoda KU, Tokyo 101 (☎ 03-810 3325)
Portugal
    Rua Artilharia Un 79 85 Lisbon (☎ 01- 685871)
Spain
    Calle Quintana No 2, 28008 Madrid (☎ 91-542 7431, 91-541 2995; fax 247 0466)

UK
   205 Regent St, London W1R 7DE (☎ 0171-437 0073)
USA
   420 East 46th St, Suite 1201, New York 10017 (☎ 212-9498184; fax 9498148)

USEFUL ORGANISATIONS

The following organisations in Morocco may prove useful:

Fédération Royale Marocaine des Auberges de Jeunes
   The head office of this, the Moroccan youth hostel organisation (☎ 524698), is on Blvd Oqba ben Nafii in Meknès. There is another office in Casablanca (☎ 970952) in the Parc de la Ligue Arabe.
Division de la Cartographie
   This section of the Conservation and Topography department (☎ 705311; fax 705885), at 31 Ave Moulay Hassan in Rabat, sells detailed survey maps of interest to people doing serious hiking or travelling well off the beaten track. Maps of the most popular areas of the High Atlas can be obtained on the spot (Dr 30 a sheet); for other areas you may need your passport and an official request – the whole process can take days.
Club Alpin Français
   BP 6178, Casablanca 01 (☎ 270090; fax 297292) This organisation is useful if you want to book refuges in the High Atlas Mountains for trekking.
Fédération Royale Marocaine de Ski et Montagne
   Parc de la Ligue Arabe, BP 15899, Casablanca 01 (☎ 203798)

BUSINESS HOURS

Although a Muslim country, Morocco adheres, for business purposes, to the Western Monday-to-Friday working week. In Muslim countries, Friday is the equivalent of Sunday for Christians, and hence is usually the main day off during the week. During Ramadan, office hours are reduced.

Banks

In the bigger centres at least, banks tend to be open Monday to Thursday from 8.30 to 11.30 am and again from 2.30 to 4.30 pm. On Friday, the midday break generally runs from 11.15 am to 3 pm to take the main Friday prayers into account. These hours can vary slightly from bank to bank, but usually not more than by a quarter of an hour or so either way.

The BMCE usually maintains an exchange bureau open out of normal banking hours at its main branches in the big cities. These booths are good for exchange and cash advances on Visa and MasterCard and open from 10 am to 2 pm and 4 to 8 pm. This service usually runs seven days a week.

Offices

Government offices, should you have any need to tangle with Moroccan bureaucracy, are generally open Monday to Thursday from 8.30 am to noon and 2 to 6.30 pm. On Fridays, the midday break lasts from about 11.30 am to 3 pm. As with the banks, these times are generally adhered to in the main centres, but should be taken with a pinch of a salt.

Museums & Monuments

Most museums are closed on Tuesdays and otherwise loosely follow office hours, which means they are usually closed from about 11.30 am to 3 pm. Not all of the sights follow this rule, however. Some of the medersas (former Qur'anic schools) have the irritating habit of closing at noon on Friday and not opening again in the afternoon.

Shops & Souqs

Shops tend to be open from about 8 am to 6 pm, often closing for a couple of hours in the middle of the day, but there are no strict rules about this. Most shops apart from grocery stores and the like tend to close over the weekend. Medina souqs and produce markets in the villes nouvelles of the bigger cities tend to wind down on Thursday afternoon and are usually dead on Fridays but, again, there is no law fixing this.

Ramadan

Typically, the office working day runs from about 9 am to 3 pm during Ramadan, but this does vary.

HOLIDAYS
Secular Holidays

There are five national secular holidays:

New Year's Day	1 January
Feast of the Throne	3 March
Labour Day	1 May
Anniversary of the Green March	6 November
Independence Day	18 November

Islamic Holidays

Of more significance to the majority of people are the principal religious holidays tied to the lunar Hijra calendar. The word 'hijra' refers to the flight of the prophet Mohammed from Mecca to Medina in 622 AD, which marks the first year of the Islamic calendar (so the year 622 AD is the year 1 AH). The calendar is about 11 days shorter than the Gregorian calendar, meaning that the holidays fall on different days each year (see the table below). Although most business hours and daily life are organised around the Gregorian calendar, the religious rhythms of Muslim society are firmly tied to the lunar calendar. Predicting the exact day the holidays will begin is impossible, as this depends on when the new moon is sighted – the decision rests with the religious authorities in Fès.

Ras as-Sana This means New Year's day, and is celebrated on the first day of the Hijra calendar year, 1 Moharram.

Achoura This is a day of public mourning observed by Shiites on 10 Moharram. It commemorates the assassination of Hussein ibn Ali, the grandson of the Prophet Mohammed and pretender to the caliphate, which led to the schism between Sunnis and Shiites. For children, however, it can be a joyous occasion. They receive toys and sweets and parade through the streets to the beating of drums.

Mawlid an-Nabi This is a lesser feast celebrating the birth of the Prophet Mohammed on 12 Rabi' al-Awal. For a long time it was not celebrated at all in the Islamic world. In the Maghreb this is generally known as Mouloud.

Ramadan & 'Eid al-Fitr Most Muslims, albeit not all with equal rigour, take part in the fasting that characterises the month of Ramadan, a time when the faithful are called upon to renew their relationship with God as a community. Ramadan is the month in which the Qur'an was first revealed. From dawn until dusk, Muslims are expected to refrain from eating, drinking, smoking and sex. This can be a difficult discipline, and only people in good health are asked to participate. Those who are travelling or are engaged in exacting physical work are considered exempt. Every evening is, in a sense, a celebration. *Iftar* or *ftur*, the breaking of the day's fast, is a time of animated activity, when the people of the local community come together not only to eat and drink, but also to pray.

The Arabic for fasting is *sawm*. You may find yourself being asked *inta sa'im?* – 'Are you fasting?' – and encouraged to do so if your answer is *la, ana faatir* – 'No, I am breaking the fast'. Non-Muslims are not expected to participate, even if more pious Muslims suggest you do. Sharing the suffering involved is an important symbolic social element of Ramadan, and the peer pressure on unenthusiastic Muslims is considerable.

Restaurants and cafés that are open during the day may be harder to come by, and at any rate you should try to avoid openly flouting the fast.

Islamic Holidays

Hejira Year	New Year	Prophet's Birthday	Ramadan Begins	'Eid al-Fitr	'Eid al-Adha
1415	10.06.94	19.08.94	01.02.95	04.03.95	10.05.95
1416	31.05.95	09.08.95	22.01.96	22.02.96	29.04.96
1417	19.05.96	28.07.96	10.01.97	10.02.97	18.04.97
1418	09.05.97	18.07.97	31.12.98	31.01.98	08.04.98
1419	28.04.98	07.07.98	20.12.99	20.01.99	28.03.99
1420	17.04.99	26.06.99	–	–	–

The end of Ramadan, or more accurately the first days of the following month of Shawwal, mark the 'Eid al-Fitr, the Feast of the Breaking of the Fast (also known as the 'Eid as-Sagheer, the Small Feast), which generally lasts four or five days, during most of which just about everything grinds to a halt. This is not a good time to travel, but it can be a great experience if you are invited to share in some of the festivities with a family. It is a very family-oriented feast, much in the way Christmas is for Christians.

The Hajj & 'Eid al-Adha The fifth pillar of Islam, the sacred duty of all who can afford it, is to make the pilgrimage to Mecca – the Hajj. It can be done at any time, but at least once it should be accomplished in Zuul-Hijja, the 12th month of the Muslim year. At this time, thousands of Muslims from all over the world converge on Islam's most holy city.

The high point is the visit to the Ka'aba, the construction housing the stone of Ibrahim (Abraham) in the centre of the *haram*, the sacred area into which non-Muslims are forbidden to enter. The faithful, dressed only in a white robe, circle the Ka'aba seven times and kiss the black stone. This is one of a series of acts of devotion carried out by pilgrims.

Once great caravans set out from Cairo and Damascus, their ranks swollen by pilgrims from all over the Muslims world, to converge on Mecca amid great circumstance and fanfare. Now the national airlines of Muslim countries put on hundreds of extra flights to jet in the faithful, although many Arabs still head for the sacred city overland. Moroccans often drive or take the bus all the way across North Africa to Cairo and the Red Sea, where they take a boat to Aqaba in Jordan and then continue on into Saudi Arabia. Some get boats direct to Jeddah from Suez. It can be a long and frustrating journey.

The hajj culminates in the ritual slaughter of a lamb (in commemoration of Ibrahim's sacrifice) at Mina. This marks the end of the pilgrimage and the beginning of the 'Eid al-Adha, or Feast of the Sacrifice (also known as the 'grand feast' or 'Eid al-Kabeer). Throughout the Muslim world the act of sacrifice is repeated, and the streets of towns and cities seem to run with the blood of slaughtered sheep. The holiday runs from 10 to 13 Zuul-Hijja.

CULTURAL EVENTS
Moussems & Amouggars
Festivals are often held in honour of marabouts (local saints). Sometimes no more than an unusually lively market day, quite a few have taken on regional and even national importance. These festivals are common among the Berbers and are usually held during the summer months.

This is one of those religious frontiers where orthodoxy and local custom have met and compromised. The veneration of saints is frowned upon by orthodox Sunni Muslims, but Islam, no less than Christianity, is made up of many parts and sects (see Religion in the Facts about the Country chapter) and so such festivals, which take some of their inspiration from a mix of pre-Islamic Berber tradition and Sufi mystic thought, continue.

Wedding Procession

Some of the more excessive manifestations, such as self-mutilation while in an ecstatic trance, once not an unusual sight at such gatherings, have all but disappeared in the face of official disapproval of such 'barbarism'.

It's worth making enquiries to determine when moussems and other such festivals are due to happen. The most important, in chronological order, are as follows:

March
  Moussem of Moulay Aissa ben Driss in Beni Mellal
May
  Moussem of Moulay Abdallah ben Brahim in Ouezzane
  Fête des Roses (rose festival) at Kélâa des M'Gouna in the Dadès Valley. It is held late in the month.
  Moussem of Sidi Bou Selham south of Larache. This festival sometimes takes place in June.
  Moussem of Sidi Mohammed M'a al-'Ainin at Tan Tan is an occasion to see the so-called blue people, Moors from the Sahara. It also acts as a commercial gathering of tribes and is usually held at the end of May or in early June.
June
  National Folklore Festival in Marrakesh. This festival runs for 10 days and is held early in the month.
  Moussem at Goulimime. With its big camel market, this is as much a trade affair as a religious get-together.
  Fête des Cerises (Cherry Festival) in Sefrou.
July
  Moussem at Mdiq, north-west of Tetouan. This festival takes place early in the month.
August
  Moussem of Moulay Idriss in Zerhoun, north of Meknès.
  Moussem of Moulay Abdallah south of El-Jadida. The festival takes place late in the month.
  Moussem of Sidi Ahmed in Anti-Tiznit. This celebration of prayer is held towards the end of the month.
  Moussem of Setti Fatma in the Ourika Valley, south of Marrakesh.
  International Arts Festival in Asilah.
September
  Fête des Fiancés in Imilchil. The festival is held late in the month.
  Moussem of Sidi Moussa or *Quarquour* near El-Kelas du Straghna, north of Marrakesh.
  Moussem of Moulay Idriss in Fès. It is sometimes held in early October.

Moussem of Sidi-Allal in Arbaoua, north of Meknès.
October
  Fête du Cheval (Horse Festival) in Tissa, north-east of Fès. This takes place in early October.
  Fête des Dattes (Date Festival) in Erfoud. This takes place in late October.

The Folklore Festival at Marrakesh, usually held around the end of May or early June, is essentially a tourist event, although it attracts many Moroccans. Nevertheless, it's colourful and well worth attending, since groups of dancers, musicians and other entertainers are invited from all over the country.

RESPONSIBLE TOURISM
There are a few common-sense rules to keep in mind when traipsing around Morocco. By African standards, the Moroccans keep their city streets pretty clean, and if you have been travelling around elsewhere in Africa and developed the habit of chucking junk anywhere, try to chuck the habit instead. Even where locals don't seem terribly concerned about rubbish, there's no need to add to it. This is particularly important at beaches and other natural beauty spots.

At open-air sites like Volubilis and Lixus, take care not to trample over the ruins needlessly.

Everybody likes to take a photo, but be aware of local sensibilities. Not everyone wants to be immortalised on film, and in some areas people are afraid of being captured by what to them seems the evil eye (or at least a prying eye). For more information, see the Film & Photography section.

POST & TELECOMMUNICATIONS
Few towns don't have a post office (PTT, or Postes, Télégraphes et Téléphones). A colourful new logo has recently been introduced – La Poste (*al-barid* in Arabic). All services are housed in the one or adjacent buildings.

Postal Rates
Although the postal system is fairly reliable, it is not terribly fast. It can take about a week for letters to get to their European destinations (it depends a little on the efficiency of

Erg Chebbi, Merzouga (DS)

Top Left: Public fountain, Talaa as-Seghir, Fès el-Bali (DS)
Top Right: Great Mosque seen from the Medersa Bou Inania, Meknès (DS)
Bottom Left: Fès el-Bali (HF)
Bottom Right: Chefchaouen seen from the roof of the kasbah (DS)

individual European postal services too!), and two weeks or so to get to Australia and North America. Occasionally you get lucky and mail moves faster. It's about the same going in the other direction. Standard letters and postcards to Europe cost from Dr 4.40 (France) to Dr 4.80 (UK). Postcards to Australia and North America cost Dr 6 and standard letters Dr 11. In the main tourist centres it is not unheard of to be charged above the standard rates.

You can buy stamps at some *tabacs*, the small tobacco and newspaper kiosks you see scattered about the main city centres. This is useful, as post office counters are often besieged.

Sending Mail

Parcels The parcel office (indicated by the sign 'Colis postaux') is generally in a separate part of the building. Take your parcel unwrapped for customs inspection. You had better have your own wrapping materials, as more often than not there is nothing in the parcel office. There is a 20-kg limit and parcels should not be longer than 1.5 metres on any side.

A 10-kg parcel to Australia will cost Dr 780 by surface mail and Dr 1500 by air. The same parcel to the UK is Dr 270 by surface mail and Dr 352.80 by air.

Express Mail There is usually an Express Mail Service (EMS), or Poste Rapide in the same office as parcel post. You can send up to 500 grams to France, Spain and Portugal for Dr 160, to the rest of Europe for Dr 200, to the Americas for Dr 300 and to Australia for Dr 400. Your letter or package should arrive within 24 hours in Europe and within two to three days elsewhere, but don't depend on such speed.

Receiving Mail

Having mail addressed to 'Poste Restante, La Poste Principale' of any big town should not be a problem. There is generally a small charge for picking up any items you receive. Note, however, that some offices don't hang on to parcels for more than a couple of weeks before returning them to the sender. Remember to take your passport as proof of identity, as no other document will be accepted.

Possibly more reliable for receiving mail is American Express, which has four branches in Morocco (see Money for addresses). To qualify for the client mail service, you are supposed to have American Express travellers' cheques or an Amex card. In practice, you are usually asked only to produce a passport for identification. There is no charge for any letters you receive.

Telephone

The business of making a phone call is getting easier in Morocco as hundreds of millions of dollars are being poured into the system. Although the number of lines has more than doubled in the past 10 years, fewer Moroccans have phones than in practically any other Middle Eastern or North African state. According to one report, only 43% of local calls get through, and less than 30% of international calls, although this seems to be an overly pessimistic assessment. The defects of the system are most obvious to the user making local calls, as lines are frequently so bad that you can't hear the person on the other end.

Most cities and towns have at least one phone office (increasingly known by its Arabic title – Itissalat al-Maghrib), and in the main centres they are open round the clock, seven days a week.

Public phones are not hard to find around the bigger cities, but become scarcer in more out-of-the-way locations. Card phones are becoming more common and are generally the easiest way to make a call.

Costs To make a local call in a coin-operated phone, you must insert a minimum of Dr 1.50. Costs are worked out in terms of units (one unit equals 80 centimes), and your initial Dr 1.50 gets you about 12 minutes. You can phone from hotels, but they generally charge about Dr 5 for a local call!

For long-distance calls within Morocco, one unit gets you from two minutes (35 km or under) to 12 seconds (300 km or more).

Calls are half-price from midnight to 7 am, 40% off any other time on Sundays and holidays as well as from 12.30 pm to midnight on Saturdays and 8.30 pm to midnight on other days. There is a 10% discount from 12.30 to 2 pm on weekdays.

International calls are *expensive*. The cheap rate (40% off) operates all-day Sunday and on holidays, all-day Saturday except from 7 am to 12.30 pm and from midnight to 7 am on weekdays. On weekdays the rate is 20% off from 10 pm to midnight.

There are six international zones for telephone purposes, and rates range from Dr 8.20 a minute in Zone 1 (just under US$1) to Dr 32 (just over US$3) in Zone 6. France, for instance, lies in Zone 2 (Dr 13.70 a minute), as do most other Western European countries. Australia and New Zealand, naturally, are in Zone 6, while the USA and Canada lie in Zone 5 (Dr 27.40 a minute).

It makes no difference whether you use a phonecard or place a call through a telephone office. There is, thankfully, no three-minute minimum, but in the telephone offices you'll pay for every minute or part thereof.

Card Phones These are becoming increasingly widespread, and are generally the easiest way to make calls, especially if you're calling abroad. You can buy the cards at phone offices and occasionally in newspaper kiosks and tabacs. *Télécartes* (phonecards) sell for Dr 68.50 (50 units), Dr 93.50 (70 units) and Dr 156 (120 units – this one seems to be a rarity). When your card runs out during a call, you are technically supposed to be able to insert another without losing the call, but in practice this does not work all the time.

You will notice enterprising lads outside phone offices, trying to sell units on cards. This 'service' may suit some locals who cannot afford to buy a full card and only want to make short calls, but for outsiders it is a perfect way to get done.

Reverse Charges It is possible to make reverse-charge (collect) calls from Morocco, but it can involve painfully long waits in phone offices. If you want to do this, say 'Je voudrais téléphoner en PCV' (pronounced peh-seh-veh) – the French expression for this service.

An increasingly popular international service known as 'country direct' or 'home direct' is barely acknowledged as yet in Morocco, but before you leave home it might be worth investigating whether such a link exists between your country and Morocco. It involves calling a toll-free number that connects you with operators in your home country, through whom you can then request reverse-charge calls and the like. You can do this from any phone direct. The only country that appeared to have such a link with Morocco at the time of writing was Spain, for which you dial (☎ 002 802828); however, more countries are bound to be linked up in good time.

Calling from Hotels The bigger hotels usually offer international phone and fax services should you want to avail yourself of them. Remember that it can easily cost double the normal amount, depending on the type of call you make, so it is really only for the desperate or those on expense accounts.

Telephone Directories There is one standard phone book for all Morocco in French – the *Annuaire des Abonnés au Téléphone*. Most phone offices have a copy lying around. Since 1993 a slimmer volume containing just fax numbers has also been available. Look up the city first, then the person you want.

A kind of Yellow Pages, *Télécontact*, is sporadically available in some bookshops – try the Librairie Farairre in Casablanca.

If your French is OK, you could dial ☎ 16 for Information (Renseignements).

Telephone Area Codes When calling abroad from Morocco, dial ☎ 00, your country code and then the city code and number.

When calling Morocco from abroad, dial the international access code, then 212

(Morocco's country code), the city code and the local number.

For telecommunications purposes, Morocco is divided up into regions. Roughly from north to south, the area codes are as follows (remember when calling from within Morocco to dial 0 first):

9: Tangier, Tetouan, Al-Hoceima, Larache, Asilah
6: Nador, Oujda, Bouarfa, Figuig
5: Fès, Meknès, Taza, Er-Rachidia
7: Rabat, Kenitra, Ouezzane
2: Casablanca and immediate vicinity
3: El-Jadida, Beni Mellal
4: Marrakesh, Essaouira, Safi, Ouarzazate
8: The rest of the country south (including all of the Western Sahara) of a line running roughly east to west and including Agadir, Taroudannt and Tata

Fax, Telex & Telegraph

Only the main post offices in any given town have telex and telegraph services. They can be sent from special counters in the post (not phone) office. Few, if any, post offices offer fax – the central post and phone offices in Rabat flatly denied that the Moroccan post and telecommunications system offered any such service, although one or two phone offices in the country claim they *can* send a fax for you.

Ceuta & Melilla

Although situated in North Africa, the two enclaves of Ceuta and Melilla are Spanish territory and so their post and phone services are part of the Spanish system.

Post Post offices are called *Correos y Telégrafos*. Don't expect a superfast service. Post can take a good week or more to arrive from just about anywhere – distance seems to make little difference.

Postcards and letters up to 20 grams cost 45 pta to other countries of the European Union and 65 pta elsewhere. Aerograms are 65 pta wherever they go.

Parcels Parcels up to a maximum weight of 20 kg can also be sent from the post office. It costs 440 pta to send a two-kg parcel abroad via surface mail. Charges for larger packages vary considerably.

Express Mail Express Mail Service also goes by the name of *postal expres*. You can send up to one kg for 3200 pta to Europe, Turkey and the countries of the Maghreb. The same parcel would cost 5300 pta to North and Central America and most Middle Eastern countries, and 6000 pta to the rest of the world. Each extra 500 grams up to a maximum of 20 kg costs 650, 1300 and 1550 pta respectively.

Receiving Mail Poste restante is in the main post office of each of the enclaves. Ask for the *lista de correos*.

Telephone The Telefónica is a separate organisation from the Correos y Telégrafos. Phoning is generally no problem. Telefónica either has its own phone office, or has contracted the service out to bureaux known as *locutorios*, which are generally open from 10 am to 10 pm, with a three-hour afternoon break from 2 pm.

You can buy phonecards in post offices and selected newsstands and kiosks. They cost 1000 and 2000 pta. Most phones accept cards and coins.

There is nothing cheap about the phone in Spain (and hence its enclaves). The standard day rate for international calls will make that clear. A five-minute call costs 657 pta to other EU countries, 792 pta to the rest of Europe and the Maghreb, 1163 pta to the Americas, and 2286 pta to the rest of the world. There is no minimum call time, but you pay for every minute or part thereof. The cheap rate (about 30% to 40% off) for international calls is from 10 pm to 8 am.

For calls within Spain, there are three different bands: urban, provincial and interprovincial calls. There are three rates: morning, evening and night. The latter is the cheapest, and runs from 10 pm to 8 am on weekdays, and from 2 pm on Saturday until 8 am on Monday.

Making reverse-charge calls is possible from phone offices, but a growing number of countries are linked to Spain in the *país directo* (home direct) service. The home direct numbers are listed on the newer telephones.

To call outside Spain dial ☎ 07, then the country code and number. Spain's international dialling code is 34. Ceuta's area code is 56 (same as Algeciras) and that of Melilla 5 (same as M laga). If calling from within Spain, dial 9 first.

Fax, Telex & Telegram All these services are available in the post office. Ordinary telegrams to the rest of Europe and the Mediterranean basin cost 42 pta per word, with a fixed minimum charge of 1300 pta. Elsewhere it's 135 pta a word. Urgent telegrams cost about double that. Telexes cost 60 pta a minute to Europe and the Maghreb, 300 pta to North America and 370 pta to more distant destinations.

Faxes cost from 750 to 1650 pta for the first page, depending on where you are sending it, and slightly less for each subsequent page. Receiving incoming faxes from abroad will cost 350 pta for the first page and 205 pta for each following one.

TIME
Morocco is on GMT/UTC all year round. So (not taking account of daylight-saving time elsewhere) when it's noon in Morocco it's the same in London, 1 pm in Western Europe, 7 am in New York, 4 am in Los Angeles, 8 pm in Perth and Hong Kong, 10 pm in Sydney and midnight in Auckland. Remember if travelling between Morocco and Spain that the latter is two hours ahead in summer, which can affect plans for catching ferries and the like.

On the subject of time, Moroccans are not in nearly as much of a hurry to get things done as Westerners. Rather than letting yourself be frustrated by this, it pays to learn to go with the flow a little (although not necessarily to surrender altogether).

ELECTRICITY
Throughout most of the country, electricity supply is 220 V at 50 Hz AC, although in

some places you'll still find 110 V. Sockets are of the European two-pin variety.

WEIGHTS & MEASURES
Morocco uses the metric system. There is a standard conversion table at the back of the book.

LAUNDRY
Self-service laundrettes are hard to find. You will inevitably be directed to dry cleaners, which are rather expensive. Even hotels don't seem to know the difference half the time. So unless you have lots of money to waste on dry-cleaning bills, the simplest option is to do it yourself in your room! If you do have your laundry done, remember to leave yourself time, as it always takes them a few days.

BOOKS
Because of Morocco's colonial heritage under the French, and the continued importance of French in Moroccan society, works in that language have been added to the suggested reading list that follows. Some Moroccan writers choose to write in French rather than Arabic – one sign of how deep a mark the French protectorate left on the country.

Islamic, Arab & North African History
For those wanting to become generally acquainted with the wider Arabic-speaking world, there are several books to recommend. Among these is Philip Hitti's work, *History of the Arabs* (MacMillan paperback), which is regarded as a classic and is very readable.

A more recent but equally acclaimed work is Albert Hourani's *A History of the Arab Peoples* (Faber, 1991). It is as much an attempt to convey a feel for evolving Muslim Arab societies as a straightforward history, with extensive, if largely generalised, treatment of various aspects of social, cultural and religious life.

If you want a more comprehensive reference source on the whole Muslim world (although it's weak on more recent history), you could try delving into the two hardback or four paperback volumes of *A Cambridge History of Islam*. Volume 2A has a section devoted to North African history.

Maghreb: Histoire et Société (SNED, Algiers, 1974), is one of a number of studies by Jacques Berque, who is regarded as one of the better historians of the region in the French language.

In an attempt to get away from a French interpretation of Maghreb history, Abdallah Laroui wrote *The History of the Maghreb* (translated from the French by Ralph Manheim, Princeton University Press, New Jersey, 1970). He strives to assert an indigenous view and is regarded by some Moroccans as the best there is. Unfortunately, the book is out of print and hard to track down. It is as much an analysis of how historians have dealt with Maghreb history as an account of events, and so not as useful an introduction to the country.

For a completely different perspective, *L'Afrique du Nord au Féminin* (Gabriel Camps, Perrin, Paris, 1992) presents stories of famous women of the Maghreb and the Sahara from 6000 BC to the present. Camps has written several works dealing with various aspects of Maghreb history.

Moroccan History

Histoire du Maroc (Bernard Lugan, Critérion, Paris, 1992) is a reasonable potted history of the country, although it rather falls back into the category Abdallah Laroui was combatting.

Les Almoravides by Vincent Lagardare (L'Harmattan, Paris, 1988) traces the history of this great Berber dynasty from 1062 to 1145.

The Conquest of the Sahara by Douglas Porch (Jonathan Cape, London, 1985) describes France's attempts to gain control of the Sahara and subdue the Tuaregs. His *Conquest of Morocco* (Jonathan Cape, London, 1986; Papermac, London, 1987) examines the takeover of Morocco by Paris, which led to the establishment of the protectorate.

A Country with a Government and a Flag by C R Pennell (Menas, 1986) is an account of the anticolonial struggle in the Rif from 1921 to 1926 which threatened the French and Spanish hold over their respective protectorates.

In *Lords of the Atlas: the Rise and Fall of the House of Glaoua 1893-1956* (Arrow Books, London, 1991), Gavin Maxwell recounts the story of Thami el-Glaoui, the Pasha of Marrakesh. The book relates some of the more extraordinary events linked with this local despot, who even after WW II ordered that the heads of his enemies be mounted on the city gates.

The Western Sahara desert, which Morocco claims and to all intents and purposes now controls, remains a contentious issue. There are a few books on this issue in English and French. Claiming the territory has been an important feature of the government's policy and if you want to read its side of the story you could try *Hassan II présente la Marche Verte* (Plon, Paris, 1990). The title refers to the Green March, when Moroccan troops and civilians moved in to take control of the territory in 1975 as Spain pulled out.

The Western Saharans, by Virginia Thompson & Richard Adloff (Croom Helm, London, 1980), takes a less government-friendly view of the conflict.

On contemporary Morocco, the French writer Gilles Perrault caused a diplomatic storm with his none-too complimentary *Notre Ami Le Roi* (Gallimard, Paris). Don't be seen carrying this one around with you in Morocco!

People & Society

Peter Mayne's highly readable *A Year in Marrakesh* (Eland, London, 1991), first published in 1953, is his account of time spent living among the people of the city and observations on their lives.

The House of Si Abdallah – The Oral History of a Moroccan Family, recorded, translated and edited by Henry Munson Jr, Yale University Press, 1984, is a unique insight into the daily lives and thoughts of Moroccans, mainly seen through the eyes of a traditional pedlar in Tangier and his Westernised cousin, a woman living in the USA.

A fascinating, non-academic book examining the lives of Moroccan women is Leonora Peets's *Women of Marrakesh* (C Hunt & Co, London, 1988). Although she is not Muslim, Peets became very close to the women she met in the 40 years she spent in Morocco from 1930. The book has been translated from the Estonian.

For a comparatively recent study of the Berber population of Morocco, you could do worse than consult *Les Berbères*, by Gabriel Camps (Éditions Errance, Paris, 1987).

Another account is Salem Chaker's *Berbères Aujourd'hui* (L'Harmattan, Paris, 1989).

Moroccan Fiction

Literary genres such as the novel and drama, long taken for granted as an integral part of Western culture, are a comparatively recent development in the Arab world, where the bulk of literature until the late 19th century consisted of traditional poetry, much of it in imitation of older classics. For a full treatment of literature, past and present, in the Arab world, you might like to consult the three-volume *Cambridge History of Arabic Literature* (Cambridge University Press, 1992).

Egypt has tended to lead the way in the past 100 years, but Morocco too has seen a growth of modern talent. Output in neighbouring Algeria, however, is considerably greater. Many Moroccan authors still write in French, although more and more are turning to their native tongue, even at the risk of not gaining wider recognition for want of translation into French or other European languages. Little Moroccan writing has been translated into English.

Year of the Elephant, by Leila Abouzeid (1989), has been put out by the Center for Middle Eastern Studies of the University of Texas in Austin, which has embarked on a programme of translation of Middle Eastern and Arabic literature. The stories recount the life of Zahra, a Moroccan woman who, in the face of an unsympathetic society, carves out a degree of independence for herself, without abandoning the pillars of her upbringing, including the Islamic faith.

In *Si Yussef* (Quartet, London, 1992), Anouar Majid evokes Moroccan life through the eyes of a man who looks back on his life in Tangier. A bookkeeper for years, he started his apprenticeship in survival as did most of the port city's urchins, as a guide for foreigners.

One of Morocco's better known authors (and winner of the 1994 Prix Méditerranée) is Tahar ben Jelloun, resident in France since 1971. At least two of his works, which he writes in French, have appeared in English. *Solitaire* (Quartet, London, 1988) explores the seemingly insurmountable difficulties encountered by a Moroccan migrant in France.

In *Silent Day in Tangier* (Quartet, London, 1991) an elderly and bedridden man ruminates over his past. Although the book is largely a personal exploration, the many allusions to the history of Tangier and Morocco from about the time of the Rif war on are unobtrusively woven into the observations of an old and angry man.

Abdel Krim Ghallab, editor-in-chief of *Al-'Alam* newspaper, is considered one of Morocco's finer modern writers. Although he writes in Arabic, some of his works, including *Le Passé Enterré*, have been translated into French.

Ahmed Sefrioui, a writer of Berber origin who grew up in Fès, aims in his short stories and particularly his novel *La Boîte à Merveilles* (Éditions du Seuil, Paris, 1978) to relate the life of ordinary Moroccans through the eyes of his characters, such as little Mohammed in *La Boîte à Merveilles*. Here is all the hubbub and local colour of Fès half a century ago.

An important representative of Moroccan émigré literature is Driss Chraïbi, who was born in El-Jadida and now lives in France. A prolific author, his novels tend to be politicised, which sets him at odds with Sefrioui (who prefers to deal with what he sees as more essential human issues). His works include *Le Passé Simple* and *Mort au Canada*. One work that appears in English translation is *Heirs to the Past* (Heinemann, London, 1986). A couple of other novels have also been translated into English, but are hard to come by.

Mohammed Khaïr-eddine, who writes in French and Arabic, is one of Morocco's ground-breaking authors. His poems, novels and other writings express a desire for revolt and change, not only in the context of Moroccan society and traditions, but in his own methods of writing. One of the better known anthologies is *Ce Maroc!* (Éditions du Seuil, Paris, 1975).

For something closer to the pulse of traditional society, *Contes Berbères de l'Atlas de Marrakech*, a series of Berber tales edited by Alphonse Lequil (L'Harmattan, Paris, 1988) might be worth perusing.

Foreign Writers

Of foreigners who have written in or about Morocco, Paul Bowles, who still lives in Tangier, is probably the best known. *The Sheltering Sky* (Paladin, London, 1990), made into a film by Bernardo Bertolucci in 1990 (in which Bowles makes a cameo appearance), tells the story of an American couple who arrive in North Africa shortly after WW II and try to put their relationship back together. The early stages of the film were shot in Morocco, although in the novel the action takes place in Oran (Algeria).

The film served to bring the author back to public prominence. Other books by Bowles include *The Spider's House* and *Let It Come Down*, the latter of which is set in Tangier. *Their Heads Are Green* (Abacus, London, 1990) is a collection of travel tales set in several countries, including Morocco, and provide some interesting insights to the country.

Bowles also translated a series of oral tales from Moroccan Arabic into English. The tales were compiled by Mohammed Mrabet, Mohammed Choukri and Larbi Layachi (whose work was published under the pseudonym Driss ben Hamed Charhadi). Among Mrabet's works are *Love with a Few Hairs*

and *M'Hashish*. His is an uncompromising account of the life of Tanjawi street lads, and the sometimes irksome activities they undertook to earn a crust.

Choukri's main work is *For Bread Alone: An Autobiography*, in which he describes the seemingly unbearable saga of his family, one of many families forced by drought in the Rif during the early 1940s to seek opportunities in Tangier and largely crushed by its indifference.

Layachi's best known work is *A Life Full of Holes*. Layachi, of as humble origins as the other two, is said to have wanted to use a pseudonym because he didn't want anyone to know who he was: jobless and living in 'a rotten country in rotten times'.

Iain Finlayson's *Tangier – City of the Dream* (Flamingo, London, 1993) is an intriguing look at some of the Western literati who found a new home in Morocco at one time or another. The single greatest entry deals with Paul and Jane Bowles and those around them, but there is interesting material on William Burroughs and the Beat movement writers, Truman Capote, Joe Orton and others. It is a highly readable account of the life of this 'seedy, salacious, decadent, degenerate' city.

Elias Canetti, a foremost novelist in the German language, ended up in Marrakesh in 1954 in the company of a film team and penned his recollections in a slim but moving volume of short and elegantly simple stories entitled *Die Stimmen von Marrakesch*, Fischer, Frankfurt, 1989. It has appeared in English as *The Voices of Marrakesh*, Marion Borays/Farrar Straus & Giroux.

From the 1890s to the early 1930s, *The Times'* correspondent Walter Harris lived through the period that saw Morocco fall under the growing influence of France. His whimsical and highly amusing, if not always totally believable *Morocco That Was* (Eland, London, 1983), first appeared in 1921.

At the beginning of the century, Budgett Meakin made one of the first serious attempts by a Westerner at an overall appraisal of Moroccan society and history. First published in 1901, Darf Publishers in

London thought *The Land of the Moors* interesting enough to bring out again in 1986.

Equally interesting, but potentially very irritating for modern readers is Frances Macnab's *A Ride in Morocco* (Darf Publishers, London, 1987), a British woman's rather strident account of her adventures on horseback from Tangier to Marrakesh at the turn of the century.

If the writing on Morocco from this period appeals, another book of casual interest, mainly for its reflection on the ideas of the more zealous Westerners living in the Orient, is Donald Mackenzie's *The Khalifate of the West*, Darf Publishers, London, 1987 (first printed in 1911).

Travel Guides

Michelin's *Guide de Tourisme – Maroc* is a detailed and excellent route guide through Morocco. The bad news is that it's only available in French. If this is not an obstacle, you can find it in some London bookstores outside the Francophone world, including Stanford's bookshop in London (see Bookshops).

For English speakers there is a fairly thin *Blue Guide* on Morocco, which lays the emphasis on historical and urban cultural detail, with only limited information on natural beauty spots.

Quite a number of travel guide publishers have books on Morocco, including Frommer's, Fodor's (not for the budget traveller), Cadogan and Insight (attractive and well written, but not too hot on practicalities).

For people planning any desert driving in Morocco and beyond into Algeria, the *Sahara Handbook* by Simon Glen (Roger Lascelles, Middlesex, 1990) offers detailed advice on how to plan such adventures. The same publishers have put out another book in a similar vein called *Africa Overland*.

Morocco – The Traveller's Companion, by Margaret & Robin Bidwell (I B Tauris, New York, 1992), is a compilation of excerpts from the writings of Westerners who in one way or another have come into contact with Morocco. The line-up ranges from the likes of Leo Africanus to Samuel Pepys and George Orwell.

One of the first attempts at a travel guide to the country was undertaken by Edith Wharton, who arrived in 1917 and three years later had *In Morocco* published. Century brought it out again in 1984.

An entertaining account of a Westerner's travails in Morocco more than a century ago is *Morocco – its People & Places* by Edmondo de Amicis (translated by C Rollin-Tilton and published by Darf, London, in 1985), which first appeared in 1882.

Arts & Architecture

A Practical Guide to Islamic Monuments in Morocco (Richard Parker, Baraka Press, 1981) is exactly what its title suggests and is full of town maps, pictures and ground plans of important monuments.

Titus Burckhardt's *Fès, City of Islam* (Cambridge UP, 1992) is a pictorial treasure, including many of the art historian's own B&W shots of the city from his visits in the 1930s.

Islamic Architecture – North Africa, Antony Hutt, Scorpio Publications, 1977, is a pictorial overview of the great buildings of the Maghreb.

Zillij – The Art of Moroccan Ceramics, by John Hedgecoe & Salma Sanar Damluji (Garnet, Reading, 1992), is a decent study of an important aspect of Moroccan decoration, also often known as *zellij*.

Les Tapis, Solar, Paris, 1993, has all you ever wanted to know (in French), about Moroccan carpets and rugs.

Living in Morocco (Lisl & Landt Dennis, Thames & Hudson, London, 1992), is a sumptuous coffee table book with a lot of material on Moroccan arts and crafts.

For an aerial approach, try *Maroc Vu d'en Haut*, Anne & Yann Arthus-Bertrand (Editions de la Martinière).

Culture

If traditional Moroccan dancing fascinates you, a look at *Danses du Maghreb* by Viviane Lièvre (Karthala, Paris, 1987) will give you a deeper insight into the meaning and history behind it.

Musique du Maroc, by Ahmed Aydoun, Eddif, Casablanca, 1992, seems to be about the only serious book dealing with Moroccan music, and is hard to find outside Morocco.

Food
The Taste of Morocco by Robert Carrier (Century, London, 1987) is an excellent illustrated guide to Moroccan cuisine.

Also good is *Good Food From Morocco*, by Paula Wolfert (John Murray, London, 1989). Wolfert loves the food, but says there are only half a dozen good Moroccan restaurants in Morocco. The best way to learn the joys of the cuisine, she writes, is to try home cooking or get invited to a banquet.

If there are not enough recipes in the latter, another possibility is *240 Recettes de Cuisine Marocaine* by Ahmed Laarri (Jacques Grancher, Paris, 1982).

Phrasebooks
For an introduction to the complexities of Moroccan Arabic, pick up a copy of Lonely Planet's *Moroccan Arabic Phrasebook*, by Dan Bacon.

Bookshops
In Morocco Morocco is not exactly bursting with good bookshops, and you will certainly be much better served if you can read French, as the better stores have a far wider selection both on Morocco and general subjects as well. Branches of the American Language Center in Rabat, Marrakesh and Casablanca have small bookshops dedicated mainly to English literature and learning English. In addition, there is an English bookshop in both Rabat and Fès. Rabat probably has the best general bookstores (which mostly stock works in French, though you'll find the occasional book on Morocco in English), but there are one or two good bookshops in Casablanca, Tangier, Fès and Marrakesh. For details, see the relevant chapters.

Outside Morocco Most of the books in French are not readily available outside

France, although one exception is the small Maghreb Bookshop (☎ 0171-388 1840) at 45 Burton St, London (WC1H 9AL), which leans towards the academic side.

For a good range of travel guides and literature and a wide selection of maps, Stanford's bookshop (☎ 0171-836 2121), 12-14 Long Acre, London, WC2E 9LP, is one of the best shops of its kind in the UK. Some of the bigger mainstream bookstores also have a range of material on Morocco. Another very good source of travel literature is The Travellers' Bookshop (☎ 0171-836 9132), at 25 Cecil Court, London WC2N 4EZ.

If you are interested in literature on Islam, Moroccan history and politics, or a wide range of subjects pertinent to the Muslim world, Al Hoda (☎ 0171-240 8381; fax 0171-497 0180) at 76-78 Charing Cross Rd is a useful resource.

A couple of specialist shops in Paris are worth exploring if you have more than a passing interest in things North African. L'Harmattan (☎ 1-46.34.13.71), at 21 Rue des Écoles in the Latin Quarter is probably the best. They publish a lot of Maghreb literature in French. Another place worth trying in the same part of town is Le Tiers Mythe (☎ 1-43.26.72.70) at 21 Rue Cujas.

MAPS
Few decent maps of Morocco are available in the country itself, so you are advised to get one before leaving home if you require any degree of detail and accuracy.

North-West Africa
There are several reasonable maps covering all of North-West Africa, taking in parts of Egypt and the Sudan in the east. Kümmerley & Frey publish one called *Africa, North and West* (UK£6.95) on a scale of 1:4,000,000. At the same price comes another map by VWK, with the same title and of virtually the same quality. Michelin map number 953 (UK£4.45) covers much the same area and is perfectly adequate.

Morocco

There are several possibilities for maps of Morocco, and the choice depends partly on what you want from the map. Michelin's map number 959 (UK£4.45) is the best. In addition to the 1:4,000,000 scale map of the whole of Morocco, which includes the disputed territory of Western Sahara, there is a 1:1,000,000 enlargement of Morocco proper and 1:600,000 enlargements of the Marrakesh, Casablanca, Rabat, Middle Atlas and Meknès areas.

If you want six small city maps included, you could try Kümmerley & Frey's *Morocco* (UK£5.45), but this does not cover all of the Western Sahara on its 1:1,000,000 scale main map.

GEOprojects, based in Beirut, produces *Maroc* (UK£6), a very basic map of the country which includes half a dozen fairly detailed city plans and some information about the country and individual cities. The 1:2,000,000 scale main map and the 1:500,000 area enlargements are thin on detail.

Hallwag's *Morocco* (UK£3.95), aside from being cheap, is distinguished by its comparatively detailed maps of the Canary Islands. The main map is on a scale of 1:1,000,000.

Survey Maps & Air Charts The Ministère de l'Agriculture et de la Réforme Agraire in Rabat produces highly detailed survey maps on a scale of 1:100,000. However, only a series of 15 from the centre of the country around Marrakesh and stretching to Zagora in the south-east is made available outside Morocco and even so can be difficult to obtain. You can get these and other maps from the office in Rabat, but most are too detailed to be of interest to travellers. See the Rabat section for more information.

Operational Navigation Charts on a scale of 1:1,000,000 cost UK£7.50 each. Charts G-1, H-1, H-2 and J-1 cover all Morocco. They are each subdivided into four Tactical Pilotage Charts at 1:500,000, again for UK£7.50 each. While of topographical interest and of obvious use to fliers, most

travellers will not need them. They are available at Stanford's in London.

MEDIA
Local Newspapers & Magazines

Morocco possesses a diverse press in both Arabic and French. The bulk of the daily papers owe their allegiance to one or other political party or grouping. Although censorship does not take the form of blobs of black ink appearing in your morning paper, none of the papers rocks the boat much. Even those run by opposition parties rarely, if ever, say anything that could be construed as anti-monarchist. It is quite all right for the parties to attack one another, and for the opposition to criticise the government, but the country's real power – the royal family – is another kettle of fish.

None of the papers makes riveting reading, and none has a huge circulation. The government-run French-language daily, *Le Matin du Sahara et du Maghreb* (which also appears in Arabic and Spanish) is an extremely turgid read yet sometimes manages a print run of 100,000. Most papers put out under 50,000 copies.

Among the French papers (most of which have an Arabic equivalent), *l'Opinion*, which is Casablanca based and attached to the opposition Istiqlal Party, is perhaps the most interesting for getting an idea of some of the points of contention in Moroccan society.

Libération, the Union Socialiste des Forces Populaires' daily, produced in Rabat, is similar if less punchy. *Al Bayane*, another opposition daily, is not too bad for foreign news. All have listings pages for the Casablanca and Rabat cinemas, airport shuttle timetables, Royal Air Maroc arrivals and departures and a list of late-night pharmacies that work on a rotating roster.

There is a plethora of sports papers and magazines, fashion rags and the like, and a surprising number of weeklies dedicated purely to economics.

For readers of French who happen to be trying to learn Arabic, the monthly *La*

Tribune du Maroc is worth getting a hold of. It culls the local Arabic and French language press to cover the main events of the month, and runs articles in both languages.

There is virtually nothing produced locally in English. A tiny monthly put out in Fès, *The Messenger of Morocco* (Dr 3), is of minimal interest.

Foreign Press

In the main centres, a reasonable range of foreign press is available at central newsstands and in some of the big hotels. News magazines like *Newsweek* and *Time*, along with the *International Herald Tribune*, are usually fairly easy to find, along with a range of UK papers and their Continental European equivalents. The French press is about as up to date and easy to obtain as in France itself, and is by far the cheapest – there seems to be virtually no added charge for import costs.

Tourist Publications

A useful booklet loaded with practical information, listings and the like is called *La Quinzaine du Maroc*, which appears every fortnight. Unfortunately, it is hard to find outside Casablanca, although it is supposed to be available in the bigger hotels around the country. It costs from nothing to Dr 15, depending on where you stumble across it.

Radio

Local radio is an odd mix. There is only a handful of local AM and FM stations, the bulk of which broadcast in Arabic and French. At least one of the FM stations plays quite reasonable contemporary music. The frequencies change from one part of the country to another.

Throughout northern Morocco and along much of the Atlantic coast you can pick up a host of Spanish stations, especially on the AM band. In fact, you can usually tune into Spanish radio just about anywhere in Morocco, although reception can be patchy.

None of this is much use if you don't understand Spanish, but it may give you a choice in music terms.

On the north coast around Tangier and across to Ceuta, you can often pick up English-language broadcasts from Gibraltar.

The Voice of America has long had a presence just outside Tangier, and in September 1993 opened its biggest transmitter outside the USA at a cost of US$225 million. You can tune into VOA on various short-wave frequencies.

The other short-wave option in English is the BBC. It broadcasts into the area on MHz 15,070, 12,095 and 9410, and several other frequencies. The bulk of the programmes are broadcast from about 8 am to 11 pm.

TV

As with radio, Moroccans in the north of the country can pick up the full gamut of Spanish stations, and the more risqué stations like Télé 5 are extremely popular. It is a rare thing to see Moroccan TV on the screens in Tangier cafés.

In the rest of the country, the choice is fairly limited. There are basically two government-run stations, RTM-1 (also known as TVM) and 2M. The first is the more staid of the two. Both broadcast in Arabic and French, and RTM-1 also has the news in Spanish at 7 pm. The third choice is basically a European satellite import from the Francophone world – TV5. It is an all-French station with programs from France, Belgium, Switzerland and Canada .

Should it be of interest, you can see Algerian TV in the east of the country.

FILM & PHOTOGRAPHY

Most of the usual brands of film, including slide film, are readily available in the big cities and towns. It costs about as much as it would in Europe, so you won't save anything by not bringing your own. If you do buy it in Morocco, be sure to check expiry dates. A 36-frame roll of Kodak 100 ASA print film will cost around Dr 45 to Dr 50. A 36-frame roll of Kodak Ektachrome slide film (100 ASA) goes for about Dr 70. There are quite a few processing shops in the cities and larger towns. It costs about Dr 82 to have a 36-frame roll of colour prints developed, and as little as Dr 55 to have unmounted slides done.

For most daylight outdoor shooting, 100 ASA is quite sufficient, and generally it is best to shoot in the morning and afternoon, as the light in the middle of the day is harsh and can give your pictures a glary washed-out look.

It is worth keeping a few rolls of 200 and even 400 ASA handy for lousy weather (especially in the north in winter) and for shots in the medinas, which tend to let in a minimum of sunlight.

Morocco is full of photo opportunities, but there are a couple of warnings. Don't point your camera at anything that is vaguely military or that could be construed as 'strategic'. This includes airports, bridges, government buildings and members of the police or armed forces. Generally there is little trouble with taking still shots or filming in Morocco, although some travellers are unlucky enough to come up against officials with a superiority complex who rip out films for little or no apparent reason – this is an exception rather than the rule.

The second point is to be careful whom you aim your lens at. Some people, women in particular, dislike it intensely, and their wishes should be respected. It is always best to ask first. The other side of this coin is the growing tendency in the main tourist centres for people to demand payment for photos. Water-sellers make more money from tourists taking photos of them than they could ever hope to from merely selling water. It is not uncommon for them to run up to you, claiming you took their picture and demanding payment, even if it's plain that you did not. Deal firmly but politely with this nonsense. The Djemaa el-Fna in Marrakesh is full of this sort of thing. It has to be said there is something amusing about watching an unwitting tourist cheerfully getting an oh-so-obliging snake-charmer to pose for that perfect happy snap, only to be pursued halfway around the medina for absurdly high payments. Try not to be one of them.

HEALTH

Travel health depends on your predeparture preparations, your day-to-day health care while travelling and how you handle any medical problem or emergency that may develop. While the list of potential dangers can seem quite frightening, with a little luck, some basic precautions and adequate information, few travellers experience more than upset stomachs.

Don't forget that you should always see your doctor for medical advice before heading off for a trip overseas.

Travel Health Guides

There are a number of books on travel health:

Staying Healthy in Asia, Africa & Latin America, Volunteers in Asia. This is probably the best all-round guide to carry, as it's compact but very detailed and well organised.

Travellers' Health by Dr Richard Dawood (Oxford University Press, 1992), is comprehensive, easy to read, authoritative and also highly recommended, though it's rather large to lug around.

Also recommended is *The Traveller's Health Guide* by Dr Anthony C Turner (Lascelles, Middlesex, 1991).

Travel with Children by Maureen Wheeler (Lonely Planet Publications) includes basic advice on travel health for younger children.

Predeparture Preparations

Health Insurance A travel insurance policy to cover theft, loss and medical problems is a wise idea. There are a wide variety of policies and your travel agent will have recommendations. The international student travel policies handled by STA Travel or other student travel organisations are usually good value. Some policies offer lower and higher medical expenses options but the higher one is chiefly for countries like the USA which have extremely high medical costs. Check the small print

• Some policies specifically exclude 'dangerous activities' which can include scuba diving, motorcycling, even trekking. If such activities are on your agenda you don't want that sort of policy.

A locally acquired motor cycle licence may not be valid under your policy.

- You may prefer a policy which pays doctors or hospitals direct rather than you having to pay on the spot and claim later. If you have to claim later make sure you keep all documentation. Some policies ask you to call back (reverse charges) to a centre in your home country where an immediate assessment of your problem is made.
- Check if the policy covers ambulances or an emergency flight home. If you have to stretch out you will need two seats and somebody has to pay for them!

Medical Kit A small, straightforward medical kit is a wise thing to carry. A possible kit list includes

- Aspirin or Panadol – for pain or fever.
- Antihistamine (such as Benadryl) – useful as a decongestant for colds, allergies, to ease the itch from insect bites or stings or to help prevent motion sickness.

  Antihistamines may cause sedation and interact with alcohol so care should be taken when using them.

- Antibiotics – useful if you're travelling well off the beaten track, but they must be prescribed and you should carry the prescription with you.

  Some individuals are allergic to commonly prescribed antibiotics such as penicillin or sulfa drugs. It would be sensible to always carry this information when travelling.

- Kaolin preparation (Pepto-Bismol), Imodium or Lomotil – for stomach upsets.
- Rehydration mixture – for treatment of severe diarrhoea. This is particularly important if travelling with children, but is recommended for everyone.
- Antiseptic such as Betadine, which comes as impregnated swabs or ointment, and an antibiotic powder or similar 'dry' spray – for cuts and grazes.
- Calamine lotion – to ease irritation from bites or stings.
- Bandages and Band-aids – for minor injuries.
- Scissors, tweezers and a thermometer (note that mercury thermometers are prohibited by airlines).
- Insect repellent, sunscreen (such as Caladryl, which is also good for sunburn, minor burns and itchy bites), suntan lotion, chap stick and water purification tablets.
- A couple of syringes, in case you need injections in a country with medical hygiene problems. Ask

your doctor for a note explaining why they have been prescribed.

Ideally antibiotics should be administered only under medical supervision and should never be taken indiscriminately. Take only the recommended dose at the prescribed intervals and continue using the antibiotic for the prescribed period, even if the illness seems to be cured earlier. Antibiotics are quite specific to the infections they can treat. Stop immediately if there are any serious reactions and don't use the antibiotic at all if you are unsure that you have the correct one.

Many of these or similar items, other than water sterilisation tablets and insect repellent, are cheaper in Morocco than in the West. Condoms are also available but are not good quality. The pill, although around, is still harder to get, and obtaining your particular prescription will be difficult indeed.

Always check the expiry date of any medication. Bogus drugs are common and it's possible that drugs that are no longer recommended, or have even been banned, in the West are still being dispensed in many Third World countries.

In many countries it may be a good idea to leave unwanted medicines, syringes etc with a local clinic, rather than carry them home.

Health Preparations Make sure you're healthy before you start travelling. If you are embarking on a long trip make sure your teeth are OK; there are lots of places where a visit to the dentist would be the last thing you'd want to do. In Morocco, your best bet is to reach a bigger city and get a recommendation for a good dentist at a consulate. As with doctors, most of them are French-speaking.

If you wear eyeglasses, carry a second pair or at least a copy of your prescription in case of loss or breakage.

If you wear glasses take a spare pair and your prescription. Losing your glasses can be a real problem, although in many places you can get new spectacles made up quickly, cheaply and competently.

If you require a particular medication take an adequate supply, as it may not be available locally. Take the prescription or, better still, part of the packaging showing the generic rather than the brand name (which may not be locally available), as it will make getting replacements easier. It's a wise idea to have a legible prescription with you to show you legally use the medication – it's surprising how often over-the-counter drugs from one place are illegal without a prescription or even banned in another.

Public toilets in Morocco are bad news: they're fly-infested, dirty and smelly. Some toilets are still of the squat-over-a-hole variety. Always carry a roll of toilet paper with you; it's easy to buy throughout Morocco.

Immunisations Vaccinations provide protection against diseases you might meet along the way. For some countries no immunisations are necessary, but the farther off the beaten track you go the more necessary it is to take precautions.

It is important to understand the distinction between vaccines recommended for travel in certain areas and those required by law. Essentially the number of vaccines subject to international health regulations has been dramatically reduced over the last 10 years. Currently yellow fever is the only vaccine subject to international health regulations. Vaccination as an entry requirement is usually only enforced when coming from an infected area.

On the other hand a number of vaccines are recommended for different areas of travel. These may not be required by law but are recommended for your own personal protection.

All vaccinations should be recorded on an International Health Certificate, which is available from your physician or government health department.

Plan ahead for getting your vaccinations: some of them require an initial shot followed by a booster, while some vaccinations should not be given together. It is recommended you seek medical advice at least six weeks prior to travel. In London, there are several places where you can get advice and vaccinations. Trailfinders (see Air in the Getting There & Away chapter) has an inoculation centre, as does British Airways at its Victoria Station office. The Travel Clinic of the Hospital for Tropical Diseases (☎ 0171-637 9899) at Queen's House, 180-182 Tottenham Court Rd is open from 9 am to 5 pm for consultations and shots. It also runs a recorded information line (☎ 0839-337733) on specific destinations.

If you are in Melbourne, Australia, the Travellers' Medical & Vaccination Centre (☎ 03-650 7600) can help you.

Most travellers from Western countries will have been immunised against various diseases during childhood but your doctor may still recommend booster shots against measles or polio, diseases that are still prevalent in many developing countries. The period of protection offered by vaccinations differs widely and some are contraindicated if you are pregnant.

People planning extended stays in Morocco, particularly in more remote areas, are advised to consider taking a pre-exposure rabies vaccine, along with cover for tuberculosis and hepatitis B. Also recommended is the polio vaccine.

Malaria is not a significant problem in Morocco, or indeed anywhere in the Maghreb, but if you are contemplating a long stay, especially in out-of-the-way places, you will want to consult your doctor about prophylactics. Note that they are hard to come by in Morocco – some pharmacists seem indignant at the suggestion that malaria could even be thought of as a potential problem in Morocco.

A list of other possible vaccinations includes:

Cholera Not required by law but occasionally travellers face bureaucratic problems on some border crossings. Protection is poor and it lasts only six months; the vaccine is contraindicated in pregnancy. It is important to note, however, that the disease has been a problem in the Meknès area since 1971. In

1990, 214 people reportedly died out of a total 2500 who had contracted the disease in Meknès, Fès, Taza and the Sebou River valley. There have been several smaller outbreaks since.

Hepatitis This is the most common travel-acquired illness that can be prevented by vaccination. Protection can be provided in two ways – either with the antibody gammaglobulin or with a new vaccine called Havrix.

Havrix provides long-term immunity (possibly more than 10 years) after an initial course of two injections and a booster in the one year. It may be more expensive than gammaglobulin but certainly has many advantages, including length of protection and ease of administration. It is important to know that the vaccine will take about three weeks to provide satisfactory protection.

Gammaglobulin is not a vaccination but a ready-made antibody which has proven very successful in reducing the chances of hepatitis infection. Because it may interfere with the development of immunity, it should not be given until at least 10 days after administration of the last vaccine needed; it should also be given as close as possible to departure because it is at its most effective in the first few weeks after administration and the effectiveness tapers off gradually between three and six months.

Smallpox Smallpox has now been wiped out worldwide, so immunisation is no longer necessary.

Tetanus & Diphtheria Boosters are necessary every 10 years and protection is highly recommended.

Typhoid Available either as an injection or oral capsules. Protection lasts from one to three years and is useful if you are travelling for long in rural, tropical areas and is recommended for Morocco. You may get some side effects such as pain at the injection site, fever, headache and a general unwell feeling. A new single-dose injectable vaccine, which

appears to have few side effects, is now available but is more expensive. Side effects are unusual with the oral form but may occasionally cause stomach cramps.

Yellow Fever Protection lasts 10 years and is recommended where the disease is endemic, chiefly in Africa and South America. You usually have to go to a special yellow fever vaccination centre. Vaccination is contraindicated during pregnancy but if you must travel to a high-risk area it is probably advisable.

Basic Rules
Care in what you eat and drink is the most important health rule. Stomach upsets are the most likely travel health problem (between 30% and 50% of travellers in a two-week stay experience this) but the majority of these upsets will be relatively minor. Don't become paranoid – trying the local food is part of the experience of travel, after all.

Water The number one rule is don't drink the water and that includes ice. If you don't know for certain that the water is safe always assume the worst. In Morocco's cities tap water is generally chlorinated and safe to drink, although the chlorination doesn't always agree with people. In the countryside the water is not so safe.

Reputable brands of bottled water or soft drinks are generally fine. Only use water from containers with a serrated seal – not tops or corks. Make sure the seals have not been tampered with, as it is not unheard of for bottles to be refilled with tap water. Take care with fruit juice, particularly if water may have been added. Milk should be treated with suspicion, as it is often unpasteurised. Boiled milk is fine if it is kept hygienically; the same goes for cream. In Morocco you can buy pasteurised milk in cartons. It is usually OK, but if it tastes at all funny, give it a miss. Yoghurt is always good.

Tea or coffee should also be OK, since the water should have been boiled.

Water Purification The simplest way of purifying water is to boil it thoroughly. Vigorously boiling for five minutes should be satisfactory. Remember that at high altitude water boils at a lower temperature, so germs are less likely to be killed and water may need to be boiled longer.

Simple filtering will not remove all dangerous organisms, so if you cannot boil water it should be treated chemically. Chlorine tablets (Puritabs, Steritabs or other brand names) will kill many but not all pathogens, including giardia and amoebic cysts. Iodine is very effective in purifying water and is available in tablet form (such as Potable Aqua), but follow the directions carefully and remember that too much iodine can be harmful.

If you can't find tablets, tincture of iodine (2%) or iodine crystals can be used. Four drops of tincture of iodine per litre or quart of clear water is the recommended dosage; the treated water should be left to stand for 20 to 30 minutes before drinking. Iodine crystals can also be used to purify water but this is a more complicated process, as you have to first prepare a saturated iodine solution. Iodine loses its effectiveness if exposed to air or damp so keep it in a tightly sealed container. Flavoured powder will disguise the taste of treated water and is a good idea if you are travelling with children.

Food There is an old colonial adage which says: 'If you can cook it, boil it or peel it, you can eat it......otherwise forget it'. Contaminated food or water can cause dysentery, giardia, hepatitis A, cholera, polio and typhoid – all of which are best avoided!

Fruit should be washed with purified water or peeled where possible. It is preferable to avoid salad unless you're sure it has been properly washed.

Thoroughly cooked food is safest but not if it has been left to cool or if it has been reheated. Shellfish such as mussels, oysters and clams should be avoided as should undercooked meat, particularly in the form of mince. Steaming does not make shellfish safe for eating. Ice cream is usually OK if it is a reputable brand name.

If a place looks clean and well run and if the vendor also looks clean and healthy, then the food is probably safe. In general, places that are packed with travellers or locals will be fine, while empty restaurants are questionable. Busy restaurants mean the food is being cooked and eaten quite quickly with little standing around and is probably not being reheated.

Nutrition If your food is poor or limited in availability, if you're travelling hard and fast and therefore missing meals, or if you simply lose your appetite, you can soon start to lose weight and place your health at risk.

Make sure your diet is well balanced. Eggs, tofu, beans, lentils and nuts are all safe ways to get protein. Fruit you can peel (bananas, oranges or mandarins for example) is always safe and a good source of vitamins. Try to eat plenty of grains (eg rice) and bread. Remember that although food is generally safer if it is cooked well, overcooked food loses much of its nutritional value.

Morocco is hardly a vegetarian's delight, and sticking to a limited range of food could result in vitamin deficiencies. Even those not so handicapped may find they are not eating as well as they could, and in both cases a course of multivitamins is worth considering to supplement the local diet.

In hot climates make sure you drink enough – don't rely on feeling thirsty to indicate when you should drink. Not needing to urinate or very dark-yellow urine is a danger sign. Always carry a water bottle with you on long trips. Excessive sweating can lead to loss of salt and therefore muscle cramping. Salt tablets are not a good idea as a preventative, but in places where salt is not used much adding salt to food can help.

Everyday Health A normal body temperature is 98.6°F or 37°C; more than 2°C higher is a 'high' fever. A normal adult pulse rate is 60 to 80 per minute (children 80 to 100, babies 100 to 140). You should know how to take a temperature and a pulse rate. As a general rule the pulse increases about 20 beats per minute for each °C rise in fever.

Respiration (breathing) rate is also an indicator of illness. Count the number of breaths per minute: between 12 and 20 is normal for adults and older children (up to 30 for younger children, 40 for babies). People with a high fever or serious respiratory illness (like pneumonia) breathe more quickly than normal. More than 40 shallow breaths a minute usually means pneumonia.

In Western countries with safe water and excellent human waste disposal systems we often take good health for granted. In years gone by, when public health facilities were not as good as they are today, certain rules attached to eating and drinking were observed, eg washing your hands before a meal. It is important for people travelling in areas of poor sanitation to be aware of this and adjust their own personal hygiene habits.

Clean your teeth with purified water rather than straight from the tap. Avoid climatic extremes: keep out of the sun when it's hot, dress warmly when it's cold. Avoid potential diseases by dressing sensibly. You can get worm infections through walking barefoot or dangerous coral cuts by walking over coral without shoes. You can avoid insect bites by covering bare skin when insects are around, by screening windows or beds or by using insect repellents. Seek local advice: if you're told the water is unsafe due to jellyfish, crocodiles or bilharzia, don't go in. In situations where there is no information, discretion is the better part of valour.

Medical Problems & Treatment

Self-diagnosis and treatment can be risky, so wherever possible seek qualified help. Although we do give treatment dosages in this section, they are for emergency use only. Medical advice should be sought before administering any drugs. An embassy or consulate can usually recommend a good place to go for such advice. So can five-star hotels, although they often recommend doctors with five-star prices. (This is when that medical insurance is really useful!) In some places standards of medical attention are so low that for some ailments the best advice is to get on a plane and go somewhere else.

Climatic & Geographical Considerations
Sunburn In the tropics, the desert or at high altitude you can get sunburnt surprisingly quickly, even through cloud. Use a sunscreen and take extra care to cover areas which don't normally see sun – eg, your feet. A hat provides added protection, and you should also use zinc cream or some other barrier cream for your nose and lips. Calamine lotion is good for mild sunburn. Remember that when you're on the beach or in the water you will burn quite quickly, so wear a shirt while snorkelling or swimming.

Prickly Heat Prickly heat is an itchy rash caused by excessive perspiration trapped under the skin. It usually strikes people who have just arrived in a hot climate and whose pores have not yet opened sufficiently to cope with greater sweating. Keeping cool and bathing often, using a mild talcum powder or even resorting to air-conditioning may help until you acclimatise.

Heat Exhaustion In some parts of Morocco, especially in the south, it can be difficult to gauge how quickly you are losing body water, because the climate is dry. Dehydration or salt deficiency can cause heat exhaustion. Take time to acclimatise to high temperatures and make sure you get sufficient liquids. (Note that the caffeine in coffee and tea also contributes to dehydration).

Salt deficiency is characterised by fatigue, lethargy, headaches, giddiness and muscle cramps and in this case salt tablets may help. Vomiting or diarrhoea can deplete your liquid and salt levels. Anhydrotic heat exhaustion, caused by an inability to sweat, is quite rare. Unlike the other forms of heat exhaustion, it is likely to strike people who have been in a hot climate for some time rather than newcomers. You will stay cooler by covering up with light, cotton clothes that trap perspiration against your skin rather than by wearing brief clothes.

Heatstroke This serious, and sometimes fatal, condition can occur if the body's heat-regulating mechanism breaks down and the body temperature rises to dangerous levels. Long, continuous periods of exposure to high temperatures can leave you vulnerable to heatstroke. You should avoid excessive alcohol intake or strenuous activity when you first arrive in a hot climate.

The symptoms are feeling unwell, little or no sweating and a high body temperature (39°C to 41°C). Where sweating has ceased, the skin becomes flushed and red. Severe, throbbing headaches and lack of coordination will also occur, and the sufferer may be confused or aggressive and will eventually become delirious or convulse. Hospitalisation is essential, but meanwhile get victims out of the sun, remove their clothing, cover them with a wet sheet or towel and fan them continually.

Fungal Infections Hot weather fungal infections are most likely to occur on the scalp, between the toes or fingers (athlete's foot), in the groin (jock itch or crotch rot) and on the body (ringworm). You get ringworm (a fungal infection, not a worm) from infected animals or by walking on damp areas, like shower floors.

To prevent fungal infections wear loose, comfortable clothes, avoid artificial fibres, wash frequently and dry carefully. If you do get an infection, wash the infected area daily with a disinfectant or medicated soap and water, and rinse and dry well. Apply an antifungal powder like Tinaderm. Try to expose the infected area to air or sunlight as much as possible and wash all towels and underwear in hot water as well as changing them often.

Cold Too much cold is just as dangerous as too much heat, particularly if it leads to hypothermia. Although not generally a problem in Morocco, take care when trekking high up in the Atlas Mountains (especially in winter) or indeed when taking an overnight bus through the mountains.

Hypothermia occurs when the body loses heat faster than it can produce it and the core temperature of the body falls. It is surprisingly easy to progress from being very cold to dangerously cold through a combination of wind, wet clothing, fatigue and hunger, even if the air temperature is above freezing. It is best to dress in layers; silk, wool and some of the new artificial fibres are all good insulating materials. A hat is important, as a lot of heat is lost through the head. A strong, waterproof outer layer is essential, as keeping dry is vital. Carry basic supplies, including food containing simple sugars to generate heat quickly and lots of fluid to drink.

Symptoms of hypothermia are exhaustion, numb skin (particularly toes and fingers), shivering, slurred speech, irrational or violent behaviour, lethargy, stumbling, dizzy spells, muscle cramps and violent bursts of energy. Irrationality may take the form of sufferers claiming they are warm and trying to take off their clothes.

To treat hypothermia, first get victims out of the wind or rain, remove their clothing if it's wet and replace it with dry, warm clothing. Give them hot, nonalcoholic liquids and some high-kilojoule, easily digestible food. This should be enough for the early stages of hypothermia, but if it has gone further it may be necessary to place victims in warm sleeping bags and get in with them. Do not rub patients, place them near a fire or remove their wet clothes in the wind. If possible, place them in a warm (not hot) bath.

Altitude Sickness Acute Mountain Sickness or AMS occurs at high altitudes and can be fatal. The lack of oxygen at high altitudes affects most people to some extent.

A number of measures can be adopted to prevent acute mountain sickness

Ascend slowly – have frequent rest days, spending two to three nights at each rise of 1000 metres. If you reach a high altitude by trekking,

- acclimatisation takes place gradually and you are less likely to be affected than if you fly direct.
- Drink extra fluids. The mountain air is dry and cold and moisture is lost as you breathe.
- Eat light, high-carbohydrate meals for more energy.
- Avoid alcohol as it may increase the risk of dehydration.
- Avoid sedatives.

Even with acclimatisation you may still have trouble adjusting – headaches, nausea, dizziness, a dry cough, insomnia, breathlessness and loss of appetite are all signs to heed. Mild altitude problems will generally abate after a day or so but if the symptoms persist or become worse the only treatment is to descend – even 500 metres can help. Breathlessness, a dry, irritative cough (which may progress to the production of pink, frothy sputum), severe headache, loss of appetite, nausea, and sometimes vomiting are all danger signs. Increasing tiredness, confusion, and lack of coordination and balance are real danger signs. Any of these symptoms individually, even just a persistent headache, can be a warning.

There is no hard and fast rule as to how high is too high: AMS has been fatal at altitudes of 3000 metres, although 3500 to 4500 metres is the usual range. Jebel Toubkal is the highest point of the High Atlas Mountains, at 4165 metres. It is always wise to sleep at a lower altitude than the greatest height reached during the day.

Motion Sickness Eating lightly before and during a trip will reduce the chances of motion sickness. If you are prone to motion sickness, try to find a place that minimises disturbance – near the wing on aircraft, close to midships on boats, near the centre on buses. Fresh air usually helps – reading and cigarette smoke don't. Commercial anti-motion-sickness preparations, which can cause drowsiness, have to be taken before the trip commences; when you're feeling sick it's too late. Ginger is a natural preventative and is available in capsule form.

Jet Lag Jet lag is experienced when a person travels by air across more than three time zones (each time zone usually represents a one-hour time difference). It occurs because many of the functions of the human body (such as temperature, pulse rate and emptying of the bladder and bowels) are regulated by internal 24-hour cycles called circadian rhythms. When we travel long distances rapidly, our bodies take time to adjust to the 'new time' of our destination, and we may experience fatigue, disorientation, insomnia, anxiety, impaired concentration and loss of appetite. These effects will usually be gone within three days of arrival, but there are ways of minimising the impact of jet lag

- Rest for a couple of days before departure; try to avoid late nights and last-minute dashes for travellers' cheques, passport etc.
- Try to select flight schedules that minimise sleep deprivation; arriving late in the day means you can go to sleep soon after you arrive. For very long flights, try to organise a stopover.
- Avoid excessive eating (which bloats the stomach) and alcohol (which causes dehydration) during the flight. Instead, drink plenty of noncarbonated, nonalcoholic drinks such as fruit juice or water.
- Avoid smoking, as this reduces the amount of oxygen in the aeroplane cabin even further and causes greater fatigue.
- Make yourself comfortable by wearing loose-fitting clothes and perhaps bringing an eye mask and ear plugs to help you sleep.

Diseases of Poor Sanitation

Diarrhoea A change of water, food or climate can all cause the runs; diarrhoea caused by contaminated food or water is more serious. Despite all your precautions you may still have a bout of mild travellers' diarrhoea but a few rushed toilet trips with no other symptoms is not indicative of a serious problem. Moderate diarrhoea, involving half-a-dozen loose movements in a day, is more of a nuisance. Dehydration is the main danger with any diarrhoea, particularly for children where dehydration can occur quite quickly. Fluid replacement remains the mainstay of management. Weak black tea with a little sugar, soda water, or soft drinks allowed to go flat and diluted

50% with water are all good. With severe diarrhoea a rehydrating solution is necessary to replace minerals and salts. Commercially available ORS (oral rehydration salts) is very useful; add the contents of one sachet to a litre of boiled or bottled water. In an emergency you can make up a solution of eight teaspoons of sugar to a litre of boiled water and provide salted cracker biscuits at the same time. You should stick to a bland diet as you recover.

Lomotil or Imodium can be used to bring relief from the symptoms, although they do not actually cure the problem. Only use these drugs if absolutely necessary – eg, if you travel. For children Imodium is preferable, but under all circumstances fluid replacement is the main message. Do not use these drugs if the person has a high fever or is severely dehydrated.

In certain situations antibiotics may be indicated

- Watery diarrhoea with blood and mucous. (Gut-paralysing drugs like Imodium or Lomotil should be avoided in this situation.)
- Watery diarrhoea with fever and lethargy.
- Persistent diarrhoea for more than five days.
- Severe diarrhoea, if it is logistically difficult to stay in one place.

The recommended drugs (adults only) would be either norfloxacin 400 mg twice daily for three days or ciprofloxacin 500 mg twice daily for three days.

The drug bismuth subsalicylate has also been used successfully. It is not available in Australia. The dosage for adults is two tablets or 30 ml and for children it is one tablet or 10 ml. This dose can be repeated every 30 minutes to one hour, with no more than eight doses in a 24-hour period.

The drug of choice in children would be co-trimoxazole (Bactrim, Septrin, Resprim) with dosage dependent on weight. A three-day course is also given.

Ampicillin has been recommended in the past and may still be an alternative.

Giardiasis The parasite causing this intestinal disorder is present in contaminated water.

The symptoms are stomach cramps, nausea, a bloated stomach, watery, foul-smelling diarrhoea and frequent gas. Giardiasis can appear several weeks after you have been exposed to the parasite. The symptoms may disappear for a few days and then return; this can go on for several weeks. Tinidazole, known as Fasigyn, or metronidazole (Flagyl) are the recommended drugs for treatment. Either can be used in a single treatment dose. Antibiotics are of no use.

Dysentery This serious illness is caused by contaminated food or water and is characterised by severe diarrhoea, often with blood or mucus in the stool. There are two kinds of dysentery. Bacillary dysentery is characterised by a high fever and rapid onset; headache, vomiting and stomach pains are also symptoms. It generally does not last longer than a week, but it is highly contagious.

Amoebic dysentery is often more gradual in the onset of symptoms, with cramping abdominal pain and vomiting being less likely; fever may not be present. It is not a self-limiting disease: it will persist until treated and can recur and cause long-term health problems.

A stool test is necessary to diagnose which kind of dysentery you have, so you should seek medical help urgently. In case of an emergency the drugs norfloxacin or ciprofloxacin can be used as presumptive treatment for bacillary dysentery, and metronidazole (Flagyl) for amoebic dysentery.

For bacillary dysentery, norfloxacin 400 mg twice daily for seven days or ciprofloxacin 500 mg twice daily for seven days are the recommended dosages.

If you're unable to find either of these drugs then a useful alternative is co-trimoxazole 160/800 mg (Bactrim, Septrin, Resprim) twice daily for seven days. This is a sulfa drug and must not be used in people with a known sulfa allergy.

In the case of children the drug co-trimoxazole is a reasonable first line treatment. For amoebic dysentery, the recommended adult dosage of metronidazole (Flagyl) is one

750 mg to 800 mg capsule three times daily for five days. Children aged between eight and 12 years should have half the adult dose; the dosage for younger children is one-third the adult dose.

An alternative to Flagyl is Fasigyn, taken as a two-gram daily dose for three days. Alcohol must be avoided during treatment and for 48 hours afterwards.

Cholera Cholera vaccination is not very effective. The bacteria responsible for this disease are waterborne, so that attention to the rules of eating and drinking should protect the traveller.

Outbreaks of cholera are generally widely reported, so you can avoid such problem areas. As noted above, it can be a minor problem in parts of Morocco, particularly in the Meknès region.

The disease is characterised by a sudden onset of acute diarrhoea with 'rice water' stools, vomiting, muscular cramps, and extreme weakness. You need medical help – but treat for dehydration, which can be extreme, and if there is an appreciable delay in getting to hospital then begin taking tetracycline. The adult dose is 250 mg four times daily. It is not recommended in children aged eight years or under nor in pregnant women. An alternative drug would be Ampicillin. Remember that while antibiotics might kill the bacteria, it is a toxin produced by the bacteria which causes the massive fluid loss. Fluid replacement is by far the most important aspect of treatment.

Viral Gastroenteritis This is caused not by bacteria but, as the name suggests, by a virus. It is characterised by stomach cramps, diarrhoea, and sometimes by vomiting and/or a slight fever. All you can do is rest and drink lots of fluids.

Hepatitis Hepatitis A is a very common problem among travellers to areas with poor sanitation. With good water and adequate sewage disposal in most industrialised countries since the 1940s, very few young adults now have any natural immunity and must be protected. Protection is through the new vaccine Havrix or the antibody gamma-globulin. The antibody is short-lasting.

The disease is spread by contaminated food or water. The symptoms are fever, chills, headache, fatigue, feelings of weakness and aches and pains, followed by loss of appetite, nausea, vomiting, abdominal pain, dark urine, light-coloured faeces, jaundiced skin and the whites of the eyes may turn yellow. In some cases you may feel unwell, tired, have no appetite, experience aches and pains and be jaundiced. You should seek medical advice, but in general there is not much you can do apart from rest, drink lots of fluids, eat lightly and avoid fatty foods. People who have had hepatitis must forego alcohol for six months after the illness, as hepatitis attacks the liver and it needs that amount of time to recover.

Hepatitis B, which used to be called serum hepatitis, is spread through contact with infected blood, blood products or bodily fluids, for example through sexual contact, unsterilised needles and blood transfusions. Other risk situations include having a shave or tattoo in a local shop, or having your ears pierced. The symptoms of type B are much the same as type A except that they are more severe and may lead to irreparable liver damage or even liver cancer.

Although there is no treatment for hepatitis B, an effective prophylactic vaccine is readily available in most countries. The immunisation schedule requires two injections at least a month apart followed by a third dose five months after the second. People who should receive a hepatitis B vaccination include anyone who anticipates contact with blood or other bodily secretions, either as a health care worker or through sexual contact with the local population, and particularly anyone who intends to stay in the country for a long period of time.

Hepatitis Non-A Non-B is a blanket term formerly used for several different strains of hepatitis, which have now been separately identified. Hepatitis C is similar to B but is less common. Hepatitis D (the 'delta particle') is also similar to B and always occurs in concert with it; its occurrence is currently limited to intravenous drug users. Hepatitis E, however, is similar to A and is spread in the same manner, by water or food contamination.

Tests are available for these strands, but are very expensive. Travellers shouldn't be too paranoid about this apparent proliferation of hepatitis strains; they are fairly rare (so far) and following the same precautions as for A and B should be all that's necessary to avoid them.

Polio This is another disease spread by insanitary conditions and found more frequently in hot climates. There is an oral vaccine against polio – three doses of drops taken at four to eight week intervals. If you were vaccinated as a child you may only need a booster.

Typhoid Typhoid fever is another gut infection that travels the faecal-oral route – ie, contaminated water and food are responsible. Vaccination against typhoid is not totally effective and it is one of the most dangerous infections, so medical help must be sought.

In its early stages typhoid resembles many other illnesses: sufferers may feel like they have a bad cold or flu on the way, as early symptoms are a headache, a sore throat, and a fever which rises a little each day until it is around 40°C or more. The victim's pulse is often slow relative to the degree of fever present and gets slower as the fever rises – unlike a normal fever where the pulse increases. There may also be vomiting, diarrhoea or constipation.

In the second week the high fever and slow pulse continue and a few pink spots may appear on the body; trembling, delirium, weakness, weight loss and dehydration are other symptoms. If there are no further complications, the fever and other symptoms will slowly go during the third week. However you must get medical help before this because pneumonia (acute infection of the lungs) or peritonitis (perforated bowel)

are common complications, and because typhoid is very infectious.

The fever should be treated by keeping the victim cool and dehydration should also be watched for.

The drug of choice is ciprofloxacin at a dose of one gram daily for 14 days. It is quite expensive and may not be available. The alternative, chloramphenicol, has been the mainstay of treatment for many years. In many countries it is still the recommended antibiotic but there are fewer side affects with Ampicillin. The adult dosage is two 250 mg capsules, four times a day. Children aged between eight and 12 years should have half the adult dose; younger children should have one-third the adult dose.

People who are allergic to penicillin should not be given Ampicillin.

Worms These parasites are most common in rural, tropical areas and a stool test when you return home is not a bad idea. They can be present on unwashed vegetables or in undercooked meat and you can pick them up through your skin by walking in bare feet. Infestations may not show up for some time, and although they are generally not serious, if left untreated they can cause severe health problems. A stool test is necessary to pinpoint the problem and medication is often available over the counter.

Diseases Spread by Animals & Humans

Tetanus This potentially fatal disease is found in undeveloped tropical areas. It is difficult to treat but is preventable with immunisation. Tetanus occurs when a wound becomes infected by a germ which lives in the faeces of animals or people, so clean all cuts, punctures or animal bites. Tetanus is also known as lockjaw, and the first symptom may be discomfort in swallowing, or stiffening of the jaw and neck; this is followed by painful convulsions of the jaw and whole body.

Rabies Rabies is found in many countries and is caused by a bite or scratch by an infected animal. Dogs are noted carriers as are monkeys and cats. Any bite, scratch or even lick from a warm-blooded, furry animal should be cleaned immediately and thoroughly. Scrub with soap and running water, and then clean with an alcohol solution. If there is any possibility that the animal is infected medical help should be sought immediately. Even if the animal is not rabid, all bites should be treated seriously as they can become infected or can result in tetanus. A rabies vaccination is now available and should be considered if you are in a high-risk category – eg, if you intend to explore caves (bat bites could be dangerous) or work with animals.

Meningococcal Meningitis Sub-Saharan Africa is considered the 'meningitis belt' and the meningitis season falls at the time most people would be attempting the overland trip across the Sahara – the northern winter before the rains come. Although throughout most of Morocco it is not an issue, people penetrating to the very south of the country or going beyond should be aware of the potential danger. The disease is spread through close contact with people who carry it in their throats and noses, spread it through coughs and sneezes, and may not be aware that they are carriers.

This very serious disease attacks the brain and can be fatal. A scattered, blotchy rash, fever, severe headache, sensitivity to light and neck stiffness which prevents forward bending of the head are the first symptoms. Death can occur within a few hours, so immediate treatment is important.

Treatment is large doses of penicillin given intravenously, or, if that is not possible, intramuscularly (ie, in the buttocks). Vaccination offers good protection for over a year, but you should also check for reports of current epidemics.

Tuberculosis (TB) Although this disease is widespread in many developing countries, it is not a serious risk to travellers. Young children are more susceptible than adults and vaccination is a sensible precaution for chil-

dren under 12 travelling in endemic areas. TB is commonly spread by coughing or by unpasteurised dairy products from infected cows. Milk that has been boiled is safe to drink; the souring of milk to make yoghurt or cheese also kills the bacilli.

Bilharzia Bilharzia is carried in water by minute worms. The larvae infect certain varieties of freshwater snails, found in rivers, streams, lakes and particularly behind dams. The worms multiply and are eventually discharged into the water surrounding the snails.

They attach themselves to your intestines or bladder, where they produce large numbers of eggs. The worm enters through the skin, and the first symptom may be a tingling and sometimes a light rash around the area where it entered. Weeks later, when the worm is busy producing eggs, a high fever may develop. A general feeling of being unwell may be the first symptom; once the disease is established abdominal pain and blood in the urine are other signs.

Avoiding swimming or bathing in fresh water where bilharzia is present is the main method of preventing the disease. Even deep water can be infected. If you do get wet, dry off quickly and dry your clothes as well. Seek medical attention if you have been exposed to the disease and tell the doctor your suspicions, as bilharzia in the early stages can be confused with malaria or typhoid. If you cannot get medical help immediately, praziquantel (Biltricide) is the recommended treatment. The recommended dosage is 40 mg per kg in divided doses over one day. Niridazole is an alternative drug.

Diphtheria Diphtheria can be a skin infection or a more dangerous throat infection. It is spread by contaminated dust contacting the skin or by the inhalation of infected cough or sneeze droplets. Washing frequently and keeping the skin dry will help prevent skin infection. A vaccination is available to prevent the throat infection.

Sexually Transmitted Diseases Sexual contact with an infected person spreads these diseases. While abstinence is the only 100% preventative, using a condom is also effective. Gonorrhoea and syphilis are the most common of these diseases; sores, blisters or rashes around the genitals, discharges or pain when urinating are common symptoms. Symptoms may be less marked or not observed at all in women. The symptoms of syphilis eventually disappear completely but the disease continues and can cause severe problems in later years. Treatment of gonorrhoea and syphilis is by antibiotics.

There are numerous other sexually transmitted diseases, for most of which effective treatment is available. However, there is no cure for herpes or AIDS.

HIV/AIDS HIV, the Human Immunodeficiency Virus, may develop into AIDS, Acquired Immune Deficiency Syndrome. HIV is a major problem in many countries. Any exposure to blood, blood products or bodily fluids may put the individual at risk. In many developing countries transmission is predominantly through heterosexual sexual activity. This is quite different from industrialised countries where transmission is mostly through contact between homosexual or bisexual males or contaminated needles in intravenous drug users. Apart from abstinence, the most effective preventative is always to practise safe sex using condoms. It is impossible to detect the HIV-positive status of an otherwise healthy-looking person without a blood test.

HIV/AIDS can also be spread through infected blood transfusions; most developing countries cannot afford to screen blood for transfusions. It can also be spread by dirty needles – vaccinations, acupuncture, tattooing and ear or nose piercing are potentially as dangerous as intravenous drug use if the equipment is not clean. If you do need an injection, it may be a good idea to buy a new syringe from a pharmacy and ask the doctor to use it. You may also want to take a couple of syringes with you, in case of an emergency.

Insect-Borne Diseases

Malaria This serious disease is spread by mosquito bites. If you are travelling in endemic areas it is extremely important to take malarial prophylactics. Symptoms include headaches, fever, chills and sweating which may subside and recur. Without treatment malaria can develop more serious, potentially fatal effects. Although malaria is a minimal problem in Morocco, if you're in remote regions, and especially in the south, during the summer months, it's far better to be safe than sorry.

Antimalarial drugs do not prevent you from being infected but kill the parasites during a stage in their development.

There are a number of different types of malaria. The one of most concern is falciparum malaria. This is responsible for the very serious cerebral malaria. Falciparum is the predominant form in many malaria-prone areas of the world, including Africa, South-East Asia and Papua New Guinea. Contrary to popular belief, cerebral malaria is not a new strain.

The problem in recent years has been the emergence of increasing resistance to commonly used antimalarials like chloroquine, maloprim and proguanil. Newer drugs such as mefloquine (Lariam) and doxycycline (Vibramycin, Doryx) are now recommended for chloroquine and multidrug-resistant areas. Expert advice should be sought as to whether an antimalarial is required and what drug if any is suitable for the individual. The main messages are:

1. Primary prevention must always be in the form of mosquito-avoidance measures. The mosquitoes that transmit malaria bite from dusk to dawn and during this period travellers are advised to:

- wear light-coloured clothing
- wear long pants and long sleeved shirts
- use mosquito repellents containing the compound DEET on exposed areas
- avoid highly scented perfumes or aftershave
- use a mosquito net – it may be worth taking your own

- sleep near a fan (mosquitoes hate fast-moving air)

2. While no antimalarial is 100% effective, taking the most appropriate drug significantly reduces the risk of contracting the disease.

3. No-one should ever die from malaria. It can be diagnosed by a simple blood test, so a traveller with a fever or flu-like illness should seek examination as soon as possible.

Contrary to popular belief, once a traveller contracts malaria he/she does not have it for life. One of the parasites may lie dormant in the liver but this can also be eradicated using a specific medication. Malaria is therefore curable, as long as the traveller seeks medical help when symptoms occur, either at home or overseas.

Bugs, Bites & Cuts

Cuts & Scratches Skin punctures can easily become infected in hot climates and may be difficult to heal. Treat any cut with an antiseptic such as Betadine. Where possible avoid bandages and Band-aids, which can keep wounds wet.

Bites & Stings Things to look out for in Morocco include scorpions, which often shelter in shoes and the like and pack a powerful sting, and snakes. Bee and wasp stings are usually painful rather than dangerous. Calamine lotion will give relief and ice packs will reduce the pain and swelling. There are some spiders with dangerous bites but antivenenes are usually available.

Snakes To minimise your chances of being bitten always wear boots, socks and long trousers when walking through undergrowth where snakes may be present. Don't put your hands into holes and crevices, and be careful when collecting firewood.

Snake bites do not cause instantaneous death and antivenenes are usually available. Keep the victim calm and still, wrap the bitten limb tightly, as you would for a sprained ankle, and then attach a splint to

immobilise it. Then seek medical help, if possible with the dead snake for identification. Don't attempt to catch the snake if there is even a remote possibility of being bitten again. Tourniquets and sucking out the poison are now comprehensively discredited.

Bedbugs & Lice Bedbugs live in various places, but particularly in dirty mattresses and bedding. Spots of blood on bedclothes or on the wall around the bed can be read as a suggestion to find another hotel. Bedbugs leave itchy bites in neat rows. Calamine lotion may help.

All lice cause itching and discomfort. They make themselves at home in your hair (head lice), clothing (body lice) or pubic hair (crabs). You catch lice through direct contact with infected people or by sharing combs, clothing and the like. Powder or shampoo treatment will kill the lice and infected clothing should then be washed in very hot water.

Women's Health

Gynaecological Problems Poor diet, lowered resistance through the use of antibiotics for stomach upsets and even contraceptive pills can lead to vaginal infections when travelling in hot climates. Maintaining good personal hygiene and wearing cotton underwear and skirts or loose-fitting trousers will help to prevent infections.

Yeast infections, characterised by a rash, itch and discharge, can be treated with a vinegar or even lemon-juice douche or with yoghurt. Nystatin suppositories are the usual medical prescription. Trichomonas is a more serious infection; symptoms are a discharge and a burning sensation when urinating. Male sexual partners must also be treated and if a vinegar-water douche is not effective medical attention should be sought. Metronidazole (Flagyl) is the prescribed drug.

Pregnancy Most miscarriages occur during the first three months of pregnancy, so this is the most risky time to travel as far as your own health is concerned. Miscarriage is not uncommon, and can occasionally lead to severe bleeding. The last three months should also be spent within reasonable distance of good medical care. A baby born as early as 24 weeks stands a chance of survival, but only in a good modern hospital. Pregnant women should avoid all unnecessary medication, but vaccinations and malarial prophylactics should still be taken where possible. Additional care should be taken to prevent illness and particular attention should be paid to diet and nutrition. Alcohol and nicotine, for example, should be avoided.

Women travellers often find that their periods become irregular or even cease while they're on the road. Remember that a missed period in these circumstances doesn't necessarily indicate pregnancy. There are health posts or Family Planning clinics in many small and large urban centres in developing countries, where you can seek advice and have a urine test to determine whether you are pregnant or not.

Moroccan Hospitals & Doctors

The standards of health care in Morocco vary considerably, and some hospitals are quite off-putting. Nevertheless, the better doctors are generally well trained. If you must go to hospital, the Hôpital Avicenne (☎ 672871) in Rabat is one of the better options and is fully functional around the clock. The French-language newspapers publish lists of hospitals with 24-hour emergency services ('les urgences') in Rabat and Casablanca. The best advice, where possible, is to seek recommendations from a foreign consulate.

WOMEN TRAVELLERS

Sexual harassment by men of women seems to be something of a Mediterranean problem, so you may as well be prepared for it. Morocco is no different from other countries where this is an issue, but assertions that it is a specifically Muslim quirk are not justified – plenty of women have ugly tales to tell

about offensive males in countries such as Spain, Portugal, Italy and Greece.

Western (and especially blonde, fair-skinned) women will find they have constant male company at various times during their stay in Morocco. This may go no further than annoying banter or proposals of marriage and declarations of undying love (or considerably less noble suggestions). Harassment usually takes the comparatively harmless form of leering, sometimes being followed and occasionally being touched up (there are, as you can probably imagine, a million variations on this theme). Strange as it may sound, some of these charming fellows are not in the least bit deterred by the sight of husband and kids in tow.

You cannot make this problem go away, but plenty of women travel through Morocco, many of them without male companions and some even alone, and enjoy it. The best thing is to ignore this pubescent idiocy or you will end up letting a few uncouth individuals spoil your entire trip.

The first rule of thumb is to respect standard Muslim sensibilities about dress – cover the shoulders, upper arms and legs at least – and not with skin-tight apparel. Your respecting local custom doesn't guarantee you'll get any respect in return; in the main tourist attractions especially, efforts to please by covering hair and the like seem to be wasted on the lads, who are all too used to such attempts to ward them off, but it's a start.

Use your common sense. When dealing with men, avoid overdoing eye contact, as it's amazing what can be read into a glance. In some of the bigger cities, slick Western fashions are popular among many of the local women too, and so the kind of dress sense you are more accustomed to will tend not to raise eyebrows as often. It is noticeable that local women in cities like Casablanca who wear more modern clothes are not immune to the kind of attention Western visitors are subjected to. Their attitude appears to be to laugh them off with a good deal of scorn.

There is a variety of methods for dealing with lewd and unpleasant behaviour. As often as not it is probably better to let pass unnoticed remarks you wish you hadn't heard, and some women find it's not worth the energy to acknowledge, say, being brushed up against. Other behaviour may well warrant a bit of a scene. There's no more reason to let yourself be intimidated in Morocco than anywhere else.

The best way for female travellers to meet and talk to local women is to go to a *hammam* (bathhouse). Every town has one, and if there is not one that is exclusively for women there are times set aside each day for women and men.

Indeed, this could be a particularly interesting time to get to know Moroccan women. In the 1993 national elections Morocco got two women MPs – a first. In addition, some changes have been made to the Mudawwana, the marital law code. A man can now technically no longer repudiate (effectively divorce) his wife without producing some valid reasons before a judge, who is expected to be a little more generous now when awarding compensation *(mut'a)* to the woman concerned. It may not sound a lot, but it is a step towards improving the legal status of women, who are still much disadvantaged in Moroccan society.

TRAVELLING WITH CHILDREN

Travelling with children generally poses no problems in Morocco. If they are already about four or older, and so past the age where you have to worry about preparing special food and the like, having a young child with you can sometimes be a great plus. Moroccans love children and are very indulgent towards them. Don't be surprised to have the odd local bowling up out of nowhere with a sweet or something for your little one. In this way, children can often break the ice between you and locals, opening up unexpected opportunities for getting to know people. Food poses no real problems, although to stay on the safe side, it is probably wiser to give some of the cheaper street stall food a miss.

Although your child won't need all that many toys, it's worth bringing along his or her favourite teddy bear or equivalent, a couple of colouring books and a small bag of little bits and pieces to play with. Most Moroccan children don't have any of that sort of thing – the teddy bear alone will probably attract attention.

Some, but by no means all, hotels will charge little or nothing extra for a young child, but you shouldn't count on this.

Travelling with Children

Geoff Crowther, who did several trips into Morocco for earlier editions of Lonely Planet's guides to the region, has some useful observations for those wanting to take younger children (of one to two years of age) into Morocco.

The three biggest considerations with children of this age are finding suitable food and bathroom facilities and keeping them amused on long journeys. Where your child is already eating solids, you shouldn't have too much trouble. Certain things will be out though, such as street stall food, if you want to minimise the risks of diarrhoea and the like. Soups, tajines (stews), couscous, fried or grilled fish, omelettes/boiled eggs and fruit (washed and peeled, of course) should all be OK. For liquids, you can get powdered milk in many places and mix it with bottled mineral water. Where this isn't possible, on long journeys, for example, you may have to stick to the mineral water alone.

As for nappies (diapers), it's impractical to take along more than half a dozen of the washable variety. Disposable nappies, despite their environmentally unfriendly nature, are the only practical solution. These are readily available all over Morocco but they aren't cheap (about US$5 for a packet of 10). Babidou is the only decent brand.

Keeping infants and their clothes clean is the biggest constraint. You may find you have to take rooms in hotels with private showers and hot water most of the time.

Geoff Crowther

EMERGENCY

Throughout Morocco, you can contact the police on ☎ 19 and the fire brigade (sapeurs-pompiers) on ☎ 15.

DANGERS & ANNOYANCES

When all is said and done, Morocco is a comparatively safe place to travel, and the great majority of people are friendly and honest. Nevertheless, the country does have a few traps for the unwary.

Theft & Violence

On the whole, theft is not a huge problem in Morocco but travellers who have spent time in other Arab countries may feel a little less secure. The moral is not to give your belongings away – more often than not it is in moments of laxness that things go missing.

When wandering around the streets, keep your valuables to a minimum, and what you must take around with you well hidden. External money pouches attract attention, but neck pouches or money belts worn under your clothes do not – and that's where you should keep your money, passport and other important documents. Pouches made of cotton are much more comfortable than nylon ones.

In some of the medinas, such as the Djemaa el-Fna in Marrakesh and Tangier, which have a particular reputation for petty theft, a common tactic is for one guy to distract your attention while another cleans out your pockets. There is no point walking around in a state of permanent alert, but it is worth keeping an eye open.

Other valuables such as cameras should be left with the hotel reception when you don't want to use them. If you prefer to keep things in your room, nine times out of 10 you'll have no trouble. Where you can, lock everything up. Leaving anything in a car, even out of sight, is asking for grief.

In places like Tangier, physical attacks on foreigners are not entirely unheard of. There are some desperate people in the bigger cities, and some feel no compunction about trying to extract money from tourists. Treat the medinas with particular caution at night.

Drugs & Dealers

For some people, Morocco means only one thing – dope. The place has heaps of the stuff, and it is much cheaper than in Europe, where the bulk of it is exported. Stories abound of travellers being led down Tangier alleyways, lured by offers of large quantities of hash, only to find themselves paying off unpleasant characters not to denounce them to the police (a threat they'd be highly unlikely to carry out). Tangier's lowlife is for the initiated only. If you feel you know the lie of the land, fine. New arrivals should ignore late-night offers of hash and grass – these people have a sixth sense for greenness, and won't miss an opportunity to squeeze ridiculous amounts of money out of frightened people. Much the same goes for Tetouan, and care should be taken in places like Casablanca and Marrakesh, too.

It doesn't matter where you go, offers are a part of the daily routine. More often than not, hash is referred to as 'chocolate', the Spanish slang. You may also have offers of 'shit', which Moroccans apparently feel refers to the same substance. If you do want it, you should get a feel for where it's safe to go ahead and where not.

On the opposite end of the scale is Ketama and the Rif Mountains – kif-growing heartland. If you don't want trouble, don't hang about here. The standard game consists of going to great lengths to sell vast amounts of the stuff to people, especially those in their own vehicles. The buyers then find themselves at the mercy of the next police roadblock. At best the kif will be confiscated and you'll get a hard time before being sent on your way, but Westerners are doing time for trafficking in Morocco, and who knows whether any of them simply got unlucky in this way.

Always bear in mind that it is illegal to sell or consume hash in Morocco – although in practice, except for the Ketama capers, this usually means little if you're discreet. Smoking it in public is inviting trouble.

Another phenomenon is drugged-out kids (often glue-sniffers), whose antics can be unsettling. Marrakesh seems to be the biggest problem city on this score.

A lot has been said about taking personal supplies of drugs through customs into Spain. Possession of small amounts of cannabis for personal use was made legal in Spain in 1983, but that law was later revoked. In general, although the police attitude in Spain is relaxed in respect of small amounts of cannabis, Spanish customs will come down hard on people entering the country from Morocco if they find any. Plenty of people take the risk, but it is hardly recommended. If you're taking a car across, the chances are high that it will be searched.

If you are going to Algeria, there is a simple message: leave your dope in Morocco. If they find the stuff on you here, you could wind up in very deep trouble.

Touts, Guides & Hustlers
What hasn't already been written about the now legendary hustlers (or *faux guides* – false guides) of Morocco? As soon as you arrive in cities like Marrakesh, Fès, Tangier or Tetouan, people are offering you their services. The 'guides' come in all shapes, sizes and humours, and there is no one method of dealing with them. While it may be true that they are not as troublesome as they once were, they remain an unavoidable part of the Moroccan experience.

Your first days in any of these places are bound to be the worst. After you've been around for a bit, they'll begin to recognise your face and leave you alone – other prey will have arrived in the meantime anyway.

It often starts at train and bus stations. As soon as you alight, people are there to guide you to a hotel, restaurant or anything else. Although sometimes easier said than done, the best you can do is politely decline and head off with the appearance of knowing what you're after. If you don't, make for a café where you can sit down and get your bearings. Beware of taxis at Marrakesh and Fès train stations, as some of them are not the real McCoy and others have their own ideas on where you might like to stay. They are a small minority, but they are there.

It is best to assume that friendly offers to show you a great restaurant, hotel, useful bus stop or just about anything else, especially if unsolicited by you, will be accompanied by requests, and sometimes short-tempered demands, for baksheesh.

Drivers should note that motorised hustlers operate on the approach roads to Fès and Marrakesh. These motorcycle nuisances are keen to find you a hotel, camp site and so on, and can be just as persistent as their colleagues on foot.

You'll encounter the next battery of these people when you're heading into medinas. It *is* possible to get around even the most complicated of the medinas (Fès and Marrakesh) without a guide. If you're irretrievably lost, a few dirham will be enough to get someone to lead you out. The point in taking a guide (provided you get a good one) is to save time and avoid further hassle – the one thing about having a guide is that they deter other helpful hopefuls. This alone can make it worth your while to hire one.

Official guides can be hired through tourist offices or bigger hotels, though you'll sometimes find them hanging around in the medina. Ask to see their brass badge. They

Majoun
You may occasionally come across someone offering you *majoun*, a kind of sticky, pasty mass (not unlike molasses) made of crushed seeds of the marijuana plant. A small ball of this can send your head into a bit of a spin (see Paul Bowles' *Their Heads Are Green* or *Let It Come Down* for descriptions), and anyone with a slight tendency to paranoia when smoking dope should take note that this is a common reaction among first-time majoun-munchers. One quote suggests 40 grams of the stuff is worth Dr 100. This is not a recommendation. It is, of course, illegal. ∎

generally charge between Dr 30 and Dr 50 for half a day (make sure you agree on the definition of a half-day). The unofficial guides, who invariably introduce themselves as students, will charge less and *can* be just as good.

Whether you're dealing with official or unofficial guides, establish exactly where you want to go. If that does not include shops, make it clear from the start, because all these people make much of their living from commissions on sales in shops and will be anxious to show you some. Make sure your guide-to-be speaks your language well enough to offer decent explanations of what you are seeing.

A common phenomenon is the last-minute help you really don't need. Just as you're about to enter a hotel or shop, you find some character by your side congratulating you and himself on having got you there. The hotel and shop owners generally don't go along with these games, so make sure everyone's aware that your new-found 'friend' is not with you at all.

If you are adamant about not wanting a guide, you will have to develop a reasonably thick skin, in Fès and Marrakesh at any rate. In both cities, they tend to congregate in various parts of the villes nouvelles (such as hotels, and on roads leading to the medina) and then by the gates into the medina itself.

Chances are you'll be pretty much left alone if you manage to get inside the medina without taking on a guide.

Approaches How to shake them off? There is no easy answer. Bear in mind that many are unemployed and in some cases have families to support. Patience, politeness and firmness are the three necessary ingredients. Talk to them. There's nothing they hate more than the brush-off, which incites some to launch into a torrent of abuse.

On the other hand, others will stick to you like glue no matter how much you talk or how polite you are in declining their services. They don't like the word 'police' very much, but you'll have to look like you have every intention of going to them.

Never believe the one about 'the Berber market, today only'. For 'Berber market' read 'carpet shop'.

Don't have anything to do with people who want you to take letters or parcels for them out of Morocco – you don't know what you're getting yourself mixed up in. Less sinister requests for help with translating letters and the like are a typical means of latching on to you.

Streets & Medinas

A minor irritation is the ever-changing street name in Moroccan cities. For years now, there has been a slow process of replacing old French and Spanish names with Arabic ones. The result so far is that, depending on whom you talk to, what map you use or which part of the street you are on, you are likely to see up to three different names.

The general Arabic word used is *sharia* (*zankat* for smaller ones), for which you'll still find the Spanish *calle* quite often in the north, and more commonly the French *avenue*, *boulevard* or *rue*. In some cases the Arabic seems to have gained the upper hand. This is reflected in this guide, in which some streets appear as 'sharia' or 'zankat' if local usage seems to justify it.

Street names won't help much in the labyrinthine medinas, but one rule might help if you feel you are getting lost. If you stick to the main paths (which generally have a fair flow of people going either way), you will soon reach a landmark or exit. It's really only when you dive into the maze of little alleys that it becomes more difficult – some would say more fun!

Police Roadblocks

See the Car & Motorbike section of the Getting Around chapter for details on this somewhat irritating phenomenon.

False Hitchhikers

Professional hitchhikers operate on some of the more popular tourist routes. They get in your car and oblige you to accept their thanks for your help with a glass of tea at their house and the inevitable carpet-sales session – or something worse. See the Car & Motorbike section of the Getting Around chapter for more information.

WORK

Morocco is not the most fruitful ground for digging up work opportunities. A good command of French is usually a prerequisite, and a knowledge of Arabic would certainly not go astray. If you do secure a position, your employer will have to help you get a work permit and arrange residency, which can be an involved process. There is some very limited scope for teaching English and voluntary work.

Teaching English

It is technically possible to get this kind of work here, but the openings are limited. The British Council has only one branch in Morocco, in Rabat, but as a rule it recruits all its staff directly from London. You could try them for supply work and they might have suggestions on smaller local outfits.

The only really credible alternatives are the American Language Center and the much smaller International Language Centre. The former has schools in Rabat, Casablanca, Fès, Marrakesh, Tangier, Tetouan and Kenitra. See the individual entries for addresses. Don't get your hopes up though. These are all fairly small operations and the chances of just walking into a job are not high. Obviously, qualified teachers of English as a Foreign Language (TEFL) will have a better chance. The minimum qualification is generally the RSA Certificate. The best time to try is around September-October (the beginning of the academic year) and, to a lesser extent, early January. Casablanca has about half a dozen outfits and so is the best hunting ground.

ALC rates (about the highest) in 1994 ranged from Dr 82 per teaching hour for someone with a Bachelor of Arts degree and no prior experience to Dr 123 for a teacher with 12 years' experience and at least a Masters degree in a relevant field.

Voluntary Work

There are several organisations in Morocco that organise voluntary work on regional development projects. They generally pay nothing, sometimes not even lodging, and are aimed at young people looking for something different to do for a few weeks over the summer period. If this sort of thing interests you, a couple of possible sources of information in Morocco may be:

Les Amis des Chantiers Internationaux de Meknès, BP 8, Meknès

Chantiers Jeunesse Maroc, BP 1351, 31 Rue du Liban, Rabat

Chantiers Sociaux Marocains (☎ 791370), BP 456, Rabat

ACTIVITIES
Trekking

Morocco is becoming increasingly popular as a trekking destination, and while the possibilities are not as breathtaking as in Nepal, there is some good walking to be done in the High and Middle Atlas mountains. Various outside tour companies organise trips, or you can do things more haphazardly and organise something on the ground in Morocco. You can do relatively easy walks, such as the two-day trek up Jebel Toubkal in the High Atlas, or get together guides, porters and mules for longer adventures through the mountains. For more detailed information and some suggested reading, see the High Atlas Trekking section in the High Atlas chapter.

Skiing

Although no match for Europe's Alpine offerings, skiing is a viable option in winter. The higher slopes and peaks usually have decent cover from December to March. Oukaïmeden, about 70 km south of Marrakesh, is a popular ski station and boasts the highest ski lift in Africa. A day lift pass costs Dr 80 and full equipment hire is usually around Dr 100 a day, although it's not always of the greatest quality. There are a couple of other spots dotted around the Middle Atlas equipped for snow sport, the best known and equipped being Mischliffen and Ifrane (18 km apart from one another).

Skiing is possible in the Rif, but the business has all but died with the increased problem of dope dealers. Jebel Tidirhine, near Ketama, is one such spot. Another possibility is Bou Iblane, north of Taza, but not much is organised here either.

White-Water Rafting
Morocco will never be one of the world's great rafting centres, but some specialist adventure companies do organise this kind of activity, particularly on some of the rivers in the High Atlas near the Bin el-Ouidane lake, in the area around Azilal and Afourer. People do it here as much for the setting as for the sport itself.

Surfing
With thousands of km of ocean coastline, Morocco is not a bad place to take your board. Surfing has had little or no attention in Morocco, but you would not be the first to abandon the chill of the European Atlantic for something a little warmer. **Essaouira** has been singled out by some surfers, partly for the town's qualities, but there is no reason not to explore farther afield. One Californian surfer found the beaches around **Kenitra** a safe and enjoyable bet. It has to be said that

in a lot of places the wind makes a mess of the waves.

Windsurfing
The winds off **Essaouira** are still better for windsurfers than their wax-and-board colleagues. Although probably quite a number of beaches up and down the Atlantic coast would make equally good spots, this has definitely been singled out as *the* place to do it. It is possible to hire equipment there on the beach.

Golf
Believe it or not, golf is high on the list of Morocco's advertised attractions, and it seems quite a few holidaymakers are not averse to a round or two. The oldest course, laid out in 1917, is the Royal Country Club of Tangier (938925), an 18-hole course that one golfing writer has described as 'adventurous'. The Royal Dar es-Salam (☎ 754692/3), 10 km out of central Rabat, is the most modern course and was the scene of the Moroccan Open in 1987. There are other courses in Casablanca (Royal Golf d'Anfa; ☎ 251026), Marrakesh (☎ 444341), Ben Slimane, Mohammedia and Agadir (12 km out of town).

Fishing
Fishing is permitted in most rivers, lakes and on the coast, but only from sunrise to sunset. You will need a licence, which must be organised through the Service des Eaux et Forêts. They supposedly have an office in all the big cities. Surfcasting in the area around Dakhla, in the south, has been recommended. Some of the creeks around Marrakesh aren't bad, but the artificial lake created by the Moulay Youssef dam, purposely stocked with fish such as black bass, is better.

Language Courses
The business of learning Arabic is quite undeveloped in Morocco, and the possibilities for doing so are strictly limited. Apart from possible summer courses at the university in Rabat, your best bet would be to head for the Arabic Language Institute in Fès

(☎ 624850) at 2 Rue Ahmed Hiba. The institute has been going since 1983 and is attached to the American Language Center. Until now classes have been quite small, so each student can expect a reasonable amount of individual attention. The institute offers three levels of Modern Standard Arabic (MSA) and Moroccan dialect *(darija)*, and offers a series of intensive courses that run over six weeks and cost Dr 5900 per course.

The institute can also help with accommodation, either in hotels or on a homestay basis with Moroccan families.

Some branches of the Centre Culturel Français run Arabic courses. This is the case in Tangier.

HIGHLIGHTS

In all of Africa, Morocco offers possibly the greatest variety of attractions. The Imperial Cities are the biggest drawcard, and each of them is distinctly different from the other. The medina of **Fès**, brooding in the foothills of the Middle Atlas, will swallow you up in its countless winding and twisting alleyways, taking you past exquisite monuments and labyrinths of souqs selling everything from edible delicacies to the range of souvenir items that Morocco's artisans can offer. Nearby **Meknès**, only briefly the capital, presents a more open aspect, and in its ambitious dimensions has often been compared with Versailles.

The red city of **Marrakesh**, nuzzling the snowcapped High Atlas Mountains, is another world again, and while the stamp of France's protectorate is clearly evident in the villes nouvelles of the northern capitals, Marrakesh offers an altogether different and somehow wilder picture. With its city walls and rambling medina, basking in the bright sun and clean air (the climate is reputedly perfect for anyone with respiratory problems) and dominated by the minaret of the great Koutoubia mosque, Marrakesh has long been one of North Africa's most popular destinations. The focal point is its main square, the Djemaa el-Fna, one of the last redoubts of a more traditional Moroccan 'nightlife', which throngs with storytellers, snake charmers, food stalls and herbalists selling cures for colds and all sorts of charms.

The fourth of the imperial cities, **Rabat**, and its sister town of Salé, once home to the corsairs, is a curious mix of remnants of the past and aspects of the new. Along with the booming economic capital of Casablanca to the south, Rabat presents Morocco's most modern and progressive face.

With thousands of km of Atlantic coast, Morocco is blessed with dozens of good spots for a beach holiday. While **Agadir** is an up-market resort for Europeans tired of the European Mediterranean resorts, **Essaouira** to the north is a laid-back place favoured by windsurfers and backpackers.

Inland, trekkers can find plenty of satisfying challenges in the **High Atlas** Mountains, and those haunted by desert fantasies can head south-east of Marrakesh through the extraordinary landscape of kasbahs and oases to reach the edge of the **Sahara**, which stretches on into the vast expanses of Algeria to the east.

ACCOMMODATION
Camping

Provided you have the site owner's permission, you can camp practically anywhere in Morocco. There are also quite a few official camp sites dotted around the country. Most of the bigger cities have one, often located well out of town and of more use to people with their own transport. Some of them are brilliantly located and worth the extra effort to get to them, but many offer little shade and are hardly worth what you pay. Most have water, electricity, a small restaurant and grocery store. Water and electricity generally come with a charge. Where there is hot water, you will pay at least Dr 5 for a hot shower.

As a rule, you'll be up for Dr 10 per person, plus a charge for pitching your tent (also often around Dr 10), along with charges for cars, motorbikes and caravans. For two people travelling by car, the total costs can easily come to nearly Dr 30 a head, so there are times when it will be better to spend a little more for a hotel.

Hostels

Hostelling International (HI) recognises 10 hostels in the country, which are located in Asni, Azrou, Casablanca, Chefchaouen, Fès, Marrakesh, Meknès, Rabat and Tangier. The head office of the Fédération Royale Marocaine des Auberges de Jeunes (☎ 524698) is on the Blvd Oqba ben Nafii in Meknès. The organisation has another office in Casablanca (☎ 970952) on the Parc de la Ligue Arabe. A bed usually costs from Dr 20 to Dr 30 (a little more without a membership card). Generally they are not too bad – those in Marrakesh, Meknès and Casablanca are among the better ones.

Hotels

About the cheapest hotel rooms you're likely to find anywhere will cost around Dr 30/50 for a single/double. As a rule you get what you pay for, and most of these unclassified hotels tend to be clustered in certain parts of the medinas of the bigger cities. For a little more, you can often find better unclassified or one-star hotels outside the medinas. This is especially the case in the high season, when the unclassified hotels tend to crank up prices as high as they think possible.

It is always worth looking around, but most of these places are clean if basic. In some cases the single biggest objection is the size of the rooms, as they can be tiny. Hot water is either not available or costs Dr 5 per gas-heated shower. Where there is no hot water at all, hotel staff can point you in the direction of a local public shower (douche) or hammam. You should not get too excited by claims of hot water in the cheapies either, as this sometimes amounts to little more than a warm trickle.

If you have a little flexibility on the money front, you can dig up some very good hotels in the one and two-star range. In the better cases, you are looking at good, clean rooms with comfortable beds and, with a bit of luck, a halfway decent shower. Hot water tends to be available only at certain times.

In the three and four-star bracket you will sometimes come up with a gem of an older place left over from more elegant days and which may have been tastefully renovated. In the upper bracket you're more likely to be confronted with more modern and sterile places.

At the top end of the scale are the five-star places. Many of the worldwide chains are represented, and prices and amenities are on a par with what you would expect of such places elsewhere.

For an idea of prices in the classified hotels, refer to the Classified Accommodation Costs table on the following page. There has been some suggestion that hotels are no longer required to stick to these maximum room rates, but there is little evidence of any hotels overstepping their set rates. Some charge a little less, and some clearly don't deserve their rating. Five-star hotels are not governed by this system and can charge what they like.

Although many unclassified places in the most popular locations increase their prices in the high season, it is fair to say that cities like Marrakesh offer a reasonable choice of places to stay. Not-so-popular destinations like Tetouan offer little and the quality of what's there is poor.

If you are resident in Morocco, you are entitled to a 25% discount on the classified hotel rates in some establishments. Always ask.

You will almost always be asked to leave your passport with reception so they can fill in their hotel registers. There is no reason for not asking to have it back when they're done, although this occasionally sparks requests for advance payment.

Classified Accommodation Costs

Category	Room	Shower (Dr)	Shower & Toilet (Dr)
1 star B	Sing/Doub	75/90	87/111
1 star A	Sing/Doub	86/110	110/127
2 star B	Sing/Doub	97119	119/144
2 star A	Sing/Doub	121/142	153/179
3 star B	Sing/Doub	153/195	195/240
3 star A	Sing/Doub	179/225	226/273
4 star B	Sing/Doub	247/303	302/377
4 star A	Sing/Doub	297/387	362/460

A third bed in these rooms costs from Dr 43 (one-star) to Dr 98 (four-star). Breakfast is also extra, costing from Dr 19 a person (one-star) to Dr 40 (four-star). There is also an additional tourist tax, which ranges from Dr 3 to Dr 8 per person.

FOOD

At its best, Moroccan cuisine is a delight to the palate, and offers a great range, from the traditional staples such as couscous and *tajine* to occasionally excellent seafood. For the budget traveller especially, the day-to-day truth can be a bit of a letdown. As so often with African and Middle Eastern cooking, the best examples are to be found either in restaurants outside the region or in private homes.

The basics are starch and meat, and in the more out of the way places you'll find little variety. Those looking for a splurge will find plenty of restaurants serving local cuisine and a variety of European (particularly French) food in the bigger and more popular centres. Menus are generally in French and/or Arabic, so a smattering of either or both will be useful in the eating department.

The French influence is strong, and in the cities, the most common breakfast remains a croissant or other pastry with coffee; pâtisseries abound.

A reasonable meal in a mid-range restaurant will set you back about Dr 60 to Dr 80. Moving up a little and indulging in non-Moroccan cuisine (at the occasional Italian, Chinese or Vietnamese restaurants) will generally cost around Dr 80 to Dr 100. If you want to eat in one of the cavernous restaurants decorated like the inside of some of the monuments you have visited and be treated to something of a folkloric music show or Egyptian-style belly-dancing, the bill per person will be Dr 200 plus. If you want to go any higher than that, it's most easily done in the hotel restaurants.

Snacks

One of the biggest growth industries is kebab and kefta fast-food outlets. What you get is a serving of barbecued kebab or *kefta* wrapped in bread with or without salad, and a dose of hot sauce plus chips. They're popular, essentially forming a meal in themselves, and cost as little as Dr 10 (about US$1). There are quite a few variations on this theme, and a growing array of Western-style hamburger places. Some of these are not bad at all, although you'll be looking at Dr 20 or more for a meal.

McDonald's opened its first Moroccan restaurant near the lighthouse in Casablanca in 1992, and plans a network of at least 12 franchises around the country – so if you're hankering for a Big Mac, head for Casablanca!

One item stands out. If you like olives, trawl a few vegetable markets and you'll soon find more varieties than you ever dreamed existed. Not surprisingly, olives are a common condiment in most meals.

Soups & Starters

Soups (*chorba* or *harira*) are usually tasty and filling. Based on a meat stock, they have macaroni and vegetables as the other main ingredients. Any flavours these might impart are often cunningly concealed by a hefty dose of pepper or chilli. Harira is by far the best and is based on lentils. With a chunk of bread, it makes a good meal in itself. It's usually only available in the late afternoon/early evening. Grocery stores all over the country sell Maggi Harira in a packet – one can only hope that that's not what is served in the restaurants! It's probably fine, but it would detract from the authenticity of the Moroccan eating experience!

Salad is a great catch-all that can include anything from a limp piece of lettuce and a tired tomato right through to a tasty mix of chopped vegetables and herbs, olives, anchovies, tuna and spicy dressing. All in all, you are more likely to get a good one than a bad one, although some of the cheapest restaurants are stingy. Coriander leaves and parsley are the most common herbal ingredients.

If you have just arrived from Europe, you may find the salads don't agree with you, as the vegetables are not always properly washed. After a while, when your stomach has had a chance to acclimatise, you should be able to handle them without any problem.

Main Dishes

Most of the dishes are starch based, which usually means couscous, spaghetti or rice.

Couscous is the staple food and is an enormous bowl of steamed semolina topped with a meat and vegetable sauce. It is available virtually everywhere, but the sauce varies widely and can make or break the meal. It has become a commonplace that the often disappointing couscous you'll get in Moroccan restaurants is not a patch on the home-cooked variety – so take up any invitations to eat in private homes!

If you want to cut costs and aren't too bothered about not eating meat, ask how much the dishes are without meat (sans viande), as you still get the rest of the sauce and the price drops significantly.

Chicken is popular and is usually roasted and served with chips, which are often cold if you don't ask to have them warmed up.

Brochettes are one of the most basic meals and are available just about everywhere.

They're essentially kebabs – pieces of meat on a skewer barbecued over hot coals. A chilli sauce is usually provided.

Seafood is big on the coast and many restaurants specialise in it. The fish you get in the Atlantic towns is generally good as it's straight from the day's catch. What's more, the culinary traditions of Portugal and Spain have long been assimilated into the art of preparing seafood dishes, so you're looking at something more exotic than plain fish and chips; however, if that's what you want, you can get that too.

Other than couscous, the big dish here is tajine. This is basically a meat and vegetable stew cooked slowly in an earthenware dish over hot coals. The meat is usually lamb, goat or chicken, but is sometimes beef or rabbit.

The vegetables commonly cooked with the meat are potatoes, onions, carrots and squash, but it's not unusual for fruits such as prunes, apricots and raisins to be included, and you would definitely expect this in a better restaurant. Depending on the restaurant, tajines range from being absolutely delicious to almost tasteless.

Another dish worth trying, though not so widely available, is *pastilla (bastaila* in Arabic). It is a delicious and incredibly rich pigeon pie, made in layered *ouarka* pastry (like filo pastry) with nuts and spices, coated with sugar and baked. It is common in Fès, where you just get a chunk from a stall, but it is also served in restaurants in other cities.

Desserts & Pastries

Desserts and sweets are more often available from pâtisseries than in restaurants, but things such as *crème caramel*, cakes and fruit are often served in the better restaurants. The European pastries, most of which cost Dr 3 to Dr 5, are generally very good. In the north of the country especially, ordering tea or coffee and a pastry or two in a café or salon de thé is a pleasant way to pass an hour or two.

A great local version of, for want of a better comparison, the Spanish *churro*, is a light, deep-fried doughnut called a *sfinj*.

They cost practically nothing, are not sweet and go perfectly with coffee. Since European-style pastries have become an integral part of Moroccan life, you won't see the rich variety of oriental pastries (such as *baqlawa*) that you get in other Arab countries. There are a few though, including the *cornes de gazelle*, which are typically dripping in liquid sugar and are very good.

English	Arabic	French
Soup		
soup	*chorba*	*potage*
spicy lentil soup	*harira*	

Salads & Vegetables		
carrots	*kheezoo/ gazar*	*carottes*
chips	*ships*	*frites*
cucumber	*khiyaar*	*concombre*
green beans	*loobeeya*	*haricots verts*
haricot beans	*fasooliya*	*haricots blancs*
lentils	*'aads*	*lentilles*
lettuce	*khess*	*laitue*
mixed salad	–	*salade marocaine*
olives	*zeetoun*	*olives*
onion	*besla*	*oignon*
peas	*zelbana/ bisila*	*petits pois*
potatoes	*batatas*	*pommes de terre*
tomato	*mataisha/ tamatim*	*tomate*

Meat		
camel	*lehem jemil*	*chameau*
chicken	*farooj/dujaj*	*poulet*
kidneys	*kelawwi*	*rognons*
lamb	*lehem ghenmee*	*agneau*
liver	*kebda*	*foie*
meat	*lehem*	*viande*

Fruit		
apple	*teffah*	*pomme*
apricot	*mesh-mash*	*abricot*
banana	*banan/moz*	*banane*
dates	*tmer*	*dattes*
figs	*kermoos*	*figues*
fruit	*fakiya*	*fruits*
grapes	*'eineb*	*raisins*
orange	*leemoon*	*orange*
pomegranate	*remman*	*grenade*
watermelon	*dellah*	*pastèque*

Miscellaneous		
bread	*khubz*	*pain*
butter	*zebda*	*beurre*
cheese	*fromaj*	*fromage*
eggs	*bayd*	*œufs*
oil	*zit*	*huile*
pepper	*filfil/lebzaar*	*poivre*
salt	*melha*	*sel*
sugar	*sukur*	*sucre*
yoghurt	*zabadee/ laban/ danoon*	*yaourt*

DRINKS

Tea & Coffee

As throughout North Africa and the Middle East, these fluids keep the wheels of daily life in motion. They are drunk in huge amounts and are quite strong.

Tea (*atay*, or 'Moroccan whisky' according to the local wits) is served in large glasses or pots and heavily sweetened. A glass generally costs Dr 2. The Moroccan touch is the sprig of mint *(nanaa')* that accompanies it. In other countries you usually have to request it specifically. It seems that the locals can spend endless amounts of time over tea and backgammon, the newspaper or just having a good gossip, but if you just want to sit down for a while and do some people-watching, the cafés (more often than not called *salons de thé*) are a great place to do it, especially those that put chairs out onto the footpath.

Qahwa, coffee, tends to be served strong, black and in small cups. Alternatively you can have white coffee in larger cups. If you do want it with milk ask for *café au lait* or *qahwa bil-haleeb*. A strong coffee with a dash of milk is a *café cassé*. Turkish-style coffee is nonexistent. A glass of water is invariably served with the coffee. A cup of coffee will normally be Dr 3 to Dr 4.

Cafés are predominantly gathering places for men, except for some of the more chic, European-style establishments in the big cities. Local women would not dream of entering one in the more conservative areas, but Western women can get away with it – albeit often with the uncomfortable feeling that it's not the done thing.

Soft Drinks & Bottled Water

Coca-Cola, Pepsi and other soft drinks are well established in Morocco, but remember that in hot weather, they don't do an awful lot to quench your thirst. They generally come in bottles of 300 to 500 ml for about Dr 5.

There are several brands of bottled water, including Sidi Harazem. The bigger bottles contain 1.5 litres and cost Dr 4 to Dr 5. Smaller bottles cost Dr 2.50.

Juices

The best places to get freshly squeezed juices are in the occasional small shops that do nothing else, although most cafés and restaurants can make them for you too. At juice stands you can get orange juice or something a little more exotic like strawberry juice. The former costs about Dr 3 for a tall glass.

A particularly tasty local concoction is something called *sharba* – a mix of orange juice, banana extract, lemon and caramel colouring. It may sound horrid but is really very good.

Alcohol

Drinking alcohol is frowned upon in Islam, but that doesn't stop quite a lot of Moroccans from indulging in the odd tipple. Some of the better (or at least more expensive) restaurants are licensed but many are not. The cheapest places are rarely licensed unless they have a bar attached.

There are more bars around than is at first obvious. They tend not to advertise themselves and most are pretty basic set-'em-up-and-knock-'em-down places. The bigger cities have the occasional liquor store,

where you can get beer, wine and spirits for considerably less than in the bars or restaurants.

Beer The two main locally produced beers, Flag Spéciale (brewed in Tangier) and Stork (brewed in Fès & Casablanca) are quite drinkable without being anything to write home about. Smallish bottles cost between Dr 6 and Dr 8 in the liquor stores, and Dr 12 to Dr 15 in the bars and restaurants. Amstel and Heineken are also produced in Morocco under licence, and you can come across the odd imported brand, such as US Budweiser, in the liquor stores.

Wine Some quite reasonable wines are produced in Morocco. The bulk of wine production used to be in the hands of the Jewish population, but the business has moved into Arab hands since 1948, when many Jews left for Israel. Sincomar, based in Casablanca, produces quite a few labels, including Rabbi Jacob and Toulal (reds), Coquillage (white) and various others.

The plains around Meknès are good grape and wine country and Les Celliers de Meknès is another reasonable company. Guerrouane Rouge is not bad. Another good Meknès red is Aït Souala (Dr 35 in the liquor stores). For those with a more expensive palate, a recommended red is Beau Vallon (Dr 80).

Spirits Various spirits can be had, although they are hardly cheap. There is a French emphasis, especially in the northern half of the country. If you like the aniseed-based *pastis*, one of the more well known brands, sells in Morocco for Dr 120.

ENTERTAINMENT

Morocco is not the last word in night life. In fact your choices are fairly limited. The bigger centres have cinemas, some of which are quite good. Bars are scarce in small towns, but, again, the big cities have enough to keep you going. Beyond that it's discos and nightclubs, mostly of little interest, and the odd folkloric show, which can be interesting the first time round.

Cinemas

The best cinemas are in Rabat and Casablanca. It's pretty cheap entertainment, with seats costing from Dr 7 to Dr 12, depending on where you want to sit. The better cinemas get some quite up-to-date films, but if they're not French films, they are almost invariably dubbed into French. It is interesting to note that half the time they don't seem to bother with Arabic, not even subtitles.

Every town has at least one cinema specialising in Kung Fu-style movies, often with a sprinkling of the vague Indian equivalent of the genre. If you can believe the posters, some cinemas show porn films – another surprise in a Muslim country.

Bars

There are two kind of bars. The majority are pretty basic, and tend to be discreet about their existence. Many have a Flag Spéciale sign outside – push the door open and there you are. In Casablanca, some go by the name of *drogueries*. The local punters will probably be surprised to see you. Note that most of these bars close pretty early.

The other version is the expensive hotel bar. These stay open a little later, are considerably more expensive and not terribly interesting.

Discos & Nightclubs

Discos are discos, and the difference between them and nightclubs is not always clear. Generally you'll have to pay at least Dr 50 to get in, which usually includes a drink, and subsequent drinks cost an average of Dr 50. Many discos are decidedly overpopulated with local lads; a couple of the more chic jobs in the Casablanca suburbs are better, but very dear.

Some of the sleazier nightclubs, particularly in central Casablanca, put on a cabaret or floor show, usually of the belly-dancing variety. Though rarely captivating, they can be a curious experience. Some of these

places are clearly the stamping gro... prostitutes.

Folkloric Shows

Some of the big hotels and tourist restaurants put on folkloric performances. Those in the restaurants are probably preferable, since the settings are often quite sumptuous. The shows themselves can be a mixed bag, but are entertaining enough if reasonable musicians have been engaged to play traditional Andalusian or Berber music. The dancing is more often than not Egyptian-style belly-dancing (it's not really a Moroccan genre). A few of the top hotels opt for Western-style cabarets.

THINGS TO BUY

The souvenir hunter could spend weeks, if not longer, trawling through the souqs of Morocco. From leather goods to copper and brassware and the myriad collections of rugs and carpets, there is an enormous choice. Obviously a lot of rubbish is produced alongside the higher-quality objects, and it pays to take your time before buying. For a better idea of what to look for, see the following Arts & Crafts colour section.

For some people the big attraction is the herbs and spices. Besides the cumin, saffron, ginger and so on that are usually displayed in huge colourful mounds, there are occasionally stands selling all sorts of obscure things for medicinal purposes. The Djemaa el-Fna in Marrakesh is a good place for this. If you've got a cough, cold or other ailment, point to the part that hurts and you'll soon have a small plastic bag with the wonder herb in your hand. Directions for use vary, so try to get an explanation of how to take your herbal remedy. The locals swear by these *'ashaab* (herbs).

Markets

In common with most African and Middle Eastern countries, Moroccan towns and villages have a special weekly market day (sometimes twice a week) when people from the surrounding area come to sell their wares

...cannot produce for them-

...s are different from the per-
...d markets you'll find in most
...ually provide a lively opportu-
...rve the distinctive customs and
clothing of local tribespeople. Some of the
most interesting include:

Agadir: Saturday and Sunday
Figuig: Saturday
Ifrane: Sunday

Khenifra: Sunday
Larache: Sunday
M'Hamid: Monday
Midelt: Sunday
Moulay Idriss: Saturday
Ouarzazate: Sunday
Ouezzane: Thursday
Oujda: Wednesday and Sunday
Sefrou: Thursday
Tafraoute: Wednesday
Taroudannt: Friday
Tinerhir: Monday
Tinzouline: Monday
Zagora: Wednesday and Sunday

Evil Eye

The evil eye, whether you happen to believe in it or not, is a potent force in the minds of many Moroccans. A common symbolic means of warding it off is to show the open palm of the hand, fingers pointing upwards. You may well notice hand prints on the walls of people's houses. Often applied on the occasion of some festivity, such as a wedding, it is one way of trying to avert misfortune befalling the inhabitants of the house concerned.

There are more powerful methods of dealing with the evil eye, and you may come across one of them in the herb and spice markets – the chameleon (al-boua). This highly adaptable little creature is great to have in the home for eating flies and mosquitoes, but if you feel you have been struck by misfortune from a spiritual source beyond your control, throw one into a small wood-fired oven, walk around it three times and, if the chameleon explodes, you're in the clear. If it just melts down to goo, you're still in trouble, and will have to get yourself another chameleon. ∎

Arts & Crafts

Since the 16th century, merchant ships have been leaving Moroccan shores laden with exotic goods bound for Europe. *Maroquinerie* (leatherware) was the single most prized item in those days, and the word became synonymous with quality leather goods throughout the fashionable courts and houses of Europe.

That tradition lives on, accompanied by a rich heritage in the production of all sorts of goods – from carpets to fine pottery, heavy silver jewellery to elegant woodwork.

The traditional crafts of Morocco are the living embodiment of its preindustrial manufacturing industry. Although much of what is made today is aimed at tourists and is for decorative use, it all has its roots in the satisfaction of the everyday needs of people – from the humblest person to the most elevated.

The government goes to some lengths to keep these arts alive because they are as important to the economy as phosphates and agriculture. As far back as 1918, the then resident-general of the French protectorate over Morocco, General Lyautey, set up the Office des Industries d'Art Indigène to promote craft sales abroad. No doubt some of what is produced today is garbage – quick, cheap souvenirs that end up in the hands of tourists too impatient to look around for quality – but there is plenty of decent stuff to be found.

Moroccan tourism took a battering during the Gulf War, and although the number of visitors is back to prewar levels, craft sales in 1993 were still only a quarter of what they had been in 1990. It sounds a little selfish, but this can be good news for the patient bargainer, as shopkeepers are more anxious than ever to make a sale.

Many of the products that attract visitors, such as rugs and chased brass and copperware, owe at least some of their visual appeal to a meeting of religious precept and traditional tribal design.

Considering the depiction of all living beings an affront to God, Islam imposed strictures on the artist. There was no question of art imitating life (let alone life imitating art). Consequently, public art had little choice but to follow an abstract and decorative path which inspired the serene contemplation of seemingly endlessly repeated and interlaced motifs.

Alongside variations on floral designs, geometry developed as a prime tool of the artist. In Morocco and throughout the Islamic world, artisans have, over the centuries, perfected the creation of

Detail of rug, Tangier (DS)

Top: Quartier des
Potiers, Safi (DS)

Bottom: Detail of
mausoleum in the
garden of the
Saadian tombs,
Marrakesh (DS)

intricate geometrical patterns, many of which are elaborations on tribal themes long known in Morocco.

Added to this came calligraphy, which made of the Arabic language, and particularly the sacred words of the Qur'an, an artistic medium in itself. For although it was sacrilegious to portray the image of God, it was praiseworthy to have His words on display for all the world to see. The calligraphy you see in great religious buildings in Morocco is generally composed of extracts from the Qur'an or such ritual declarations as *la illah illa Allah* ('There is no god but Allah').

An artistic peak was reached in the 13th century under the Merenids. This dynasty seemed to specialise in sponsoring the construction of theological colleges (medersas) in all the great cities, and they are the most richly decorated of all of Morocco's historical buildings. Visiting these, you will soon notice that not a centimetre of the interior wall surfaces is left bare. The base of the walls is covered in zellij tiles – fragments of ceramic tiles in hues

Bab Bou Jeloud,
Fès (DS)

of green, blue and yellow interspersed with black on a white background. Above these tiles, the stylised decoration is continued in lacework stucco, topped finally by carved wood (often cedar) panels, which are continued on the ceiling.

Geometric finesse and harmony in design (much of it introduced by Arabs from Muslim Spain) spread through all levels of artisanal handicrafts, although the origins of many Berber designs, especially in textiles and jewellery, predate the emergence of Islam. Carpets and rugs almost always feature some geometric decoration; of course today you will find items depicting animals and the like, but they have nothing to do with traditional artistic norms. More often than not the popular copper and brass trays boast flurries of calligraphic virtuosity. The beauty of the most intricate of jewellery is in the sum of its many simply shaped parts.

Although much craftwork is now aimed at tourists, little of it has been specifically designed *for* them. Rugs and trays, silver jewellery and swords were being made for local use long before tourism became a phenomenon. There are exceptions. Much of the leatherware is more inspired by an attempt to imitate popular

Tuareg bags,
Taroudannt (DS)

European tastes than it is by tradition. The same can be said of most woollen products, such as caps, multicoloured coats, sweaters and the like – you'll be lucky to see a Moroccan wearing any of these items. A lot of woodwork, especially thuya-wood carvings from the Essaouira region, is a reaction to the influx of tourists hungry for original souvenirs.

IN THE SOUQ

The most useful tool when hunting for crafts is patience. Morocco is crawling with craft souqs, and tourists often find themselves subjected to heavy sales pressure. Before you even get to the shops in many cities you will have to deal with 'guides' and touts of various types. Once inside the shops, you will, in the best circumstances, be caught up in the age-old mint tea ritual, in which gentle but persistent pressure is applied to you to purchase something. Less scrupulous (or more desperate) shopkeepers tend to go for more strong-arm tactics, and badger unsuspecting visitors into buying things they barely even wanted to look at – this species is a minority and mainly inhabits the bigger tourist cities like Marrakesh. Most shopkeepers are perfectly all right, although some can put on childish long faces if you leave with your hands empty and wallet full.

Before buying anything, you should look around. You may be taken with the first items you see, but if you buy them you may well be disenchanted with them by the time you leave. Every big city has an Ensemble Artisanal. These are government-run 'supermarkets'. Prices are generally higher than those you would pay if you bargained in the souqs, but here you can check out the goods in peace and get an idea of what good-quality items are like. It might also be an idea to visit some of the various Moroccan traditional arts museums, where you can admire classical pieces of work, be they rugs or rings.

WEAVING & TEXTILES
Carpets & Rugs

Carpet shops. The words themselves evoke for many the sum total of their Moroccan experience. All the touts in Morocco seem to assume the first (and only) thing the tourist wants is a carpet.

The selling of carpets is exclusively men's business and the same can be said for practically all arts and crafts. The big difference between carpets and other crafts is that making them is virtually a women's preserve. Good rugs and carpets can take months to make, and the women see little cash for their labours.

The heavy woollen carpets and throw rugs vary greatly in design and colouring from region to region. Rabat is reputed to be one of the best centres and maintains a tradition inspired by the carpet-makers of the Middle East. Carpets here come in rich blends of blues, reds, greens and yellows. They generally feature a central motif and an intricate border – the wider and more complicated the work in the border, the more the carpet is worth.

Outside Rabat, most of the carpets and rugs are the work of Berber tribes, each of which (when the work is at its best) pass down certain designs and colour combinations. If browns dominate in the Middle Atlas, the famous carpets of Chichaoua (on

Inside Raissouli Palace, Asilah (DS)

Top, Middle & Bottom: Detail of cushion, Meknès (GB)

the road from Marrakesh to Essaouira) are almost always a stunning red to dark-red wine colour. Unlike the highly prized Rabat carpets, most of those made by the Berbers do not have a frame around the edges.

The value of a carpet is based not only on the intricacy of design, but also on its age, the number of knots and, perhaps most importantly, the strength of the wool. The tougher and more wiry the wool, the longer the rug is likely to last – many Moroccan soft-wool carpets will not stand up well to much foot traffic.

A handmade carpet can become something of an antique if it's well made, and those done by masters are much sought after by connoisseurs and are hard to come by. A square metre of carpet contains tens of thousands of knots and it's basically a case of the more the better, as they indicate a product is more likely to last. Top-class examples will have some 150,000 knots per square metre. These are comparatively rare, and glib claims that the item in front of you has several hundred thousand knots per square metre can, as a rule, be confidently discounted.

For decades, chemical colours have been used instead of vegetable dyes, but despite what you may be told, they tend to fade too, sometimes quite dramatically. Vegetable dyes are still used, and tend to fade more slowly. A wide range of products are used to create different colours, including almond leaves, bark, iron sulphate and cow urine.

For the locals, carpets are utilitarian as much as works of art, and the brilliant colours of a new rug are not expected to retain their intensity. If you find a genuinely old piece (of 40 or so years), you can be fairly confident that it *won't* change colour significantly.

Kilims

More suitable as wall-hangings or bedspreads than carpets are the flat-weave kilims. What sets kilims apart from other rugs is the fact that they are woven rather than knotted. While knotted woollen rugs tend to have great splashes of colour, kilims are characterised by a finer design. One or two colours may dominate, but they are always interwoven in delicate, rectilinear patterns. As with knotted carpets, there are any number of variations in design, motif and choice of colour, depending on the region or tribe that produces them.

Detail of Berber rug, Erfoud (GB)

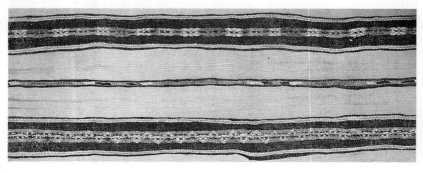

Buying Carpets

You will hear many absurd asking prices while bargaining in Morocco. A high but not insane starting price for good wool carpets is Dr 100 per square metre. If you hold out and the item is not of great quality, the price will soon come down. Kilims require more work and are generally more expensive. Dr 500 for two square metres is a not unreasonable price, but insistent bargaining would bring it down to Dr 300 or perhaps less. Again, much depends on the quality of the handiwork and the eagerness of the shopkeeper to sell.

Kilim, Tangier (DS)

Other Wool Products

There are plenty of other good woollen purchases to be made. Chefchaouen and Ouezzane are in flourishing wool country, and in the former especially all manner of garments can be found. Perhaps the best are thick sweaters, which tend to cost from Dr 50 up, depending on quality and thickness. Jackets, head gear and woven bags are further items. Inspect the goods closely. The most attractive coats made of superb wool can look great, but if they're of poor quality, you'll find them unravelling within weeks. Another item popular with some visitors are the heavy, hooded cloaks (burnouses), worn by Berbers from all over the country. They are practical in the cold mountain weather, but Westerners look a little silly in them.

Textiles

Although Morocco does not have Egypt's reputation for producing cotton, many visitors are tempted by jellabas, the full-length cotton garments worn by men, and similar clothing items worn by women, which are very comfortable in hot climes.

Various materials are used to produce a whole range of what for Berber households are useful floor covers and the like. Depending on the designs, they can be as attractive a buy as the carpets.

Fès is reputedly Morocco's great silk and brocade centre, but both these artforms are apparently heading for extinction and so are increasingly hard to find.

LEATHERWORK

The bulk of contemporary leatherware is aimed solely at tourists. The tanneries of Fès provide raw material for about half the country's total production in leather goods, but several other big cities maintain their own tanneries.

The most 'authentic' of these items are *babouches*, slippers that

Above: Kilim, Tangier (DS)

Right: Detail of leatherwork on bag, Marrakesh (GB)

are still the most common footwear among Moroccans of both sexes. Men wear yellow or white ones, while all the bright colours or more ornate styles are reserved for women.

A whole range of products designed for Westerners in search of leather goods more affordable than in the designer stores at home can be found in Fès, Marrakesh, Rabat and Tetouan. They include jackets, bags of all descriptions, wallets, belts and poufs. The latter are a genuinely traditional item and are made of goat leather. If camel saddles are your thing, try Marrakesh. Some of the best shoulder bags are made in the Rif and find their way into the markets of Tetouan and Chefchaouen. Tiny bags designed to carry around personal minicopies of the Qur'an form popular souvenir items.

The leather is often of a high quality, and to this extent the fame of maroquinerie remains justified. Unfortunately, the artisanship of many items leaves a lot to be desired – check the links, stitching and so on of anything you're interested in.

POTTERY & CERAMICS

The potteries of Safi have long been touted as the main centre of ceramic production in Morocco, but smaller cooperatives are springing up in other parts of the country, and the cities of Fès and Meknès have a centuries-old heritage of ceramics production. A lot of it is prosaic, such as the ubiquitous green roof tiles that are largely made in these two Middle Atlas cities and to some extent in Safi.

Safi's pottery makers have taken their inspiration from the ceramics once produced in Málaga (southern Spain), which are

Detail of large decorative bowl, Safi (GB)

Top: Tajine bowls and vase, Safi (GB)

Middle: Potters' souq, Safi (DS)

Bottom: Cache-pots (flowerpot holders) and candlestick, Safi (GB)

identified by a characteristic metallic sheen. The arrival of many potters from Fès has led to an increasing mixture of that city's traditional designs, which were mostly handed down by artisans exiled from Al-Andalus.

Fès's ceramics are dominated by browns, blues or yellow and green on a white background. You can see fine examples of jars, pots and other household items (for well-to-do households!) in most of the museums of Moroccan art in the big cities. Meknès inherited much of its skills from Fès, and its pottery industry really only began to flourish in the 18th century.

Among the handiest commercially available souvenirs are decorative ceramic plates or coffee and tea sets. The rougher examples can sell for as little as Dr 50, but expect to pay several hundred for a decently made plate.

A uniquely Moroccan item is the *tajine*, the casserole dish with the conical cover used to cook the meal of the same name (and indeed other meals, too). You can get a classy decorative tajine, or settle for the locally used product. One of the latter can cost as little as Dr 10 or Dr 20.

One way to tell the difference between something of value or production-line tourist trash is the gaudiness of colour and brightness of finish. The more precious pottery tends to be muted in colour, decoration and finish. This doesn't make the other stuff intrinsically bad, but it *does* mean you should not pay an arm and a leg for it.

In contrast to the largely urban and sophisticated pottery are the rougher, rustic products of the Berbers. Although simpler, they have their own charm, and are characteristic of the regions in which they are made. In the High Atlas south of Marrakesh, ochre is the dominant colour, the exception being down by Zagora, where you can find pots, jars and cups with a green finish. Water vessels are often decorated with a mysterious black substance that is said to purify the water.

BRASS & COPPERWARE
One of the best things about brass and copperware is that it is

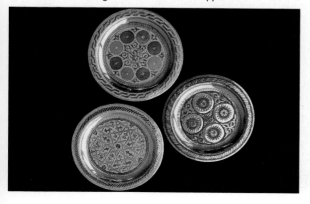

Bottom: Brass plates, Fès (GB)

comparatively hard to cheat on quality. Probably the most commonly bought items are plates and trays of chased copper and sometimes brass. You can start at about Dr 10 for saucer-sized decorative plates of low quality to several hundred for large, heavy trays. The latter are lavishly decorated and can be used to make a coffee table or hung on the wall as decoration.

There are plenty of other souvenirs. Candlesticks and lamp bases come in all shapes and sizes, and are best looked for in Marrakesh, Fès and Tetouan. Tetouan can be quite a good place to pick up these products, provided you are not accompanied by guides and hangers-on. Also worth buying are brass mirror frames,

Top left: Copper utensils (AC)

Top right: Copper jug (GB)

Bottom: Brass plate detail, Fès (GB)

often sporting patterns and designs reminiscent of what you will see in the best of Moroccan Islamic architecture.

For hammered rather than chased copper items, Taroudannt is about the best place.

JEWELLERY

Much of the jewellery around is not what it is claimed to be. Gold and silver are more often than not plated, and amber is plastic (put a lighted match to it and smell). Unless you are sure of your stuff, you should be cautious about what you buy and be prepared for disappointment.

This is not to say that genuinely good jewellery cannot be found, but you have to look for it. The making of jewellery in Morocco was once the preserve of the country's Jewish population, and it is said that Muslims at one stage had a superstitious aversion to metal-work. Whatever the truth of that, the Jews have left and Muslims have been fashioning jewellery for centuries.

Silver jewellery,
Tiznit (DS)

Gold

Fès is traditionally *the* place to buy gold jewellery, as much because of the sophisticated, urban and well-off clientele as anything else. Some of the city's artisans started a minor migratory wave to Essaouira a century ago, making the Atlantic town a secondary centre for the production of gold. Gold markets are to be found in various other big cities too – the one in Meknès, which is not overwhelmed by gold-hunting tourists, is worth investigating.

Classic jewellery made in Fès and Tangier remains largely faithful to Andalusian recherché lines, and is often ostentatious and

Top & bottom: Silverware and jewellery, Taroudannt (DS)

beyond the means of most. The Meknès products are generally more modest.

Essaouira, apart from the contribution made by the jewellers from Fès, boasts a local style dominated by floral designs and enamel work, although little of the jewellery produced has any gold content.

Silver

You can find cheap silver-plated jewellery just about anywhere. If you're looking for slightly more valuable and characteristically Moroccan items, you should head south to Tiznit, Rissani, Tan Tan or Taroudannt. Silver has long been highly prized by Berber women – a look in some of the museums of Moroccan art will soon convince you of that. The reason for this is that few peasant families, however powerful in their own stamping ground, could afford the luxury of gold.

Silver necklaces, bracelets, rings and earrings are invariably quite chunky, and often enlivened with pieces of amber or comparatively cheap precious stones. A particular item you will see in jewellery souqs is the hand of Fatima. The open palm is supposed to protect its wearer from ill fortune.

OTHER METALWORK

While down around Tiznit and Taroudannt, you might be interested in other silverwork. Specialities in both towns are silver-encrusted

Top: Guns, Taroudannt (DS)

Bottom: Tin box to carry the Qur'an (GB)

sabres and muskets. You can also come across silver daggers and silver (or silver-plated) scabbards.

For wrought iron, the place to hunt around is the ironsmiths' souq in Marrakesh. Here you can find heavy frames for mirrors, fire screens, lanterns and the like. There is little of this sort of work outside Marrakesh, and it is generally classed among the artisanal arts originally imported from Muslim Spain.

Top: Berber painted wooden box, Rabat (GB)

Bottom: Thuya wood table, Essaouira (DS)

WOODWORK

The artisans of Tetouan, Salé and Meknès continue to produce veritable works of art in wood. Painted and sculpted panels for interior decoration are commonplace, and the infinitely more intricate work required to produce the stalactite-like decoration that graces the interior of various medersas and other religious build-

ings and private houses of the rich also survives. Nor has the *mashrabiyya* (sometimes also spelled *mousharabiyya*) been consigned to history. These screens were and are designed to allow women to observe the goings-on in the street without being seen themselves. Fès and Meknès are the main centres of production.

While these items don't make likely candidates for souvenirs, they do serve to show that Moroccan crafts are not completely dependent on floods of tourists.

Pleasantly perfumed cedar is used for most woodwork, and in some of the better workshops you will find beautiful bowls, candlesticks, painted cribs, chests, jewellery boxes and the like. Fès is particularly good for this sort of work. Tetouan produces some interesting pieces too.

For marquetry, inlaid chessboards, caskets and all sorts of trinkets, you should wait until you get to Essaouira. The artisans here mainly use thuya wood *(Tris articuta)*, the most common tree in Essaouira's hinterland, but virtually unknown outside Morocco. The wood is so coveted that it is valued like a precious metal. From little jewellery boxes right through to enormous wooden statues, the range of thuya products is almost unlimited. The remarkable natural patterns that show up in the grain of better-quality items are found in the roots of the thuya tree.

STONE & PRECIOUS STONES

In Taroudannt you can pick up lamps, paperweights and boxes made of stone. Various kinds of softer stone are also sculpted into all sorts of shapes and sold for a pittance.

Throughout the Middle and High Atlas you'll pass roadside

Top: Stone statue, Er-Rachidia (GB)

Bottom: Stone masks, Er-Rachidia (GB)

stands with people offering clumps of all sorts of semiprecious stones such as quartz and amethyst.

In the desert around Erfoud are black marble quarries that furnish the base element for that town's souvenir industry. There are several stores there selling everything from statues to paperweights in black marble, as well as plenty of kids trying to unload more modest trinkets.

Fossils in rock, especially ammonite, are occasionally offered alongside the semiprecious stones. Morocco is full of fossils, and more enterprising souvenir merchants convert them into all sorts of things, including bowls and superb table-top sections.

MUSICAL INSTRUMENTS
It is possible to pick up traditional Moroccan instruments in a few places. One of the best places to look around is in the Bab el-Jedid area of the Meknès medina, where you'll find various string, wind and percussion instruments. For more information on Moroccan music and instruments see Music in the Arts section of the Facts about the Country chapter.

BASKETWARE
Throughout Morocco you will come across basketware, a wide term that covers everything from the Rif-style straw hats of the north to baskets with cone-shaped covers used by Berbers to carry dates and other merchandise. They make cheap souvenirs and are obviously not made to last forever.

Wooden tambourine and ceramic darbukas (drums) with goatskin heads, Safi (GB)

Getting There & Away

However you're travelling, it's worth taking out travel insurance. Work out what you need. You may not want to insure that grotty old army surplus backpack – but everyone should be covered for the worst possible case: an accident, for example, that will require hospital treatment and a flight home. It's a good idea to make a copy of your policy, in case the original is lost. If you are planning to travel for a long time, the insurance may seem expensive – but if you can't afford it, you certainly won't be able to afford to deal with a medical emergency overseas. It's also sensible to buy travel insurance as early as possible. If you buy it the week before you fly, you may find, for example, that you're not covered for delays to your flight caused by industrial action.

Once you have your ticket, keep a separate record of its details or photocopy it. If the ticket is lost or stolen, this will help you to get a replacement.

Morocco is a popular holiday destination with Europeans, and is well linked by air and sea with its northern neighbours. Most of the ferries running between Morocco and Spain and France can carry vehicles, making it relatively easy to tour the country in your own transport and push on into the rest of Africa.

Before deciding to head off yourself overland via Spain (which is where the majority of travellers usually start out for Morocco), it is worth checking out cheap deals with flights, particularly to southern Spain. From London for instance, you can sometimes get to Málaga for much less by air (even if you have to buy a return charter flight ticket and ditch the return half) and then proceed by boat rather than doing the whole trip by bus or train.

AIR

Morocco is well served by air from Europe, the Middle East and west Africa. Mohammed V Airport, the main international airport, is south of Casablanca, but there are also flights from some European cities to Tangier, Agadir and Marrakesh. In the high season most of these are charters. Of the regular flights, the bulk go via Mohammed V. Although there is a small airport 10 km north-east of Rabat, the capital is increasingly served by Mohammed V, to which it is directly linked by train and bus shuttles.

Oujda is linked to Paris and several other French cities as well as to Amsterdam, Brussels, Düsseldorf, Frankfurt, Munich and Stockholm. There are connections from the USA to Casablanca. You can get direct flights from various cities including Paris, Geneva, London, Rome and Munich to Marrakesh and, less frequently, Fès. There are direct flights between Paris and Ouarzazate.

Laayoune, the capital of the disputed territory of Western Sahara, is linked to Abidjan (Côte d'Ivoire) and Libreville (Gabon) by the national carrier, Royal Air Maroc (RAM), and to the Canary Islands.

Most Middle Eastern capitals can also be reached from Casablanca.

RAM and Air France take the lion's share of flights, but other airlines operating to Morocco include Lufthansa, KLM, Iberia, GB (Gibraltar) Airways, Swissair, TAT European Airlines, Sabena, British Airways, Alitalia, Air Algérie, Royal Jordanian, EgyptAir and Tunis Air. RAM has had some rather unflattering reports from travellers, particularly on the subject of lost luggage.

The northern summer months are the high season, as is the Christmas-New Year period and the weeks around Easter.

Air Travellers with Special Needs

If you have special needs of any sort – you've broken a leg, you're a vegetarian, are travelling in a wheelchair, taking the baby or terrified of flying – you should let the airline know as soon as possible so that they can make arrangements accordingly. You should remind them when you reconfirm your booking (at least 72 hours before departure) and again when you check in at the airport. It may also be worth ringing round the airlines before you make your booking to find out how they can handle your particular needs.

Airports and airlines can be surprisingly helpful, but they do need advance warning. Most international airports will provide escorts from the check-in desk to the plane if necessary, and there should be ramps, lifts and accessible toilets and phones. Aircraft toilets, on the other hand, are likely to present a problem; travellers should discuss this with the airline at an early stage and, if necessary, with their doctor.

Guide dogs for the blind will often have to travel in a specially pressurised baggage compartment with other animals, away from their owner, though smaller guide dogs may be admitted to the cabin. All guide dogs will be subject to the same quarantine laws (six months in isolation etc) as any other animal when entering or returning to countries currently free of rabies, such as Britain or Australia.

Deaf travellers can ask for airport and in-flight announcements to be written down for them.

Children under the age of two travel for 10% of the standard fare (or free, on some airlines), as long as they don't occupy a seat. They don't get a baggage allowance either. 'Skycots' should be provided by the airline if requested in advance; these will take a child weighing up to about 10 kg. Children between two and 12 can usually occupy a seat for half to two-thirds of the full fare, and do get a baggage allowance. Push chairs can often be taken as hand luggage.

Discount Travel Agencies

The plane ticket will probably be the single most expensive item in your budget, and buying it can be an intimidating business. It is worth putting aside a few hours to research the state of the market. Start early: some of the cheapest tickets have to be bought months in advance, and popular flights sell

out early. It's also worth talking to other travellers, as they may be able to stop you making some of the same old mistakes. Look at the ads in newspapers and magazines, consult reference books and watch for special offers. Then phone round travel agents for bargains. Airlines can supply information on routes and timetables; however, except at times of inter-airline war, they do not supply the cheapest tickets. Find out the fare, the route, the duration of the journey and any restrictions on the ticket (see the Air Travel Glossary). Then sit back and decide which is best for you.

You may discover that those impossibly cheap flights are 'fully booked, but we have another one that costs a bit more...' Or the flight is on an airline notorious for its poor safety standards and leaves you in the world's least favourite airport in mid-journey for 14 hours. Or they claim only to have the last two seats available for that country for the whole of July, which they will hold for you for a maximum of two hours. Don't panic – keep ringing around.

The fares quoted in this book are intended as a guide only. They are approximate and based on the rates advertised by travel agents at the time of going to press. Quoted airfares do not necessarily constitute a recommendation for the carrier.

If you are travelling from the UK or the USA, you will probably find that the cheapest flights are being advertised by obscure bucket shops whose names haven't yet reached the telephone directory. They sell airline tickets at up to 50% less where places have not been filled, and although airlines may protest to the contrary, many of them release tickets to selected bucket shops – it's better to sell tickets at a huge discount than not at all. Many such firms are honest and solvent, but there are a few rogues who will take your money and disappear, to reopen elsewhere a month or two later under a new name. If you feel suspicious about a firm, don't give them all the money at once – leave a deposit of 20% or so and pay the balance when you get the ticket. If they insist on cash in advance, go somewhere else. And once you have the ticket, ring the airline to confirm that you are booked on the flight.

You may decide to pay more than the rock-bottom fare by opting for the safety of a better known travel agent. Firms such as STA Travel, who have offices worldwide, Council Travel in the USA or Travel CUTS in Canada are not going to disappear overnight, leaving you clutching a receipt for a nonexistent ticket, but they do offer good prices to most destinations.

Moroccan Airports

Morocco's main international point of entry is the Mohammed V Airport, 30 km southeast of Casablanca, which also serves for the majority of flights to Rabat. Shuttle trains and buses link Casablanca and Rabat to the airport. International flights also land at Tangier, Marrakesh, Agadir, and occasionally at several other airports, including Fès, Oujda and Ouarzazate.

Mohammed V Airport Most flights to Morocco arrive at the sparkling, modern Mohammed V Airport. Passport control and customs formalities are straightforward. You will find representatives of the main international car rental agencies in the arrivals hall, along with representatives for some of the big hotels.

The tourist office information is on the 1st floor, just inside the departure lounge. It's open daily from 8.30 am to 7 pm – or at least that's what they say.

The BMCE bank has a branch in both the arrivals and departures lounges, but you cannot count on either being open all the time. They should change cash and travellers' cheques, but quite a few travellers have reported trouble – there are often long queues and sometimes they'll only take cash. Both branches have ATMs as well, so if you have a Visa or MasterCard, you could well save yourself a lot of trouble.

There are several cafés and newsstands dotted around the airport. For details on getting to and from the airport, see the Casablanca and Rabat Getting Around entries.

Other Airports Many of those arriving from overseas at Morocco's other airports will have already organised deals on accommodation, including transfers to and from the airport.

Marrakesh's airport is five km south-west of town, and the No 11 bus runs irregularly into the city centre. The taxi ride should not exceed Dr 50, but you'll probably end up paying more. The *grands taxis* can take up to six people – the fare is for the cab, not per person.

Tangier's tiny airport is about 16 km south-west of the city. No buses run directly there, so you'll have to battle with taxis. The fare should not exceed Dr 100.

Agadir's modern airport is about 28 km south-west of the town. A taxi will cost about Dr 100. Otherwise there are a couple of possibilities by bus – see the section on Agadir for more details.

To/From North America

The *New York Times*, the *LA Times*, the *Chicago Tribune* and the *San Francisco Examiner* produce weekly travel sections in which you'll find any number of travel agents' ads. Council Travel and STA Travel have offices in major cities nationwide.

The magazine *Travel Unlimited* (PO Box 1058, Allston, Massachusetts 02134) publishes details of cheap air fares.

In Canada, Travel CUTS has offices in all major cities. The *Toronto Globe & Mail* and the *Vancouver Sun* carry travel agents' ads. The magazine *Great Expeditions* (PO Box 8000-411, Abbotsford, British Columbia V2S 6H1) is also useful.

The cheapest way from the USA or Canada to Morocco and North Africa is usually a return flight to London or Paris and a bucket-shop deal from there.

RAM flies from New York to Casablanca. It also has flights from Montreal to Casablanca, via New York. The standard one-way fare from New York is US$839, or US$1678 return. Youth fares are 25% cheaper, and an excursion fare valid for six months costs US$918 return. From Montreal the standard economy fares are C$1386 one way and

C\$2772 return, while the excursion fare is exactly the same as the economy one-way ticket.

To/From the UK

London is one of the best centres in the world for discounted air tickets. The price of RTW tickets, especially, is about the best available anywhere and tickets can be had for well under UK£1000, although Morocco rarely figures in such a ticket.

For the latest fares, check out the travel page ads of the Sunday newspapers, *Time Out*, *TNT*, *City Limits* and *Exchange & Mart*. All are available from most London newsstands. A good source of information on cheap fares is the magazine *Business Traveller*.

Most British travel agents are registered with the ABTA (Association of British Travel Agents). If you have paid for your flight with an ABTA-registered agent who then goes out of business, the ABTA will guarantee a refund or an alternative. Unregistered bucket shops are sometimes cheaper but are also riskier.

The Globetrotters Club (BCM Roving, London WC1N 3XX) publishes a newsletter called *Globe* that covers obscure destinations and can help in finding travelling companions.

One of the most reliable London agents is STA Travel (☎ 0171-937 9962), which has offices at 86 Old Brompton Rd, London SW7; 117 Euston Rd, London NW1; and 38 Store St, London WC1. Another is Trailfinders (☎ 0171-938 3366, 938 3939), 42-50 Earls Court Rd, London W8. It has another office around the corner at 194 Kensington High St, London W8. The latter offers an inoculation service and a research library for customers. The US agent, Council Travel (☎ 0171-287 3337), has an office at 28a Poland St, London W1V 3DB.

The Africa Travel Shop (☎ 0171-387 1211), at 4 Medway Court, Leigh St, London WC1, caters to the growing number of travellers interested in Africa. It is ABTA bonded, has a free video library and can organise overland safaris and cater to most other travel requirements.

At the time of writing, RAM's cheapest return Superpex fares in the low season from London to Tangier were UK£190 for one month and UK£234 for two. RAM also has direct flights from London to Casablanca, Marrakesh and Agadir. RAM offers various other fares, including a special youth ticket.

A quick ring around a few bucket shops soon reveals big differences, so it is worth shopping around. Many travellers use GB Airways, which flies from London and Manchester via Gibraltar to three Moroccan destinations: Tangier, Casablanca and Marrakesh. At the time of writing, return tickets, valid for one month, were being offered by various agents for UK£120 to UK£180. GB Airways has four flights a week to Casablanca from Manchester and London Heathrow via Gibraltar. There are two weekly flights to Tangier and two others from London Gatwick to Marrakesh.

At the time of writing, Air France and KLM had tickets valid for three months return to Casablanca for about UK£230, and it was possible to fly British Airways return to Casablanca for UK£173 in the low season.

Some agents also have charter flights, usually requiring that you return within one or two weeks, and starting at UK£100 return. If you can get one at the bottom range, it's generally cheaper to throw away the return half than to buy a regular one-way ticket. Some charters and scheduled flights also leave from cities other than London, such as Manchester.

If you only want to go for a short time, consider taking a hotel or fly-drive package. Three nights in, say, Marrakesh in a reasonable hotel near the medina, half-board, optional escorted tours, flights and transfers can cost well under UK£300. See Tours for more information.

If you are not in too much of a hurry and counting pennies, the most efficient way to get to Morocco is generally to fly to Málaga in southern Spain and either get a boat from there to the Spanish enclave of Melilla or a bus round to Algeciras and from there a boat across to Ceuta or Tangier (refer to the Sea section for details).

There are any number of flights virtually all year round to Málaga and many other Spanish destinations. It is feasible to get a one-way ticket to Málaga for around UK£60, and sometimes less. Return fares generally start at about UK£100 for scheduled flights, but deals on charters and the like abound, so look around. Agents specialising in travel to Spain often have ridiculously cheap return flights for short breaks in early November and early December. These are in the range of UK£40 to UK£60 for practically any destination. You'll forfeit the return half, but it's still cheap.

Sometimes charter tickets for either Morocco or Spain are tied to specific accommodation, but some agents are prepared to give you bogus vouchers for the accommodation, enabling you to benefit from the cheap flight.

The cheapest, but most unpredictable, way to fly to Morocco from London is to carry a package for an air courier service. DHL no longer offers this possibility, apparently for security reasons, but it may be worth hunting around for other courier companies.

To/From Europe

France There is no shortage of flights from Paris (and many other French cities) direct to Casablanca, Agadir, Rabat, Tangier, Fès, Marrakesh, Oujda and Ouarzazate. Most travel agents can do deals, and fly-drive arrangements are an attractive option. Given the sheer volume of traffic from France, deals here are often better than in traditional bucket-shop paradises like London or Amsterdam. RAM alone has four to five flights a day from Paris to Casablanca. Air France boasts some 50 weekly connections between a range of Moroccan and French destinations.

Various agencies sometimes offer charter flights at very low prices, and it is possible to get one-way flights or deals including accommodation. At the time of researching,

some of the cheapest return charter flights from Paris were to Marrakesh (1100FF) and Agadir (1200FF), with a maximum stay of four weeks, but in general prices are somewhat higher. You could try looking at Sélection Informations Vacances (☎ 1-42.60.83.40) at 9 Rue de l'Échelle, 75001 Paris, or Nouvelles Frontières (☎ 1-41.41.58.58) at 87 Blvd de Grenelle, 75015 Paris.

If you are looking for something more organised on the ground or desert expeditions, then a couple of places that might be worth tracking down are Explorator (☎ 1-42.66.66.24), 16 Place de la Madeleine, 75008 Paris, and Déserts (☎ 1-46.04.88.40), 6-8 Rue Quincampoix, 75004 Paris.

The possibilities are much more limited from Morocco. Despite the plethora of travel agents in central Casablanca, there seems to be little discounting. A standard one-way fare to Paris is Dr 4305 – hardly a bargain.

Spain Despite its proximity, Spain is not the ideal place from which to fly to Morocco, unless perhaps you are in a hurry and want to take an organised tour (for details see Tours).

Among the cheaper tickets available from Madrid at the time of writing was one for about 30,000 pta return to Tangier or 44,800 pta to Marrakesh, with a maximum stay of six months. Such prices are not always easy to find, and flights can easily cost 20,000 pta more. However, it is possible to find package deals that come in a lot cheaper. At the time of writing, Juliatours was offering a return flight and one night's stay in Morocco for 19,500 pta. You'd have to do some hunting around to see if you could extend the time you can stay before using the return flight.

In the high season there are flights from numerous Spanish cities direct to Agadir.

Travel agents in Madrid tend to be clustered in the vicinity of the Gran Vía, and budget travellers should try Unijoven at Calle San Bernardo 98 and Mundojoven at Calle Hortaleza 8.

The options *from* Morocco are more limited still. A one-way ticket to Madrid from Casablanca, regardless of the airline, comes to about Dr 2750. Spain's national carrier, Iberia, has four weekly flights between Madrid and Casablanca and two between Madrid and Tangier.

About the only scheduled flights worth a serious look are those between Málaga and the Spanish enclave of Melilla. One way costs 8800 pta, and there are quite a few daily flights.

Gibraltar Few travellers will want to fork out large sums of money to fly from 'the Rock' across the strait to Morocco, but it can be done. GB Airways has four weekly direct flights to Casablanca and two each to Tangier

---

Air Travel Glossary

Apex Apex, or 'advance purchase excursion' is a discounted ticket which must be paid for in advance. There are penalties if you wish to change it.

Baggage Allowance This will be written on your ticket and usually includes one 20-kg item to go in the hold, plus one item of hand luggage.

Bucket Shop This is an unbonded travel agency specialising in discounted airline tickets.

Budget Fare These can be booked at least three weeks in advance but the travel date is not confirmed until seven days prior to travel.

Bumped Just because you have a confirmed seat doesn't mean you're going to get on the plane – see Overbooking.

Cancellation Penalties If you have to cancel or change an Apex ticket there are often heavy penalties involved; insurance can sometimes be taken out against these penalties. Some airlines impose penalties on regular tickets as well, particularly against 'no-show' passengers.

Check-In Airlines ask you to check in a certain time ahead of the flight departure (usually one to two hours on international flights). If you fail to check in on time and the flight is overbooked, the airline can cancel your booking and give your seat to somebody else.

Confirmation Having a ticket written out with the flight and date you want doesn't mean you have a seat until the agent has checked with the airline that your status is 'OK' or confirmed. Meanwhile you could just be 'on request'.

Discounted Tickets There are two types of discounted fares – officially discounted (see Promotional Fares) and unofficially discounted. The lowest prices often impose drawbacks like flying with unpopular airlines, inconvenient schedules, or unpleasant routes and connections. A discounted ticket can save you other things than money – you may be able to pay Apex prices without the associated Apex advance booking and other requirements. Discounted tickets only exist where there is fierce competition.

Full Fares Airlines traditionally offer first class (coded F), business class (coded J) and economy class (coded Y) tickets. These days there are so many promotional and discounted fares available from the regular economy class that few passengers pay full economy fare.

ITX An 'independent inclusive tour excursion' (ITX) is often available on tickets to popular holiday destinations. Officially it's a package deal combined with hotel accommodation, but many agents will sell you one of these for the flight only. They'll give you phoney hotel vouchers in the unlikely event that you're challenged at the airport.

Lost Tickets If you lose your airline ticket an airline will usually treat it like a travellers' cheque and, after enquiries, issue you with another one. Legally, however, an airline is entitled to treat it like cash and if you lose it then it's gone forever. Take good care of your tickets.

MCO A 'miscellaneous charge order' (MCO) is a voucher that looks like an airline ticket but carries no destination or date. It is exchangeable with any IATA (International Association of Travel Agents) airline for a ticket on a specific flight. Its principal use for travellers is as an alternative to an onward ticket in those countries that demand one, and it's more flexible than an ordinary ticket if you're not sure of your route.

No-Shows No-shows are passengers who fail to show up for their flight. Full-fare passengers who fail to turn up are sometimes entitled to travel on a later flight. The rest of us are penalised (see Cancellation Penalties).

On Request This is an unconfirmed booking for a flight (see Confirmation).

Open Jaws This is a return ticket where you fly out to one place but return from another. If available, this can save you backtracking to your arrival point.

and Marrakesh. The one-way flight to Tangier costs from UK£49 to UK£69. To Marrakesh, the range is UK£143 to UK£180 (UK£270 return). There are plenty of travel agents in Gibraltar (and Algeciras) through which you can book tickets. For reservations with the airline in Gibraltar, call ☎ 79300.

GB Airways has various agents in Morocco (noted under the city entries). A one-way ticket from Tangier costs Dr 520. The full return fare from Tangier costs Dr 1225, although there is a one-day excursion fare for Dr 620.

Germany In Munich, a great source of travel information and equipment is the Darr

---

Overbooking Airlines hate to fly empty seats and since every flight has some passengers who fail to show up (see No-Shows), airlines often book more passengers than they have seats. Usually the excess passengers make up for those who fail to show up, but occasionally somebody gets bumped. If this happens, guess who it is most likely to be? The passengers who check in late.

Point-to-Point This is a discount ticket that can be bought on some routes in return for passengers waiving their rights to stopover.

Promotional Fares These are officially discounted fares like Apex fares, available from travel agents or direct from the airline.

Reconfirmation At least 72 hours prior to departure time of an onward or return flight, you must contact the airline and 'reconfirm' that you intend to be on the flight. If you don't do this the airline can delete your name from the passenger list and you could lose your seat. You don't have to reconfirm the first flight on your itinerary or if your stopover is less than 72 hours. However, it doesn't hurt to reconfirm more than once.

Restrictions Discounted tickets often have various restrictions on them – advance purchase is the most usual one (see Apex). Others are restrictions on the minimum and maximum period you must be away, such as a minimum of 14 days or a maximum of one year. See Cancellation Penalties.

Round-the-World An RTW ticket is just that. You have a limited period in which to circumnavigate the globe and you can go anywhere the carrying airlines go, as long as you don't backtrack. These tickets are usually valid for one year, the number of stopovers or total number of separate flights is worked out before you set off and they often don't cost much more than a basic return flight.

Stand-By A discounted ticket where you only fly if there is a seat free at the last moment. Stand-by fares are usually only available on domestic routes.

Tickets Out An entry requirement for many countries is that you have an onward or return ticket, in other words, a ticket out of the country. If you're not sure what you intend to do next, the easiest solution is to buy the cheapest onward ticket to a neighbouring country or a ticket from a reliable airline which can later be refunded if you do not use it. (See also MCO.)

Transferred Tickets Airline tickets cannot be transferred from one person to another. Travellers sometimes try to sell the return half of their ticket, but officials can ask you to prove that you are the person named on the ticket. This is unlikely to happen on domestic flights, but on an international flight tickets may be compared with passports.

Travel Agencies Travel agencies vary widely and you should choose one that suits your needs. Some simply handle tours, while full-service agencies handle everything from tours and tickets to car rental and hotel bookings. A good one will do all these things and can save you a lot of money, but if all you want is a ticket at the lowest possible price, then you really need an agency specialising in discounted tickets. A discounted ticket agency, however, may not be useful for other things, like hotel bookings.

Travel Periods Some officially discounted fares, Apex fares in particular, vary with the time of year. There is often a low (off-peak) season and a high (peak) season. Sometimes there's an intermediate or shoulder season as well. At peak times, when everyone wants to fly, not only will the officially discounted fares be higher but so will unofficially discounted fares and there may simply be no discounted tickets available. Usually the fare depends on your outward flight – if you depart in the high season and return in the low season, you pay the high-season fare. ■

Travel Shop (☎ 089-282032) at Theresienstrasse 66. Aside from producing a comprehensive travel equipment catalogue, they also run an Expedition Service with current flight information available.

In Berlin, ARTU Reisen (☎ 030-310466), at Hardenbergstrasse 9, near Berlin Zoo is a good travel agent and has five branches around the city.

Netherlands Amsterdam is a popular departure point for Morocco. Some of the best fares are offered by the student travel agency NBBS Reiswinkels (☎ 020-620 5071), which has seven branches throughout the city. The fares are comparable to those of London bucket shops. NBBS Reiswinkels has branches in Brussels, Belgium, as well.

To/From Australasia
There are no direct flights between Australia or New Zealand and Morocco. Your best bet is to get a flight to Europe and make your way to Morocco from there. Most people tend to head for London or Amsterdam first.

STA Travel is one of the more reliable travel agents and has branches around Australia. Flight Centres International is another reasonable place to check out.

To/From Asia
Hong Kong and Bangkok are the main two centres for cheap air tickets in south-east Asia, although there's not a huge market for Morocco. If you can't find anything direct, get a cheap ticket to Europe and head down from there.

To/From Algeria & Tunisia
Air Algérie and RAM have flights to Algiers, but there is not much in the line of discounts. One-way and return tickets go for Dr 1560 and Dr 2170. The trip to Tunis with Tunis Air costs Dr 2465/3445 one-way/return. They also offer an excursion fare of Dr 2740.

To/From Mauritania
At the time of writing, the only way you could get a visa for Mauritania was to arm yourself with a return air ticket on Air Mauritanie for Dr 4745.

To/From South Africa
As a sign of South Africa's increasing acceptability in Africa, RAM is considering options for direct flights to Johannesburg.

LAND
Taking your own vehicle to Morocco is comparatively straightforward. There is no need for a *carnet de passage en douane* when taking your car to Morocco, or indeed into Algeria or Tunisia, but this is a document required in many other African countries and worth getting if you think you'll be driving on beyond the Maghreb.

The UK Automobile Association (and most other such organisations) requires a financial guarantee for the carnet, which effectively acts as an import-duty waiver, as the vehicle could be liable for customs and other taxes if its exit is not registered within a year. The deposit they require can be well in excess of US$1000. The carnet costs UK£57.50 to UK£67.50 in the UK, depending on the number of countries you want to cover (up to 25). It is essential to ensure that the carnet is filled out properly at each border crossing, or you could be up for a lot of money. The carnet may also need to list any expensive spares you plan to carry, such as a gearbox.

In addition to such obvious papers as vehicle registration and an International Driving Permit (although many foreign licences are acceptable), a Green Card is required from the car's insurer. Not all insurers will issue one to cover Morocco. If yours does not, you must arrange insurance at the border. You can do this in Spain before embarkation on a ferry in Algeciras or on arrival in Morocco. Beyond Morocco, the Green Card is accepted in Tunisia but you are obliged to arrange local third-party insurance upon entering Algeria.

If you must arrange the insurance on arrival in Morocco, note that the liability limits on such policies are often absurdly low by Western standards and if you have any bad accidents you could be in deep water.

It may be advisable to arrange more comprehensive and reliable cover before you leave. If you're starting from the UK, a company often recommended for insurance policies and for detailed information on carnets is Campbell Irvine Ltd (☎ 0171-937 9903), 48 Earls Court Rd, London, W8 6EJ.

To/From the UK & Europe

Bus It is possible to get a bus ticket to destinations in Morocco from as far away as London. A one-way ticket with Eurolines (in conjunction with CTM, Morocco's national line) to Tangier or Marrakesh costs UK£128 or UK£208 return. The service leaves Victoria coach station (☎ 0171-730 0202), 164 Buckingham Palace Rd, London SW1, four to six days a week, depending on the season (summer is the high season) at 10 pm and arrives at Paris's Gare Routière Internationale (metro Galieni) at Porte de Bagnolet the next day at 7 am. There you change buses and leave at 10.30 am or noon, depending on the service you have been booked onto. The Eurolines office in London (☎ 0171-730 8235) is at 52 Grosvenor Gardens, London SW1W 0AU; in Paris (☎ 1-49.72.51.51) it's at 3-5 Ave Porte de la Villette.

The bus travels via Tours and Bordeaux and arrives in Algeciras in southern Spain the next evening for the crossing to Tangier, where you supposedly land by 9.30 pm.

It is possible to book a ticket right through to one of about 30 destinations, although the timetable for some of these is limited (as few runs as one a week) and it would seem better to stick to the main centres such as Tangier, Rabat, Marrakesh and the like. Indeed after so much time spent on buses, you may want to get off at the earliest possible moment (Tangier), have a rest and proceed by train or local bus.

From Paris, the fares vary according to the final destination and the season. One-way tickets to Tangier, Kenitra, Rabat and Casablanca cost 730 and 880FF in the high season (15 May to 7 August). The return fares are 1250 and 1400FF respectively.

To Marrakesh, Agadir, Taroudannt, Tiznit and other destinations in between, the one-way/return fares are 880/1500FF and 1030/1650FF (high season).

To Meknès, Fès, Taza, Oujda, Nador and Ouarzazate the respective one-way/return fares are 930/1600FF and 1080/1780FF.

Children between the ages of four and 12 travel for half-price.

Whether you're starting in Paris or coming from elsewhere (such as London), you must pay a 30FF embarkation tax. Passengers are allowed to carry 30 kg of luggage free. Each extra kg is another 10FF.

One of the big drawbacks with this trip is that the ticket is for a through trip without stops, whereas travellers taking the train have two months to use the ticket and can stop along the way. If you are in a hurry, it would be worth hunting around for a good airfare, given the time and cost involved with the bus journey.

If you're in **Madrid**, you can take a train (see the next section) south to Algeciras or a bus from the Estación Autobuses Sur (☎ 1-527 9927), which is not too far from Atocha train station. From Algeciras you can take a boat to Ceuta (Spanish Morocco) or Tangier (refer to the Sea section). With Enatcar (Spain's national bus line), the bus goes via Málaga, Torremolinos, Fuengirola, Marbella and Estepona and takes about 10 hours. There are departures from Madrid at 9.30 am and 11 pm. From Algeciras, buses doing the reverse route leave at 6 and 9 pm. The one-way fare is 3385 pta. The 6 pm bus also stops in Granada. Enatcar has long-distance buses from Algeciras's Estación Marítima to Paris (16,900 pta one way) and London (18,500 pta one way) departing on Tuesdays (and Fridays in summer). For information by phone, call ☎ 1-527 9927 in Madrid or ☎ 956-665067 in Algeciras.

From **Morocco**, CTM operates buses from Casablanca and most other main cities and towns to France (Paris, Toulouse, Marseilles, Lyons and several other cities), Belgium (Brussels and one or two other stops) and northern Italy (Milan, Turin and a couple of other intermediate stops).

Most of the services originate in Casablanca and pass through various other Moroccan cities before crossing the Strait of Gibraltar. You must book at least a week in advance to get a seat. Frequency varies depending on your starting point, but on average there are four or five runs to Paris every week. Buses to Belgium and Italy leave once a week as a rule.

The buses to Paris stop at several places: Gennevilliers (☎ 1-47.98.64.98), 9 Route Principale du Port; Porte de Clichy (☎ 1-42.70.99.99), 14 Blvd Victor Hugo; and Galieni (☎ 1-49.72.51.51), Ave du Général de Gaulle.

Fares vary little, regardless of your point of departure. To most of France (including Paris) and Italy you pay about Dr 1200. To Belgium and northernmost France it's Dr 1440.

One or two other private companies, particularly in Fès, claim to have buses running not only to the European destinations already mentioned, but on to Amsterdam (Dr 1350 with SAT) and other northern European cities. It should be possible to book right through to London (given that you can do the reverse) if you really want to.

Train From Victoria station, **London**, you could get a train ticket to take you all the way through to a number of Moroccan destinations. It is more expensive than the bus, but the tickets are good for two months, which means you could make Morocco part of a wider trip through France and Spain. A one-way/return ticket to Algeciras is UK£137/225. This trip, which leaves at 9.25 am, takes about 48 hours all up, including a 12-hour wait to change trains in Madrid. To Tangier the fares are UK£164/278.

People under 26 can get 30% off with a Wasteels or BIJ (billet de jeunesse) ticket. Such tickets have to include travel across at least one frontier, and you can't make stops until you have left the country of purchase. At Victoria station the Wasteels office (☎ 0171-834 7066) is near platform two. You can also buy Wasteels tickets in Morocco for travel to Spain and beyond.

Wasteels offers Eurodomino passes, which entitle the holder to three, five or 10 days' travel on a specific country's network within a month. The fares for 2nd/1st-class passes in Morocco are UK£25/35, UK£38/52 and UK£75/103 respectively. The tickets cannot be purchased in Morocco itself, and are only worth it in 2nd class and if you are sure you'll want to do a lot of train travel in a short time.

Morocco is part of the Inter-Rail network. For UK£249, travellers under the age of 26 can purchase an Inter-Rail ticket entitling them to a month of free 2nd-class travel on trains in up to 26 countries in Europe, including Morocco. To do this, they have to be able to prove they have been resident in a European country for at least six months. In practice this rule is often interpreted leniently. In the unlikely event that you will want, or be able, to get an Inter-Rail ticket in Morocco, they cost Dr 3150.

Train travel is not that expensive in Morocco, so buying an Inter-Rail pass just for Morocco would be of dubious value. Although people over 26 can now also buy Inter-Rail passes, they are not valid in Morocco.

From **Paris**, your best bet is probably to take the TGV from the Gare Montparnasse, changing at Irun for Madrid and on to Algeciras. If you want to do it in one hit, take the 6.55 am train. The trip takes at least 25 hours and the standard adult fare is 715/1430FF one way/return. The SNCF (French Railways) timetable includes a train from Gare d'Austerlitz to Algeciras at 10.15 pm every day. This journey takes about 33 hours and is more expensive.

From **Madrid**, RENFE, the Spanish rail network, has a daily train (the Estrella del Estrecho) going from Chamartín station to Algeciras, which leaves at 10 pm and arrives at about 9 am the following day. The one-way 2nd-class fare is 5300 pta. Alternatively, you could depart from Atocha station at 3.25 pm, changing at Bobadilla and arriving in Algeciras at 10.25 pm. The fare, including a 1000 pta supplement, is 6900 pta. From there you can connect for the boat ride to Ceuta or

Tangier. Going in the other direction, the direct train to Chamartín leaves at 9 pm and arrives in Madrid at around 8.45 am. The Estrella Media Luna also leaves at 9 pm for Hendaye on the Spanish-French border. There are a couple of morning trains to Bobadilla, from where you can get connections to other destinations.

Alternatively, you could head for Málaga or Almería and take the boat from there to the Spanish Moroccan enclave of Melilla. There are four trains a day from Chamartín station to Málaga, taking from seven to nine hours and costing 4600 pta. The luxury Talgo 200 train runs three times daily between Madrid and Málaga, taking just four hours and forty minutes. The fare is 6000 to 9700 pta, depending on what class you choose and when you travel.

Two trains a day run between Almería and Madrid. The faster (Talgo) takes about seven hours to/from Madrid's Atocha station and costs 5700 pta. The slower train leaves from Chamartín station in Madrid, takes 10 hours and costs 4000 pta. From Almería, the Talgo to Madrid leaves at 2.15 pm and the slower train at 10.05 pm. There are also three trains a day to Granada (1065 pta).

Again, those under 26 could invest in a Wasteels ticket. The trip from Madrid to Marrakesh, including the Algeciras ferry crossing, is 8710/16,030 pta one way/return.

You can book international tickets in Morocco up to two months ahead.

To/From North Africa

Bus CTM has a weekly bus to Tripoli (Libya) for Dr 1000 from Casablanca on Saturdays, via Algeria and Tunisia. At least one private company, Rostoum, offers a similar run for Dr 750.

From Oujda there are local buses and grands taxis to the border, and several daily buses (US$1.50) and taxis to and from Tlemcen on the Algerian side – the latter take about an hour.

Train The rail link between Morocco and Algeria (and on to Tunisia), long suspended, has been up and running for several years now.

The Al-Maghreb al-Arabi, as it is known, leaves Casablanca (Casa-Port) every night at 8.35 pm. The journey to Algiers takes about 24 hours, and it's about another 20 hours to Tunis. You have to change trains at the Algerian border and again in Algiers (the latter stop takes about half an hour). Going the other way, the train leaves Tunis at 10.20 am (Tunisian time), arriving at 6.55 am (Algerian time) in Algiers the following day and at 8.20 am (Moroccan time) in Casablanca the day after (there's a 3½ hour wait at Oujda on this leg). Note that these times can vary because of seasonal changes. Algeria and Tunisia both have daylight-saving time, whereas Morocco does not. For the rest of the year, Algeria is on GMT/UTC (as is Morocco) and Tunisia is an hour ahead.

The train runs via Rabat and Fès to Oujda, where Moroccan passport control and customs are carried out. It is also possible to hook up with the train coming from Tangier, which involves a three-hour wait at Fès. Going the other way, you have a four-hour wait at the intermediate station of Sidi Slimane.

Examples of 2nd/1st-class fares from Rabat are Dr 222.50/299.50 to Oran, Dr 273.50/368.50 to Algiers, Dr 336.50/452.50 to Constantine (Algeria), Dr 446.50/600.50 to Tunis and Dr 474.50/640.50 to Sousse (Tunisia). For the run to Oujda you can get a couchette for an extra Dr 46.50/56 (2nd/1st class), which is a worthwhile investment. It is also possible to pay for the more expensive *voiture lit* (sleeper).

Car There are two crossing points between Morocco and Algeria: between Oujda and Tlemcen in the north near the coast and between Figuig and Beni Ounif some 300 km farther south.

In the past, it used to be necessary for people bringing their own vehicle into Morocco from Algeria to have a telex from their embassy in Rabat guaranteeing that they would take the vehicle out of the country. This may now have lapsed but it's worth checking out well in advance, as it used to take up to a couple of weeks to get such a telex. This telex was in addition to a Green Card.

To/From Mauritania

Although a UN ceasefire has kept the Western Sahara quiet since September 1991, it is still difficult to cross the border into Mauritania. Since early 1994, the Moroccans have been issuing travel permits in Dakhla and escorting civilian convoys to the border, but the Mauritanian embassy in Rabat will not issue visas for overland travel, which for most would seem to put the mockers on any such ideas. The French do not need visas, and so probably can get through. It is worth checking the latest situation with the Mauritanian embassy, and it may also be worth trying to get an overland visa at a Mauretanian embassy outside Morocco.

SEA
To/From Spain

Various car ferries are operated by Compañía Trasmediterranea, Islena de Navigación SA, Comarit, Limadet and Transtour. Jetfoils also make the crossing from Algeciras to Tangier and Ceuta. The most popular service is the Algeciras-Tangier route, although for car owners the service to Ceuta might be more worthwhile because of the availability of tax-free petrol in the enclave. The others are Tarifa-Tangier, Almería-Melilla (Spanish Morocco) and Málaga-Melilla. The majority are car ferries of the drive-on and drive-off type.

On most routes, more boats are put on in the high season, which is from 15 June until 15 September.

If you want the latest information on Trasmediterranea's services before turning up at one of the ports, you could contact Southern Ferries (☎ 0171-491 4968) at 179 Piccadilly, London W1V 9DB, or the Trasmediterranea offices in Madrid (☎ 1-431 0700) at Calle Pedro Muñoz Seca, 2, and in Barcelona (☎ 3-412 2524) at the Estación Marítima, Muelle Barcelona, 1.

Various reductions are available on some of the services. Pensioners of EU nations and people under 26 should enquire about them before buying tickets.

Algeciras-Tangier Trasmediterranea, the Spanish government-run company, runs at least nine daily car ferries between Algeciras and Tangier in tandem with Islena de Navigación, Limadet and Comarit. Depending on demand, the number of boats can rise to about 20. It doesn't matter whose boat you end up on, the fares remain the same, although there are a few variations: on Comarit's boats children up to the age of four go for free, whereas the limit is two on Trasmediterranea's boats (in both cases children up to 12 years pay half-fare). What difference this makes in practice is anyone's guess. In addition to each line's official outlet at the Estación Marítima, there is a plethora of other ticket offices at the port and along the waterfront.

The one-way adult fare is 2700 pta. If you happen to be considered a Moroccan resident, the fares are reduced. The fee for cars is between 8500 pta and 14,000 pta, depending on the dimensions of the car. Motorcycles and bicycles cost 2400 pta. The crossing takes 2½ hours. Eurail and Inter-Rail pass holders are entitled to a 20% discount on ferry tickets between Algeciras and Tangier and should make a point of asking for it. This can prove more problematic on the Moroccan side. You can usually pay for your ticket with a credit card on the Spanish side.

If you don't have a vehicle, Trasmediterranea's jetfoil service is a quicker (some would say more nauseating) deal. It leaves Algeciras daily at 9.30 am and Tangier at 3.30 pm. In the high season there is usually a second service in the afternoon. The run takes an hour and the fare is the same as for the ferry.

The fare per person from Tangier on ferry and jetfoil is Dr 196. Cars up to six metres long cost Dr 618, and Dr 290 for every metre extra. Bikes and motorcycles attract a charge of Dr 175.

Spanish passport control is quite straightforward if you're leaving Algeciras, but customs can be slow if you're coming from Morocco. Leaving Tangier, you must get an exit form to fill in before getting your passport stamped and boarding. You should be given one when you buy your ticket. There are lot of people pretending to be officials of one sort or another – most of them *écrivains publics* (public scribes!) – who will try to get one last dirham out of you before you leave. One of their services is to give you an exit form and lend you a pen to fill it out. If you approach the port at Tangier on foot, there'll usually be a few of them around trying to create a sense of urgency and bustling you about, or guiding you to a boat (not all dock at the main port). All these characters want money, so if you're not feeling overly generous, watch out for them.

You can buy tickets in the main port building, although the booths are not always open (this is when the public scribes come into their own, producing tickets as if from nowhere). You must pay for the ticket in cash. There are a few banks represented just outside the terminal, and you'll have to change a bit more of your hard-earned money if you don't have enough dirhams to buy a ticket. They should open by 7 am (before the first departure), but this rarely happens.

Tangier is swamped with agencies where you can buy tickets, but as a rule, you are probably best advised to go to the port early and get a ticket on the spot.

Algeciras-Ceuta (Spanish Morocco) There
are at least six ferry and six jetfoil crossings on this route in either direction, except on Sundays, when there are only four. Around Easter and Christmas the number of services can rise to 10 each way.

The ferry trip takes 1½ hours and the fare is 1625 pta (1700 pta in the high season; children between two and 11 pay half-fare). Vehicles between 2.5 and six metres long cost from 7500 to 13,650 pta, depending on dimensions. Motorcycles cost from 1700 to 2550 pta depending on engine size.

The jetfoil costs adults 2650 pta one way and double return (2700 pta in the high season). The trip takes about 30 minutes.

Tarifa-Tangier There is a daily ferry from
Tarifa to Tangier (one hour; 2700 pta/Dr 196 per person) at 10 am (9 am on Fridays). It sets off from Tangier at 4 pm Monday to Thursday and at 7 am and 4 pm on Saturdays. Costs for cars are identical to those for the Algeciras-Tangier ferries. In Tarifa, you can buy your tickets on the morning at the dock or from Viajes Marruecotur (☎ 681821; fax 680256), Calle Batalla del Salado, 57.

You can catch buses from Tarifa to various other cities in Spain.

Almería-Melilla (Spanish Morocco) The
timetable for services between Almería and the Spanish enclave of Melilla is not quite so straightforward. In the low season there is generally a ferry from Almería at 1 pm every day but Sunday and Monday, and at 11.30 pm on Sunday. There is no boat on Mondays. Going the other way, there is a departure every day but Sunday at 11.30 pm.

In the high season (from mid-June to mid-September), the timetable operates on a system of alternating weeks, under which there are two ferries four days a week (Monday, Wednesday, Friday and Sunday) at 2 am and 6 pm and one at 10 am on the other days one week, and the reverse on alternate weeks.

The trip takes 6½ to eight hours. The cheapest fare *(butaca turista* or deck) fare is 3050 pta (3150 pta in the high season) each way. You can also get beds in cabins of four or two, some with toilets. Prices range from 5000 pta a head for four to 8500 pta for single occupation of a twin-berth. Fares are a little higher in the high season. Children from two to 12 years of age travel for half-price (infants go free). A car can cost from 7550 to 22,650 pta in the low season, depending on its dimensions. You also pay to take across motorbikes. You can buy tickets at the Estación Marítima (about a 10 to 15-minute walk from the train and bus stations) or at travel agents in the centre of town. You can pay by credit card.

If you arrive in Almería from Morocco, you can push on into Spain by train or bus . The train station is about 10 minutes' walk off to the right from the port. The bus station is five minutes' walk farther down the road in front of the train station.

Málaga-Melilla (Spanish Morocco) Also operated by Trasmediterranea, ferries leave Málaga Monday to Saturday in the low season at 1 pm and Melilla at 11 pm. An exceptional Sunday service is occasionally put on. In the high season the Sunday service is permanent. The journey time is 7½ to 10 hours and fares are the same as for the Almería-Melilla ferry. As in Almería, you can buy tickets most easily at the Estación Marítima, which is more or less directly south of the town centre.

You could do worse than arrive in Málaga from Morocco if you want to proceed to other destinations in Spain and the rest of Europe. Check out charter flight possibilities for London and other European capitals.

The main bus and train stations are within five minutes' walk of each other to the west of the town centre (about 20 minutes' walk).

Almería-Nador A UK maritime group, Cenargo, has for some time been planning a rival service from Almería to Nador, just east of the Spanish enclave of Melilla. The Spaniards, flying in the face of EU competition rules, are doing their best to block the new service, but Morocco is quite happy about the idea.

To/From Gibraltar
Gibraltar-Tangier Twice a week, the *Idriss I* ferry links Gibraltar with Tangier. The voyage costs UK£16/27 one way/return. The ferry can carry up to 30 cars (the charge is UK£30) and runs all year, leaving Gibraltar at 8.30 am on Mondays and 6.30 pm on Fridays. From Tangier, it leaves at 9 am on Fridays and 5 pm on Sundays. The Gibraltar agents are Tourafrica Int Ltd (☎ 79140; fax

76754), 2a Main St. The ferry departs from the nearby North Mole. Several Tangier travel agents can sell you tickets for the Gibraltar ferry. They cost Dr 220 per person and Dr 480 for a car up to 4.5 metres long. On Fridays you can pay the one-way fare for a same-day return excursion. The trip takes about two hours.

Gibraltar-Tetouan Jasmine Lines sometimes runs a catamaran to Restinga Smir (a little north of Tetouan), usually in the summer, but inclement weather often leads to cancellations. The boat used until 1993 carried 250 people, but the owners planned to put a bigger, sturdier boat into service in 1994. When the going is good (in summer), it runs four or five times a week, costing UK£16.50/27.70 one way/return. The agents are Parodytur (☎ 76070; fax 70563), in the Cazes Arcade, 143 Main St.

Leaving Gibraltar If you arrive in Gibraltar from Morocco, you will probably want to head out soon after going through the British enclave's passport and customs control (and perhaps a quick look around). Apart from flights to the UK, your only choice is to cross into Spain. It's a 15-minute walk to the border (La Linea) across the airstrip, or you can get the No 9 bus from Casemates Square.

Passport control and customs are pretty much a formality on the Gibraltar-Spanish border, but remember that citizens of some countries who have no trouble entering Gibraltar may require a visa to proceed into Spain. Once through Spanish customs, it's a five-minute walk to the Estación de Autobuses (bus station), from which there are buses to various destinations in Spain.

To/From France
Sète-Tangier This car ferry service, which is considerably more luxurious (swimming pool, night club of sorts on board) than those linking Spain and Morocco, and commensurately more expensive, is operated by the Compagnie Marocaine de Navigation (Comanav). The crossing is made six or seven

times a month, usually once every four to five days. As a rule the *Marrakesh*, which can carry 634 passengers, leaves Sète at 7 pm and Tangier at 6 pm (local time).

The trip takes 36 to 38 hours and the fare, depending on the class, is between 1250 and 2100FF one way (or 2130 and 3570FF return) in shared cabins of two to four people. If you want to have a cabin to yourself, you'll be up for about another 1000FF. There are sometimes supplements to be paid on top of the fare. Children between two and 11 travel for half-price. Cars under four metres long cost 1540FF. There is room for 220 vehicles on board. There are special reduced fares per passenger and vehicle for students and people under 26. A berth in a cabin of four costs 880 to 950FF.

You can book tickets for this service at Southern Ferries (☎ 0171-491 4968; fax 0171-491 3502) at 179 Piccadilly, London W1V 9DB, or in France at the SNCM Ferryterranée office (☎ 1-49.24.24.24; fax 1-91.56.36.66), 12 Rue Godot de Mauroy, Paris 75009. The Sète office (☎ 67.74.96.96; fax 67.74.93.05) is at 4 Quai d'Alger, 34202 Sète. The port agency in Sète is the Compagnie Charles Leborgne (☎ 67.46.61.70; fax 67.74.33.04), at 3 Quai de la République. There are agents in Germany, Italy, Belgium, Holland, Switzerland and several other European countries.

In Morocco, Comanav's main office (☎ 302412; fax 300790) is in Casablanca, at 7 Blvd de la Résistance. In Tangier, the office (☎ 932649; fax 943570) is at 43 Ave Abou al-Alaa al-Maari.

Sète-Nador The same company runs a similar service at much the same rates between Sète and Nador in the high season (mid-June to mid-September).

TOURS

A growing number of operators are putting more effort into organised trips to Morocco. More than 40 agencies operate out of the UK alone, and although the ONMT (Moroccan tourist office) in London keeps a list of them,

the Paris equivalent does not. One employee there simply said that everyone arranges tours to Morocco! Before diving into something, it pays to do a bit of research. The ONMT in your country is a good place to begin. They may be able to advise you on particular tour operators. Possibilities range from the more traditional style of tour of the Imperial Cities to beach holidays, golf trips, trekking, bird-watching and desert safaris.

The following information is intended as a guide to the options only, and not as a recommendation of these over other operators.

It should be remembered that the programs on such trips are usually tight, leaving little room for roaming around on your own. But they do take much of the hassle off your plate. Shop around and check itinerary details, accommodation, insurance and tour conditions carefully. Also find out who will organise the ticketing, visas and other documentation.

Tours from the UK
Morocco Specialists In the UK, Best of Morocco (☎ 01380-828533; fax 01380-828630), at Seend Park, Seend, Wiltshire SN12 6NZ, is one of the better established tour operators for Morocco. They offer horse-trekking tours, Land Rover safaris in the Sahara and a host of other possibilities. Their seven-day tour of the imperial cities costs about UK£700, depending on the season, and includes flights, transfers, four-star hotels (treat this with a pinch of salt) and meals. Two days of white-water rafting in the Middle Atlas can cost as little as UK£300, depending on numbers.

The Moroccan-run Moroccan Sun (☎ 0171-437 3968; fax 0171-287 9127) and Morocco Bound (☎ 0171-734 5307; fax 0171-287 9127), both at Triumph House, 189 Regent St, London W1R 7WB, apart from organising classic itineraries such as circuits of the Imperial Cities, offer holidays ranging from golf trips to bird-watching and trekking. Morocco Bound has a series of possible short trips for people who want a quick escape from the UK and a taste of Morocco.

Adventure Tours Quite a few adventure travel specialists organise tours to Morocco. Several organise long trips crossing the length and breadth of Africa and going through Morocco along the way. These trips usually involve a group of people travelling in communal fashion on board an overland truck. You share tents, food and time, and considering that some of these trips can last several months, there is a certain amount of risk involved that it won't be quite what you were hoping for. If you don't get on with your fellow travellers (or they don't get on with you!), or you simply want to branch off on your own, the money's gone and you have to live with it. On the other hand, such trips can remove much of the bureaucratic hassle of traipsing through Africa, and you benefit from the experience of tour leaders who have (usually) been around before and can anticipate problems.

You could try the Africa Travel Shop in London (see To/From the UK under Air) or read *TNT* for a selection of operators to Africa. Encounter Overland (☎ 0171-370 6951; fax 0171-244 9373), at 267 Old Brompton Rd, London SW5 9JA, is one such operator. Other names worth looking out for are Africa Explored and Dragoman.

Guerba Expeditions (☎ 01373-826689; fax 01373-858351) runs shorter (usually about two weeks) trips for trekking in the Atlas or slightly longer Saharan 'experiences'. Their tours start at about UK£500.

Other Tours For a more exclusively cultural holiday, you could do worse than find out what British Museum Tours (☎ 0171-323 8895; fax 0171-436 7315), 46 Bloomsbury St, London WC1B 3QQ, has to offer. Tours of the imperial cities are the speciality, accompanied by expert lecturers. You'd be looking at more than UK£1000 for 11 days.

Ramblers Holidays Ltd (☎ 01707-331133; fax 01707-333276), Box 43, Welwyn Garden, Hertfordshire AL8 6PQ, is one of several UK tour operators that organises walking holidays in the Atlas.

Tours from France
As already noted, there are any number of agencies and tour operators to turn to in France. A couple of travel agencies and adventure specialists appear in the Air section.

In addition, a number specialise in trekking tours to Morocco. Terres d'Aventure (☎ 1-43.29.94.50), 16 Rue Saint-Victor, 75005 Paris, has been running walking trips to various parts of Morocco, including the High Atlas and the southern oases, since 1976. Allibert (☎ 1-48.06.16.61), 39 Rue du Chemin Vert, Paris 75011, is another such operator.

Tours from Spain
If you're in Spain, the best way to experience Morocco is simply to head down yourself through southern Spain (see the Land section). However, if your time is limited, it might be worth considering a package tour, of which there are plenty on offer, particularly through the summer.

Solafrica, for instance, has four-day weekends in Marrakesh from about 60,000 pta, depending on the quality of the hotel.

Juliatours offers a range of eight-day and 15-day tours ranging from 60,000 to 90,000 pta, which include flights and accommodation.

Mundojoven and Akali Joven are among the operators offering bus trips for younger people into Morocco from Madrid and other Spanish cities. These tours typically start at 35,000 pta for about a week; two-week tours cost about 60,000 pta. Some of them concentrate on less challenging elements like the beaches, while others follow what are becoming fairly well trodden routes around the imperial cities, into the Atlas Mountains or the Sahara.

LEAVING MOROCCO
There is no departure tax upon leaving Morocco, and departure formalities are

straightforward. You must fill in an exit card and have your passport stamped before exiting.

WARNING

The information in this chapter is particularly vulnerable to change: prices for international travel are volatile, routes are introduced and cancelled, schedules change, special deals come and go, and rules and visa requirements are amended. Airlines and governments seem to take a perverse pleasure in making price structures and regulations as complicated as possible. You should check directly with the airline or a travel agent to make sure you understand how a fare (and ticket you may buy) works. In addition, the travel industry is highly competitive and there are many lurks and perks.

The upshot of this is that you should get opinions, quotes and advice from as many airlines and travel agents as possible before you part with your hard-earned cash. The details given in this chapter should be regarded as pointers and are not a substitute for your own careful, up-to-date research.

Getting Around

AIR

If time is limited, it's worth considering the occasional internal flight offered by RAM (Royal Air Maroc) or its subsidiary, RAI (Royal Air Inter).

Several reductions are available. If you buy a return ticket for internal flights, you get 25% off the normal one-way fares. If you're under 22 or a student under 31, you are entitled to 25% off all fares. There are group reductions and children aged two to 12 travel at half price. Generally these reductions can only be had through Royal Air Maroc offices and not through travel agents. Beware of 'Discover Morocco' vouchers which are sometimes offered by the airline in its overseas offices. They are supposed to give you a set number of discounted internal flights, but travellers have reported that airline staff in Morocco simply won't accept them.

For an idea of what you'll pay, the standard one-way fare from Casablanca to Fès is Dr 405 (about US$45). Fès to Agadir is Dr 810 (US$90) one way. Casablanca to Marrakesh is Dr 340 (US$38) one way.

Internal airports serviced by RAM and RAI are Agadir, Al-Hoceima, Casablanca, Dakhla, Er-Rachidia, Fès, Goulimime, Kenitra, Laayoune, Marrakesh, Ouarzazate, Oujda, Rabat, Smara, Tangier, Tan Tan and Tetouan. About the longest flight you could take is the weekly Dakhla-Tangier run via Casablanca, which takes six hours 50 minutes (the return flight is shorter because there's no stop in Marrakesh en route).

The bulk of internal flights involve making a connection in Casablanca.

Among direct flights, there are at least two daily runs between Marrakesh and Casablanca (35 minutes). Four times a week there is a direct flight from Marrakesh to Agadir (45 minutes), and once a week to Fès (1¼ hours). Agadir is also connected by two weekly direct flights to Laayoune and Dakhla, and one to Tan Tan. Up to three flights connect Tangier with Casablanca most days (55 minutes). You can pick up a full timetable for free at most RAM offices.

BUS

A dense network of buses operates throughout Morocco, and many private companies compete for business alongside the main national carrier, CTM (Compagnie de Transports Marocains). The latter is the only firm to have a truly national service. In most cities or towns there is a single central bus station *(gare routière)*, but in some places CTM maintains a separate terminal. Occasionally there are other stations for a limited number of fairly local destinations. CTM tends to be a little more expensive than the other lines, but often there are only a few extra dirhams in it. Bus fares work out to about Dr 1 for every four or five km, and are comparable to 2nd-class fares on normal trains.

Supratours runs a subsidiary bus service in conjunction with the railways (see Train).

Compagnie de Transports Marocains (CTM)

The main national carrier is the best and most secure bus company in Morocco, and serves most destinations of interest to travellers. As part of Morocco's program of economic reform, CTM was privatised in May 1994. It is difficult to say what effect this might have on its service.

CTM offers different classes: *mumtaz* (excellent), and 1st and 2nd class, but the distinction seems to be made mostly on longer routes away from the big centres. Always ask about different fares, but where there is only one the official line is usually that you are getting a mumtaz bus. On CTM buses, children four years old and up pay full fare.

Where possible, especially if services are infrequent or do not originate in the place you want to leave, it is not a bad idea to book ahead. Unfortunately, they do not always allow you to do so. Of the more popular places travellers get to, Chefchaouen can be one of the most painful to get out of again.

CTM buses are fairly modern and comfortable. Mumtaz buses have videos (a mixed blessing) and heating in winter (they sometimes overdo this). The first 20 seats are theoretically reserved for nonsmokers.

Sample (mumtaz) fares are as follows:

From	To	Fare (Dr)	Hours
Casablanca	Agadir	117.50	10
	Marrakesh	57.50	4½
Fès	Casablanca	69	5
	Oujda	60	6
	Tangier	77.50	6
Marrakesh	Agadir	63	4
	Fès	115	9
	Ouarzazate	49	3
Tangier	Agadir	205.50	15
	Casablanca	88	7
	Marrakesh	146	11

There is an official charge for baggage on CTM buses. Once you have bought your ticket you get a baggage tag, which you should hang on to, as you'll need it when you arrive. The charge for an average backpack is about Dr 3 to Dr 4.

CTM also operates international buses from all the main Moroccan cities to Paris, Brussels and other destinations abroad. See the Getting There & Away chapter for details.

Other Companies

The other bus companies are all privately owned and only operate regionally. The biggest of them is SATAS, which operates from Casablanca south and is every bit as good as CTM. Some of the others are two-bit operations with one or two well-worn buses, so the degree of comfort is a matter of pot luck. Some of the stations seem like madhouses, and touts run about screaming out any number of destinations for buses about to depart. Occasionally, you will find would-be guides, anxious to help you to the right ticket booth – for a small consideration of course.

Some companies offer 1st and 2nd class,

although the difference in fare and comfort is rarely great. On the secondary runs you can often buy your tickets on the bus, but if you do you'll probably have to stand. The buses also tend to stop an awful lot. More often than not you'll be charged for baggage, especially if it's going on top of the bus. You should not pay more than Dr 2, but foreigners frequently find themselves obliged to hand over Dr 5 per item.

These buses rarely have heating in winter, even when crossing the High Atlas, so make sure you have plenty of warm clothing with you. Occasionally buses are held up by snow drifts in mountain passes; then you'll really feel the cold. The Marrakesh-Ouarzazate road is prone to this.

TRAIN

Morocco has in its Office National des Chemins de Fer (ONCF) one of the most modern rail systems in Africa, linking most of the main centres. The trains, mostly Belgian-made, are generally comfortable, fast and preferable to buses. Present lines go as far south as Marrakesh, but a new one is planned from there to Agadir and on to Laayoune. Buses run by Supratours link up with trains to further destinations with no rail line, so that the ONCF can get you as far south as Dakhla.

Classes

There are two types of train (normal and *rapide*) and two classes on each (1st and 2nd), giving four possible fares for any given trip. The main difference between the normal trains and the rapides is not, as the name suggests, speed (there is rarely any difference), but comfort and air-conditioning. Second class is more than adequate on any journey, and on normal trains 2nd-class fares are commensurate with bus fares.

Tickets & Fares

You are advised to buy tickets at the station as a supplement is charged for doing so on the train. Although you can buy a ticket up to six days in advance, there are no reserved seats, so it seems a little pointless. A ticket is technically valid for five days, so that you can use it to get off at intermediate stops before reaching your final destination. You need to ask for a *bulletin d'arrêt* at the inter-mediate stop. Always hang on to tickets, as inspectors check them on the trains and they are collected at the station on arrival.

Children under four travel for free. Those up to 12 years old get a reduction of 10% to 50%, depending on the service.

Sample 2nd-class fares in normal and rapide trains are as follows:

From	To	Fare	Hours
Tangier	Casablanca	81.50/103	6
	Fès	66/84	6
	Marrakesh	134/169	10
Casablanca	Marrakesh	52.50/66.50	4
	Oujda	142/179.50	11
Rabat	Fès	59.50/62.50	3½
	Marrakesh	71/90	4½
	Tangier	62.50/79	5

Sleepers
You can get couchettes on the overnight trains from Marrakesh to Tangier and from Casablanca to Oujda. They are worth the extra money and cost Dr 46.50/56 in 2nd/1st class.

On the Al-Maghreb al-Arabi train from Casablanca to Oujda and on to Algeria you can also get a proper sleeper (single or twin). The full fare per person to Oujda is Dr 359 in the twin and Dr 406 in the single.

Shuttles
In addition to the normal and rapide trains, there are express shuttles (TNR) running frequently between Kenitra, Rabat, Casablanca and Mohammed V Airport. In 1994, Belgium's ACEC Transport supplied six new locomotives for this service. From Rabat to Casablanca you pay Dr 19 in 2nd class normal and Dr 24 in 2nd class for rapide and TNR. The 1st-class fares are Dr 28 (normal); Dr 34 (rapide) and Dr 43 (TNR). For more on airport connections, see the Getting Around sections under Casablanca and Rabat.

Supratours Buses
The ONCF runs buses through Supratours to widen its network. Thus Nador, near Melilla on the Mediterranean coast, is linked to the Oujda-Casablanca lines by a special bus to Taourirt station. Tetouan is linked to the main line from Tangier by bus to Tnine Sidi Lyamani. Train passengers heading further south than Marrakesh link up with buses at Marrakesh station for Essaouira, Agadir, Smara, Laayoune and Dakhla.

Timetables
Timetables for the whole system are posted in French at most stations. It is occasionally possible to get hold of a handy pocketbook timetable called the *Indicateur des Horaires*.

TAXI
Shared taxis (*grands taxis* or *taxiat kebira* in Arabic) link towns to their nearest neighbours in a kind of leap-frogging system. Usually ageing Mercedes imported from Europe, they take six passengers and leave when full. There are fixed-rate fares, generally a little higher than on the buses, but attempts to extract more from foreigners are not uncommon – try to see what other passengers are paying. When asking about fares, make it clear you want to pay for a *plasa* ('place', presumably a corruption of the Spanish *plaza)* in a *taxi collectif* (shared taxi). Another expression that helps explain you don't want to hire a taxi for yourself is that you wish to travel *ma'a an-nas* ('with other people').

As a rule they are faster on shorter runs than the buses because they don't make as many stops. There are, however, certain disadvantages. Six people is a tight fit, and longer trips can be quite uncomfortable.

Another problem is that although the bigger cities are littered with grand taxi stops, there are several subspecies of this particular beast, which are impossible for the outsider to differentiate. They either do set routes *within* a town or behave more or less like normal urban taxis (*petits taxis* – see Local Transport).

Now, if it were just a matter of asking and

being told, no, this is not where to get the inter-urban grands taxis to such-and-such a destination, it would not be so bad. The fact is, they will almost all tell you they are prepared to take you wherever you want to go – for a price. And they won't tell you where the inter-urban grand taxi stand is for the destination you want. To hire a grand taxi (these special rides are called *corsa*, presumably because many city taxis have Italian meters displaying the *prezzo della corsa* – the 'price of the trip', or fare) in this way can be a reasonable idea if you have six people and you can organise to have the driver stop along the way for photo opportunities. Otherwise it's no help at all. The Ziz and Drâa valleys and the Tizi n'Test Pass are particularly good to visit in a shared taxi, and there are many other scenic routes.

Appropriate grand taxi stops have been marked on maps and fares mentioned in individual city entries.

PICK-UP TRUCK & LAND ROVER
In some of the remoter parts of the country, especially in the Atlas mountains, about the only way you can get around from village to village is by local Berber market pick-up trucks, which is how the locals do it. This is a bumpy but adventurous way to get to know the country and people a little better, but can mean waiting days at a time for the next lift.

Land Rover taxis also operate on more remote *pistes* (tracks) that would destroy normal taxis.

CAR & MOTORBIKE
The roads connecting the main centres are pretty good in most of Morocco, and plenty of people bring their own cars and motorbikes into the country. There are many places that you simply cannot reach without private transport, so a vehicle can be a definite advantage.

Road Rules
In Morocco you drive on the right, as in Continental Europe. Daylight driving is generally no problem, and even in the bigger cities it is not too stressful in the villes nouvelles. You'd need to have your head read if you wanted to drive into the medinas. When in towns note that you should give way to traffic entering a roundabout from the right when you're already on one, which is quite a departure from prevailing rules in Europe. Speed limits in built-up areas range from 40 to 60 km/h.

Outside the towns there is a national speed limit of 100 km/h, rising to 120 km/h on the only stretch of motorway, which lies between Rabat and Casablanca. A new motorway is being built between Rabat and Tangier. The Rabat-Casa run is actually a tollway – you pay Dr 10 about halfway along.

Many minor roads are too narrow for normal vehicles to pass without going onto the shoulder. You'll find yourself hitting the dirt a lot in this way. Stones thrown up by on-coming vehicles present a danger for windscreens – locals (drivers or front-seat passengers) press their hands against the inside of the windscreens to reduce the chances of debris shattering the glass. This also makes night driving on many roads fraught.

Be aware that driving across the mountain ranges in winter can easily involve negotiating a passage through snow and ice. This kind of driving is obviously dangerous. If a strong chergui wind is blowing and carrying a lot of dust, you'll have to wait until it eases off if you don't want to do your car considerable damage.

Fuel

Petrol is readily available just about everywhere. Super and unleaded (sans plomb – found only sporadically) cost Dr 6.98 a litre, and diesel is Dr 3.99 a litre. Regular petrol (essence) is not so commonly available. Costs rise the further you go from the northwest of the country. Super costs up to Dr 7.11 south of Marrakesh and towards Oujda in the east. The big exception is the territory of Western Sahara, which is still awaiting a UN-administered plebiscite on whether it is to be integrated into Morocco, but to all intents and purposes already is. Petrol here is sold by the Atlas Sahara service station chain, is tax free and costs about a third less than in the rest of Morocco. Heading south, the first of these stations is just outside Tarfaya, on the road to Laayoune. If you're heading north, stock up as much as you can here.

The same situation applies in the Spanish enclaves of Ceuta and Melilla, so drivers heading to Morocco and mainland Spain via the enclaves should do their best to arrive there with a near-empty tank.

Warning

When driving into Fès, Marrakesh and one or two other spots you are likely to be accosted by hustlers on motorbikes. They will try to direct you to hotels and the like and are every bit as persistent as their colleagues on foot; dodging around these guys can be downright dangerous.

There have been reports of hitchhiking hustlers too. You pick them up and they try to lead you to their 'home' – often a carpet factory or the like. The road south from Ouarzazate is particularly bad, as is the road from Asni to Imlil in the High Atlas.

In the Rif Mountains around Ketama, stories abound of tourists being stopped and having large wodges of hash foisted on them by particularly unpleasant characters, only to land in the poo further on when they reach the next police road block they've been shopped to.

Road Blocks

Morocco's roads are festooned with police and customs road blocks. Be sure to stop at all of them and put on your best sunny smile – with luck you should be waved through in about half the time. For the rest, you'll have to show your passport and answer lots of silly questions – not knowing how to speak French or Arabic may well speed up the process! Some of these blocks come with tyre-eating traps, so keep your eyes peeled.

Parking Attendants

In most towns there are parking zones watched by gardiens. The going rate is a few Dr for a few hours and Dr 10 overnight. The parking attendants are not a guarantee of safety, but they do provide some peace of mind.

Mechanics & Repairs

Moroccan mechanics are generally pretty good, but if you need help and are in a position to do so, get a Moroccan sufficiently well disposed towards you to help with buying parts, such as replacement tyres, as this may help to keep the price closer to local levels.

Car Rental

Most of the major rental companies have representatives throughout Morocco, including Hertz, Avis, Budget and Europcar/InterRent. You will find a lot of local agencies, too. Addresses of the international companies and a couple of local ones appear under individual city entries but, in Casablanca especially, it is worth doing some legwork.

Renting a car in Morocco is not cheap, but you can strike bargains with some of the smaller dealers, and if there are four of you it becomes affordable. The competition is greatest in Casablanca, and there are many agencies in Marrakesh, Tangier and Fès. The cheapest cars are the Renault 4 and Fiat Uno.

Cars rented from a major company are not

necessarily better than those from a local company; what differs is the degree of service or help you can get in the event of a breakdown. Major companies will replace a car from their nearest depot if there are problems, whereas local companies often don't have branch offices so there isn't much they can do. In any event, make an effort to get a look at the car yourself before you sign up.

In many cases you can hire the car in one place and leave it elsewhere, although this usually involves a fee if you want to leave it in a city where the company has no branch.

Always haggle for a discount when renting a car, especially if it's for an extended period. Most companies offer excellent discounts for rentals over one month. Many will automatically offer 25% off their quoted rates on longer rentals.

It's also advisable to take out collision damage waiver insurance (around Dr 40 to Dr 100 a day, depending on the make of car and the company), otherwise you'll be liable for the first Dr 3000 to Dr 5000 (depending on the company) in the event of an accident. You may also want to take out personal insurance (around Dr 30 a day).

Most companies demand a (returnable) deposit of Dr 3000 to Dr 5000 in cash when you hire the car, unless you're paying by credit card, in which case it's waived. Minimum age for drivers is 21 years, with at least one year's driving experience. An International Driving Permit is technically required, but most agencies will accept your national licence.

All companies charge from Dr 35 to more than Dr 100 (depending on make) per hour that you go over time on the return date. After the first two or three hours this becomes a full extra day's rent.

Virtually all cars take premium petrol (super). Keep receipts for oil changes and any mechanical repairs, as these costs should be reimbursed.

Few companies seem to offer motorcycle hire. In Agadir you'll find plenty of booths in among the big hotels that hire out motorcycles and scooter – you're looking at about Dr 80 a day.

The Car Rental table below is intended as a general guide only. For example, some of the models are put into different categories by different companies. The rates shown

CAR RENTAL

Major companies

category	model	cost with km......		unlimited km	
		per day	per km	3 days	7 days +
A	Renault 4	Dr 250	Dr 2.50	Dr 1962	Dr 3437
B	Fiat Uno	Dr 280	Dr 2.80	Dr 2400	Dr 4200
C	Peugeot 205	Dr 330	Dr 3.30	Dr 2826	Dr 4949
D	Peugeot 309	Dr 440	Dr 4.40	Dr 3768	Dr 6594
E	Renault 19	Dr 525	Dr 5.25	Dr 4500	Dr 7875
F	Peugeot 405	Dr 600	Dr 6.00	Dr 5139	Dr 8995

Local companies

category	model	cost with km......		unlimited km	
		per day	per km	3 days	7 days +
A	Renault 4	Dr 170	Dr 1.70	Dr 1270	Dr 2265
B	Fiat Uno	Dr 210	Dr 2.10	Dr 1670	Dr 2985
C	Peugeot 205	Dr 250	Dr 2.50	Dr 1985	Dr 3450
D	Peugeot 309	Dr 320	Dr 3.20	Dr 2290	Dr 3950

here do not include the 19% government tax that you must pay on all rentals.

BICYCLE

There's no reason not to take a bicycle into Morocco – there is no better way to see some of the beautiful countryside. However, you need to be pretty fit to cover a lot of the territory. The biggest problem on secondary roads is that they tend to be narrow and dusty, and the traffic is none too forgiving. It is possible to transport bikes on trains and buses, although on the latter they may well take a beating.

On the whole, bicycles are not much help in cities like Marrakesh and Fès, which are best explored on foot.

Remember to take decent supplies, especially lots of drinking water, and a good repair kit whenever you are on the road. When you are in more remote parts of the country, you will need to be pretty well self-sufficient.

Mountain biking is another possibility. There are plenty of trails away from the well-worn tourist paths to explore. If you don't want to take your own bike, you'll find some hotels in Marrakesh that organise mountain bike trips into the High Atlas.

HITCHING

Hitching is never entirely safe in any country in the world, and we don't recommend it. Travellers who decide to hitch should understand that they are taking a small but potentially serious risk. However, many people do choose to hitch, and the advice that follows should help to make their journeys as fast and safe as possible.

Hitching in Morocco is OK, but demands a thick skin and considerable diplomatic expertise in the north because of aggressive hustlers. They simply won't take 'no' for an answer and feign outrage if you express lack of interest in whatever they're trying to sell you – usually drugs. It's particularly bad on the road between Tetouan and Tangier. Giving lifts to people in these areas is similarly a bad idea. See Road Rules.

It goes without saying that people, especially women, attempting to hitch are placing themselves at risk.

More often than not drivers expect some money for picking you up, so it's as well to offer a little – it may be refused, but it's more likely not to be. Keep in mind what public transport fares would be so that, should you strike someone trying to extort silly amounts from you, you'll know what *not* to give.

WALKING

There is plenty of good walking and trekking in the Middle and High Atlas. See the section on High Atlas Trekking.

LOCAL TRANSPORT
To/From Airports

As Mohammed V international airport is 30 km south-east of Casablanca and serves Rabat as well, the connections are not really a matter of local transport. For details see the Casablanca and Rabat Getting Around entries.

Bus

The bigger cities, such as Casablanca, Rabat, Marrakesh, Fès and Meknès, have public bus services. They are especially good for crossing from the ville nouvelle of a city to the medina, and there are a few other useful runs. Tickets usually cost around the Dr 2 to Dr 3 mark.

Taxi

Cities and bigger towns have local 'petits taxis', which are a different colour for every city. They are licensed to carry up to three passengers and are often metered. They are not permitted to go beyond the city limits. Where they are not metered (or don't use the meter), you'll have to set a price in advance. It's like everything else: many of the drivers are perfectly honest and some are rotten. As already noted, many grands taxis will do city runs too. They certainly do not have meters and you'll have to set a price. Multiple hire is the rule rather than the exception, so you can get half-full cabs if they are going your way. From 8 pm, there is a 50% surcharge.

TOURS

There are plenty of travel and tour agents scattered around the big cities, but most seem quite surprised by individuals walking in off the street asking about tours. If you want an organised tour around Morocco, do it from home (see Tours in the previous chapter).

One exception to the rule is Marrakesh, from where you can organise trips down to Ouarzazate, Zagora and the like through agencies and hotels. They also put together walking, mountain bike and other excursions into the High Atlas. Agadir is another centre for package excursions. For more information, refer to the Marrakesh and Agadir entries.

The Mediterranean Coast & the Rif

From those two bastions of Spanish tenacity, the enclaves of Ceuta and Melilla, to the cosmopolitan hustle and hassle of Tangier and the contrasting laid-back ambience of Chefchaouen in the Rif Mountains, northern Morocco offers a diverse range of experiences for the independent traveller.

East of Chefchaouen, the Rif presents a spectacular mountain crest trip through the unfortunately dodgy Ketama area – the heartland of kif cultivation. Those who brave the hustlers will be rewarded by the views, and a couple of modest Mediterranean resorts where the Rif makes a rare concession and gives way to beaches – Al-Hoceima and Saidia.

Tangier

For more than 2500 years people have inhabited this strategic point on the straits separating Europe from Africa. And just about every race or power that ever had any interests in this corner of the Mediterranean has left its mark. The world-weary port has seen them all come and go: Phoenicians, Romans, Visigoths, Arabs, Portuguese, British and Spaniards among others. For some 40 years under the dubious control of an international council, Tangier (Tanja to the locals) today is like an ageing libertarian – propped up languidly at a bar, he has seen it all.

In the days of what William Burroughs called Interzone , every kind of questionable activity was carried on. Smugglers, money-launderers, currency speculators, gun-runners, prostitutes and pimps formed a good part of the Moroccan and foreign population. And in its way, Tangier (often erroneously referred to as Tangiers) flourished.

Since its incorporation into the rest of independent Morocco, the city has lost much of its attraction. But the odd cruise ship still calls in and new activities are always to be

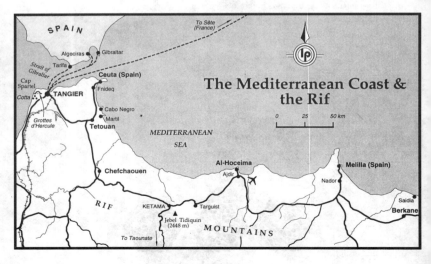

150

discovered. Alongside the exploding business of drug-running (including a growing contribution from South American cocaine barons), there is the commerce in people, many of whom come from sub-Saharan Africa. Moroccan and Spanish boat captains charge them as a much as US$1000 a person to smuggle them into Spain. Often the boats are so small and overcrowded that they don't make it – bodies of those who have risked and lost all frequently wash up on the Spanish and Moroccan coasts. The Socco Chico (also known as the Zoco Chico or Petit Socco) in the heart of Tangier, long *the* place for transactions of the greatest diversity, is one of the centres for organising this nasty trade.

King Hassan II has his own plans for the port, and has poured money into infrastructure programs and set the city up as an international offshore banking zone. His hope is that it will compete for international funds with Gibraltar, Tunis and Cyprus. Only the big banks need apply, for, as the king said: 'We don't want banks that create scandals. We do not want banks that come here to launder drug money'.

Little of this may be obvious to travellers passing through, but they are soon aware of what makes the place tick – money. From shoeshine boys up, everyone is on the make, and for the small-time hustlers the main trade is in tourists, especially those newly arrived from Europe. In Tangier, a city of half a million, it was always so but today a veritable army of multilingual hustlers prey on unsuspecting newcomers and can be quite implacable. You may have them in your taxi, 'finding' you a hotel, or accompanying you on foot. Many will want to be your 'guide' or have something to sell, more often than not dope. Most visitors cannot wait to get out, which is a pity, because it is a unique city – hardly truly Moroccan, and not really belonging anywhere else. After the first few days you are generally left alone; you can finally breathe easier and absorb the faded atmosphere of this mongrel creation.

There are days when all of the hassle can seem just that much more irritating – when the *chergui* (east wind) is blowing. Tahar ben Jelloun, a leading Moroccan writer who grew up in Tangier, claims that if the chergui arrives on a Friday during the midday prayers, it will keep blowing for seven days and nights.

History

Tangier has been coveted for millennia as a strategic site commanding the Strait of Gibraltar. The area was settled by the ancient Greeks and Phoenicians, for whom it was a trading port, and its early days are shrouded in myth. Paradise on earth, the Garden of the Hesperides, supposedly lay nearby, and it was here that Hercules slew the giant Antaeus and fathered a child, Sophax, by the giant's widow, Tinge – no prizes for guessing where the city's original name, Tingis, comes from. The name has changed little since, and also gave rise to the name of the citrus fruit tangerine, although the tree was imported by either the Romans or Arabs at a later date.

Since those early days, the port has been one of the most contested in the Mediterranean. During the Roman period, Diocletian made it the capital of the province of Mauretania Tingitana, garrisoned by British (ie Celtic) cavalry. Not long after, it became part of the Christian episcopal see of Spain, and in fact may have been the seat of the bishops.

Following the break-up of the Roman Empire, the Vandals arrived from Spain in 429 AD. Whether they ever took Tangier is uncertain. The Byzantines took an erratic interest in the port, but for the most part they contented themselves with their strongly fortified outpost at Ceuta. Apart from them and scant reports suggesting the Visigoths from Spain occupied it for a time in the 7th century, little was recorded about the area until the arrival of the Arabs in 705 AD. This may have been partly due to a smallpox epidemic that wrought havoc throughout Europe and North Africa not long after the Byzantines left the scene; continual warfare between the indigenous Berber tribes and the conquering Arabs may not have helped.

Once Arab supremacy had been established, however, Tangier became a bone of contention between the Umayyads of Spain and the Idrissids of Morocco, and was even occupied by the Fatimids of Tunis in 958. A little over 100 years later, it was taken by the Almoravids as they swept across Morocco from their Mauretanian desert strongholds; it eventually passed to the Almohads in 1149. As the Almohad regime gradually reached its nadir, the city elected to be ruled by the Hafsids of Tunis, but passed to Merenid control shortly afterwards in 1274.

Following the victories of the Christian armies in the Iberian peninsula, the Portuguese attempted to take Tangier in 1437. Unsuccessful at first, they finally made it in 1471. The city passed to Philip II of Spain in 1580 when Spain and Portugal were united. It reverted to Portugal when that country regained its independence, only to be passed to England in 1661 as part of Catherine of Braganza's dowry to Charles II.

The English were not to remain long. Tangier was besieged by Moulay Ismail in 1679 and the English abandoned the city seven years later (after destroying the port and most of the city), following a dispute

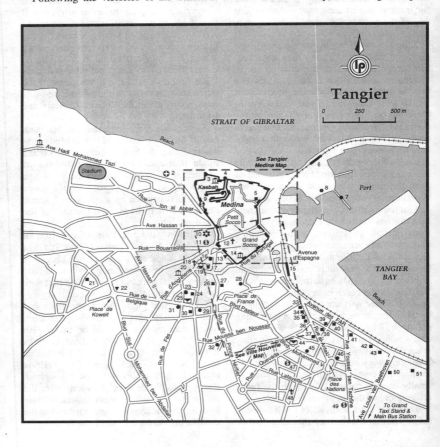

Tangier

between parliament and the king in which the former refused to fund the reinforcement of the garrison in Tangier.

The Moroccans were left in control until the mid-19th century, when Tangier became the object of intense rivalry between the French, Spanish, Italians, British and Germans. The situation was partially resolved by the Treaty of Algeciras in 1906, whereby the British were bought off with Egypt and the Italians with Libya, leaving the remaining three European powers intriguing for the spoils. The status of the city was finally resolved only in 1923, when Tangier and the surrounding countryside was declared an 'international zone' controlled by the resident diplomatic agents of France, Spain, Britain, Portugal, Sweden, Holland, Belgium, Italy and the USA. Even the Moroccan sultan was represented by an agent, although the latter was appointed by the French resident-general (by this time France and Spain had divided Morocco into protectorates). In fact, much of the administration of Tangier had been in European and American hands since the late 19th century, and their hold had been progressively tightened by the Treaties of Madrid (1880) and Algeciras.

Tangier was to remain an international zone until a few months after Morocco became independent, when it was reunited with the rest of the country (although it was some years before all its economic and financial privileges were removed). In the meantime it became one of the most fashionable Mediterranean resorts, and a haven for freebooters, artists, writers, refugees, exiles and bankers; it was also renowned for its high profile gay and paedophile scene. Each of the countries represented in Tangier maintained its own banks, post offices and currency, and took a share in the policing of the city. Banks, in particular, made fortunes out of manipulating the currency markets. All this came to an end in 1956, but the legend of notoriety lingers on.

Orientation

The square known as the Grand Socco (officially renamed Place du 9 Avril 1947) is the centre of things and the link between the

---

PLACES TO STAY		
5	Hôtel Continental	
21	Hôtel Inter Continental	
24	Pension Holland	
26	Pension Gibraltar	
27	Hôtel El Minzah	
30	Pension Safari	
33	Hôtel Marco Polo	
34	Hôtel El Djenina	
35	Hostel	
36	Hôtel Bristol	
37	Pension Omar Khayam	
38	Hôtel El Farabi	
39	Hôtel Charf	
40	Hôtel Rif	
41	Hôtel Miramar	
42	Hôtel Shéhérazade	
43	Hôtel Les Almohades	
50	Hôtel El Oumnia	
51	Hôtel Solazur	

PLACES TO EAT	
13	Cafés & Snack Stands
22	Guitta's Restaurant

OTHER	
1	Forbes Museum of Military Miniatures
2	Hôpital al-Kortobi
3	Dar el-Makhzen
4	Bab el-Raha
6	Tanger Port (railway station)
7	Hydrofoil Dock
8	Ferry Terminal
9	Banque Populaire (exchange)
10	Mendoubia Gardens
11	BMCE (ATMs)
12	Spanish Church
14	Old American Legation Museum
15	Main Railway Station
16	Cinéma Rif
17	Dean's Bar
18	St Andrew's Church
19	Local Bus Terminal
20	Musée d'Art Contemporain
23	American Language Center
25	Post Office
28	Gran Teatro de Cervantes
29	Instituto Cervantes
31	Ensemble Artisanal
32	Club Regina
44	Post Office (PTT)
45	UK Consulate
46	Europcar
47	Bank al-Maghrib
48	Church
49	BMCI (ATMs)

medina and the new city. The small and rather hilly medina lies to the north. Rue Semmarine leads off the Grand Socco almost immediately into Rue as-Siaghin, which quickly takes you to the modest central square inside the medina – the Petit Socco (also known as the Zoco Chico, and officially Place Souq ad-Dakhil). The kasbah occupies the north-west corner of the medina and is built in a dominating position on top of the cliff.

East of the medina lie the port and ferry terminal. A little to the south of the port are the main train station and the CTM bus station.

The ville nouvelle spreads out west, south and south-east of the medina, but the heart of it, Blvd Pasteur, Blvd Mohammed V and the immediately surrounding area, is compact and close to the medina. It contains the main post office, banks, some of the consulates, many of the restaurants and bars and the bulk of the middle and top-end accommodation.

Farther south is the bus station (gare routière) and grand taxi stand. They are on Place Jamia el-Arabia, at the end of Ave Louis van Beethoven. It's a good half-hour walk to the Grand Socco and the bulk of the cheap hotels.

Farther out, to the north-west, is the Marshan, a modestly elevated plateau where the rich once maintained (and in some cases still maintain) their palatial villas. Dominated by 'the Mountain', it has a prominent place in the legends and myths surrounding the colourful band of expatriates that has passed through here.

Information

Tourist Office The Délégation Régionale du Tourisme (☎ 938239), at 29 Blvd Pasteur, has the usual limited range of maps and brochures. The staff speak several languages (you can usually rely on English, French, German and Spanish), but they seem not to want to make more use of them than necessary. The office is open Monday to Friday from 8.30 am to noon and 2.30 to 6 pm. As if sensing you're unlikely to get much joy from the office, there is usually at least one chap waiting outside with a solicitous air, enquiring 'did you find it?' or some such nonsense. Of course, it's another 'faux guide' – a brisk pace and a display of healthy disinterest are usually enough to shake these fellows, who seem a little less energetic than their harbourside colleagues.

Money There are plenty of banks along Blvd Pasteur and Blvd Mohammed V as well as a quick and efficient BMCE branch on the bottom side of the Grand Socco at the junction of Rue d'Italie. Mid-range hotels can also change money at much the same rate as the banks.

The BMCE head office is on Blvd Pasteur and has ATMs. It also has an exchange booth where you can change cash or cheques and get cash advances on Visa and MasterCard. The booth is open seven days a week from 10 am to 2 pm and 4 to 8 pm.

The agent for American Express is Voyages Schwartz (☎ 933459/71), 54 Blvd Pasteur. It's open from 9 am to 12.30 pm and 3 to 7 pm.

Post & Telecommunications The main post office is on Blvd Mohammed V, 15 to 20 minutes' walk from the Grand Socco. Go to the right end of the counter for poste restante. The office is open from 8.30 am to 12.15 pm and 2.30 to 6.45 pm.

The phone and fax office is around the corner to the right of the main post office entrance and appears to be open much the same hours. A less helpful crew of people it would be hard to find. If you have a phone-card, there are card phones outside both the phone and post offices. There are a few late-night phone offices dotted about the new city. One, on the corner of Blvd Pasteur and Rue du Prince Moulay Abdallah, is open daily from 7.30 am to 10.30 pm. They don't have card phones, but you can book overseas phone calls. They also have telex and fax services.

Foreign Consulates Quite a few countries have diplomatic representation in Tangier, including the following:

Belgium
   Consulate: Immeuble Jawara (apartment 5a), 83 Place al-Medina (☎ 943234; fax 935211)
   Visa office: 97 Blvd Sidi Mohammed Abdallah (☎ 933163)
France
   Place de France (☎ 932039/40)
Germany
   47 Ave Hassan II (☎ 938700)
Italy
   35 Rue Assad ibn al-Farrat (☎ 931064). The consulate is open Monday to Friday from 9.30 am to noon.
Netherlands
   Immeuble Miramonte, 42 Ave Hassan II (☎ 931248)
Spain
   85 Ave Président Habib Bourghiba (☎ 935625, 937000; fax 932381)
UK
   4 Ave Mohammed V (☎ 941563)

Cultural Centres The Centre Culturel Français (☎ 942589; fax 940937), 41 Rue Hassan el-Ouezzane, puts on a rich variety of films, exhibitions and the like, as well as classes in Arabic. They use the Galerie Delacroix on Rue de la Liberté for art exhibitions.

The Spanish are well represented in Tangier, too, which is hardly surprising. The Instituto Cervantes and its Biblioteca Española (☎ 931340; fax 947630) are at 9 Rue de Belgique. The library was founded in 1941. The complex is open Monday to Friday from 10 am to 1 pm and 4 to 7 pm and in the morning only on Saturdays. The library has a varied collection of material on Tangier (some in English) as well as Moroccan, Spanish and Gibraltarian phone books.

Language Schools The American Language Center (☎ 933616) is at 1 Rue M'sallah. You might be able to pick up work here teaching English.

If you want to learn Arabic, see Cultural Centres.

Bookshops & Books The *Rogue's Guide to Tangier* is (or was) a humorous alternative guide to the city. At best it was only ever sporadically available from some of the larger hotels, and now seems to have disappeared altogether.

A much easier guidebook to obtain is the thoroughly enjoyable and well-written *Tangier – City of the Dream* by Iain Finlayson, which dwells on some of the 'luminaries' that have graced Tangier since 1923.

By far the best bookshop in Tangier is the Librairie des Colonnes (☎ 936955), on Blvd Pasteur. It has material on the city itself, including Finlayson's book, although it concentrates more on Francophone literature. The shop was founded in the interwar years and taken over by the prestigious French publisher Gallimard. It was run for a long time by a couple of august French women, Yvonne and Isabelle Gerofi, who played host to pretty well all the high and low-life of European Tangier – most found their way into the bookshop at one time or another.

Emergencies The police can be contacted in an emergency on ☎ 19 and the fire brigade on ☎ 15.

For an all-night chemist, or information on where to find one, ring ☎ 932619. Alternatively, buy a copy of the local rag in French, *Le Journal de Tanger*, which usually lists the day's 'pharmacies de garde', which are open late, if not all night. The pharmacies in Morocco operate a rotating roster for late-night service.

Film & Photography There are plenty of places along Blvd Pasteur where you can buy films or have them developed.

Ensemble Artisanal This government-backed arts and crafts centre on Rue de Belgique is not a bad place to browse and get an idea of what crafts you might like to buy in the souqs. On the whole, Tangier is not a great place for souvenir hunting, as the quality is not too hot and prices are inflated. Still, you can get an idea of top end of the price scale at the Ensemble and do so in relative peace.

Street Names As in many other Moroccan cities, street names are being changed in Tangier, largely to replace foreign with home-grown names. Not all of these have caught on with equal success, and the process seems somewhat haphazard. You may well come across more than one name for the same street.

Grand Socco

The Grand Socco was once as full of life as the Djemaa el-Fna in Marrakesh, with make-shift shops, snake charmers, musicians, storytellers and food stalls filling the night air with cacophonous activity. It is still a busy place, and on Thursday and Sunday, when Riffian peasants come to market, the area comes alive.

Medina

You enter the medina from the Grand Socco by Rue Semmarine and quickly veer right onto **Rue as-Siaghin**. This was once Tangier's principal gold market (some jewellery stores remain), located on the northern flank of what was once the Jewish quarter, or mellah. On your right you soon pass the Spanish **Church of the Immaculate Conception** (closed), which was built in 1880, at a time when Spaniards made up one-fifth of the city's population. A few doors down is what used to be the residence of the sultan's agent (naib), who was the point of contact between the Moroccan leader and European legations until 1923. From you here you emerge on to the **Petit Socco**.

Gone are the days when William Burroughs could cheerfully write of the endless stream of louche offers from young boys and men around the Petit Socco, but it is still a buzzy little square and a great place to sit over a mint tea, watch the world go by and contemplate its colourful past. And just in case you feel disappointed about the passing of Tangier's sleazy era, there's enough still going on to give you a taste of what it was like. Whispers of 'something special, my friend' are still a feature of the area, and one of the cheap pensions overlooking the

square, the Fuentes, is a brothel. It is perhaps difficult to imagine now, but the Fuentes was one of Tangier's luxury hotels at the end of the 19th century. At that time there was little more to the town than the medina and, as the Europeans became more influential, the city's administration was established here, including the Spanish postal service and the main banks.

If you head down Ave Mokhtar Ahardan (formerly Rue de la Poste), you will probably find it equally hard to believe that some of the little pensions here were classy hotels squeezed in among such important offices as the Spanish Legation and French post office. (From here you can descend a series of stairways and walk down to the railway station and port.) This era came to an end as the new city was built and the administration was transferred out of the medina in the early 20th century.

At the end of Rue Jemaa el-Kebir (ex-Rue de la Marine) you come to a small belvedere overlooking the port. You could easily miss the **Grand Mosque** on the corner. The building itself is of little interest, but it is said to have been the site of a Roman temple and at one time housed a church built by the Portuguese.

From the Petit Socco Rue des Almohades (formerly Rue des Chrétiens) takes you north past some very determined shopkeepers and a hammam to the kasbah.

Kasbah The kasbah is on the highest point of the city and isolated from the rest of the medina by its walls; you enter from Bab el-Assa (one of four gates) at the end of Rue Ben Raissouli in the medina. The gate gives onto a large open courtyard, to the right of which once stood the fort's stables. Around to the right of them is Bab Haha, which leads back into the medina. Directly in front of you is Bab ar-Raha (Gate of Rest), which leads onto to a windswept viewpoint across to Spain.

Off to the left is the Dar el-Makhzen, the former sultan's palace and now a good museum devoted to Moroccan arts. There is also a small archaeological collection, most of the exhibits of which come from Volubilis. You can see a modest pavilion that served as the Beit al-Mal (the Treasury).

The museum is open from 9 am to noon and 3 to 6 pm in winter and 9 am to 3.30 pm in summer (closed Tuesday). Entry is Dr 10.

The palace was built by Moulay Ismail in the 17th century and enlarged by later sultans. The interior has some beautifully carved wooden ceilings and a marble court-yard. Parts of the palace are being restored by Rif craftsmen and will eventually host an artisanal gallery and rooftop café.

The future café may provide some competition for the Café Détroit on the 2nd floor in the walls, which you can reach if you leave the present museum by the gardens. It was set up by Brion Gysin, the 1960s writer and friend of the Rolling Stones, and was called The Thousand & One Nights. It became famous for the trance musicians who played here in the 1960s and released a record produced by Brian Jones.

Musicians still play here, but it's a tourist trap. The tour groups are all brought here, and after the obligatory mint tea they file out to the tune of songs like 'Roll Out the Barrel'. The views are good, but the tea is expensive.

Quite a few of the houses inside the kasbah are owned by wealthy foreigners, only some of whom live here for much of the time. Just outside the kasbah is the Calle Amrah, where Paul Bowles bought himself a small house in 1947. Not far away was the Sidi Hosni palace where Barbara Hutton, the Woolworth heiress, lived and gave some of her grandest parties. It is said that when things were going well, she had an annual income of US$3 million, but by the time she died in 1979 in Los Angeles, she had less than US$4000 in the bank.

Old American Legation Museum An intriguing relic of the international zone is the former US legation, now a museum funded by the Americans. The three-storey building was donated to the USA in 1820 by Sultan Moulay Suleyman. The Americans had sent a representative there late in the previous century, as Morocco was the first nation to recognise the new country. The museum houses archives and interesting material on the history of Tangier, and it was here that American and British agents did much of the local planning for the Allied landings in North Africa in 1942.

The easiest way to find it is to turn into Rue du Portugal from Rue Salah ed-Din el-Ayoubi and enter the medina at the first gate on your left. The museum is a little way down the lane, after the dogleg turn. Getting in might prove harder. It is supposedly open on Monday, Wednesday and Thursday from 10 am to 1 pm and 3 to 5 pm, or by appointment (☎ 935317). It may not be open even at the advertised times, but knock on the door to be sure. Entrance is free.

Musée d'Art Contemporain

Housed in the former British Consulate on Rue d'Angleterre, this art gallery is devoted to modern Moroccan art, some of which leaves a little to be desired. Nevertheless, the place itself is pleasant and occasionally they have good exhibitions. It's open from 8.30 am to noon and 2 to 6.30 pm (closed Tuesday). Entry is Dr 10.

Forbes Museum of Military Miniatures

A half-hour walk from the Grand Socco, heading north-west from town along the coast is the villa (a former palace of the Mendoub, or sultan's representative in Tangier) owned by the family of the American tycoon Malcolm Forbes (of Forbes Magazine), who died in 1990. The villa, still occasionally used by Forbes's family, now houses a military miniatures museum, with an 'army' of 120,000 miniatures and diora-mas depicting all sorts of unrelated conflicts, from the Battle of the Three Kings (1578) to the Green March (1975), with stops in the Sudan, various WW I battlefields and several sea engagements along the way. You can also wander around the gardens outside, but the swimming pool is out of bounds.

It's open from 10 am to 5 pm and entry is free, although the Spanish-speaking atten-dant may want a tip. Apparently the Forbes family gets to see the visitors' book – so maybe you should sign it so that they don't shut the place down for want of visitors.

Ville Nouvelle

The core of the new city, largely unchanged since its heyday in the 1930s, is worth a wander. The area around Place de France and Blvd Pasteur, with its cafés and pâtisseries, still retains something of its glamour. There is a lively **market** along a lane down from Rue de la Liberté near the Hôtel El Minzah. It is not a tourist market, but rather concentrates on food, household products and all sorts of bits and bobs.

A remnant of the days when Spaniards formed the largest non-Moroccan community in Tangier is the **Gran Teatro de Cervantes**, in a side street off Rue Salah ed-Din el-Ayoubi (also known as Rue de la Plage). Opened in 1913, the theatre enjoyed its heyday in the interwar years. You can't miss the dazzling Art Deco façade. The building has long been in decline but is now being restored with Spanish funding.

Ever since Tangier passed to British control for about 20 years in 1661, Britons have had a special relationship with the city, immortalised by some of the literary figures who have graced the city with their presence. There was a small English church in Tangier as far back as the 1660s. The present church, **St Andrew's**, on Rue d'Angleterre, was consecrated in 1905 on ground donated by the Sultan Moulay al-Hassan in the 1880s. The caretaker, Mustapha Chergui, will be pleased to show you around the building, which was largely constructed in the Moroccan style,

---

Literary Tangier

Ever since Paul Bowles first landed in Tangier in 1931, the port city has exercised a fascination on the minds of many writers. For some it was an exotic break, for others a more lasting refuge. Not that Bowles was the first – as far back as the 17th century, Samuel Pepys was complaining of the sleaziness and debauchery of the then British possession, and Mark Twain visited in 1867.

Bowles returned to stay in 1947 with his wife Jane. Both travelled a great deal, but while Paul and his writing flourished, Jane suffered and eventually died in a Málaga hospital in 1973.

Bowles, now in his eighties, gets a lot of unsolicited visitors and has become something of an unofficial tourist attraction. He was first encouraged to come to Tangier by the American writer Gertrude Stein, whom he met in Paris after she herself had a made a trip to Tangier in the 1920s. In those days, Bowles was a composer, and although he would later turn his focus to writing books, he never abandoned music. One of his services to Moroccan culture was a job he undertook to research and record the gamut of traditional Berber music. His account of the assignment appears in *Their Heads Are Green*.

Music was Bowles' link with the American playwright, Tennessee Williams, for whom he used to write scores and whom he managed to entice to Tangier for a time. A somewhat more outrageous character, Truman Capote, could not resist the temptation and visited Tangier for several months in 1949.

Not long afterwards, the first of the Beat writers arrived on the scene. William Burroughs, who spent much of his early days in Tangier pushing himself as close to the edge as he could, ended up becoming one of the port's longer-term literary residents. As he wrote to his friend and mentor, Allen Ginsberg, he found Bowles a rather tricky character, but did not let this stop him from developing an uneasy rapport with the old hand. Ginsberg himself visited Burroughs several times in Tangier, on one occasion bringing Jack Kerouac along, but neither liked it sufficiently to stay.

One of England's more iconoclastic modern playwrights, Joe Orton, spent the summer of 1966-67 just outside Tangier with his lover, Kenneth Halliwell. Orton's growing success and insatiable appetite for young boys irked Halliwell, who showed his displeasure by killing Orton and himself in London after their second trip. A gay French contemporary of Orton's, the much tormented Jean Genet, had a similar affection for Tangier and visited the city frequently.

Samuel Beckett also spent a lot of time here with his wife, apparently leading a considerably quieter and more introspective existence than some of his colleagues.

All of them came and went, but Bowles has remained, seeming more and more like Tangier's patron saint of authors. ■

with the Lord's Prayer in Arabic atop the chancel. At the western end of the church is a plaque to the memory of Emily Kean, an English woman who married the sherif of Ouezzane and spent many years of her life introducing vaccination to the people of northern Morocco. Others buried here include Walter Harris, the British journalist who chronicled the goings-on here from the late 19th century, and 'Caid' Maclean, a military adviser to the sultans who, like Harris, was at one time imprisoned and held to ransom by the Rif bandit Raissouli.

Virtually across the road stands the closed **Grand Hôtel Villa de France**. The French impressionist painter Henri Matisse stayed here in the early years of this century, his imagination captured and his brush driven by the African light. He had been preceded in 1831 by Delacroix, although the latter mainly produced sketches during his time in Tangier.

There is a story that the **mosque** on Place de Koweit was built after a rich Arab Gulf sheikh sailed by Tangier and noticed that the modern cathedral's spire overshadowed all the minarets of Tangier. Shocked, he paid for the mosque and now the spire plays second fiddle to the new minaret.

The **beaches** of Tangier, although not too bad, are hardly the best in Morocco. Women will not feel at ease sunning themselves here. The much reduced European gay population still frequents certain of the beachside bars, some of which can be fun in summer. The beach is not a good place to be in the evening, however.

Places to Stay – bottom end

Camping Campers have a choice. The most convenient of the two sites is *Camping Miramonte* (☎ 937133), or *Camping Marshan* as it's also known. It lies three km west of the centre of town, facing the Mountain near Jews' Bay. It's a good site, close to the beach, and there's a reasonable restaurant. To get there, take bus Nos 12, 21 or the combined 12/21 (Dr 2) from the bus terminal near the Grand Socco and get off at the Café Fleur de la Montagne. Don't leave valuables unat-

tended here – things disappear. It costs Dr 15 a person plus Dr 10 to pitch a tent and Dr 8 for a car. There is hot water, and they have some low-quality rooms for Dr 100/150.

The other site is *Caravaning Tingis*, about six km east of the town centre. It is much more expensive but includes a tennis court and swimming pool. To get there, take bus No 15 from the Grand Socco.

Hostel The *youth hostel* (☎ 940127) is on Rue al-Antaki, just up past the hotels Marco Polo and El Djenina. Beds cost Dr 20 with ID card and Dr 22.50 without. Dr 5 will get you a hot shower. The dorms are almost an open-plan arrangement, meaning minimal privacy. The hostel is open from 8 to 10 am, noon to 3 pm and 6 to 10.30 pm.

Hotels Most of the traditional Moroccan-style hostelries are in the medina around Petit Socco and on Ave Mokhtar Ahardan, which connects the Petit Socco and the port area. They run the gamut from flophouses to two-star hotels.

If you arrive by ferry, walk out of the port until you reach the main railway station on your left. Then take the road on the extreme right-hand side, which goes uphill until you get to a set of steps just past the junction with Rue du Portugal. Go up the steps and you'll find yourself at the bottom of Ave Mokhtar Ahardan.

Alternatively, once out of the port gates, carry on past the railway station and take the first street on your right, Rue Salah ed-Din el-Ayoubi, which has a string of cheapies. Better are some of the unclassified, one and two-star, hotels farther along or just back from the waterfront, as well as up the narrow Rue Magellan in the ville nouvelle.

Some unclassified places simply charge per head, and singles often mean getting a small double to yourself. People travelling in pairs who want a bit of extra space might want to try turning up separately in one of these places and each asking for a single rather than paying the same price to share a room. Of course the risk is that one of you will get a room and the other might find there are none left!

Hotels – medina There are plenty of cheap pensions to choose from here. Most are basic and you won't get much more than a bed and shared bathroom facilities, although some have hot water (for a small extra charge). Prices vary slightly and you're looking at Dr 30 to Dr 40 for singles and Dr 50 to Dr 80 for doubles. Some are grubby, whereas others are well maintained.

One of the better places on the Petit Socco (on Rue as-Siaghin) is the *Pension Maurita-* nia (☎ 934677). The best rooms look out on to the Socco. Clean rooms with washbasin and bidet cost Dr 50/70. Toilets are shared and there are only cold showers. The entrance is just off the Socco.

A little farther along Rue des Almohades is the *Pension Ifrikia* (☎ 933821). This is a good example of a place to avoid. They charge Dr 40 a head and claim to have hot water, but the grubby little rooms are like prison cells. A little better, and just around the corner up a lane, is the *Pension Agadir* (☎ 938084). They also charge Dr 40 a person and hot water is Dr 5 extra.

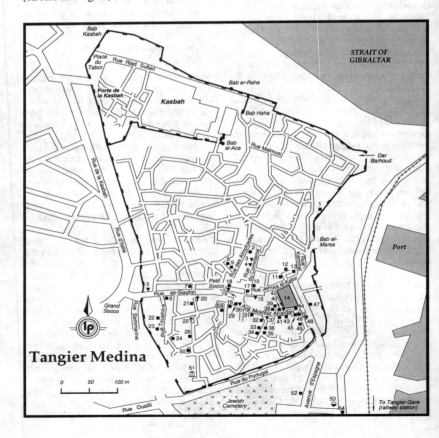

Tangier Medina

0   50   100 m

Back on the square, the *Pension Fuentes* (☎ 934669) is basically a knock-up shop. If this doesn't bother you, you can get an adequate room for Dr 40 a head. There is a lively café on the 1st floor. A little way up a lane off the square behind the Fuentes are the pensions *Essaada* and *Al-Massira*.

Others scattered about inside what was once the mellah (in the western part of the medina) include the pensions *Marisa, Lillian, Regina, Marrakesh* and, on Rue as-Siaghin, the *Touahine*.

Across the Petit Socco from the Fuentes is the *Pension Becerra* (☎ 932369). The rooms are a little better than in the Fuentes, and cost the same.

Down Rue Jemaa el-Kebir (formerly Rue de la Marine) and in a side alley are a few others: the *Hôtel Larache*, *Pension Amar* and the *Pension el-Wedad*. The *Pension Lixus* is a little farther on to the left on Rue Kammal.

The main street for accommodation, however, is Ave Mokhtar Ahardan. In the lower range, two of the best options are the *Pension Palace* (☎ 936128), at No 2, and the *Hôtel Olid* (☎ 931310), at No 12. They both charge Dr 40/80 for singles/doubles. The Palace's rooms are small but otherwise reasonable, and many of them front on to a quiet, verdant courtyard. There are shared toilets and hot showers for Dr 5. The Olid has seen better days, but the rooms come with private shower, from which you can occasionally coax out some hot water. The *Pension Amal* is a pokey place that has the gall to ask Dr 50 a head and Dr 5 extra for hot water.

Others along this street, few with anything more to recommend them than the Amal, include the pensions *Fès, Karlton, Maarifa, Tan Tan, Victoria* and *Américain*.

In a side street running south of Ave Mokhtar Ahardan next to the Restaurant Ahlan you will find four others of the flophouse variety: the pensions *Bahja, Colon, Touzoni* and *Aziz*.

There is also a hammam here, which may come in handy given the scarcity of hot water in many of the pensions. A few other cheapies with nothing in particular going for them are noted on the map.

Also worth checking out is the *Hôtel du Grand Socco*, just outside the medina in the square of the same name, which has basic singles/doubles with shared bathroom facil-

PLACES TO STAY

1	Hôtel Continental
6	Pension Touahine
7	Pension Monaco
8	Pension Agadir
9	Pension Ifrikia
10	Hôtel Larache
11	Pension Amar
12	Pension el-Wedad
13	Pension Lixus
16	Pension Essaada
17	Pension Becerra
18	Pension Mauritania
21	Pension Monaco
22	Pension Marrakech
23	Pension Regina
24	Pension Lillian
26	Pension Marisa
28	Pension Al-Massira
29	Pension Fuentes
31	Pension Palace
32	Pension Aziz
33	Pension Bahja
35	Pension Colon
36	Pension Touzoni
38	Pension Amal
39	Pension Maarifa
40	Hôtel Mamora
41	Pension Karlton
43	Hôtel Olid
44	Pension Tan Tan
45	Pension Fès
46	Pension Victoria
47	Pension Nahda
49	Pension Américain
52	Pension Avenida

PLACES TO EAT

3	Grèce Restaurant
4	Restaurant Andalus
5	Restaurant Mamounia
15	Cheap Snack Bar
19	Café Central
37	Restaurant Ahlan
42	Restaurant Moderne
48	Restaurant Granada

OTHER

2	Hammam
14	Grand Mosque
20	Spanish Church
25	Spanish Church
27	Place Takadoum
30	Café
34	Hammam
50	Hammam
51	Old American Legation Museum
53	CTM Bus Station
54	Port Entrance

ities for Dr 42/55. They have no phone and no shower.

The absence of showers is not a huge problem, as there's a hammam opposite the entrance, which is in a backstreet behind the Grand Socco. There is another hammam at 80 Rue des Almohades. It costs Dr 5 for a shower, and is open from 8 am to 8 pm.

Hotels – ville nouvelle First up are the unclassified hotels and pensions along Rue Salah ed-Din el-Ayoubi, but most are no better than the cheapies in the medina and some are decidedly characterless. Most offer basic accommodation with shared bathroom and toilet facilities for Dr 30 to Dr 40 for singles and Dr 50 to Dr 60 for doubles. Some have hot water.

Heading up from the waterfront you strike four in a row on the left-hand side – they seem to improve as you climb. The first of them, the *Royale*, is cheap and basic. Rooms go for Dr 30/60 and they have no shower. Next is the slightly better *Madrid*, which charges Dr 40 a head but does have hot water (Dr 5 a shower). *Le Détroit* (☎ 934838) offers clean, simple rooms for Dr 40/60 and hot showers for Dr 5 extra. The *Miami* (☎ 932900) offers much the same deal. Around the corner is the *Pension Chams*, a slightly grubbier place with beds for Dr 30. The last place on the left side of Rue Salah ed-Din el-Ayoubi is the *Pension Talavera* (☎ 931474). Its rates are Dr 40 per person plus Dr 5 for a hot shower.

Of the three places on the right side of the street, the *Pension Atou* possibly has the most going for it. Some of its 150 (!) rooms are not bad, and as it is fairly high up, the sundeck has sweeping views of the city. Singles/doubles/triples cost Dr 30/60/90. There's a public shower, *Douche Cléopatra*, just by the Hôtel Valencia. A shower costs Dr 5.

If none of these appeals, or you just want to be a bit farther away from the medina walls, you could try some of the places along Ave d'Espagne. Among the cheapest are the *Pension Majestic*, the *Pension Mendez* and the *Hôtel L'Marsa* (☎ 932339). The latter is

the most expensive of the three at Dr 60/100. The rooms are quite clean and comfortable, but some look straight on to a café – there's something irksome about a bunch of noisy people sitting virtually next to your bed through the day and night. Of the other two, the Majestic is extremely basic and not recommended. The rooms are bearable, but there's no shower at all – at Dr 40/70 there are better deals around. The Mendez is little better at Dr 50/80.

If you have a little more dosh, one that is considerably better is the *Hôtel Biarritz* (☎ 932473), 102-104 Ave d'Espagne. For Dr 70/133 you can get comfortable, spacious old rooms overlooking the sea. Slightly better are the front rooms with balcony in the *Hôtel Cecil* (☎ 931087), at 112 Ave d'Espagne. Most of them are big and self-contained and also have a phone. They charge Dr 83 per person, but this appears to be negotiable.

The little lane heading uphill between these last two is Rue Magellan. There are a couple of good places here. The first two you come across, the *Hôtel Family* and *Pension Excelsior* are nothing special. The latter has rooms for Dr 50/90, and although they are roomy, with big beds, the loos stink. Keep winding up the hill until you reach the *Hôtel L'Amor* and the *Hôtel Magellan* (☎ 938726). They have big, clean, carpeted rooms for Dr 40/80. The latter has a hot trickle pretty much whenever you ask, though it's difficult to describe it as a shower. The staff are friendly, and if you can get a front room, it's a good deal.

Head farther up around to the left and you strike two more places opposite each other. Both the *Hôtel Ibn Batouta* (☎ 937170) and the British-run *Hôtel El Muniria* have spotless rooms. The latter is probably a better bet, although on the expensive side for the budget wallet at Dr 100/120. This is where William Burroughs wrote *The Naked Lunch*. The Tanger-Inn downstairs is a popular haunt for a beer, particularly for Anglo-Saxons, and one of the last remnants of the Tangier of yesteryear.

Close by and with wonderful views over

the harbour (assuming you get a front room) is the one-star *Hôtel Panoramic Massilia* (☎ 935015), on the corner of Rue Ibn Joubair and Rue Targha. The staff here are friendly and singles/doubles with private shower, toilet and hot water (in the morning) cost Dr 80/130. This is definitely one of the better deals in Tangier.

Heading back down the price scale, there are a number of other cheap pensions scattered about the ville nouvelle, but they are not overly convenient. The *Pension Omar Khayam* is past the youth hostel heading south up Rue al-Antaki from Ave d'Espagne. The *Pension Holland* is simple but OK and in a pleasant shady spot in a backstreet behind the French Consulate. Unfortunately, the manager seems to speak only Moroccan Arabic and a Berber dialect. Another slightly out-of-the-way place is the *Pension Safari*, on Rue de Hollande.

A little more accessible, but less pleasant, are the pensions *Atlal* and *Al Hoceima* on Rue al-Moutanabi and the *Pension Gibraltar* on Rue de la Liberté, virtually opposite the El Minzah. For the truly desperate, there are a few more south of Rue Moussa ben Noussair, but you shouldn't need them.

Places to Stay – middle

Medina Area If you prefer a modicum of luxury but still want to stay in the medina area then one place to stay is the two-star *Hôtel Mamora* (☎ 934105), 19 Ave Mokhtar Ahardan, which offers spotlessly clean singles/doubles with shower for Dr 110/127 in the low season and Dr 135/152 in the high season. There's hot water in the mornings. Some of the rooms overlook the Grand Mosque, which means an early morning wake-up call unless you're a sound sleeper.

The pick of the crop and a good choice by any standards is the *Hôtel Continental* (☎ 931024; fax 931143). Used for some scenes in the film version of Paul Bowles's *The Sheltering Sky*, it is full of character, even if it is ragged around the edges. Some of the long-term residents are a little ragged themselves, but what stories they could tell. The best of the 56 rooms are those overlook-

ing the port. Singles/doubles cost Dr 150/200. It's popular with tour groups and film crews, so book ahead if possible. The entrance is off Dar Barhoud, and the best way to get there from the port is to head *up* the street past the Pension Avenida and continue along past the Grand Mosque, veering right at the fork (don't take the covered lane). The entrance is about 100 metres up on the right, shortly after *Jimmy's* perfume shop – 'patronised by film stars and the jet set'.

Ville Nouvelle There are a few possibilities at the lower end of this scale (where a single will cost a little more than Dr 100). One of the better ones is the *Hôtel de Paris* (☎ 931877), virtually opposite the tourist office at 42 Blvd Pasteur. Good, comfortable rooms with private shower and breakfast thrown in cost Dr 107/130. A few rooms have toilets too and cost somewhat more.

Back along the waterfront, you could stay at the popular *Hôtel Valencia* (☎ 930770), 72 Ave d'Espagne. It's not the most salubrious location, but a reasonable place and close to transport. It's often booked solid. Singles/doubles cost Dr 122/150.

At the junction of Ave des FAR and Ave Youssef ben Tachfine, the *Hôtel Miramar* (☎ 941715) is not bad for what you pay, but definitely on the tatty side. Singles/doubles with private shower are Dr 102/144, including the obligatory breakfast. Rooms with private toilet cost Dr 106/149. The prices can go up quite a lot in summer in this undeservedly three-star hotel.

Where Rue al-Antaki heads up from Ave d'Espagne (and where Ave d'Espagne becomes Ave des FAR) is the spotless German-run *Hôtel Marco Polo* (☎ 938213, 941124). It has quite impeccable rooms as well as a restaurant and bar service. It charges Dr 157/187/244 for singles/doubles/triples.

Next door is the two-star *Hôtel El Djenina* (☎ 942244), 8 Rue al-Antaki. It also has decent rooms, which at Dr 106/131 are a little cheaper than next door, along with a restaurant and bar. A couple of doors up is the two-star *Hôtel Bristol* (☎ 931070), 14

MEDITERRANEAN COAST

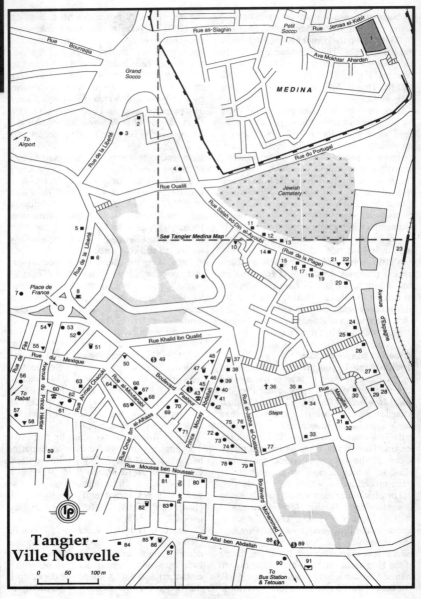

Rue Bourragia

Rue as-Siaghin

Petit
Socco

Rue   Jemaa el-Kebir

Ave Mokhtar Ahardan

Grand
Socco

MEDINA

To
Airport

Rue de la Liberté

Rue du Portugal

Rue Oualili

Rue Salah ed-Din el-Ayoubi

Jewish
Cemetery

See Tangier Medina Map

(Rue de la Plage)

Rue de la Liberté

Place de
France

Rue Khalid ibn Qualid

Fès

Rue de

Rue   du   Mexique

Avenue d'Espagne

Avenue du Prince Héritier

To
Rabat

Rue Ahmed Chaouki

Boulevard

Rue al-Moutanabi

Rue Omar   Ibn al-Alhass

Pasteur

Prince   Moulay   Abdallah

Rue el-Jabha el-Oualania

Steps

Rue   Magellan

Avenue d'Espagne

Rue Moussa ben Noussair

Rue   du

Tangier –
Ville Nouvelle

Rue Allal ben Abdallah

To
Bus Station
& Tetouan

0   50   100 m

Rue al-Antaki. It has 33 rooms with shower, and some with toilet. Doubles with shower or shower and toilet are Dr 144/149, which includes an obligatory breakfast. The hotel has a restaurant and bar.

Across from the Bristol, a side street runs off Rue al-Antaki leading to another good deal, the *Hôtel El Farabi* (☎ 943473), 8 Rue Saidia. Singles/doubles are Dr 90/120 and some rooms have sea views. Across the intersection is the pricey two-star *Hôtel Charf*

(☎ 943340). If you can afford it, the self-contained rooms are very good and have magnificent views, as does the 4th-floor restaurant. Singles/doubles are Dr 166/185.

In the heart of the ville nouvelle are some more expensive alternatives to the Hôtel de Paris. The *Hôtel Astoria* (☎ 937201), 10 Rue Ahmed Chaouki, has been renovated and offers 27 attractively furnished, mostly self-contained rooms for Dr 113/133 in the low season.

PLACES TO STAY

2	Hôtel du Grand Socco
5	Pension Gibraltar
6	Hôtel El Minzah
11	Pension Atou
12	Pension Playa
13	Pension Azzeraf
14	Pension Talavera
15	Pension Chams
16	Pension Miami
17	Pension Le Détroit
18	Pension Madrid
19	Pension Royale
20	Hôtel Valencia
24	Pension Mendez
25	Pension Majestic
26	Hôtel L'Marsa
27	Hôtel Biarritz
28	Hôtel Cecil
29	Hôtel Family
30	Pension Excelsior
31	Hôtel Magellan
32	Hôtel L'Amor
33	Hôtel Panoramic Massilia
34	Hôtel Ibn Batouta
35	Hôtel El Muniria & Tanger-Inn
38	Hôtel Bar Restaurant Maroc
39	Hôtel Lutetia
59	Hôtel Atlas
63	Hôtel Astoria
64	Pensions Atlal & Al Hoceima
70	Hôtel de Paris
77	Hôtel Rembrandt
79	Hôtel Tanjah-Flandria
80	Hôtel Africa
81	Hôtel Ritz
84	Hôtel Chellah

PLACES TO EAT

8	Café de Paris
10	Restaurant Le Bon Goût
21	Restaurants Africa & Hassi Baida
22	Restaurant/Bar La Paix
24	Restaurant Mendez
26	Restaurant L'Marsa
41	Morocco Palace
45	Romero's Restaurant
46	Restaurant Damascus
48	Restaurant Les Ambassadeurs
50	Big Mac
54	Café de France
55	Restaurant Negresco & English Bar
58	Restaurant Andalou
61	La Pagode
71	Eric's Hamburger Shop
76	Restaurant La Grenouille
85	Lee Wong

OTHER

1	Grand Mosque
3	Covered Market
4	Glacier Liberté
7	French Consulate
9	Gran Teatro de Cervantes
23	Tanger-Gare (railway station)
36	Church
37	Bar
40	Budget
42	Limadet Boat Ticket Office
43	Telephone & Fax Office
44	Tourist Office
47	Bar
49	BMCE (Late Bank & ATMs)
51	Bar Lisba
52	Discothèque Monocle
53	Royal Air Maroc
56	Cinéma Le Paris
57	Club Troya
60	Telephone & Fax Office
62	Laundry
65	Scott's Nightclub
66	Koutoubia Palace Nightclub
67	Churchill's Nightclub
68	Gospel Nightclub
69	The Ranch Club
72	Librairie des Colonnes
73	Avis
74	Voyages Schwartz (American Express agent)
75	Iberia
78	Cinéma Flandria
82	The Pub
83	Cinéma Goya
86	Bar
87	Cinéma Roxy
88	Banque Populaire
89	Wafabank
90	Hertz
91	Main Post Office

On Rue du Prince Moulay Abdallah is the fairly popular *Hôtel Lutetia* (☎ 931866). Rooms with shower and toilet cost Dr 144/194, including breakfast. There are cheaper rooms with toilet and some without shower or toilet. The hotel has parking facilities.

The *Hôtel Atlas* (☎ 936435; fax 933095), 50 Rue Moussa ben Noussair, is a little out of the way, but not bad in its class. Singles/doubles with shower cost Dr 161/207 while rooms with complete bathroom are Dr 202/249.

Heading into what most people would consider the top range is the inconveniently located and depressing *Hôtel Chellah* (☎ 943388; fax 945536), 47-49 Rue Allal ben Abdallah. They have characterless but perfectly comfortable rooms for Dr 326/373, or Dr 100 less in the low season.

Places to Stay – top end
With a tourist trade the size of Tangier's, there is a good choice of top-range hotels.

In the four-star category with some character is the ageing *Hôtel Rif* (☎ 935908/09/10) on Ave des FAR. Singles/doubles cost Dr 402/477.

A cheaper option is the *Hôtel Rembrandt* (☎ 937870), at the junction where Blvd Pasteur becomes Blvd Mohammed V. They charge Dr 360/470. Across the road, the *Hôtel Tanjah-Flandria* (☎ 933279) offers all the mod-cons for Dr 411/495.

Another four-star joint is the *Solazur* (☎ 940264), down on Ave des FAR. Not far away are a couple of also-rans relegated to the three-star division, the *El Oumnia* (☎ 940366), Ave Louis van Beethoven, and the *Shéhérazade* (☎ 940500), on Ave des FAR, next to the four-star *Hôtel Les Almohades* (☎ 940026; fax 946371). Also in the four-star category is the *Hôtel InterContinental* (☎ 936053; fax 937945), Park Brooks.

The only five-star hotel in Tangier that deserves this ranking is the *El Minzah* (☎ 935885; fax 934546), 85 Rue de la Liberté. A well-maintained reminder of the 1930s, when it was patronised by anyone who was anyone in the transient and not-so-transient European community, the hotel is beautifully conceived along the lines of a Moroccan palace. In 1931 the US businessman Ion Perdicaris, who at one point spent an uncomfortable spell as a prisoner of the Rif bandit Er-Raissouli, converted what had been the Palmarium casino into a hotel. The building was once the mansion of a certain Lord Bute. During WW II, as Tangier turned into a vipers' nest of spies and mercenaries of all types, the hotel hosted a mainly American clientele. It has all the amenities you would expect of a hotel in this category, including a swimming pool, bars and a couple of rather expensive restaurants.

Places to Eat
Medina Area There are several cheap eating possibilities in and around the Petit Socco, in between the cafés. There's a good takeaway snack bar just where Rue Jemaa el-Kebir begins. Huge rolls filled with meat, salad and pickles cost about Dr 10. Heading north of the Socco on Rue du Commerce there are two small sit-down places, the *Restaurant Andalus* and the *Grèce Restaurant*, which offer the standard fare – a meal won't cost more than Dr 30. The *Restaurant Ahlan* on Ave Mokhtar Ahardan offers a filling meal of brochettes, salad and a drink for Dr 25. Virtually across the road is the *Restaurant Moderne*, which is similar. Down the first flight of stairs towards the port is an oddly louche place, the *Restaurant Granada*. You can get meals of indifferent quality for about Dr 50, but few of the locals seem interested in the food. There are good views over the port, and the Moroccan men and women who find their way in here bring plenty of local colour.

There are a few food stalls at the bottom of the steps at the end of Ave Mokhtar Ahardan. They serve up fried fish and one or two other things for a few dirham.

More expensive is the *Restaurant Mamounia* on Rue as-Siaghin, which offers full Moroccan feasts in more sumptuous surroundings than any of the other medina eateries.

Ville Nouvelle A good place for snacks is the *Restaurant Le Bon Goût* on Rue Salah ed-Din el-Ayoubi. Farther down this street, towards Ave d'Espagne, are two reasonably priced sit-down restaurants, the *Africa* (No 83) and, next door, the *Hassi Baida*. Both offer set meals for around Dr 40 or main courses of fairly generous proportions for Dr 25 to Dr 35. The *Restaurant/Bar La Paix*, right on the corner of Ave d'Espagne is more a bar than restaurant.

The *Restaurant Mendez*, in front of the pension of the same name on Ave d'Espagne, serves mediocre fish and is a little expensive at Dr 50 for a set menu. You can do better for this price in the centre of town.

If you feel like Western-style fast food, you could do worse than *Big Mac*, which is on the corner of Blvd Pasteur and Rue Ahmed Chaouki. They do good hotdogs for Dr 20. Also in this line is the unlikely-sounding *Eric's Hamburger Shop*, which claims to be open 24 hours a day. It's in the arcade between Blvd Pasteur and Rue al-Moutanabi. For as little as Dr 10 you can get a decent imitation of a basic burger.

The stretch of Rue du Prince Moulay Abdallah around the corner from the tourist office is laden with eating possibilities. *Les Ambassadeurs* and the *Restaurant Damascus* are good for Moroccan food, whereas *Romero's* concentrates on fairly pricey Spanish cuisine. *Brenda's Tea Shoppe*, between the Hôtel Lutetia and the Hôtel Bar/Restaurant Maroc, serves good old baked beans, but at the time of writing looked like shutting down. Next door is a tiny pizza place. The *Morocco Palace* is the best choice in town for a full Moroccan spread and show featuring Moroccan music and belly-dancing. You'll be looking at well over Dr 100 a head for the whole evening. A few prostitutes operate here.

The *Restaurant Negresco*, on Rue du Mexique, is a posh place serving French and Moroccan cuisine. A full meal will come close to Dr 100 per person.

The *Carrousel* caters for homesick Brits hungry for pub grub (at about Dr 40 for mains) and a beer. It's more or less opposite

the expensive *La Pagode* Chinese restaurant, just off Rue du Prince Héritier.

On the subject of Asian food, you could also try *Lee Wong* for Vietnamese food, near the Hôtel Chellah on Rue Allal ben Abdallah. Mains are about Dr 60.

Restaurant La Grenouille, on Rue el-Jabha el-Ouatania, serves up quite a decent French set meal for Dr 80.

A bit of a walk from Blvd Pasteur is another leftover from the days of the international zone, *Guitta's*, on Place de Koweit. They do no-nonsense food, with main courses starting at about Dr 50.

The *Restaurant Andalou*, in a side street between Rue de Fès and Rue du Prince Héritier, has Spanish *tapas*.

For ice cream, you should try the Glacier Liberté on Rue de la Liberté.

Entertainment
Cafés & Bars In the heart of the medina, the *Café Central* on the Petit Socco was a favourite hang-out for William Burroughs and others and today is a good place to have a glass of tea, watch the world go by or catch up on Spanish TV. There are a couple of other cafés on the square, including upstairs in the Pension Fuentes.

There are several cafés on the Grand Socco where you can while away the time, or you could take a walk up to Blvd Pasteur, which is lined with elegant, European-style cafés, their tables spilling out onto the footpaths. Of these the pick of the crop has to be the *Café de Paris*, an ageing grande dame of Tangier coffee society. Take a seat inside and you're likely to have an odd assortment of characters for company – remnants of the Spanish population, genteel Moroccans and the odd ageing northern European – all in all an atmosphere redolent of bygone days. Your Dr 4 coffee will be served by the most correct of waiters, making it well worth the little extra. There are plenty of others to try for variety along the rest of the street. A coffee and cake or croissant from one of the pâtisseries make a great start to the day.

There are numerous bars around the ville nouvelle. *Restaurant/Bar La Paix* on Ave d'Espagne has been mentioned – it seems to be a preferred rest stop for some of the city's 'working girls', but is quite all right. A couple of local spit and sawdust bars are located near each other on Rue du Prince Moulay Abdallah and Rue Omar ibn al-Alhass. Another of the species, the *Bar Lisba* is on a side street between Blvd Pasteur and Rue du Mexique. There is also one near the Hôtel Chellah.

Anyone who has done any reading about Tangier will have come across *Dean's Bar*, on Rue Amérique du Sud. Hardly a Westerner of any repute (or ill-repute) did not prop up this bar at some time. It's not all that interesting now, but may be worth a drink if you've steeped yourself in Tangier mythology. Others of the same ilk, such as the Parade Bar (a favourite haunt of Jane Bowles), have long since disappeared.

For something a little more up-market, you could try the *English Bar*, next to the Restaurant Negresco. Apart from the not-so-cheap pint glasses, there's nothing very English about the place. A pint of Flag Spéciale with Spanish-style bar snacks will set you back Dr 36. Another similar place, but slightly more English, is *The Pub*, also known as *Le Pub*.

A place well worth investigating is the *Tanger-Inn*, next to the Hôtel El Muniria. It's open from 9 pm to about 1 am; knock on the heavy grill door to get in. It's a tiny place where the clientele can give you a taste of Interzone.

Many of the middle and top-range hotels have bars. The *Caid's Bar* in the Hôtel El Minzah is good for an expensive tipple.

Cinema There are a few cinemas around town, a couple of which have been marked on the maps. The *Cinéma Rif* on the Grand Socco serves up a rigid diet of kung fu-style movies.

Discos & Nightclubs There is a quite a collection of late-night places in the ville nouvelle, although they are not necessarily to be recommended. Rue al-Moutanabi has a cluster of them; *Scott's, Gospel* and

Churchill's (with the London Underground sign) can be vaguely interesting. The first of them has a reputation as a gay bar. Also here is the *Koutoubia Palace*, where you can see some tacky Egyptian belly-dancing into the wee hours. The *Morocco Palace* puts on a better version with a full meal. Some other discos and clubs are marked on the maps, but most are mainstream local hang-outs that generally have little promise, and can be unpleasant for unaccompanied women. They include the *Discothèque Monocle*, *Club Troya*, the *Ranch Club* and the *Club Regina*.

Getting There & Away

Air RAM (☎ 935505) has an office on Place de France. With the exception of two weekly flights to Al-Hoceima, all RAM's internal flights from Tangier go via Casablanca. The one-way fare to Casablanca is Dr 430. To Marrakesh it's Dr 705 and Dr 940 to Agadir.

RAM has connections to several European destinations, as do the following airlines:

Air France
    7 Rue du Mexique (☎ 936477)
British Airways
    Rue de la Liberté (☎ 935211)
GB Airways
    83 Rue de la Liberté (☎ 935877). GB Airways has flights to Gibraltar leaving at 11.05 am on Saturday and Sunday mornings. They go on to London Heathrow. The one-way fare is Dr 520. They also have a same-day return fare for Dr 620.
Iberia
    35 Blvd Pasteur (☎ 936177/8/9). Iberia has two flights a week from Tangier to Madrid.
KLM
    7 Rue du Mexique (☎ 938926)
Lufthansa
    7 Rue du Mexique (☎ 931327)

Bus – CTM The CTM office is near the port entrance, opposite the Tanger Gare railway station, although it runs some buses from the main bus station (gare routière), which is on Place Jamia el-Arabia, a good half-hour walk from the Grand Socco. There are six departures for Casablanca from 11 am to midnight (Dr 88; seven hours). They stop at Rabat (Dr

67; 5½ hours) and Kenitra (Dr 57). At 6 pm there is a bus to Meknès (Dr 63) and Fès (Dr 77.50; six hours). The CTM booth at the main station advertises a bus to Fès for only Dr 66 at 12.30 pm. At 4.30 pm a bus sets off for Marrakesh (Dr 146), Agadir (Dr 205.50) and Tiznit (Dr 228.50).

CTM has 13 buses a day to Tetouan (Dr 13) from the main bus station. Four buses also leave for Larache (Dr 22; about 2½ hours), three going via Asilah (Dr 10, one hour). They leave at 10 am, noon, 5.15 and 7 pm. The last is direct to Larache, but there is a fourth bus to Asilah at 7.45 pm. At 12.30 pm a bus leaves for Chefchaouen (Dr 27) and Ouezzane (Dr 39).

Bus – Non-CTM The other companies run buses from the main bus station. They have departures for Casablanca, Rabat, Fès, Meknès, Tetouan, Larache and Asilah. Some put on 'de luxe' buses for a few extra dirham. Fares vary but tend to be lower than the CTM fares (in some cases as much as Dr 20 lower, as with the fare to Casablanca).

Transports L'Étoile du Nord offers buses to Ketama (Dr 49) that go on to Al-Hoceima (Dr 74) and Nador (Dr 106). Transports Bradley runs buses to the Ceuta border (Dr 19).

Train There are two railway stations – Tanger Gare and Tanger Port. Most trains leave from the Gare station, although more seem to proceed to the Port station on arrival from elsewhere. All trains leaving from the port stop at Tanger Gare on the way out.

There are two direct trains to Marrakesh. The morning service departs from Tanger Gare at 8.10 am (about 9½ hours) and the night run from Tanger Port at 11.30 pm (about 10½ hours).

Both stop in Rabat and Casablanca. Three other trains head for Casablanca and Rabat too, departing at 9.45 am, 1.40 pm (Tanger Gare only) and 4.05 pm. You have to change at Sidi Kacem on the first two of these (a wait of about 40 minutes). The trip to Casablanca takes about six hours on the direct trains.

There are five daily trains to Fès via Meknès. They depart at 12.55, 8.10 and 9.45 am, and 1.40 and 4.05 pm. Only the last of these starts at Tanger Port. You have to change on three of these runs, with a wait not exceeding 40 minutes. The direct train takes about six hours to Fès. All but the 4.05 pm train go on to Oujda (about 12 hours).

The 2nd-class fares to Casablanca are Dr 81.50 in the normal trains and Dr 103 in the rapide; to Fès (Dr 63.50/84); Marrakesh (Dr 134/169); Rabat (Dr 62.50/79); and Oujda (Dr 142/179.50). All trains from Tangier stop at Asilah (Dr 10/12.50).

Taxi Grands taxis leave from a lot next to the main bus station. The main destinations are Tetouan (Dr 20) and Asilah (Dr 19). You may have to wait a while for Asilah-bound taxis to fill up. The bus is a better bet given that it's half the price.

Car The following are among the car rental agencies in Tangier:

Avis
    54, Blvd Pasteur (☎ 938960)
    Airport (☎ 933031)
Budget
    7 Ave Prince Moulay Abdallah (☎ 937994)
Europcar
    87 Blvd Mohammed V (☎ 941938)
Goldcar
    Hôtel Solazur, Ave des FAR (☎ 940164, 946568)
Hertz
    36, Blvd Mohammed V (☎ 709227, 707366)

Sea If you're heading to Spain or Gibraltar by boat you can buy tickets from the company offices down at the dock (closed weekends), in the terminal building (unreliable on weekends), or from virtually any travel agency around town. The Wasteel agency by the port entrance is a popular one. The prices are always the same (if someone tries to add on extras, go elsewhere). For more details see the Getting There & Away chapter.

There are ferries to Algeciras and Tarifa (Spain), Gibraltar and Sète (France). When the weather is calm, hydrofoils also make the run to Algeciras.

Getting Around

To/From the Airport Tangier's rather tiny Boukhalef Airport is 15 km from the town centre. From here you must arrange taxis into town, as there is no direct bus service.

Bus The local bus terminal is just up from the Grand Socco on Rue d'Angleterre.

Petits Taxis The price for a standard petit taxi journey around town is about Dr 5. Remember that fares go up by 50% after 8 pm.

AROUND TANGIER
Cap Spartel

A 14-km drive west of Tangier (there is no public transport) lies Cap Spartel, the north-western extremity of Africa's Atlantic coast, marked by a lighthouse and fish restaurant. If you're driving, take Rue de Belgique, cross Place de Koweit and head west for La Montagne. The road beyond this to Cap Spartel is heavily wooded. Below it, **Robin-son Plage** stretches off to the south. Four km away are the so-called **Grottes d'Hercule** (about 100 metres from the Robinson Plage Village de Vacances), which have been something of a tourist trap since the 1920s. You may be heavied into paying a few dirham to get into this hole in the rock that looks onto the ocean. For a long time locals quarried stone here, but tourists are more profitable business. Early morning is the best time to arrive, as the hasslers are still in bed. There are several overpriced cafés around the entrance to the grotto which overlook the Atlantic.

About one km inland are the remains of a tiny Roman settlement, **Cotta**. Like the more important town of Lixus farther south, it was a centre for producing garum – a kind of fish-paste delicacy. Walk about 200 metres down the road (which continues seven km south-east to the main Tangier-Rabat highway) past the camp site on the left and you'll find a track with a barrier. Ignore the latter and proceed down the track – the sparse ruins are about 800 metres in front of you.

You can stay at the *Robinson Plage Village de Vacances* (☎ 938765) near the caves or *Camping Robinson*. The former is pleasant enough but pricey at Dr 156/212/268 in the low season (and quite a bit more in the high season). They have no hot water and the restaurant is a rip-off. The camp site is spartan and has no showers. Despite this it costs Dr 15 per person, Dr 20 to pitch a tent and Dr 12 for a car. If it's open, the *Restaurant/Bar Mirage* by the grotto might be a better alternative.

Road to Ceuta

If you have your own transport, the drive along the wild and hilly 'coast' road to Fnideq and Ceuta is an attractive alternative route if you are thinking of heading to Tetouan and Chefchaouen from Tangier, although it will add a couple of hours to the trip.

Spanish Morocco

For hundreds of years, Spain has controlled the two North African enclaves of Ceuta and Melilla. It has also controlled five islets that have served as military bases and prisons: the three Jaafariya Islands off the Cap de l'Eau, about 25 km west of Saidia; the Peñon de Alhucemas, just off the coast near Al-Hoceima; and the Peñon de Velez de la Gomera, some 50 km west of the same town. Moroccan independence in 1956 brought no change, as Spain claims a historical right to the enclaves. Curiously, it does not recognise any such historical British right to control Gibraltar. Morocco has made several half-hearted attempts to have the enclaves returned. Rabat is not keen to rock the boat, however, as Spain is an increasingly important trading partner.

By the end of 1993, a process of granting Spain's regions a large degree of political autonomy was complete, except in the enclaves, which were still waiting to have their statutes approved. In mid-1994, however, it appeared that Melilla would accept a limited self-government agreement without legislative powers by the end of the year.

Moroccans fear that autonomy would mean Rabat could no longer negotiate the enclaves' future with Madrid, but would have to talk directly to the enclaves' political leaders, who will have no interest in restoring Moroccan rule. Indeed, many of the enclaves' Muslim inhabitants, mostly of Rif Berber origin, would themselves regard such a transfer with mixed feelings.

Because of its distance from Ceuta, Melilla has been included in the East Coast section later in this chapter.

CEUTA (SEBTA)

With a population of 75,000, about a third of which is made up of Muslims (to all intents and purposes Berbers, but officially 'Spanish Muslims'), the island is devoted to the military (almost half of its 19 sq km is owned by the army), duty-free shopping and a lot of shadier cross-border commerce. Although Spanish citizens get huge tax breaks for residing in Ceuta (and Melilla), the enclave's uncertain future has led some to migrate to the Spanish mainland.

Ceuta has an Andalusian feel to it, but the presence of so many Muslims (clearly treated as second-class citizens) gives it an other-wordly air. Just as it is odd to hear the bobbies of Gibraltar speaking English *and* Spanish, so it strikes you to hear the bus drivers of Ceuta speaking Spanish and Arabic.

Although Ceuta is pinning hopes on its tourist potential, there is not an awful lot here. If you're driving, stock up on duty-free petrol before leaving. The duty-free liquor is also worth a look before heading on to Morocco.

Many people enter Morocco via Ceuta to avoid the touts who hang around in Tangier, and you can easily push straight on from Ceuta to Tetouan (and on to Chefchaouen) in the same day.

History

Ceuta's Arabic name, Sebta, stems from the Latin Septem. Two heroes of Greek mythol-

ogy, Hercules and Ulysses, are both supposed to have passed through here, but more certainly it served as one of the Roman Empire's coastal bases. The city later passed into the control of the Byzantine empire and, in 931, was taken by the Arab Umayyad rulers of Muslim Spain. In 1083 it fell to the Almoravids and remained under direct Moroccan control until 1309, when James II of Aragon took it. In 1415 Portugal grabbed Ceuta and, when Portugal and Spain united under one crown in 1580, it passed by default to Spain. When the two countries split in 1640, Ceuta remained Spanish, as it has ever since.

Orientation & Information

Ceuta is a peninsula jutting into the Mediterranean. Most of the hotels, restaurants and offices of interest are gathered around the narrow spit of land linking the peninsula to the mainland. The port is a short walk to the west.

Tourist Office There are two tourist offices: the main one in the middle of town by the local bus terminus, and the other by the ferry terminal (☎ 509275). They have a decent brochure, a tiny map and an out-of-date accommodation list. The town office is open Monday to Friday from 8 am to 3 pm, but the one near the ferry sometimes also opens in the late afternoon and on Saturday.

Money There are plenty of banks along the main street, Paseo de Revellín, and its continuation, Calle Camoens. It's sometimes possible to buy Moroccan dirham, but there's no need, as you can change easily at the border (so long as you have *cash*). Banks are open from 8 am to 2 pm. Outside business hours you can change money at the Hotel La Muralla. If you have a credit card, there are plenty of ATMs around. Most of the banks charge about 1% commission on travellers' cheques, with a minimum of 650 pta per transaction.

At the border you'll find a few informal moneychangers on the Spanish side and branches of the BMCE bank and Banque

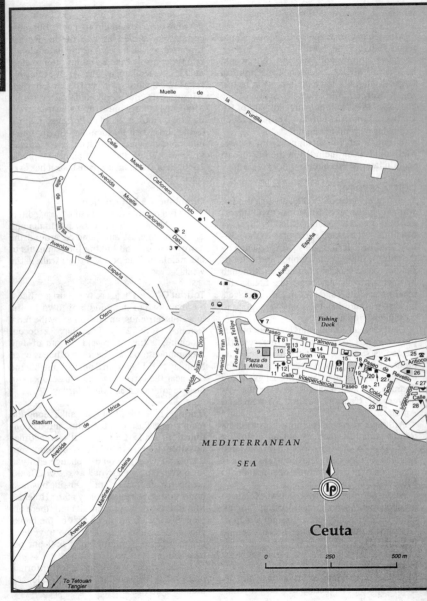

Ceuta

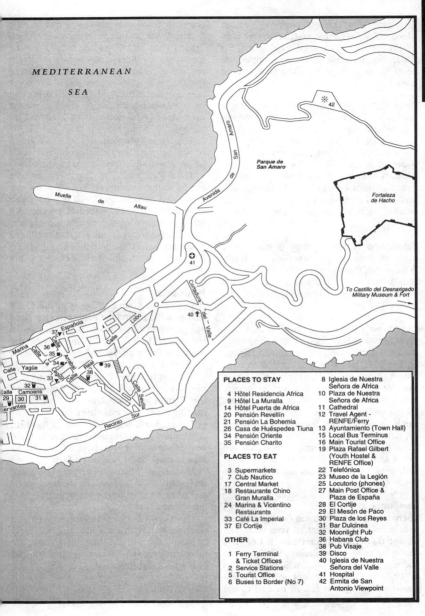

MEDITERRANEAN
SEA

Parque de
San Amaro

Fortaleza
de Hacho

To Castillo del Desnarigado
Military Museum & Fort

Muelle   de   Alfau

Avenida de San Amaro

Cortadura del – Valle

Española

Calle

Marina
Calle

Calle   Yagüe

Camoens

Recinto   Sur

PLACES TO STAY

4 Hôtel Residencia Africa
9 Hôtel La Muralla
14 Hôtel Puerta de Africa
20 Pensión Revellín
21 Pensión La Bohemia
26 Casa de Huéspedes Tiuna
34 Pensión Oriente
35 Pensión Charito

PLACES TO EAT

3 Supermarkets
7 Club Nautico
17 Central Market
18 Restaurante Chino
   Gran Muralla
24 Marina & Vicentino
   Restaurants
33 Café La Imperial
37 El Cortije

OTHER

1 Ferry Terminal
   & Ticket Offices
2 Service Stations
5 Tourist Office
6 Buses to Border (No 7)

8 Iglesia de Nuestra
   Señora de Africa
10 Plaza de Nuestra
   Señora de Africa
11 Cathedral
12 Travel Agent -
   RENFE/Ferry
13 Ayuntamiento (Town Hall)
15 Local Bus Terminus
16 Main Tourist Office
19 Plaza Rafael Gilbert
   (Youth Hostel &
   RENFE Office)
22 Telefónica
23 Museo de la Legión
25 Locutorio (phones)
27 Main Post Office &
   Plaza de España
28 El Cortije
29 El Mesón de Paco
30 Plaza de los Reyes
31 Bar Dulcinea
32 Moonlight Pub
36 Habana Club
38 Pub Visaje
39 Disco
40 Iglesia de Nuestra
   Señora del Valle
41 Hospital
42 Ermita de San
   Antonio Viewpoint

Populaire (which change *cash only*) on the Moroccan side. The moneychangers are only useful for changing leftover dirhams for which you have no exchange receipts into pesetas at an average rate. Otherwise, use the banks.

Post & Telecommunications The main post office (Correos y Telégrafos) is the big yellow building on Plaza de España, a square just off Calle Camoens, in the centre of town. For letters it's open Monday to Friday from 9 am to 8 pm. You can send telegrams Monday to Friday from 8 am to 9 pm and on Saturday from 9 am to 7 pm. Spanish public servants take the siesta seriously, so it may be hard to get anyone's attention from about 2 to 4 pm.

Telephone There are plenty of blue public phones around. They accept coins and cards. A locutorio, from where you can book overseas calls, has been marked on the map. It's open from 10 am to 10 pm daily, but is closed from 2 to 5 pm.

Duty-Free Ceuta is a duty-free zone, although nothing seems extravagantly cheap. If you are heading to mainland Spain, duty of 10% to 14% may be slapped on items worth more than 6840 pta. Going to Morocco, the main attraction is petrol. Normal and diesel cost 45 pta a litre, super 64 pta and unleaded 60 pta. If you want to stock up on goodies, there are a couple of supermarkets on Calle Muelle Cañonero Dato (Dumaya and Eurospar) which are worth a browse. Liquor is the best deal. A couple of service stations are on the same street.

Museums
There are a few museums in Ceuta, although none are worth too much of your time. The **Museo de la Legión**, on Paseo de Colón, is perhaps the most intriguing. Dedicated to and run by this army unit, which was set up in 1920 as Spain's answer to the French Foreign Legion, it is full of medals of the brave fallen and memorabilia of various commanders. These guys are a little on the fanatical side, and the reverence with which Franco's bits and pieces are treated (by the guide) is a reminder of how strong the Right remains in certain quarters of Spain. Most of the legion's actions have been in North Africa – the Rif war of 1921-26 being the most disastrous campaign. The museum is open Monday to Saturday from 11 am to 1.30 pm and 4 to 6 pm. Entry is free.

The **Museo Municipal**, which contains a tiny room with local archaeological finds from Palaeolithic times on, is on the corner of Calle Real and Calle Ingenieros. It was closed at the time of writing. Another one that seems perpetually closed is the **Museo de la Catedral**, in the cathedral, which has a small collection of ecclesiastical paraphernalia and paintings. There is a small **military museum** at the Castillo del Desnarigado on the south-eastern tip of the peninsula. It's only open at weekends.

Peninsula
If you have a couple of hours to spare, it's easy to walk around the peninsula (the No 4 bus goes part of the way), which is capped by Monte Hacho, said by some to be the southern Pillar of Hercules (Jebel Musa, west of Ceuta along the coast towards Tangier, is the other contender. Gibraltar is the northern pillar). From the **Convent of the Ermita de San Antonio** there is an excellent view towards Gibraltar.

The convent, originally built in the 17th century and reconstructed in the 1960s, is the venue for a large festival held annually on 13 June to mark Saint Anthony's Day.

Monte Hacho is crowned by the **Fortaleza de Hacho**, a fort first built by the Byzantines and added to since by the Moroccans, Portuguese and Spanish.

The **Castillo del Desnarigado** on the south-eastern end of the peninsula was built as a coastal battery in the 19th century, but there are remnants of earlier Spanish and Portuguese fortifications.

City Walls
The most impressive leftovers of the city

walls and the navigable **Foso de San Felipe** date back to Almohad times, although they were largely reconstructed by the Spaniards at the end of the 17th century.

Places to Stay – bottom end

Camping Camping Ceuta (☎ 503840) is a good four km west of the town centre, and hardly worth the effort if you don't have your own transport.

Hostel The Residencia de la Juventud is not an HI hostel and, at 1663 pta a bed, is hardly cheap. It is nevertheless often full. Tucked away on Plaza Rafael Gilbert, it opens in the early morning and late afternoon (no precise time). Turn up the stairs off Paseo de Revellín by the Restaurante China Gran Muralla. The hostel is on your right as you enter the square.

Hotels There is no shortage of fondas and casas de huéspedes, easily identifiable by the large blue-and-white 'F' or 'CH' on the entrances. The cheapest of these is the small Pensión Charito (☎ 513982), on the 1st floor at 5 Calle Arrabal, about 15 minutes' walk along the waterfront from the ferry terminal. The only indication that it is a guesthouse is the 'Chambres' sign, and the 'CH' sign on the wall. Basic singles/doubles cost 800/1400 pta. There are no hot showers. Just up the hill a little is the Pensión Oriente (☎ 511115). It has five rooms and was closed at the time of writing. They normally charge 1200/2000 pta. There are quite a few others in this category. If you're having trouble, pick up a list from the tourist office.

Conveniently situated in the centre, the Pensión Revellín (☎ 516762) is on the 2nd floor at 2 Paseo de Revellín. The doorway is right in the middle of the busy shopping street and, again, can be identified by the 'CH' sign. It is opposite the Banco Popular Español. Singles/doubles cost 1200/2200 pta, and hot showers are available in the morning. It's OK but the manager is none too friendly.

If you can afford a little more, the two best deals in town are the Casa de Huéspedes Tiuna (☎ 517756), at 3 Plaza Teniente Ruiz, and the Pensión La Bohemia (☎ 510615), 16 Paseo de Revellín. They both charge 2000/3000 pta for good singles/doubles, but the Bohemia (look for the small sign in the shopping arcade) is definitely the better of the two. It has piping-hot showers in spotless shared bathrooms.

Should you be stuck, the Pensión Real (☎ 511449), 1 Calle Real, offers singles/doubles for 2500/3000 pta.

Places to Stay – middle

A conveniently located place just near the ferry terminal is the Hotel Residencia Africa (☎ 514140), on Calle Muelle Cañonero Dato. In the low season it has singles/doubles for 3900/7000 pta (breakfast 500 pta), but in summer prices go up to 5500/8500 pta.

Places to Stay – top end

The premier establishment is the entirely characterless four-star Hotel La Muralla (☎ 514940; fax 514947), at 15 Plaza de Africa. It'll set you back 10,000/12,500 pta for singles/doubles with private bath. It has a restaurant, bar, parking and swimming pool.

Just east of the square a new place is being built, the Hotel Puerta de Africa. Another four-star joint is the Hotel Ulises (514540), 5 Calle Camoens. They charge marginally less than La Muralla.

Places to Eat

You won't find food as cheap here as in neighbouring Morocco. There are plenty of cafés that serve snacks, such as bocadillos and pulgas, which are basically rolls with one or two fillings in them. They are simple and reasonably good but hardly constitute a proper meal.

Café La Imperial at 27 Calle Real has some set menus (platos combinados) – standard Spanish fare, comprising meat, chips and salad or cooked vegetables) for 750 pta. It closes at 10 pm. Farther east along the same street are a few cheap tapas bars. Closer to the centre, the Marina and Vicentino restaurants have pricey mains for 1300 to 1500 pta. They are in a side street connecting the Paseo de Revellín and Marina Española.

The *Club Nautico* (☎ 514440), Paseo de las Palmeras, is a simple place overlooking the fishing port and offers solid fish meals for about 1300 pta.

The *Restaurante Chino Gran Muralla* is Ceuta's only Asian food place. It's on the Paseo de Revellín, just off Plaza de la Constitución.

Entertainment
Cafés & Bars The Marina and Vicentino restaurants are good places for a coffee and tostada (toasted sandwich) for breakfast.

In the evening, *El Cortije* and *El Mesón de Paco* are a couple of bright, lively, slightly up-market places for a coffee or beer. Slightly more posh is *Bar Dulcinea* on Calle Sargento Coriat. A caña (small glass of beer) costs an expensive 200 pta.

Nightclubs If you want a late night, the *Moonlight Pub* on Calle Camoens has a kind of beer garden-cum-disco out the back. Other places you might try include the *Habana Club* on Calle Arabal or the *Pub Visaje*, which has a disco next door.

Getting There & Away
To/From Morocco Buses to the border run every 15 minutes or so from Plaza de la Constitución. The No 7 bus costs 60 pta and takes 20 minutes.

If you arrive by ferry and want to head straight for the border, there is a bus stop for the No 7 just past the tourist booth and off to the right opposite the ramparts.

You walk across the border. The Spaniards barely take any notice of you going out, but are more meticulous if you're going the other way. On the Moroccan side you must fill in a white or yellow entry card. If you have a car you must also fill out a green one; keep the green customs slip they give you as you'll need it on the way out again. Just beyond the banks there are plenty of grands taxis to Tetouan. A seat costs Dr 15. The whole trip

from Ceuta to Tetouan should take no more than two hours and it often takes a good deal less.

Occasional buses run from various towns, such as Chefchaouen, to the Ceuta border, but it's a matter of luck whether any happen to be there when you arrive. You're best off taking a taxi and arranging further transport from Tetouan. If you set off early enough, you could conceivably make it to Fès or Meknès, and certainly to Chefchaouen, in the one day.

To/From Mainland Spain The Estación Marítima (ferry terminal) is west of the town centre on Calle Muelle Cañonero Dato, and there are frequent ferry and jetfoil departures to Algeciras. See the Getting There & Away chapter for details. You can purchase through train tickets to European destinations at the RENFE office on Plaza Rafael Gilbert, or at one of the travel agencies dotted about town. The bus between the ferry terminal and the centre is marked 'Puerto-Centro'. Be aware that Tetouan touts send a small advance guard to Ceuta – you're bound to meet some of them on debarkation.

The Rif Mountains

TETOUAN
For more than 40 years the capital of the Spanish protectorate established in 1912, Tetouan is unique for its mixed Hispanic-Moroccan look and feel. The medina, a conglomeration of cheerfully whitewashed and tiled houses, shops and religious buildings set against the brooding Rif Mountains, shows off its Andalusian heritage. The Spaniards added the new part of town, where even now you can buy a bocadillo and more people speak Spanish than any other foreign language.

Unfortunately for travellers and Tetouan's shopkeepers, the town remains a painful introduction to Morocco (most visitors come from Ceuta). Although not as bad as it once was, Tetouan is an active hive of touts, false guides and hustlers. Wandering around the medina at night is a definite no-no – you can stumble across some decidedly inhospitable individuals. Many visitors simply stop here to change buses and push on, which is a shame, because the medina is interesting and even the modern part of the city, although neglected, is worth a quick look.

History

Tetouan's ancient predecessor was Tamuda, a Mauretanian city founded in the 3rd century BC. Destroyed in the 1st century AD after a local revolt, the Romans built a fortified camp in its place, remnants of which are visible about five km from the modern town.

In the 14th century, the Merenids created the new city of Tetouan as a base from which to control rebellious Rif tribes, but the city was destroyed by Henry III of Castile in 1399.

Reoccupied in the 16th century by Muslim and Jewish refugees from Granada, Tetouan prospered, and was the last of the Muslim kingdoms in Spain to fall to the Christians. Part of that prosperity was due to piracy, to which the Spanish put an end by blockading Tetouan's port at Martil. They succeeded in stopping the piracy, but legitimate trade suffered too.

Moulay Ismail built Tetouan's defensive walls in the 17th century, and the town's trade links with Spain improved and developed on and off until 1859, when Spanish forces occupied it for three years during a punitive campaign against Rif tribes aimed, it was said, at protecting Ceuta. In 1913 the Spanish made it the capital of their protectorate, which they only abandoned in 1956, when Morocco regained independence.

Orientation & Information

The medina makes up about two-thirds of the city, while the modern town is tucked into the south-western corner. It is in the latter that you'll find the hotels, banks, most of the restaurants and cafés, bus station and taxi stands. Many streets, called 'calles', still advertise the town's Spanish heritage, but this is changing as, alongside Arabic, French takes over as Morocco's semiofficial second language.

Tourist Office The Délégation Régionale du Tourisme (☎ 964407, 967009) is at 30 Calle Mohammed V, just near the corner of Rue Youssef ben Tachfine. The guy here is helpful and speaks quite a bit of English. Don't be talked into hiring a guide (unless, of course, you want one), as the medina is manageable on your own. If you get lost, it's never far to the walls or a gate. The office is open from 8.30 am to noon and 2.30 to 6.30 pm Monday to Thursday; on Friday it's open the same hours but closes from 11.30 am to 3 pm.

Money There are plenty of banks along Calle Mohammed V. The most useful is the BMCE, which has a branch with ATMs on Place Moulay el-Mehdi, in the new city.

Post & Telecommunications The post office is also on Place Moulay el-Mehdi, and open from 8.30 am to 12.15 pm and 2.30 to 6.45 pm. The telegram section is open from 7 am to 9 pm.

The main telephone office is around the corner from the main entrance to the post office, on Rue al-Ouahda.

Foreign Consulates Spain has a consulate in Tetouan at Avenida al-Massira (☎ 973941/2; fax 973946) and a visa office at Carretera Martil, km 3 (☎ 971325; fax 971326). They are open Monday to Friday from 9 am to noon.

Language School The American Language Center has a branch at 1 Rue Maerakate Zelaka.

Ensemble Artisanal On Ave Hassan II south of the town walls is a large government-sponsored emporium of Moroccan arts and crafts. It is not a bad place to get an idea of the upper range of prices of Moroccan crafts without the pressure of souq sales

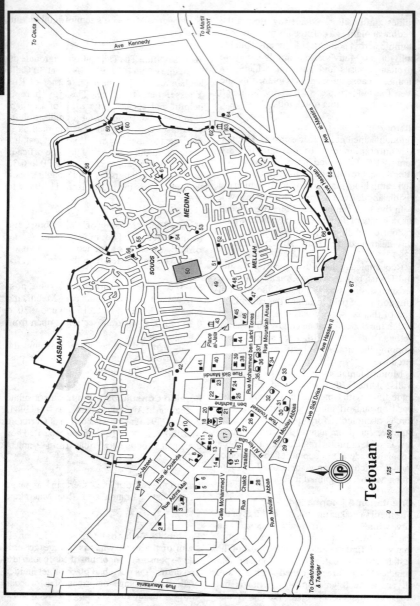

Tetouan

tactics. It is open Monday to Friday from 9 am to 12.30 pm and 3.30 to 6.30 pm.

Medical Services & Emergencies There is a night pharmacy (☎ 966777) on Rue al-Ouahda. The police can be called on ☎ 19 and the fire brigade on ☎ 15.

Film There is a Kodak store on Rue Youssef ben Tachfine, just up from the El Yesfi Snack bar.

Medina & Around
Place Hassan II, which links the medina to the new city, is the heart of the city. It has traditionally been a meeting place, and there are a couple of cafés where you can sit and watch the world go by. Heading west, Calle Mohammed V is a pedestrian zone right up to Place Moulay el-Mehdi, and is lined with shops, cafés, restaurants and the odd hotel.

The main entrance into the medina is Bab er-Rouah ('Gate of the Winds'), to the right of the former Spanish consulate. The medina is a bustling place, great for just wandering at random. It is quite unlike the great medinas farther south, in that the Spaniards had a hand in some of the building in the 19th century. In any case, most of its inhabitants from the 16th century on were refugees from what had been Muslim Spain. There are some 20 **mosques** within the medina, of which the Great and Saidi mosques stand out a little more than the others. As is usual in Morocco, non-Muslims may not enter.

The north-eastern area of the medina, north of Bab el-Okla, was the up-market end of town. Some of the fine houses built by the city's residents in the last century still stand

PLACES TO STAY		OTHER			
2	Hôtel Oumaima	1	Bab Noider	37	Grands Taxis to Martil
12	Pension Rio Jana	3	Café	39	Café Détroit
14	Pensions Fès, Bienvenida & Florida	4	Café & Cinema Avenida	42	Bab Tout
		5	Bar Ideal	43	Museum
23	Hôtel Regina	6	Café/Pâtisserie	47	Cinema Español
26	Hôtel Príncipe	7	Drycleaners	48	Cafés
27	Pension Iberia	9	Grands Taxis to Tangier & Chefchaouen	49	Place Hassan II
28	Hôtel Paris			50	Royal Palace
31	Hôtel Trebol			51	Bab er-Rouah
38	Hôtel Nacional	10	Modern Hammam (Duchas y Sauna)	52	Gold Souqs
40	Pension Cosmopolita			53	Dyers
41	Hôtel Persa	13	Café	55	Leather
44	Hôtel Bilbao	15	Wafabank	56	Carpentry
		16	Cathedral	57	Bab M'Kabar (Bab Sebta)
PLACES TO EAT		17	Place Moulay el-Mehdi		
				58	Bab Sfli
8	Picinic Snack Bar	18	Telephone Office	59	Bab as Saida
11	Bakery	19	Post Office	60	Saidi Mosque
22	El Yesfi Snack	20	Men's Hammam	61	Great Mosque
24	Restaurant Restinga	21	Tourist Office	62	Bab el-Okla
34	Sandwich Ali Baba	25	Voyages Hispamaroc	63	Musée Marocain
36	Restaurant Zarhoun	29	Bus to Martil	64	Artisanat School
45	Restaurant Granada	30	Taxis to Tangier	65	Spanish Consulate
46	Restaurant Saigon	32	Taxis to Ceuta	66	Bab Remouz
54	El Yesfi Snack	33	Bus Station	67	Ensemble Artisanal (Artefact Emporium)
		35	Grands Taxis to Ceuta		

here and several have been turned into carpet showrooms and extravagant tearooms. You'll probably stumble across them yourself, but there are plenty of touts around who will gladly take you to one, particularly the carpet shops.

Although the shopkeepers don't do a roaring tourist trade here, wood and leatherwork are two local artisanal specialities. It might be worth wandering up towards Bab M'Kabar (or Bab Sebta) for a look. You'll also come across other shops dedicated to the tourist trade, selling copper and brassware, babouches and a limited selection of souvenirs. If you're interested in Tetouan carpets, go first to the Artisanat school to get an idea of what to look for.

Musée Marocain Also known as the Museum of Moroccan Art, this collection of traditional clothing, instruments, carpets, arms and household implements is a pleasing and peaceful stop built in a bastion in the town wall, just south of Bab el-Okla – cannon are still in place in the garden. Unfortunately, most of the labelling is in Arabic. The chap following you around to turn lights on and off will expect a small tip when you've finished.

It is open Monday to Friday from 8.30 am to noon and 2.30 to 6 pm. The entry fee is Dr 10.

Artisanat School Just opposite Bab el-Okla is the artisan school, where you can see children being taught traditional crafts such as carpet-weaving, leatherwork, woodwork and the making of enamel zellij tiles. Their work is on display but not for sale. The building itself is worth a visit. The school is open from 8.30 am to noon and 2.30 to 5.30 pm (closed weekends). Entry is Dr 10.

Archaeology Museum There is a small archaeology museum opposite the end of Rue Prince Sidi Mohammed but it is only for the dedicated. It has a few prehistoric stones, some Roman coins and a number of small mosaics and other artefacts from Lixus. It is open Monday to Saturday from 8.30 am to

noon and 2.30 to 5.30 pm; closed weekends. Entry costs Dr 10 but the enclosed gardens in front of the museum, where many of the larger exhibits have been set up, are free.

Places to Stay – bottom end
Camping The nearest camp site is by the beach at Martil, about eight km away (see the Around Tetouan section). There's also a site not far from Club Med, about halfway between Tetouan and the (Ceuta) border.

Hotels There are plenty of cheap, very basic pensions available in Tetouan, most of which charge from Dr 50 for a single. Little store seems to be set by quality. Few have hot water, and even at the upper end of the price scale, most of the staff at these places seem to be exceptionally ill-humoured.

Some of the pensions could be straight out of Spain, with their wrought-iron balconies overlooking the street. Others are flophouses or straight-out brothels. The pensions *Fès, Bienvenida, Florida* and *Rio Jana* all fall into this category, and want about Dr 50/80 (they may ask for more) for singles/doubles. The Florida has small but clean and comfortable rooms. The Rio Jana is a brothel, but they'll let you have a room if you really want one.

One pension that can be recommended is the *Pension Iberia* (☎ 963679), on the 3rd floor above the BMCE on Place Moulay el-Mehdi. Although there are only a few rooms, it has a homey atmosphere and some rooms have great views over the square. They cost Dr 60/70 for singles/doubles with shared bathroom. They don't seem to have hot showers.

The *Hotel Bilbao* (☎ 967939), 7 Calle Mohammed V, is a good cheap alternative to the pensions and has a lot of character, especially if you can get one of the front rooms. It costs Dr 52 for a room, regardless of whether one or two people occupy it, with shared bathroom and cold showers.

If you're looking for something a little better, but not too expensive, try the one-star *Hotel Trebol* (☎ 962018), which is close to the bus station. It has singles/doubles without private shower for Dr 50/80 or Dr

70/103 with shower. There is hot water in the morning and a dry-cleaner's next door.

Another possibility is the undeservedly two-star *Hotel Príncipe* (☎ 962795) at 20 Rue Youssef ben Tachfine. Clean singles/doubles/triples are Dr 59/98/145. They only have cold water and are basic. Since the prices don't reflect the star-rating, however, it's not bad value.

Hammams Given that so few of the cheaper hotels offer hot water, the public baths may well come in handy. The hammam off Rue al-Jazeer is pretty new. The sign says 'Duchas y Sauna', and men and women can go from 6 am to 9.15 pm, seven days a week. A shower costs Dr 5, a sauna is Dr 30 and a massage and sauna cost Dr 60. There is a second public shower (men only) on Rue Youssef ben Tachfine across the road from the El Yesfi Snack bar, and another behind the post office.

Places to Stay – middle
The *Hotel Persa* (☎ 964215) is a dusty old place with a cavernous café on the ground floor. It offers ill-lit doubles with private shower, toilet and sagging beds for Dr 84.

Better is the *Hotel Nacional* (☎ 963290), 8 Rue Mohammed ben Larbi Torres, which has singles/doubles with private shower and toilet for Dr 71/108 including taxes. The rooms are a little gloomy, but are otherwise quite good.

A particularly unhelpful crew run the *Hotel Regina* (☎ 962113), 8 Rue Sidi Mandri. Doubles with private shower and toilet here cost Dr 109 and there's hot water in the morning. The rooms themselves are on a par with those in the Nacional.

Better, but considerably more expensive (especially for lone travellers) and devoid of character, is the *Hotel Paris* (☎ 966750), 11 Rue Chakib Arsalane, where singles/doubles with private shower, toilet and hot water are Dr 151/171 including taxes. The management is friendly but you'll need to hassle for soap and toilet paper.

The pick of the bunch in Tetouan itself is the *Hotel Oumaima* (☎ 963473), Rue Achra Mai. It has rooms for Dr 151/190/241, and they are considerably better than those at the Paris. The staff even turn on the central heating in winter – sometimes.

Places to Stay – top end
The four-star *Hotel Safir* (☎ 970144/77), Ave Kennedy, is the only top-range hotel in Tetouan. It has 98 rooms, a swimming pool, tennis courts and a nightclub, but is a long way out of the centre of town.

Places to Eat
The best place to get a cheap, filling and nutritious meal is *El Yesfi Snack*. They do great baguette sandwiches with various meats, potato salad, chips and salad for Dr 10.

The *Picnic* snack bar, on Rue Achra Mai, does an average version of a hamburger. Another reasonable and cheap snack place is *Sandwich Ali Baba* on Rue Mourakah Anual. Despite the name, they also have chicken, chips, soups and tajines. It's popular and you practically have to fight through the crowd at the front to get to the seating area in the back.

A good-value restaurant is the *Restaurant Saigon* on Rue Mohammed ben Larbi Torres, although there's nothing Vietnamese about it. You can get a huge serve of tasty couscous or brochettes for Dr 20, preceded by a big bowl of chunky soup for Dr 4. It's justifiably popular.

Close by, down a lane opposite the Cinema Español, is the *Restaurante Moderno*. It's a bit more down to earth, but the prices are much the same. Locals recommend it, and there are a couple of lively cafés in the same spot.

Not so good is the *Restaurant Restinga*, which you get to through a small alley off Calle Mohammed V. You can eat inside or in a partly open courtyard. The staff are friendly and the menu is about the same as at the Saigon, though many items are not available. The big plus, however, is that they serve beer. A bottle of Amstel costs Dr 13.

The *Restaurante Granada*, on Calle Mohammed V at Place al-Jala, is clean and cheap and serves the usual tajines, couscous and soups.

The best restaurant in Tetouan by far is the *Restaurant Zarhoun*, on Rue Mohammed ben Larbi Torres. They do a great pastilla (pigeon pie). At Dr 55, it's pricey but good. The rest of the limited menu features the usual couscous, tajine and brochettes for about Dr 45 a serve. You can get beer and wine, and some locals clearly use it as an up-market bar. The interior is like something from *A Thousand and One Nights*.

Entertainment
Cafés & Bars There appears to be only one bar, the *Ideal* – look for the Flag Spéciale sign off Rue Achra Mai. It's a spit-and-sawdust place. The *Zarhoun* and *Restinga* restaurants are about the only other places where you can get a drink.

On the other hand, Spanish-style cafés (without alcohol) abound, and the coffee and tea are good. There are a lot along the Calle Mohammed V pedestrian zone and Rue Achra Mai. On the latter, the *Avenida* and another café closer to Place Moulay el-Mehdi are slightly chic and very pleasant. The *Café Détroit* on Calle Mohammed V is another rather European-style spot that does a good cup. The cafés on Place Hassan II are more down to earth and Moroccan in flavour. There are plenty of others to choose from, and quite a selection of cake shops too.

Cinema The *Cinema Avenida*, on Rue Achra Mai, is the main movie house in Tetouan and offers four sessions a day.

Getting There & Away
Bus The bus station is at the junction of Rue Sidi Mandri and Rue Moulay Abbas. It is a dark and gloomy place with the ticket windows upstairs, buses downstairs and touts all over.

CTM has six buses to Chefchaouen a day, starting at 5 am and finishing at 10 pm. They cost Dr 16.50. Buses for Tangier leave at 5.30 am and 2.30, 4.15 and 6.15 pm, take about an hour and cost Dr 13.

At 10.30 pm there is a bus to Casablanca

(Dr 91.50) via Rabat. The trip takes about seven hours. There is a second bus nonstop to Casablanca at 11 pm. There is one bus to Fès at 11.30 am, which stops in Ouezzane on the way. It takes about five hours and tickets cost Dr 55.

Four buses a day head for Al-Hoceima (about seven hours), and two of them go on to Nador (close to 10 hours).

If you can't get on a CTM bus, there are plenty of other private lines. These buses are often not in such great shape, but the competition means you have quite a few choices. There are regular departures for Chefchaouen and Tangier, and some of these companies cover destinations CTM doesn't. Transports AMA, for instance, goes to Oujda for Dr 117.65. It also has a bus every three hours to Cabo Negro for Dr 3.

A local bus to Martil (Dr 2) leaves from Rue Moulay Abbas, not far from the bus station.

Train There is no train station at Tetouan but the ONCF runs two Supratours buses to Tnine Sidi Lyamani at 7.30 am and 3.30 pm to link up with trains to and from Tangier. The Supratours office is on Rue Achra Mai, near the Cinema Avenida.

Taxi Grands taxis for the Spanish enclave of Ceuta leave frequently from the corner of Rue Mourakah Anual and Rue Sidi Mandri, just up from the bus station. A seat costs Dr 15 for the 20-minute trip to Fnideq on the Moroccan side. Although the border is open 24 hours a day, transport dries up from about 7 pm to 5 am.

On the Spanish side of the border, the No 7 public bus runs every half-hour or so to the centre for 60 pta.

Local grands taxis to the beach at Martil leave from farther up Rue Mourakah Anual and cost Dr 3.

Grands taxis to Chefchaouen leave frequently from a rank on Rue al-Jazeer (Dr 20). There are less frequent departures from the same rank for Tangier (Dr 30).

Car Rental Zeit (☎ & fax 961664) is at Immeuble Yacoub el-Mansour.

Getting Around

Taxi It's unlikely you'll need one, but a petit taxi ride around town should not be more than about Dr 6. If you need to get to or from the airport (also fairly unlikely), you'll pay Dr 15 for the four-km run.

AROUND TETOUAN
Martil & Cabo Negro

About eight km east of Tetouan is the beach town of Martil. Once Tetouan's port and home to pirates, there is little to it now but a reasonable beach and a couple of waterfront cafés. Farther north up the coast is Cabo Negro (or Ras Aswad in Arabic), a headland jutting out into the Mediterranean clearly visible from Martil beach.

Places to Stay & Eat *Camping Martil* is the closest camping ground to Tetouan, but it's a sparse affair. It costs Dr 6 a person, Dr 6 for a car and Dr 10 for pitching a big tent. There are cold showers and electricity costs an extra Dr 2. *Camping Ch'bar*, on the road from Martil up to Cabo Negro, is a little better.

As Martil is so close to Tetouan, there is hardly any need to stay here, but you could try the *Charaf Pension*. In summer they charge a hefty Dr 70/90/120/160 for a room with beds and basin. Another place is the *Pension Badia*, near the bus stop.

An up-market place is the *Hotel Estrella del Mar* (☎ 979276), which has modern rooms for Dr 157.50/204/273 including breakfast. In summer they impose half-board, which takes a double to Dr 340. Apart from the hotel restaurant, there are a few nondescript cafés and small eateries scattered about.

Getting There & Away The local bus to Tetouan leaves from a dirt patch near the camping ground, but it'll stop for you on the main road back to Tetouan.

Road to Ceuta

The stretch of coast between Cabo Negro and Fnideq (the border with Ceuta) is littered with expensive chalets, small-scale beach resorts and a Club Med. Just near Restinga Smir (where, by the way, a catamaran occasionally lands from Gibraltar during summer) is the *Camping Fraja*.

CHEFCHAOUEN

Also called Chaouen, Chechaouen and Xauen, this delightful town in the Rif Mountains is a favourite with travellers for obvious reasons: the air is cool and clear, the people are noticeably more relaxed than in Tangier or Tetouan, there's more kif than you can poke a stick at, and the town is small and manageable. All this makes it a great place to hang out for a few days.

Founded by Moulay Ali ben Rachid in 1471 as a base from which to attack the Portuguese in Ceuta, the town prospered and grew considerably with the arrival of Muslim refugees from Spain. It was these refugees who built the whitewashed houses with blue painted doors and window frames, tiny balconies, tiled roofs and patios with a citrus tree planted in the centre that give the town its distinctive Hispanic flavour. The obvious intention was to re-create at the base of Jebel al-Qala'a (1616 metres) what they had been forced to leave behind in Spain.

The town remained isolated, and almost xenophobic, until occupied by Spanish troops in 1920, and the inhabitants continued to speak a variant of medieval Castilian. In fact, Christians were forbidden entry to the town and only did so on pain of death. Two managed to do so in disguise: the French adventurer Charles Foucauld in 1883 and, five years later, the British wanderer and journalist Walter Harris (disguised as a Jew).

The Spanish were briefly thrown out of Chefchaouen by Abd el-Krim between 1924 and 1926 during the Riffian rebellion but returned to stay until independence in 1956.

Despite being firmly on the tourist circuit, Chefchaouen (Chaouen means 'peaks', referring to the Rif heights around the town, and Chefchaouen 'look at the peaks') is

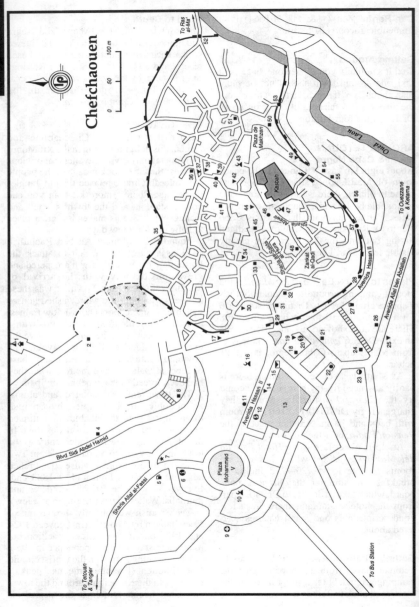

Chefchaouen

remarkably easy-going, with only a few touts around. The new bus station is a 20-minute hike south-west of the town centre, which is downhill when you leave but a rather steep incline on arrival. The main street in the new town is Avenida Hassan II. At Bab al-'Ain it swings south and follows the medina wall around towards Oued Laou.

Information

Tourist Office There is a syndicat d'initiative in a lane just north of Plaza Mohammed V, open Monday to Friday from 9 am to noon and 3 to 6 pm, but it is of limited use. They have a sketch map of the town with hotel phone numbers, but that's it.

Post & Telecommunications The post office (PTT) is on Avenida Hassan II, about 50 metres west of the Bab al-'Ain entrance to the medina. It's open from 8.30 am to 12.15 pm and 2.30 to 6.45 pm Monday to Saturday (on Friday it is closed for noon prayers from 11.30 am to 3 pm). You can make international phone calls from here but there are no card phones.

Money The BMCE and the Banque Populaire are both on Avenida Hassan II. You can change cash and travellers' cheques and get cash advances on Visa and MasterCard at both. There are no ATMs.

Newspapers There is a reasonable newsstand between the Banque Populaire and the Pâtisserie Magou on Avenida Hassan II. It has the odd publication in French, English, Spanish and German.

Market

The market (see map) is much the centre of things on Mondays and Thursdays, when merchants come from all over the Rif to trade. The emphasis is on food and second-hand clothes, although there are sometimes a few interesting souvenirs.

Medina

The old medina is small, uncrowded and

PLACES TO STAY	PLACES TO EAT	
		9 Hospital
		10 Mosque
1 Camping Ground &	14 Café	11 Newsstand
Youth Hostel	17 Restaurants Zouar &	12 BMCE Bank
2 Hôtel Asma	Moulay Ali ben	13 Market
4 Residencia La	Rachid	15 Post Office (PTT)
Estrella	19 Pâtisserie Magou	16 Sidi Ali ben Rachid
8 Auberge Granada	25 Café Ahlan	Mosque
18 Hôtel Magou	30 Restaurant Assaada	20 Banque Populaire
21 Hôtel Sahra	34 Restaurant El Baraka	22 Kodak Shop
24 Hôtel Ketama	37 Restaurant Granada	23 Grands Taxis to
26 Hôtel Sevilla	38 Restaurant Chez	Ouezzane
28 Hôtel Rif	Fouad	27 Bar
31 Hôtel Bab El Ain	39 Restaurant Maravilia	29 Bab al-'Ain
32 Hôtel Abie Khanda	42 Restaurant Tissemlal	35 Bab Djenan
33 Hôtel Andaluz	44 Cafés & Restaurants	40 Fountain
36 Pension Valencia	49 Restaurant	43 Mosque
41 Pension Znika	Chefchaouen	46 Plaza Uta
45 Pension Castilliano		el-Hammam
48 Pension Mauritania	**OTHER**	47 Great Mosque
50 Hôtel Parador		52 Bab al-Ansar
51 Pension al-Hamra	3 Cemetery	53 Bab al-Muqaddam
54 Hôtel Marrakech	5 Mobil Service Station	57 Bab Hammar
55 Hôtel Salam	6 Syndicat d'Initiative	
56 Hôtel Madrid	7 Police	

easy to find your way around in. For the most part, the houses and buildings are a blinding blue-white and, on the northern side especially, you'll find many with tiny ground-floor rooms crowded with weaving looms. These are a legacy of the days when silkworms were introduced by Andalusian refugees and weaving became the principal activity of families living here. Most of the weaving done now is of wool, which is one of the biggest products of the area. The people working these looms are friendly and, to break the monotony of their work, they may well invite you in for a smoke and a chat.

There is also a fair smattering of tourist shops, particularly around Plaza de Makhzen and Plaza Uta el-Hammam – the focal points of the old city.

Plaza Uta el-Hammam & Kasbah The shady, cobbled Plaza Uta el-Hammam, with the kasbah along one side, is at its busiest in the early evening, when everyone starts to get out and about after the inactivity of the afternoon. It's a great time to sit in one of the cafés opposite the kasbah and relax. The atmosphere is sedate and almost medieval, except for the cars and, unfortunately, the tour buses.

The red-hued ruins of the 17th-century kasbah dominate the square and its walls enclose a beautiful garden. It was built by Moulay Ismail to defend the town against unruly Berber tribes as well as outsiders such as the Spaniards. For a time it was Abd el-Krim's headquarters, but, in one of those twists of history, he ended up being imprisoned here by the Spaniards.

To the right of the entrance to the kasbah are the cells, complete with neck chains at floor level, where Abd el-Krim was imprisoned in 1926. To the left is a small museum containing a collection of traditional arms, instruments, textiles and some old photos of the town. It also houses a small Andalusian studies centre. You can climb up a couple of storeys onto the roof for some good views of the town.

The kasbah is open from 9 am to 1 pm and 3 to 6.30 pm, and entry costs Dr 10.

Great Mosque Next door to the kasbah is Chefchaouen's Great Mosque, built in the 15th century by the town's founder, Ali ben Rachid. Non-Muslims may not enter.

Plaza de Makhzen The Plaza de Makhzen is the lesser of the two town squares; it has a large old gum tree in the centre. Instead of cafés, it has mostly tourist shops. However, on market days you still get people squatting under the tree selling bundles of mint and vegetables grown in the surrounding area.

If you take the lane heading north-east from the square you'll eventually come out at Bab al-Ansar; after this comes the river, Oued Laou, with a couple of agreeable shady cafés on its banks. Off to the left is Ras al-Ma', the spring at the source of the Oued Laou's clear, fresh water. This is also where women come to do the washing while the men busy themselves drinking tea.

Activities
Hiking The hills around Chefchaouen offer some good hiking possibilities. If you want to do anything ambitious, you should probably consider engaging a guide – ask at your hotel. It is supposedly possible to organise small hikes in the hills on donkey-back, if you like that sort of thing. Again, the best place to start making enquiries is at your hotel.

Music Chefchaouen occasionally hosts a modest festival of traditional Andalusian music in August.

Places to Stay – bottom end
Camping & Hostel Right up on the side of the hill behind the Hotel Asma is the *camp site* and *youth hostel* (☎ 986031). They are only really worth considering if you have your own vehicle, as it's quite a hike to get to them. It's a steep 30-minute walk by the road (follow the signs to the Hotel Asma), or a 15-minute scramble up the hill through the cemetery; you shouldn't attempt the latter on a Friday, as the locals don't take kindly to it.

The camping area is shady and costs Dr 5 per person, Dr 10 per vehicle and Dr 10 to

Dr 15 to pitch a tent, depending on how big it is. Showers are Dr 5. The hostel is extremely basic and poor value at Dr 20 per person.

Hotels If you've come from Tetouan, you'll find the standard of accommodation considerably better and cheaper here. There are plenty of places around, but in peak periods especially they can all fill up quickly. In winter (when it can be very cold) the main problem is that, with a couple of exceptions, no-one has considered the idea of heating.

The cheapest places are the pensions in the medina. For the most part they are OK, if a little gloomy and claustrophobic at times. It all depends on what you are offered, but some of them are very popular with budget travellers so, if you want a good room, get there early in the day.

The *Pension Castilliano*, just off the western end of Plaza Uta el-Hammam, is a popular travellers' hang-out, with beds for Dr 20 a person and hot showers for Dr 5 more. At that price, some of the other places are definitely better. One of these is the *Hotel Andaluz*, which costs Dr 30 a double; there are no singles. The rooms all face an internal courtyard and while those on the upper floor are light and airy, the ones on the ground floor are dark and gloomy. Hot showers are available for Dr 5.

Another place travellers zero in on is the *Pension Mauritania*, Zankat al-Qadi, which offers singles/doubles for Dr 25/50 including a good breakfast. The staff are friendly and there's a beautiful traditional lounge area. Also good value is the *Pension Znika*, north of the kasbah, which is spotlessly clean, light and airy and costs Dr 20 a person. Hot showers are available on the ground floor.

Up in the higher reaches of the medina, with good views and the chance of a breeze, is the *Pension Valencia*. The doubles and triples are clean, simple and good value at Dr 35/50, but the singles are glorified cupboards. The communal showers and toilets are well maintained. To find the Valencia, take the lane off to the north from Plaza Uta el-Hammam; it twists back and forth up the hill but after a few minutes you come to the Restaurant Granada. From there take the left fork and follow it around to the right.

Just inside the Bab al-'Ain on the right is the *Hotel Bab El Ain* (☎ 986935), which is a little expensive at Dr 50 a head, but is clean and comfortable with occasional hot water. A little farther up is the *Hotel Abie Khanda* (☎ 986879). The rooms are clean and bright and there is a roof terrace and hot water some of the time. The beds are a little on the rock-hard side, but it's not a bad deal at Dr 30 a person.

Outside the medina area below (south of) the Bab al-'Ain is the *Hotel Sahra*, which also has singles/doubles for Dr 20/30. It's a little gloomy and doesn't have the atmosphere of the pensions in the medina. Farther south is the noisily located *Hotel Ketama*, which doesn't have a whole lot to recommend it either, especially at Dr 30/40 – the medina places are better.

North-east of Plaza de Makhzen is the *Pension al-Hamra* (☎ 986362). It's a quiet place away from the bulk of the tourist trade and is OK at Dr 30/60. Hot showers are Dr 5. A bit farther along towards Bab al-Ansar is the *Hostal Gernika* (☎ 987434), which is run by two Spanish women. It has 10 rooms, some with private shower. They have hot water and prices range from Dr 60 for a single to Dr 120 for a double.

Outside the medina again is the *Hotel Salam* (☎ 986239) on Avenida Hassan II. At Dr 40/58, it is a pretty good deal. It has hot water most of the time and its own restaurant. If you're lucky, you'll get a room with a decent view over the valley to the south, or you can get the same view from the terrace.

The *Hôtel Marrakech* (☎ 987113) opened virtually next door in 1992 and provides tough competition for the Salam. Rooms without private shower go for Dr 50/100 and with shower for Dr 60/120. They are a little small, but modern, clean and comfortable. Breakfast costs an extra Dr 15.

Off to the north-west of the town centre on the long and winding road to the Hotel Asma is the *Residencia La Estrella* (☎ 986526) on Blvd Sidi Abdel Hamid. It's some way out and doesn't have a lot of character, but the rooms, at Dr 60 a head, are quite comfortable and the place has a homey atmosphere. It's equipped with a kitchen, so those wanting to do their own cooking could find it ideal.

Places to Stay – middle

The *Hotel Sevilla* (☎ 986911) on Avenida Allal ben Abdallah is a good choice if you can pay just a little extra. Rooms are basically Dr 70 per person, but in the low season management can be persuaded to lower the price. The rooms are modern and comfortable, and reasonably spacious. Some have private toilet and others have a shower as well. The main problem seems to be hot water – they promise it all day, but it never happens. The tearoom downstairs has an extremely low ceiling and satellite TV.

A long-time favourite with travellers has been the *Hotel Rif* (☎ 986207), just below the city walls on Avenida Hassan II. They've jacked their prices up considerably, so it's not the good value it once was. Rooms, some with a valley view, cost Dr 100/150/235 with hot water and the obligatory breakfast.

For a little more you can go to the *Hotel Magou* (☎ 986275), near the market at 23 Calle Moulay Idriss. In the low season it charges Dr 117/145/205 for decent rooms that sometimes have central heating; there is hot water in the mornings. Prices go up considerably in summer.

Another recent addition to Avenida Hassan II's hotel population is the *Hotel Madrid* (☎ 987498). The rooms are spotless and have heaters in winter. You pay Dr 120/184/246.

Places to Stay – top end

The cheapest of the top-end hotels is the three-star *Hotel Asma* (☎ 986002, 986265), a huge concrete structure overlooking the town, above the cemetery. It has 94 very pleasant, self-contained rooms, a bar and restaurant, though meals in the restaurant are very pricey at a minimum of Dr 100. The rooms are Dr 226/273. The disadvantage of staying here is the distance from town. The advantage is the views – especially at night.

Avoid having laundry done here, however, as the rates are extortionate.

The most expensive hotel in Chefchaouen is the four-star *Hotel Parador* (☎ 986324, 986136), on Place de Makhzen, which costs Dr 302/377 for singles/doubles. The hotel has its own bar and restaurant and all the usual facilities you would expect of a hotel at this price.

Places to Eat

Among the cafés on Plaza Uta el-Hammam are a number of small restaurants that serve good local food. You are looking at about Dr 20 for a full meal with soft drink.

Up near the Pension Valencia, the *Restaurant Granada* is run by a cheery character who cooks a variety of dishes at reasonable prices. A block back down is a reasonable place recommended by locals, the *Restaurant Chez Fouad*. Prices are roughly the same as in the Granada and the food is equally good. Another one worth checking out if you're in the area is the *Maravilia*, opposite the fountain on the tiny square.

The *Restaurant Assaada*, just inside the Bab al-'Ain to the left, serves decent food at modest prices.

Outside the medina, just up the hill from the Bab al-'Ain, are Chefchaouen's best eateries: the *Restaurant Moulay Ali ben Rachid* and the *Restaurant Zouar* – take your pick. They are simple and very good – and usually full of Spaniards down for a short holiday. The Zouar has a filling set menu for Dr 25, and both offer good mains for around Dr 15. Even if the food were bad, it would be hard to argue with the price.

For something of a splurge, try the *Restaurant Chefchaouen* on the street leading up to Plaza de Makhzen. It's pleasantly designed in traditional style, but don't come here for breakfast as it will take forever to arrive. A full meal (soup, tajine/couscous and fruit) for lunch or dinner costs Dr 50.

More expensive is the *Restaurant Tissemlal*, 22 Rue Targui, just up from Plaza Uta el-Hammam and off to the right. Like the Chefchaouen, this restaurant has been beautifully conceived and even has an upstairs balcony running the whole way around. The service is quick but the food, unfortunately, is only average. You're looking at Dr 70 for a full lunch.

A cheerfully enough decorated but over-priced (for what you get) restaurant is the *El Baraka*, near the Hotel Andaluz. At Dr 70, the rather ordinary set menu is hardly breath-taking.

The hotels *Rif*, *Salam*, *Marrakech* and *Madrid* all have decent restaurants, although the Madrid is pricier than the rest. For those with fatter wallets, there are also the top-end hotels.

Drinkers have few choices. Aside from the bar on Avenida Hassan II, you are virtually obliged to try the two big hotels.

The *Pâtisserie Magou* on Avenida Hassan II has good pastries and fresh bread.

Most of the cafés on Plaza Uta el-Hammam have seedy rooms upstairs where the hard smoking goes on – you can just about cut the air with a knife in some of them – and there are certainly worse ways to pass a few hours than to sit around playing dom-inoes with the locals.

Getting There & Away

Bus The new bus station is about a 20-minute walk south-west of the town centre. CTM and all other buses leave from here but be warned: many of them are through ser-vices from elsewhere and are often full on arrival. Since it is not always possible to book, you could easily be in for a long wait.

CTM has a bus to Casablanca (Dr 79) via Ouezzane (Dr 16.50), Souq Arba'a, Kenitra and Rabat at 6.30 am. There are buses to Fès (Dr 42; 4½ hours) via Ouezzane at 1.15 and 3.30 pm. You can book in advance for the first but not the second service. They come from Tetouan, and CTM only has six seats reserved in advance from Chefchaouen.

The easiest place to get to is Tetouan (departures at 7.30 and 8.45 am, and noon, 3, 4 and 7 pm). The fare is Dr 16.50. There is a bus at 3 pm to Tangier.

Three buses a day head to Ketama and Al-Hoceima; two of them continue on to Nador. There is one bus to Taza.

Other companies are represented at three other windows. The timetables are posted and it's all quite easy to follow. However, you can't *book* to, say, Fès (the most popular destination), for which all services are through buses from Tetouan.

At window No 2 they sell tickets for Fès buses at 9.30 and 11.45 am and 1.15 pm. Since you can't book and they often arrive from Tetouan full (in spite of what they will tell you at the window), you could be in trouble. If this happens and you decide only then that you want one of the above CTM buses, you will have to fight with everyone else to get one of the six seats on the 1.15 pm bus or just wait and hope for the 3.30 pm bus. It is easy to see how you could end up stuck at the station for the day trying to get to Fès!

At window No 2 they also have eight runs to Tetouan (Dr 15); three to Fnideq (Ceuta) at 6 and 11.15 am and 12.30 pm (Dr 22); and two to Tangier via Tetouan (Dr 26) at 9.30 am and 2.45 pm. Window No 4 has another six buses to Tangier via Tetouan.

Window No 3 has seven runs to Ouezzane (Dr 15; 1½ hours) and five to Tetouan. At 7.30 am they have a bus to Casablanca (Dr 62) via Souq Arba'a, Kenitra and Rabat.

There are three buses to Meknès, at 6 am, noon and 4 pm (Dr 45; four hours). The first and last of these stop at Moulay Idriss. These buses are far less likely to be full than the Fès buses, and a lot of locals catch them and link up with the frequent transport to Fès from Meknès. This is not a bad tip if the morning bus to Fès comes and goes without you on it and you're staring at a day spent fruitlessly at Chefchaouen bus station.

If you get the feeling the Fès *and* Meknès buses are all going to be full, catch a bus (or grand taxi in the morning) to Ouezzane and try again from there.

Taxi Grands taxis go to Tetouan (Dr 20) and Ouezzane only (from near the old CTM offices, about 50 metres west of the Hotel Sevilla). To Ouezzane they cost about Dr 25 per person. They don't go all that often, so be there early. For any other destinations you'll have to bargain for a special deal.

Ouezzane is a bit of a transport hub, so it could be worth the trip there just to pick up something going farther your way (Fès or Rabat for instance).

OUEZZANE

Lying in the plains at the southern edge of the Rif, Ouezzane is another town to which Andalusian refugees, many of them Jews, fled in the 15th century. Muslims regard it as a holy city, with a zawiyya dedicated to the memory of Moulay Abdallah ben Brahim, one of several contenders for supremacy in the chaotic Morocco of the early 18th century. His moussem is celebrated in late March. Jews too make an annual pilgrimage (around May) to visit the tomb of Rabbi Amrane ben Diwan, an Andalusian 'miracle worker' who died in about 1780 and whose tomb lies nine km north-west of Ouezzane off the road to Rabat, in the Jewish cemetery of Azjem.

The bus and grand taxi lot is a huge dirt patch to the north-west of the central Place de l'Indépendance. The small medina, the southern half of which forms the old Jewish quarter (the mellah), lies to the south-east. North of the medina are the **Moulay Abdallah Sherif Mosque** and the **Mosque of the Zawiyya**, which is also known as the Green Mosque. If you enter the Bab ash-Shurfa, the main gate in the south-eastern corner of the square, you'll find yourself walking through the metalworkers' market and soon after across into the woodworkers' market. There are a few places where rugs and the like can be bought, and you're bound to meet one of the town's two or three guides pretty soon. With so few travellers coming through, you could well strike a good bargain for a carpet.

Information

There is a bank and post office on the main road leading north off Place de l'Indépendance.

Places to Stay & Eat

Of the three hotels on the southern end of Place de l'Indépendance, the *Hôtel El Alam* is possibly the best. It has clean rooms around an open courtyard on the top floor and shared cold showers and toilets for Dr 30/50/70. The *Grand Hôtel* is also OK but *L'Horloge*, at Dr 30 for awful rooms, is to be avoided.

There are a few cafés and snack stands on the square. For a classy view of the northern plains, head through Bab ash-Shurfa and after a couple of hundred metres you'll come to the *Café Bellevue* on your right.

Getting There & Away

Bus The station is a mucky old affair, and confusion seems to reign. There are buses

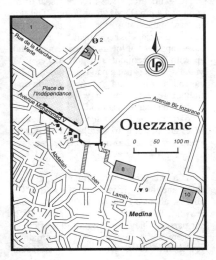

Ouezzane

0   50   100 m

1	Bus & Grand Taxi Station
2	Bank
3	Post Office
4	Hôtel l'Horloge
5	Hôtel El Alam
6	Grand Hôtel
7	Bab ash-Shurfa
8	Mosque of the Zawiyya
9	Café Bellevue
10	Moulay Abdallah Sherif Mosque

from Ouezzane to Casablanca, Rabat, Fès, Meknès, Chefchaouen (Dr 15 to Dr 16.50), Tetouan and Tangier.

Ouezzane is a bit of a crossroads and if you are losing hope of getting out of Chefchaouen to head south, it might be worth trying your luck here. There is no guarantee, and the earlier you start the better. There are virtually no buses after 5 pm.

Taxis Grands taxis run from the bus station to Fès (Dr 60), Rabat (Dr 50) and Chefchaouen (Dr 25). They are not that frequent, but if you get there in the morning you should be able to pick up something, as most people just pass through Ouezzane.

KETAMA

Instead of heading south out of the Rif from Chefchaouen towards Ouezzane and on to the coast or the Middle Atlas, you could turn east instead and plunge into the heart of the Rif and on to a couple of minor Mediterranean resorts. Buses head right across to Al-Hoceima and Nador via Ketama, and the ride along what is virtually the backbone of the Rif is among the most breathtaking trips in the country. The first stop might be Ketama, but there is little reason for getting off here, and you could be inviting hassles. This is the centre of kif country, and it will be assumed you've come to buy a load, which might have unpleasant consequences (see Dangers & Annoyances in the Facts for the Visitor chapter).

AL-HOCEIMA

Set on a bay at one of the rare points along the coast where the Rif drops away and makes a little room for beaches, Al-Hoceima is a relaxed and largely modern town. Founded in 1920 by a Spanish officer, General Sanjuro, it was known initially as Villa Sanjuro. The fact that the Rif rebel Abd el-Krim had, from 1921 to 1926, one of his main bases only 10 km away at Ajdir shows how tenuous was Spain's hold over this part of its protectorate after 1912.

Orientation

Al-Hoceima only began to grow after Spain pulled out in the wake of Morocco's accession to independence in 1956, and now numbers about 60,000 inhabitants. The Spanish influence remains – all the streets seem to be 'calles' here – but all new construction is resolutely cheap North African style. The main attraction is the couple of small beaches, making Al-Hoceima a pleasant stop while en route east or west through the Rif. In high summer it fills up with Moroccan holiday-makers and European charter tourists. What attracts the latter is hard to guess (boastful tourist-office pamphlets?), for while it is a pleasant enough place to rest up while touring the country, it's hardly one of the Mediterranean's great package resorts.

Most of the banks, better hotels and restaurants are on or near Calle Mohammed V, the main road in from Nador. Just east of this road, as you enter the town proper, is the old village centre, with the budget hotels and eateries, as well as all transport. Apart from the town beach, Plage Quemado, there are a couple of quieter ones a few km out of town on the Nador road. From some vantage points you can see the Spanish-controlled islet of Peñon de Alhucemas off the coast. It may look pretty, but it has served mainly as a prison and military base.

Information

Tourist Office The Délégation Régionale du Tourisme (☎ 982830) is on Calle Tariq ibn Ziad, and is open Monday to Thursday from 8.30 am to noon and 2.30 to 6.30 pm, and Friday from 8.30 to 11 am and 3 to 6.30 pm. They have colourful brochures but little else.

Money There are plenty of banks along Calle Mohammed V, where you can change cash and travellers' cheques. You can get cash advances on Visa and MasterCard at the BMCE and BMCI.

Post & Telecommunications The post and telephone office is on Calle Moulay Idriss

Alkbar, a few blocks west of Calle Moham-med V.

Beaches

The town beach, Plage Quemado, is OK but with the large ugly hotel of the same name forming the main backdrop, it is a little off-putting. Better are the small beaches at **Cala Bonita** (where there is a camp site), before the southern entry into town, and **Plage Sebadella**, about a two-km walk to the north-west. **Plage Espalmadero**, four km from the centre of town along the road to Nador, and **Plage Asfiha**, five km farther on,

are usually fairly quiet, especially in late spring. Local buses to Ajdir run by the turn-offs for both. Neither will win beautiful beach prizes, but they're OK.

Places to Stay – bottom end

Camping The *Camping Cala Bonita* is right on what is probably the prettiest little beach in Al-Hoceima (the name is Spanish for 'pretty cove'). Unlike at other camp sites in the country, there is a simple flat fee of Dr 45 for a place. This includes tent space, car and amenities. About a km from the town centre on the road to Ajdir, it is a nice spot.

Al-Hoceima

PLACES TO STAY
8 Hotel Quemado
13 Hôtel/Café Marrakech
21 Hôtel Al-Maghreb el-Jadid
24 Hôtel National
26 Hôtel Rif
27 Hôtel Karim
30 Hôtel de Station
31 Hotel Florido
32 Hôtel Al Manar
33 Hôtel Afrique
36 Hôtel Ketama
37 Hôtel Assalam
38 Hôtel Oriente
39 Hôtel Populaire
40 Hotel Bilbao

PLACES TO EAT
4 Snack Aladin
6 Restaurant La Belle Vue
7 Café Hyatt Regency
14 Café Agadir
17 Café La Perle
19 Restaurant Al-Maghreb al-Kabir
20 Pâtisserie Maghreb al-Fain
22 Snack Assaada
34 Restaurant Mabrouk
35 Restaurant Al-Hoceima
41 Restaurant Paris
42 Restaurant Familial

OTHER
1 Tourist Office
2 Football Ground
3 Sûreté Nationale (Police)
5 Bank al-Maghrib
9 BMCE
10 Church
11 Post & Telephone Office (PTT)
12 Salon de Thé Badr
15 Banque Commerciale du Maroc
16 Baño Popular (Hammam)
18 Mosque
23 Liquor Store
25 CTM Bus Station
28 Total Service Station
29 BMCI
32 Grands Taxis
34 Grands Taxis

Hotels There is no shortage of budget hotels in the area immediately around Place du Rif, but things can still get crowded in midsummer. The *Hôtel Populaire* is about as cheap as they come at Dr 20 a person, but that's all you can really say about the place.

A fairly decent choice is the *Hôtel Rif* (☎ 982268) on Calle Sultan Moulay Youssef, which is away from the chaos of the square. Simple rooms with a washbasin cost Dr 30/40. There are cold communal showers.

On the square itself is a curious Art Deco building called the *Hotel Florido* (☎ 982 235). The better rooms look on to the square, and it was getting a paint job at the time of writing. Rooms cost Dr 30 a head and there are cold showers along the corridor.

Although the beds are a tad hard, the nearby *Hôtel Afrique* (☎ 983065) can be recommended. The rooms are clean and bright and cost Dr 31/42. Again, it has only cold showers. Not so great is the *Hôtel Assalam*, which has singles/doubles for Dr 40/60. Others to choose from around here are the *Hotel Oriente*, *Hôtel de Station*, *Hôtel al-Manar*, *Hôtel Ketama* (dive) and *Hotel Bilbao*.

Places to Stay – middle

About the cheapest of the mid-range hotels and good value is the *Hôtel Marrakech* (☎ 983025) on Calle Mohammed V. Rooms with comfortable beds, sea glimpses and en suite bathroom (hot water 24 hours a day) cost Dr 110/127.

For a little more (Dr 123/152), the *Hôtel Karim* (☎ 982184; fax 984340), 27 Calle Hassan II, is also a decent investment in comfort. Rooms have en suite bathrooms and phone and the staff are obliging.

The *Hôtel National* (☎ 982681), closer to public transport, is perfectly all right, with singles/doubles/triples costing Dr 157/187/299.

Not spectacularly better than the others, but considerably pricier, is the *Hôtel Al-Maghreb el-Jadid* (☎ 982504) on Calle Mohammed V. It has self-contained rooms for Dr 196/237 in the low season and Dr 226/273 in the high season. All prices are

exclusive of taxes. The hotel has a bar on the 4th floor.

If you want to pay that much, you may as well head for the *Hotel Quemado* (☎ 983315) on the beach, where the rooms are not quite as good but you do wake up next to the Mediterranean.

Places to Stay – top end

There is a *Club Med* about 11 km south-east of town near Ajdir.

Places to Eat

For breakfast and a spot of people-watching, you could do worse than the *Pâtisserie Maghreb al-Fain* on Calle Mohammed V. Several other cafés and salons de thé are scattered about the town.

There are numerous little restaurants serving up the usual fare for about Dr 25 to Dr 30 on or near Place du Rif. Two that are reasonable are the *Restaurant Familial* and *Restaurant Paris* on Calle Mohammed V. *Snack Assaada* on Calle Hassan II serves various meats by weight. A filling meal with salad, chips and a soft drink will cost about Dr 25.

A generous meal of brochettes on a bed of rice, with chips, costs about Dr 35 in the *Restaurant Al-Maghreb Al-Kabir* next door to the pâtisserie. The *Restaurant La Belle Vue*, also on Calle Mohammed V, is another option, or you could try one of the better hotels. One of the few bars around is in the *Hôtel Al-Maghreb el-Jadid*. There's also a liquor store around the corner from the Hôtel Rif on Calle Hassan II.

Getting There & Away

Air RAM has one or two weekly flights from Al-Hoceima to Tangier, Tetouan and Casablanca. There is also a weekly flight to Amsterdam (why?). In summer the airport, 17 km to the south-east, plays host to charter flights, mainly from France.

Bus All the bus companies have their offices on or near Place du Rif. CTM has buses to Nador at 5.30 am and 12.30 pm (Dr 35.50; 3½ hours). Its services to Tetouan (Dr

102.50; eight hours) via Chefchaouen (Dr 49; about five hours) leave at 9 and 10 pm. At 8 pm a CTM bus leaves for Casablanca (Dr 140.50; 11 hours) via Fès, Meknès and Rabat.

There are three or four other small companies. As always, it's best to turn up in the morning and check out what's going. Nador is the most frequently served destination, with at least six departures apart from the CTM ones. Fares range from Dr 29 to Dr 32. Buses to Fès (Dr 63.50) via Ketama (Dr 30) and Taounate (Dr 46) along the Route de l'Unité highway (a spectacular drive over the Rif) leave at 3.15 and 9.45 am; obviously, the first of these is not much good for enjoying the scenery. There is a bus for Oujda at 11 am (Dr 55; about six hours). Alternatively, go to Nador and pick up further transport there. Buses to Tetouan via Chefchaouen leave at 7 and 8 am and 7 pm. Another goes through to Tangier at 8 am (Dr 74; about 11 hours). Buses to Targuist leave four times a day and cost Dr 16.50.

Taxi The best time to try to get a grand taxi is the morning, but you may find yourself hanging about for one to fill up. They line up on the street in front of the Hôtel al-Manar and Restaurant Mabrouk. The fare to Taza and Nador is Dr 50.

The East Coast

MELILLA

Melilla is marginally smaller than its Spanish sister enclave to the west, Ceuta, with about 70,000 inhabitants, a third of whom are Muslims of Rif Berber origin. The presence of 10,000 troops provides a boost to the local economy, but Melilla lives mainly from contraband trade. Anything up to 80% of the goods that arrive in the enclave end up not only in Morocco, but in countries throughout north-west Africa. Some people within Melilla's business community worry that a free-trade agreement between the EU and Morocco could kill this business, leaving

Melilla in deep trouble – it already has an unemployment rate higher than any city in the EU.

Relations between the Muslim population, worst hit by the unemployment, and the rest of the enclave's inhabitants are strained. The ill-feeling bubbled over into violent protests in the 1980s when new citizenship laws threatened to leave many Muslims without proper papers in limbo.

Spaniards in the enclave also worry that the Muslims will one day push for the enclave to be handed over to Morocco. Most of the Muslims say this is rubbish, that as Rif Berbers they owe no allegiance to the Moroccan king and that in any case they would prefer to be under Spanish rule. Other Spaniards fear that, with their big families, the Muslims will eventually outnumber the Christians and gain power. Melilla, like Ceuta, lives under a cloud of uncertainty.

The city also leaves the visitor with equally ambiguous impressions. Uncompromisingly Spanish in look and feel, and not a little run down, the presence of so many Muslims (some of them Moroccans who have slipped across the border), most of whom are underemployed or jobless, lends it an atmosphere quite unlike that of any city on the peninsula.

History

The port and peninsula of Melilla have been inhabited for more than 2000 years. The Phoenicians and Romans both counted it among their network of Mediterranean coastal bases – it was then known as Russadir. After the departure of the Romans, the city fell into obscurity until it was captured by Abd ar-Rahman III of Cordova. In 1496 it was taken by a Spanish raiding party and has remained in Spain's hands ever since. Abd el-Krim's rebels came close to taking the town during the Rif war in 1921, and it was from here that Franco launched the Spanish Civil War in 1936.

Its excellently preserved medieval fortress gives the city a lingering fascination. Right up until the end of the 19th century virtually all of Melilla was contained within these

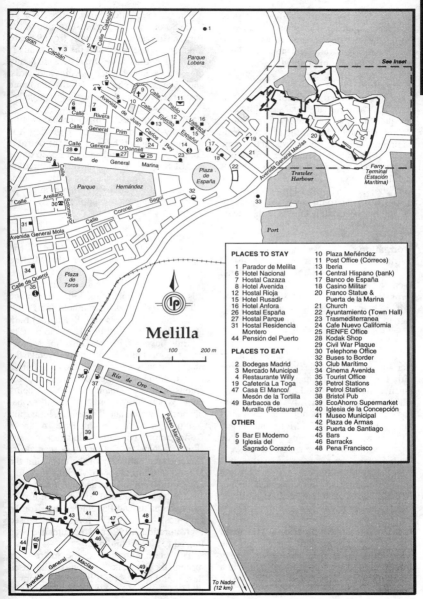

Melilla

0   100   200 m

To Nador
(12 km)

PLACES TO STAY

1 Parador de Melilla
6 Hotel Nacional
7 Hostal Cazaza
8 Hotel Avenida
12 Hotel Rioja
15 Hotel Rusadir
16 Hotel Anfora
26 Hostal España
27 Hostal Parque
31 Hostal Residencia
   Montero
44 Pensión del Puerto

PLACES TO EAT

2 Bodegas Madrid
3 Mercado Municipal
4 Restaurante Willy
19 Cafetería La Toga
47 Casa El Manco/
   Mesón de la Tortilla
49 Barbacoa de
   Muralla (Restaurant)

OTHER

5 Bar El Moderno
9 Iglesia del
   Sagrado Corazón
10 Plaza Meñéndez
11 Post Office (Correos)
13 Iberia
14 Central Hispano (bank)
17 Banco de España
18 Casino Militar
20 Franco Statue &
   Puerta de la Marina
21 Church
22 Ayuntamiento (Town Hall)
23 Trasmediterranea
24 Cafe Nuevo California
25 RENFE Office
28 Kodak Shop
29 Civil War Plaque
30 Telephone Office
32 Buses to Border
33 Club Marítimo
34 Cinema Avenida
35 Tourist Office
36 Petrol Stations
37 Petrol Station
38 Bristol Pub
39 EcoAhorro Supermarket
40 Iglesia de la Concepción
41 Museo Municipal
42 Plaza de Armas
43 Puerta de Santiago
45 Bars
46 Barracks
48 Pena Francisco

massive defensive walls. This old part of town has a distinctly Castilian flavour, with its narrow, twisting streets, squares, gates and drawbridges, and the area has been declared a national monument.

Orientation

Plaza de España is the heart of the new part of town, which was largely designed by Don Enrique Nieto, a contemporary of Gaudí. Most of the hotels are in the grid of streets leading north-west of the plaza. In the same area you'll find banks and other offices, and most of the restaurants and bars. East of Melilla la Vieja (the old town) lies the ferry port; the frontier with Morocco is a 20-minute bus ride south, over the trickle of effluent inappropriately known as the Río de Oro.

Information

Tourist Office The tourist office (☎ 684013) is at the junction of Calle de Querol and Avenida General Aizpuru, close to Plaza de Toros (the bullring). It's well stocked and the staff are helpful. Opening hours are roughly 9 am to 2 pm Monday to Friday, and to noon on Saturday.

Money You'll find several banks along or near Avenida de Juan Carlos I Rey, starting with the Central Hispano on Plaza de España, which is as good as any. They buy and sell dirham at a slightly inferior rate to that found in Morocco, but as good as anything you'll get from the Moroccan dealers in the streets. The latter hang about Plaza de España and deal in Algerian dinar as well. Don't believe their stories about the atrocious bank rates – check them first. This will of course be difficult with Algerian dinar, but for these you are better off waiting until you get to Oujda or even Figuig.

Post & Telecommunications The main post office (Correos y Telégrafos), on Calle Pablo Vallescá, is open Monday to Friday from 9 am to 8 pm for ordinary mail, and a little longer for telegrams. It is also open on Saturday mornings.

The main public phone offices are on Calle Sotomayor, on the western side of the Parque Hernández (open daily from 9 am to 2 pm and 6 to 9 pm), and the Teléfonica is just north of the Río de Oro. There are plenty of public phones that accept coins and cards, and from which you can also use the home direct service to make reverse-charge calls.

Petrol & Supplies Remember that Melilla is a duty-free zone. If you are driving it is worth waiting to fill up here, as the petrol is about a third cheaper than in Morocco or the rest of Spain. The EcoAhorro supermarket on the road to the border post of Beni-Enzar is open from 10 am to 10 pm and might be worth checking out for supplies on your way south.

Melilla la Vieja

Under normal conditions, Old Melilla (or, according to some guides, the Medina Sidonia) is well worth exploring for a half-day or so. Perched over the Mediterranean, it is a good example of the kind of 16th and 17th-century fortress stronghold the Portuguese (and in this case the Spaniards) built along the Moroccan littoral. At the time of writing, however, it looked like the Moroccans had just launched an attack to retake the place. Virtually all of the old town is buried in scaffolding and rattles to the sounds of the reconstruction and maintenance work being done. When they've finished, it will probably be a very pleasant, if sanitised, little spot.

Worth a look are the **Iglesia de la Concepción**, with its gilded reredos and shrine to Nuestra Señora la Virgen de la Victoria (the patroness of the city), and the **Museo Municipal** (open Monday to Saturday from 10 am to 1 pm and 5 to 7 pm; entry free), which has a good collection of historical documents and Phoenician and Roman ceramics and coins. The former was closed for restoration in 1994 and the latter had been moved to a new building.

The main entrance to the **fortress** is through the Puerta de la Marina on the Paseo de General Macías (you'll also see a monument to Franco here). After your visit, you could leave by the **Puerta de Santiago**, which takes you west over a couple of draw-bridges and the Plaza de Armas and out by the Foso de Hornabeque.

New Town
Construction of the new part of town, to the west of the fortress, was begun at the end of the 19th century. It was laid out by Don Enrique Nieto, who, following Gaudí's lead, is considered by some to have made of Melilla Spain's 'second modernist city' after Barcelona – a somewhat inflated boast. A combination of shiny duty-free shopfronts and general decay has failed to rob the area entirely of its charm, and travellers arriving from Morocco (especially the likes of Nador) will hardly fail to notice the difference.

A walk around can be instructive in the city's more recent past. A statue on Avenida de Juan Carlos I Rey and a plaque you can see opposite the Parque Hernández on Calle de General Marina celebrate 7 July 1936, the day Franco began the campaign against the government in Madrid, with the cry of 'Viva España'.

Beaches
For the desperate, there is a string of beaches south of the Río de Oro to the border. They are hardly special – you would be better off heading for mainland Spain or continuing on into Morocco.

Places to Stay – bottom end
If you're coming from Morocco, you'll know you've arrived in Europe when you look for a place to stay. Hotels at all levels charge a little more in the high season (summer and Easter week). The cheapest option is the *Pensión del Puerto*, a largely Moroccan establishment just back from Paseo de General Macías. A bed should cost less than 1000 pta, but it's a little rough and seems to serve as a brothel too.

Easily the best place for the tight budget is the *Hostal Rioja* (☎ 682709), at 6 Calle Ejército Español. It has decent singles/doubles for 2000/3000 pta outside the high

season, with communal hot showers. It's a friendly place with a homey atmosphere.

Another decent alternative for about the same money is the *Hostal Parque* (☎ 682 143), which fronts the Parque Hernández and is often full. Not such good value, but acceptable, is the *Hostal Cazaza* (☎ 684648) on Calle Rivera. Gloomy doubles with basin only are 3850 pta. Those with shower cost 4500 pta. A block west and a little better, depending on which rooms you end up with, is the *Hotel Nacional* (☎ 684540/1) on Calle Rivera. Pokey singles start at 2200 pta, and comfortable doubles with en suite bathrooms and balconies range from 4500 to 5700 pta, depending on the season. The *Hotel España*, on Avenida de Juan Carlos I Rey, seems to be closed.

Places to Stay – middle
Heading up the price scale is the *Hotel Avenida* (☎ 684949), on Avenida de Juan Carlos I Rey. It has singles/doubles for 3970/6930 pta. In a similar bracket is the *Hotel Anfora* (☎ 683340), on Calle Pablo Vallescá. Across the road is the still more expensive *Hotel Rusadir* (☎ 681240).

Places to Stay – top end
The *Parador of Melilla* (☎ 684940; fax 683486), one of a series of top-class hotels around Spain, is the top of the tree here, with a pool and views over the Mediterranean, but with an uninspired concrete exterior. Singles (without a sea view) start at 6900 pta and doubles go up to 12,000 pta.

Places to Eat
Any of the bars is decent for a morning coffee and pastry, but if you want churros and hot chocolate, head for *Cafetería La Toga* on Plaza de Don Pedro de Estopiñán.

The best area to search for good cheap bocadillos and the like is along Calle Castelar, not far from the Mercado Municipal (food market). The *Bodegas Madrid*, with its old wine casks for tables, is easily the most popular spot here for a beer and a bite.

For mostly seafood snacks, the *Bar El Moderno* is open until midnight, when most of the rest are firmly shut. Across the road is a pretty decent pizza place, the *Restaurante Willy*, where a filling small pizza will cost from 450 to 550 pta.

There are countless other bars and the odd restaurant where you can get a meal in the streets around Avenida de Juan Carlos I Rey.

In Melilla la Vieja, search out the *Casa El Manco/Mesón de la Tortilla*. Like the whole area, it was closed for refurbishment at the time of writing, but it's worth tracking down when open.

For a splurge, you can't beat the *Barbacoa de Muralla*, in the southernmost corner of Melilla la Vieja.

Entertainment

Apart from exploring the many bars and cafés around the centre of town and joining in the evening *paseo* (promenade), you could try a folk-music club such as the *Peña Francisco* (or *Peña Flamenca)* inside the fortress (see map). The *Bristol* is a popular drinking hole on the road to the border. Of the various discos and disco-pubs (a Spanish speciality), *Logüeno*, on the Carretera de Alfonso XIII, and *El Paraíso*, on Calle de General Polavieja, are locally recommended.

The *Casino Militar*, on Plaza de España, has a Centro Cultural de los Ejércitos, which occasionally stages little art exhibits.

Getting There & Away

Air Iberia, the Spanish national carrier, has an office on Avenida de Juan Carlos I Rey. The one-way fare to Málaga is 8800 pta, and there are numerous daily flights (except in bad weather) on 46-seat Fokkers. There's a flight a day to Almería (8500 pta). To Madrid there are up to six daily flights, and tickets cost 23,000 pta one way.

Bus & Taxi Local buses (catch the one marked for 'Aforos') run between Plaza de España and the Beni-Enzar border post from about 7.30 am to late evening. From where the buses stop, it's about 150 metres to Spanish customs and another 200 metres to Moroccan customs. Spanish checks seem largely cursory both ways, but the Moroc-

cans can hold things up for quite a while. Remember that some nationalities require visas to enter Spain (see Foreign Embassies in the Rabat section). If they don't stop you here, they will when you try to move on to the mainland.

Don't give in to Moroccan customs officers suggesting that you'd like to give them a few hundred of your excess dirham 'for a coffee'. Just change it at the bank (if you have an exchange receipt) or deny having any and change it to pesetas in Melilla. You can buy dirham in Melilla or at the Moroccan side of the border (the latter accepts *cash only).*

From Beni-Enzar there are Moroccan local buses (No 19; Dr 2) and grands taxis (Dr 4) to Nador, from where you can catch other buses and grands taxis to a host of destinations farther inside the country (see the following section). If driving in, remember to retain the green customs slip, which you must present when you (and your vehicle) leave Morocco.

Sea Trasmediterranea ferries leave Melilla every night but Sunday for Málaga and Almería. For details, see the Getting There & Away chapter. You can buy tickets at the Trasmediterranea office on Plaza de España (open Monday to Friday from 9 am to 1 pm and 5 to 7 pm, and 9 am to noon Saturday), or direct at the port (Estación Marítima). You can also buy rail tickets for mainland Spain and beyond at the RENFE office on Calle de General O'Donnell. Ferries are sometimes cancelled because of bad weather.

There are fairly thorough passport and customs checks at Melilla (although technically you're travelling inside Spain). Cars are all searched, and the process can delay departure considerably. Similar but less rigorous checks are carried out on arrival in Málaga and Almería.

NADOR

Only the traveller with plenty of time and a love of unloved places would want to do more than catch the first bus or grand taxi out of Nador, a sprawling town set on a lagoon

13 km south of Melilla and earmarked, officially at least, for development as a business centre. Luckily, most of the transport is located in the one place, which makes arriving and leaving comparatively painless tasks. Should you get stuck and have to stay overnight, there is no shortage of hotels of all classes, and quite a few of them are near the bus and grand taxi lots.

Information
The tourist office (☎ 606518) is at 80 Blvd Ibn Rochd. Spain has a consulate in Nador at 12 Rue Mohammed Zerktouni (☎ 606136; fax 606152).

Getting There & Away
Bus The bus station (gare routière) is down by the lagoon, south of the city centre. CTM and other lines run from here. Heading westwards, there are bus services to Al-Hoceima at 7 and 9.30 am, and noon, 2.45, 4.45 and 5 pm. The trip takes about 3½ hours. Beyond Al-Hoceima, there are buses to Tetouan via Ketama and Chefchaouen at 5.30 and 8 am, and 6, 7 and 9.30 pm. Even if you're only going to Chefchaouen this is a long trip, and breaking it up with a stop in Al-Hoceima is worth thinking about.

Buses to Taza leave at 1 and 1.40 pm. For those who are in a hurry, there are through services to Fès (6.30 and 8 am, noon, 4 pm and midnight), Meknès (5, 9 and 10.30 am), Rabat (2, 7 and 8 pm), Casablanca (4, 5, 8 and 8.30 pm) and Tangier (4.15 am and 4, 5 and 9.30 pm). There are at least 10 runs a day to Oujda (about 2½ hours) between 6 am and 5 pm.

CTM's fares include Al-Hoceima (Dr 35.50), Oujda (Dr 23.50), Chefchaouen (Dr 84), Rabat (Dr 131) and Casablanca (Dr 152.50).

Train It is possible to get a Supratours bus to Taourirt to catch connecting trains going west to Fès and beyond or east to Oujda. The bus leaves Nador at 7.30 pm and you buy a ticket for the bus and train to the destination you want. The same trip can be done in the other direction (leaving Taourirt at 5 am). As

a rule, it's easier to use buses and grands taxis.

Taxi The main grand taxi lot is across the road from the bus station. Taxis cost Dr 100 per person to Fès, Dr 50 to Taza and Al-Hoceima, and Dr 35 to Oujda. There are usually taxis available to most of these and other destinations until about 8 pm.

To/From Melilla The local bus lot is next to the main bus station. The No 19 regularly makes the 20-minute run to Beni-Enzar for Melilla, but stops operating by about 8 pm. Unfortunately, the grands taxis to the border (Dr 4 for a place) use a lot that is a fair distance from the main grand taxi station. The best way to get between the two is by petit taxi.

SAIDIA
A couple of km short of the Algerian border (you can't cross here) is the charming little seaside town of Saidia. In summer it is often packed with Moroccans, especially during the August traditional music festival, but out of season it's empty and offers a fine sandy beach and crystal-clear water.

There are a few hotels in the town, but they only open for the summer season from mid-June. Saidia's distance from the main Moroccan cities thankfully makes it a spot unlikely to become a huge resort.

Places to Stay & Eat
There are two one-star hotels: the *Hôtel Select* (☎ 623120) and *Hôtel Al-Kalaa* (☎ 625123). If you have a little more money, the *Hôtel Hannour* (☎ 625115), in the centre of town, is probably a better bet, although you're looking at about Dr 100 a head.

There are quite a few little restaurants in the centre of town. The *Restaurant Coq Magique*, which specialises in seafood, and the *Restaurant En-Nassim*, which serves pizzas and crêpes, are both on Blvd Hassan. You can get a drink in a couple of bars, and such nightlife as there is in summer seems to revolve around the Hôtel Hannour and the

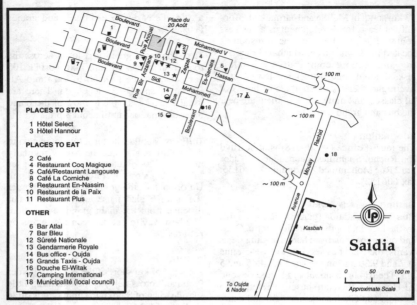

Saidia

PLACES TO STAY
1 Hôtel Select
3 Hôtel Hannour

PLACES TO EAT
2 Café
4 Restaurant Coq Magique
5 Café/Restaurant Langouste
8 Café La Corniche
9 Restaurant En-Nassim
10 Restaurant de la Paix
11 Restaurant Plus

OTHER
6 Bar Atlal
7 Bar Bleu
12 Sûreté Nationale
13 Gendarmerie Royale
14 Bus office - Oujda
15 Grands Taxis - Oujda
16 Douche El-Witak
17 Camping International
18 Municipalité (local council)

Kiss disco, which is about a km west along the beach.

Getting There & Away

Without your own transport, the easiest access to Saidia is from Oujda by bus (Dr 11; at least four a day throughout the year) or grand taxi (Dr 15). See also the Oujda section.

The Middle Atlas & the East

A visit to the Middle Atlas can take in such diverse activities as snow skiing in the exclusive mountain resort of Ifrane, visiting Morocco's best preserved Roman ruins at Volubilis, trekking or simply relaxing in Azrou in the mountains, wandering through the labyrinthine medina of Fès, and visiting Moulay Ismail's huge palace complex at Meknès. From Fès, a natural route leads via Taza and Oujda on the border to Algeria. The road south from Oujda is the easiest way to get to the frontier oasis town of Figuig, reputedly the hottest place in Morocco, and an alternative gateway to Algeria.

Meknès

Although Meknès is thought of by some as the Versailles of Morocco, you could be forgiven for thinking that it hardly warrants that kind of hyperbole. Had the enormous build-ing projects of the Alawite sultan, Moulay Ismail, survived the ravages of time, the comparison might not seem so outlandish today. Although for most people Meknès runs third behind its more illustrious sisters, Marrakesh and Fès, it was the heart of the Moroccan sultanate for a short time and is worth at least a couple of days' exploration. Moreover, it is a convenient base for visiting Volubilis, and the intriguing village of Moulay Idriss, a holy site that contains the tomb of the founder of Morocco's first imperial dynasty.

Surrounded by the rich plains that precede the Middle Atlas Mountains, Meknès is blessed with a hinterland that provides abundant cereal crops, olives, wine, citrus and other agricultural products that have long been the city's economic backbone. The comparative prosperity of the city and the surrounding countryside continues to fuel its population – at last count 735,000 inhabitants and growing.

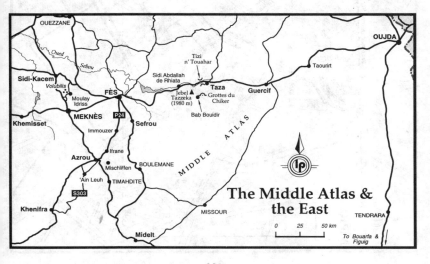

MIDDLE ATLAS

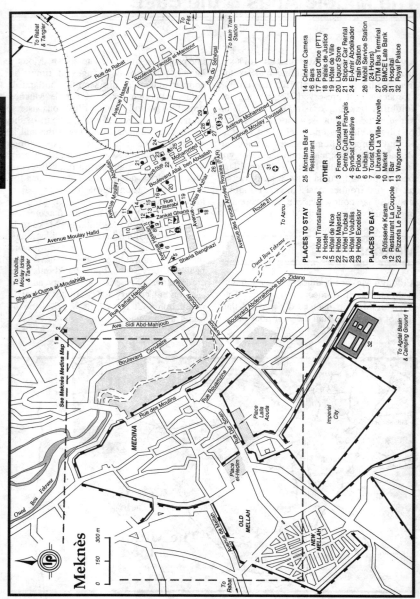

Meknès

0   150   300 m

PLACES TO STAY

1 Hôtel Transatlantique
2 Hostel
15 Hôtel de Nice
25 Hôtel Majestic
27 Hôtel Toubkal
28 Hôtel Volubilis
29 Hôtel Excelsior

PLACES TO EAT

9 Rôtisserie Karam
12 Restaurant La Coupole
23 Pizzeria Le Four

25 Montana Bar & Restaurant

OTHER

3 French Consulate & Centre Culturel Français
4 Syndicat d'Initiative
5 Police
6 Uniban
7 Tourist Office
8 Librairie La Ville Nouvelle
10 Market
11 Bar
13 Wagons-Lits
14 Cinéma Camera
16 Bars
17 Post Office (PTT)
18 Palais de Justice
19 Hôtel de Ville
20 Liquor Store
21 Stopcar Car Rental
24 El-Amir Abdelkader Train Station
26 Mobil Service Station (24 Hours)
27 CTM Bus Terminal
30 BMCE Late Bank
31 Hospital
32 Royal Palace

History

Meknès is a good thousand years old. The Berber tribe of the Meknassis (hence the city's name) first settled here in the 10th century. Under the Almohads and Merenids, the medina was expanded and defensive walls and some of the city's oldest remaining monuments were built. The fall of the Merenids brought a hiatus in the city's fortunes.

It was the accession to power of Moulay Ismail in 1672 on the death of his brother and founder of the Alawite dynasty, Moulay ar-Rashid, that yanked Meknès back from obscurity. He reigned for 55 years and selected Meknès as his capital, which he endowed with an enormous palace complex (which was never finished) and 25 km of imposing walls pierced by monumental gates. That he was able to devote so much energy to construction was partly due to his uncommon success in subduing all opposition in Morocco and keeping foreign meddlers well at bay.

His death in 1727 also struck the death knell for Meknès, as his grandson Mohammed III (1757-90) moved back to Marrakesh. Meknès again became a backwater, and its monuments were, as so often happened in the course of Moroccan history, stripped for materials to build elsewhere. The 1755 earthquake that devastated Lisbon had already dealt Meknès a heavy blow.

The arrival of the protectorate in 1912

Moulay Ismail

Moulay Ismail, the second sultan of the Alawite dynasty (which still rules today), marked his ascent to power at the age of 25 in 1672 in an unforgettable manner. As a warning to unruly tribes, he sent the heads of 10,000 slain enemies to adorn the walls of the two great imperial capitals, Fès and Marrakesh. He had presumably collected these earlier during battles against insurgents in the north of Morocco.

It was the beginning of a particularly gruesome period of rule, even by Moroccan standards, but Moulay Ismail is one of the few Moroccan sultans ever to get the whole country under his control. His cruelty was legendary, and the cheerful ease with which he would lop off the heads of unfortunate servants who displeased him or labourers not working hard enough probably contributed much to his hold over the country.

His first 20 years of rule were taken up with bloody campaigns of pacification. It is difficult to know just how much blood was spilt, but more than 30,000 people are said to have died at his hands alone.

The core of his military success lay in the infamous Black Guard. Having brought some 16,000 slaves from Black Africa, Moulay Ismail guaranteed the continued existence of his elite units by providing the soldiers with women and raising their offspring for service in the guard. By the time of his death, the Black Guard had grown tenfold and resembled a huge family whose upkeep was paid for by the treasury.

In addition to quelling internal rebellion, he chased the Portuguese and English out of Asilah, Larache, Mehdiya and Tangier. Spain managed to hang on to Ceuta, Melilla and Al-Hoceima in spite of unrelenting sieges. Moulay Ismail disposed of the Ottoman Turk threat from Algeria, securing a stable eastern frontier with a string of fortifications centred on Taza, and established a virtual protectorate over modern Mauritania.

A contemporary of Louis XIV of France, the Sun King, Moulay Ismail was at least partly inspired by descriptions of Versailles when he planned the construction of his imperial palace and other monuments in Meknès. For decades he tried to secure an alliance with France against Spain, but continued attacks by the corsairs of Salé on French merchant shipping effectively scuppered his hopes. Although both monarchs bestowed presents on each other, Louis XIV stopped short of acceding to Moulay Ismail's request to marry one of his daughters, the Princess of Conti. Not that the sultan was in need of more female company – it is reckoned he had 360 to 500 wives and concubines (depending on which source you believe) and 800 children by the time he died.

To carry out his building plans, he needed plenty of labour, and it is said he used 25,000 Christian prisoners as slave labour in Meknès, in addition to 30,000 common criminals. His great stables (Heri as-Souani) could house 12,000 horses. ■

gave the town a fillip, as the French made it their military headquarters. The army was accompanied by a corps of French farmers, attracted by the good land around the city. Most of their properties were taken over by the Moroccan government after independence in 1956 and leased out to local farmers.

It is only in the past few decades, as the tourist potential of the city has become obvious, that any serious attempts at restoration have taken place.

Orientation

The old medina and the French-built ville nouvelle are neatly divided by the valley of the Oued Bou Fekrane. The (usually dry) riverbed also marks an administrative boundary. The Wilayat Ismailia covers the medina side and the Wilayat al-Menzah the modern side.

Train and CTM bus connections are in the new city, as are most offices and banks. All the more expensive hotels and most of the better restaurants are also in the new city.

All the private bus lines and the main intercity grands taxis use a station on the west side of the medina. The cheap hotels, camping ground and sights are in the old city. It's a 20-minute walk between the old and new cities, but there are regular (and very crowded) local buses as well as petits taxis.

Information

Tourist Office The Délégation Régionale du Tourisme (☎ 524426) is next to the main post office facing Place de France (or Place Administrative) in front of the Hôtel de Ville. It has the usual brochures, and staff will try to answer any questions you may have. Interestingly enough, it has a police list of hustlers (faux guides) operating in the medina, but it seems there is little anyone can or wants to do to haul them into line. It's open Monday to Friday from 8.30 am to noon and 2.30 to 6.30 pm; on Friday it's closed from 11.30 am to 3 pm. The syndicat d'initiative seems to be closed for good.

Money The banks are concentrated in the new city, mainly on Ave Hassan II, Ave Mohammed V and Blvd Allal ben Abdallah. As usual, the BMCE, on Rue Rouamzine near the Hôtel de Paris, is the best bet. Its main branch operates an out-of-hours change office on Ave des FAR, opposite the Hôtel Excelsior, open daily from 10 am to 2 pm and 4 to 8 pm. It also has a couple of ATMs.

The Banque Populaire has a branch on Rue Dar Smen in the old city and the Crédit du Maroc has a branch on the medina side of Ave Moulay Ismail.

Post & Telecommunications The main post office is in the new city on Place de France. It's open from 8.30 am to 12.15 pm and 2.30 to 6.45 pm. The phone office is in the same building and is open daily from 8.30 am to 9 pm. The parcel post and EMS department is around the corner to the left.

There is another large post office in the medina, on Rue Dar Smen, near the corner of Rue Rouamzine.

French Consulate & Cultural Centre The Centre Culturel Français is on the corner of Ave Moulay Ismail and Rue Farhat Hachad. It has a program of films and lectures and a small library. It's open Monday to Saturday from 9 am to noon and 3 to 7 pm. The consulate (☎ 522227) does *not* issue visas – you'll have to go to Fès.

Bookshops & Newsstands If you don't read French or Arabic, there's not much around in terms of books. The Librairie La Ville Nouvelle on Ave Hassan II is one of the better French-language bookshops. There are several newsstands where you can get hold of English-language press, as well as the usual full range of French press. One that is OK is virtually across the road from the Hôtel Majestic on Ave Mohammed V.

Medical Services & Emergencies There are two hospitals in Meknès: the Hôpital Mohammed V (☎ 521134) and the Hôpital Moulay Ismail (☎ 522805). A reasonable pharmacy is the Pharmacie El Kadi Soussi on Ave Hassan II.

Film & Photography There are several places around the ville nouvelle where you can have film developed. There's a Kodak place next door to the Hôtel Majestic.

Travel Agencies Wagons-Lits (☎ 521995) has an office at 1 Zankat Ghana. Wasteels (☎ 523062) is at 45 Ave Mohammed V.

Old City

From the ville nouvelle, you get to the old city by crossing Oued Bou Fekrane along Ave Moulay Ismail.

On the other side, you follow the street up into a little square as it veers to the right. This is Rue Rouamzine, which you take until you get to the post office, at which point you turn left into Rue Dar Smen. Follow this until a great square opens up on your right, Place el-Hedim. The heart of the old medina lies to the north (with the old Jewish quarter, the mellah, to the west). On your left (to the south) Moulay Ismail's imperial city opens up through one of the most impressive monumental gateways in all Morocco, the Bab el-Mansour. Although not as bad as, say, Fès, there are 'guides' in Meknès. If they're going to get you it will most likely be around Rue Dar Smen and Place el-Hedim. Once inside the medina itself, they are few and far between.

Medina

Dar Jamaï Museum Bab el-Mansour opens onto Place el-Hedim. On the far north side of this square is the Dar Jamaï, a palace built in 1882 by the powerful Jamaï family. Two of their number were viziers to Sultan Moulay al-Hassan I in the late 19th century. When the sultan died in 1894, the Jamaï family fell into disgrace, as so often happened in the fickle political atmosphere of the Moroccan court. They lost everything, including their Meknès palace, which went to Al-Maidani al-Glaoui. The French turned it into a military hospital in 1912 and since 1920 it has housed the Administration des Beaux Arts.

The building, which boasts a peaceful Andalusian garden and courtyard, is as interesting as the exhibits. The latter consist largely of Fès ceramics, jewellery (note the silver *sebsi*, for smoking kif), rugs, textiles and woodwork. The domed reception room upstairs is furnished in the style of a well-to-do salon, complete with plush rugs and cushions. It is open daily, except Tuesdays and holidays, from 9 am to noon and 3 to 6.30 pm. Entry costs Dr 10.

Medina Souqs Before plunging into the heart of the old medina from Place el-Hedim, you might want to take a look at the food market west of the square (behind the rows of barber shops), which borders on the old mellah. If you like olives, you'll think you've died and gone to heaven.

The easiest route into the medina proper is through the arch to the left of the Dar Jamaï. If you plunge in here, you will quickly find yourself in among the **carpet shops**. As you walk along the streets, you will occasionally notice covered market areas (or qissariat) off to your right or left. A couple of these are devoted to carpets, and the hard sell is not as hard here as elsewhere. Keeping more or less to the lane you started on, you will emerge at Rue Najarine. Here the carpets give way to textiles and to quite a few shops specialising in babouches. If you follow the street west and veer with it left into Rue Sekkakine, you will find yourself at an exit in the west wall of the medina leading onto the mellah. Virtually opposite it is the **Qissariat ad-Dahab**, the gold and jewellery market.

If you take the exit and follow the lane north hugging the city wall on the outside, you'll go past the colourful nuts and spices souq, a flea market and, a bit farther to the west, Meknès's tanneries. Enter the city again at Bab el-Jedid, and as you pass inside the gate you'll find yourself in a small **musical instruments souq**. Turning left up Rue el-Hanaya, the local-produce markets open up in front of you – this is a cheap place to do your grocery shopping. Eventually, if you continue north, you will arrive at the

Berdaine Mosque and, just beyond it, the city's northernmost gate, **Bab Berdaine**. Outside is a Muslim cemetery, in which is located the tomb and **koubba** (sanctary) of Sidi ben Aissa, who gave rise to one of the more extreme religious fraternities in Morocco. At his moussem, entranced followers would cheerfully digest anything from glass to snakes, but nowadays such practices have been all but suppressed.

You could then proceed straight back down Rue Zaouia Nasseria (which becomes Rue Souika) to get to the Great Mosque and the nearby Medersa Bou Inania.

Medersa Bou Inania The Great Mosque is, of course, closed to non-Muslims, but you can enter the medersa, which was built in the 14th century during the reign of the Merenids. Completed in 1358 by Bou Inan (after whom a more lavish medersa in Fès is also named), the Meknès version of the Qur'anic school is typical of the exquisite interior design that distinguishes Merenid monuments from those of other periods. For some general ideas on the use and layout of the medersa, see the Arts entry in the Facts about the Country chapter. The standard zellij-tile base, stucco middle and carved olive-wood top of the interior walls (only the ceiling is made of cedar) is repeated here in all its elegance. Students aged eight to 10 once lived two to a cell on the ground floor, while older students and teachers lived on the 1st floor. You can climb on to the roof and see the green-tiled roof and minaret of the Great Mosque next door.

The medersa is open daily from 9 am to noon and 3 to 6 pm. Entry is Dr 10. A guide will probably want to show you around for a fee. It's a quick walk back to Place el-Hedim.

Imperial City
Bab el-Mansour The focus of the old city is the massive gate of Bab el-Mansour, the main entrance to Moulay Ismail's 17th-century imperial city that stands opposite Place el-Hedim. The gate is well preserved and lavishly decorated, with (faded) zellij tiles and inscriptions that run right across the

top. The gate was completed by Moulay Ismail's son, Moulay Abdallah.

Koubbat as-Sufara' After passing through Bab el-Mansour and along the *mechouar* (parade ground), where Moulay Ismail reviewed his famed Black regiments, the road runs straight ahead and then round to the right. On the right is an open grass area with a small building, the Koubbat as-Sufara', which was once the reception hall for foreign ambassadors. It's very plain and hardly worth visiting, but beside it is the entrance to an enormous underground granary complete with vents that open onto the surface of the lawn. The popular story has this as a huge prison in which thousands of Christians (most captured by corsairs operating out of Salé) were held captive as slave labour on Moulay Ismail's building schemes. This story has largely been discredited, but it dies hard. Entry to the vaults and the reception hall, open daily from 9 am to noon and 3 to 6 pm, costs Dr 10. Almost directly opposite are royal gardens, which form part of what was Moulay Ismail's imperial city complex. It's off limits.

Mausoleum of Moulay Ismail To the left of the gardens is a more imposing gateway, through which you proceed to the resting place of the man who elevated Meknès to capital in the 17th century. He is generally considered one of the greatest figures in Moroccan history, and perhaps because of this non-Muslims are allowed in to the sanctuary, although only Muslims can visit the tomb itself. The mausoleum, except for the inner sanctuary, is modestly decorated. Entry is free but it's customary to tip the guardian. The mausoleum is open from 9 am to noon and 3 to 6 pm. It's closed on Friday. On the opposite side of the road are a number of craft and carpet shops belonging to a cooperative of artisans. It's worth having a look in these shops because there's an excellent selection of Meknassi specialities and little pressure to buy.

Heri es-Souani & Agdal Basin If you turn

left on leaving the mausoleum and pass under the Bab er-Rih (Gate of the Wind), you have about a 20-minute walk around what remains to this day an official royal residence (no visitors). The complex was known as the Dar el-Makhzen ('the House of the Government'). Follow the street to the end and turn right (you have no choice) and head straight down past the main entrance of the Royal Palace (on the right) and on past the camping ground (on the left). Virtually in front of you are the Heri es-Souani granaries and vaults. The storerooms are impressive in size, and wells for drawing water can still be seen. The first few vaults have been restored, but the stables, which once housed 12,000 horses, stand in partial ruin with no roof, seemingly stretching forever. Such is the atmosphere here that the place vies with Aït Benhaddou (near Ouarzazate) as one of the country's favourite film sets. It is open daily from 9 am to noon and 3 to 6 pm. Entry costs Dr 10.

Another doorway farther around to the Agdal Basin leads upstairs to a charming rooftop café, from where you have sweeping views back towards the Royal Palace and of the Agdal Basin below.

The basin is an enormous stone-lined lake about four metres deep that was once fed by the Oued Bou Fekrane and served as both a reservoir for the sultan's gardens and a pleasure lake.

Places to Stay – bottom end

Camping There is a good, shady camping ground near the Agdal Basin on the south side of the imperial city. It's a long walk to *Camping Agdal*, and a taxi from the train, CTM or private bus stations will cost about Dr 12. The camping ground is a little expensive. It costs Dr 17 per person (Dr 12 for children), Dr 10 to pitch a tent, Dr 17 for a car (Dr 20 camper van), Dr 7 for a hot shower and Dr 10 for electricity.

Hostel The *youth hostel* (☎ 524698) is close to the large Hôtel Transatlantique in the ville nouvelle, about one km from the centre. It's open from 8 to 10 am, noon to 3 pm, and 6 to 10.30 pm except on Sundays, when it's open from 6 to 10 pm only. A dormitory bed costs Dr 20. They also have family rooms for three and four people, which come to Dr 25 per person. Hot water is available.

Hotels – medina Most of the cheapest places are clustered together in the old city along Rue Dar Smen and Rue Rouamzine. The best of the lot and excellent value for money is the *Hôtel Maroc* (☎ 530075), on Rue Rouamzine. It's quiet, clean, pleasantly furnished (all rooms with a washbasin) and most rooms face a well-kept courtyard. The (cold) showers and toilets are clean and well-maintained. It's a bargain at Dr 30/60/70 for singles/doubles/triples. Not as good, but acceptable, is the *Hôtel de Paris*, also on Rue Rouamzine. This is an older hotel with large airy singles/doubles, with a table, chair and washbasin, for Dr 30/50. There are no showers and the loo is decidedly stinky.

The rest of the cheapies are nothing special, and many don't have showers. The *Hôtel Agadir*, Rue Dar Smen, is clean but the rooms are tiny and there are no showers. Rooms cost Dr 30/50. Slightly better but rather gloomy is the nearby *Hôtel Regina*, a cavernous edifice with the air of a Dickensian workhouse. Rooms are overpriced at Dr 40/70, and the bed linen could do with more regular changing. The ground-floor rooms are even darker and danker than those upstairs. Again, there are no showers. The *Hôtel de Meknès*, a few doors away from the Regina, is similar, and charges Dr 30/60. The *Hôtel Nouveau*, opposite the Banque Populaire, is little better and charges Dr 30/50.

You'll be pleased to know the local hammam is close by. It's down an alley between the Hôtel de Paris and the BMCE bank. Look for the yellow signs marked 'Douche' and 'Bain'. The showers are for men only (7 am to 7 pm); they cost Dr 4 and there are small towels and soap if you forget your own. The actual baths are open from noon to 8 pm for women and 8.30 pm to 2 am for men. Another hammam for men only is at the northern end of Rue Ben el-Maacer.

MIDDLE ATLAS

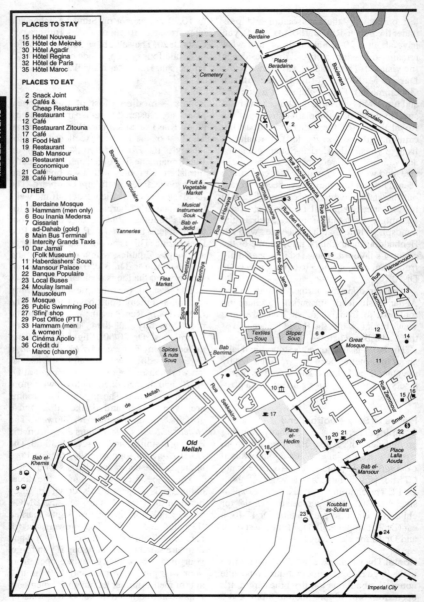

PLACES TO STAY
15 Hôtel Nouveau
16 Hôtel de Meknès
30 Hôtel Agadir
31 Hôtel Regina
32 Hôtel de Paris
35 Hôtel Maroc

PLACES TO EAT
2 Snack Joint
4 Cafés &
   Cheap Restaurants
5 Restaurant
12 Café
17 Restaurant Zitouna
17 Café
18 Food Hall
19 Restaurant
   Bab Mansour
20 Restaurant
   Economique
21 Café
28 Café Hamounia

OTHER
1 Berdaine Mosque
3 Hammam (men only)
6 Bou Inania Medersa
7 Qissariat
   ad-Dahab (gold)
8 Main Bus Terminal
9 Intercity Grands Taxis
10 Dar Jamaï
   (Folk Museum)
11 Haberdashers' Souq
14 Mansour Palace
22 Banque Populaire
23 Local Buses
24 Moulay Ismail
   Mausoleum
25 Mosque
26 Public Swimming Pool
27 'Sfinj' shop
29 Post Office (PTT)
33 Hammam (men
   & women)
34 Cinéma Apollo
36 Crédit du
   Maroc (change)

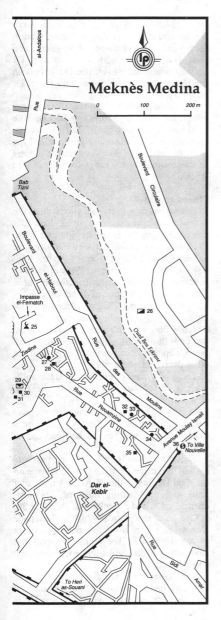

Meknès Medina

0   100   200 m

Hotels – ville nouvelle One of the cheapest places to stay is the *Hôtel Central*, 35 Ave Mohammed V, close to the CTM bus station and El-Amir Abdelkader train station. Inside, the place is quite attractively arranged around a central courtyard and has reasonable rooms for Dr 40/70/85/125. The mattresses are thin, the showers cold and the toilets basic. It has been said that the place is used as a brothel and the sheets aren't always changed.

In the same price range is the *Hôtel du Marché* on Ave Hassan II. At Dr 40/80 you can't expect too much, but some of the rooms are crumbling away. Others are better and have balconies. The bed linen is dubious and there are only cold showers.

Considerably better, but a little dearer, is the *Hôtel Toubkal* (☎ 522218), back on Ave Mohammed V. The rooms have big beds, the showers and toilets are clean and occasionally there is hot water. The staff are a friendly lot. It costs Dr 60 per person in a single or double.

There's also the *Hôtel Guillaume Tell*, down an alleyway next to the Hôtel Volubilis. However it rarely gets Western guests and seemed unwilling to name a price for the rather basic rooms.

The one-star *Hôtel Touring* (☎ 522951), 34 Blvd Allal ben Abdallah, is quite adequate and reasonably good value at Dr 79/98, although the 'hot' water in the showers is only ever lukewarm. The rooms are a decent size and some have private showers, but the beds are on the saggy side.

Virtually overlooking the railway is the *Hôtel Excelsior* (☎ 521900), 57 Ave des FAR. It's in the same category as the Continental but somewhat better. Rooms without shower cost Dr 86/110, while those with bathroom are Dr 110/127. Add a few dirhams in taxes.

An altogether better deal is the *Hôtel Majestic* (☎ 522035), 14 Ave Mohammed V. It has a bit of character, and although the beds are rather narrow the rooms with washbasin, bidet and sometimes balcony are fine. Rooms without private shower cost Dr 86/111 for singles/doubles, Dr 169 for triples, plus taxes. The shared showers are clean and the water piping hot. They even have central heating which sometimes works in winter. There are some rooms with private shower and toilets for more.

Quite reasonable (except for the lack of hot water) is the more modern *Hôtel Panorama* (☎ 522737), just off Ave des FAR. For a big room with a private shower and very comfortable beds you pay Dr 114/135.

Places to Stay – middle

At the lower end of this category is the two-star *Hôtel Moderne* (☎ 524228), 54 Ave Allal ben Abdallah, which has singles/doubles with shower and shared toilet for Dr 157/187.

Farther up the line and not bad value in its class is the *Hôtel Palace* (☎ 525777), 11 Zankat Ghana, which has rooms with private bathroom for Dr 195/240 or Dr 153/195 without.

Those looking for guaranteed creature comforts and a full range of private facilities couldn't do better than the popular *Hôtel de Nice* (☎ 520318), 10 Zankat Accra, a three-star hotel with singles/doubles/triples for Dr 201/252/344.

There are three three-star hotels within a stone's throw of each other around Ave des FAR and Ave Mohammed V. The *Hôtel Bab Mansour* (☎ 525239; fax 510741), 38 Rue El-Amir Abdelkader, has clean and modern, if somewhat sterile, rooms with carpet and phone. Those with bath cost Dr 226/273, while those without are Dr 179/225. A bit older and not so good is the *Hôtel Volubilis* (☎ 525082), 45 Ave des FAR, which has rooms at the same prices (including triples for Dr 377). Unfortunately, it is on a noisy intersection.

Quieter and newer is the *Hôtel Akouas* (☎ 596768; fax 515994). It has some excellent self-contained rooms, and others that are not nearly so good, so ask to see a few. They charge Dr 232/285/377.

Places to Stay – top end

The four-star *Rif Hôtel* (☎ 522591; fax 524428), Zankat Accra, and the *Hôtel Zaki*

(☎ 521140), Blvd al-Massira, both have similar facilities, including swimming pool, restaurant, bar and air-con throughout, and cost Dr 297/387 without bath and Dr 362/460 with bath, plus taxes. Outsiders can use the pool at the Rif for a daily fee of Dr 50.

Top of the line is the five-star *Hôtel Transatlantique* (☎ 525051; fax 520057), Rue el-Mériniyine, which has 120 air-con rooms, tennis courts, a swimming pool and all the other facilities you would expect of a hotel of this nature. Rooms range from Dr 700 to Dr 900.

Places to Eat

If you are staying in the old town, there are a few simple restaurants along Rue Dar Smen between the Hôtel Regina and Place el-Hedim. Two of the best are the *Restaurant Economique*, at No 123 (one of the few with a sign), and a little closer to Place el-Hedim, *Restaurant Bab Mansour*. In either of these you can point to a range of dishes on display and so put together a filling meal for about Dr 25.

A few doors down from the Economique, just after the café, is a good hole-in-the-wall place, nameless but perhaps better than the other two mentioned.

There is a mass of cheap-eats stalls spilling out in the lanes just outside the Bab el-Jedid.

In the ville nouvelle, there are a few cheap eats along Ave Mohammed V, including a roast-chicken place close to the Hôtel Excelsior.

There are two good little restaurants around the corner from the Hôtel Majestic on the road leading to the El-Amir Abdelkader train station. A filling meal of, say, brochettes, salad and a drink costs about Dr 30.

One place that stands out is the *Rôtisserie Karam*, at 2 Zankat Ghana, near the corner of Ave Hassan II. The chips are good and most main meals (typically brochettes) cost about Dr 20.

The *Restaurant Marhaba*, next to the Empire Cinema (about 100 metres south of the Hôtel Majestic) on Ave Mohammed V, is a modestly touristy restaurant, with somewhat kitsch décor but reasonable food. You'll leave about Dr 60 lighter, but the fact that it advertises itself as recommended in guide books is hardly a good sign for the future.

For Western-style fast food, try *Free Time* on Ave Hassan II, where a small hamburger plus chips goes for Dr 18.

La Coupole, also on Ave Hassan II, is a popular local restaurant with set menus for Dr 70 and comparatively cheap main meals à la carte. There is also a bar and, at night, a rather noisy and tacky nightclub.

Many travellers go to the *Restaurant Metropole Annexe*, 11 Rue Charif Idrissi, around the corner from the junction of Ave Hassan II and Ave Mohammed V. A three-course, Moroccan-style set meal costs about Dr 80. The food is excellent, the service quick and beer and wine are available. Next door on the corner is the *Restaurant Gambrinus*, which offers a set menu for Dr 50.

Pizzeria Le Four is a favourite meeting place for chic Meknassis, and you can get surprisingly good pizza for Dr 30 to Dr 40. Wine and beer are also available. Watch out for the 19% taxes. Across the road is the *Montana*, which is a bar downstairs and a Moroccan restaurant upstairs – a good meal will cost Dr 40 to Dr 60. Another place for pizza is the *Pizzeria La Mama*, around the corner from the Hôtel de Nice.

If you are desperate for Asian food, you could do worse than the licensed *Restaurant Tangerois-Hai Phong* (☎ 515091) in Zankat Beyrouth. A main meal will cost you at least Dr 60 plus taxes. Across the road is a rather good bakery, pâtisserie and café.

For a splurge in traditional Moroccan surroundings, check out the *Restaurant Zitouna* (☎ 532083), 44 Jamaa Zitouna, in the medina. This is a veritable palace of a restaurant with an atmosphere as enjoyable as its Moroccan specialities. Meknès is full of places like this, but despite its definite tourist orientation, it can make a pleasant once-off. There's a set menu for Dr 100 or à la carte mains, which makes it quite cheap compared

with its Fès counterparts. Alcoholic drinks are not available. There's a similar place just south of where Rue Souika and Rue Ben el-Maacer meet.

If you want to really lash out, there's the formal *Palais Terrab* (☎ 521456), 18 Ave Zerktouni, in the ville nouvelle east of the El-Amir Abdelkader train station. A full meal here costs around Dr 350 per person.

Entertainment
Cafés & Bars There are cafés all over the old city and the ville nouvelle. *La Comtesse* café under the Hôtel de Paris on Rue Rouamzine is a new, lively place; it has ice cream in summer. Just by the Restaurant Economique on Rue Dar Smen is a lovely old café with an interior décor of smoky wooden beams. The cafés on Place el-Hedim are good for people-watching. The *Café Hamounia* on Rue Rouamine is also not bad, and just down from it is a hole-in-the-wall selling freshly fried sfinj – a kind of light, deep-fried doughy doughnut great for dunking in coffee. You buy a few at a time and they are tied together with a strand of palm frond.

The ville nouvelle, especially on and around Ave Mohammed V, is full of French-style cafés good for a relaxing coffee or tea and cake.

There are a few basic bars around the Ave Mohammed V end of Blvd Allal ben Abdallah. There's nothing particular to recommend them, and you may want to try the highly discreet liquor store farther up Blvd Allal ben Abdallah for some take-home alcohol. As noted, some of the restaurants in the ville nouvelle are licensed. There is a bar in the Restaurant Montana and the bigger hotels all have bars.

Discos & Cinemas The Rif Hôtel has a disco in which it stages an 'Oriental show'. Otherwise, there are a couple of dubious nightclubs about, including one in the Hôtel Volubilis and one a bit farther east along Ave des FAR, the *Café de France Club de Nuit*. Entrance to these places starts at Dr 50, including your first drink, but subsequent tipples are in the order of Dr 50 a go.

There are a few cinemas around town.

Getting There & Away

Air RAM has several representatives, including Wasteels and Wagons-Lits, mentioned in the earlier Information section. It also has an office (☎ 520963) at 7 Ave Mohammed V. There is a small airstrip just outside Meknès, but no regular flights.

CTM Bus The CTM terminal is on Ave Mohammed V near the junction with Ave des FAR. There are nine departures daily to Casablanca (Dr 55) and Rabat (Dr 33), the first at 5.30 am and the last at 8 pm; seven a day to Fès (Dr 14.50), the first at 11 am and the last at 11 pm; two daily to Er-Rachidia (at 10 and 11.30 pm – the first continues on to Rissani); two daily to Ifrane and Azrou, at 4 and 8 pm; one daily to Tangier (Dr 63), at 7 pm; and one daily to Taza (Dr 45), at 5 pm.

CTM also operates international buses to Paris and Brussels – for details see the Getting There & Away chapter.

Other Buses The main bus terminal for all other companies is just outside Bab el-Khemis on the northern side of the new mellah along Ave du Mellah. There is a left-luggage office, a café and phone office. The various companies are represented at nine windows, but almost all the information posted up is in Arabic. At Window 9 you can get tickets for a 6.30 am bus to Marrakesh (Dr 96). For Moulay Idriss, go to Window 8 (Dr 7). There are fairly regular buses to Kenitra, Rabat and Casablanca – tickets can be bought at Window 5.

Window 6 has tickets for Tetouan (Dr 56) and Chefchaouen (Dr 45), which leave at 5 am and noon, with a third service to Chefchaouen only at 6 am. Buses for Ouezzane leave at 5, 6, 7, 8, 11 am and noon (Dr 30). Finally, you can also get tickets for Tangier (Dr 50) at this counter. The Tangier buses leave at 6.45, 8, 10 am, noon and 3 pm. The trip takes about six hours.

Fès bus tickets (Dr 12) can be purchased at Window 7. Buses leave every hour or so until 4 pm, after which there are a few more at uncertain times in transit from Rabat.

From the same window, you can also get tickets for Taza (Dr 35; 6.30 and 8.30 am); Sefrou (Dr 48; 7 am); Oujda (Dr 84.50; 5.30 am) and Nador (Dr 78 to Dr 82; 4.30, 8.30 and 9.30 am).

Train The main train station is some way from the centre of the new city, on Ave du Sénégal. It's much more convenient to use the El-Amir Abdelkader station, one block down from and parallel to Ave Mohammed V, as all trains stop here. All trains to or from Fès also stop in Meknès.

A total of 11 trains go to Fès (one hour), six of which go on to Oujda (6½ hours), and at least nine to Casablanca (4¼ hours) via Rabat. There are seven services to Marrakesh, three of them direct (7½ hours).

Second-class fares on normal and rapide services include: Fès (Dr 12/15); Tangier (Dr 55.50/70); Casablanca (Dr 56.50/72.50) and Marrakesh (Dr 109/137.50).

Taxi All the grands taxis leave from a dirt lot between Bab el-Khemis and the main bus station. You can't miss it. There are regular departures to Fès (Dr 15), Rabat (Dr 38), Moulay Idriss (for Volubilis, Dr 7), Sidi Kacem and Beni Slimane. As always, it's best to arrive in the morning.

Car Zeit (☎ and fax 525918) has an office at 4 Rue Anserabi. Stopcar (☎ 525061) is at 5 Rue de la Voûte.

Getting Around

Bus There are local buses between the medina and the new city, but they are invariably crowded and hard to get on at times.

Useful routes include the No 2 (Bab el-Mansour to Blvd Allal ben Abdallah, returning to the medina along Ave Mohammed V) and No 7 (Bab el-Mansour to the CTM bus station).

Taxi A useful urban grand taxi route, which connects the new and old cities, starts in the new city from Zankat Ghana near the corner of Ave Hassan II, directly opposite the Rôtisserie Karam. The grands taxis are silver Mercedes with black roofs. The fare is Dr 5 per person. Pale-blue petits taxis covering the same distance would cost about Dr 10. A petit taxi ride from the main bus station to El-Amir Abdelkader train station is Dr 12.

AROUND MEKNÈS

Volubilis

About 33 km from Meknès is the site of the largest and best preserved Roman ruins in Morocco. Volubilis dates largely from the 2nd and 3rd centuries AD, although excavations have revealed that the site was originally settled by Carthaginian traders in the 3rd century BC.

Volubilis (Oualili in Arabic) was one of the Roman Empire's most remote outposts. Direct Roman rule lasted for only 240 years after the area was annexed in about 40 AD. According to some historians, Rome imposed strict controls on what could or could not be produced in its North African possessions, according to the needs of the empire. One result was massive deforestation and the large-scale planting of wheat.

MIDDLE ATLAS

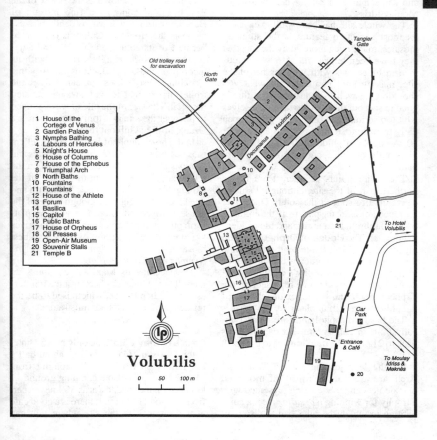

1 House of the
  Cortege of Venus
2 Gardien Palace
3 Nymphs Bathing
4 Labours of Hercules
5 Knight's House
6 House of Columns
7 House of the Ephebus
8 Triumphal Arch
9 North Baths
10 Fountains
11 Fountains
12 House of the Athlete
13 Forum
14 Basilica
15 Capitol
16 Public Baths
17 House of Orpheus
18 Oil Presses
19 Open-Air Museum
20 Souvenir Stalls
21 Temple B

Old trolley road for excavation

Tangier Gate

North Gate

Decumanus Maximus

To Hotel Volubilis

Car Park

Entrance & Café

To Moulay Idriss & Meknès

Volubilis

0   50   100 m

The sweep of largely treeless plains around Volubilis certainly makes such a thesis plausible.

Volubilis' population of Berbers, Greeks, Jews and Syrians continued to speak Latin and practise Christianity right up until the coming of Islam. Unlike Lixus, to the north-west, which was abandoned shortly after the fall of the Roman Empire, Volubilis continued to be inhabited until the 18th century, when its marble was plundered for the building of Moulay Ismail's palaces in Meknès.

If you like ancient ruins, Volubilis is worth a visit. It is an easy day trip from Meknès, and you can also take in the nearby town of Moulay Idriss.

The whole site has been well excavated. Its most attractive feature is the stunning mosaics, made even more so by the fact that they have been left *in situ*. A few officious men in blue coats with whistles patrol the site, making sure you don't do what you shouldn't (ie walk on the mosaics); this is good to see, but they tend to take themselves a bit too seriously at times. The site is open daily from sunrise to sunset and entry is Dr 20. A couple of guides will offer their services at the entrance, but they don't try very hard.

The major points of interest are in the northern part of the site, although it's more convenient to start in the south. Once over the Oued Fertassa, the path from the entrance takes you through an unremarkable residential quarter. The **House of Orpheus**, a little higher up and identifiable by the three pine trees growing in the corner, was a sumptuous mansion for one of the city's wealthier residents. Its two mosaics, one representing the Orpheus myth and the other the chariot of Amphitrite, are still in place.

The basilica, capitol and forum are, typically, built on a high point. The **capitol** dates back to 217 AD; the **basilica** lies to the north of it.

On the left, just before the Triumphal Arch, are a couple of roped-off **mosaics**. One depicts an athlete being presented with a trophy for winning a *desultor* race, a competition in which the rider had to dismount and jump back on his horse as it raced along. Opposite these mosaics are the remains of an aqueduct and fountain.

The **Triumphal Arch** on the Decumanus Maximus road, built in 217 AD in honour of Emperor Caracalla and his mother, Julia Domna, used to be topped with a bronze chariot. The arch was reconstructed in the 1930s, and the mistakes made then were rectified in the 1960s.

The **Decumanus Maximus** stretches up the slope to the north-east. The houses lining either side of the road contain the best mosaics on the site. The first house on the far side of the arch is known as the House of the Ephebus and contains a fine mosaic of Bacchus in a chariot drawn by panthers. Next along is the House of Columns (so named because of its columned façade), and adjacent to this is the Knight's House, with its incomplete mosaic of Bacchus and Ariadne.

Behind these houses you can still see the trolley tracks laid to cart away excavated material. The size of the pile of waste moved to uncover the site is astonishing – there's a sizable artificial hill out there.

In the next couple of houses are excellent mosaics entitled the *Labours of Hercules* and *Nymphs Bathing*. The best collection on the whole site, however, is in the House of the Cortege of Venus, one block farther up and one block to the right. Although some of the house is roped off, there is a viewing platform built along the southern wall that gives you a good vantage point over the two best mosaics – the *Abduction of Hylas by the Nymphs* and *Diana Bathing*.

The Decumanus Maximus continues up the hill to the Tangier Gate, past the uninteresting Gordien Palace, which used to be the residence of the city's administrators.

Places to Stay & Eat The only nearby hotel is the four-star *Hôtel Volubilis*, about half a km farther on from the site coming from Meknès. There is also a camping ground 11 km back on the road towards Meknès. Apart from the hotel restaurant, there is a good café at the entrance to the site where you can rehydrate and nourish yourself – at a price (a glass of tea costs Dr 5).

Getting There & Away To get to Volubilis from Meknès, take one of the infrequent buses or more frequent grands taxis to Moulay Idriss from the bus station outside Bab el-Khemis. Get off at the turn-off to Moulay Idriss. From there it's about a 30-minute walk – extremely pleasant when it's not too hot – and follow the turn-off to the left for Oualili.

Getting back can be a little more problematic, but if you don't fancy hitching, your best bet will be to walk up to Moulay Idriss (a good hour away) and wait for a bus or grand taxi back. Do so early in the day, as transport dries up in the mid-afternoon. The last option is to get a group together and a hire a grand taxi for half a day, which will probably come to about Dr 150.

Moulay Idriss

The other main place of interest outside Meknès is Moulay Idriss, about 4.5 km from Volubilis. The town is named after Morocco's most revered saint, a great-grandson of the Prophet and the founder of the country's first real dynasty. Moulay Idriss fled Mecca in the late 8th century AD in the face of persecution at the hands of the then recently installed Abbassid Caliphate, which was based in Baghdad. Idriss settled at Volubilis, where he managed to convert the locals to Islam and made himself their leader. From there he went on to establish Morocco's first imperial dynasty.

Moulay Idriss is an attractive town from a distance, nestled in a cradle of verdant mountains, and for Moroccans it's a place of pilgrimage. Non-Muslims may well get the feeling that they are only grudgingly tolerated (it has been open to them only for the past 70 years or so). You cannot visit any of the mosques or shrines and you are not allowed to stay overnight.

Things to See Although the twin hilltown is a veritable maze of narrow lanes and dead ends, it is not hard to get around to the few points of interest.

First to the **Mausoleum of Moulay Idriss**, the object of veneration and the reason for the country's greatest annual moussem in late August. From the main square (where buses and grands taxis arrive), walk up the street that starts to the left of the bus ticket booths. This brings you into the main street, which is lined on both sides by cafés and cheap food stands; those on the right overlook the square from which you have just emerged. Proceed straight down this street and under the arch – the increasing number of quite unnecessary guides and package-tourist groups should reassure you that you're getting warm. About 50 metres on to your left you'll see a three-arched gateway. Go through it and continue straight ahead – you'll soon come up against the barrier that marks the point beyond which non-Muslims may not pass. The mausoleum that stands here today was built by Moulay Ismail, although various additions have since been made.

You can now head left into the maze of streets and try to find your way to a couple of vantage points that give you a **panoramic view** of the mausoleum and the town – plenty of guides will offer to help.

If you don't feel like being guided, there is an alternative. Head back to the beginning of the main street, which you reached coming up from the bus station square. Looking again in the direction of mausoleum, you'll notice a side street heading uphill to your left and signposted 'Municipalité'. Follow it, and just before the Agfa photo shop on the left take the cobbled street to the right. As you climb up you'll notice the only **cylindrical minaret** in Morocco. The green tile décor spells out in stylised script the standard Muslim refrain, *la illah illa Allah* – 'There is no god but Allah'.

Proceed another couple of hundred metres and you're close. This is where you have to ask a local for the 'grande' or 'petite terrasse' – this should produce no problem. The terraces are nothing of the sort, but are simply vantage points high above the mausoleum and a good part of the town.

Saturday is market day and so a more lively time to be in Moulay Idriss; it's also easier to get there on a Saturday.

Places to Eat There is nowhere to stay in Moulay Idriss. The main battery of cheap restaurants and cafés is in the main street above the bus station. There are a few cafés on the square and its approaches too.

Getting There & Away Occasional buses and more frequent grands taxis run from the bus station outside Bab el-Khemis in Meknès. The ride costs Dr 7. Note that it can be extremely difficult getting out of Moulay Idriss after about 3 pm. There are few services and often a lot of customers. The occasional bus stops here en route to or from such places as Casablanca.

Fès

The oldest of the imperial cities, Fès is arguably the symbolic heart of Morocco. Founded shortly after the Arabs swept across North Africa and Spain, it quickly became the religious and cultural centre of Morocco. Even in those periods when it was not the official capital of the whole country, Fès could not be ignored and never really ceased to be considered the northern capital.

All the great dynasties left their mark on the city, but it owes much of its magnificence to the people who from the start made up its cosmopolitan population. In the early days, thousands of families from Muslim Spain came, followed by Arabs from farther east along the North African littoral. Despite the arrival over the centuries of some Berbers from the interior, Fès has retained a distinctly Arab identity.

It has also long considered itself the centre of Islamic orthodoxy, and its allegiance, or at least submission, has always been essential to Morocco's rulers. With such symbolic importance attached to their city, Fassis (the people of Fès) have always been conscious of the power they wield. The city has, up to the present day, acted as a barometer of popular sentiment: Morocco's independence movement was born in Fès, and when there are strikes or protests, they are always at their most vociferous here.

The medina of Fès el-Bali (Old Fès) is one of the largest living medieval cities in the world and the most interesting in Morocco. With the exception of Marrakesh, Cairo and Damascus, there is nothing remotely comparable anywhere else in the Arab world.

Its narrow winding alleys and covered bazaars are crammed with every conceivable sort of craft workshop, restaurant, meat, fruit and vegetable market, mosque and medersa, as well as extensive dye pits and tanneries – a veritable assault on the senses as you squeeze past recalcitrant donkeys and submit to the sounds and smells of this jostling city.

The gates and walls that surround the whole are magnificent, all the more so because, unlike many other medieval walled cities, Fès el-Bali has not burst its banks. The expanding population instead has filled out the ville nouvelle to the south-west and spread to the hillsides in an arc stretching principally north and south of the new city.

But Fès is a city in trouble. Its million or so inhabitants are straining it to the utmost, and the old city especially, some experts have warned, is slowly falling apart. UNESCO has done a lot to stop this deterioration, and is working on a cultural heritage plan for the city, but in the long term it will need huge investment if its unique beauty is to be preserved.

For now, it still represents an experience you are unlikely to forget. You could easily spend a week wandering through this labyrinth and still not be ready to leave. In spite of the hordes of tourists that pile through, Fès gives the impression of living largely in the centuries-old traditions that have shaped it.

The ville nouvelle and its chic, café-lined avenues provide a jarring contrast – the modern flipside to the ancient city. Sipping coffee and watching the passers-by along

Blvd Mohammed V, you could just about be forgiven for thinking you're in a southern French city.

Young Fassis, like young Moroccans in the other big cities, appear to have cast aside the trappings of their parents' lives, instead adopting fashions and lifestyles more readily identified with the West. The downside is that many are without work. The smart, clean centre of the ville nouvelle disguises the sad lot of the poorer people living on the periphery. This aspect of the city's life will be most evident to travellers in the touts, hustlers and beggars who will undoubtedly be encountered. Most of them operate in the area stretching from the centre of the ville nouvelle to the old city gates. Once inside Fès el-Bali you will largely be left alone.

History

There is some dispute over who founded Fès. Some say that Idriss I, who founded Morocco's first imperial dynasty, decided Oualili (Volubilis) was too small for the role of capital and began work on a new one here in 789 AD. Others claim his son, Idriss II, was responsible. In any event, a town was well established here by 809. The town's name is believed to come from the Arabic word for 'axe', and one tale relates that a golden pickaxe was unearthed at the beginning of construction around Oued Fès.

The city started off modestly enough as a predominantly Berber town, but its complexion changed with the arrival on the east bank of 8000 families fleeing Al-Andalus. They were later joined by Arab families from Kairouan (or Qayrawan – in modern Tunisia), who set up home on the west bank – the quarter of the Kairaouine (people from Kairouan). They brought with them the religious, cultural and architectural heritage of two great Muslim centres, thereby forming a solid foundation for future greatness. As his father is venerated still in the village of Moulay Idriss, so the memory of Idriss II is perpetuated in his zawiyya in the heart of Fès el-Bali.

Idriss II's heirs split the kingdom up, but

for a while Fès continued to enjoy peace and prosperity. In the 10th century, Berber tribes descended on the city, which was torn by a bitter civil war and was also experiencing a famine.

The chaos continued until the arrival of the Almoravids in 1070. For 80 years they ruled the city, which was second in importance only to Marrakesh, the chosen capital of their greatest leader, Youssef bin Tachfin. The Almoravid stay was short, however, for a still more ascetic movement arose to take their place – that of the Almohads.

In their conquest of Fès in about 1154, the Almohads destroyed the walls of the city and only replaced them when they were assured of the inhabitants' loyalty. Large sections of the walls of Fès date from this period. Although Marrakesh remained the imperial capital, Fès continued to be a crucial crossroads and, with the importance of the Kairaouine mosque and university already well established, it became *the* centre of learning and culture in an empire that stretched from Spain to Senegal.

Fès recovered its political status only much later, with the arrival of the Merenid dynasty. They took the city around 1250, but it took them another 20 years to wrest control of Marrakesh from the Almohads and so definitively remove their predecessors from power.

Never sure of his subjects' loyalty, the second Merenid sultan, Abu Youssef Yacoub (1258-86), built a self-contained walled city outside the old one – Fès el-Jdid (New Fès) – and there stationed loyal troops, most of whom were Syrian and Christian mercenaries.

In the 14th century, the Jewish community was relocated from Fès el-Bali to the new city. In this way the first Jewish ghetto, or *mellah*, was created in Morocco. Although regarded as second-class citizens, the Jews were important economically in the life of the nation and were to become increasingly so. The records suggest that the move was partly inspired by a desire to offer the Jews greater protection from pogroms. Whatever the truth of this, they enjoyed the protection

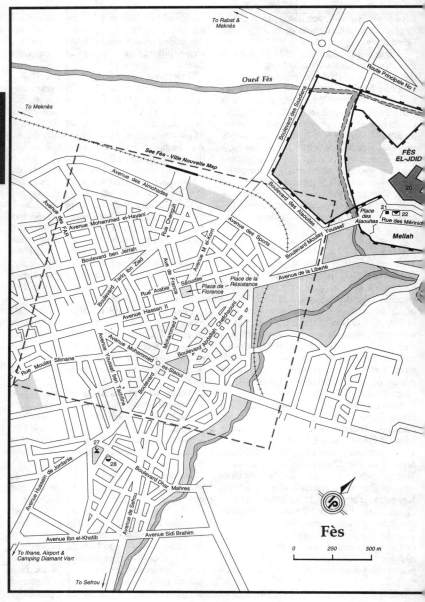

To Rabat &
Meknès

Oued Fès

Route Principale No 1

To Meknès

Boulevard des Saadiens

FÈS
EL-JDID

20

See Fès - Ville Nouvelle Map

Avenue des Almohades

Avenue Mohammed el-Hayani

Rue Chenguit

Avenue des Sports

Boulevard des Alaouites

Boulevard Moulay Youssef

Place
des
Alaouites

21

22

Rue des Mérinid

Mellah

Boulevard ben Jerrah

Avenue M. el-Korri

Avenue des FAR

Boulevard Tariq Ibn Ziad

Ave de France

Saôudite

Rue Arabie

Place de la
Résistance

Place de
Florence

Avenue de la Liberté

Avenue Hassan II

Rue Moulay Slimane

Avenue Mohammed
es-Slaoui

Mohammed V

Boulevard Abdallah Chefchaouni

Avenue Mohammed

Boulevard
Youssef ben Tachfine

27

28

Boulevard Dhar Mahres

Avenue Hussein de Jordanie

Avenue de Sefrou

Avenue Ibn el-Khatib

Avenue Sidi Brahim

To Ifrane, Airport &
Camping Diamant Vert

To Sefrou

Fès

0   250   500 m

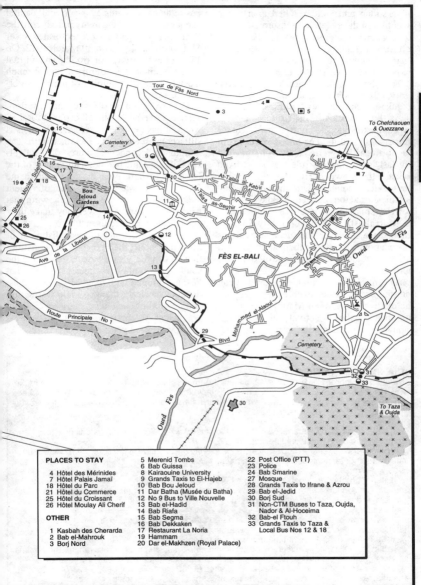

MIDDLE ATLAS

PLACES TO STAY

4 Hôtel des Mérinides
7 Hôtel Palais Jamaï
18 Hôtel du Parc
21 Hôtel du Commerce
25 Hôtel du Croissant
26 Hôtel Moulay Ali Cherif

OTHER

1 Kasbah des Cherarda
2 Bab el-Mahrouk
3 Borj Nord

5 Merenid Tombs
6 Bab Guissa
8 Kairaouine University
9 Grands Taxis to El-Hajeb
10 Bab Bou Jeloud
11 Dar Batha (Musée du Batha)
12 No 9 Bus to Ville Nouvelle
13 Bab el-Hadid
14 Bab Riafa
15 Bab Segma
16 Bab Dekkaken
17 Restaurant La Noria
19 Hammam
20 Dar el-Makhzen (Royal Palace)

22 Post Office (PTT)
23 Police
24 Bab Smarine
27 Mosque
28 Grands Taxis to Ifrane & Azrou
29 Bab el-Jedid
30 Borj Sud
31 Non-CTM Buses to Taza, Oujda,
   Nador & Al-Hoceima
32 Bab-el Ftouh
33 Grands Taxis to Taza &
   Local Bus Nos 12 & 18

of the sultan, and could be relied upon to side with him in the event of an insurrection.

Few Jewish families remain in Fès. Most left for Israel during the 1950s and '60s, and their synagogues have been converted into carpet warehouses and the like.

The Merenids' single greatest gift to posterity, in Fès as in several other cities, is the exquisite medersas they built.

As the Merenids in their turn collapsed, two dynasties vied for power, the Saadians in the south and the Fès-based Wattasids in the north. Although the latter won, they did not last long. Saadian rule was short-lived too, and the Alawites arrived on the scene in 1664. The second of their sultans, Moulay Ismail, shifted the capital to Meknès in 1672; however, his successors chose to move back to Marrakesh. Fès never really lost its importance, however, and successive sultans made a point of residing there at intervals in order to maintain some control over the north.

As central power crumbled and European interference increased over the 19th century, the distinction between Marrakesh and Fès diminished – they effectively both served as capitals of a fragmented country. If anything,

Fès retained its status as the 'moral' capital and it was here that the treaty introducing the French and Spanish protectorates over Morocco was signed on 30 March 1912. On 17 April, three days of rioting and virtual revolt against the country's new French masters proved a reminder of the city's volatile history.

Largely because of the insurrection, France moved the political capital to Rabat, where it has remained ever since, but Fès is still a constituency to be reckoned with. The Istiqlal (Independence) Party of Allal al-Fassi was established here, and many of the impulses towards ejecting the French came from Fès. Fès was also the scene of violent strikes and riots in the 1980s, showing that Morocco's rulers, wherever they make their capital, must still reckon with Fès.

In 1916, following the establishment of the protectorate, the French began construction of the ville nouvelle on the plateau to the south-west of the two ancient cities. That Fès, in common with most Moroccan cities, did not experience the wholesale destruction and rebuilding that characterised colonial practice in Algeria is largely due to General (later Marshal) Lyautey.

The 1912 Insurrection

The insurrection of 17-19 April, 1912, caught the French somewhat by surprise, although in the wake of the violence it appeared a fairly predictable reaction to the signing of the Treaty of Fès, which ushered in the protectorate. Several French journalists were in Fès at the time. *L'Illustration* reported:

The Mellah, the Jewish quarter, was the first to be sacked – still a Moroccan tradition. How many corpses have been swallowed up in its ruins?

There were only some 1400 to 1500 troops to bring the situation under control, colonial infantry and sharpshooters camped at Dar Debibagh, some of whom were still engaged in operations around Sefrou.

Throughout the afternoon the struggle between the rebels and our soldiers continued in the streets. By nightfall, all the Europeans who had escaped the insurgents' assaults were safe. Our officers and non-commissioned officers had many an occasion to display their courage and sangfroid...

The following day, however, the rebels dared attack Dar Debibagh. They were pushed back, but Captain Bourdonneau was mortally wounded.

It was only on the 18th that the uprising was brought under control; General Dalbiez's troops, called in from Meknès, arrived and quickly overcame the last sparks of resistance...By the time General Moinier had arrived at a forced march beneath the ramparts of Fès, it was all over.

Losses among the rebels have been estimated at 800 dead. For our part, we can only deplore the deaths of nine civilians...Among the military, it has been a bloodbath. ∎

Orientation

Fès is comprised of three distinct parts: Fès el-Bali, Fès el-Jdid and the ville nouvelle. The first two form the medina, while the last is the administrative area built by the French.

Fès el-Bali is the original medina and the area of most interest to visitors. Its walls encircle an incredible maze of twisting alleys, blind turns and souqs. Finding your way around, at least at first, can be difficult but this is no problem: you can either take a guide or, if you do get lost, pay an eager kid a couple of dirham to guide you at least as far as a familiar landmark. In spite of what you'll hear, it is not at all necessary to take a guide to find your way around if you don't want to.

The wall has a number of gates, of which the most spectacular are Bab Bou Jeloud, Bab el-Mahrouk and Bab Guissa. Bab Bou Jeloud, in the south-west corner of the old part of the city, is the main entrance to the medina. You will probably pass through it many times during your stay, and there is a cluster of cheap pensions in the area. For a good view over the medina, walk up to the Merenid tombs on the hill north of the Bab.

Next to Fès el-Bali is the less interesting Merenid city of Fès el-Jdid, which houses the old Jewish quarter. There are a couple of hotels here, where you can stay if you want to be close to the medina and the hotels around Bab Bou Jeloud are full.

The new city lies south-west of Fès el-Jdid and is laid out in typical French colonial style with wide, tree-lined boulevards, squares and parks. Here you'll find the majority of restaurants and hotels, as well as the post office, banks and most transport connections. It lacks the atmosphere of the medina, but pulses to the rhythm of modern Morocco and is where you'll stay if you're looking for something other than a medina cheapie. There are local buses connecting the ville nouvelle with various parts of the old city. They run regularly and don't take long, so there's no great disadvantage in staying here. It is also quite possible to walk between the two – set aside about half an hour to go from Place de Florence in the ville nouvelle to Bab Bou Jeloud.

Information

Tourist Offices The ONMT office (☎ 623460, 626279) is on Place de la Résistance (Immeuble Bennani) in the new city. It has little of interest other than the usual brochures, although if pressed can be helpful with specific local information. You can supposedly hire official guides to the medina at about Dr 35 for a half-day here. The problem is they will tell you to arrange it at the syndicat d'initiative on Place Mohammed V, which appears to be permanently closed. You don't absolutely need a guide, but if you want an official one and get no joy at the tourist offices, try one of the big hotels.

The ONMT is open Monday to Friday from 8.30 am to noon and 2.30 to 6.30 pm, and in the morning on Saturday.

Money Most of the banks are in the new city on Blvd Mohammed V. The BMCE branch on the corner of Blvd Mohammed V and Ave Mohammed es-Slaoui has ATMs. Several other banks have branches in the ville nouvelle and the medina. The RAM office has a booth where you can change cash and cheques. The Restaurant Mounia and several of the bigger hotels will also change money.

Post & Telecommunications The main post office is in the new city on the corner of Ave Hassan II and Blvd Mohammed V. It is open Monday to Friday from 8.30 am to 6.45 pm, and on Saturday from 8 to 11 am. Poste restante is at window No 9. The parcels office entrance is on Ave Hassan II.

The telephone office next to the post office on Blvd Mohammed V is open daily from 8.30 am to 9 pm.

There is another post office in the medina near the Dar Batha.

Guides In addition to the official guides, a host of unofficial guides are waiting for your business. They tend to hang about some of the hotels, and at various strategic points approaching Fès el-Jdid and Bab Bou Jeloud. On a good day, you'll hardly notice any, and once inside the medina you are generally OK. Drivers should note a Fès speciality; motorised hustlers and guides on the approach roads to the city.

Foreign Consulates France maintains a consulate (☎ 625547) in Fès at Ave Obaid Bnou el-Jarrah.

Cultural Centre The Centre Culturel Fran-

çais (☎ 623921) at 33 Rue Loukiki puts on films, lectures and sometimes offers classes in Arabic.

Bookshops The English Bookshop, at 68 Ave Hassan II, close to Place de la Résistance, has a wide range of textbooks and novels. It has some books on Morocco in English and French, but its main market is students of English. The shop closes at lunch times.

The best place to find foreign newspapers

Fès in the 19th Century

Entering Fès el-Bali today is like stepping into a time warp back to the Middle Ages, not so different from the city discovered by Edmondo De Amicis on a diplomatic visit from Italy in the 1880s. He described his experiences in *Morocco – Its People & Places* (Darf Publishers, London, 1985), and had this to say about Fès:

The first impression is that of an immense city fallen into decrepitude and slowly decaying. Tall houses, which seemed formed of houses piled one upon the other, all falling to pieces, cracked from roof to base, propped up on every side, with no opening save some loophole in the shape of a cross; long stretches of street, flanked by two high bare walls like the walls of a fortress; streets running uphill and down, encumbered with stones and the ruins of fallen buildings, twisting and turning at every thirty paces; every now and then a long covered passage, dark as a cellar, where you have to feel your way; blind alleys, recesses, dens full of bones, dead animals, and heaps of putrid matter; the whole steeped in a dim and melancholy twilight. In some places the ground is so broken, the dust so thick, the smell so horrible, the flies so numerous, that we have to stop to take breath. In half an hour we have made so many turns that if our road could be drawn it would form an arabesque as intricate as any in the Alhambra. Here and there we hear the noise of a mill, a murmur of water, the click of a weaver's loom, a chanting of nasal voices, which we are told come from a school of children, but we see nothing...We approach the centre of the city; people become more numerous; the men stop to let us pass, and stare astonished; the women turn back, or hide themselves; the children scream and run; the larger boys growl and shake their fists at a distance...We see fountains richly ornamented with mosaics, arabesque doors, arched courts...We come to one of the principal streets, about six feet wide, and full of people who crowd about us...There are a thousand eyes upon us; we can scarcely breathe in the press and heat, and move slowly on, stopping every moment to give passage to a Moor on horseback, or a veiled lady on a camel, or an ass with a load of bleeding sheep's heads. To the right and left are crowded bazaars; inn courtyards encumbered with merchandise; doors of mosques through which we catch a glimpse of arcades and figures prostrate in prayer...The air is impregnated with an acute and mingled odour of aloes, spices, incense and kif; we seem to be walking in an immense drug-shop. Groups of boys go by with scarred and scabby heads; horrible old women, perfectly bald and with naked breasts, making their way by dint of furious imprecations against us; naked, or almost naked, madmen, crowned with flowers and feathers, bearing a branch in their hands, laughing and singing...We go into the bazaar. The crowd is everywhere. The shops, as in Tangier, are mere dens opened in the wall...We cross, jostled by the crowd, the cloth bazaar, that of slippers, that of earthenware, that of metal ornaments, which altogether form a labyrinth of alleys roofed with canes and branches of trees.

Essentially, the only way in which Fès has changed since then is that the moderate affluence Fassis now enjoy has enabled them to restore many of the buildings and clean up the streets. However, that hasn't radically altered the atmosphere; Fès is still worlds apart from anything you will find north of the Strait of Gibraltar. ■

and magazines is along Blvd Mohammed V. The stand virtually across the road from the police building is not bad.

There are a few decent bookshops if you read French. One of the best is the Librairie Papeterie du Centre (☎ 622569), at 134 Blvd Mohammed V.

Language Schools The American Language Center (☎ 624850) and its affiliated Arabic Language Institute are at 2 Rue Ahmed Hiba in the ville nouvelle, near the youth hostel. This is one of the few places in Morocco set up for the systematic teaching of Arabic to foreigners. For more details, refer to Activities in the Facts for the Visitor chapter. If you're interested in teaching English, you could look up the International Language Centre rep, Mme Bassou (☎ 641408), at 15 Blvd el-Joulan.

Medical Services & Emergency There is a night pharmacy (☎ 623380) on Ave Abdelkrim el-Khattabi.

For the police, call ☎ 19. The fire brigade is on ☎ 15.

Film & Photography There are quite a few places around the ville nouvelle and the well-trodden parts of the medina where you can buy film. For developing films you could try the Kodak store on Blvd Mohammed V, a block in from Ave Hassan II.

Fès el-Bali

According to one count, about 9400 streets and lanes twist and turn their way through the original old medina of Fès el-Bali (Old Fès). Because there are many cemeteries outside the walls, and also as a result of the enlightened policies of General Lyautey in siting the ville nouvelle well away from the old city, nothing has been built immediately outside the walls.

Finding your way around can be confusing but a delightful way to get lost and found. Although it is easy to become quickly disoriented, one 'rule' is worth bearing mind while navigating. Through the labyrinth are threaded a few main streets that will bring

you to a gate or landmark sooner or later. It is not always evident whether you are on one of these, but the density of crowds moving up and down them is a clue. The easiest stretch is from Bab Bou Jeloud down At-Talaa al-Kebir or At-Talaa as-Seghir to the Kairaouine Mosque area – it is virtually downhill all the way. Heading back therefore, you'll know you aren't far wrong if you follow the crowds and head uphill. Similarly, if you want to get towards the Hôtel Palais Jamaï and the northern gates, keep heading *up*. If this fails, you can always ask shopkeepers for directions or pay someone a few dirham to lead you to where you want to go.

It will take you at least a couple of days to get around and appreciate the city's sights to any degree. And, even though notable buildings such as mosques and medersas are interesting, they form only part of the essence of Fès. You're much more likely to find the real Fès by letting your senses lead you slowly through the crowded bazaars,

Woodwork in the medina

MIDDLE ATLAS

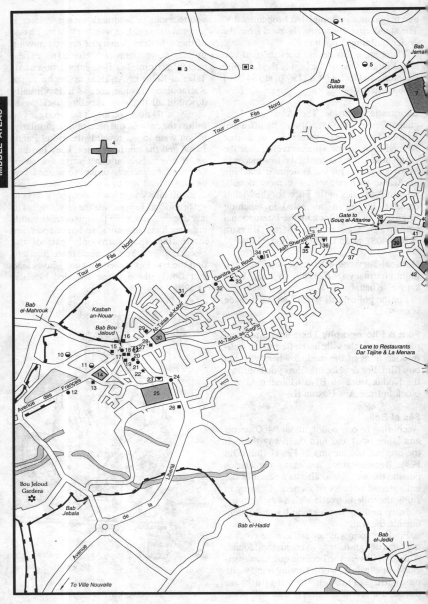

Fès el-Bali

0   250   500 m

PLACES TO STAY

3 Hôtel des Mérinides
7 Hôtel Palais Jamaï
13 Hôtel du Jardin Public
15 Hôtel National
16 Hôtel al-Watani
17 Hôtel Mauritania
18 Hôtel Cascade
19 Hôtel Erraha
26 Hôtel Batha
28 Hôtel Lamrani
61 Hôtel Andalous
62 Hôtel Bahia
64 Hôtel Moulay Idriss

PLACES TO EAT

6 Restaurant Al-Firdaous
8 Restaurant Les Remparts de Fès
36 Restaurant Palais des Mérinides
38 Restaurant Dar Saada
46 Restaurant Palais de Fès

OTHER

1 Bus No 10 to Railway Station & No 12 to Bab Bou Jeloud
2 Merenid Tombs
4 Borj Nord (Arms Museum)
5 Petits Taxis to Ville Nouvelle
9 Terminal, Local Bus No 10
10 Grands Taxis to El-Hajeb
11 Bus Terminal
12 College Moulay Idriss
14 Bou Jeloud Mosque
20 Hammam
21 Cinema
22 Police
23 Branch Post Office
24 Place de l'Istiqlal
25 Dar Bartha (Musée du Batha)
27 Banque Commerciale du Maroc (exchange)
29 Water Clock
30 Medersa Bou Inania
31 Fountain
32 Hammam (Men & Women)
33 Gazleane Mosque
34 Hammam
35 Sherabliyin Mosque
37 Souq an-Nejjarine (Carpenters' Souq)
39 Zawiyya Moulay Idriss
40 Medersa el-Attarine
41 Souq el-Attarine
42 Medersa Cherratin
43 Qur'anic School
44 Funduq Tsetouanien
45 Tanners' Souq
47 Kairaouine Mosque
48 Place as-Seffarine
49 Hammam
50 Medersa as-Seffarine
51 Bronze & Silver Souq
52 Bein al-Mudun Bridge
53 Dyers' Souq
54 Er-Rsif Mosque
55 Local Bus No 19 to Ville Nouvelle
56 Wafabank
57 Hammam (Men & Women)
58 Medersa es-Sahriji
59 Andalus Mosque
60 Pottery Souq
63 CTM Garage Office
65 Non-CTM buses to Taza, Oujda, Al-Hoceima, Nador
66 Grands Taxis to Taza
67 Local Buses Nos 12 & 18

pausing wherever the mood takes you to watch something of interest, rummage through the articles for sale, or simply sit down over a glass of tea and take it all in.

Like any Moroccan medina, Fès el-Bali is divided into areas representing different craft guilds and souqs interspersed with houses. It is replete with fascinating old buildings, mostly of a religious nature, but many are closed to non-Muslims. Because of the compact nature of this part of the city, little can be seen of them from the outside either. No-one particularly minds if you discreetly peer through the doorways, but that's the limit.

What follows can be interpreted as a suggested itinerary for an excursion into the medina, taking you from Bab Bou Jeloud to the area around the Kairaouine Mosque and finishing with several options for exiting the medina. The medina's souqs are virtually empty on Thursday afternoon and Friday.

Bab Bou Jeloud Bab Bou Jeloud is the main entrance to Fès el-Bali. Although you will probably encounter people offering to be guides, they are not nearly as bad here as they can be farther out from the medina. You are bound to be warned by would-be guides in the ville nouvelle, for instance, that you should accept their services now to avoid the packs of man-eating guides circulating by the Bab and inside the medina. Should they be persistent, tell them you're staying at one of the cheap hotels just inside the gate.

Bab Bou Jeloud, unlike much of the rest of the city walls and gates, is a recent addition, which was built in 1913. When you pass through it you come upon a cluster of cheap hotels and cafés – this area is a hive of activity and a great place to sit and watch people's comings and goings.

Medersa Bou Inania Not far from the Bab Bou Jeloud is the Medersa Bou Inania, built by the Merenid sultan Bou Inan between 1350 and 1357, and said to be the finest of the theological colleges built by the Merenids. The entrance is on At-Talaa al-Kebir. You can't really miss it, as the minaret is visible from the moment you enter the city by Bab Bou Jeloud.

The medersa has been restored in recent years with a degree of skill proving that Moroccans have lost none of the talents for which they are justly famous. The carved woodwork and stucco are magnificent. There are excellent views over Fès from the roof (closed at the time of writing for further restoration work).

This medersa differs in a number of ways from others you may have seen already; most of those that can be visited in Morocco were built under the Merenids and all betray a common artistic inspiration. A comparison with its namesake in Meknès is sufficient to get the point across. All medersas come equipped with what we might call a prayer hall, but what Muslims would still call a mosque *(masjid)* – of admittedly modest dimensions and containing a simple mihrab. Here, opposite the entrance, the 'mosque' is more elaborate, and the outstanding feature is its minaret. This distinguishes it from other medersas, as they rarely come equipped with minarets.

One explanation is that the medersa required something approaching a full-scale mosque of its own because of the absence of a nearby mosque at the time it was built. As this little mosque is still in use, non-Muslims may not pass the barrier marked by a tiny tributary of the Oued Fès.

Opposite the entrance to the medersa, to your left, is a water clock designed by a clockmaker who was said to be a part-time magician. Unfortunately, it, too, was covered up for restoration at the time of writing.

The medersa is open between 8 am and 5 pm (except at prayer times), and closed on Friday mornings. Entry costs Dr 10.

Towards the Zawiyya Moulay Idriss II Turn right out of the medersa and head down At-Talaa al-Kebir. About 150 metres down the street on a bend you will pass a **fountain** on your left and a little farther on a **hammam**, which precedes one of the medina's 300 or so mosques, the **Gazleane Mosque**. At-Talaa al-Kebir continues right down to the Medersa el-Attarine, but changes its name along the way. At the Gazleane Mosque it is known as the Qanitra Bou Rous. About 100 metres farther down, at an unmistakable dogleg (there is another **hammam** on the left just after it), it becomes Ash-Sherabliyin ('the slippermakers'); the **mosque** you pass on the right another 200 or so metres farther down has taken the same name. Note on the right also, a little way past the mosque, one of the numerous 'traditional' Moroccan restaurants that Fès boasts, the Restaurant Palais des Mérinides (see Places to Eat).

Another 100 metres on, At-Talaa as-Seghir (the parallel artery from Bab Bou Jeloud) joins this street and takes you on to an unassuming gate, beyond which it makes a slight incline into the Souq el-Attarine (the spice market). Just past the gate on the left is another restaurant and café worth noting, the **Dar Saada**. It doubles as a carpet warehouse, and is a useful landmark. Virtually across the road and down a short narrow alley is the **henna souq**, where you can buy, well, henna. It is used as a hair dye and, more importantly, to paint complicated tattoo-like designs on women's hands and feet. Certain designs are associated with particular events, such as weddings.

In the jumble of back lanes and small

squares just south of where At-Talaa as-Seghir and Ash-Sherabliyin meet is the **Souq an-Nejjarine** (carpenters' souq), through which you will come across a pretty little square, **Place an-Nejjarine**, dominated by one of the city's most beautiful fountains and an impressive *funduq* – a former caravanserai for travelling merchants who would store and sell their goods below and take lodgings on the floors above.

Zawiyya Moulay Idriss II Son of the founder of Morocco's first dynasty, Moulay Idriss II is often credited with having founded the city of Fès. In fact it is probable that his father took that decision, but there is no doubt that Moulay Idriss II brought the city to life. He is almost as highly revered as his father, and his zawiyya is an object of pilgrimage. You can get to two gates leading into the sanctuary. From Place an-Nejjarine, a lane leads off the south-east corner to the women-only gateway into sanctuary. Alternatively, from the Dar Saada (see the previous section) you can continue a few metres east into the Souq el-Attarine and take the first alley to the right – this leads to the main entrance. Both usually have bars across them marking the point beyond which non-Muslims may not pass. With discretion, you can go up to the gates and get a look inside. Next to the

Kairaouine mosque and university, it is one of the main monuments in the heart of Fès. From vantage points overlooking the city, its green-tiled roof stands out with those of the Kairaouine against the white-grey backdrop of the surrounding houses and buildings.

Medersa el-Attarine The street that leads through the Souq el-Attarine continues another 200 metres or so (past a qissaria, or covered market, on the right) until it ends in a T-junction. Right in front of you is the Medersa el-Attarine. It was built by Abu Said in 1325 and follows the traditional pattern of Merenid artisanship. The central courtyard is flanked by halls for teaching and the modest masjid. The zellij tile base, intermediate stucco work and cedar wood completion at the top of the walls and the ceiling cede nothing in elegance to the artistry of the Medersa Bou Inania. It's open from 9 am to noon and 2 to 6 pm (closed Friday mornings and often Thursday afternoons, too). Entry costs Dr 10. There are good views of the courtyard of the Kairaouine Mosque from the roof, if you're allowed up there.

Kairaouine Mosque Emerging again from the medersa, turn left. You'll see Rue Bou Touil on the left with a few snack stalls. The walls of the great Kairaouine (or Qayrawin)

Ibn Khaldoun

Although Fès cannot count him as one of its own, Ibn Khaldoun, one of the Arab world's greatest thinkers, was one of many luminaries attracted to Morocco's centre of learning, where he studied in the Kairaouine University for some years.

Considered the greatest of Arab historians, Ibn Khaldoun developed the first philosophy of history not based on religion. Called the *Muqaddimah* (Introduction to History), his book is regarded as a classic. The 20th-century historian Toynbee has called it 'a philosophy of history which is undoubtedly the greatest work of its kind that has ever yet been created by any mind in any time or place'. Ibn Khaldoun also wrote a definitive history of Muslim North Africa.

He was born in Tunisia in 1332 and spent the early years of his life there, but by the age of 23, after completing his studies at the Kairaouine, he had become a secretary to the sultan of Fès. After having been imprisoned for two years on suspicion of being involved in a palace rebellion, Ibn Khaldoun moved to Granada, then Bejaia, Tlemcen, Biskra and Fès before ending up back in Granada.

In 1375 he gave up the world of business and politics and retired to the village of Frenda in Algeria where, under the protection of the local emir, he spent four years writing the *Muqaddimah*.

He spent the later years of his life teaching at the Kairaouine's eastern counterpart, the Al-Azhar in Cairo. He died in 1406. ■

mosque and university stretch down this street and ahead of you on the left-hand side (the qissaria opens up on your right).

The mosque is said to be capable of holding 20,000 people, and the university, one of the oldest in the world, has for centuries been one of the most highly regarded centres of Muslim religious learning, surpassed in reputation only by the Al-Azhar in Cairo.

It was built between 859 and 862 by Fatma bint Mohammed ben Feheri for her fellow refugees from Tunisia. It was enlarged in 956 and brought to its present size by the Almoravid sultan Ali ben Youssef. The Almohads and Saadians also contributed to its detail. The buildings include one of the finest libraries in the Muslim world, and there are usually 300 students in residence in the university. Unfortunately, non-Muslims may not enter, and it's so hemmed in by other buildings that little can be seen of it from the outside.

You can follow the walls right around it and occasionally get a look inside.

Around the Kairaouine If you head down Rue Bou Touil, following the university walls, you will be obliged to make a right turn. Just on your left is the 14th-century **Funduq Tsetouanien** (Tetouan Funduq). For centuries it served as a hotel and warehouse for travelling merchants; the name suggests that it was originally the preserve of businessmen from Tetouan. Mohammed Bouzoubaa, who runs a carpet factory in the former funduq, will be happy to tell you a bit about the place, but may be a little disappointed if you don't stay a while for some tea and a look at his wares.

A little way down and still on the left is a wonderful 14th-century merchant's mansion that has been converted into a carpet shop and restaurant, the **Palais de Fès**. The rooftop café has superb views over the Kairaouine University. Proceeding along the university walls, you emerge on another small square, Place as-Seffarine (Brassmakers' Square). With the university walls still on your right (the entrance to its library

opens on to this square), there is a small and not particularly captivating **medersa**, named after the square, on your left – look for the heavy studded cedar door. Built in 1280, it is the oldest in Fès, but is in an advanced state of disrepair. Across the main street leading east off the square (away from the Kairaouine) is a **hammam**.

Itinerary Options You could now continue to follow the walls of the Kairaouine back to where you started and head back to Bab Bou Jeloud, ideally taking At-Talaa as Seghir and perhaps winding up the day's visit with a look at the Dar Batha museum. On the way, if you're interested, you could get off the beaten track south of the Kairaouine University to have a quick look at the **Medersa Cherratin**, which was built in 1670 under Moulay ar-Rashid, the first of the Alawites. It is far less interesting than its Merenid precursors.

There are other options from Place as-Seffarine. You can head off north-east to see Fès's famous tanneries (from where you could push on over the Oued Fès towards the Andalus quarter, south to the Bab el-Ftouh and buses to the ville nouvelle) and then return to the square before setting off for the dyers' souq, Er-Rsif mosque and an alternative bus stop for rides back into the ville nouvelle.

Yet another possibility would be to return to the gateway into the Souq el-Attarine for an excursion north towards Bab Guissa, the Hôtel Palais Jamaï and perhaps beyond to the Merenid tombs (see that entry). You can also pick up a bus to the ville nouvelle from Bab Guissa.

Tanneries From Place as-Seffarine, take the lane just north of the medersa on the square. Take the left fork after about 50 metres and follow your nose – or the directions locals are bound to give you. You will probably be led to a platform overlooking the tanners' pits through a leather shop. It's also fairly likely that someone will ask you for a donation (Dr 10) for a 'workers' fund'. They can be quite insistent about this, although it's all rather dubious.

The tanneries are best visited in the morning, when the pits are awash with the colours used in the tanning and dyeing process. It doesn't smell good, but is not quite as bad as you might be led to believe.

Dyers' Souq & Er-Rsif Mosque From Place as-Seffarine, take the main lane heading east away from the Kairaouine, and south of the medersa on the square, and you will quickly find yourself in the Dyers' Souq by the Oued Fès. There are two small bridges over the fairly filthy-looking stream, whose water is used in the dyeing of textiles. If you cross either one and head off to the right you will emerge on to a wide square by the Er-Rsif Mosque. From here you can get the No 19 bus back to the ville nouvelle.

Andalus Quarter The only real attractions here are the Andalus Mosque and the Medersa es-Sahriji next door. To get there from Place as-Seffarine, take the lane for the tanneries, but turn right instead of left at the fork and you will reach the Bein al-Mudun ('Between the Cities') bridge over the Oued Fès. It will not be immediately obvious how to proceed from here, and you may want to enlist someone's help. There are at least two ways to choose from. The first is as follows. As soon as you cross the bridge, turn right and then take the first left (which starts out as a covered street). At the T-junction turn right and then take the first left; about 100 metres up on your right is a hammam for men and women. As you head up to an archway over the street, you pass a small square on the left and a mosque on the right. Once through the arch (you emerge on a small square), turn left. Dead ahead is the women's entrance to the Andalus Mosque and, shortly before on the right, the entrance to the medersa. The main entrance to the mosque is around the corner to the left of the women's entrance.

The **medersa** was built in 1321. The basic structure of this college is simple, but the inside is richly decorated and there are good views from the roof. Much of the structure lay in ruins until fairly recently, but restoration work is still continuing. It is open daily from 8.30 am to 5 pm, usually with a break from noon to 3 pm. It is closed on Friday morning. Entry is Dr 10.

The **mosque** was founded as a small local place of worship in the 9th century and was expanded by the Almohads in the 13th century, not long before the arrival of the Merenids, who also added to the decoration and installed a library.

If you want to leave the medina at this point, you can return to the small square, turn left and follow the wide street heading south off the square. It leads right down to Bab el-Ftouh, where you can catch local buses to the ville nouvelle.

Northern Medina The best way to reach Bab Guissa and the Hôtel Palais Jamaï in the north of the medina is to start off at the gateway to Souq el-Attarine. Take the street just on the west side of the gate. If you stick to the wider streets and keep going *up*, you really can't go wrong. You'll know you're on the right track if you pass by a little square with a cinema on its northern side. From there you will probably arrive at Bab Guissa, from which you can easily see the Hôtel Palais Jamaï to the east. What is now a luxury hotel was built in the late 19th century by the Grand Vizier to Moulay al-Hassan I, Sidi Mohammed ben Arib al-Jamaï. (He and his brother also had a palace built in Meknès, on Place el-Hedim, which now houses a museum.) The Jamaï brothers fell from grace at the rise of Sultan Abd al-Aziz, and lost all their properties. Set in lush gardens, the palace is a wonderful place to take a refreshment – if you can afford Dr 20 for a cup of coffee!

Across the road from Bab Guissa you can pick up local buses back into the ville nouvelle. There are also petits taxis.

Fès el-Jdid

Fès el-Jdid was built next to Fès el-Bali by the Merenids in the 13th century. It has some spectacular buildings and the old Jewish quarter and, although less interesting than the older city, is much easier to explore. No-one will hassle you for guide services (except perhaps to suggest that you engage a guide here to take you into Fès el-Bali).

The entrance to the Dar el-Makhzen (Royal Palace) on Place des Alaouites is a stunning example of modern restoration. The grounds cover some 200 acres and house palaces, pavilions, medersas, mosques and pleasure gardens; the complex has been used to host an Arab League conference. It used to be possible to visit the palace with prior permission from the tourist office, but this is no longer the case unless you have political or cultural elbow.

At the northern end of the main street, Sharia Moulay Suleiman (formerly Grande Rue de Fès el-Jdid), is the **Petit Mechouar**, a parade ground for the sultan's troops, and the enormous Merenid gate of **Bab Dekkaken**, once the main entrance to the royal palace. Between it and Bab Bou Jeloud are the well-maintained and relaxing **Bou Jeloud Gardens** (or Jnan Sebil), though the partially dried-up lake is used as a rubbish dump. Through the gardens flows the Oued Fès, still the city's main source of water. North of the gate is the **Grand Mechouar**, leading up to Bab Segma. Behind the western wall of the Grand Mechouar was the royal arms factory, established in 1886 by Moulay al-Hassan. It now serves as a carpet factory.

Sharia Moulay Suleiman is lined with shops and a few hotels and cafés, but lacks the atmosphere of the main streets in Fès el-Bali. South of it is the old **mellah**, the Jewish quarter. Few Jews live here now, but their houses, with windows and balconies looking into the streets, are in marked contrast to the usual Muslim practice of having windows opening on to an internal courtyard. They were transferred from the centre of the old city by the Merenids. Some say they were moved for their own protection, others maintain that it made it easier to keep an eye on their activities, and others believe it was to provide the Merenids with a loyal bulwark against possible rebellions from

---

Mellah

The word 'mellah' (from the Arabic for salt) appears to have referred to the area of Fès el-Jdid to which the city's Jewish population was transferred under the Merenids. Some say it was watered by a salty tributary of the Oued Fès, whereas other describe something more along the lines of a salty swamp. The word 'mellah' eventually took on the same meaning in Morocco as ghetto in Europe – the Jewish quarter. According to a more colourful explanation, the area in which the Jews lived derived from a job some of them were assigned by the Muslim city authorities – salting the heads of criminals, rebels and the like before they were hung up to adorn the city's gates and walls. ■

Fassis of the old city, whose loyalty they were unsure of.

Dar Batha

One place on the border of Fès el-Jdid and Fès el-Bali that you should not miss is the Dar Batha, now the Musée du Batha (also known as the Museum of Moroccan Arts). It is on Place de l'Istiqlal, about five minutes' walk from Bab Bou Jeloud. Built as a palace about 100 years ago by Moulays al-Hassan and Abd al-Aziz, it houses historical and artistic artefacts from ruined or decaying medersas, fine Fassi embroidery, tribal carpets and ceramics dating from the 14th century to the present. As usual, the explanations are in Arabic and French. It's open from 8.30 am to noon and 2.30 to 6.30 pm (closed Tuesday). Entry costs Dr 10.

Outskirts

For a spectacular overview of Fès, head through the Grand Mechouar and Bab Segma, cross the highway (Route Principale No 1), veer off to the left and walk around the old Kasbah des Cherarda (which now houses secondary schools, a university and hospital), following the road behind the cemetery to the Borj Nord. The Borj (like its counterpart on the southern side of the city) was built by the Saadian sultan Ahmed al-Mansour in the late 16th century to keep a watch on the potentially disloyal populace of Fès.

It now houses a military museum, which consists mainly of endless rows of muskets, rifles and cannon, many of them taken from Riffian rebels in 1958. Opening hours are the same as for the Dar Batha and entry is Dr 10.

Merenid Tombs

Farther along here, a short way past the Hôtel des Mérinides, are the Merenid tombs. These date from the time when the Merenids abandoned Chellah in Rabat as their necropolis. Unfortunately, they're in an advanced state of ruin and little remains of the fine original decoration. There are good views over Fès from here, but watch out for stone-throwing kids.

Places to Stay

Fès is a large city, so where you stay on arrival will depend largely on the season and the time of day you arrive. In summer, when many of the smaller hotels tend to fill up quickly, there's little point in heading for Fès el-Bali if it's getting late. Take something close to where you are for the first night and have a look around the following morning. In summer many of the cheapies in Fès el-Jdid and Fès el-Bali hike up their prices, and you end up paying the same as you would for better accommodation in the ville nouvelle. At this time, too, single rooms in the cheapies are almost impossible to find, as hoteliers make more money by letting them out to two or three people at corresponding double and triple prices.

Places to Stay – bottom end

Camping Camping isn't really feasible unless you have your own transport, as the nearest site is at 'Ain Chkef, some six km out of town off the Ifrane road. It's known as *Camping Diamant Vert* and sits at the bottom of a valley through which a clean stream runs. There's plenty of shade. Facilities include a swimming pool and disco. Camping costs Dr 15 per person (Dr 5 for children), Dr 10 for a car, Dr 15 for a caravan and Dr 10 to pitch a tent. Motorised 'guides'

tend to hang about here. Bus No 218 will get you here from Fès. Bus No 17 to 'Ain Chkef will also get you close to the camp site. You can pick it up in the ville nouvelle on Blvd Tariq ibn Ziad, near the mosque.

There are other camp sites in the region, in Sefrou for instance, but they are hardly practical for Fès.

Hostel The cheapest place in the new city is the *youth hostel* (☎ 624085), 18 Rue Mohammed el-Hansali. It costs Dr 15 per person in dormitory accommodation (Dr 17 without membership card) and there are cold showers. It's a fairly new building, and you can sleep on the roof if there are no beds left. They are planning to add family rooms and a communal kitchen. The hostel is open from 8 to 9 am, noon to 3 pm and 6 to 10 pm.

Hotels – Fès el-Bali (Bab Bou Jeloud) The most colourful places to stay are the bunch of cheapies clustered around Bab Bou Jeloud. They're basic and the shower situation is grim, but there are hammams all over the city. The cheapest are the hotels *Erraha* and *Al-Watani* (Arabic for 'hotel') opposite each other just outside Bab Bou Jeloud. Singles/doubles cost Dr 30/50 and the Al-Watani claims to have hot water. Better is the *Hôtel du Jardin Publique*, which is in a quiet location and has rooms for the same price. There are a couple of rooms on the 3rd floor with windows in the outside wall. These are preferable to the more claustrophobic lower rooms which face the internal courtyard, although the upper ones are hotter in summer. There is no hot water.

Just inside the Bab is the *Hôtel Cascade*. It has simple but clean rooms for Dr 50/80, and occasionally there is hot water. Next door is the *Hôtel Mauritania*, which charges Dr 40 per person and Dr 10 for a hot, shared shower.

Closer to the Medersa Bou Inania is the *Hôtel Lamrani*, a friendly place with acceptable rooms but still higher prices at Dr 60/80 (or Dr 50 for singles on the roof).

Various hammams have been marked on

the Fès el-Bali map, and there are others to be discovered. Ask at your hotel.

Hotels – Fès el-Bali (Bab el-Ftouh)
If you want to be near the buses that leave from Bab el-Ftouh, or happen to be desperate for a cheapie, you could look at the handful of hotels down here.

The *Hôtel Moulay Idriss*, with rooms for Dr 20/40, is about as cheap as you'll find. It's simple but clean. Farther up the road, the *Hôtel Andalous* is also basic and quiet, with cold showers. They charge Dr 30/50. Another nearby possibility is the *Hôtel Bahia*.

Hotels – Fès el-Jdid
There are at least four cheap hotels spread out in this area, if you have no luck around Bab Bou Jeloud or don't want to be quite so close to the action. The *Hôtel du Parc*, nearest the Bab, is a clean, cheap deal at Dr 20 a head on Sharia Moulay Suleiman. Down near Bab Smarine (Semmarin), also on Sharia Moulay Suleiman, the *Hôtel du Croissant* has beds for the same price, cold showers and somewhat smelly loos. The rooms are on several floors gathered around a sunny courtyard behind a café. Virtually around the corner is the *Hôtel Moulay Ali Charif*, which is much the same, but a bit noisier.

Practically in the ville nouvelle is the *Hôtel du Commerce* on Place des Alaouites. It's nothing special, but OK at Dr 60 for two people.

If showers prove a problem, there is a hammam on Sharia Moulay Suleiman.

Hotels – ville nouvelle
The cheapest hotels here are the *Hôtel Moghreb* (also called *Hôtel du Maghreb*), 25 Ave Mohammed es-Slaoui, the *Hôtel Regina*, 25 Rue Moulay Slimane, and the *Hôtel Renaissance*. The Moghreb and the Regina are basic but clean and the latter has cold, shared showers. They cost Dr 40 to Dr 60 for a single, Dr 80/100 for a double/triple. The Renaissance is an old, cavernous place with an lobby resembling a decrepit art gallery. It's friendly and

clean, has no showers and costs the same as the two other hotels.

Slightly better are the *Hôtel Volubilis*, Blvd Abdallah Chefchaouni, and, just round the corner, the *Hôtel Savoy* (☎ 620608). Both have good, clean, airy rooms with washbasins and there are communal showers (cold water). Singles/doubles/triples cost around Dr 30/70/90.

There are several hammams and public showers (douches) around the ville nouvelle if hot water is a problem. In the lane behind the CTM bus station is a modern place called Douche el-Fath. You pay Dr 4.50 for 30 minutes. Men can go from 6 am to 8.30 pm and women from 8 am to 8 pm. Soap and towels are available.

Places to Stay – middle
The ville nouvelle has plenty of one and two-star hotels. Among the cheapest is the *Hôtel CTM* (☎ 622811). It offers singles/doubles with communal shower for Dr 72/86, or rooms with private shower for Dr 83/100 plus taxes. The rooms are OK, but the beds are a little dodgy. They occasionally come up with hot water.

Not far away is the *Hôtel Central* (☎ 622333), 50 Rue du Nador, at the junction with Blvd Mohammed V. It's friendly, very clean and secure. Rooms with private shower (hot water in the mornings and evenings), bidet and washbasin cost Dr 72/86/130 plus taxes. Baggage can be safely left in reception if you're catching a late bus or train. Unfortunately, guides hang about outside the front door in the mornings.

The *Hôtel Excelsior* (☎ 625602), on Blvd Mohammed V, is not bad either. Singles/doubles cost Dr 76/94 with shower, toilet and a little furniture in the room. Hot water is sporadically available and they have a TV lounge on the first floor.

Closer to the railway station and particularly good value in comparison with most other places in this range is the *Hôtel Kairouan* (☎ 623596), 84 Rue du Soudan. It has spacious rooms with big clean beds, basin and bidet for Dr 70/111. Rooms with private shower cost Dr 107/129. Not bad at

Fès - Ville Nouvelle

0   100   200 m

all is the nearby two-star *Hôtel Royal* (☎ 624656), 32 Rue du Soudan, although it is more expensive at Dr 117/146 for rooms with private shower.

Also in the two-star range is the *Hôtel Lamdaghri* (☎ 620310), 10 Kabbour el-Mangad. It is a friendly place with good singles and twins (no double beds) for Dr 120/146. There are showers in the rooms and shared toilets. The hotel also has a pleasant dining area on the first floor. Although it was not obvious at the time of researching, travellers have written in to say it is used as a brothel.

Not as good is the *Hôtel Amor* (☎ 623304), 31 Rue Arabie Saoudite. It has rooms for the same prices and hot water in the evenings, but cockroaches are a bit of a problem.

Going up in price again and reasonable without being spectacular is the *Hôtel Olympic* (☎ 624529), around the corner from the covered market on Blvd Mohammed V. Singles/doubles/triples go for Dr 150/179/233 and the clean rooms come with private bathroom and toilet. There is hot water for a few hours in the evening.

Moving up to the three-star range, a good

PLACES TO STAY

3	Hôtel Moussafir
10	Hôtel Sofia (closed for repairs)
12	Hôtel Amor
16	Hôtel Royal
17	Hôtel Kairouan
23	Hôtel de la Paix
30	Hôtel Olympic
32	Hôtels Savoy & Volubilis
33	Hôtel Zalagh
34	Youth Hostel
38	Hôtel Excelsior
39	Hôtel Lamdaghri
42	Grand Hôtel
46	Hôtel Renaissance
48	Hôtel Splendid
49	Hôtel Palais de Fès
50	Fès Motel
51	Hôtel Regina
52	Hôtel Central
61	Hôtel CTM
62	Hôtel Jnan Palace

PLACES TO EAT

7	Restaurant La Cheminée
11	Cracos & Venisia
36	Central Market
37	Pizzeria Oliverdi
41	Restaurant Chamonix
43	Restaurant du Centre
47	Restaurant Mounia
56	Restaurant Oued La Bière
58	Restaurant Golding Palm

OTHER

1	Railway Station
2	Grands Taxis to Meknès
4	Swimming Pool
5	Café
6	Café
8	Mosque
9	Hertz
13	Bar Lala Iris
14	Bank al-Maghrib
15	BMAO (Exchange)
18	Centre Culturel Français
19	Budget
20	ONMT Office
21	English Bookshop
22	ABM Bank (Visa & Eurocheques)
24	Uniban (Exchange)
25	Europcar
26	Main Post & Telephone Office (PTT)
27	Police
28	Newsstand
29	Kodak Shop
31	Bar
35	American Language Center
40	Goldcar
44	BMCE (ATMs)
45	Bar
53	Place Mohammed V
54	French Consul's Residence
55	Church
57	Bar
59	Grands Taxis to Rabat & Casablanca
60	Douche el-Fath
61	CTM Bus Station

choice is the *Hôtel Zalagh* (☎ 625531), on Rue Mohammed Diouri, not far from the youth hostel. Many of the big rooms have wonderful views across to Fès el-Bali. Singles/doubles with toilet but shared shower cost Dr 171/215 plus tax or Dr 216/256 with shower and toilet. In winter they have heating. If you have a bit of money to spend, this is a good deal.

The *Grand Hôtel* (☎ 625511; fax 653 847), on Blvd Abdallah Chefchaouni, is an older place with a little character. It has rooms with shower and toilet for Dr 202/250. It is a reasonable place and has a basement parking lot.

More modern, with large carpeted, comfortable rooms and en suite bathrooms is the *Hôtel Splendid* (☎ 622148) at 9 Rue Abdelkrim el-Khattabi. Prices are Dr 216/261/342 plus taxes. The hotel also has a small swimming pool.

The *Hôtel Mounia* (☎ 62 4838), 60 Rue Azilah, is not so hot, but a little cheaper and handy for the CTM bus station. They have their own bar and hammam. Rooms cost Dr 192/241/328.

The *Hôtel de la Paix* (☎ 625072; fax 626880), 44 Ave Hassan II, near the Place de la Résistance, has slightly more expensive rooms at Dr 222/273/360. The rooms are self-contained, quiet and comfortable.

Right by the railway station is the *Hôtel*

Moussafir (☎ 651902; fax 651909). It is part of a chain of modern hotels located at railway stations and rooms come with all the mod-cons. The big plus is its proximity to the trains. Singles/doubles cost Dr 216/261 plus taxes.

Places to Stay – top end
An excellent location within quick strolling distance of the medina is the four-star *Hôtel Batha* (☎ 636441) on Place de l'Istiqlal (or Place Batha, depending on whom you talk to). It is not the cheapest hotel in this category but has good, modern rooms for Dr 380/420.

A little cheaper but located in the ville nouvelle at the opposite end of town, not really within quick strolling distance of anything, is the *Fès Motel*, formerly known as *Hôtel Volubilis* (☎ 621126; fax 621125) on Ave Hassan II. It has singles/doubles/triples for Dr 355/460/565.

At the five-star end of the spectrum, there are two places near the Fès Motel in the ville nouvelle. On the corner of the Ave Hassan II and Ave des FAR, the *Hôtel Palais de Fès* (☎ 623006; fax 620486) has rooms ranging from Dr 525 to Dr 1600 plus taxes. Farther out still is the extremely posh *Hôtel Jnan Palace* (☎ 653965; fax 651917), on Rue Moulay Slimane, where rooms start at Dr 1300/1500.

More interesting is the recently rebuilt *Hôtel des Mérinides* (☎ 645226; fax 645 225), with its sweeping views of the old medina from near the Merenid tombs. It has a swimming pool and two restaurants, and rooms start at Dr 820/1040.

If you had the money, the most interesting place to stay in Fès would without doubt be the *Hôtel Palais Jamaï* (☎ 634331; fax 635096), once the pleasure dome of a late 19th-century grand vizier to the sultan. Set in a lush Andalusian garden, its rooms start at Dr 900 and head for the sky. Along with the Mamounia in Marrakesh, it is a jewel of another epoch.

Places to Eat
Medina The restaurants around Bab Bou Jeloud in Fès el-Bali remain among the most popular places to hang out in the medina. Although the quality-price relationship is not always as good as it might once have been, enough Moroccans eat here to reassure the wary diner.

The *Restaurant Bouayad*, which has been going since 1939, is definitely one of the better ones, although not the cheapest place in Morocco to get a meal. Pastilla (pigeon pie), when they have it, costs Dr 50. On the other end of the scale, you can get a steaming bowl of harira for just Dr 2; ordering just harira does not always endear you to the owners, but this shouldn't deter you. Most of the other mains cost about Dr 40. Watch out if you start ordering side dishes and extras from the display – they don't appear on the menu and prices can be inflated.

The *Restaurant des Jeunes*, closer to the gate, also has good set meals but it has been reported that they have two menus and give you the one they think you can afford, even though the food is the same!

There are some great-value snack stands interspersed among the restaurants and cafés. For Dr 10 you can get a huge sandwich stuffed with meat, sausage, chips, salad and various other condiments – easily a satisfying lunch.

There are similar restaurants along Sharia Moulay Suleiman, close to Bab Smarine. For something better check out *La Noria*, in the Bou Jeloud Gardens. This is popular with young Moroccans, but you can expect to pay more for a meal here (a glass of tea alone costs Dr 4).

If you get hungry down around the Kairaouine Mosque, there is a small huddle of cheap food stands and an ice-cream stall between the Kairaouine and the Medersa el-Attarine.

Ville Nouvelle There are a few cheap eats on or just off Blvd Mohammed V, especially around the municipal market. They are mixed in with pâtisseries, cafés and the like. A couple of these food places are on the same side street off Blvd Mohammed V as the Hôtel Olympic. Watch the prices.

The *Restaurant Chamonix*, in a side street a block south, offers a limited range of good food, including a tasty set menu for Dr 42.50. Across the street is the *Pizzeria Oliverdi* (☎ 620231), a pizza place that does home delivery. Most of the pizzas are around Dr 35 and they also do some pasta dishes.

If you want a drink with your meal, you could do worse than the *Restaurant du Centre*, not far from the Chamonix but directly on Blvd Mohammed V (there's a Crédit du Maroc bank opposite). They prepare good, simple French fare which washes down nicely with some wine or beer.

Farther south and just opposite the Hôtel Central is another restaurant in a similar vein, the *Oued La Bière*. Despite its name, it doesn't serve beer, but there's a bar next door. A lively bar/restaurant, the *Golding Palm*, is a little farther south on Blvd Mohammed V, just short of the CTM station. It's popular with Moroccans, but mostly for drinking, as the meals start at about Dr 50.

By comparison, the *Restaurant Mounia* (☎ 626661), at 11 Blvd Mohammed Zerktouni, is a class act. It offers good serves of Moroccan food for Dr 50 to Dr 70 (main course only). They have a decent wine list and the waiters even wear bow ties. If you're skint or sick of couscous, you could try the spaghetti for Dr 15. You can even change money here and they accept credit cards for payment.

La Mamia on Place de Florence does eat-in and takeaway pizzas and hamburgers. The pizzas cost from Dr 30 to Dr 50 and are not bad at all.

Around the corner to the left of the Hôtel Amor on Ave de France, among the cafés and shops, are a couple of hamburger joints, *Cracos* and the *Venisia*. They are similar, although you get a better serve of chips at the Cracos. A decent hamburger will set you back about Dr 15. There are a few other such places scattered about the ville nouvelle, particularly in the side streets off Blvd Mohammed V.

Splurges Fès is dotted with a good half-dozen restaurants housed in old mansions

and the like offering expensive Moroccan meals in grand 'traditional' surroundings. Many of these also stage shows, including Moroccan music and Oriental dancing. The idea is to create something of the atmosphere of a Thousand and One Nights, and although it is a bit artificial, one extravagant evening along these lines can be good fun. You'll be looking at about Dr 200 per person. These places are at their best in the evening and when reasonably well patronised. If it's just you, the expensive menu and some desultory singing, they can be rather depressing.

There are two such restaurants in Fès el-Bali near the Hôtel Palais Jamaï: *Al-Firdaous* (☎ 634343) and *Les Remparts de Fès*. The latter offers set menus ranging from Dr 170 to Dr 220 and puts on a nightly music and dance show.

In the winding lanes near the Er-Rsif mosque are another couple of the genre. *La Menara* and the *Dar Tajine* (☎ 634167), 15 Ross Rhi, are signposted from the main road – the latter is much easier to find. They are both in a part of town you would otherwise have little cause to visit. They are open only for dinner, and if business is slow may not be open at all.

The *Dar Saada* (☎ 633343), down in the Souq el-Attarine in the heart of the medina, has already been mentioned (see Fès el-Bali). They offer set menus up to Dr 220 and à la carte. The *Restaurant Palais des Mérinides* (☎ 634028), near the Ash-Sherabliyin mosque, has somewhat cheaper menus.

Possibly the pick of the crop is the *Palais de Fès*, a gracious 14th-century mansion housing a restaurant and roof terrace café. The coffee costs Dr 5 a shot, but is worth it for the views. It is open for lunch.

You could also head for the *Hôtel Palais Jamaï*, which has a terrace overlooking the medina. The food is excellent and there's a choice of French or Moroccan cuisine, but you'll be up for about Dr 200 per person for food alone.

Entertainment
Cafés & Bars There is no shortage of cafés and salons de thé. There are a few inside Bab

Bou Jeloud, and an innumerable collection of them along the main streets of the ville nouvelle, particularly on Blvd Mohammed V. Take your pick. You could buy yourself some croissants or cakes in one of the pâtisseries and then settle down for breakfast at one of the outdoor tables and watch the morning slide by.

There are a few bars scattered around the ville nouvelle. Some have already been mentioned, as they are part of or just next door to restaurants. They are generally spit and sawdust places and some of the clientele can get a bit rowdy towards the end of a night's drinking. In addition to those already referred to, there's one next to the Hôtel Olympic and another next to the BMCE. The *Lala Iris*, on Ave Hassan II, is another well-patronised bar. Apart from these, which have little enough going for them, especially for women, there are bars in the middle and top-range hotels. Again, however, the company is more often than not all male.

Some of the bigger hotels have nightclubs or discos. Entry generally costs at least Dr 50, drinks are expensive and decent dress is expected. After going to all that effort, you often find they are little more than a glorified version of some of the bars with mirror balls. Among these is the *Salam Nightclub* in the Hôtel Zalagh.

The expensive 'traditional' Moroccan restaurants listed earlier sometimes put on a show with music and dance. *Al-Firdaous* does this every night (see Places to Eat).

Getting There & Away

Air The airport serving Fès is at Saiss, 15 km to the south. There are five flights a week to Casablanca, five a week to Marrakesh (all but one via Casablanca), nine a week to Agadir (all but one via Casablanca), three to Tangier (all via Casablanca) and a weekly direct flight to Er-Rachidia. There are also a couple of weekly direct flights to Paris.

Royal Air Maroc (☎ 625516) is at 54 Ave Hassan II. The one-way fare to Casablanca is Dr 405. To Marrakesh (direct flight on Tuesday), it costs Dr 590 one way. The same flight goes on to Agadir. The one-way fare is

Dr 810. The office is open Monday to Friday from 8.30 am to 12.15 pm and 2.30 to 7 pm; on Saturday mornings from 8.30 am to noon and 3 to 6 pm; and on holidays from 9 am to noon and 3 to 6 pm. You can only use credit cards to purchase air tickets.

Bus – CTM The CTM station is in the ville nouvelle on Blvd Mohammed V. Demand is high, especially on the Fès-Tangier and Fès-Marrakesh runs, so where possible you should buy tickets in advance.

There are eight daily departures to Casablanca, starting at 7 am and finishing at 7 pm (Dr 69; five hours). All but the 7 am bus call at Rabat (Dr 47.50; 3½ hours). They also call at Meknès (Dr 14.50; one hour), except for the 9.30 am service. There is an additional Meknès run at 6 pm.

Two buses a day depart for Marrakesh, at 6.30 am and 9 pm (Dr 115; nine hours), and for Tangier, at 11 am and 6 pm (Dr 77.50; six hours). There are two daily buses for Tetouan, which leave at 8 and 11 am (Dr 55; five hours).

Once a day a bus leaves for Oujda (Dr 62; six hours) at 12.30 pm via Taza (Dr 30.50; two hours). Another one heads for Taza at 6.30 pm.

There are international departures at 8 pm on various days of the week for Paris and Brussels as well as other French and Belgian destinations. For more details, see the Bus section of the Getting There & Away chapter.

Bus – Non-CTM The bulk of the non-CTM departures are from a station at Place Baghdadi, near Bab Bou Jeloud. There are various companies doing regular runs to such destinations as Meknès (about Dr 13), Rabat (about Dr 39) and Casablanca (Dr 55). There are at least four daily departures to Tangier for Dr 60 and two to Marrakesh for Dr 92. It's all very higgledy-piggledy, so the best thing to do is get there as early as you can and get yourself shepherded to the right window and on to the right bus.

Three CTM buses leave from here: one to Meknès at 3.30 pm, one to Ouezzane at 7.30 am (via ville nouvelle station) and another to

Taza at noon (via the ville nouvelle and Bab el-Ftouh).

Buses for Oujda (about Dr 60), Chefchaouen, Al-Hoceima and Taza (Dr 23 to Dr 30.50) leave from the station at Bab el-Ftouh, the south-eastern gate. Get here early, as the runs are quite irregular.

It appeared in early 1994 that a new bus station was being built at the foot of the cemetery next to the kasbah. How long this will take to complete is anyone's guess.

Train The railway station is in the ville nouvelle, 10 minutes' walk from Place de Florence. Trains are the best bet if you are headed for Casablanca, Marrakesh, Meknès, Oujda, Rabat or Tangier.

There are at least nine daily departures to Casablanca (five hours), all of which stop at Rabat (four hours) and Meknès (one hour) en route. There are two direct runs to Marrakesh (7.20 and 9.40 am; about 8¼ hours) and four other services requiring changes at Casa-Voyageurs or Kenitra. The longest wait is about 50 minutes. There are two direct trains (coming from Oujda) for Tangier (1.10 and 4.10 pm; 6½ hours). Three other trains (heading south) require changes at Sidi Kacem or Sidi Slimane. They all stop at Meknès and Asilah. Direct trains for Oujda (6½ hours) via Taza (2½ hours) leave six times a day.

Examples of 2nd-class fares (normal and rapide) include: Casablanca (Dr 69/87); Marrakesh (Dr 121.50/153.50); Meknès (Dr 12/15); Oujda (Dr 74/93.50); Rabat (Dr 49.50/62.50) and Tangier (Dr 63.50/84).

Taxi Grands taxis on fixed-price routes leave for Rabat (Dr 50) and Casablanca (Dr 80) from a rank near the CTM bus station. Taxis for Meknès (Dr 15) leave from Ave des Almohades in front of the railway station.

Others for Taza (Dr 30) leave from just outside Bab el-Ftouh.

Local ones run to places like El-Hajeb from a rank near the Place Baghdadi bus station and if you want to get to Ifrane (Dr 16) or Azrou (Dr 21), there is a rank behind the mosque on Blvd Dhar Mahres in the ville nouvelle.

For any other destination you will have to negotiate a corsa (special) fare.

Car The following are among the car rental agencies located in Fès:

Avis
    50 Blvd Chefchaouni (☎ 626746)
Budget
    On the corner of Ave Hassan II and Rue Bahrein (☎ 620919)
    Hôtel Palais Jamaï, Bab Guissa (☎ 634331)
Europcar
    41 Ave Hassan II (☎ 626545)
Goldcar
    Rue Abdelkrim el-Khattabi (☎ 620495)
Hertz
    Blvd Lalla Maryam (☎ 622812)
    Airport (☎ 651823)
Zeit
    35 Ave Mohammed es-Slaoui (☎ & fax 654063)

Getting Around
To/From the Airport There is a regular bus service between the airport and the railway station. Look for No 16. The fare is about Dr 3. Otherwise you'll have to get a grand taxi, which will cost Dr 70.

Bus Fès has a fairly good local bus service, although the buses are like sardine cans at certain times of the day. The route number is usually displayed on the side of the bus, near the back door, or at the front. You get on the back and off at the front door. There's a conductor sitting at the back. Fares hover around the Dr 1.70 mark.

Useful routes include:

No 2
    Bab Smarine – Ave Hassan II – Hay Hussein
No 9
    Place de l'Atlas – Ave Hassan II – Dar Batha
No 10
    Railway station – Bab Guissa – Sidi Bou Jidda
No 12
    Bab Bou Jeloud – Bab Guissa – Bab el-Ftouh
No 16
    Railway station – Airport
No 17
    Blvd Tariq ibn Ziad – 'Ain Chkef

No 18
    Bab el-Ftouh – Dar Batha
No 19 & 29
    Ave Hassan II – Bab el-Jedid – Bab er-Rsif
No 47
    Railway station – Bab Bou Jeloud
No 50
    Bab Smarine – Ave Hassan II – Soukarin

Taxi The red petits taxis are cheap and plentiful. The drivers generally use the meters without any fuss. Expect to pay about Dr 10 to go from the CTM station to Bab Bou Jeloud. Only grands taxis will go out to the airport and although it's only 15 km they're virtually impossible to beat down to less than Dr 70.

SOUTH OF FÈS
For travellers heading south, there are two main options from Fès. You can take highway P24 towards Marrakesh, stopping in at the odd alpine village of Ifrane and then Azrou on the way. A detour from Beni Mellal on this route would also allow you to take in the impressive Cascades d'Ouzoud (see the Around Marrakesh section for more on this) before finally reaching the southern imperial capital.

Alternatively, you could make a stop at Sefrou on your way along highway P20 to the southern valleys, including a tour through the Ziz Gorges before reaching Er-Rachidia. From there you could head east to Figuig, south to Erfoud or west to Ouarzazate via the still more impressive Todra and Dadès valleys.

Ifrane
Just 17 km short of Azrou on highway P24 from Fès is Ifrane (altitude 1650 metres), where you would be hard-pressed not to do a double-take and wonder whether you hadn't just left Morocco. Built by the French in the 1930s as an Alpine resort, the red-tiled roofs of this highly un-Moroccan looking place are a bit of a shock when they come into view. The place is popular with Moroccans though, and more villas are being jerry-built in much the same style. Outside the uncertain winter ski season and high

summer weekends, when the better-off flock to their holiday homes to escape the heat of the big cities, the place is a bit of a ghost town. Many of the grander villas are actually company hotels – the post office, Banque Populaire and CTM are among those that have 'hotels' here for staff holidays.

Ifrane could make a reasonable base for those with their own vehicles to explore the surrounding gentle countryside, and for walkers too, although a better option would probably be the somewhat more lively Azrou to the south-west. If you have a decent car, a pleasant **lakes** circuit starts at a turn-off 17 km north of Ifrane ('Tour Touristique des Lacs'). First up is Dayet Aoua, after which the road deteriorates badly. At the far end of the lake turn off away from it, or you'll end up doing a circle and finish up where you started.

Information The tourist office (☎ 566038) is in the Hôtel Michlifen (see the next section).

Places to Stay & Eat Other than the *camp site* on Blvd Mohammed V, which is not bad at all, there is no budget accommodation in

1 Hôtel Michlifen
2 Hôtel/Restaurant Chamonix
3 Post Office (PTT)
4 Grand Hôtel
5 Bus & Grand Taxi station

To Meknès
To Camping Ground
Blvd Mohammed V
To Azrou (17 km)

Route de la Source
Avenue de l'Atlas
Avenue de la Poste
Rue des Catalpas
Avenue Prince Moulay Abdallah
Rue des Robiniers
Avenue Mosquée du Niger
Avenue des Cèdres
Vittel

Ifrane

0   100   200 m

Top Left: Tour Hassan, Rabat (DS)
Top Right: Brassware, El-Jadida (DS)
Bottom: Walls of Chellah, Rabat (DS)

Top: Moulay Idriss (HF)
Middle: Market scene, Fès (HF)
Bottom: Ramparts, Asilah (DS)

Ifrane. The camp site, west of the bus station, costs Dr 5 a person and the same each for car, tent place and electricity. It's a pleasant, leafy spot.

The surly individuals at the *Hôtel/Restaurant Chamonix* (☎ 566028), on Ave de la Marche Verte in what could be described as the centre of town should be enough to put you off taking a room here. The rooms cost Dr 150 and there are no showers! You can also rent antediluvian ski equipment here.

Inside the *Grand Hôtel* (☎ 566203; fax 566407), Ave de la Poste, you would swear you were in the Alps. Built in 1941, it's the most characterful of Ifrane's hotels and has its own bar and restaurant. Singles/doubles are Dr 226/273 – you'd need to book ahead in winter.

The top of the range is the *Hôtel Michlifen* (☎ 566607; fax 566623), north of the town centre. It overlooks and dominates the town, and its five-star prices will do much the same to your wallet.

Outside the hotels, the eating choices are limited. There are a few small restaurant cafés in the centre of town near the Chamonix.

Getting There & Away The main bus and grand taxi station is on Blvd Mohammed V, west of the town centre. Occasional buses between Fès and Marrakesh stop here, and there are two CTM runs a day from Meknès but otherwise bus activity is slow.

Grands taxis are a better bet. They run to Azrou (Dr 6), Sefrou (Dr 17.50), Fès (ville nouvelle) for Dr 16 and Meknès for the same amount.

Mischliffen

This is the premier ski playground of the Middle Atlas, but apart from a couple of lifts, café and nice views, there's precious little to be seen here. Both Ifrane (17 km to the north) and Azrou (24 km west) make decent bases. The uneven season – snow is not always reliable – runs more or less from December to March. You can hire antiquated gear in Ifrane.

Azrou

The green-tiled rooftops of central Azrou are in total contrast to Ifrane, and this primarily Berber town is a cheerful, hassle-free little place – and full of life in a way that Ifrane is not. Surrounded by pine and cedar forests, which are ideal for exploring either on foot or by car, the cool mountain air helps make this a good location to relax after the pressure-cooker of Fès. The Tuesday market is a lively affair, and the centre of the town busy enough to hold your interest, but there's not much to do in Azrou, which is part of its charm. The cheaper hotels and most of the little restaurants are on or near Place Mohammed V or just south of it in the narrow lanes of the old town. The banks and post office are also on Place Mohammed V. The bus and taxi stations are five minutes' walk to the north, beyond the big new mosque that seems destined to remain forever 'under construction'.

Azrou means 'rock', and the clump of stone that gives the town its name, below which the weekly market takes place, lies near Blvd Mohammed, to the west of the town centre.

Information You can change money at the BMCE or Banque Populaire on Place Mohammed V. The post office is next to the Banque Populaire, just east of the square.

Places to Stay – bottom end The cheapest place to stay, and probably the least convenient, is the *youth hostel* (☎ 562496). It's a couple of km from the bus station, east of the town centre on the Midelt road. Cardholders pay Dr 15 and nonmembers Dr 20. The showers are cold and there's no kitchen.

Of the little places around Place Moulay Hachem ben Salah, the cheapest is *Hôtel Beau Séjour*, at Dr 20 a person. Cold showers are available. Try for a room overlooking the square. The *Hôtel Atlas* next door was closed at the time of writing. The *Hôtel Ziz* (☎ 562362) has rooms ranging from Dr 20 to Dr 50. A big bed in a windowless cell costs Dr 25. The same room with a tiny window is Dr 30. The *Hôtel Salam* (☎ 562562) is the best of the cheapies. A small but decent single is Dr 30. Bigger rooms range up to Dr 70. Some of the rooms smell a little too lived in, and again showers are cold.

In winter, none of these places would be much chop – blankets are always in short supply and you can forget about heating.

Places to Stay – middle By far the best value for money (and often full), is the one-

PLACES TO STAY

18 Hôtel des Cèdres
23 Hôtel Salam
28 Hôtel Ziz
30 Hôtels Beau Séjour & Atlas
33 Hôtel Panorama

PLACES TO EAT

3 Food Market
4 Juice Stands & Pâtisseries
8 Restaurant Atlas
9 Restaurant Echaab

10 Cheap Restaurants
11 Café
14 Café Rex
15 Café Atlas
17 Restaurant Relais Forestier
22 Café Salam
24 Cheap Eats
26 Cheap Eats
27 Cheap Eats

OTHER

1 Grands Taxis (Main Station)
2 Bus Station

5 Hôtel de Ville
6 The Rock ('Azrou')
7 Grands Taxis for 'Ain Leuh
12 Place Hassan II
13 Salon de Thé Azrou
16 BMCE
19 Place Mohammed V
20 Banque Populaire
21 Post Office (PTT)
25 Great Mosque
29 Place Moulay Hachem ben Salah
31 Small Bar
32 Ensemble Artisanal

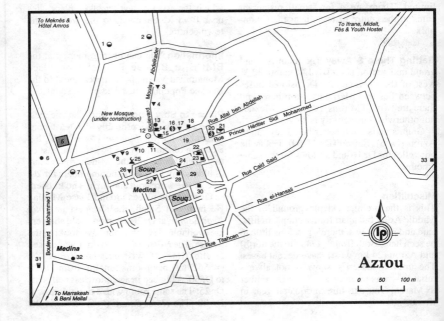

Azrou

star *Hôtel des Cèdres* (☎ 562326), Place Mohammed V, which has large, airy, comfortable and spotlessly clean rooms for Dr 90/112/149. Rooms have a basin, table and chairs and a balcony overlooking the square. The bathroom has a big tub, and when the water is steaming makes for a wonderful hot bath (yes, there's a plug!).

There's also the one-star *Hôtel Azrou* (☎ 562116), Route de Khenifra, which costs the same as the Cèdres but is quite a way from the centre of town and not so easy to find.

. Further up the scale, and a long walk or olive green petit-taxi ride from the bus station is the pricier *Hôtel Panorama* (☎ 562010). The 40 rooms (heated in winter) cost Dr 153/195 without shower (but with private loo) and Dr 193/240 with en suite, plus taxes. The hotel has a restaurant and bar.

Places to Stay – top end About five km out on the road to Meknès is the four-star *Hôtel Amros* (☎ 563663; fax 563680). It has all the amenities you would expect of a top-class hotel, including a pool, tennis courts and a nightclub. Singles/doubles cost Dr 362/460, plus taxes.

Places to Eat There is no shortage of cheap eats in Azrou – a couple are scattered through the old town and there is a string of at least 10 of them across the road from the big unfinished mosque. Of these, the *Restaurant Echaab* is pretty decent value. They sometimes have a huge pot of steaming harira by the entrance in the evenings – a bowl of this is just what the doctor ordered on a cool evening. A big meal of harira, brochettes, chips, salad and a drink comes to Dr 26. Pricier but with good food is the *Restaurant Relais Forestier* on Place Mohammed V.

The numerous cafés around here are great for breakfast – the one opposite the Hôtel des Cèdres does bread, jam and tea for Dr 6. There are a few juice stands and pâtisseries on Blvd Moulay Abdelkader.

Things to Buy A visit to the Ensemble Artisanal on the right-hand side on the road to Khenifra (signposted) is worthwhile. Here you can find work in cedar and iron, as well as Berber carpets typical of the Middle Atlas.

Getting There & Away Azrou is a crossroads, with one axis heading north-west to south-east from Meknès to Er-Rachidia and the other north-east from Fès to Marrakesh in the south-west. The bus station (gare routière) and taxi station are located just north of the mosque construction site.

Bus CTM has departures to Fès at 2.30 pm (Dr 22); Casablanca (Dr 76) via Rabat at 4 and 7.30 am, Marrakesh (Dr 82) at 8.30 am; Meknès (Dr 16) at 7.30 and 9 am; and Midelt and Beni Mellal at 8 am. The other lines have buses to these destinations at other times and for a dirham or two less. All up, there are plenty of departures for Fès and Meknès, but for places like Marrakesh you'd want to book ahead. There is at least one bus to Er-Rachidia (Dr 62) at 3.30 pm; otherwise you would be better off getting one of the more frequent Midelt buses and hooking up with transport there.

Taxi Grands taxis leave the lot behind the bus station regularly for Fès (Dr 21), Meknès (Dr 16), Ifrane (Dr 6), Immouzer (change for Sefrou), Midelt and Khenifra. From the last two you could arrange further transport on to Er-Rachidia and Beni Mellal (or even Marrakesh) respectively.

Around Azrou

If you have your own transport, a good drive takes you through some of the best of the Middle Atlas greenery along a forest lane to the Berber village of 'Ain Leuh. Leave Azrou by the Midelt road and take the first right (the S3398). Once in the village, you could continue south into the heart of the Middle Atlas along the S303 – be warned that some of the tracks here are difficult and impassable in or after foul weather. This route would eventually take you to Khenifra, from where you could continue south towards Marrakesh, or you could simply follow the S303 north from 'Ain Leuh to head back to Azrou.

Sefrou

At 28 km from Fès, Sefrou is much easier to contemplate as a day trip than either Ifrane or Azrou, and with virtually no accommodation at the time of writing, a dubious choice for an overnight stop on the way south to the Ziz Valley and Er-Rachidia.

About the size of Chefchaouen, this picturesque Berber town is well worth the effort. With the exception of the odd Fès-trained 'guide' hanging about the gates near the bus station, you will be left in complete peace to wander the compact medina. Sefrou once had one of the largest Jewish communities of any Moroccan city and it was here, in a nearby ksar (fortified stronghold), that Moulay Idriss II lived while he planned the development of Fès.

The walled medina and mellah lie on either side of the garbage-strewn Oued Aggaï, across which there are a number of bridges. The best points of entry/exit are the Bab Taksebt, Bab Zemghila and the Bab Merba. The town walls that stand today were built in the 19th century.

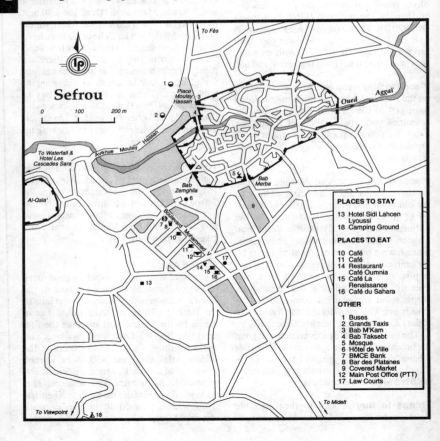

Sefrou

0   100   200 m

To Fès

To Waterfall & Hotel Les Cascades Sara

To Viewpoint

To Midelt

PLACES TO STAY
13 Hotel Sidi Lahcen Lyoussi
18 Camping Ground

PLACES TO EAT
10 Café
11 Café
14 Restaurant/ Café Oumnia
15 Café La Renaissance
16 Café du Sahara

OTHER
1 Buses
2 Grands Taxis
3 Bab M'Kam
4 Bab Taksebt
5 Mosque
6 Hôtel de Ville
7 BMCE Bank
8 Bar des Platanes
9 Covered Market
12 Main Post Office (PTT)
17 Law Courts

Once you've visited the walled town, walk up the gorge of the river to the waterfall about 1.5 km from town. To get there, follow the Ave Moulay Hassan over the bridge which spans the river and turn left at the first turn-off (signposted 'Cascades'). Follow this road around to the right (north side) of Al-Qala' (a sort of semiwalled ksar) and follow the dirt road alongside the river until you get to the waterfall.

Information The main post office and a branch of the BMCE bank are along Blvd Mohammed V.

Places to Stay Somebody doesn't want anyone to stay in Sefrou. About the only option is the *camp site* on the hill overlooking the town. It's a long, steep walk (take a taxi), but a pleasant spot. There are toilets and cold showers; it costs Dr 5 per person, Dr 5 to pitch a tent and Dr 5 for a car. The guy who runs it is a laid-back sort of a chap. If you continue a little farther up the hill, you'll find a magnificent viewpoint over Sefrou and the plains below.

The unclassified *Hôtel les Cerises*, on Blvd Mohammed V, has been firmly shut since 1991. The two-star *Hôtel Sidi Lahcen Lyoussi* (☎ 660497) was also shut at the time of writing. Another one, the *Hôtel Sara Les Cascades*, right by the waterfall, was not a bad little place in a peaceful location. Even if it ever re-opens, though, you may not want to stay. The authorities shut it in 1993 after the bodies of a couple of young local girls were discovered there, apparently after a night's revelry with off-duty soldiers turned nasty.

Places to Eat There's a good choice of small, cheap restaurants on either side of the covered market and at the entrance to the Bab Merba. Otherwise, pickings are slim. You could try the *Restaurant Café Oumnia* up near Blvd Mohammed V in the new part of town. There's a string of cafés and a bar on the same street, all near the post office.

Getting There & Away There are regular buses between Fès and Sefrou (Dr 5) which drop you off at Place Moulay Hassan in front of Bab M'Kam and Bab Taksebt. Grands taxis (Dr 7) can also be found here. Grands taxis go to Immouzer (Dr 10), from where you can pick up others for Azrou. A few taxis heading south leave from the law courts on Blvd Mohammed V.

The East

TAZA

Despite its tempestuous history, Taza is a relatively quiet city these days. Nevertheless, it is worth a visit if you are passing through the area going to or coming from Algeria, if only for the views and the crumbling fortifications. And, if you have your own transport, the drive around Jebel Tazzeka with a visit to the Gouffre du Friouato – one of the most incredible open caverns in the world – is superb.

Since it was an important French military and administrative centre during the protectorate, Taza too has a ville nouvelle which, as usual, is separate from the old town. However, the two are quite some distance from each other – three km in fact – although urbanisation is rapidly closing the gap.

History

The fortified citadel of Taza, built on the edge of an escarpment overlooking the only feasible pass between the Rif Mountains and the Middle Atlas, has been important throughout Morocco's history as a garrison town from which to exert control over the eastern extremities of the country. The Taza Gap, as it is known, has provided the traditional invasion route for armies moving west from Tunisia and Algeria. The Romans and the Arabs entered Morocco via this pass, and the town itself was the base from which the Almohads, Merenids and Alawites swept down on Fès to conquer lowland Morocco and establish their respective dynasties.

All the various Moroccan sultans had a

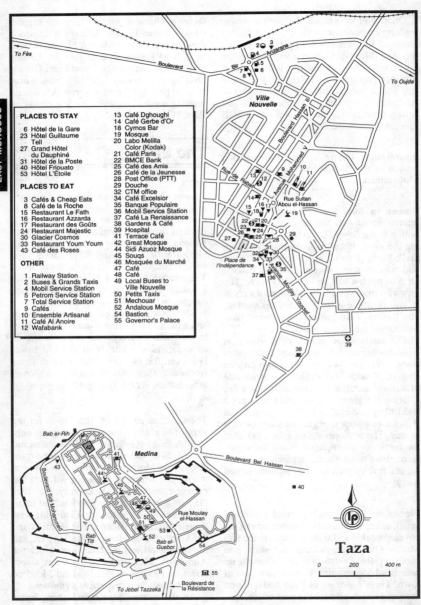

PLACES TO STAY
6 Hôtel de la Gare
23 Hôtel Guillaume Tell
27 Grand Hôtel du Dauphiné
31 Hôtel de la Poste
40 Hôtel Friouato
53 Hôtel L'Étoile

PLACES TO EAT
3 Cafés & Cheap Eats
8 Café de la Roche
15 Restaurant Le Fath
16 Restaurant Azzarda
17 Restaurant des Goûts
24 Restaurant Majestic
30 Glacier Cosmos
33 Restaurant Youm Youm
43 Café des Roses

OTHER
1 Railway Station
2 Buses & Grands Taxis
4 Mobil Service Station
5 Petrom Service Station
7 Total Service Station
9 Cafés
10 Ensemble Artisanal
11 Café Al Anoire
12 Wafabank
13 Café Dghoughi
14 Café Gerbe d'Or
18 Cymos Bar
19 Mosque
20 Labo Melilla Color (Kodak)
21 Café Paris
22 BMCE Bank
25 Café des Amis
26 Café de la Jeunesse
28 Post Office (PTT)
29 Douche
32 CTM office
34 Café Excelsior
35 Banque Populaire
36 Mobil Service Station
37 Café La Renaissance
38 Gardens & Café
39 Hospital
41 Terrace Café
42 Great Mosque
44 Sidi Azuoz Mosque
45 Souqs
46 Mosquée du Marché
47 Café
48 Café
49 Local Buses to Ville Nouvelle
50 Petits Taxis
51 Mechouar
52 Andalous Mosque
54 Bastion
55 Governor's Palace

EAST MOROCCO

hand in fortifying Taza. Nevertheless, their control over the area was always tenuous, since the fiercely independent and rebellious local tribes were always willing to exploit any weakness in the central power in order to overrun the city.

Never was this more the case than in the first years of the 20th century, when 'El-Rogui' (the pretender to the sultan's throne), Bou Hamra, held sway over Taza (although he was based largely in Selouan, 24 km south of Melilla) and most of north-eastern Morocco. After some early successes, his claims to the throne were revealed to be a sham and he met a colourfully grizzly end at the hands of Sultan Moulay Abd al-Hafiz.

The French occupied Taza in 1914 and thereafter made it the main base from which they fought the prolonged rebellion against their rule by the tribes of the Rif and Middle Atlas.

Orientation

Arriving by bus (except CTM) or train, you'll find yourself on the main Fès-Oujda road, which might appear to be in the centre of town but is actually quite some distance away.

Place de l'Indépendance is the heart of the ville nouvelle. On it or nearby are the banks, post office and most of the hotels and restaurants. If you arrive by CTM bus, you're in luck because the terminal is right on this square. The old town is another three km to the south. Local buses and petits taxis run regularly between the two parts of the town.

Information

Tourist Office The tourist office (☎ 672737) is in the Immeuble des Habous, Ave Hassan II, but seems to be defunct.

Post & Telecommunications The post and telephone offices are on the south-eastern corner of Place de l'Indépendance. Both are open during normal office hours only.

Money There are a couple of banks in Taza, including the BMCE on Ave Mohammed V and the Banque Populaire on Ave Moulay Youssef, on the way from the ville nouvelle to the medina.

Film & Photography Across the road from the Restaurant Majestic is Labo Melilla Color, where you can stock up on film (check the dates).

City Walls

Most of the city walls, which are about three

Bou Hamra

Bou Hamra (the 'Man on the She-Ass'), or Jilali ben Driss as he came into the world, was one of a host of colourful and violent characters who strode across the Moroccan stage at the turn of the century as central power evaporated and the European powers prepared to take greater control.

Born in 1868 in the Jebel Zerhoun area, he became a minor government official in Fès. In 1894, he was jailed for forgery, but managed to escape to Algeria six years later.

In for a penny, in for a pound, Bou Hamra decided on a more ambitious fraud – claiming with conviction to be Sultan Abd al-Aziz's elder brother Mohammed. He acquired his name by dint of his custom of travelling around on a she-donkey and staked a claim in eastern Morocco as the legitimate pretender to the throne – 'El-Rogui'. As the British journalist Walter Harris wrote, he had learned 'a few conjuring tricks' – but surely the best was having himself proclaimed sultan in Taza in 1902.

Another character of a different style, Er-Raissouli, who at this time held sway in the Tangier area of northern Morocco, placed an each-way bet by signing a deal with Bou Hamra recognising him as sultan. In the end he needn't have worried, for in 1908 the real Mohammed stood up and the Rif tribes that had backed Bou Hamra turned on him. He soon fell into the hands of the new sultan, Moulay Abd al-Hafiz. Bou Hamra was paraded around the country for a month in a one-metre-high cage on the back of a camel before being thrown to the lions of the sultan's menagerie in Fès in March 1909. ■

km in circumference, date from the time of the Almohads (12th century). Having withstood so many sieges, they are ruined in parts. There's also a bastion built by the Saadians in the 16th century in a part of the walls that juts out to the east of the medina.

The most interesting section of a trip around the walls is the **Bab er-Rih** (Gate of the Wind), with its superb views over the surrounding countryside. On the extreme left you can see the wooded slopes of Jebel Tazzeka and before that, across the Oued Taza, the terraced gardens and dry ravines of the foothills of the Rif. On the right, below the park, is the ville nouvelle, with the Rif Mountains in the distance.

Great Mosque

Not far from Bab er-Rih is the Great Mosque, which was begun by the Almohads in 1135 and added to by the Merenids in the 13th century. Non-Muslims are not allowed to enter, and it is difficult to get much of an impression of the outside of the building. Stretching from here down to the far end of the old town is the main thoroughfare (Rue Kettanine/Rue Nejjarine/Rue Koubet/Rue Sidi Ali Derrar). This is perhaps the most interesting part of town: there are many examples of richly decorated doorways and, occasionally, windows high up in the walls guarded by old, carved cedar screens.

Souqs

The souqs are about halfway down the street, around the Mosquée du Marché. Although some of the shops offer mats and carpets woven by the Beni Ouarain tribe in the surrounding mountains, the souqs are virtually bereft of tourist shops. The place is devoid of 'guides' and the like, meaning you can wander around the souqs observing the workings of a normal Berber market without looking constantly over your shoulder or being distracted by one irritant after another.

Most of the shops cater for household necessities and foodstuffs, as do the ones in the nearby qissaria (the commercial centre of the medina). While in this part of the city, don't miss the minaret of the **Mosquée du Marché**, which is perhaps unique in Morocco in that its upper part is wider than its base.

Andalous Mosque

Right at the end of the main street, close to the mechouar, is the Andalous Mosque, constructed in the 12th century. Nearby is a ruined house once occupied by Bou Hamra, and the Merenid Bou Abu al-Hassan Medersa. It may be possible to gain entry to the latter if you ask around and enlist the help of a guide.

Places to Stay – bottom end

Medina In the medina itself about the only choice is the fairly basic *Hôtel de l'Étoile*, inside Bab el-Guebor on the left along Rue Moulay el-Hassan. It costs Dr 35 and has no shower (the manager suggests that the only hotel in town with a shower is the up-market Hôtel Friouato, a slight exaggeration).

Ville Nouvelle Down by the traffic lights on the main Fès-Oujda road, more or less in front of the railway station, is the *Hôtel de la Gare* (☎ 672443). It has cheap and not overly inviting rooms (some of them decidedly on the nose) without shower for Dr 42/60, and substantially better rooms with en suite shower for Dr 70/85. It's convenient for the transport but not for the centre of the new town or the medina.

The remaining moderately priced hotels are around Place de l'Indépendance. About the cheapest and most reasonable is the *Hôtel Guillaume Tell* (☎ 672347), which offers big, simple rooms with double beds for Dr 41/62. Some have cold showers in the room, otherwise there is a shared shower which is just as cold.

Just off Ave Moulay Youssef is the *Hôtel de la Poste* (☎ 672589), which has small but clean and comfortable rooms for Dr 48/64 but no shower at all and somewhat smelly loos. If you need a shower, there's a public one for men and women not far away (Dr 4.80 a go). Ask the hotel employees for directions.

Places to Stay – middle

The *Grand Hôtel du Dauphiné* (☎ 673567) is a two-star hotel, to the left of Place de l'Indépendance, housed in an attractive colonial-style building. It is the best place to stay if you have the money, as it's comfortable and old-fashioned, with period bathrooms, and balconies overlooking the square. You can get rooms without bathroom for Dr 70/92 and others with private shower for Dr 96/120. There's hot water in the evenings only. Downstairs there's a lively bar and a sedate dining hall with a limited choice of food. Meals here are fairly expensive.

Places to Stay – top end

The only top-end hotel in Taza is the *Hôtel Friouato* (☎ 672593/8), set in its own well-maintained grounds between Place de l'Indépendance and the old town. It's part of the Salam chain and, although quite an ugly concrete building and awkwardly located, it is a quiet and pleasant enough place. Self-contained singles/doubles go for Dr 194/245. The hotel has a bar, restaurant, swimming pool and tennis courts.

Places to Eat

Medina A pleasant place to have breakfast is the *Café des Roses* on Rue Riad Azmag in the medina.

While wandering around the medina, there are numerous small stands where you can pick up a snack, and some of the cafés sometimes do food as well.

Ville Nouvelle There is a series of cafés and cheap eateries by the grand taxi lot on Blvd Bir Anzarane (the Fès-Oujda road).

Probably the best choice for a meal remains the *Restaurant Majestic*, on Ave Mohammed V. Here you can get a filling dish of chicken and chips, with a plate of beans and another side dish of a sort of pea salad for Dr 30.

Around the corner from the Hôtel de la Poste is the *Restaurant Youm Youm*, a reasonable alternative. Apart from these places, you could also try the more expensive hotel restaurants.

For dessert you could do worse than head to *Glacier Cosmos* for an ice cream.

Entertainment

Cafés & Bars There is no shortage of cafés and salons de thé in both the ville nouvelle and the medina, but probably the best is the nameless terrace café on the eastern side of the medina. From here you have sweeping views of the new town and the countryside.

In addition to the hotel bars, you could try the locals' *Cyrnos Bar*, on Ave d'Oujda in the ville nouvelle.

Getting There & Away

Bus The CTM bus terminal is on Place de l'Indépendance, but it offers only a few services. At 7 am there are two buses: one to Casablanca (Dr 99.50, 7½ hours) via Fès, Meknès and Rabat; the other is a mumtaz run to Fès for Dr 30.50. At 2.30 pm there is another bus to Fès for Dr 23, and half an hour later a service to Oujda for Dr 39.

All other buses gather near or pass by the grand taxi lot on the main Fès-Oujda road. There are quite a few to Oujda (Dr 35 to Dr 40) and Fès (mostly to Bab el-Ftouh; you'll need to take a local bus or petit taxi from there to Bab Bou Jeloud or the ville nouvelle – see the Fès Getting Around section). Many of the buses on these runs just pass through Taza, so getting a seat is sometimes problematic.

There are three buses a day to Nador, at 11.30 am and 2.30 and 5.30 pm; they cost Dr 40. At 1 pm (more or less), a bus leaves for Al-Hoceima (Dr 35). As there is no organised bus station as such, it can be a bit chaotic. The best bet is to turn up as early as you can and choose between the buses and grands taxis – taking whichever leaves first.

Train Going east or west, the train is a more reliable and comfortable option. There are daily trains to Fès and Meknès at 12.52, 1.47 (summer only) and 10.51 am and 1.20, 5.08 and 11.08 pm. The 12.52 am and the 1.20,

5.08 and 11.08 pm trains go through to Casablanca; the others turn north to Tangier. To Oujda there are daily trains at 3.37, 6.07 and 8.55 am (this last one in summer only) and 5, 6.19 and 10.07 pm. The 2nd-class fares in standard/rapide trains are: Dr 49.50/62.50 to Oujda; Dr 25/31.50 to Fès and Dr 93/119 to Casablanca. There are no through trains to Marrakesh from Taza.

Trains to Oujda pass through Taourirt, from where there is a once-daily Supratours connection to Nador, but this is really doing it the hard way – buses and grands taxis are simpler.

Taxi Grands taxis all leave from a lot near the railway station on the main Fès-Oujda road. They depart fairly regularly for Fès (Dr 30; they take you to Bab el-Ftouh – see the preceding Bus section) and Oujda (Dr 50) throughout the day, but the morning is best. Less regular taxis go to Nador and Al-Hoceima for Dr 50 a person.

AROUND TAZA
Jebel Tazzeka Circuit

If you have your own transport (hitching isn't really feasible), you can make a fascinating day trip around Jebel Tazzeka, which takes in the Cascades de Ras el-Oued (waterfalls), the Gouffre du Friouato (cavern), Daïa Chiker (a lake) and the gorges of the Oued Zireg. There's a good sealed road the whole way. If you don't have your own transport it would be worthwhile getting a small group together and hiring a taxi for the day.

Having negotiated the long, winding road up from Taza onto the plateau, you'll find yourself in a different world. It's almost eerie in its apparent emptiness, with small patches of farmland, a few scattered houses and, closer to Jebel Tazzeka itself, dense coniferous forests. There are superb views from many points, including the semiderelict hamlet of Bab Bouidir (this hamlet must have been a beautiful retreat at one time, with its tiled Alpine-style houses, but it appears to have been largely abandoned – weekend picnickers notwithstanding).

The **waterfalls** are the first stop. Shortly before you reach the Daïa Chiker plateau, you'll see a sign on your left for Ras el-Ma ('headwater'). The waterfalls are here, but they are really only worth a stop after the winter rains. By the summer they have usually slowed to a trickle.

A little farther on, where the road flattens out, you take a right fork and have the odd depression of the **Daïa Chiker** on your left. The lake bed is usually pretty dry, but the earth is good and is used for grazing and crops. Daïa Chiker is a geological curiosity associated with fault lines in the calciferous rock structure. It is connected to a subterranean reservoir, the water of which is highly charged with carbon dioxide. Depending on the season and the state of affairs in the subterranean reservoir, the surface of the lake can change dramatically. The nearby **Grottes du Chiker** (caves) at the northern end of the lake have been explored and are said to give access to a five-km-long underground river, but they are not open to casual visitors.

A little farther along the road, the **Gouffre du Friouato** is signposted off to the right. You can drive up or take a steep, 20-minute walk to the entrance. It is the main attraction of this circuit and a must at any time of the year.

This vast cavern is said to be the deepest and possibly the most extensive in the whole of North Africa and has only been partially explored to date. The main part plummets vertically some 100 metres to a floor below, from where various chambers break off and snake away to who knows where. Several flights of precipitous steps with handrails lead you to the floor of the main cavern, and since there's a large hole in the roof of the cavern letting in light, you can get this far with ease. At the bottom of the steps is a hole through which you can drop to start exploring the more interesting chambers below. Here you will need your own light. Some of the stalactite formations are extraordinary. Speleologists have made explorations to a depth of 300 metres, and it is believed a fossil river runs another 500 metres below.

There is usually a guardian at the cavern entrance who will expect to be paid. He may ask for all sorts of sums, but Dr 10 a head will be enough (and seems reasonable as it's the same as the official monument entry price throughout the country). If it's locked, wait around, as someone will soon appear to open it up for you. You may be offered guide services too, but if you have your own light you should be OK.

As you leave the Daïa Chiker behind, the road begins to climb again into coniferous forests past Bab Bouidir. Along the way you can catch good views of the snowcapped Atlas. About eight km past Bab Bouidir, a poor piste branches nine km off to the right (north). If you can get your car up the incline, you'll find the TV relay station at the top of Jebel Tazzeka (1980 metres) and wonderful views all around, to the Rif in the north and the Atlas in the south.

The main road continues around for another 38 km back to the main Fès-Taza road at Sidi Abdallah de Rhiata. On the way you will wind your way around hairpin bends through some dense woodland and then down through the pretty **gorges** of the Oued Zireg.

From the intersection at Sidi Abdallah de Rhiata, you can take the main highway back east to Taza, pausing at Tizi n'Touahar on the way for some more views. If you're coming from Fès, take the *left* turn signposted for Bab Bouidir. This road curves round and under the main highway to head south. There is often a police checkpoint here.

OUJDA

This is the last town before the Algerian border. If you have just come from Algeria, make the most of the relaxed atmosphere – there is no hassling, apart from the occasional offers to change money.

The town boasts a busy but small medina

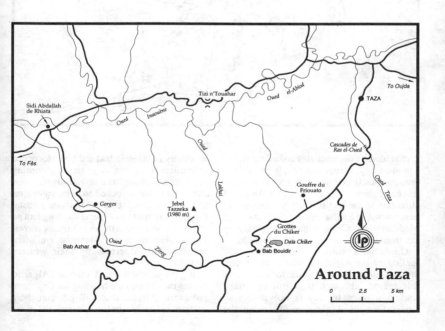

Around Taza

0   2.5   5 km

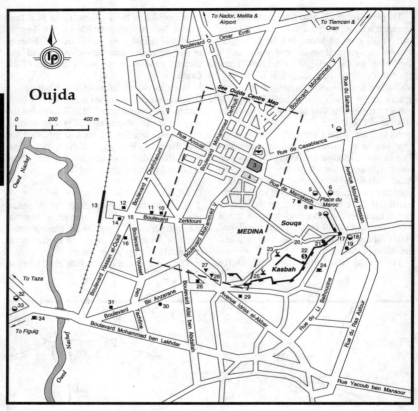

Oujda

0   200   400 m

To Nador, Melilla & Airport

To Tlemcen & Oran

Boulevard Omar Errifi

Boulevard Mohammed V

Rue du Sahara

See Oujda Centre Map

Rue Anoual

Boulevard Mohammed Darfoufi

Rue de Casablanca

Rue de Marrakech

Avenue Moulay Hassan

Oued Nachef

Boulevard A. Chefchaouni

Place du Maroc

13

12

11   10

15

14

Boulevard Zerktouni

16

Boulevard Hassan el-Ouikili

Boulevard Youssef

MEDINA

Souqs

Boulevard Mohammed V

20

21   17   18

19

23

22

Kasbah

24

27

26

25

28

To Taza

31

30

Bir Anzarane

Boulevard Tachfine ben

Boulevard Allal ben Abdallah

29

Avenue Idriss el-Akbar

32

33

34

To Figuig

Boulevard Mohammed ben Lakhdar

Oued Nachef

Rue du Lt Belhouche

Rue du Ras Asfour

Rue Yacoub ben Mansour

surrounded by the undistinguished sprawl of a modern city. Essentially, Oujda has little to interest travellers, but it is not a bad place to just hang about in for a day or two. An added attraction is the fact that the Mediterranean beach town of Saïdia (see the chapter on the Mediterranean Coast & the Rif) is only 58 km from Oujda and relatively accessible.

Oujda has a bustling atmosphere, mostly fuelled by the Algerians who come to buy products unavailable at home for resale. For this reason, although it is full of hotels, finding a place to stay is not always so straightforward. At the time of writing, the problems in Algeria had led the Moroccan authorities to tighten controls on incoming Algerians, slowing the usual steady stream – even hotels are supposed to keep an eye on the activities of their Algerian guests. Oujda's proximity to Algeria has long had an influence on its affairs, and Oujdans travelling farther west into Morocco are often mistaken for Algerians by their western cousins.

If you arrive from Tlemcen (Algeria) during the day and are heading for Fès, there are evening trains that will get you there extremely early (before dawn) the next

EAST MOROCCO

PLACES TO STAY

7	Hôtel Nouvel
8	Hôtel el Menzeh
10	Hôtel Rofaïda
11	Hôtel Al-Manar
12	Hôtel Moussafir
14	Hôtel Terminus
16	Hôtel Lutetia
28	Hôtel Riad
29	Hôtel Al Massira
31	Hôtel Chafik

PLACES TO EAT

26	Restaurant Quick Food
27	Iris Sandwich

OTHER

1	Buses to Algerian Border
2	Main Post Office (PTT)
3	Town Hall & Clock Tower
4	Place du 16 Août 1953
5	Petits Taxis
6	Grands Taxis to Algerian Border & Saidia
9	Grands Taxis to Nador
13	Railway Station
15	Place de l'Unité Africaine
17	Bab el-Ouahab
18	Local Buses
19	Douche (Men Only)
20	Place el-Attarine
21	Qissaria
22	BMCE
23	Great Mosque
24	Café El Maghrib El Arabi
25	Mosque
30	Algerian Consulate
32	Grands Taxis to Taza & Fès
33	Bus Station
34	Café de la Foire

morning – otherwise you could try the buses and grands taxis.

History

The site of Oujda has long been important, lying as it does on the main axis connecting Morocco with the rest of North Africa (the Romans built a road through here). Like Taza, it has been a key in controlling the east and often a step towards seizing control of the heartland around Fès.

The town was founded in the 10th century by the Meghraoua tribe, and it remained independent until the Almohads overran it in the 11th century. All the subsequent dynasties left their mark on its fate. Under the Merenids, however, Algerian rulers based in Tlemcen took the town on several occasions, and in the 17th century it fell under the sway of the Ottoman administration set up in Algiers. Moulay Ismail put an end to this in 1687, and Oujda remained in Moroccan hands until 1907, when French forces in Algeria crossed the frontier in one of a series of 'incidents' and occupied the town. The protectorate was still five years away, but the sultan was powerless to oppose the move.

The French soon expanded the town, which has since swelled in size as provincial capital and in its role as the main gateway for commerce with Algeria. Its industrial role rests on mining, particularly zinc, which is carried out farther to the south.

Orientation

Although quite large, only the centre of Oujda is of any interest to travellers. The main street is Blvd Mohammed V, along or near which you'll find banks, the post and tourist offices, and many of the better budget and mid-range hotels and restaurants. About a five-minute walk to the west along Blvd Zerktouni is the railway station. A farther 15 minutes to the south-west, across Oued Nachef, is the main bus station (gare routière). Also here, on the Taza exit road, are grands taxis for Taza and Fès. Buses and taxis to the Algerian border leave from Place du Maroc, just outside the medina.

Information

Tourist Office The tourist office (☎ 689089, 684329) is on Place du 16 Août 1953 at the junction with Blvd Mohammed V. It has the usual brochures and the staff try to help out.

Money Most Moroccan banks have branches in Oujda. The BMCE and BMCI on Blvd Mohammed V have ATMs and give cash advances. The Banque Populaire on Blvd Mohammed Derfoufi should also be good for cash advances and most banks will change cash and cheques.

There is no shortage of people lurking around Place du Maroc and Blvd Mohammed V offering to change money. They will buy and sell dirham or Algerian dinar. Don't go looking for them – they'll soon find you. Take your time about changing, and compare offers. At the time of writing, it appeared you could get about eight dinar for each dirham, but this is bound to change. Ideally, if you come across travellers coming from Algeria ask them what the minimum should be. Equally, people coming from Algeria should get an idea of dirham and hard-currency rates in the banks before unloading unwanted dinar. The street dealers also buy and sell hard currency, which might is only useful if you want to dispose of dinar.

Post & Telecommunications The main post office is in the centre of the ville nouvelle on Blvd Mohammed V. It's open from 8.30 am to 12.15 pm and again from 2.30 to 6 pm. The phone office, next door to the right of the main entrance to the post office, is open seven days a week from 8.30 am to 9 pm. There are card phones outside.

Foreign Consulates The following countries have foreign consulates in Oujda:

Algeria
11 Blvd Bir Anzarane (also known as Blvd de Taza; ☎ 683740/1). Nonresidents of Oujda can apply for visas here (UK citizens must apply in Rabat), but even when things are going well you can easily wait a month for a response. You may be able to get a 10-day visa more easily, but don't count on it. There have been reports that visas are issued on the spot for Dr 100; you will need three passport photos. The consulate is open from 8 am to 3 pm Monday to Thursday and from 8 am to

noon on Friday. You may well meet an enterprising chap outside who claims to have a friend working on the inside. For a consideration (and some business on the money-changing front), he says he can help you get a visa within 10 days. You obtain and fill in all the papers and then leave it to him. Who knows whether or not this works?

France
16 Rue Imam Lechaf (☎ 682705)
Sweden
Ave Allal al-Fassi, B23 Apt 2 (☎ 685753)

Film & Photography There's a place where you can have film developed just by the Hôtel L'Oasis on Blvd Mohammed V.

Swimming Pools There is a municipal pool in the south of the city, or you could try the Hôtel Al Massira, which will let you into its pool for a daily fee of Dr 30.

Emergencies There is an all-night chemist (☎ 683490) on Rue de Marrakech.

Medina

Although hardly the most fascinating of medinas, Oujda's old centre warrants a bit of stroll at least. The most animated part is the area inside and outside the eastern gate, **Bab el-Ouahab**. Also known as the Gate of Heads – local pashas had a habit of having the heads of criminals and renegades hung here – it is full of food stalls, beggars, shoppers and all the noise and bustle of a typical North African market. Plunging deeper into the medina you'll find mainly clothes shops and a few hotels. The **Great Mosque**, built in the 14th century by the Merenids, is in bad shape and in any case is closed to non-Muslims.

Places to Stay – bottom end

Oujda is armed to the teeth with hotels. Although many of them may be full of visiting Algerians when you arrive, you would be unlucky not to find a room sooner or later.

Medina & Around The medina has a few fairly simple places, but there are so many hotels just outside it that it hardly seems worth the effort of searching them out. For the die-hard lovers of medina living, they include the *Ifriquia* (☎ 682095), *En-Nasr* (☎ 683932), *Rissani*, *Du Peuple* and *Al-Kasbah*. As a rule of thumb, rooms in these places cost about Dr 30/60, usually with shared cold showers. They are adequate without being exciting.

Closer to the centre, on and around Rue de Marrakech, is another bunch of similar places, the main difference being that they are easier to find. Among the better ones here is the *Hôtel du 16 Août* (☎ 684197), on Rue de Figuig. Rooms cost Dr 30/60 and hot showers are supposedly included in the price. Farther down the street at No 10 is the rather grand sounding *Hôtel-Résidence Gharnata* (☎ 681541). It is a little depressing. Rooms cost Dr 40/70; the shared cold showers are the combined shower/squat loo arrangements, which are sensible but unpleasant. At the same price, the *Hôtel Marrakech* (☎ 681556) is better but unspectacular (hot showers cost an extra Dr 5). The rooms could do with a bit more fresh air. Other similar places here include the *Hôtel el Menzeh* and the *Hôtel Nouvel* (nothing new about it at all).

Slightly pricier, but the best of this lot, is the *Hôtel Al-Hanna* (☎ 686003) at 132 Rue de Marrakech. Singles/doubles with basin (shared shower) cost Dr 48/64. Clean rooms with private shower are Dr 64/77. Try to get one of the rooms upstairs, as the lower floors are a little gloomy.

Ville Nouvelle A better hunting ground for cheap hotels is the pedestrian zone off Blvd Mohammed V and the area nearby.

A popular, cheap but showerless place is the *Hôtel Majestic* (☎ 682948). The rooms are big and have a basin, and cost Dr 30/60. Around the corner, the *Hôtel El-Andalous* (☎ 684491) also has quite decent rooms, and again is without a shower. Rooms cost Dr 35/50.

Right on Blvd Mohammed V is the *Hôtel Victoria* (☎ 685020). At Dr 40/60/90 it is fairly cheap too, and it does have cold communal showers. It is often full.

A pretty good deal is the *Hôtel Isly* (☎ 683928) at 24 Rue Ramdane el-Gadhi, which has rooms a cut above the budget average for Dr 45/70/90. The hot water in the showers is hit and miss, however. A place to avoid is the *Hôtel de Nice*, which charges Dr 35/60 for crummy, crumbly rooms. It has no shower.

A little more money will get you a considerably better deal. The *Hôtel Simon* (☎ 686304), 1 Rue Tarik ibn Ziad, for example, has rooms with private shower, bidet, basin and (some of them) wrought iron balcony for Dr 60/93. This hotel, with its restaurant/café, has a busy, friendly air.

Better still is the *Hôtel Afrah* (☎ 686533), 15 Rue de Tafna. Rooms for Dr 60/120 are small but comfortable and contain spotless en suite bathrooms and the promise of hot water.

Others you can try in the area include the *Hôtel Zegzel*, *Hôtel d'Alger* (a dump), *Hôtel En-Nazaha*, *Hôtel Bahia*, *Hôtel Tlemcen* and the *Hôtel Chic* (I kid you not).

Two places on the other side of Blvd Mohammed V are really only for hard-luck situations. The *Hôtel Ziri* in particular is pretty awful value, even at Dr 30/50/75. The beds are falling apart, as are the en suite showers (cold only).

The *Hôtel L'Oasis* (☎ 683114) is not much better but often full nonetheless. Rooms cost Dr 40/60. There is a cramped restaurant and bar opposite, and the hotel does have limited parking.

Not far away, at 13 Blvd Zerktouni, is one of the best lower-end deals in Oujda. The one-star *Hôtel Royal* (☎ 682284) is excellent value at Dr 60/90 for rooms without shower and Dr 105/121 with private shower and toilet (hot water more or less all day). The hotel has limited guarded garage parking (Dr 12 a night).

If you have shower problems, the Douche Moderne in the pedestrian area is an alternative.

Places to Stay – middle

There's a small group of hotels to the north-

EAST MOROCCO

west of the post office. The *Grand Hotel* (☎ 680508/9) on Rue Beni Merine is not as grand as it might once have been, but it's not too bad at Dr 75.50/92.50. It's a big place and unlikely to be full. A block farther north is the more expensive *Hôtel/Restaurant Mamounia* (☎ 690072; fax 690073). It has perfectly comfortable, carpeted rooms with phone for Dr 95/147, which is probably straining most wallets on a tight budget. A couple of other hotels around here include the *Iris* and the *Ghilane*.

Another very good deal in its range is the *Hôtel Lutetia* (☎ 683365), 44 Blvd Hassan el-Oukili. It is directly opposite the railway station, and has comfortable, carpeted rooms with phone. They even put towels in the bathrooms without your having to ask. Rooms with shower but shared toilet are Dr 85/111 and rooms with full bathroom are Dr 109/129.

New hotels are going up all over Oujda. One that claims to have opened in 1993 but looks like it's been around for quite some time is the *Hôtel Rofaïda* (☎ 703768), at 44 Blvd Zerktouni. The taciturn manager offers mediocre rooms with showers and stinking squat loos for Dr 100/120. Avoid this place.

On the other end of the new hotel scale there's the *Hôtel Al Fajr* (☎ 702293), just off Blvd Mohammed Derfoufi. This place opened in early 1994 and it has 48 sparklingly clean and modern rooms with central heating, en suite bathroom and telephone. At the time of writing they were inexplicably operating as a one-star hotel and charging Dr 109/129. The prices will probably rise, but it might be worth checking out if you have a slightly more generous budget.

Back in the pedestrian precinct is the overpriced *Hôtel Angad* (☎ 681452). Apart from the cockroaches, there is nothing intrinsically wrong with the place, and they will probably bargain down quickly from their stated room rates of Dr 140/170.

Better value but a bit farther away and heading up the price scale is the *Hôtel Riad* (☎ 688353), on Ave Idriss el-Akbar. It's another new place and it appears that the bar

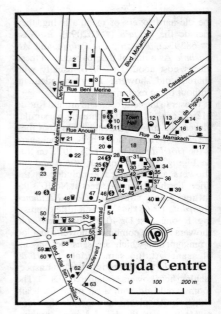

Oujda Centre

doubles as a pick-up joint. The rooms on the higher floors are quite good though, with phone and en suite bathroom. They cost Dr 146/171 plus taxes.

Older and crustier is the *Hôtel La Concorde* (☎ 682328), on Blvd Mohammed V. Rooms with private bathroom and phone cost Dr 140/200 and, although a bit ragged around the edges, the place has a bit of character. The bar especially has the grittiness of typical local drinking houses but with just a slight edge in atmosphere.

Places to Stay – top end

There are a few hotels in the three-star bracket and up. Right near the railway station, the *Hôtel Moussafir* chain (☎ 688202; fax 688208) has one of its standard and fairly reliable hotels for people who want to be near railway stations. Rooms, as usual, are modern and well kept at the standard Dr 216/261 plus taxes.

PLACES TO STAY

1	Hôtel Ghilane
2	Hôtel Mamounia
3	Hôtel Iris
4	Grand Hotel
13	Hôtel Al-Hanna
14	Hôtel Résidence Gharnata
16	Hôtel du 16 Août
17	Hôtel Marrakech
27	Hôtel Ziri
29	Hôtel Victoria
30	Hôtel de Nice
31	Hôtel Zegzel
32	Hôtel Tlemcen
33	Hôtel Chic
34	Hôtel Isly
36	Hôtel Afrah
37	Hôtel Angad
38	Hôtel En-Nazaha
39	Hôtel d'Alger
40	Hôtel Bahia
43	Hôtel & Bar EL-Andalous
44	Hôtel & Bar Majestic
45	Hôtel Simon
51	Hôtel Al Fajr
53	Hôtel L'Oasis
54	Hôtel/Bar/Restaurant La Concorde
56	Hôtel des Lilas
58	Hôtel Royal
63	Hôtel Oujda

PLACES TO EAT

5	Restaurant aux Delices
7	Restaurant Marius
21	Restaurant du Palais
26	Brasserie Restaurant de France
41	Restaurant/Café Holiday
42	Restaurant Tourisme
55	Restaurant China Town
60	Sandwich Taroudannt
62	Restaurant Le Printemps

OTHER

6	Main Post Office (PTT)
8	Café Le Trésor
9	Uniban (exchange facilities)
10	Hertz
11	Wafabank
12	CTM Bus Terminal
15	Café Fath
18	Place du 16 Août 1953
19	Crédit du Maroc
20	Wagons Lits/Europcar
22	Market
23	Budget
24	BMCI (ATM)
25	BMCE (ATM)
28	Tourist Office
35	Douche Moderne
46	Bank al-Maghrib
47	Cinema
48	Bar Cinq Etoiles
49	Banque Populaire
50	Sûreté Nationale (police)
52	Bar Chanteclair
55	Banque Commerciale du Maroc
57	Société Générale Marocaine de Banques
59	Café/Bar des Anciens Combattants
61	Maroc Voyages/Avis
63	Royal Air Maroc

The *Hôtel Terminus* across the square is closed.

A little way up Blvd Zerktouni is yet another brand-new place, with staff eager to please. The *Hôtel Al-Manar* (☎ 697037; fax 681670) has air-con rooms with en suite bathrooms, direct-line phones and satellite TV for Dr 186/229. Parking is also available.

Older and not as gleaming is the *Hôtel des Lilas* (☎ 680840), at Rue Jamal ed-Din el-Afghani. It has 38 rooms and 10 suites. The rooms are good, with private bathroom and TV, and cost Dr 216/261. Parking is available.

The two top hotels are the *Hôtel Oujda* (☎ 684093; fax 685064), on Blvd Mohammed V, and the *Hôtel Al Massira* (☎ 685300/1), off Ave Idriss el-Akbar. They both charge Dr 222/273 and have their own restaurants and bars. The latter has been taken over by the government, and it now has something of the air of an Intourist establishment of the Cold War era.

Places to Eat

Probably the cheapest place to eat snack food is at the stalls set up inside Bab el-Ouahab, providing you have a taste for broiled sheep heads, deep-fried intestines and very large bags of snails. Fortunately, you can also find slightly more standard meals along the lines of cooked potatoes and omelettes.

Otherwise, there's not an oversupply of cheap eating places in Oujda. *Iris Sandwich* is a good snack-food place on Ave Idriss el-Akbar. You can get a baguette stuffed with meat, salad and chips for Dr 12 to Dr 16. Virtually next door is the *Restaurant Quick Food*, which offers a common Middle

Eastern dish, shawarma (lamb's meat cooked on a huge, upright rotisserie) – something of a rarity in these parts.

There are other cheap places in the pedestrian area off Blvd Mohammed V which are OK. The *Café Holiday*, for instance, does an unexciting tajine for Dr 25. There are also a few nondescript places along Rue de Marrakech.

A good place is *Sandwich Taroudannt*, on Blvd Allal ben Abdallah, just around the corner from the Hôtel Royal. It serves generous portions of the usual dishes, although it's not the cheapest place to eat – Dr 45 to Dr 50 will get plenty of meat, chips and salad.

A little farther afield, the *Restaurant aux Délices*, on Blvd Mohammed Derfoufi and close to the Grand and Mamounia hotels, offers hamburgers, brochettes, salads and pizzas, all priced at around Dr 20.

For a splurge in air-conditioned comfort, with black-suited waiters and starched white linen, try the *Brasserie Restaurant de France*, on Blvd Mohammed V. The food here is of uneven quality and can cost you about Dr 100 a head with wine, but on a good night it's good. The extensive menu includes a rather watery spaghetti bolognese (Dr 42), pizza and a range of fish dishes. A small bottle of beer costs Dr 17 or more, depending on your poison.

Not far behind this place in price, but with equally good food on a good night, is the *Restaurant Marius*, just off Blvd Mohammed Derfoufi. A full meal will cost about Dr 80 a head. The *Restaurant du Palais*, a block south, has a noisy all-male bar next door. The Palais is nothing special.

Entertainment
Cafés & Bars There is no shortage of cafés all over the ville nouvelle and in the area around the medina. Some have been marked on the maps, but it is hard to particularly recommend one over the other. A couple of those on Blvd Mohammed V have a definitely more swish air about them. *Le Trésor* is one.

The few bars marked on the maps are of the usual discreet spit-and-sawdust variety. The bigger hotels have bars and some of these double as dubious discos.

Getting There & Away
Air The airport serving Oujda is 15 km from the town centre (about a Dr 50 petit taxi ride). RAM (☎ 683909), which has an office below the Hôtel Oujda, has six flights a week to Casablanca (Dr 715 one way; one hour 40 minutes). There is also a weekly direct flight to Rabat/Salé (Dr 625) and a flight to Agadir via Casablanca (Dr 1290). There is one direct flight a week to Paris (Dr 4115 one way) on Saturday at 8 am. Air France also has a weekly flight to Paris, departing on Sunday at 3.55 pm.

Bus CTM has a small office behind the town hall. There are only two departures from here: Casablanca (Dr 158.50) via Rabat (Dr 131) at 8 pm and a mumtaz run to Fès (Dr 83.50) at 8.30 pm. The SAT bus company has an office across the road for its Casablanca and Rabat runs at 6 and 8 pm.

All other buses, including CTM's other services, leave from the bus station (gare routière) across Oued Nachef on the southwestern edge of town, about 15 minutes' walk from the railway station. Advance booking is available on the main runs.

Several companies operate buses to most destinations, including Fès at 5, 8.30 and 11 am (Dr 60; six hours); Meknès at 2.30 pm; Taza at least five times daily (Dr 39); Figuig at 4.30, 6, 7 and 10 am and 3 pm (Dr 66.50 – check departure times carefully in advance as the information seems unreliable at best); Bouarfa at the same times (Dr 47.50); Nador up to 13 times daily (Dr 23.50); Al-Hoceima via Nador at 2 pm; and Saidia four or five times a day (Dr 11).

CTM has daily departures to Taza and Fès at 5 and 11 am, and to Taza and Nador at 7 and 10 am and 1 and 3.30 pm. Ligne du Sahara has departures to Figuig (via Bouarfa) at 6 am and 1.30 pm (Dr 61.60; seven hours). Transports des Hauts Plateaux has departures to Figuig at 10 am and 3 pm, and to Bouarfa at 7 am. Ligne de Casablanca has departures to Fès at 2.30 pm and to Casablanca/Rabat at 6 am and 5, 6, 7.30 and 8.30 pm.

Train The railway station is fairly close to the centre of town, at the western end of Blvd Zerktouni. There are departures for the west of the country at 7.05 and 9.55 am and 1.15, 7.30, 9.25 and 10.20 pm (the last of these services runs in summer only). All these trains call at Taza (four hours), Fès (6½ hours) and Meknès (7½ hours). The 7.05 am and 10.20 pm trains continue on to Tangier, while the others continue on to Rabat and Casablanca. First and 2nd-class sleepers are available on the evening trains.

Second-class fares on normal/rapide services include: Taza (Dr 49.50/62.50); Fès (Dr 74/93.50); Casablanca (Dr 142/182.50); Tangier (Dr 142/179.50); and Marrakesh (Dr 194.50/246, no direct trains).

There's a weekly train to Bouarfa. See below for details.

Supratours has an office at the station, should you want to book rail/coach tickets to destinations south of Marrakesh.

Taxi Grands taxis to Taza and Fès leave fairly regularly from outside the main bus station. The fares per person are Dr 50 and Dr 80 respectively. Taxis to Fès take you to Bab el-Ftouh (see the Getting Around section for Fès).

Grands taxis to Nador leave from Place du Maroc (Dr 35). Others travelling to Saidia on the Mediterranean coast leave from the other side of the square, but they are infrequent outside summer (Dr 15). Taxis from here also serve other regional towns.

To/From Algeria There are buses to the Algerian border (13 km) every half-hour throughout the day from near Place du Maroc; the cost is Dr 3.

The train to Algeria and on to Tunisia leaves Oujda at 8.30 am. The Moroccan section of the journey is a short ride to the border, where you must change to an Algerian train. One-way fares include Tlemcen (Dr 33), Oran (Dr 47), Algiers (Dr 81) and

Tunis (Dr 217). You can get off at the border and change for a taxi if you want to, but you still pay a minimum of the Tlemcen fare.

Grands taxis to the Algerian border leave from Place du Maroc and cost Dr 7 (day rate) and Dr 10 (night rate).

There are plenty of taxis at the border. Allow two hours for border formalities.

Car Rental The following agencies can be found in Oujda:

Avis
    (Maroc Voyages), 110 Blvd Allal ben Abdallah (☎ 683993)
Budget
    Immeuble Kada, Blvd Mohammed V (☎ 682437)
Europcar
    (Wagons-Lits), Place Mohammed V (☎ 682520)
Hertz
    Blvd Mohammed V (☎ 683802)

AROUND OUJDA
Sidi Yahia Oasis
About seven km east of Oujda is the fairly unexciting oasis village of Sidi Yahia. If you happen to be in Oujda in September, however, it might be worth enquiring about the annual moussem held there. It is one of the bigger celebrations of this type in the country.

BOUARFA
There is an argument for skipping the Oujda crossing to Algeria and heading first to the oasis of Figuig, 376 km to the south, especially for those who see the desert routes through the Sahara as the main attraction of Maghreb travel. Figuig itself warrants a visit, but the towns on the way down from Oujda do not. Bouarfa is no exception, and the only thing that separates it from the others is the fact that it is a minor transport hub.

Places to Stay & Eat
Should you get stuck here, or want to stay for some perverse reason, the best accommodation bet is the *Hôtel Tamlalte*, on the town's main street and about 100 metres from the bus lot. Rooms are clean but basic and cost

Dr 30/60. The *Hôtel des Hauts Plateaux* is better known, more expensive and poorer value. It's located at the Oujda exit of town. Neither of these places has showers, but they do have basins. There is supposedly a third hotel lost in the warren of streets to the west of the bus lot. A few cafés and snack stands are scattered around town.

Getting There & Away
Bus Buses to Oujda cost Dr 47.50, and leave at 6.30, 7, 7.30 and 10 am and 2 and 4 pm. Departures to Figuig are at 10.30 am and 3, 5.30 and 7 pm. The fare is Dr 19. Heading west to Er-Rachidia there is a bus for Dr 50 at 12.45 pm.

Train Believe it or not there is a weekly passenger train between Bouarfa and Oujda. It leaves Oujda on Saturday night at 10.42 pm and takes about eight hours. It then turns around at 9.20 am on Sunday to return to Oujda.

Taxi Few grands taxis run these routes, but you might get lucky if you need one. Grands taxis leapfrog the towns north to Oujda, but you should be covered by the through buses if you need a connection.

FIGUIG
Some 100,000 palm trees are fed by artesian wells in this oasis on the edge of the Sahara. Figuig was once the last stop before crossing the Sahara for Moroccan pilgrims heading to Mecca, and as the second border post with Algeria after Oujda, it retains the feel of a frontier town. There are several ksour of varying interest throughout the palmeraies (palm groves), and from some vantage points you can get great views across the extent of the oasis.

Figuig's greatest charm is as a place to simply unwind. It would be hard to find a more laid-back place, although in summer this is due more than anything to the oppressive heat. The main road from Bouarfa goes right through the oasis and on to Beni Ounif, on the Algerian side of the frontier. The

hotels, along with such cafés and eating places as there are, are all along this road.

Information
There is a Banque Populaire here, especially handy for those entering the country from Algeria. There is a mild black market in Algerian dinar and Moroccan dirham in the oasis – ask about discreetly. There is also a post and phone office set back off the main road. Note the police post (Sûreté Nationale) where the street makes a dogleg, shortly before the Hôtel Diamant Vert on the way to the frontier. People leaving and arriving must stop here to have their passports stamped.

Places to Stay & Eat
The *Hôtel Diamant Vert* is the best option – it's a good 20 minutes' walk from the roundabout where the buses usually stop on the road to the border. You can camp here for Dr 10 a head, or take a room for Dr 30/40. There are cold showers and a pool.

The *Hôtel Sahara*, about 50 metres on from where the buses stop, has basic rooms for Dr 25 a head. There is a hammam opposite (Dr 5 a go; women during the day and men in the evening). The worst place is the *Hôtel El-Meliasse* at the Shell service station, which you'll see on the right entering the town from Bouarfa. Rooms are Dr 30/60.

For food there's a small, nameless place by the roundabout where the buses stop, where you can eat brochettes for about Dr 4 each. The *Café Fath* and *Café Oasis* (the latter just short of Moroccan customs on the border) are other possibilities.

Getting There & Away

Bus There are buses to Oujda at 6 and 8 am every day, and occasionally at 2 pm. They all stop at Bouarfa (in case you want to link up with the Er-Rachidia bus there at 12.45 pm). The fare is Dr 66.50 to Oujda.

To/From Algeria It's a three-km walk to Moroccan customs, another km to Algerian customs and three more km to the first Algerian town, Beni Ounif. With luck you might get a lift part of the way. Coming or going, be sure to have your passport stamped by the Moroccan police in Figuig, on the right just before the Hôtel Diamant Vert on the way to the border. Be prepared for long waits on the Algerian side, and thorough searches.

The North Atlantic Coast

From Tangier to the Mauritanian border, Morocco boasts an Atlantic seaboard of some 2500 km (including the still-disputed territory of the Western Sahara, which is under Rabat's control). If Tangier is a unique mix of Moroccan and European influences, the cities and towns of the coast, too, present a different face from those of the interior. Most were occupied, or even founded, by European powers over the centuries, and this is reflected in their appearance and feel. Long used to the sight of foreigners among them, the people of the coastal cities have been handed down a legacy quite different from that of the long-xenophobic interior.

Rabat and Casablanca, the political and economic capitals since the French installed their protectorate in 1912, are cosmopolitan centres at the heart of modern Morocco. They are flanked up and down the coast by towns that at one time or another served as bridgeheads for European merchant empires. Such was the case in Asilah and Larache, which changed hands several times before ending up as part of Spain's zone in the protectorate. What remains is a curious combination of European and Moroccan fortifications and medinas. In between lie hundreds of km of beaches, many of them crowded in summer. Foreigners tend to head still farther south, to Essaouira and Agadir.

North Coast

ASILAH

A 46-km drive south of Tangier through soft, verdant country along a stretch of Atlantic beaches lies the small port of Asilah. Small it may be, but, over two millennia, it has had a tumultuous history far out of proportion to its size.

The first settlers were the Carthaginians, who named the port Zilis. Next were the Romans. Forced to deal with a population that had backed the wrong side during the Punic Wars, Rome decided to move the inhabitants to Spain and replace them with Iberians.

Asilah featured again in the 10th century, when it held Norman raiders from Sicily at bay. In the following century it became the last refuge of the Idrissids. The town's most turbulent period, however, followed the Christian victories over the forces of Islam on the Iberian peninsula in the 14th and 15th centuries. In 1471 it was captured by the Portuguese, and the walls around the city date from this period, although they have been repaired from time to time.

In 1578 King Dom Sebastian of Portugal chose Asilah as the base for an ill-fated crusade, which resulted in his death and the subsequent passing of Portugal (and its Moroccan possessions) into the hands of Spain.

Asilah was captured by the Moroccans in 1589, lost again to the Spanish, and then was recaptured by Moulay Ismail in 1691. In the

The North Atlantic Coast

0   25   50 km

ATLANTIC OCEAN

TANGIER
ASILAH
M'Soura
Lixus
LARACHE
KSAR-EL-KEBIR
OUAZZANE
SOUK EL-ARBA DU-RHARB
Oued
Sebou
Kenitra
SIDI-KACEM
SALÉ
RABAT
MOHAMMEDIA
CASABLANCA
BEN SLIMANE
Meknès

19th century, as a result of pirate attacks on its shipping, Spain sent in the navy to bombard the town.

Early this century, Asilah was used as a base by one of the most colourful bandits ever produced by the wild Rif mountains – Er-Raissouli (see the aside below). Shortly after the end of WW I he was forced to abandon Asilah, and within a few years had lost everything.

Asilah has found its niche in the late 20th century as a bijou resort town. Money has been poured into gentrifying the houses within the city walls by both affluent Moroccans and Europeans. Consequently, the streets gleam with fresh whitewash, ornate wrought-iron work adorns windows, and chic craft shops have sprouted along virtually every alley. A new harbour is under construction and should soon be providing berths for pleasure yachts and the small local fishing fleet. A little farther north along the

beaches, camping resorts have mushroomed, catering to European summer holiday-makers.

Despite the changes mass tourism has brought (including the arrival of a handful of touts and guides), it is worth staying in Asilah for a while, especially in the low season, when there are hardly any tourists around.

Information

Money Both the BMCE and Banque Populaire will change cash and travellers' cheques and issue cash advances on credit cards. There are no ATMs.

Post & Telecommunications The post and telephone office is on the east side of town, just in off the Tangier-Rabat road. It is open during regular office hours. There are a couple of card-operated telephones outside the office.

NTH ATLANTIC COAST

Er-Raissouli

Moulay Ahmed ben Mohammed er-Raissouli (or Raisuni) began his career in the late 1800s as a petty mountain bandit but soon progressed to murder on such a scale that the whole countryside around Tangier and Tetouan lived in fear of him. At this time, however, he had been made pasha of Asilah, which was to become his main residence and base. In 1899, when Er-Raissouli was 23 years old, the sultan lost patience (or summoned up the nerve to act against the 'pasha') and had him arrested and jailed in Mogador (modern Essaouira) for several years.

When he was let out he returned home, but was soon at it again. His most profitable game became kidnapping Westerners. He and his band held various luminaries to ransom, including US businessman Ion Perdicaris, who was ransomed in 1904 for US$70,000. In return for promising good conduct, Er-Raissouli was made governor of the Tangier region. His conduct, however, was anything but good, and by 1907 the European powers were sufficiently worried by his antics that they compelled the Moroccan government to attack him. It did, but failed to capture him.

Things were looking grim for Er-Raissouli, but in 1909 Moulay Abd al-Hafiz became sultan, and Er-Raissouli – whose influence over the Rif tribes was still great – proclaimed his allegiance to the new sultan immediately. In return he was made governor of most of north-west Morocco except Tangier.

Spain, which took control of the north under the deal that cut Morocco up into protectorates in 1912, tried to make use of Er-Raissouli to keep order among the Rif tribes. Madrid invested considerable money and military hardware in the effort, but in vain. Er-Raissouli as often as not used the arms against the Spanish, inflicting several stinging defeats.

Having obtained promises from Germany that he would be made sultan after WW I, he found himself at loggerheads with everyone when Germany lost, in 1918. The Spaniards forced him to flee Asilah, but for the following few years he continued to wreak havoc in the Rif hinterland.

The final irony was his arrest and imprisonment at the beginning of 1925 by a Rif rebel with a slightly broader political outlook, Abd el-Krim. Er-Raissouli, who had submitted to the medical attention of a Spaniard, stood accused of being too closely linked to the Spanish! He died on 10 April 1925. ■

NTH ATLANTIC COAST

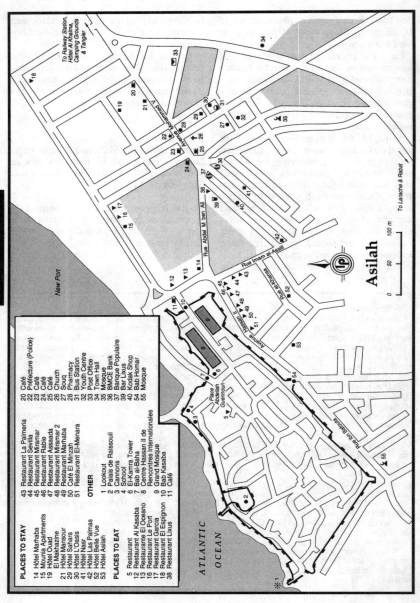

Asilah

PLACES TO STAY
14 Hôtel Marhaba
15 Mounia Apartments
19 El Makhazine
21 Hôtel Ouad
29 Hôtel Mansour
30 Hôtel Sahara
41 Hôtel L'Oasis
42 Hôtel Nasr
52 Hôtel Las Palmas
53 Hôtel Belle Vue
    Hôtel Asilah

PLACES TO EAT
5   Restaurant
12 Restaurant Al Kasaba
16 Restaurante El Oceano
17 Restaurant Le Port
18 Restaurant Garcia
38 Restaurant Lixus

43 Restaurant La Palmeria
44 Restaurant Sevilla
45 Restaurant Miramar
46 Restaurant Rabie
47 Restaurant Assaada
48 Restaurant Miramar 2
49 Restaurant Marhaba
50 Café El Minzah
51 Restaurant El-Menara

OTHER
1   Lookout
2   Palais de Raissouli
3   Cannons
4   School
6   El-Kamra Tower
7   Bab al-Baha
8   Rentre Hassan II de
    Rencontres Internationales
9   Grand Kiosque
10 Bab Kasaba
11 Café

20 Café
22 Prefecture (Police)
23 Café
24 Café
25 Café
26 Church
27 Souq
31 Pharmacy
32 Bus Station
33 Post Office
34 Youth Centre
35 Town Hall
36 Mosque
37 BMCE Bank
39 Banque Populaire
40 Bar Lixus
54 Kodak Shop
54 Bab Homar
55 Mosque

Medical Services Asilah has several pharmacies. The easiest one to find is just down from the bus station.

Ramparts & Medina
The impressive 15th-century Portuguese ramparts are largely intact, partly a result of modern restoration work. Access is limited, since many private houses abut them. The two prongs that jut out into the ocean, however, can be visited at any time and these afford the best views. It's reminiscent of the old towns enclosed behind the walls of El-Jadida and Essaouira and there are plenty of photographic opportunities.

The bright medina is worth a wander around. You'll notice a lot of cheery **murals** on many of the houses. Of more historical note is the **Bab Homar** (also known as Bab al-Jebel or, to the Spaniards, Puerta de la Tierra), topped by the much-eroded Portuguese royal coat of arms. On Place Abdellah Guennoun is an interesting-looking **tower** known as the El-Kamra. There are a few old cannons left just inside the seaward wall, although you can only see them from a distance – access has been cut off by another cement wall.

Palais de Raissouli (Raissouli Palace)
Undoubtedly one of the town's most interesting sights, this beautifully preserved three-storey building was constructed in 1909 and includes a main reception room with a glass-fronted terrace overlooking the sea. It was from this terrace that Er-Raissouli forced convicted murderers to jump to their deaths onto the rocks 30 metres below. Unfortunately, all the furniture has been removed, so it's hard to get an idea of the sumptuousness of Er-Raissouli's life at the height of his power. Access is through a door just inside the seaward wall; a guardian will open it up, for a small tip. Entry is free. The palace is the venue for an international arts festival held in August each year.

Beaches
Other than the medina, the beaches to the north of town are the main attraction. During the summer months they are awash with tourists from Europe. A whole service industry has grown up to cater for the needs of these people, including camp sites, restaurants, discos and the like. It's a smaller-scale version of Agadir at this time of year, and you can meet people from as far afield as Brisbane and Bremen.

Places to Stay – bottom end
Camping For campers, there are a number of resorts/sites along the beach, all of them north of town. The first two you come across walking out of town are *Camping As-Saada* (Dr 12 per person and Dr 10 for a car) and *Camping Echrigui*. They are much of a muchness, and both have small grocery shops and claim to have hot water. Just beyond the Hôtel El Khaima and about one km inland is *Camping El Minzah* – its location makes it a rather unlikely candidate for most popular camp site in Asilah.

Closer to the Mohammed V Bridge, which lies about 10 km north of Asilah, are at least three more Atlantic coast camps, *L'Océan*, the *Atlas* and the *Sahara*. They tend to be pretty full in summer and at Easter, as they are often block-booked by tour groups from Europe. At other times of the year, you'll virtually have the place to yourself. They all have guarded camping facilities, shower and toilet blocks, and restaurants and bars.

Hotels About the cheapest place is said to be the *Hôtel Nasr*, which offers small, basic rooms. However, it was closed at the time of writing. Next up is the *Hôtel Marhaba* (☎ 917144), which overlooks Place Zelaka, in front of the main entrance (Bab Kasaba) to the old town, and is quite adequate for most travellers. It costs Dr 70 for a single or double. Each room has a double bed with clean sheets and a washbasin, but you share the bathroom. Hot showers are Dr 5 extra. Try for a room at the front, as some of the ones farther back are a bit pokey. The *Hôtel Asilah* was another reasonably cheap place, but it was closed for refurbishment at the time of writing.

Another similarly priced hotel is the *Hôtel*

Sahara (☎ 917185), 9 Rue Tarfaya, which is on a par with the Marhaba, although a little more expensive at Dr 80/100. Showers are Dr 5 extra. Nearby is yet another closed hotel, *L'Oasis*.

Places to Stay – middle

There are a few mid-range options in Asilah. The *Hôtel Belle Vue* (☎ 917747), Rue al-Khansa, offers comfortable, clean rooms with shared shower and toilet and plenty of hot water. Rooms cost Dr 100/120, although you can be fairly sure they'll ask more in summer. It also has self-contained apartments with lounge, kitchen and refrigerator (Dr 300), or larger ones which can accommodate up to six people (Dr 400).

A rather characterless place with spacious, comfortable rooms is the *Hôtel Ouad El Makhazine* (☎ 917090; fax 917500), on Ave Melilla. The rooms have carpet, showers, toilets and phones and cost Dr 115/137.

The *Hôtel Mansour* (☎ 917390) is a cosy little place with sparklingly clean rooms, all with shower and toilet. The small dining area is almost reminiscent of an English tea room. Rooms cost Dr 153/181 and the staff are helpful.

Another mid-range place, *Las Palmas*, was closed at the time of researching.

Places to Stay – top end

The three-star *Hôtel El Khaima* (☎ 917428; fax 917566) is beside the road heading north, just out of town on the right-hand side. Singles/doubles here cost Dr 266/273 (plus taxes). Breakfast costs Dr 34. The hotel has 110 rooms, a restaurant, a pool and a disco.

Out near the camp sites by the Mohammed V Bridge are a couple of other hotels, the *Club Solitaire* and the *Atlantis*, which are more important for the pools, restaurants and discos they offer campers than for their accommodation.

Long-Term House Rentals

Because many people have bought houses in the old town and converted them into holiday homes, it is possible to find long-term rentals outside the high season. Ask around and the grapevine will do the rest. What you pay for these houses will depend on the standard of accommodation offered, but they won't be cheap. References or a substantial deposit for wear and tear or breakages would be normal.

Places to Eat

You'll find a string of restaurants and cafés on Ave Hassan II, and around the corner on Rue Imam al-Assili. A main course in any of them will cost around Dr 30. There is a small restaurant inside the medina near the El-Kamra tower. It's nothing special either, but is a change of location if nothing else.

There are two slightly more expensive restaurants across from Bab Kasaba: *Restaurante El Oceano* and *Restaurant Al Kasaba*. Both specialise in fish (which is quite good), and a full meal at either will cost around Dr 70. Heading north along the waterfront (the views are not so hot, as the esplanade is wide and construction work is underway) are three more restaurants, again offering fish as a speciality. A little cheaper is the more straightforward *Restaurant el-Noujoum*, under the Hôtel Marhaba. It serves standard Moroccan fare.

The *Restaurant Le Port* and the *Restaurant Garcia* are right next to each other, while the *Restaurant El Espigon* is at the end of the street. All three are a little more expensive than the two by the city gates.

There are a couple of other nondescript places around, and several cafés near the grand taxi stand.

If it's a drink you're after, try the locals' *Bar Lixus* or head out to the Hôtel El Khaima. There is also a small liquor store next to the Hôtel Marhaba.

Getting There & Away

Bus Your best bet for getting to and from Asilah is the bus. All buses leave from the same lot, with just the one ticket window. There are lots of buses to Tangier (Dr 10), and about eight a day that stop in Larache (Dr 10), although there is nothing between 12.45 and 6 pm. Pay on the bus. The trip either way takes just under an hour.

There are two buses a day to Meknès and

two to Rabat (Dr 40 to Dr 50, depending on the company), although the more numerous runs to Casablanca (about Dr 80) usually stop there too. There are about six buses to Fès (Dr 52 or more, depending on the company).

Train This is the painful way to get to Asilah, as the station is 2½ km north of town. Rapide/2nd-class ordinary fares are Dr 67/53 to Rabat, Dr 91/72 to Casablanca and Dr 12.50/10 to Tangier.

Taxi Grands taxis to Tangier cost Dr 19, and you might be able to get one to Larache for Dr 10 a person, although they seem to be a rarity.

AROUND ASILAH
Monoliths of M'Soura
An ancient and little-understood stone circle stands on a desolate patch of ground some 25 km (by road) south-east of Asilah. The stones range from 50 cm to six metres in height, and some historians believe they surround the tomb of a noble, perhaps dating back to Punic times. To get to it you must first reach the village of Souq Tnine de Sidi el-Yamani, off highway P37, which branches east off the main Tangier-Rabat road. From here, six km of bad piste lead north to the site. You need a good vehicle, and a local guide would help.

LARACHE
Most people come to Larache to visit the Roman ruins of Lixus, four to five km out of town to the north, but it's worth staying a night or two just for its own sake. Bigger and scruffier than Asilah and with a more substantial fishing port, Larache is a tranquil town where you'll have few hassles.

The old town was once walled, but the kasbah and ramparts are now in almost total ruin. What remains intact are the old medina, a fortress known as the Casbah de la Cigogne and a pocket-sized, Spanish-built citadel that houses the archaeological museum. The medina, a tumbledown affair, is worth walking around to get a feel for a typical,

living Moroccan town without any of the tourist trappings and hassle. The heart of the new town is Place de la Libération (formerly the Plaza de España), a typical example of Spanish colonial urban planning. The white-washed town, inside the medina and out, is dominated by one other colour – the blue used on doors and window frames.

One thing that makes Larache interesting is the nightlife. Although it's a long time since the Spanish left, the social institution of the evening stroll lives on in the warmer months. Between the hours of 5.30 and 9 pm, everyone emerges from the woodwork to promenade, drink coffee or beer, play cards and talk about the day's events. Not so Spanish, however, is the fact that by 10 pm the streets are virtually empty. Naturally, there's some good seafood available in the restaurants.

Information
Money Across the road from the post office is a cluster of banks, all of which accept cash and travellers' cheques. There are no ATMs.

Post & Telecommunications The post and telephone office is on Blvd Mohammed V and is open normal office hours. There are some card-operated phones outside.

Foreign Consulates Spain has a consulate at 1 Rue Casablanca (☎ 913302). It's open from 8 am to 1 pm Monday to Friday and from 10 am to 12.30 pm on Saturday.

Musée Archéologique
The tiny archaeological museum contains a small collection of artefacts, mostly from nearby Lixus, including coins, ceramics, utensils and the like from Phoenician and Roman times. The display is on two floors but is so small that, if you are on a tight budget and want to save yourself the tenner, you could probably skip it. The explanations are in Arabic and French only. The building itself is a former Spanish citadel and bears the arms of Charles V above the main door. It's open daily from 9 am to 12.30 pm and 3 to 6 pm (closed Tuesday). Entry costs Dr 10.

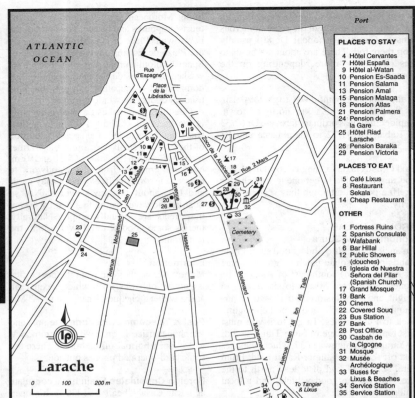

PLACES TO STAY
4 Hôtel Cervantes
7 Hôtel España
9 Hôtel al-Watan
10 Pension Es-Saada
11 Pension Salama
13 Pension Amal
15 Pension Malaga
18 Pension Atlas
21 Pension Palmera
24 Pension de
   la Gare
25 Hôtel Riad
   Larache
26 Pension Baraka
29 Pension Victoria

PLACES TO EAT
5 Café Lixus
8 Restaurant
   Sekala
14 Cheap Restaurant

OTHER
1 Fortress Ruins
2 Spanish Consulate
3 Wafabank
6 Bar Hillal
12 Public Showers
   (douches)
16 Iglesia de Nuestra
   Señora del Pilar
   (Spanish Church)
17 Grand Mosque
19 Bank
20 Cinema
22 Covered Souq
23 Bus Station
27 Bank
28 Post Office
30 Casbah de
   la Cigogne
31 Mosque
32 Musée
   Archéologique
33 Buses for
   Lixus & Beaches
34 Service Station
35 Service Station

Larache

0   100   200 m

NTH ATLANTIC COAST

The Old Town

The only intact fortification here is the **Casbah de la Cigogne** (built by the Spaniards under Phillip III in the 17th century), which is out of bounds to visitors. The old city walls and ruined kasbah (the *Qebibat*, or cupolas) built by the Portuguese in the 16th century, while not out of bounds, are made dangerous by the possibility of falling masonry.

The old cobbled **medina**, on the other hand, is alive and well and, although not comparable with the medinas of the imperial cities, is worth exploring. No-one will hassle

you about guide services and there are good photographic possibilities. As you enter by the large, unmistakable Mauresque arch on Place de la Libération (the Bab al-Khemis), you come immediately into a colonnaded market square, the **Zoco de la Alcaiceria**, built by the Spaniards during their first occupation of Larache in the 17th century. It is the busiest part of the medina, full of vendors displaying their wares.

You can also get into the heart of the medina through a similar arch opposite the archaeological museum. If you want to go down to the port, head for the eastern corner

Woman wearing ceremonial headdress

of the Zoco and turn past the Pension Atlas down Rue 2 Mars, which will take you through, among other things, the wood-workers' market.

Beaches

The nearest beaches are north of Larache, across the other side of the Loukkos estuary. To get there, you can take a small boat across the estuary from the port, or go by the more circuitous road route (seven km), using the No 4 bus, which you can also pick up from the main bus stop opposite the Casbah de la Cicogne. The buses run approximately every hour throughout the day.

There are a number of simple restaurants at the beach, offering the usual range of seafoods.

Places to Stay – bottom end

There's a good choice of budget accommodation to be found in Larache. Inside the medina there are at least three extremely basic places: the *Pension Atlas, Pension Victoria* and *Hôtel al-Watan*. They are all close

to the Zoco, but you're really better off staying in one of the places in the new part of town.

If you want to be right near the bus station, you could try the *Pension de la Gare*, which has singles/doubles for the pretty much standard Dr 30/50, but no hot water.

The bulk of the other cheapies are on or near Ave Mohammed ben Abdallah. The three best, all with hot water, are the *Pension Baraka* (☎ 913127), which has clean and comfortable rooms for Dr 40/60; the *Pension Malaga* (☎ 911868), which is virtually the same, although doubles cost a little more at Dr 70; and the *Pension Amal* (☎ 912788), which has good rooms for Dr 30/60 and hot showers for Dr 5.

Not so good is the *Pension Es-Saada*, which is closest to Place de la Libération. The cramped rooms (Dr 30/50) have only cold water and, on the ground floor, are very noisy. Better, but still without hot water, are the *Pension Palmera* (☎ 911220) and the *Pension Salama*, both of which charge Dr 30/60.

For Dr 60/90 you could try the *Hôtel Cervantes*, possibly once a decent Spanish hotel but now quite frankly a dump. They claim to have hot water in the shared showers, and some of the rooms do have ocean glimpses.

If you have problems with showers, you could try the public showers (Dr 5) on Ave Mohammed ben Abdallah.

Places to Stay – middle

Once *the* place to stay during Spanish colonial times, the two-star *Hôtel España* (☎ 913195), which fronts onto Place de la Libération, still exudes an air of grandness. It has 50 rooms, some with private bathroom and balcony. The cost is Dr 130/150 for singles/doubles with private bathroom and Dr 80/130 without. It is a reliable, well-maintained place and all of the rooms have phones.

A few km south of Larache on the road to Rabat, the *Hostal Flora* is of little use to anyone without a car.

Places to Stay – top end

The only top-end hotel in town is the three-star *Hôtel Riad Larache* (☎ 912626; fax 912629), Ave Mohammed ben Abdallah, apparently once the private home of some French nobles, and now part of the Kasbah Tours Hotels chain. Set in its own somewhat neglected grounds with swimming pool and tennis courts, the hotel offers spacious, self-contained rooms at Dr 270/450 plus taxes. As well as a beer garden, there's an internal bar and restaurant that offers expensive meals. Breakfast, by the way, is included in the room price.

Places to Eat & Drink

There are a number of small eateries around Place de la Libération and the Zoco, inside the medina, where you can get cheap Spanish-style meals. The best of them by far, the *Restaurant Sekala*, is on your left just before you enter the Zoco through Bab al-Khemis. For Dr 25 you get a big serve of paella-style rice, chicken, fish, salad and a soft drink.

There are a few eateries among the cafés along Ave Hassan II as you head away from Place de la Libération. One block up from the Hotel España is a good, cheap brochette and sandwich joint.

Apart from the cafés around Place de la Libération and along Ave Hassan II and Blvd Mohammed V, the only other kind of drinking institution is the *Bar Hillal*, for a soothing beer with the locals. You could also try the bar and beer garden at the Hôtel Riad.

Getting There & Away

Bus Larache is most easily reached by bus. CTM and several private lines run buses through here. Since booking is not always possible, the best bet is to turn up in the morning and get the first service you can.

CTM has a daily bus to Fès (Dr 55.50), at 7.30 am; four to Tangier (Dr 22) at 11.15 am and 4.30, 7.30 and 11 pm; and six to Casablanca (Dr 67) via Rabat, at 12.30, 4, 6 and 11.45 pm and 12.45 and 1.30 am. There is also a daily bus to Tiznit at 6 pm.

Other buses also cover these destinations,

and a few others besides, including Tetouan and Fnideq (for the Ceuta frontier).

Taxi Grands taxis run from just outside the bus station. The main standard run is to Ksar el-Kebir, which will be of little interest to most travellers. Otherwise they seem cagey about whether anything will go anywhere except as a special corsa (ride). Should enough people want to go (the mornings are always best), you should pay no more than Dr 10 to Asilah and Dr 50 to Dr 60 to Rabat.

Getting Around

The main local bus stop is just outside the Casbah de la Cicogne. The blue and red buses could do with an overhaul, but they do work. The average ride costs Dr 2.50. Bus Nos 4 and 5 go to Lixus, and bus No 4 goes on to the beaches north of Larache, but many buses are unnumbered, so it is as well to ask. For the beach try *ash-shaata'* (Arabic), *la plage* (French) or *la playa* (Spanish).

AROUND LARACHE
Lixus

Four to five km north of Larache on a hillock overlooking the Loukkos estuary and the Tangier-Larache highway are the Roman ruins of Lixus. Although not as substantial or as well excavated as those at Volubilis, they are definitely worth a visit. An hour or so is sufficient for most people to explore these ruins. To get there, take bus No 4 or 5 (or simply ask for Lixus, as many of the local red and blue buses have no number at all) and ask to be dropped at the turn-off. There's no entry fee and the site is not enclosed, so you're at liberty to wander around on your own. If you exercise some discretion about where you enter the ruins (head down the side road a way before entering), no-one will hassle to be your guide. Otherwise, there'll be the inevitable unemployed youth offering his services.

The site was originally occupied by a pre-historic sun-worshipping people about whom little is known, except that they left a number of stones in the vicinity of the citadel. The positioning of the stones sug-

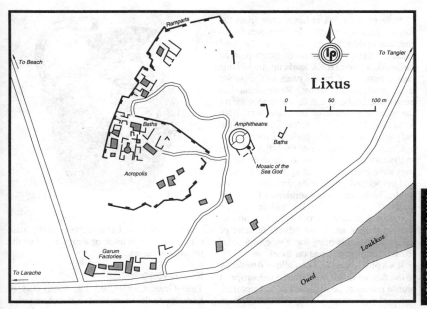

gests these people were in touch with developments in astronomy and mathematics that led to the building of stone circles in places as far apart as The Gambia and Scotland during the megalithic period.

The Phoenicians set up a colony here, known as Liks, around 1000 BC or even earlier – at about the same time they settled Cádiz (Gades or Gadera, as it was known to them) in Spain. Trade here, and through the later-established colonies of Tingis (Tangier), Tamuda (Tetouan), Russadir (Melilla) and Chella (Rabat), was principally in gold, ivory and slaves.

Nevertheless, the Atlantic colonies were never very important to the Phoenicians until the destruction of the mother city of Tyre by Nebuchadnezzar in the 6th century BC and the subsequent rise of the city-state of Carthage.

As a result of explorations as far south as the mouth of the Niger River about this time by the Carthaginian Hanno, Carthage is said to have been able to monopolise the trade in gold from West Africa and to keep its source a secret. There is some dispute as to whether or not Hanno or any other Carthaginians really did find gold. Liks was, at any rate, a key trading base, and, even when Carthage fell to the Romans in 146 BC, it continued to exert a civilising influence on this area until the establishment in 25 BC of the Roman vassal state of the Berber king Juba II.

Direct Roman rule over this part of the world came in AD 42 under Emperor Claudius, and Lixus now entered its second period of importance. Its main exports during Roman times were salt, olives, *garum* (an aromatic anchovy paste), and wild animals for the various amphitheatres of the empire.

Lixus rapidly declined following the Roman withdrawal north under Diocletian, but was not finally abandoned until some time in the 5th century AD, when the Roman Empire fell apart.

NTH ATLANTIC COAST

Most of the ruins at Lixus date from the Roman period, and include the garum factories alongside the highway. Just beyond these (at the end of a line of green-painted railings), a gravel track leads up the hillside past a number of minor ruins to the public baths and amphitheatre. Restoration has been done on these, and they're undoubtedly the most impressive of the ruins here. Also to be found is a mosaic of the Sea God – the only such mosaic to be seen at Lixus.

Carrying on to the top of the hill, you come to the citadel where most of the civic buildings were located, including the main temple and associated sanctuaries, an oratory, more public baths and what remains of the city walls. The view over the estuary of the Loukkos is excellent from here, but most of the antiquities are in an advanced state of decay and there's been some woefully amateurish restoration done on them.

It's a pity Lixus has been allowed to decay to the degree that it has. Were it in Europe, it would no doubt be regarded as an important national monument. On the other hand, there is something exhilarating about finding this place in its overgrown state, largely unprettified by human hands – nature is reclaiming the site. In winter, your only companions will be the wind and the odd goat.

To get back to Larache, you could walk (one hour), try to hitch or wait for one of the infrequent buses.

Ksar el-Kebir

The 'Great Castle', 36 km south-east of Larache on the main road to Rabat, is today a quite uninteresting town. In Almoravid and Almohad times it was a comparatively important base, but nothing much remains as a reminder of its past. It was near here that the Battle of the Three Kings was fought in

---

The Battle of Three Kings
Dynasties wouldn't be true to their nature without dynastic quarrels, but the one that began in 1574 in Morocco was destined for quite a Shakespearian end. When Mohammed al-Mutawwakil took the reins of Saadian power in 1574, on the death of his father, he contravened the family rule that the eldest *male* in the family should succeed, not the eldest *son*. Al-Mutawwakil's uncle, Abdel Malik, then in Algiers and an ally of the Ottoman Turks, decided to rectify the situation, and after two victories with the help of Turkish troops in 1576, he succeeded in evicting his nephew.

Al-Mutawwakil fled and asked Phillip II of Spain to help him regain power. Phillip declined in what turned out to be a very astute move, and sent Al-Mutawwakil to King Dom Sebastian of Portugal. Promised a virtual protectorate over Morocco in exchange for his help, Dom Sebastian could not resist. Abdel Malik went to considerable lengths to dissuade Dom Sebastian, offering Portugal a Moroccan port of its choice, but to no avail.

When, in 1578, the Portuguese army of some 20,000 landed in northern Morocco, Abdel Malik gathered a force of 50,000 to meet it. On 4 August, caught in marshy territory near Ksar el-Kebir, Dom Sebastian was routed. He and Al-Mutawwakil drowned trying to flee across the Oued Makhazin (hence the Arab name of the battle) and Abdel Malik died of an illness that had long plagued him, although some say it was a heart attack.

Ahmed al-Mansour succeeded in Morocco, but in Portugal there was no heir. Phillip II of Spain became the biggest winner of all, swallowing Portugal into his empire. ■

Top: Djemaa el-Fna, Marrakesh (GC)
Middle: Rahba Qedima, Marrakesh medina (DS)
Bottom: Palais de la Bahia, Marrakesh (DS)

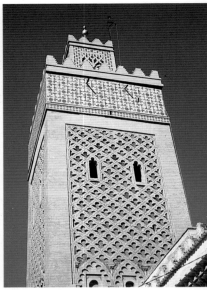

Top Left: Hassan II Mosque, Casablanca (DS)
Top Right: Minaret, Kasbah Mosque, Marrakesh (DS)
Bottom Left: Mosque south of Azilal (DS)
Bottom Right: Mosque on Jebel Tazzeka road to Taza (DS)

1578, costing the lives of the king of Portugal and two Moroccan sultans.

KENITRA
About 40 km north of Rabat lies the French-built town of Kenitra (population about 100,000), the country's sixth-largest port, known until 1958 as Port Lyautey. There is nothing in the town to attract anyone, but the nearby Plage Mehdiya and nature reserve of Lac de Sidi Bourhaba are worth a stop, for those with time.

Information
A couple of banks and the post office (PTT) are all at the junction of Blvd Mohammed V and Ave Hassan II.

Places to Stay
There are a couple of basic hotels around. The *Hôtel Marignan*, near the train station, has simple rooms for Dr 60/100, as does the *Hôtel du Commerce* (☎ 371503), near the town hall.

More expensive is the *Hôtel La Rotonde* (☎ 371401/2), at 60 Ave Mohammed Diouri (Dr 146/171 plus taxes). The *Hôtel Ambassy* (☎ 362926), at 20 Ave Hassan II, is in the same league. Back near the town hall is the fancier *Hôtel Mamora* (☎ 371775), with rooms for Dr 231/262. Top of the tree is the four-star *Hôtel Safir* (☎ 371921), near the town hall, on Place Administrative.

An alternative is the three-star *Hôtel Atlantique*, on Mehdiya beach.

Places to Eat
You'll find a few simple eateries and cafés in the town centre, especially along Ave Mohammed Diouri, but the best place is the *Restaurant L'Embouchure*, on the corner of Ave Mohammed Diouri and Rue Mohammed el-Fetouaki. They have respectable pizza imitations for Dr 35, and ice cream for dessert.

Entertainment
There seem to be a disproportionate number of bars and purported nightclubs in Kenitra.

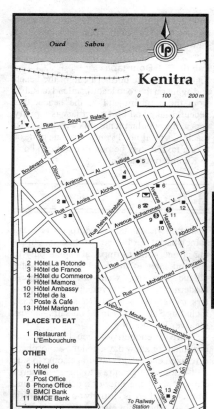

Kenitra

0   100   200 m

PLACES TO STAY
2 Hôtel La Rotonde
3 Hôtel de France
4 Hôtel du Commerce
6 Hôtel Mamora
10 Hôtel Ambassy
12 Hôtel de la
   Poste & Café
13 Hôtel Marignan

PLACES TO EAT
1 Restaurant
   L'Embouchure

OTHER
5 Hôtel de
   Ville
7 Post Office
8 Phone Office
9 BMCI Bank
11 BMCE Bank

Getting There & Away
There are regular trains and buses to Rabat, 40 km to the south. Going by train is probably the easiest bet. The one-way 2nd-class fare is Dr 10 (Dr 12.50 rapide).

AROUND KENITRA
Mehdiya
Local bus No 15 and the orange grands taxis from Ave Mohammed Diouri make the seven-km run to Mehdiya from Kenitra. Apart from the beach, which is popular with locals and not bad (though hardly Morocco's best), there are also the ruins (which you pass

on the way in from Kenitra) of a **kasbah** built by Moulay Ismail. There are some good views of the Oued Sebou estuary from here.

Lac de Sidi Bourhaba
Signposted at the northern end of the beach and again on the road leading inland to Rabat from the southern end of the beach, this peaceful lake and bird sanctuary is a pretty spot and a popular picnic area with locals. To reach it, you'll need your own transport, or take a taxi. It may be possible to hitch back to Kenitra or on to Rabat.

Rabat

The modern capital of Morocco has had somewhat of a roller-coaster history, climbing at one point to imperial capital only to descend later to the level of a backwater village. The great walls enclose a largely modern city, but there remain several quarters to remind you of Rabat's rich past, including Salé – home to the corsairs – across the river Bou Regreg.

There is enough to keep the sightseer occupied for a few days, and the atmosphere is relaxed enough to encourage some to stay a little longer. In contrast to the great tourist attractions of the interior, such as Fès and Marrakesh, there is virtually no sign of hustle and hassle here, not even in the souqs.

The new city is comparatively quiet, and although its people appear as cosmopolitan as their counterparts down the coast in Casablanca, Rabat lacks the gritty big-city edge of its economic big brother.

History
Apart from two brief spells as imperial capital, Rabat has been the capital of Morocco only since the days of the French protectorate. However, as far back as the 8th century BC, indigenous people had a settlement in the area of the necropolis of Chellah. They were followed by the Phoenicians and the Romans, who successively patrolled the coast and set up outposts of the empire.

The Roman settlement, known as Sala Colonia, was built along the river of the same name (today's Bou Regreg, which has since altered its course). Like Volubilis, it lasted long beyond the break-up of the Roman Empire and eventually became the seat of an independent Berber kingdom.

The settlement's fate is obscure enough to have given rise to varying stories about what happened next. It appears the people of Sala Colonia embraced Islam on the arrival of the Arabs in the late 7th century, but with unorthodox modifications. The first Moroccan dynasties, the Idrissids and Almoravids, largely neglected Sala Colonia, and, as its river port silted up, the town declined. By the 10th century, the new town of Salé had sprung up on the north bank of the river. Its inhabitants, of the Zenata tribe (although some sources attribute the rise of the new town to the people of the old), built a *ribat* (fortress-convent) on the present site of Rabat's kasbah, as a base for fighting a rival and heretic tribe south of the river. Whether Sala Colonia had already been emptied of its population by then or whether the process was accelerated by the fighting is unclear.

Things changed with the arrival of the Almohads in the 12th century. They put an end to the fighting and built the kasbah on the site of the ribat. Their intention was to make it the jumping-off point for campaigns against the Christian Reconquista in Spain.

It was under Yacoub al-Mansour ('the Victorious') that Rabat enjoyed a brief peak of glory. After successful campaigns in Spain, Ribat al-Fatah ('Victory Fortress') was to become a great capital. Al-Mansour had extensive walls built, added the Oudaia gate to the kasbah and began work on what was intended to be the greatest mosque in all of the Muslim west, if not in all Islam. His death, in 1199, brought an end to these grandiose schemes. The great Hassan Mosque was never completed – all that remains today are the impressive, squat (and incomplete) minaret (the Tour Hassan), and some columns that have since been re-erected on the site. The city lost all significance quickly thereafter.

Its fortunes began to change in the 17th century with the arrival of Muslim refugees from Christian Spain. At the same time, the population of the sister cities of Rabat and Salé received a colourful injection of Christian renegades, Moorish pirates, freebooters and adventurers of many nationalities. The two cities flourished as what English chroniclers called the Sallee Rovers (or corsairs) set about intercepting merchant ships and men-of-war, especially those returning to Spain and Portugal from the Americas. They brought such a rich booty in gold, Christian slave labour and other goods that the cities briefly formed the independent Republic of Bou Regreg, in the first half of the 17th century.

Although the first Alawite sultans curtailed their activities, no sultan ever really exercised control over the corsairs, who continued plundering European shipping until well into the 19th century, by which time Europe's wishes were becoming writ in Morocco. Sultan Mohammed ben Abdallah briefly made Rabat his capital at the end of the 18th century, but with little appreciable effect on its destiny.

France decided to shift the capital of its protectorate, established in 1912, from Fès to Rabat. The new capital was on the coast (and therefore easily supplied and defended), far from the hornet's nest of political intrigue and potential unrest of Fès or Marrakesh, long the two traditional choices for capital. Since independence (in 1956), Rabat has remained the seat of government and home to the king.

Orientation

Rabat is best approached by rail, since the central railway station lies on the city's main thoroughfare, the wide, tree-lined Ave Mohammed V.

Arrival by bus is inconvenient, as the bus station lies a good four or five km outside the centre and you will need to take a local bus (No 30) or taxi into the centre – not always an easy task because of the competition. If you do arrive by bus from northern destinations, it is easier to get off at Salé and take a local bus or grand taxi into central Rabat. That way you'll be looking for a hotel before the bus you were on has even made it to Rabat's main bus terminal.

All the main administrative buildings and many of the hotels lie on or just off Ave Mohammed V, although there are others farther afield. Most of the embassies are scattered around the streets to the east, between Ave Mohammed V and Place Abraham Lincoln.

The medina is divided from the ville nouvelle by the wide and busy Blvd Hassan II, which follows the line of the medina walls to Oued Bou Regreg.

Rabat is an easy and pleasant city to walk around, and you will probably need public transport only to visit the twin city of Salé.

Information

Tourist Office The extraordinarily inconvenient location of the ONMT office (☎ 775171), on Rue al-Abtal in the west of the city, renders a visit there a total waste of time unless you desperately want a fistful of the usual handouts and brochures. It's open Monday to Friday from 8.30 am to noon and 2.30 to 6 pm (closed from 11.30 am to 3 pm on Fridays). There is a tourist office on Ave al-Jazaïr, but it's an administrative centre for the ministry only (they sometimes have an odd brochure lying around). The syndicat d'initiative on Rue Lumumba is open but empty.

Money The banks are concentrated along Ave Mohammed V. The BMCE is open from 8 am to 8 pm Monday to Friday; on weekends it's open from 10 am to 2 pm and 4 to 8 pm. There are plenty of banks dotted around the ville nouvelle.

Post & Telecommunications The post office is open from 8.30 am to 6.30 pm Monday to Friday. The phone office is open 24 hours a day, seven days a week. Poste restante is not in the main post office building but in the telephone office across the

NTH ATLANTIC COAST

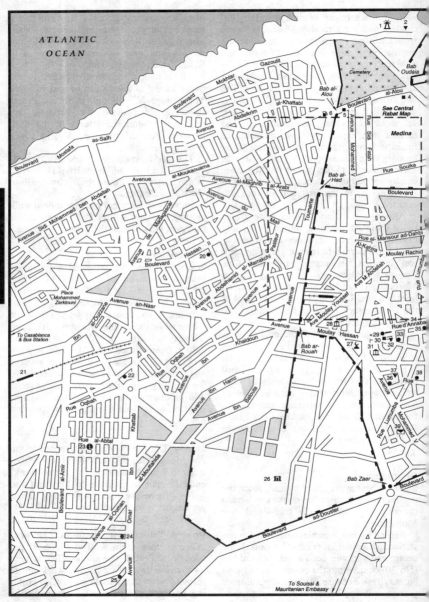

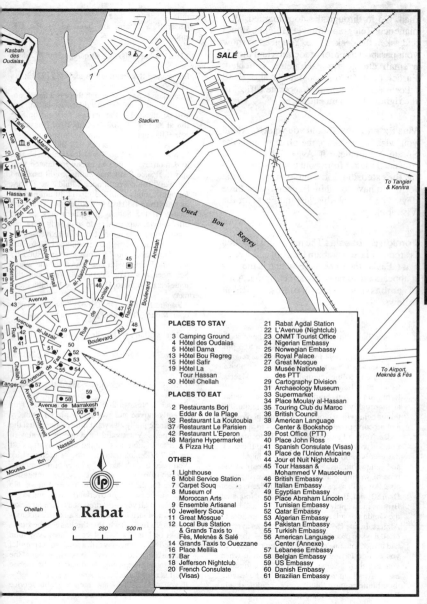

PLACES TO STAY

3 Camping Ground
4 Hôtel des Oudaias
5 Hôtel Darna
13 Hôtel Bou Regreg
15 Hôtel Safir
19 Hôtel La
   Tour Hassan
30 Hôtel Chellah

PLACES TO EAT

2 Restaurants Borj
   Eddar & de la Plage
32 Restaurant La Koutoubia
37 Restaurant Le Parisien
42 Restaurant L'Eperon
48 Marjane Hypermarket
   & Pizza Hut

OTHER

1 Lighthouse
6 Mobil Service Station
7 Carpet Souq
8 Museum of
   Moroccan Arts
9 Ensemble Artisanal
10 Jewellery Souq
11 Great Mosque
12 Local Bus Station
   & Grands Taxis to
   Fès, Meknès & Salé
14 Grands Taxis to Ouezzane
16 Place Mellilia
17 Bar
18 Jefferson Nightclub
20 French Consulate
   (Visas)

21 Rabat Agdal Station
22 L'Avenue (Nightclub)
23 ONMT Tourist Office
24 Nigerian Embassy
25 Norwegian Embassy
26 Royal Palace
27 Great Mosque
28 Musée Nationale
   des PTT
29 Cartography Division
31 Archaeology Museum
33 Supermarket
34 Place Moulay al-Hassan
35 Touring Club du Maroc
36 British Council
38 American Language
   Center & Bookshop
39 Post Office (PTT)
40 Place John Ross
41 Spanish Consulate (Visas)
43 Place de l'Union Africaine
44 Jour et Nuit Nightclub
45 Tour Hassan &
   Mohammed V Mausoleum
46 British Embassy
47 Italian Embassy
49 Egyptian Embassy
50 Place Abraham Lincoln
51 Tunisian Embassy
52 Qatar Embassy
53 Algerian Embassy
54 Pakistan Embassy
55 Turkish Embassy
56 American Language
   Center (Annexe)
57 Lebanese Embassy
58 Belgian Embassy
59 US Embassy
60 Danish Embassy
61 Brazilian Embassy

road. Go in through the door marked 'Permanence Télégraphique et Téléphonique' and ask at the desk inside. You need to show your passport as proof of identity, and there's a small charge for each letter collected. Parcel post ('Colis postaux') and EMS ('Poste Rapide') are in a separate office, to the right of the main entrance.

Visa Extensions Should you want to extend your visa in Morocco, the place to go is the Sûreté Nationale, off Ave Mohammed V. You need a letter from your embassy requesting the extension, and a photo to attach to the form you have to fill in. Expect to wait three days. For more on this, see the Facts for the Visitor chapter.

Foreign Embassies The main embassy area is around Place Abraham Lincoln and Ave de Fas ('Fas' is the same as 'Fès' and is the way it appears on some of the street signs). A list of embassies and consulates in Rabat follows:

Algeria
   46 Ave Tariq ibn Zayid (☎ 767668). The office is open Monday to Friday from 8.30 am to 3 pm, but since early 1994 total confusion has reigned and it may prove next to impossible to get a visa. This is due to the internal troubles in Algeria, which may be enough to put most people off trying to go. You should check out the situation as thoroughly as you can before setting out. All things being equal, you will need four photos and a photocopy of your passport details to apply for a visa. You will also have to provide documentation for your car if you intend to drive. If issued, the visa is valid for a month's travel in Algeria, and renewable inside the country. Costs at the time of writing were as uncertain as everything else. Australians pay nothing, US citizens about Dr 150 and Britons about Dr 350. Note that Britons must apply in person in Rabat, and not at the Oujda consulate. All applications are sent to Algiers. In late 1993, they were taking an average of 10 days to process, but by early 1994, the wait had turned into one of weeks or even months. All you can do is find out the latest position when you get there. Some travellers have found it easier to pick up the Algerian visa before leaving their home country (but if you're reading this in Rabat, it will be a bit late!).

Australia
   Australia's affairs are handled by the UK embassy.
Canada
   13 bis Zankat Jaafar as-Sadiq, Agdal (☎ 772880).
France
   Embassy: 3 Rue Fahnoun, Agdal (☎ 777222; fax 777752)
   Consulate (visas): Although there is a large consular building on Ave Allal ben Abdallah, you will be directed to the Service de Visas on Rue Ibn al-Khattib (☎ 702404), off Blvd Hassan II. Australian nationals are among those requiring a visa. A 90-day visa costs Dr 328 and takes about 48 hours to issue. You'll probably need to be able to demonstrate how you intend to finance your stay in France (bank statements, credit card and the like). The office is open Monday to Friday, for applications from 8.30 to 11.30 am and for pick-up from 1.30 to 3 pm. Note that all this may change if the Schengen agreement goes into effect; it was supposed to do so in early 1994, but was delayed. The agreement, which covers all the member states of the EU (except the UK, Ireland and Denmark), would replace visas issued by individual states with one issued for the whole Schengen area. The Service de Visas can also issue visas for Togo, Djibouti and Burkina Faso.
Germany
   7 Zankat Madnine (☎ 709662). The embassy is open Monday to Friday from 9 am to noon.
Ireland
   Ireland's affairs are handled by the UK embassy.
Japan
   70 Ave des Nations Unies, Agdal (☎ 674163/4/5).
Libya
   1 Rue Chouaib Doukkali (☎ 731888).
Mauritania
   Souissi II, Number 266, OLM (☎ 656678). This recently moved and awkwardly placed embassy has some equally awkward information. First the good news. Visas valid for a one-month stay in Mauritania are issued on the same day at a cost of Dr 70 (French nationals do not need a visa). You need two photos and a letter of recommendation from your embassy; some embassies charge for this service. Now the bad news. No visa will be issued for overland travel, and to get any visa at all you must present a *return* air ticket with Air Mauritanie, which has an office in Casablanca. To find out whether this has changed, take a taxi or bus No 1, 2, 4 or 8 down Ave John Kennedy. The embassy is in a small street parallel to the avenue (to your right as you head out of the city centre). The nearest landmark on the avenue itself is the Pharmacie al-Andalous, on the left – if you pass a Shell and then a Mobil service station (also on the left), you've gone too far. The

embassy is open from 8.30 am to 3 pm Monday to Thursday and until noon on Friday.

New Zealand
New Zealand's affairs are handled by the UK embassy.

Netherlands
40 Rue de Tunis (☎ 733512).

Niger
Niger has no diplomatic representation in Morocco.

Senegal
Rue Qadi Amadi (☎ 730636). The embassy here will direct you to the consulate in Casablanca for visas.

Spain
Embassy: 3-5 Zankat Madnine (☎ 707600, 707980; fax 707964)
Consulate: 57 Ave du Chellah (☎ 704147/8; fax 704694). Nationals of various countries require visas to enter Spain (this means Ceuta and Melilla, too), including Australians, South Africans, Israelis and Malaysians. You can ask for 30-day visas with two entries (Dr 208) or 90-day visas with three entries (Dr 320). The latter can be harder to obtain. You need to fill in three forms and attach three photos. In addition, you may be asked for photocopies of passport details, credit cards and/or bank statements. The Spaniards prefer you to apply for a visa in your country of residence – an awkward requirement, so be prepared for some diplomatic haggling. If they go along with your request, it takes at least 24 hours to issue. Apply between 9 am and noon and pick up the following day (1 to 2 pm). The consulate is open Monday to Friday. Note the observations on the Schengen agreement above, under the France entry.

Tunisia
6 Ave de Fès (☎ 730576, 730636/7; fax 727866). EU, US and Japanese citizens are among those who do not require a visa for Tunisia. Australians are among those who do (although for a one-month stay, you technically shouldn't). A visa costs Dr 56, is valid for one to three months (seemingly depending on your luck) and could take as long as a week to issue. You need two photos.

UK
17 Blvd de la Tour Hassan (☎ 731403; fax 720906). The embassy is open Monday to Friday from 8.30 am to 12.30 pm and 2 to 5 pm.

USA
2 Ave de Marrakech (☎ 762265; fax 765661). The embassy is open Monday to Friday from 8.30 am to 12.30 pm and 2.30 to 6.30 pm.

Cultural Centres Apart from those listed below as language schools, the Centre Culturel Français (☎ 701138) has a branch at 2 Zankat al-Yanboua. They put on films, theatrical performances and lectures, and have a library open Tuesday to Saturday from 10 am to noon and 2.30 to 7 pm.

The German Goethe Institute (☎ 706544) is at 10 Rue Djebli.

Spain maintains a Centro Cultural Español (☎ 708738) by its embassy, at 5 Zankat Madnine. The Istituto Italiano di Cultura (☎ 720852) is at 2 Zankat al-Aghouat, near Place de l'Union Africaine. Its library is open Monday, Wednesday and Friday from 9 am to noon.

Language Schools The British Council (☎ 760836) is at 34 Rue Tanger (or Zankat Tanja). As well as a library, which holds a stock of some 14,000 books and periodicals, they have a program of feature films and occasional lectures. The library is open from 2 to 7 pm on Monday, 9.30 am to 7 pm Tuesday to Friday and 9.30 am to 1.45 pm on Saturday.

You could try to wangle some part-time work as an English teacher here, but you need to be qualified. The chances of full-time work are low, as teachers are usually recruited in London.

Another possible source of work as an English teacher is the American Language Center (☎ 766121), at 4 Rue Tanger.

You also try your luck at the International Language Centre (☎ 709718) at 2 Rue Tihama.

Bookshops & Newsstands The English Bookshop (☎ 706593) is at 7 Zankat Alyamama and is run by Mohammed Belhaj. He's a friendly person and stocks a good selection of mainly second-hand English and American novels, guides, language books, dictionaries, etc. Books taken back in under two weeks can usually be swapped for another (for a small service charge). The American Bookstore, part of the American Language Center at 4 Rue Tanger, has a smaller collection of new books.

Rabat has the best bookshops in Morocco for Francophone readers. There are several along Ave Mohammed V and Ave Allal ben Abdallah. One of the best is the Librairie Libre Service (☎ 724495), at 46 Ave Allal ben Abdallah.

All the French press is available at newsstands scattered around the ville nouvelle. For other foreign press, there a few places – the shop inside the Rabat Ville railway station is as good as any.

Maps It is possible to get a range of maps of Morocco and some of its towns and cities from the Cartography Division of the Conservation & Topography Department (☎ 705311; fax 705885), 31 Ave Moulay Hassan. The survey maps are extremely detailed, and for the most part only of interest to hikers planning serious mountain treks. Maps of the most popular areas of the High Atlas can usually be obtained on the spot; for other areas you may need your passport and an official request. Maps cost Dr 40 a sheet. The office is open on weekdays from 8.30 to 11 am and 2.30 to 5.30 pm. These maps, if at all obtainable in places like Imlil, cost at least twice as much there as in Rabat.

Medical Services & Emergencies As throughout Morocco, the emergency police phone number is ☎ 19. For the fire brigade or ambulance call ☎ 15. To keep up to date on where there are late-night chemists, pick up one of the local French-language papers, such as *Le Riverain*. They usually have a listings page with the day's rostered 'pharmacies de garde' on it.

Film & Photography There are plenty of places along Ave Mohammed V that sell photographic supplies and develop film.

Medina

The walled medina is far less interesting than those in Fès, Meknès and Marrakesh, and dates only from the 17th century. Nevertheless, it's worth a stroll, and there is no hustling to worry about. About the most interesting medina street is Rue Souika. Starting out from Rue Sidi Fatah and heading east, you will find mainly food, spice and

general stores until you reach the area around the Great Mosque. From here to the Rue des Consuls, you are in the Souq as-Sebbat, where jewellery is the main item for sale. If you continue past the Rue des Consuls (so called because foreign diplomats lived here until 1912), you end up in a flea market before emerging at the river. Most of the stuff is junk, but you never know what a rummage might turn up.

If you head north along the Rue des Consuls on the way to the kasbah, you will find yourself surrounded on all sides by carpet and rug shops, along with the occasional leatherwork, babouche or copperwork place. The street ends in a fairly broad, open area that leads up the hill to the kasbah. In the days of the Sallee Rovers, this was the site of slave auctions.

Kasbah des Oudaias

The Kasbah des Oudaias, built on the bluff overlooking the estuary and the Atlantic Ocean, dominates the surrounding area and can be seen from some distance. It is unfortunate that a much-used city circular road runs right past the entrance. Apart from the obvious aesthetic displeasure, you can only guess at the long-term damage done to the buildings by the passing traffic.

The main entry point is the enormous Almohad gate of **Bab Oudaia**, built in 1195. This is one of the few places in Rabat where you will encounter 'guides'. It's totally unnecessary to take one – once through the gate, there's only one main street, Rue Jamaa, so you can't get lost. Most of the houses here were built by Muslim refugees from Spain. There are great views over the estuary and across to Salé from what is known as the *'plateforme du sémaphore'*, at the end of Rue Jamaa. On your left as you head towards the viewpoint is the oldest **mosque** in Rabat, built in the 12th century and restored in the 18th.

From just inside Bab Oudaia you can turn to your right (south) and walk down to a passage running more or less parallel to Rue Jamaa. Turn into this and on your right is a 17th-century palace built by Moulay Ismail.

It now serves as part of the **Museum of Moroccan Arts**, or Musée des Oudaia. To get the tickets, however, you have to proceed a little farther south into the Andalusian Gardens (actually laid out by the French during the colonial period). Built into the walls of the kasbah here are two small galleries that form part of the museum. The northernmost of these contains a small display of traditional musical instruments and the ticket desk for the whole museum, while the second gallery houses a display of traditional costumes. Back up in Moulay Ismail's palace (which later became a medersa), two of the four galleries are devoted to Fès ceramics and one to jewellery. The last has been decked out as a classic high-class Moroccan dining and reception room. Tickets cost Dr 10, and the rooms are open from 9 am to noon and 3 to 5 pm (6 pm in summer). The gardens stay open later.

The *Café Maure*, on the far side of the

gardens and overlooking the river, is a pleasant place to relax. It serves soft drinks and snacks at reasonable prices. A coffee will cost you Dr 3.50.

Tour Hassan
Rabat's most famous landmark is the Tour Hassan, which overlooks the bridge across the Oued Bou Regreg to Salé. Construction of this enormous minaret – intended to be the largest and highest in the Muslim world – was begun by the Almohad sultan Yacoub al-Mansour in 1195, but abandoned on his death some four years later. Meant to reach a height of more than 60 metres, it only made it to 44 metres. The tower still stands, but little remains of the adjacent mosque, which was all but destroyed by an earthquake in 1755. Only the re-erected but shattered pillars testify to the grand plans of Al-Mansour.

On the same site is the **Mausoleum of Mohammed V**, the present king's father. Built in traditional Moroccan style and richly decorated, the tomb of the king is located below ground in an open chamber. Above, visitors enter a gallery from which they can see the tomb below. Entry is free, but you must be dressed in a respectful manner.

Chellah
Beyond the city walls, at the end of Ave Yacoub el-Mansour at the junction with Blvd ad-Doustour, are the remains of the ancient Roman city of Sala Colonia, enclosed within the walls of the necropolis of Chellah, built here by the Merenids in the 13th century. The city of Rabat had by this time fallen on hard times, and this pretty spot south of the city gates was as close as the Merenids came to taking an interest in it.

The construction has a defensive air about it, and this is no coincidence. The sultan who completed it, Abu al-Hassan Ali, was intent on protecting his dynasty from possible attack or interference.

After entering through the main gate, you are pretty much obliged to follow a path heading diagonally away from the gate. You can see what little remains of the Roman city,

Guard at Mausoleum of Mohammed V

NTH ATLANTIC COAST

but it is all fenced off. Around you, fig, olive and banana trees and all sorts of other vegetation prosper, almost wild, amid the tombs and koubbas. At the bottom of this short walk are the remains of a mosque. A couple of fairly half-hearted would-be guides hang about here – you're in no way obliged to take up their offers. Penetrate into the mosque: behind it a chunk of wall is still standing and in front of it are a couple of tombs. Here lie Abu al-Hassan Ali and his wife.

You will have already noticed a minaret topped by a stork's nest (hardly anything in here *isn't* topped by a stork's nest). At one point this was a small medersa that functioned as an endowment of Abu al-Hassan Ali. You can make out where the students' cells were on either side of the building, as well as the mihrab (prayer niche) at the end opposite the minaret.

This peaceful, half-overgrown monument is open daily from 8.30 am until sunset. Entry costs Dr 10.

Archaeology Museum
The best museum in Morocco, at least among those dealing with the country's ancient past, is Rabat's modern Archaeology Museum, almost opposite the Hôtel Chellah on Rue al-Brihi, off Ave Moulay Hassan. The ground floor is given over to displays of implements and other finds from the oldest known civilisations in Morocco. Some of the material dates back 350,000 years to the Pebble Culture period. In a courtyard to the right are some prehistoric rock carvings. On the 2nd floor you can see finds from various periods in Moroccan history, from the Roman era to the Middle Ages. There are some more in-depth studies on several towns, but the explanations are all in French. In a separate building (ask to have it opened) is the Salle des Bronzes. Most of the ceramics, statuary and implements in bronze and other metals date from the period of Roman occupation and were found at Volubilis, Lixus and Chellah. There are various bronze plates with Latin texts, including a 'military diploma' awarded by the emperor to a local worthy.

The museum is open daily (except Tuesday) from 8.30 am to noon and 2.30 to 6 pm (9 am to noon and 3 to 5.30 pm in winter). Entry costs Dr 10.

Royal Palace
Of the four remaining Almohad gates in Rabat's city walls, by far the most impressive is Bab ar-Rouah (Gate of the Winds), which forms the north-west corner of the walls around the Royal Palace complex.

You can get into the palace grounds by several entrances. The main one is off Ave Moulay Hassan, a little way inside Bab ar-Rouah. It takes you south towards the *mechouar* (parade ground), on the east side of which is the Ahl al-Fas (People of Fès) Mosque. If you're lucky, you might catch the king making a grand entry for the Friday prayers around noon. All the palace buildings, which were built in the last century, are off-limits, so you're not likely to be tempted to hang around here for long. It makes a pleasant enough walk on the way from the centre of town out towards Chellah.

Musée Nationale des PTT
There is a small and much-ignored postal museum on Ave Mohammed V whose collection of stamps and first-day covers goes back to preprotectorate days. Entry is free, and the museum is open during office hours.

Places to Stay – bottom end
Camping The nearest camp site is the *Camping de la Plage* (☎ 782368), back in from the beach at Salé; it's well signposted from the Salé end of the bridge over the Oued Bou Regreg. It's open all year and costs Dr 10 per person, plus Dr 5 for a car, Dr 10 for a power line and Dr 5 for water (for two people). There's very little shade – just a few small trees – but the snack bar can provide food if you order in advance. The facilities include showers and toilets.

There are several more camp sites on the road south towards Casablanca. The first of them is the *Palmeraie*, about 15 km south of Rabat, on the beach at Temara. Another 10 km south, near Ech-Chiahna beach, are two others: *Camping Gambusias* (☎ 749142) and *Camping Rose Marie* (☎ 749251). Both are OK, and the location is pleasant enough.

Hostel The *youth hostel* (☎ 725769) is on Ave de l'Egypte, opposite the walls of the medina. It's a pleasant place to stay, costing Dr 25 per night in dormitory accommodation, including a small, obligatory breakfast. There are cold showers but no cooking facilities. The hostel is open from 8 to 10 am, noon to 3 pm and 6 to 10 pm. You need a membership card.

Hotels – medina There are several basic budget hotels on or just off the continuation of Ave Mohammed V as it enters the medina. Few make any concessions to creature comforts and some don't even have showers, cold or otherwise. An extra dollar or two will buy you better accommodation outside the medina.

The best by a mile is the *Hôtel Dorhmi* (☎ 723898, at 313 Ave Mohammed V. The hotel, which has been completely renovated, is in a good location and has rooms for Dr 70/100. Hot showers are Dr 7 more.

As for the rest, there's not an awful lot in it. The *Hôtel de Marrakech*, on Rue Sebbahi just off Ave Mohammed V, costs Dr 40/70 for singles/doubles and is OK. The *Hôtel des Voyageurs*, just off Ave Mohammed V, is similar and costs Dr 40/60 but there are no showers and it's often full. Beds at the *Hôtel du Marché* are overpriced at Dr 40 a head. They claim to have hot showers for Dr 5. The *Hôtel France* costs Dr 30 or Dr 35 for a single, depending on whether you want a double bed. Doubles/triples cost Dr 50/60, which is certainly cheap. The *Hôtel d'Alger* (☎ 724829) has a pleasant courtyard but no shower. Singles/doubles/triples/quads cost Dr 35/60/90/110. The *Hôtel Chaab* (☎ 731 351), in the first lane inside the medina wall between Ave Mohammed V and Rue Sidi Fatah, is nothing special but is cheap (Dr 25/40).

The *Hôtel du Centre*, on the right just as you enter the medina, also costs Dr 60 for a double (there are no singles). The rooms are clean, with table, chair and washbasin, but there are no showers.

Others in this area include the hotels *Al Alam, Regina, Magreb al-Jadid, Du Midi, National* and *Renaissance*, and the *Hôtel Nouvel*, which is anything but new.

If you end up in one of these places and need a good hot wash, there is a public douche next door to the Hôtel National and a couple more with a hammam (for men and women) in the lane one block north of Rue Sebbahi.

Right up at the kasbah end of the medina is a quiet little place, the *Hôtel des Oudaias* (☎ 732371), at 132 Blvd al-Alou (it's in a bit of a laneway just parallel to the main street). It's not top value for money, at Dr 60/100 for basic rooms and Dr 10 for hot showers, but it is in a pleasant location. They have a nice little tea room downstairs.

A little more expensive is the *Hôtel Darna* (☎ 736787), 24 Blvd al-Alou. The rooms come with shower or full bathroom and cost Dr 100/120. Reception is in the busy café downstairs.

Hotels – ville nouvelle West of Bab al-Had, there is a small clutch of hotels on and around Blvd Hassan II. The area is nothing special, but close enough to the action to consider if you are having trouble elsewhere.

The best of the cheapest is the *Hôtel d'Alsace* (☎ 721671), a quiet place in a back lane just off Blvd Hassan II. Most of the rooms, which cost Dr 36/60, look onto a peaceful internal courtyard. Hot showers cost Dr 5.

The *Hôtel Afrique*, on Ave al-Maghrib al-Arabi, is basic, but quite acceptable at Dr 40/70. Hot showers are Dr 5. On the intersection facing Bab al-Had is the *Hôtel Paris*, and in a lane just behind it another cheapie, the *Hôtel Rif*.

Heading into the middle range, the most expensive of this little pocket of places is the spotlessly clean *Hôtel Dakar* (☎ 721671), on the street of the same name. Rooms with shower cost Dr 108/127.

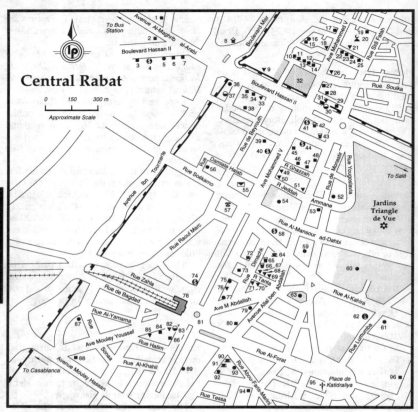

Central Rabat

To Bus Station

Avenue Al-Maghrib al-Arabi

Boulevard Hassan II

Boulevard Misr

Boulevard Hassan II

Rue de Beyrouth

Rue Damiate Halab

Rue Soekarno

Rue Raoul Marc

Rue Zahia

Rue de Bagdad

Rue Al-Yamama

Rue Al-Khahil

Ave Moulay Youssef

Sonea

Rue Hatim

Ave Moulay Hassan

To Casablanca

Rue Tessa

Rue Abou-Faris-Marini

Ave Allal ben Abdallah

Ave M Abdallah

Avenue Allal ben Abdallah

Rue Al-Forat

Rue Dimachk

Rue R Tanta

Rue Al-Mansour ad-Dahbi

R Ghazzah

R Jeddah

Ammane

Rue de Monastir

Rue de Yougoslavia

To Salé

Rue Souika

Ave Mohammed V

Rue Sidi Fatah

Rue Al-Kahira

Rue Limumba

Place de Katidraliya

Jardins Triangle de Vue

Avenue Ibn Tournerte

Ave Mohammed V

0   150   300 m

Approximate Scale

NTH ATLANTIC COAST

Back inside the city walls, a couple of places along Blvd Hassan are worth considering. The *Hôtel Petit Vatel* (☎ 723095) is modest, but the rooms are not bad. Singles/doubles go for Dr 50/70 (or Dr 80 with two double beds) and showers are Dr 5. Virtually next door is the *Hôtel Majestic* (☎ 722997), 121 Blvd Hassan II. Through the dust, you can almost see that it might once have been majestic, but it's still not a bad deal at Dr 86/98 for rooms with private shower, Dr 76/88 without. Try for one at the front.

A block south of these is a quiet, reason-able place to stay. The *Hôtel Mamounia* (☎ 724479), 10 Rue de la Mamounia, is clean and offers bright rooms for Dr 50/72. Hot showers are Dr 5 extra.

Long a popular place and still one of the best budget deals, the *Hôtel Central* (☎ 707356), 2 Zankat al-Basra, has spacious rooms with basin, bidet, wardrobe, table and chairs for Dr 63/103. The (shared) showers are not cheap at Dr 9 but they are steaming hot (mornings only).

A little more expensive for single rooms but a definite rival for value in doubles is the *Hôtel Velleda* (☎ 769531), 106 Ave Allal ben

PLACES TO STAY

1	Hôtel Dakar
2	Hôtel Afrique
3	Hôtel Touring
6	Hôtel d'Alsace
7	Hôtel Paris
8	Youth Hostel
10	Hôtel de France
11	Hôtel d'Alger
12	Hôtel Essaada
13	Hôtel du Marché
14	Hôtel des Voyageurs
15	Hôtel National
17	Hôtel du Midi
19	Hôtel Renaissance
22	Hôtel Maghreb al-Jadid
23	Hôtel al-Alam
24	Hôtel de Marrakech
25	Hôtel Regina
27	Hôtel Dorhmi
28	Hôtel du Centre
29	Hôtel Chaab
34	Hôtel Petit Vatel
35	Hôtel Majestic
38	Hôtel Mamounia
39	Hôtel Gaulois
45	Hôtel Berlin
46	Hôtel Splendid
47	Hôtel de la Paix
48	Hôtel Capitol
53	Hôtel Royal
72	Hôtel Central
73	Hôtel Balima
80	Hôtel Velleda
84	Hôtel d'Orsay
86	Hôtel Terminus
88	Hôtel Bélère
94	Hôtel Les Oudayas
96	Grand Hôtel

PLACES TO EAT

9	Seafood Restaurants
18	Restaurant de l'Union & Restaurant de la Libération
21	Restaurant Taghazout
26	Café de la Jeunesse
29	Juice Stand
31	Restaurant El Bahia
33	Fax Food
45	Restaurant Hong Kong
48	Restaurant Capitol
49	Restaurant Tagardit (Hamburgers)
50	Restaurant La Comédie
51	Café L'Empire
67	La Bidoche (Hamburgers)
68	Dolce Vita (Ice Cream)
69	Pizza La Mamma
70	Restaurant La Bamba
71	Pizza Hot
76	Restaurant Le Fouquet's
82	Café de la Paix
85	Restaurant/Brassrie Français
96	Café Restaurant Chantilly

OTHER

4	BMCI Bank (ATM)
5	Hammam
16	Douche (Public Showers)
20	Mosque
30	Petit Taxi Stand
32	Municipal Market
36	Douche al-Mamouniya
37	Bus Nos 30 (to Bus Station) & 17 (to Temara via Zoo)
40	BMCE Bank (ATM)
41	Wafabank
42	Total Service Station
43	Bar Le Grillon
44	BMCE Bank (ATMs)
52	Royal Cinema
54	Ministry of Information
55	Post Office (PTT)
56	Sûreté Nationale (Immigration Office)
57	Telephone Office
58	Banque du Maroc
59	Bagdad Nightclub
60	Théâtre Mohammed V
61	Europcar
62	Syndicat d'Initiative
63	German & Spanish Embassies & Centro Cultural Español
64	Café/Bar La France
65	Bar Le Rêve
66	Bar de Tanger
74	BMCI Bank (ATM)
75	International Language Centre
77	Royal Air Maroc
78	Rabat Ville Railway Station
79	Wagons-Lits Office
81	Place des Alaouites
83	Airport Shuttle Bus & Café Terminus
87	English Bookshop
89	Hertz
90	Café Lina
91	Café Krypton
92	French Consulate
93	Avis
95	St Pierre

NTH ATLANTIC COAST

Abdallah. Generous rooms with private shower cost Dr 87/109 (Dr 106/131 with toilet as well). Hot water is normally available from 9 pm to 9 am, but it's more warm than hot in the morning.

Staff at the *Hôtel Berlin* (☎ 703435), 261 Ave Mohammed V, are friendly enough, and the rooms, though quite tiny, are clean and secure. The hotel is on the 2nd floor, above a Vietnamese restaurant. Rates are Dr 71/92, plus Dr 5 for a hot shower. The Central and Velleda are better value for money.

The *Hôtel Gaulois* (☎ 730573, 723022), 1 Rue Hims, has a deceptively grand entrance, but for all the disappointment on stepping inside, it's not a bad place to stay. A single without shower costs Dr 63 and a double with shower and toilet Dr 116, which is no bargain compared with a few of the hotels listed earlier. A bit of renovation would go a long way. The one-star *Hôtel Capitol* (☎ 731216), on Ave Allal ben Abdallah, has singles/doubles with shared shower for Dr 77/101 (Dr 98/116 with private shower).

Doubles in the *Hôtel Splendid* (☎ 723 283), 8 Rue Ghazza, are overpriced at Dr 130 without shower and Dr 161 with private shower and toilet. The singles without shower are more reasonable in comparison with the competition, at Dr 80; Dr 136 for those with full bathroom is a bit much. Showers cost extra. The hotel boasts a pleasant internal courtyard.

Those with bath trouble could head for the *Douche al-Mamouniya*, just off Blvd Hassan II, near the Majestic Hôtel, or the already-noted public showers and hammam inside the medina.

Places to Stay – middle

For those in search of a tad more comfort, there are a few decent two-star possibilities.

The *Hôtel Royal* (☎ 721171/2), 1 Rue Amman, has 67 comfortable and reasonably furnished rooms with telephone and bathroom. Singles are Dr 116 with private shower, or Dr 149 with shower and toilet. Doubles cost about Dr 30 more. There is piping hot water all day. Try to get a room with views over the park.

Pretty much as good is the *Hôtel de la Paix* (☎ 722926), on Rue Ghazza. It offers attractively furnished rooms·with private toilet, shower and telephone for Dr 136/171.

Going up in price, there are two three-star hotels near the railway station at the junction of Ave Mohammed V and Ave Moulay Youssef. The cheaper of the two is the *Hôtel d'Orsay* (☎ 701319), 11 Ave Moulay Youssef. This small hotel (only 30 rooms) charges Dr 175/220 with private shower and toilet. They have cheaper rooms without toilet, too. Round the corner, the *Hôtel Ter-*

minus (☎ 700616, 709895; fax 701926), 384 Ave Mohammed V, has singles/doubles with private shower and toilet for Dr 222/272. Both these hotels are a good choice in this category.

Farther along Ave Mohammed V is the huge *Hôtel Balima* (☎ 707755, 708625; fax 707450), with self-contained singles/doubles for Dr 221/299, but it's a poor choice, with sagging beds. Avoid the overpriced breakfasts. The hotel does have a nightclub, though.

Better value, but farther afield and not really offering anything more than the better two-star hotels, is the *Grand Hôtel* (☎ 727285), 19 Rue Patrice Lumumba. It has self-contained singles/doubles for Dr 168/195 (including breakfast), a restaurant and the somewhat seedy Bar Manhattan.

Better is the *Hôtel Bou Regreg* (☎ 724110), Rue an-Nador, near the main city bus terminal, on the corner of Blvd Hassan II. The location is a little noisy, but handy for the medina and buses to Salé. Very clean, self-contained rooms with phone cost Dr 149/172. The hotel has a restaurant and a café.

Heading off into four-star territory is the *Hôtel Les Oudayas* (☎ and fax 707820, 709130), 4 Rue Tobrouk. Self-contained singles/doubles cost Dr 251/331.

Places to Stay – top end

The two high-grade four-star hotels in Rabat are the *Hôtel Bélère* (☎ 709801), 33 Ave Moulay Youssef, and the *Hôtel Chellah* (☎ 701051; fax 706354), 2 Rue d'Ifni (near the Archaeological Museum). The Bélère is a little cheaper, at Dr 358/488 including breakfast. The Chellah charges Dr 380/484 plus taxes.

There are three five-star hotels. The *Hyatt Regency* (☎ 771234; fax 772492) is out in the swish Rabat suburb of Souissi. The *Hôtel La Tour Hassan* (☎ 733815/6; fax 725408), 26 Ave Abderrahman Annegai, is a little less characterless. Finally, the best placed of them is the *Hôtel Safir* (☎ 726431; fax 722155), on Place Sidi Makhlouf. It offers

NTH ATLANTIC COAST

all you would expect from such places and charges Dr 1100/1250 a night plus taxes.

Places to Eat

If you want to eat in Rabat, don't leave it too late, as most restaurants are firmly shut by about 9 pm, and a lot of the cafés die about then, too. The exception is during Ramadan, since people don't come out to play until well after sunset during the month of fasting.

Medina Perhaps cheapest of all is the collection of small restaurants under a common roofed area directly opposite the Hôtel Majestic, on the medina side of Blvd Hassan II. In some of them you can get fried fish along with the usual chips and salad, though you will probably be offered more standard red-meat dishes. For a full meal, you are looking at around Dr 20.

Equally cheap are the restaurants close to the market on Ave Mohammed V. One that has been popular with travellers for years is the *Café de la Jeunesse*, where you can get a more-than-sufficient meal of meat, chips, rice and olives, plus a soft drink, for Dr 19. It gets quite packed with locals in the early evening. You can eat upstairs or get takeaway food downstairs.

Virtually across the road are a couple of similar places, the *Restaurant de l'Union* and the *Restaurant de la Libération*, where meals cost a fraction more than at the Jeunesse. On Rue Sebbahi is the *Restaurant Taghazout*, again in much the same vein.

Built into the medina walls on Blvd Hassan II is the *Restaurant El Bahia*. You can sit in the Moroccan-style interior section upstairs, in a shaded patio or outdoors on the footpath. Tajine with a drink costs about Dr 30, but the serves are a little stingy. Service is awful, and asking for the advertised set menu appears not to register with the waiters, whose main concern seems to be chatting with pals. If you can ignore this, it is still a pleasant spot to eat.

The place to splurge in the medina is *Dinarjat* (☎ 704239), 6 Rue Belgnaoui, off Blvd al-Alou. It's built in an old mansion and is *the* place in Rabat for a lavish 'Moroccan experience'.

Ville Nouvelle A rather good choice is the nameless snack bar and restaurant directly opposite the train station on Ave Mohammed V, next to Henry's Bar (who's Henry?). Proceed through the snack bar (about Dr 10 for a filling roll) into the cavernous and rather gloomy oval-shaped dining area. A decent sit-down meal here, with a beer thrown in, costs about Dr 25. Many locals just use it as a bar.

Another good place is the *Restaurant La Comédie*, on the corner of Ave Mohammed V, opposite the Ministry of Information. A lively café downstairs, the restaurant upstairs offers solid set menus for around Dr 30. It's popular with the locals.

The *Restaurant/Café Majestic*, next to the Librairie Libre Service on Ave Allal ben Abdallah, is one of several places in the city centre that function mostly as bars but offer food to the hungry drinker. There's nothing special about the standard fare, but it won't cost an arm and a leg and you'll obviously have no trouble ordering a cleansing ale with your food. The *Restaurant/Brasserie Français*, on Ave Moulay Youssef, and the nearby *Café de la Paix* also fall into this class.

The *Restaurant La Koutoubia*, at 10 Rue Pierre Parent, is a rather colourful place, with a fragile-looking mock Andalusian extrusion onto the footpath. The house speciality, tajine, is not especially cheap (around Dr 50), but it is good. The waiter seems in a hurry to clear the table, though, so keep an eye out or you'll find your half-eaten meal disappearing. Around the corner to the right is the *Pizzeria Napoli*.

Farther afield, near the Grand Hôtel, try the *Café Restaurant Chantilly*, which offers plats du jour and fish specialities. It's a minor splurge. They sometimes have live traditional Moroccan music.

A block behind the Hôtel Balima is a cluster of restaurants. *La Bamba* offers largely Moroccan food, including two set menus (Dr 55 and Dr 95). To justify the

Spanish name, they promise paella every night. Next door and across the road are two pizza joints, *Pizza Hot* and *La Mamma*. The latter is the more expensive, but does a fine pizza with (if you want it) real ham. Also here is the *Restaurant Baghdad*, which specialises in shish kebabs (brochettes) and has a bar, *La Bidoche* (a hamburger joint) and *Dolce Vita* (for ice cream). Another pizza place is *Pizza America*, near the American Language Center. It's not particularly cheap, but attracts a chic Rabat crowd seemingly drawn by the country and western music in the background.

On the subject of hamburger places, there is a surprising number of Western-style fast-food restaurants, where you can generally eat a filling meal for Dr 20 to Dr 30. These include the *Tagardit*, on Ave Mohammed V next to the Restaurant La Comédie, and *Fax Food*, on Blvd Hassan II.

For Chinese and Vietnamese food, try the *Hong Kong* (☎ 723594), on Ave Mohammed V, below the Hôtel Berlin. Main courses start at Dr 50 and are OK.

The *Restaurant de la Plage* and the *Borj Eddar* serve mediocre food down by the Rabat beach – to get to them, just follow Tariq al-Marsa past the kasbah. They are generally closed in winter, although the first of the two keeps a café open all year.

If you feel like something more up-market, *Le Fouquet's* is a charming and understated little French restaurant with not-so-understated prices (count on Dr 100 plus per head). It's on Ave Mohammed V, just across from the BMCI bank. A couple of similar restaurants include *L'Eperon* (☎ 725901), on Ave al-Jazaïr, and the *Restaurant Le Parisien*, around the block from the British Council.

Plenty of the more expensive hotels have restaurants. The Hôtel Balima is among them. The Hôtel Chellah has a classy French restaurant, *Le Bistrot*.

Outside town, along the coastal road to Casablanca, is a highly recommended seafood restaurant, the *Sable d'Or*. A meal here, with wine, will cost you a good Dr 200 per person.

Entertainment

Cafés & Bars Rabat is crawling with largely European-style cafés, which are great places for a morning croissant and coffee. Some of them double as bars (alcohol can be consumed inside only), and there are a few simple drinking holes around, too. Not many cafés or bars are open after about 9.30 pm.

Unfortunately, juice stands are not as commonplace in Morocco as elsewhere in North Africa. However, there is a good one by the Hôtel Petit Vatel, on Blvd Hassan II.

Many of the cafés remain predominantly male preserves, although Western women can usually drink in them without any fuss. A couple that attract a more mixed crowd are the *Café Krypton* and the *Café Lina*. The latter has a better balance of men and women. The *Café Terminus* is not a bad spot to wait for trains or airport shuttles.

Some restaurants and other eateries that also have bars have been mentioned in Places to Eat. Among the straightforward bars, you could do worse than the *Bar de Tanger* or the *Bar Le Rêve*. They are 20 metres up from the Hôtel Central on Rue Dimachk.

A rougher place is the *Café/Bar La France*. A couple of others have been marked on the map, without particular recommendation: the *Bar Le Grillon* and a bar on Place Mellilia.

If you prefer to drink at home (or in your hotel room), there is a liquor store between Café Terminus and Café de la Paix. You can also buy booze at the supermarket on the corner opposite the Restaurant La Koutoubia.

Nightclubs There's a good choice of nightclubs in Rabat, some of which are attached to the more expensive hotels, and they're all popular with well-heeled young people. The music is standard international disco fare. The normal entry fee, Dr 50, includes the first drink. Before ordering, make sure you know the prices of subsequent drinks, as they can be as high as Dr 50! Some of the best nightclubs are *Jefferson, Jour et Nuit* and *L'Avenue*, and the disco at the Hôtel Bélère.

Top: Dunes, Laayoune (DS)
Bottom: Casamar (former British trading house), Tarfaya (DS)

Top Left: Carpet shop, Agdz (HF)
Top Right: A view of the ramparts and sea from the north-west bastion, Essaouira (DS)
Bottom Left: Fishermen at work, Essaouira (DS)
Bottom Right: Chefchaouen (HF)

You need to be suitably dressed to get into any of these places. At the Jefferson and L'Avenue, men may not be allowed in without a member of the opposite sex. Discos close around 3 am.

Cinema Rabat has a wide choice of cinemas, although only a few are of any serious interest. The *Salle 7ème Art* is the closest Morocco comes to an art-house cinema, with a program that tends to change every few days. The Royal, near the hotel of the same name, usually screens doubles – the first of Jackie Chan variety but often with something more cerebral to follow. The French-language newspapers advertise what's on around town. Films, if they are not French, tend to be dubbed into that language.

Theatre The Théâtre Mohammed V puts on a wide variety of performances, ranging from classical music recitals to dance or the occasional play. The theatre is centrally located, on Rue Moulay Rachid.

Getting There & Away

Air RAM (☎ 769710 for bookings, 709766), Air France (☎ 707066) and Iberia are all on Ave Mohammed V. It's unlikely that you'll fly into Rabat's local airport, which is near Salé, 10 km north-east of town. RAM does have a few direct international flights from here, as well as daily flights to Casablanca – in other words, the Mohammed V International Airport. Most of the internal flights from Rabat-Salé go via Mohammed V, so it makes more sense to go there directly, by express train or shuttle bus.

Bus The intercity bus station (gare routière) is inconveniently situated about five km south-west of the city centre on the road to Casablanca. Fortunately, there are local buses (No 30 is the most convenient) and petits taxis (about Dr 12) into the centre. There is a left-luggage service at the station.

All the various bus companies have their offices in this cylindrical building, but *everything* is in Arabic, except for the CTM ticket office.

There are 13 ticket windows, stretching around to the left of the main entrance to the CTM window (interrupted by a café on the way). You may notice the white boards above the windows, with destinations in Arabic – the number written on each indicates the window number.

Window Nos 1 to 6 deal mainly with destinations north and east of Rabat, while Nos 7 to 13 are for southern destinations. Next to Window 13 is the CTM booth. Tickets for various destinations can be bought at the following ticket windows.

Window No 1
    Tangier, Tetouan and Ouezzane
Window No 2
    Fès, Meknès, Er-Rachidia, Kenitra, Sidi Kacem and Moulay Idriss
Window No 3
    Fès, Meknès, Er-Rachidia, Khenifra, Al-Hoceima, Sefrou, Nador and Oujda
Window No 4
    Tangier, Tetouan, Chefchaouen, Sefrou, Er-Rachidia, Nador and Oujda
Window Nos 5 & 6
    Minor destinations
Window No 7
    Mohammedia and El-Jadida
Window No 8
    El-Jadida, Safi and Essaouira
Window No 9
    Not in use
Window No 10
    Agadir (eight departures a day), Taroudannt and Ouarzazate
Window No 11
    Marrakesh (departures every hour or so) and Casablanca
Window Nos 12 & 13
    Casablanca

Some sample fares include Casablanca (Dr 18; 1½ hours), Marrakesh (Dr 58.50; 5½ hours), Essaouira (Dr 79; about eight hours), Agadir (Dr 112.50; about 10 hours), Taroudannt (Dr 127.50), Ouarzazate (Dr 106), Safi (Dr 61.40) and El-Jadida (Dr 35).

CTM has buses to Casablanca (Dr 22; six times daily), Fès (Dr 47.50, 3½ hours; seven times daily), Tangier (Dr 67; 5½ hours; six times daily), Er-Rachidia, Oujda, Tetouan and Tiznit (via Agadir).

If you arrive from the north, you're better

off alighting at Salé and catching a local bus or grand taxi from there into central Rabat.

Train This is the best way to arrive in Rabat, as the Rabat Ville station is in the centre of town, on Ave Mohammed V at Place des Alaouites. (Don't get off at Rabat Agdal.)

There are 17 shuttle trains (Train Navette Rapide – TNR) to Casablanca. The first leaves at 5.10 am and the last at 6.45 pm, and they take 50 minutes. Twelve go to the more convenient Casa-Port station and the rest to Casa-Voyageurs. This is in addition to other, slower trains passing through Rabat on the way to Casablanca and making intermediate stops.

For Fès and Meknès, there are departures at 7.23, 9.10, 10.35 and 11.59 am and 1.33, 3.15, 6.22, 9.41 and 11.23 pm. They take about three hours and 40 minutes to Fès.

There are four daily trains to Tangier, leaving at 12.27 and 8.13 am and 1.33 (change at Side Kacem) and 7.48 pm. The trip takes about 5½ hours.

To Marrakesh, there are nine trains a day via Casablanca. The 5.39 am and 3.47 and 11.42 pm services involve changes at Casablanca. The others are direct, taking a little less than six hours. There is a daily train to El-Jadida at 7.25 pm.

Some 2nd-class ordinary and *rapide* fares are: Casablanca (Dr 19/24), Fès (Dr 49.50/62.50), Marrakesh (Dr 71/90) and Tangier (Dr 62.50/79).

Taxi Grands taxis leave for Casablanca from just outside the intercity bus station. They cost Dr 22. There are other grands taxis from a lot between the main city bus station and the Hôtel Bou Regreg on Blvd Hassan II. They leave for Fès (Dr 50), Meknès (Dr 35) and Salé. You can't take petits taxis between Rabat and Salé, because they come under separate city jurisdictions.

Car The following are among the car rental agencies located in Rabat:

Avis
    7 Rue Abou Faris al-Marini (☎ 769759)

Budget
    Train station, Ave Mohammed V (767689)
Europcar
    25 bis Rue Patrice Lumumba (☎ 722328, 724141)
Hertz
    46 Ave Mohammed V (☎ 709227)

Getting Around

To/From the Airport Buses between Rabat and Mohammed V International Airport leave from outside the Hôtel Terminus, on Ave Mohammed V, at 5, 6.30, 8.30 and 10 am and 12.30, 3.30 and 6.30 pm. From the airport they leave for Rabat at 6.45, 8.15 and 10.45 am and 1.30, 4.30, 7.30 and 9.30 pm. The fare is Dr 50 and the journey takes 1½ hours.

There are now five direct shuttle trains (TNR) between Rabat and the airport via Casablanca. They leave Rabat Ville station at 5.10, 6.25, 9.50 and 10.10 am and 3 pm. Departures the other way are at 11.10 am and 1.15, 4.30, 7 and 9.35 pm. The 1¼-hour trip costs Dr 67/50 in 1st/2nd class.

The local Rabat/Salé airport is 10 km north-east of town, but it's unlikely that you'll need to use it unless you catch an internal flight to Rabat.

For more information on airport transport and services, refer to the Getting There & Away chapter and the Casablanca Getting Around section.

Bus The main city bus terminal is on Blvd Hassan II. From here, bus No 16 goes to Salé (get off at the Salé intercity bus station). Bus Nos 2 and 4 go to Bab Zaer for Chellah.

Bus Nos 30 and 17 run past Rabat's intercity bus station; they leave from a bus stop around the corner from the Hôtel Majestic, just off Blvd Hassan II, inside Bab al-Had. No 17 goes on past the zoo to Temara. Bus Nos 37 and 52 also go from the intercity bus station into central Rabat. Tickets cost Dr 2.30 to Dr 2.70 (hold onto them for inspectors).

Taxi Grands taxis to Salé leave when full from just near the Hôtel Bou Regreg, on Blvd Hassan II, and cost Dr 2 a head.

A ride around town in the blue petits taxis will cost Dr 8 to Dr 10, depending on where you want to go. It's about Dr 12 to the intercity bus station.

SALÉ

Although just across the estuary from Rabat, the white city of Salé has a distinct character. Little within the city walls seems to have changed over the centuries, and it is difficult to escape the feeling that Salé has been left by the wayside as Rabat forges ahead.

With a long history of action independent from central authorities, Salé is also a strongly traditional enclave amid the comparative liberalism of its sister city. The two elements are best symbolised by the presence here of Abdessalam Yassine, who heads the Al-Adl wal-Ihsan (Justice & Charity) religious movement and is here under house arrest. He has long been considered a threat to the king and the central government, and never more so than with the fundamentalist ferment gripping, to some extent, the rest of North Africa.

Although it's hardly the most interesting of Moroccan medinas, Salé's is pretty much free of touts, and a good introduction to

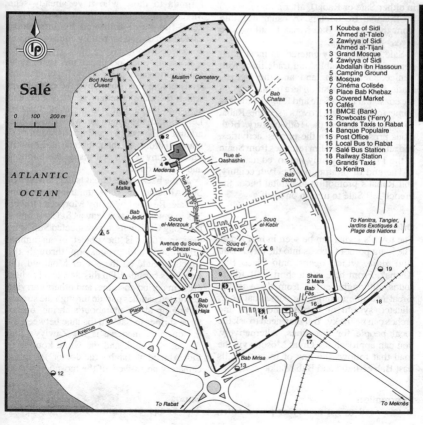

Sale

0   100   200 m

ATLANTIC OCEAN

1 Koubba of Sidi Ahmed at-Taleb
2 Zawiyya of Sidi Ahmed at-Tijani
3 Grand Mosque
4 Zawiyya of Sidi Abdallah ibn Hassoun
5 Camping Ground
6 Mosque
7 Cinéma Colisée
8 Place Bab Khebaz
9 Covered Market
10 Cafés
11 BMCE (Bank)
12 Rowboats ('Ferry')
13 Grands Taxis to Rabat
14 Banque Populaire
15 Post Office
16 Local Bus to Rabat
17 Salé Bus Station
18 Railway Station
19 Grands Taxis to Kenitra

medina navigation. If you've already been to places like Fès, it makes a tranquil change. Few tourists get around in here.

History

The origins of the town are little known, but Salé rose as Sala Colonia, south of the Oued Bou Regreg, sank into obscurity. The Almohads took control of the area in the 12th century, putting an end to local warring and establishing neighbouring Rabat as a base for expeditions to Spain. Salé's walls were not built until the following century, by the Merenids (who otherwise took little interest in either Salé or Rabat), after a raid in 1260 by Spanish freebooters. A canal was dug from the river to Bab Mrisa to allow safe access for shipping.

Salé subsequently entered its most prosperous period, establishing trade links with Venice, Genoa, England and the Netherlands. It was this position as a trading city on the coast that led to Salé and Rabat becoming home to the Sallee Rovers (see the Rabat History section) in the 16th century. Both cities prospered from the pirates' activities, and an influx of Muslim refugees from Spain in the 17th century only improved matters.

The end of pirating, in the 19th century, and Rabat's promotion to capital under the French left Salé to turn in on itself.

Orientation

The town's sights can be seen in half a day. The main point of access into the city is Bab Bou Haja, which opens onto Place Bab Khebaz. From here it's a short walk to the souqs, although getting from these to the Great Mosque through the somewhat complicated system of narrow alleyways and arches can be tricky. You may need to ask the local people for directions. Alternatively, you can approach the Great Mosque via the road that follows the line of the city walls past Bab el-Jedid and Bab Malka.

Information

If you need to get money or post a letter,

various banks and a post office are marked on the map.

Great Mosque & Medersa

These are two of the most interesting buildings in Salé. The Great Mosque, built during Almohad times, is out of bounds to non-Muslims. The medersa, on the other hand, no longer functions as such and is open to visitors. Constructed in 1333 by the sultan Abu al-Hassan Ali, it's a superb example of Merenid artistry and, although smaller, certainly the equal of the Medersa Bou Inania in Fès. It follows what will be a familiar formula to those who have already seen Merenid medersas: all the walls display a zellij-tile base, followed by intricately carved stucco and topped by equally elegant cedarwood work.

Students once occupied the small cells around the gallery. A narrow flight of stairs leads onto a flat roof above the cells, from which there are excellent views of Salé and across to Rabat. Entry to the medersa costs Dr 10, and the guardian who shows you around will expect a small tip (they don't get many visitors, so their income is limited). Photography is allowed inside the building and from the roof.

At the back of the Great is the Zawiyya of Sidi Abdallah ibn Hassoun, the patron saint of Salé. Revered by many Moroccan travellers in much the same way as St Christopher is among Christians, this respected Sufi, who died in 1604, is the object of an annual pilgrimage and procession through the streets of Salé on the eve of Mouloud, the Prophet's birthday. On this day, local fishers dress in period costume, and others carrying decorated candles parade through the streets, ending up at the marabout's shrine, one of three shrines in Salé. In the lane between the mosque and medersa is the Zawiyya Sidi Ahmed at-Tijani, and the white koubba of Sidi Ahmed at-Taleb ('the doctor') is in the cemetery north-west of the mosque.

Souqs

The souqs are connected to the Great

Mosque via Rue Ras ash-Shajara (also known as Rue de la Grande Mosquée), along which rich merchants in previous times constructed their houses. There are three souqs in all, but perhaps the most interesting of them is the Souq el-Ghezel, the wool market. Here under the shade of trees you can watch wool being bought and sold with the aid of scales suspended from a large tripod, as it has been for centuries. Close by is the Souq el-Merzouk, where textiles, basketwork and jewellery are made and sold. A little farther out is the Souq el-Kebir, featuring second-hand clothing and household items.

There are plenty of hole-in-the-wall cafés in the souqs and in the surrounding streets where refreshments and good, cheap meals can be found. It's worth calling into one or more of them to soak up the unhurried atmosphere of this timeless place.

Getting There & Away

Bus Bus No 16 passes the intercity bus station on its way to Rabat's urban bus terminal. Bus No 28 stops at the same bus station on its way north towards Bouknadel and the Plages des Nations.

Train You could get the train to Rabat if you really felt like it.

Taxi There are grands taxis to Blvd Hassan II in Rabat from Bab Mrisa (Dr 2). Note that Salé's beige petits taxis are not permitted to cross into Rabat. Grands taxis for Kenitra leave from a lot just north of the railway station.

Boat Small boats run across the Oued Bou Regreg from just below the mellah in Rabat to Salé and back. They operate all day, leaving when full. On the far side, simply follow the rest of the people up the rise to Bab Bou Haja. It costs locals half a dirham, but you'll probably find yourself paying more.

AROUND RABAT-SALÉ

Jardins Exotiques & Plage des Nations

About 13 km north of Rabat on the road to Kenitra, the Jardins Exotiques are as much a monument to one man's persistent eccentricity as anything else. Created in 1951 by one M François, a horticulturalist, the gardens contain a sampling of flora from all over the world, and although they appear disappointing when you first enter, they are quite interesting once you're farther inside. François spent a lot of time roaming the forests of Africa. His conclusion on his own efforts was that 'it is poetry that recreates lost paradises; science and technology alone are not enough'. The gardens are open from 9 am to 5.30 pm and entry costs Dr 5. Have the exact change ready, as the fellow in the ticket booth does not have any. You can get there on the No 28 bus from the bus station in Salé – ask to be let off; there's a sign to the gardens on the left-hand side of the road.

The same bus will take you part of the way farther on to the Plage des Nations, which is six km north of the gardens. A track leading from the end of the bus line will get you to the beach, which is also known as Sidi Bouknadel. There are a few cafés and a hotel here, and it's a much more pleasant place to swim than the city beaches in Rabat or Salé.

National Zoo

The Parc Zoologique National, nine km south of Rabat on the road to Temara, is a surprisingly well-kept place. Most of the animals – and there's a wide range – have more space to move around than those in many European zoos. There are snack stands and games for the kids. It's open Monday to Saturday from 10 am to 6 pm, and Sunday and holidays from 9 am to 6 pm; entry is Dr 205.

There are several buses on this route. No 17 leaves from a side street off Blvd Hassan II, just inside Bab al-Had. Ask to be let off at the zoo. From the main road, you have to walk a few hundred metres off to the left (east), as the entrance is at the back. You'll notice the rather depressing sight of a growing shantytown opposite the zoo entrance.

Casablanca

With a population of 2.9 million, Casablanca is by far Morocco's largest city, industrial centre and port. This growth is a fairly recent phenomenon, however, dating from the early days of the French protectorate, when Casa was chosen to become the economic heart of the country. The dimensions of the modest medina give some idea of just how small the place was when the French embarked on a massive building program, laying out a new city in grand style, with wide boulevards, public parks and fountains, and imposing Mauresque civic buildings.

The port handles almost 60% of Morocco's total sea traffic, the lion's share being phosphate exports. Some 20 million tonnes of goods are processed here each year. As this is not a natural haven, ships docked here are protected from the Atlantic by a 3180-metre-long jetty.

With all this economic activity, Casa became, and to an extent remains, the place to which Moroccans aspiring to fame, fortune or simply a better living tend to gravitate.

The influx of hopefuls from the countryside in search of a job has fuelled the creation of *bidonvilles* (slums), as in any other huge conurbation, although the problem has been brought under control in the past 20 years. Many of those who arrived hopeful have ended up broken – the parade of well-heeled Casablancans who have made it stands in stark contrast to the beggars, prostitutes and other less fortunate residents.

Amid the striking white medium-rise 1930s architecture – and there are many jewels, Art Deco and otherwise, of this period to be found – it is, above all, the people who strike you. You hardly ever see the veil, and it is hard to imagine the miniskirt anywhere else in the Muslim world. Men and women mix more easily here than in other Moroccan cities, especially those of the interior. On the ocean beaches and in the clubs, the bright young things strut their stuff much like the beautiful youth of many Western countries.

Casablanca has all the hallmarks of a brash Western metropolis, with a hint of the decadent languor that marks many of the southern European cities it so closely resembles. But rubbing shoulders with the natty suits, designer sunglasses and high heels are the old *jellabas* and hooded burnouses of traditional Morocco. True, the latter almost seems out of place here, but the mix of the population serves to remind you of where you are. And if you were in any doubt, laying eyes upon one of the marvels of modern religious architecture – the enormous Hassan II Mosque – should set you straight.

The mosque itself is just one element of an ambitious urban redevelopment plan that will ultimately see a lot of changes to road layout, the creation of a cultural centre in the former Sacré Cœur cathedral and the construction of a huge US$100 million marina.

Despite the pressures of urban living, it's relatively easy to strike up conversations with Casablancans, another reminder that you're not in one of the frenzied financial powerhouses of the West.

History

Settlement of the Casablanca area has a long history. Prior to the Arab conquest, what is now the western suburb of Anfa was the capital of a Berber state set up by the Barghawata tribe. The Almoravids failed to bring this state into their orbit, and it was not until 1188, during the time of the Almohads, that it was finally conquered. Some 70 years later, Anfa was taken by the Merenids, but when that dynasty became weak, the inhabitants of the area reasserted their independence, taking to piracy, and trading directly with England and Portugal.

By the second half of the 15th century, the Anfa pirates had become a serious threat to the Portuguese. A military expedition, consisting of some 10,000 men and 50 ships, was launched from Lisbon. Anfa was sacked and left in ruins. It wasn't long before the pirates were active again, however, and in 1515 the Portuguese were forced to repeat the operation. Sixty years later they arrived to stay, renaming the port Casa Branca and erecting fortifications.

Although harried by the tribes of the interior, the Portuguese stayed until 1755, when the colony was abandoned following a devastating earthquake (which also destroyed Lisbon). Sultan Sidi Mohammed ben Abdallah subsequently had the area resettled and fortified. However, its importance declined rapidly, and by 1830 it was little more than a village, with some 600 inhabitants.

It was about this time, however, that the industrialised nations of Europe began casting their nets abroad for ever-increasing quantities of grain and wool – two of the main products of the Chaouia hinterland. To secure these commodities, European agents established themselves in Casablanca (Dar el-Baïda in Arabic). Prosperity began to return, but the activities and influence of the Europeans caused much resentment among the indigenous population. In 1907, this spilled over into violence and European workers on a quarry railway that crossed a Muslim cemetery in the town were killed.

This was the pretext for intervention that the procolonialist faction in the French Chamber of Deputies had been waiting for. A French warship, along with a company of marines, was dispatched to Casablanca and proceeded to bombard the town. Accounts of what followed vary wildly, but it appears that French troops, pillaging tribes from the interior and locals collapsed into an orgy of violence. The Jews of the mellah, in particular, suffered, and many of the town's 20,000 inhabitants died in the upheaval.

The incident led to a campaign to subdue the Chaouia hinterland, and eventually to the dethronement of the sultan, Abd al-Aziz, his replacement by Abd al-Hafid, and the declaration of the French protectorate in 1912. General Lyautey, previously the French commander of Oran, was appointed the first French resident-general. He pursued a program aimed at expanding Casablanca as the main port and economic nerve-centre of the new protectorate, and it was largely his ideas on public works and the layout of the new city that made Casablanca what it is today.

The Bombing of Casablanca

Walter Harris, the London *Times'* man in Morocco at the turn of the century, was quickly on the spot after the French bombarded Casablanca. His account appears in *Morocco That Was* (now published by Eland):

A French warship arrived on the scene, and an armed party landed for the protection of the European population of the town. The forts and native quarters were at the same time bombarded. Scenes of the wildest confusion ensued, for not only was the town under the fire of the cannon of the warship, but the tribes from the interior had taken advantage of the panic to invade and pillage the place. Every sort of atrocity and horror was perpetrated, and Casablanca was a prey to loot and every kind of crime. The European force was sufficient to protect the Consulates, and the greater part of the Christian population escaped murder. When order was restored, the town presented a pitiful aspect. I saw it a very few days after the bombardment, and the scene was indescribable – a confusion of dead people and horses, while the contents of almost every house seemed to have been hurled into the streets and destroyed...Many of the houses had been burned and gutted. Out of dark cellars, Moors and Jews, hidden since the first day of the bombardment, many of them wounded, were creeping, pale and terrified...Blood was everywhere. In what had once been the poorer quarter of the town...I only met one living soul, a mad woman – dishevelled, dirty but smiling – who kept calling, "Ayesha, my little daughter; my little son Ahmed, where are you: I am calling you."

...It was the beginning of the French occupation of Morocco. ■

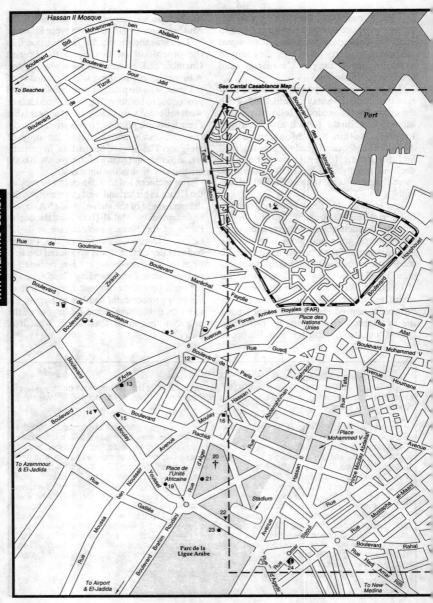

PLACES TO STAY
12 Hôtel Windsor
16 Hôtel Les Almoravides
18 Hôtel Métropole

PLACES TO EAT
14 Pizza Hut
22 Cafés

OTHER
1 Great Mosque
2 Gare du Port (Casa-Port Railway Station)
3 Red Fez bar
4 No 30 Bus Terminus
5 Cinéma Le Verdun
6 Place Oued al-Makhazine
7 Local Bus Terminus
8 CTM Bus Station
9 Grands Taxis to Rabat
10 Central Market
11 Syndicat d'Initiative & Post Office (PTT)
13 UK & Swiss Consulates
15 American Language Center & Bookshop
17 Place Paquet
19 US Consulate
20 Cathédrale du Sacré Cœur
21 Spanish Consulate & Centro Cultural Español
23 Yasmina Amusement Park
24 Tourist Office
25 Bus Station (non-CTM)

Casablanca

0   150   300 m

NTH ATLANTIC COAST

Orientation

Casablanca is a huge, modern metropolis. With few of the complications posed by the arcane medinas of the cities of the interior, however, it is easy enough to find your way around.

The heart of the city is Place des Nations Unies (formerly Place Mohammed V). From this large traffic roundabout at the southern end of the medina, the city's main streets branch out – Ave des Forces Armées Royales (FAR), Ave Moulay Hassan I, Ave Hassan II and Blvd Mohammed V.

Casa-Port railway station lies about 200 metres north of this main square, at the end of Blvd Houphouet Boigny. The CTM bus station is about 300 metres east of the square, on Rue Léon Africain. The city's main administrative buildings are clustered around Place Mohammed V. Just to the south-west are the carefully maintained lungs of the city centre – the Parc de la Ligue Arabe. West of the gardens lies the exclusive suburb of Anfa, the site of the original medieval Berber town.

The main bus station is a few km southeast of Place des Nations Unies, off Rue Strasbourg, while the principal railway station, Casa-Voyageurs, is about four km east of the town centre.

Most of Casablanca's budget and midrange hotels are in the area bounded by Ave des FAR, Ave Hassan II, Ave Lalla Yacout (named after the mother of King Mohammed V, Hassan II's predecessor) and Blvd Hassan Seghir.

An unaccustomed sight in Muslim countries is open prostitution on the streets, but Casablanca offers this dubious attraction. The 'red light' district is concentrated in the streets and lanes around Blvd Hassan Seghir and Rue Mohammed Smiha, between Ave des FAR and Place du 20 Août. There seems to be a pimp for every *fille de joie*, and the atmosphere at night is decidedly seedy. Occasional attempts by the police to clear the area appear to have made little impression.

Street Names

Casablanca is undergoing a name-change nightmare, and it is not uncommon to strike three versions for the one street. It is largely a matter of Arabisation, but there are a few other spanners in the works. The two main squares – Place des Nations Unies and Place Mohammed V – have had their names swapped around by royal decree. Worse, what is now known as Place des Nations Unies sometimes seems to take the name of the street linking it to Casa-Port railway station (Houphouet Boigny) – itself a recent change.

Where possible, the latest names (or what seem to be the latest names) appear on the maps – but be aware of the problem if you buy local street directories.

Information

Tourist Offices The Délégation Régionale du Tourisme (☎ 271177, 279533) is at 55 Rue Omar Slaoui and the syndicat d'initiative is at 98 Blvd Mohammed V. Neither will overwhelm you with useful information, but the syndicat has the advantage of being open on weekends. The ONMT is open from 8.30 am to noon and 3 to 6.30 pm Monday to Friday. The syndicat has the same hours Monday to Saturday, and is also open from 9 am to noon on Sunday.

Money There are plenty of banks in Casablanca, so changing money should pose no problems. A few are marked on the maps, including BMCE branches on Ave Lalla Yacout and Ave des FAR. They have ATMs.

American Express is represented by Voyages Schwartz (☎ 222946/7), 112 Rue Prince Moulay Abdallah. Thomas Cook is represented by KTI Voyages (☎ 398572/3/4; fax 398567), 4 Rue des Hirondelles.

Post & Telecommunications The central post office is on Place Mohammed V. This building can be confusing because the front entrance is closed. It's open from 8 am to 6.30 pm Monday to Friday and until noon on Saturday.

The poste restante counter, however, is in the same section as the international telephones. The entrance is the third door along Blvd de Paris. The telephone service is open

24 hours a day and sells phonecards. They don't have phone books, though, which seems strange considering Casablanca accounts for more than 60% of all Morocco's phone numbers! The number for telephone information is ☎ 16.

The parcel post office is farther west along Blvd de Paris, opposite the music conservatorium. The telex office is around the corner to the left.

The main building, erected in 1918, merits a look as part of the impressive array of Mauresque administrative edifices that face onto the square. Marshal Lyautey opened the post office in June 1919 – the commemorative plaque is inside, to the right of the entrance.

Touring Club de Maroc This is at 3 Ave des FAR. It's open Monday to Friday from 9 am to noon and 3 to 6.30 pm, and on Saturday from 9 am to noon.

Foreign Consulates The main consulates are in the area to the south-west of Place Mohammed V:

Austria
    45 Ave Hassan II (☎ 266904; fax 221083)
Belgium
    Consulate General: 13 Blvd Rachidi (☎ 223049; fax 220722)
    Benelux visa office: 136 Ave Moulay Hassan I
France
    Rue Prince Moulay Abdallah (☎ 265355). Hours are Monday to Friday from 8.45 to 11.45 am and 2.45 to 4.45 pm.
Germany
    42 Ave des FAR (☎ 314872). It's open Monday to Friday from 8 to 11.30 am.
Italy
    21 Ave Hassan Souktani (☎ 277558)
Netherlands
    26 Rue Nationale (☎ 221820)
Norway
    c/- Scandinavian Shipholders SA, Villas Paquet, 45 Rue Mohammed Smiha (☎ 305961).
Portugal
    104 Blvd de Paris (☎ 220214)
Senegal
    5 Rue Rouget de l'Isle (☎ 201511/2). The consulate is in a side street by the Hôtel des Almohades, and is open from 9.30 am to 3 pm Monday to Friday. EU and US citizens do not need a visa for a stay of up to three months in Senegal. Others must pay Dr 102 for a visa allowing a stay of up to one month, or Dr 236 for up to three months. You need three passport photos. Visas are generally issued on the same day.
Spain
    31 Rue d'Alger (☎ 220752, 276379; fax 205048); the consulate is open Monday to Friday from 8 am to 1 pm.
Sweden
    c/- Saida Star Auto, 88 Blvd Lalla Yacout (☎ 319003)
Switzerland
    43 Blvd d'Anfa (☎ 205856; fax 205855); the office is open Monday to Friday from 8 to 10 am.
UK
    43 Blvd d'Anfa (☎ 203316; fax 265779); the consulate is open Monday to Friday from 8 to 11 am.
USA
    8 Blvd Moulay Youssef (☎ 264550; fax 204127); the consulate is open Monday to Friday from 8 am to 1.30 pm.

Cultural Centres Several countries maintain cultural centres in Casablanca. The Centre Culturel Français (☎ 259078) is at 123 Blvd Mohammed Zerktouni. They organise films, lectures and other events, and also have a library. The German version, the Goethe Institut (☎ 200445), right on Place du 16 Novembre, is a more modest affair. They conduct German classes and also put on the occasional film. The Centro Culturale Italiano (☎ 260145) is at 22 Rue Hassan Souktani. The Centro Cultural Español (☎ 267337) is next door to the Spanish consulate, at 31 Rue d'Alger. Its library is open on weekdays from 10 am to 1 pm and 4 to 6 pm.

Language Schools The American Language Center (☎ 277765, 275270), 1 Place de la Fraternité, just down from the US consulate, might be your best hope for finding work teaching English in Casablanca.

Failing this, you could try the Centre International d'Études de Langues (☎ 441989; fax 441960), Place de la Victoire, Dar Mabrouka, 4th floor. The tiny British Centre is marked on the Central Casablanca map. It was not open at the time of writing, but could be a place to seek work or suggestions on other places to check out.

Bookshops & Newsstands Casablanca is a little disappointing for the bibliophile. For books in English, the best bet is the American Language Center bookshop. Otherwise, try the Librairie Farairre, on the corner of Blvd Mohammed V and Rue Araibi Jilali.

There are a number of reasonable newsstands around Place des Nations Unies, at Casa-Port and Casa-Voyageurs train stations, and in the big hotels. The one across the road from the Excelsior Hôtel is as good as any.

A small weekly magazine worth picking up is *7 Jours à Casa*. It has some useful local listings (not all totally reliable) and the odd interesting article (provided you read French). You can't lose anyway, as it's free. The tourist offices should have copies, and it is often lying around in hotels and more expensive restaurants. Casablanca is also the easiest place to encounter *La Quinzaine du Maroc*, a more comprehensive listings booklet covering the main centres throughout Morocco.

Music For anyone with more than a passing interest in Moroccan music, a good place to go for LPs, cassettes and CDs is Le Comptoire Marocain de Distribution de Disques (☎ 369153), 26 Ave Lalla Yacout, just west of the Hôtel Champlain. They have, or can get, a pretty substantial range of recordings of most types of traditional music.

Medical Services & Emergencies There are several decent hospitals in Casablanca. Among them is the CHU Averroès (Ibn Rochd; ☎ 224109), on Ave du Médecin Général Braun, and the nearby Hôpital du 20 Août (☎ 271459).

For medical emergencies, you could try SOS Médecins Maroc (☎ 989898). The doctors operate around the clock and can come to your hotel. A late-night pharmacy (☎ 269491) is open on Place Mohammed V. To be sure, look for the list of pharmacies de

garde in any of the local French-language newspapers.

Film & Photography There are quite a few places where you can buy film or have it developed. A couple of them are in Centre 2000, by Casa-Port train station.

Medina

The medina, although comparatively small, is definitely worth a little time. The busiest shopping areas are along Rue Chakab Arsalane and Rue de Fès. Such craft stalls as there are to see are mostly outside the city walls (along Blvd Houphouet Boigny), and just inside, on Rue Mohammed al-Hansali (which quickly changes its name to Rue de Fès). The medina is a pleasant, bright place to stroll around, and if you want to get to the Chleuh Mosque, the old city's main Friday mosque, just follow Rue Chakab Arsalane and its continuation.

If you want a new watch, this is the place to get it. Along with dope, watches seem to be the main illegal product on offer, and you're bound to be offered a good many 'Rolexes' during even a cursory visit. A pleasant spot for a cup of coffee is down on Place de l'Amiral Philibert, where the youth hostel is.

And if you're feeling bouts of wistful nostalgia for the guides of Fès and Marrakesh, you might just get the odd one or two people offering to guide you to the Hassan II Mosque.

Hassan II Mosque

Rising up on a point above the Atlantic north of the medina, the Hassan II Mosque is one of the biggest in the world. Completed in August 1993, it is well worth a visit, even though you can only get within a couple of hundred metres of it at the moment. The whole area and the access roads around it are due to be reconstructed, but whether average visitors will be able to get any closer to the mosque when everything is finished is a moot point.

The easiest way to it is along Blvd des Almohades and its extension, Blvd Sidi

Mohammed ben Abdallah, from near the Casa-Port railway station. It's about a 20-minute walk. You may run into the occasional irritating kid on the way – an unfortunate by-product of the completion not only of a new place of worship but of a new tourist attraction.

Ville Nouvelle

Place Mohammed V Formerly known as Place des Nations Unies, this animated square is flanked by what are probably the country's most impressive examples of Mauresque architecture. The French approximation of Arabo-Andalusian design produced a not-unhappy result. The main buildings of interest are the post office (on the west side), the law courts (on the east side and a little farther south) and the préfecture (police headquarters), closing off the south side of the square. What is now the fenced-off rear of the French consulate lies between the last two buildings and contains a statue of General Lyautey.

Parc de la Ligue Arabe The biggest park in the city, the Parc de la Ligue Arabe has an essentially French layout, although the flora is more faithful to its location in Africa. It is an extremely pleasant place to walk, take a leisurely coffee or enjoy the diversions of the Yasmina amusement park, entry to which costs Dr 1.

Cathédrale Sacré Cœur Built in 1930, the somewhat neglected former cathedral is an unexpected sight in the heart of a Muslim city, and symbolic of modern Casablanca's essentially European genesis. Sitting on the edge of the Parc de la Ligue Arabe, it reflects the best of the more adventurous architectural products of the Art Deco era. Deconsecrated some time ago and converted into a school, it is now destined to become a cultural centre. The first stage of this transformation will see the creation of an 800-seat theatre.

Beaches

Casablanca's beaches are west of town along Blvd de la Corniche, at the end of which (where it becomes Blvd de Biarritz) begins the affluent beachside suburb of 'Ain Diab. It's a trendy area, lined with four-star hotels, up-market restaurants, bars, coffee shops and nightclubs, and you may feel a little out of place unless you dress accordingly and have a wallet to match.

NTH ATLANTIC COAST

The Hassan II Mosque

More than 30,000 craftspeople laboured for six years to create the most remarkable homage to Allah (and perhaps also to the monarch who ordered it to be built) in recent history. The Hassan II Mosque, which was opened in grand style in August 1993, can accommodate up to 100,000 people, 25,000 of them in its main central hall. There is some dispute over whether its dimensions make it the biggest mosque in the world, but there is no doubt that it has the tallest minaret (210 metres). In the weeks after it was opened, a green laser light pierced the night sky from the top of the minaret, pointing in the direction of Mecca.

The mosque is built over the water's edge in such a way that well-placed worshippers can see the Atlantic below. Above them, a 1100-tonne central section of the roof is sliced down the middle – it can slide open, superbowl fashion, to turn the central hall into an open-air prayer stadium. The cavernous interior reveals a floor of green and gold-coloured marble, with pink granite columns rising to the ceiling. When the sliding roof is shut, 50 one-tonne chandeliers of frosted Venetian glass provide the lighting. The interior decoration is faithful to the best traditions of Moroccan-Andalusian sculpted and painted wood and stucco work.

In all, US$800 million went into the project, and from 1988 all Moroccans could feel like they had a direct part in it – a levy was imposed on them to help finance the construction. Whatever one's thoughts on the sum spent, Hassan II has achieved what the Almohad Sultan Yacoub al-Mansour set out to do in Rabat in the 12th century – building the greatest mosque in the western Muslim world. Indeed, the modern minaret is more than three times higher than Rabat's incomplete Tour de Hassan was designed to be. ■

In high summer the beaches are generally covered wall-to-wall with chic Casablancans, but for the rest of the year you can usually find some space pretty much to yourself at the southern end of 'Ain Diab. When it's not crowded, the beaches are perfectly all right, although they are better suited to a lazy afternoon than a 'beach holiday'. For the latter, you are better off heading farther south-west towards Essaouira.

Bus No 9 takes you along the southern end of the beaches at 'Ain Diab from the big bus terminal at Place Oued al-Makhazine.

Sidi Abderrahman

A few km south of the 'Ain Diab beaches, atop a tiny rocky outcrop jutting into the Atlantic, is the small marabout and settlement of Sidi Abderrahman. At high tide, it is cut off from the mainland, but otherwise you can stumble across the rocks. Non-Muslims are not allowed into the shrine itself, but you can walk past the handful of houses and sit down to look out over the ocean. It's about a half-hour walk along the beach south of the No 9 bus terminal at 'Ain Diab.

Places to Stay – bottom end

Camping Campers should head for *Camping de l'Oasis* (☎ 253367), Ave Mermoz (the main road to El-Jadida). It's a long way from the centre, so unless you have your own transport, it's hardly worth it, though bus No 31 runs past it. If you do have your own transport, you might want to get out of the big smoke altogether. About 16 km along the road to Azemmour (which starts off in town as Blvd d'Anfa) are two other camp sites: *Camping Desserte des Plages* and *Camping Tamaris*.

Hostel The *youth hostel* (☎ 226551), 6 Place de l'Amiral Philibert, faces a small, leafy square just inside the medina, off Blvd des Almohades. It's a fairly large hostel, comfortable and clean, and costs Dr 30 (or Dr 32.50 without a membership card) per person, including breakfast. They also have family rooms (Dr 5 extra per person). It's open from noon to 11 pm. A notice board

features local information, including transport timetables. From Casa-Port railway station, walk out to the first major intersection and then turn right along Blvd des Almohades. Turn left when you get to the second opening in the medina wall. Go through it and you'll see the hostel on the right.

Hotels – medina All the hotels in the medina are unclassified, cheap and quite basic. A few of them are not bad and are possibly worth considering, but in general they are not overly inviting. For a little more money, you can find something better in the centre of town. Prices are in the vicinity of Dr 30 to Dr 40 per person. A reasonable one among this lot is the *Hôtel Central*, on Place de l'Amiral Philibert. It's near the youth hostel, and if you prefer not to be in a dormitory, this is a viable alternative, especially if you can get a room overlooking the square. Rooms are clean but have only cold showers. This shouldn't pose big problems, as there is a hammam for men and women on the same square. Singles/doubles are Dr 35/70.

Equally, if you're not overly fussy about the rooms, the hotels clustered around the little square between Rue Centrale (or Rue al-Markiziya) and Rue de Fès are in an interesting bit of the medina. Places like the *Hôtel Marrakech* are typical of the area's species, with rooms at Dr 30/60 and no showers. Other hotels to choose from include the *Genève*, *Helvetia*, *Al-Nasr Widad*, *Brésil*, *Soussi*, *Gibraltar*, *Des Amis*, *De Medine*, *Candice*, *London*, *Chichaoua*, *Kaawakib Moghreb* and *De la Reine*.

In addition to the hammam on Place de l'Amiral Philibert, there are a couple of other public showers (douches) and hammams dotted about the medina.

The most convenient approach to the hotels in the medina is from the entrance on Place des Nations Unies.

Hotels – central Casablanca At any time of the year a lot of the lower-end hotels are full, so it is best to arrive in the morning.

The *Hôtel du Palais* (☎ 276191) offers

about the best value for money you will find. Located at 68 Rue Farhat Hachad, near the French Consulate, it has clean and spacious rooms, some with balconies. When the hot water is working you pay a little extra, but at Dr 51/72 without shower it's hard to beat. This place is popular and (it goes without saying) often full.

Close by is the *Hôtel Welkom* (☎ 276191), a dive with cells for Dr 52 a person.

If price is the main concern, you could try the *Hôtel Gallia* (☎ 221055), 19 Rue Ibn Batouta. It has basic singles/doubles for Dr 46/70, including (so they say) hot showers.

A couple of blocks south is the still cheaper *Hôtel de Mamora* (☎ 311511), 52 Rue Ibn Batouta. At Dr 38/52/90, it's cheap, although no better than any of the medina places. A few steps away is the *Hôtel Volubilis* (☎ 207789), 20-22 Rue Abdel Karim Diouri. Rooms, which come with a table, washbasin and bidet, are OK, if a little on the musty side, and cost Dr 60/90. If you continue south on Ave Lalla Yacout, you can't miss the *Hôtel Champlain*. It looks rather imposing from the outside, but the dingy rooms are disappointing. They cost Dr 60 per person.

Another collection of cheapies is to be found on and around Rue Allal ben Abdallah.

Virtually across the road from one another are the *Hôtel Kon Tiki* (☎ 314927) and the *Hôtel Touring* (☎ 310010). The former is pretty ordinary, with rooms at Dr 60/80 (Dr 5 extra for a hot shower). The latter is not too bad, though doubles cost Dr 5 more than in the Kon Tiki. The rooms are clean and the beds big. For others, head east and turn left into Rue Chaoui (ex-Rue Colbert). The *Hôtel Mon Rêve* (☎ 311439) is no dream, but cheap at Dr 46/62 (plus Dr 4 for a hot trickle). Like many of the cheapies, it is often full. Around the corner is the even less inspiring *Hôtel Miramar*, with rooms at similar prices.

Back on Rue Chaoui, retrace your steps and proceed south of Rue Allal ben Abdallah. On your right, at No 38, the pleasant *Hôtel Colbert* (☎ 314241) offers singles/doubles/triples without shower or toilet from Dr 47/64/99. Those with shower only are Dr

66/77/112, while others with full bathroom go for Dr 73/95/130. It may not look like much from the outside but, as one of the better-value places around, is often booked out.

Two hotels that have long been popular with travellers are the unclassified *Hôtel du Périgord* (☎ 221085), 56 Rue Araibi Jilali (ex-Rue Foucauld), and virtually next door, the *Hôtel de Foucauld* (☎ 222666), at No 52. The first has rooms for Dr 49/68/104. The singles are pretty cramped, and the place has cold showers only, but it's OK for the money. The Foucauld has singles without private shower (Dr 70) and doubles with shower (Dr 130). Again, it's reasonable without being a breathtakingly good deal.

Farther south, at 36 Rue Nationale, the *Hôtel du Louvre* (☎ 273747) is not a bad place, although some rooms are definitely better than others. Singles/doubles start at Dr 50/68; rooms with private shower cost Dr 65/78, and those with private shower and toilet cost Dr 75/90. This would all be quite good if they didn't throw in a compulsory breakfast (brought to your room at about 8 am, regardless of whether you like it). This and the taxes add about Dr 16 to the price.

Up on Blvd de Paris is the *Hôtel Moumen* (☎ 220798), which has undergone a name change (from Hôtel Lafayette), but little other visible improvement. Rooms are Dr 70/100.

A handy place if you arrive late or intend to leave early from Casa-Voyageurs railway station is the *Hôtel Terminus* (☎ 240025). It's nothing special, but at Dr 38/52/80 you can't really argue. Around the corner are a bar and a couple of decent places to eat.

Places to Stay – middle

The jump from one-star to two-star quality is quite startling. If you're prepared to pay about Dr 130/170, you can choose from a number of places and end up with a very comfortable deal.

Possibly one of the first hotels you'll notice if you're walking up from Casa-Port train station is the *Hôtel Excelsior* (☎ 200263, 262281), just off Place des

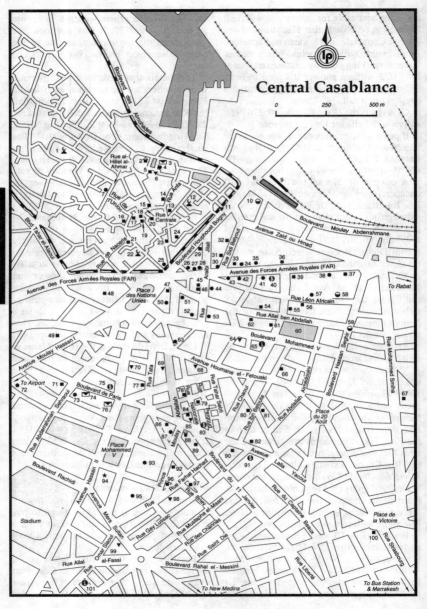

Central Casablanca

PLACES TO STAY

2 Youth Hostel
5 Hôtel Central
13 Hôtel Helvetia
14 Hôtel al-Nasr
15 Hôtels des Amis,
   de Medine & Gibraltar
16 Hôtel Marrakech
17 Hôtel Chichaoua
18 Hôtel Candice
19 Hôtel Soussi
20 Hôtel/Café London
21 Hôtel Kaawakib Moghreb
23 Hôtel de Widad
24 Hôtel Genève
29 Hôtel Plaza
31 Hôtel du Centre
32 Hôtel Toubkal
33 Hôtel Royal Mansour
36 Hôtel Marhaba
37 Hôtel Safir
39 Hôtel Sheraton
45 Hôtel de Foucauld
46 Hôtel du Périgord
47 Hôtel Excelsior
48 Hyatt Regency Hotel
49 Hôtel Basma
54 Hôtel Touring
55 Hôtel Mon Rêve
56 Hôtel Miramar
61 Hôtel Colbert
62 Hôtel Kon Tiki
66 Hôtel Gallia
67 Hôtel Métropole
71 Hôtel al Mounia
77 Hôtel Lausanne
78 Hôtel du Louvre
79 Hôtel Guynemer
80 Hôtel Volubilis
81 Hôtel de Mamora
82 Hôtel Majestic
84 Hôtel de Paris
86 Hôtel Moumen
89 Hôtel de Noailles
90 Hôtel Champlain
92 Hôtel Astrid
96 Hôtel du Palais
97 Hôtel Welcom
100 Hôtel de Sully

PLACES TO EAT

6 Café Central
11 Taverne du Dauphin
64 Restaurant Au Petit Poucet

68 Pizza Hot
69 Restaurant Le Tonkin
70 Casablanca Lights
85 Snack Bohayra
98 Restauant La Pagode
99 L'Entrecôte

OTHER

1 Chleuh Mosque
3 Post Office (PTT)
4 Hammam
7 Men's Hammam
8 Centre 2000
9 Gare du Port (Casa-Port Railway
  Station)
10 Buses for Mohammedia
12 Hassan II Mosque
22 Mosque
25 Clock Tower
26 Le Don Quichotte Nightclub
27 Touring Club du Maroc
28 Air France
30 Iberia Airlines
34 Avis
35 Comanav
38 Europcar
40 BMCI Bank (ATMs)
41 Budget
42 Royal Air Maroc
43 German Consulate
44 Hertz
50 L'Arizona Nightclub
51 Air Algérie
52 Wagons-Lits
53 Librairie Farairre
57 Wasteels Travel Agent
58 CTM Bus Terminal
59 Grands Taxis for Rabat
60 Central Market
63 Goethe Institut
65 PTT & Syndicat d'Initiative
72 Senegalese Consulate
73 Telex Office
74 Parcel Post
75 Citibank
76 Main Post Office (PTT)
83 BMCE Bank (ATMs)
87 Voyages Schwartz (American
  Express)
88 Café National
91 BMCI Bank
93 Law Courts
94 Préfecture (Police Headquarters)
95 French Consulate
101 Tourist Office

NTH ATLANTIC COAST

Nations Unies, at 2 Rue el-Amraoui Brahim (ex-Nolly). It's OK, but is cashing in on its fast-fading status as one of Casablanca's former premier hotels. Rooms come with phone, and breakfast is included, but for the price you can find better. Singles/doubles with shower cost Dr 140/220. Those with full bathroom are Dr 170/295.

The *Hôtel du Centre* (☎ 312448), just off Ave des FAR, offers better value than the Excelsior. It's been done up, and has clean, modern rooms with bathroom and phone for Dr 126/158.

If you prefer a bit more atmosphere, you should have a look at the *Hôtel Majestic* (☎ 446285), 55 Ave Lalla Yacout, whose foyer is decorated after the fashion of the Merenid era. The comfortable rooms, with shower, toilet, phone and even TV, cost Dr 150/170 plus taxes and breakfast.

Another very good place, along much the same lines as the Hôtel du Centre, is the *Hôtel de Lausanne* (☎ 268083), 24 Rue Tata (ex-Rue Poincaré). Its 31 spotless rooms with full bathroom, carpeting and phone cost Dr 138/170.

There are a couple of surprise packets away from the centre. The comparatively new *Hôtel Astrid* (☎ 277803), 12 Rue Ledru-Rollin, off Rue Prince Moulay Abdallah, has good, clean rooms with en suite bathroom for Dr 150/180. The paint job on the doors is a little on the garish side, though.

In the west of the city centre, on Place Oued al-Makhazine (near the main local bus terminal), is the *Hôtel Windsor* (☎ 200352). Though a little inconveniently located, it's good value at Dr 158/206 with private shower, or Dr 198/246 with shower and toilet. Some places claim to have central heating in winter, but this hotel actually turns it on!

Should you want to be near the main bus station (not the CTM station), you could stay at the *Hôtel de Sully* (☎ 309535), on Place de la Victoire. It's a noisy, polluted location, but could be a useful first stop if you arrive late at night. Rooms go for Dr 138/165 and are quite adequate.

Moving into the three-star bracket, there

is the excellent and well-situated *Hôtel de Paris* (☎ 298069), in the pedestrian zone off Rue Prince Moulay Abdallah. The rooms have heating, phones and plenty of hot water. They cost Dr 198/246. Not so hot, but a stone's throw from Casa-Port train station is the *Hôtel Plaza*, with singles/doubles for the same price.

At 22 Blvd du 11 Janvier, there is the somewhat more expensive *Hôtel de Noailles* (☎ 202554; fax 220589). It has spotless, elegant rooms for Dr 228/276, and the tearoom on the 1st floor is a very civilised affair indeed.

The *Hôtel Metropole* (☎ 301213; fax 305801), 89 Rue Mohammed Smiha, is a reasonable alternative to the above if you are having problems finding a room. It costs Dr 220/260 plus taxes.

As usual, the *Moussafir Hôtel* (☎ 401984; fax 400799) chain has a representative, which is just outside Casa-Voyageurs train station. Its modern, comfortable rooms go for Dr 242/286 plus taxes.

The *Hôtel Guynemer*, at 2 Rue Pergoud, used to be a good deal, but at the time of writing was being refurbished for upgrading to a three-star rating.

Places to Stay – top end

Most of Casablanca's top-end hotels are on Ave des FAR. They include the *Hôtel Sheraton* (☎ 317878), *Hôtel Safir* (☎ 311212), *Hôtel Royal Mansour* (☎ 313011) and *Hôtel Marhaba*. All are five-star hotels. Nearby is the four-star *Hôtel Toubkal* (☎ 311414). Right on Place des Nations Unies is the five-star *Hyatt Regency Hotel* (☎ 261234), and a couple of blocks south you'll find the four-star *Hôtel Basma* (☎ 223323). Still farther south along Ave Moulay Hassan I is the *Hôtel Les Almoravides* (☎ 220505). The four-star *Hôtel al Mounia* (☎ 203211) is at 24 Blvd de Paris, close to the main post office.

Most other top-end hotels overlook the beaches along Blvd de la Corniche. They include the four-star *Hôtel Tropicana* (☎ 367595), *Hôtel Tarik* (☎ 391373), *Hôtel de la Corniche* (☎ 363011) and *Hôtel Suisse*

(☎ 360202) and the five-star *Hôtel Riad Salam* (☎ 392244).

Places to Eat

Casablanca is full of places to eat; what follows is little more than a taste of what's available (a more comprehensive list appears in *La Quinzaine du Maroc*). If your budget is tight, you'll be largely restricted to the Moroccan version of fast-food joints, where you can get good sandwiches with meat, chips, salad and so on for around Dr 10, or sit-down meals for around Dr 30 to Dr 40. For anything else, you're looking at a minimum of Dr 60 for a main meal.

Central Casablanca There are a few cheap restaurants around the Place des Nations Unies entrance to the medina. No particular place stands out, but one that is clean, bright and good is the *Restaurant Widad*, attached to the hotel of the same name. They serve generous helpings of good Moroccan food. A big steaming bowl of soup costs Dr 3.50.

For those staying anywhere near the pedestrian mall (Rue Prince Moulay Abdallah), Ave Lalla Yacout has quite a number of Moroccan fast-food cafés that are popular with the locals at lunchtime and in the early evening. One is *Kwiki Sandwich*, where you can get a kefta sandwich with salad and chips for Dr 10.

A slightly more up-market version is *Snack Bohayra*, at 62 Rue Nationale, where you can get filled sandwiches for about Dr 15 or filling sit-down meals of kefta, chips, salad and a soft drink for Dr 30 to Dr 35.

For something a little better, *Las Delicias*, at 168 Blvd Mohammed V, has a good range of tajines (such as chicken with prunes and onions or beef with raisins). Watch out for the service charge and taxes here. Also good in this area is the *Restaurant Le Cardinal*, close to Place des Nations Unies.

Another place that is highly recommended by some travellers is the *Restaurant Nesma*, just off Blvd Mohammed V, at 21 Rue Ghali Ahmed. A meal of several courses costs about Dr 30.

Casablanca Lights, on Ave Hassan II, is a particularly bright and popular snack bar. When you've finished eating, you can go downstairs for a game of pool. A popular new 'self-service' restaurant, *Welcome*, is a couple of blocks in from Place des Nations Unies.

Another good place in the new city is the *Restaurant de l'Étoile Marocaine*, at 107 Rue Allal ben Abdallah, not far from the Hôtel Touring. It's a friendly place where you can eat good Moroccan food in traditional surroundings. They occasionally have serves of delicious pastilla (pigeon pie) for Dr 40.

If you're hankering after south-east Asian food, you could head for the *Restaurant Le Tonkin*, on the pedestrian mall, or *La Pagode*, which is close to the Hôtel du Palais. A decent meal at either will cost you Dr 70 or more. Alternatively, you could try the Korean restaurant, *Le Marignan*, on the corner of Blvd Mohammed V and Rue Mohammed Smiha.

For much the same money, you could have a reasonable and intimate French meal at *L'Entrecôte*, on Ave Mers Sultan, next to the RAM office.

For good but not-too-generous servings of Indian food, you could do a lot worse than the *Natraj*, at 13 Rue Chenier, just off the east side of Place des Nations Unies. They have a decent set menu for Dr 75.

A couple of blocks south-east of the Hôtel Noailles on Blvd du 11 Janvier is the *Restaurant Tout Va Bien*, which occasionally serves up a Spanish-style paella. *Pizza Hot*, on Ave Houmane el-Fetouaki, does a reasonable imitation of the real thing.

For seafood, go straight to the *Taverne du Dauphin*, on Blvd Houphouet Boigny. It may not look too inviting, but the food is pretty good and not overly expensive.

If you have at least Dr 60 handy for a main meal, there is a selection of restaurants to choose from in the Centre 2000, next to the Casa-Port railway station. They include *Le Mékong* (Vietnamese), *La Marée* (mostly French), *Le Chalutier* (Spanish seafood), *Le Tajine* (Moroccan), *Retro 1900* (expensive

French nouvelle cuisine) and a couple of others.

In the laneway running east off Rue Prince Moulay Abdallah opposite the Restaurant Le Tonkin is *Gelatino* – a good place for an after-dinner ice cream.

'Ain Diab For a totally different atmosphere, you could head out to the beaches and 'Ain Diab. You'll need a fairly fat wallet for the three up-market restaurants, *Le Cabestan, La Mer* and *La Petite Roche*, which are gathered around the El-Hank lighthouse.

If you head farther out along Blvd de Biarritz, you will find many more places to choose from. Overlooking the sea is the *Sijilmassa*, which serves the usual Moroccan fare. For a welcome variation on a theme, try the Lebanese *Restaurant Baalbek* across the road. A few metres along the boulevard heading back towards central Casablanca, *La Mama* has good pizzas for Dr 40.

The splurge of the city would have to be *A Ma Bretagne*, a few hundred metres south of Sidi Abderrahman along the coastal road. It is run by a French maître cuisinier (master chef), André Halbert, who concentrates on seafood specialities.

Western Fast Food Not far from the lighthouse is the first of the 12 *McDonald's* franchises that have been planned for Morocco. So, if it's a while since you've swallowed a Big Mac, that's the place to go. For the *Pizza Hut*, go to Place de la Fraternité, near the American Language Center.

Entertainment

Cafés & Bars There are few cafés in the medina, perhaps the most pleasantly located being the *Central*, on Place de l'Amiral Philibert.

The city centre is filled with French-style cafés, and there is little doubt that an important occupation for much of the city's male population is coffee-sipping and people-watching – and who can blame them? Although cafés are still largely the preserve of men, the sight of Western women sitting

down for a coffee, especially at the outdoor tables, is unlikely to arouse much attention. On the inside, some of these places are interesting Art Deco leftovers.

Speaking of interiors, quite a few of the cafés and bars serve alcohol inside (until about 9 pm). There is a bit of a misconception that Casablanca doesn't have many bars. Nothing could be further from the truth. Those with a taste for Flag Spéciale (or something a little stronger) will find that the city centre is riddled with drinking establishments, going by the name of cafés, bars, brasseries or drugstores. Some have been marked on the maps, but there are plenty of others. Most are pretty much spit and sawdust places, and the clientele can be a little rough around the edges (this is a port after all).

There are three in a row just east of the Restaurant de l'Étoile Marocaine. The *Red Fez*, on Blvd de Bordeaux, is nothing special, but the name appeals.

For something more genteel, the only fallback is the bars in the expensive hotels, which tend to stay open later. *Bar Casablanca*, in the Hyatt, has a happy hour from 6.30 to 7.30 pm, and is plastered with posters and other references to the Humphrey Bogart classic, *Casablanca*. The title was somewhat of a misnomer, as it was filmed entirely in Hollywood and based more on Tangier, which maintained its international status throughout WW II and was a hive of activity, crawling with spies, refugees en route from occupied Europe, and smugglers. The Hyatt bar, posters aside, is no more reminiscent of the film and wartime Tangier, or Casablanca for that matter, than the hotel itself. Still, it might be worth going to hear what the pianist plays...

Nightclubs As the bars shut down around 9 to 10 pm, the choices for kicking on are restricted to discos and nightclubs. The more up-market places are concentrated out in 'Ain Diab, but they are expensive (at least Dr 50 to get in and as much for a drink) and most expect snappy dress sense. In addition, unaccompanied women are unlikely to enjoy themselves if they just want a drink.

In the city centre, it's a man's world. The so-called nightclubs (which charge about the same as the discos, one way or another) are largely sleazy joints where you get a bit of Cairo-style belly dancing and cabaret entertainment. Quite a few hostesses and prostitutes work these places. *La Fontaine*, on Blvd Houphouet Boigny, is an unashamedly slimy hostess bar – you buy a drink for yourself and another for your company, and so on...There are a couple of slightly less tacky places opposite the Hôtel de Paris, in the pedestrian zone. Other cabaret bars include *Le Don Quichotte*, on Place des Nations Unies (Ave des FAR), and *L'Arizona*, near the Hôtel Excelsior. There are plenty of others.

If you have wads of money, and like cabarets (but not at this level), you could try the big hotels – the Hyatt and Sheraton both put on Western-style cabarets.

Cinema There are about half a dozen cinemas around the city centre, but the best of them are the twin Dawliz cinemas off Ave des FAR, a little way east of Place des Nations Unies on Rue Léon Africain. You can quite often catch films only recently released in the West, although there are no guarantees about what is cut out. Those films that are not French are generally dubbed into that language.

Getting There & Away
Innumerable travel agencies are squeezed into the same area as the bulk of the hotels. The Wagons-Lits representative is marked on the map. Trasmediterrranea and Intercona (☎ 221737) have a representative on Place 16 du Novembre. Wasteels (for cheap intercontinental rail tickets) has an agency by the CTM bus station. Comanav (☎ 312050), for boats from Tangier to France, is at 43 Ave des FAR. Supratours (☎ 277160), the ONCF's bus service, is in the Centre 2000.

Air From Casa's Mohammed V Airport (30 km south-east of the city), there are regular

connections to most of the countries of Western Europe, as well as to West Africa, Algeria, Tunisia, Egypt and the Middle East.

Internally, the vast majority of RAM's flights go via Casablanca. Consequently, you can get to any destination direct from Casablanca. For instance, there are three to five daily flights to Agadir (Dr 585, one hour), five weekly flights to Fès (Dr 405, 50 minutes), at least two daily flights to Marrakesh (Dr 340, 50 minutes) and at least one flight a day to Tanger (Dr 430, one hour).

For detailed information on airport services and transport, see the Getting There & Away chapter and the Casablanca and Rabat Getting Around sections.

Airlines flying into and out of Mohammed V International Airport include:

Aeroflot
  47 Blvd Moulay Youssef (☎ 206410)
Air Afrique
  Tour des Habous (☎ 318379)
Air Algérie
  1 Rue el-Amraoui Brahim (☎ 266995)
Air France
  15 Ave des FAR (☎ 294040)
Alitalia
  Tour des Habous (☎ 314181)
British Airways/GB Airways
  Place Zellaqa (☎ 307629)
Iberia
  17 Ave des FAR (☎ 279600)
KLM
  6 Blvd Houphouet Boigny (☎ 203222)
Lufthansa
  Tour des Habous (☎ 312371)
RAM
  44 Ave des FAR (☎ 311122)
Royal Jordanian
  Place Zellaqa (☎ 306273)
Sabena
  41 Ave des FAR (☎ 313991)
Swissair
  Tour des Habous (☎ 313280)
Tunis Air
  10 Ave des FAR (☎ 293452)

Bus – CTM The CTM bus terminal is on Rue Léon Africain, at the back of the Hôtel Safir (which is on Ave des FAR). They have a left-luggage counter.

There are regular CTM departures to Agadir (six times daily from 5.30 am to 11 pm), Essaouira (twice daily, at 5.30 am and 5 pm), Fès/Meknès (nine times daily), Marrakesh (five times daily from 7.30 am to 9 pm), Oujda (twice daily), Rabat (19 times daily), Safi (six times daily from 5.30 am to 7 pm), Tangier (six times daily), Taza (at 1 pm) and Tetouan (three times every morning). At the time of writing, CTM's services to El-Jadida had been suspended. What's weird is that buses the other way were still running! The bus to Safi does *not* go via El-Jadida.

Fares are Dr 117.50 to Agadir (10 hours), Dr 69 to Fès (five hours), Dr 57.50 to Marrakesh (4½ hours), Dr 22 to Rabat (1½ hours), Dr 60 to Safi (four hours) and Dr 88 to Tangier (seven hours).

CTM also operates international buses to France, Belgium and Italy from Casablanca. See the Getting There & Away chapter for further details.

Bus – other The station for the other lines is just off Rue Strasbourg, two blocks down from Place de la Victoire, some way from the centre of the city. There are a couple of urban buses to Place de la Victoire and down Rue Strasbourg (see Getting Around), or you could get a taxi.

Rue Strasbourg must be one of the noisiest and most air-polluted streets in North Africa, and the chaos of buses and touts could just about put you off trying to leave Casablanca. In fact, the touts are good news – they'll find you long before you find the bus you want. Nevertheless, it might be an idea to squirm your way to the ticket windows – a lot of them have prices posted, which will give you an idea of what you should pay. Some of these companies offer 1st and 2nd-class fares. The difference is usually a matter of a few Dr.

There are buses to Agadir (Dr 96), Er-Rachidia (Dr 123/114 in 1st/2nd class), Fès (Dr 55), Marrakesh (Dr 42), Midelt (Dr 80), Ouarzazate (Dr 88.50), Oujda (Dr 119/111 in 1st/2nd class), Rabat (Dr 18/16 in 1st/2nd class), Sefrou (Dr 61), Tangier (Dr 66/60 in 1st/2nd class), Tinerhir (Dr 125) and Tiznit (Dr 137).

There's a petit taxi stand next to the station – the fare into central Casablanca should not be more than Dr 10.

The No 900 bus to Mohammedia leaves regularly from a stop near Casa-Port train station. The ticket costs Dr 5.50.

Train Casablanca has five railway stations. The main one is Casa-Voyageurs, four km east of the city centre. The Casa-Port station is a few hundred metres north of Places des Nations Unies, right where you want to be. The other stations, 'Ain Sebaa, Nouvelle Medina and Mers Sultan, are of no interest to travellers.

Most departures are from Casa-Voyageurs station, which is a Dr 15 taxi ride from the centre. There are also plenty of buses between the station and the centre – it's about an hour's walk, which is silly if you're carrying luggage.

Departures include:

El-Jadida (8.50 am, 8.30 pm; 1½ hours); these trains may also go on to Azemmour
Fès (10.52 am and 12.30, 5.20 and 10.17 pm; five hours)
Marrakesh (1.30, 6.23, 7.40 and 9.48 am and 12.11, 2.05, 3.06, 5.55 and 7.28 pm; three hours 50 minutes)
Oujda (9.32 am and 1.55 and 10.17 pm; 10½ hours)
Tangier (12.30, 6.50 and 11.20 pm; 6½ hours)

Departures from the Gare du Port ('Casa-Port' on the platform signs) include Fès (8.05 am and 8.35 pm; five hours), Oujda (8.35 pm, 10½ hours) and Tangier (7.10 am; six hours).

All trains to Fès call at Meknès. Trains to Oujda call at Meknès and Fès.

All trains heading north call at Rabat. The trip takes about 1¼ hours. However, the shuttle trains between the two cities are faster. There are 17 a day (from 6.50 am to 9.59 pm): 12 from Casa-Port and the others from Casa-Voyageurs. They take 50 minutes.

Some 2nd-class normal/rapide fares include El-Jadida (Dr 24.50/31), Fès (Dr 69/87), Marrakesh (Dr 52.50/66.50), Oujda

(Dr 142/182.50), Rabat (Dr 19/24) and Tangier (Dr 81.50/103).

Taxi Grands taxis to Rabat leave from Blvd Hassan Seghir, near the CTM bus station. The fare is Dr 22.

Car The following are among the car rental agencies in Casablanca, but a plethora of smaller agencies is concentrated around Ave des Far and Blvd Mohammed V. They often employ runners to bring in business – follow some of them and you could end up with a much better deal:

Avis
  19 Ave des FAR (☎ 312424, 311135)
  Mohammed V International Airport (☎ 339072)
Budget
  Tour des Habous, Ave des FAR (☎ 313945)
  Mohammed V Airport (☎ 339157)
Europcar
  Complexe des Habous, Ave des FAR (☎ 313737)
  144 Ave des FAR (☎ 314069)
  Mohammed V International Airport (☎ 339161; fax 339517)
Goldcar
  5 Ave des FAR (☎ and fax 202510, 260109)
  81 Ave Hassan II Intermarket (☎ 202509, 220950)
Hertz
  25 Rue de Foucauld (☎ 312223)
  Mohammed V International Airport (☎ 339181)

If you do rent a car, you should be aware of Casablanca's horrendous parking problems. It is virtually impossible to find a park in the centre between 8 am and 6 pm. During these hours, cars will be parked nose to tail in every conceivable spot. How they disentangle themselves at the end of the day is anyone's guess.

Getting Around

To/From the Airport You can get from Mohammed V Airport to Casablanca or Rabat direct by shuttle bus or train (TNR).

The trains leave from below the ground floor of the terminal building, with 12 services day from 8 am to 9.35 pm to Casablanca's main station, Casa-Voyageurs; they take 24 minutes and are comfortable and reliable. Seven continue to the more convenient Casa-Port station. The other five go on to Rabat (1¼ hours) instead. The system is being expanded, and some of these fast shuttles go on to Kenitra. The first run from Casa-Voyageurs is at 6.01 am. The 2nd-class fare to Casablanca is Dr 25 and the totally unnecessary 1st-class fare (2nd is quite good enough) Dr 37.50.

There are CTM shuttle buses to Casablanca almost every hour from 5.30 am to 11 pm. They cost Dr 20 and take about half an hour.

If none of this suits you, the fare for a taxi into central Casablanca is Dr 150, or Dr 200 after 8 pm (don't let the drivers tell you anything else).

Bus The main terminal for Casablanca's city buses is on Place Oued al-Makhazine. There is even a faded route map posted up here. Some useful city routes are:

No 9
  From the terminal to 'Ain Diab and the beaches
No 5
  From the terminal to Place de la Victoire
No 30
  From Blvd Ziraoui to Casa-Voyageurs train station via Ave des FAR and Blvd Mohammed V
No 4
  Along Rue Strasbourg and down Ave Lalla Yacout to Blvd de Paris

In addition, bus No 2 regularly runs along Blvd Mohammed V to Casa-Voyageurs and beyond. Coming from the train station, you could walk up to Place al-Yassir, from where you have a greater choice of lines serving the city centre.

Taxi There's no shortage of petits taxis in Casablanca, but you'll usually find drivers unwilling to use the meters, so negotiate the fare before getting in, especially if you're going a long way. Expect to pay Dr 10 for a ride in or around the city centre.

AROUND CASABLANCA
Mohammedia
About 30 km north of Casablanca lies the

PLACES TO STAY

12 Hôtel Miramar
13 Sabah Hotel (in construction)
14 Hôtel Samir
15 Hôtel Argana
18 Hôtel Ennasr
22 Hôtel Castel

PLACES TO EAT

1 Restaurant des Sports
2 Restaurant La Friture
3 Restaurant Sans Pareil
4 Diner Grill
7 Restaurant du Parc
23 Café de Paris

OTHER

5 Total Service Station
6 Centre Culturel Français
8 Ranch Club
9 Church
10 Post Office (PTT)
11 BMCE Bank
16 Mosque
17 Royal Air Maroc
19 Douche Publique
20 BMCI Bank
21 Petrom Service Station
24 Buses to Casablanca
25 Train Station

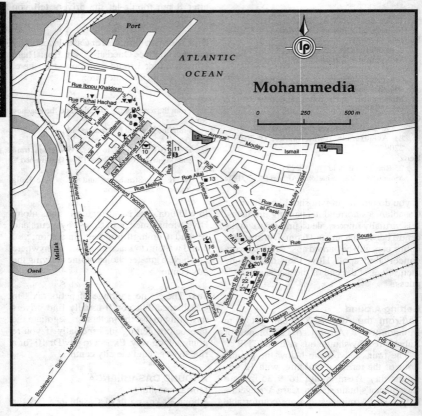

Mohammedia

local resort town of Mohammedia, which also doubles as the centre of Morocco's petrol industry. The two might seem incompatible, but Mohammedia, which until the 1960s was little more than a decaying fishing village (then known as Fedala), manages to keep the two activities apart. Site of the SAMIR oil refinery, it is one of the country's busiest ports, the traffic being almost entirely devoted to petroleum products. At the height of summer, the place tends to fill to bursting with Casablancans, but out of season it makes a pleasant place to stop off for a day or two. The walls of an old kasbah still stand, but there is nothing much to see.

It's an easy day trip from Casablanca and not hard to find your way around. When you arrive by train or bus, head down the street leading north-west directly away from the station and you arrive on Ave Abderrahmane Sarghini. Turn right and you can continue right down to the beach. Ave des FAR runs off a roundabout (note the BMCI bank) about 100 metres down Ave Abderrahmane Sarghini to the main restaurant area, the Hôtel Miramar and the western end of the beach.

Information The tourist office (☎ 324199) is at 14 Rue El-Jahid. The main post office (PTT) is on Ave Mohammed Zerktouni, a couple of blocks in from the beach. Several banks have branches in Mohammedia. BMCI is closest to the train station, just opposite the kasbah on Ave des FAR. There are no ATMs. If the banks are closed, you can change money in the Hôtel Miramar. There's even a small Centre Culturel Français, in an arcade off Rue de Fès.

Places to Stay There are three cheapies. Hôtel Castel (☎ 322584) and Hôtel Ennasr (☎ 322373), close to one another on Ave Abderrahmane Sarghini, are similar and offer only cold showers. Doubles are Dr 70; singles are Dr 40 in the Castel and Dr 60 in the Ennasr. The Hôtel Argana, down a side

street off Ave des FAR and two blocks west of the abovementioned roundabout, is much the same. There are douches for men and women a block back towards the roundabout.

Otherwise, there's the Hôtel Samir (☎ 310 770; fax 323330), with singles/ doubles for Dr 300/370, or the town's premier establishment, the Hôtel Miramar (☎ 322021; fax 324613), with rooms for Dr 620/740. Another four-star hotel, the Sabah, is being built on Ave des FAR.

Places to Eat The waterfront is lined with cafés, and there are a few standard hole-in-the-wall places on Ave des FAR and in the area around the train station. There is also a collection of decent restaurants around Rue de Fès and its continuation, Rue Farhai Hachad, west of the Miramar. Not surprisingly, fish is the theme.

The Restaurant La Friture, on Rue Ibn Tumert, offers fish and salad or tajine for as little as Dr 20. Virtually across the road is the Restaurant des Sports, a classier and very pleasant place. Farther east down the Rue Farhai Hachad is the popular Restaurant Sans Pareil, which serves a variety of food, with main courses starting at about Dr 50. The Diner Grill, a little farther on, is a more modest place, but the food is OK.

Overlooking the park at Ave Mohammed Zerktouni is the Restaurant du Parc. For a little nightlife, try the Ranch Club next door.

Getting There & Away Bus No 900 is virtually a suburban bus, running regularly between a stop by Casa-Port train station and the square in front of Mohammedia's train station. It costs Dr 5.50. The 2nd-class (normal) train fare is Dr 10.

Getting Around You're highly unlikely to need them, but there are lime-green petits taxis should you be in a hurry to get somewhere. A couple of buses run down to the beach from the square in front of the train station.

The Atlantic – South of Casablanca

From Casablanca, the Atlantic coast stretches some 350 km towards Essaouira in the south-west, where it then rounds off at Cap Sim and drops south to Agadir, before again pursuing a more south-westerly course, to the tiny coastal town of Tarfaya, just north of the Western Sahara desert.

Along the way down the coast from Casa, you're reminded of Europe's long history of interference on the Moroccan seaboard. Azemmour, El-Jadida, Safi, Essaouira and Agadir were all at one time European (mostly Portuguese) military and commercial bridgeheads, and all but Agadir retain the architectural evidence of this. Agadir, the country's premier beach resort, is where modern Europeans, in the guise of package tourists, choose to invade the country. In between these towns are plenty of beaches and some stunning, wild coastal scenery. From Agadir, you can make several excursions, such as to Taroudannt, a 'real' Moroccan city with no ville nouvelle. From there you could head on into the High Atlas and Marrakesh.

Central Coast

EL-JADIDA

Situated 96 km south of Casablanca, El-Jadida is one of history's could-have-beens. The port town, established by the Portuguese, was destined by French protectorate authorities to be made into Morocco's main port, but the foreign Casablanca merchant lobby put paid to these plans, and El-Jadida was relegated to the second division. Its principal activities revolve around maintaining sardine fishing fleets. The historic centre of this quiet, relaxed town of 150,000 is one of the best preserved examples of Portuguese military architecture in the country. Like other Atlantic towns, El-Jadida is a hassle-free and pleasant place to spend a couple of days.

History

The Portuguese founded Mazagan, as El-Jadida used to be known, in 1513, on the site of an old Almohad fortress, in the days when Portugal was building up a maritime trading empire that would stretch as far as China and Japan. Mazagan was to become their main Atlantic entrepôt in Morocco, and they held on to it until 1769, when, following a siege by Sultan Sidi Mohammed bin Abdallah, the Portuguese were forced to evacuate the fortress. Although they left with little more than the clothes they stood in, the ramparts were mined and, at the last moment, blown to smithereens, taking with them a good part of the besieging army.

The walls of the fortress lay in ruins until 1820, when they were rebuilt by Sultan Moulay Abd ar-Rahman. The Moroccans who took over the town after the Portuguese withdrawal preferred to settle outside the walls of the fortress. The medina inside the walls was largely neglected until the mid-19th century, when it was recolonised by European merchants following the establishment of a series of 'open ports' along the Moroccan coast.

A large and influential Jewish community became established at this time. The Jews controlled trade with the interior and particularly with Marrakesh. And, contrary to common Moroccan practice, the Jews of El-Jadida were not confined to their own separate quarter (the mellah).

Tourism and a prosperous agricultural hinterland have made the modern town an animated and growing commercial centre, and this is reflected in its clean look and busy atmosphere.

Orientation

El-Jadida faces north-east onto the Atlantic, and the protection this affords partly accounts for the town's suitability as a port. Coming from Casablanca, the Cité Portugaise (the old Portuguese fortress) is at the north-western end of town. The focal point of the town is the pedestrianised Place Hansali, and you'll find the post office, banks, tourist office and some of the hotels in the cluster of streets just to the south of it. The bus and grand taxi stations are a good km south-east of the town centre, and the railway station so far out as to make it useless.

Information
Tourist Office The Délégation Provinciale du Tourisme (☎ 342724, 342704) is in the Chambre de Commerce, Rue Ibn Khaldoun, and is open from 8.30 am to noon and 2.30 to 6.30 pm Monday to Friday. They have a few useful handouts, including hotel and restaurant lists – why can't more of the offices in Morocco do this? There is what appears to be a very closed syndicat d'initiative opposite the Municipal Theatre.

Money Several banks have branches here, including the BMCE and BMCI. You can change cash and cheques in the Bank al-Maghrib, but the process takes forever.

Post & Telecommunications The post and phone offices are together, on the block bounded by Ave Mohammed V and Ave Jamia al-Arabia. They are open Monday to Friday from 8.30 am to noon and 2.30 to 6 pm. There are card phones outside the office, on Ave Jamia al-Arabia.

Medical Services There's a night pharmacy (☎ 343928) at 59 Place Abdelkrim al-Khattabi.

Cité Portugaise
The Cité Portugaise is the main point of interest. Although its enclosed medina has suffered from neglect, it's still inhabited and well worth exploring. There are two entrance gates to the fortress; the southernmost one, which is more convenient, opens onto the main street through the medina. The street

The Atlantic-
South of
Casablanca

STH OF CASABLANCA

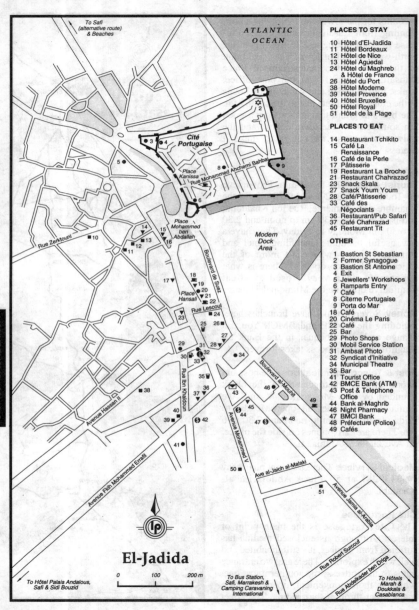

PLACES TO STAY
10 Hôtel d'El-Jadida
11 Hôtel Bordeaux
12 Hôtel de Nice
13 Hôtel Aguedal
24 Hôtel du Maghreb
   & Hôtel de France
26 Hôtel du Port
38 Hôtel Moderne
39 Hôtel Provence
40 Hôtel Bruxelles
50 Hôtel Royal
51 Hôtel de la Plage

PLACES TO EAT
14 Restaurant Tchikito
15 Café La
   Renaissance
16 Café de la Perle
17 Pâtisserie
19 Restaurant La Broche
21 Restaurant Chahrazad
23 Snack Skala
27 Snack Youm Youm
28 Café/Pâtisserie
33 Café des
   Négociants
36 Restaurant/Pub Safari
37 Café Chahrazad
45 Restaurant Tit

OTHER
1 Bastion St Sebastian
2 Former Synagogue
3 Bastion St Antoine
4 Exit
5 Jewellers' Workshops
6 Ramparts Entry
7 Café
8 Citerne Portugaise
9 Porta do Mar
18 Café
20 Cinéma Le Paris
22 Café
25 Bar
29 Photo Shops
30 Mobil Service Station
31 Ambsat Photo
32 Syndicat d'Initiative
34 Municipal Theatre
35 Bar
41 Tourist Office
42 BMCE Bank (ATM)
43 Post & Telephone
   Office
44 Bank al-Maghrib
46 Night Pharmacy
47 BMCI Bank
48 Préfecture (Police)
49 Cafés

STH OF CASABLANCA

Cité Portugaise

Place Kanissa

Rue Mohammed Ahchemi Bahbei

ATLANTIC OCEAN

To Safi (alternative route) & Beaches

Place Mohammed ben Abdallah

Rue Zerktouni

Modern Dock Area

Boulevard de Suez

Place Hansali

Rue Lescout

Boulevard al-Mouhit

Municipal Theatre

Avenue Hassan II

Rue Ibn Khaldoun

Avenue Fkih Mohammed Erratti

Avenue Mohammed V

Ave al-Jaich al-Malaki

Avenue Jamia al-Arabia

Rue Robert Surcouf

Rue Abdelkader ben Driga

To Hôtel Palais Andalous, Safi & Sidi Bouzid

To Bus Station, Safi, Marrakesh & Camping Caravaning International

To Hôtels Marah & Doukkala & Casablanca

El-Jadida

0   100   200 m

ends at the Porta do Mar, which is where, in the Portuguese era, ships used to discharge their cargo.

Citerne Portugaise About halfway down the main street of the Cité Portugaise is the famous Citerne Portugaise (Portuguese Cistern). Although the Romans built water-collection and storage cisterns similar to this, it remains a remarkable piece of architecture and engineering that has stood the test of time and is still functional. The reflection of the roof and 25 arched pillars in the water covering the floor creates a dramatic and beautiful effect. This hasn't escaped the attention of various film directors, who have staged scenes for several movies here. Perhaps best known of all is Orson Welles' *Othello*, some of whose most stunning scenes were done in the cistern. It's open seven days a week from 8.30 am to noon and 2.30 to 6 pm (sometimes later). Entry costs Dr 10. If you want, you can pay a little extra for a guide.

Medina The Portuguese built a number of churches within the medina, but unfortunately, they're all closed. You see the principal one, the **Church of the Assumption**, as soon as you enter the main gateway of the medina. Even if it were possible to visit them, however, you'd see little of their original features, since they were taken over and used for secular purposes long ago. Even the **Great Mosque**, adjacent to the Church of the Assumption, used to be a lighthouse. Just inside the Bastion of St Sebastian, on the extreme northern seaward side, you can enter a one-time synagogue; again, there is precious little to see inside nowadays.

Ramparts Entry to the ramparts, which you can walk all the way around, is through the large door at the end of the tiny cul-de-sac which is first on the right after entering the fortress. The man with the key for this is usually hanging around; if not, he won't be far away. There's no charge, but he'll expect a tip either when you enter or when he lets you out at the far side (more often than not,

the gates are open at both ends, but if the exit door is shut, you may have to hammer for several minutes before the guardian arrives).

Beaches

There are beaches to the north and south of town, although the ones to the north occasionally get polluted by oil. They're pleasant enough out of season but can get very crowded during July and August. Possibly the best of them is Sidi Bouzid (see below), about 10 km out of El-Jadida.

Places to Stay – bottom end

Camping *Camping Caravaning International* (☎ 342755), on Ave des Nations Unies, is well outside the town centre, about a 15-minute walk south-east of the bus station. It's a shame, because this is one of the better, shadier Moroccan camp sites. It costs Dr 12 a person, Dr 6.50 per car, Dr 10 to pitch a tent, Dr 5 for a hot shower and Dr 11 for electricity.

Hotels Because this is a seaside resort, you will have to be prepared to pay much higher prices in the summer months in some of the hotels – it's called market forces. The hotels also fill up quickly then, so finding a decent, cheap room will not be easy.

There is a trio of cheapies in some lanes a couple of hundred metres from the fortress. The cheapest of them is the *Hôtel Aguedal*, a very basic locanda-style place offering beds in little rooms around a courtyard for Dr 15 a head. The *Hôtel de Nice* (☎ 352272), 15 Rue Mohammed Smiha, has tidy but tiny rooms for Dr 52/80, and very much has the air of a brothel. The best of the three is the *Hôtel Bordeaux* (☎ 342356), 47 Rue Moulay Ahmed Tahiri, whose pleasant if smallish rooms are gathered around a covered courtyard. There is a hot shower on the 1st floor (Dr 5). Singles/doubles/triples cost Dr 40/60/80.

In the much busier local market area, the *Hôtel d'El Jadida* (☎ 340178), on Rue Zerktouni, offers simple rooms, with washbasins, bidets and big beds but no showers. You pay Dr 41/62/83.

There are two very cheap places just off Place Hansali, the *Hôtel du Maghreb* and *Hôtel de France* (☎ 342181), owned by the same guy. Some of the big rooms, with heavy wooden ceilings, look out to sea. They cost Dr 25/40, and a hot shower is Dr 4. All up, it's one of the better budget deals. Not so hot is the *Hôtel du Port* (☎ 342701), on Blvd de Suez. It's seedy and grubby and costs Dr 26/38.

Quite adequate but unspectacular is the *Hôtel Moderne* (☎ 343133), 21 Ave Hassan II. Rooms with basin and bidet cost Dr 52/78, but some are rather small and the whole place could do with a spring clean. Hot showers are Dr 6.

Handy for the bus station and reasonable value is the newly spruced-up *Hôtel Royal* (☎ 341100). It has some big, bright rooms, and some even have old-fashioned bathtubs. The only problem is that there is only cold water to put in them. Out-of-season prices are Dr 50/78, but they cheerfully admit to jacking them up a lot in summer. They have a bar and restaurant in a pleasant open courtyard.

The friendly *Hôtel de la Plage* (☎ 342 648), Ave Jamia al-Arabia, has more modest pretensions and is also handy for the bus station. It has clean, perfectly good rooms for Dr 45/60/85. There is hot water in the bath on the corridor (Dr 5).

Going up in price are two one-star places, both of them perfectly OK. The *Hôtel Bruxelles* (☎ 342072), 40 Rue Ibn Khaldoun, is the easier of the two to find, and offers clean if somewhat spartan rooms with private bathroom for Dr 70/100 plus taxes.

The friendly but more expensive *Hôtel Suisse* (☎ 342816), 147 Rue Zerktouni, has singles/doubles without shower or toilet for Dr 85/110 and rooms with both for Dr 105/130. It's rather awkwardly placed, about a 10-minute walk south-west of the Cité Portugaise fortress, well away from the bus station.

Places to Stay – middle

If you have the money, El-Jadida's only two-star hotel, the *Hôtel Provence* (☎ 342347; fax 352115), 42 Ave Fkih Mohammed Errafil, is still one of the most pleasant places in town. It costs Dr 121/149/204/269 (plus taxes) for rooms with private shower and toilet. Some of the rooms are definitely better than others. The hot water is very hot, and there is access to covered parking (Dr 10 a day). The Provence has a popular licensed restaurant that serves delicious food, with a choice of Moroccan, French and seafood specialities. A full meal with wine would cost about Dr 100 a head. Visa cards are accepted and English is spoken (the owner, Geoffrey Hurdidge, is English).

Places to Stay – top end

If you can afford a touch of exotic – even florid – luxury, then the three-star *Hôtel Palais Andalous* (☎ 343745), Blvd Docteur de la Lanouy, is the hotel of choice. The place was converted in 1980 into a spacious (56-bed) hotel from a local pasha's residence. There are hectares of polished marble, stunning plasterwork, comfortable salons and a bar and restaurant. The rooms, a more modest version of the same thing, cost Dr 256/332/448 plus tax – excellent value. A garage is available if you have your own transport. The hotel is a little out of the way and can be awkward to find. Follow the orange 'hotel' signs up Ave Hassan II from the city centre and you will eventually stumble across it.

Going up in price, the most expensive hotel in El-Jadida is the *Hôtel Doukkala* (☎ 343737), Ave Jamia al-Arabia. This rather grim concrete bunker of a hotel has all the amenities you would expect of a four-star establishment, including a swimming pool and tennis courts. Singles/doubles cost Dr 312/394 plus taxes. Just nearby is the *Marah Hôtel* (☎ 344170), which is cheaper but of a poorer standard. Rooms cost Dr 178/226 with shower, Dr 228/276 with full bathroom.

Places to Eat

The tourist office has a list of the more up-market restaurants in town.

Along the seafront on Blvd al-Mouhit is a whole line of cafés, which make good places to eat breakfast (coffee and pastries) for reasonable prices. There are a lot of cafés on Place Hansali, and also near Hôtel d'El-Jadida, on Rue Zerktouni.

For cheap eats, *Snack Youm Youm*, across the road from the Municipal Theatre, is a deservedly popular little place. A plate of meat (your choice of brochettes, sausages and several other items), rice, chips and tomato sauce costs Dr 13.

Fish enthusiasts should investigate the *Restaurant Tchikito*, in a side lane a short walk north-west of Place Hansali. A filling meal of fresh fried fish can cost as little as Dr 20.

Restaurant La Broche, on Place Hansali, is a homely, family-run little place that seems popular with expatriates in the area. The fish is poor but the brochettes are exceptionally good. A bowl of harira costs Dr 5 and a full meal will set you back about Dr 50.

On the other side of the cinema is the *Restaurant Chahrazad*. It's cheaper than La Broche and the food is just as good. The only problem is that most of the items on the menu aren't available.

Don't forget the restaurant at the *Hôtel Provence* for a splurge in intimate surroundings. Another place worth investigating if you have some money to burn is the *Restaurant Tit*, just behind the post office.

Entertainment

The Royal, Provence and Palais Andalous hotels all have bars; the most comfortable and 'barry' of them is the one in the Provence. There is a rough sort of bar next door to the Hôtel de la Plage, or try the *Pub Safari*, just down from the Provence. For movies, there's the Cinéma Le Paris, on Place Hansali.

Getting There & Away

Bus The bus terminal (gare routière) is south-east of town on Rue Abdelmoumen el-Mouahidi, close to the junction with Ave Mohammed V. It's a 15-minute walk along Ave Mohammed V from the fortress.

There are buses to Casablanca, Rabat and Kenitra (window No 2), Azemmour (window No 5), Oualidia and Safi (window No 7) and Marrakesh (window No 8).

CTM has three runs to Casablanca: at 8.45 am (Dr 17; 2nd class), 11.15 am (Dr 23; 1st class) and 4.30 pm (mumtaz; Dr 27). There are at least 11 runs to Marrakesh (Dr 35; about 3½ to four hours). The fare to Azemmour is Dr 3. There is one bus to Safi at 6.30 am (Dr 30), and a couple more leave later in the day.

Train The train station is about three km out of town along the Marrakesh road. It's all highly impractical. You can get a train to Oujda at 8.10 am via Azemmour, Casablanca and all subsequent main stops. At 6.10 pm, there is a train to Casa-Voyageurs. There is a free bus service from the train station to the town centre; otherwise you can take a petit taxi.

Taxi Grands taxis gather along the side street next to the bus station. A place in a taxi to Azemmour is Dr 5.

AROUND EL-JADIDA
Azemmour

While in El-Jadida, it's worth making a half-day excursion to this little-visited fortress town 15 km to the north. Here you'll find another monument to those energetic seafaring and fortress-building people, the Portuguese. Although they only stayed in Azemmour for a short while, from 1513 to 1541, it was sufficient time for them to build this fortress alongside the banks of the wide Oum er-Rbia. One of Morocco's largest rivers, the Oum er-Rbia rises in the Middle Atlas and empties into the sea about one km downriver from Azemmour. The best views of this fortress and its crumbling, white-washed medina are from the bridge across the river.

Azemmour once had a thriving Jewish community, but since their exodus to Israel, their houses have fallen into ruin, with only the façades remaining in many cases. However, there is still a synagogue here, in

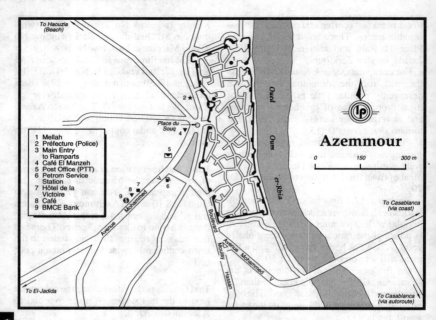

1 Mellah
2 Préfecture (Police)
3 Main Entry
   to Ramparts
4 Café El Manzeh
5 Post Office (PTT)
6 Petrom Service
   Station
7 Hôtel de la
   Victoire
8 Café
9 BMCE Bank

Azemmour

0   150   300 m

To Haouzia
(Beach)

Place du
Souq

Oued

Oum

er-Rbia

To Casablanca
(via coast)

Avenue Mohammed V

Boulevard

Avenue Mohammed V

Moulay

Hassan

To El-Jadida

To Casablanca
(via autoroute)

reasonable shape, with lettering in Hebrew and English above the door saying 'Rabbi Abraham Moul Niss'.

The ramparts are open to visitors – the main entry is on the inside to the left after you enter the fortress town from Place du Souq. You could also enter by a door on the open square at the extreme north-eastern tip of the fort, but you might have to wait for the guardian to arrive with the keys. In all probability you'll have been waylaid by kids before he gets to you, and they will take over as your guides. Whether you get them or the official guardian/guide, you'll have to pay – no more than Dr 10.

Once up on the ramparts, the guide rattles off a plethora of dates, facts and not a little fantasy and carefully steers you under a live, high-tension electricity cable that loops across the walls at waist height at one point. After that, he walks you through the medina and brings you back to where you entered. The kids steer you under the same cable, but

in terms of explanation tend to stick to the obvious ('this, cannon').

There's nothing much of interest in the new part of town outside the ramparts, but if you get here early in the day and aren't in a hurry to get back to El-Jadida, you might like to visit the **beach** (Haouzia), which is about half an hour's walk from Place du Souq (signposted). When the wind's not howling, this is a pretty good beach.

Information The post office, a branch of the BMCE bank, a hotel and some cafés are located on Ave Mohammed V, the main road in from El-Jadida.

Places to Stay & Eat There are at least two basic hotels in Azemmour, the *Hôtel de la Victoire* (☎ 347157), 308 Ave Mohammed V and the *Hôtel Moulay Bouchaib* .

The *Café El Manzeh*, on Place du Souq, is the most pleasant of a series of cafés along the main road. In summer you could try *La*

Top Left: Oued Assaka, between Tiznit and Tafraoute (DS)
Top Right: Painted Rocks, Tafraoute (DS)
Bottom Left: Aït Souka village near Imlil (DS)
Bottom Right: Oued Ouarzazate seen from the Taourirt kasbah, Ouarzazate (DS)

Top: Todra Gorge (GC)
Bottom Left: Todra Gorge (GC)
Bottom Right: Kasbah Ben Moro, Skoura (DS)

Perle, a moderately priced restaurant on the beach (it's closed out of season).

Getting There & Away Local buses connect Azemmour with El-Jadida (Dr 3), but grands taxis (Dr 5 a head) are probably an easier bet as there are plenty of them. The bus station is located east of Ave Mohammed V, near the town centre. Some of the trains that go from Casablanca to El-Jadida also stop at Azemmour.

Sidi Bouzid
About 10 km south of El-Jadida is one of the area's better beaches, Sidi Bouzid. You can get local bus No 2 there from Place Mohammed ben Abdallah, near the Portuguese fortress. There is a rather expensive place to stay, the *Motel Club Hacienda* (☎ 348311), which has a pool, a tennis court and its own restaurant. Doubles cost Dr 281.

OUALIDIA
Seventy-six km down the coast from El-Jadida lies the slow but pleasant seaside fishing village of Oualidia. The drive (there are occasional buses) is a pleasant one, at least once you get past the Jorf Lasfar (formerly Cap Blanc) phosphate port. Your first impression of Oualidia as you arrive along the highway is of just another dusty roadside town. You have to take one of the turn-offs that lead quickly down to the village proper, situated between the sea and a lagoon. There's not much to do here, and out of the summer season it's quite dead. The village's main claim to fame is the oysters grown in the lagoon.

Places to Stay & Eat
The cheapest place to stay is *Camping Oualidiya* (Dr 3 a person, Dr 2 per car and Dr 30 per tent). There is no hot water.

Up on the main road is the *Hôtel La Lagune* (☎ 366477), which offers double rooms with half-board for Dr 350. The *Hôtel Shems* (☎ 366478), back in the village proper, costs Dr 400 for the same arrangement.

About 40 km north of Oualidia is a well-located unclassified hotel looking out over the Atlantic, the *Hôtel La Brise*.

The hotel restaurants and two others, *L'Araignée* and *Les Roches*, offer seafood menus – or you could just buy some from any of the fishers getting around town with the day's catch and cook it up yourself.

SAFI (ASFI)
Largely a modern fishing port and industrial centre, Safi sits on the Atlantic coast in a steep crevasse formed by the Oued (river) Chabah. Its industrial side is pretty obvious if you arrive from the north. A lot of Morocco's raw phosphate rock and fertilisers pass through here, the latter produced in chemical plants south of the town.

The sardine fleet is one of the world's biggest, although the canning industry has declined from the peaks it reached under the French protectorate – the majority of the canneries on the southern side of the city seem to have been closed for a long time.

The city centre has a lively and charming walled medina and souq, with battlements dating from the brief Portuguese period of occupation. Safi is also well known for its traditional potteries, and even if you are not interested in buying any souvenirs, it is worth walking around the potteries to see how they work.

History
Safi's natural harbour was known to the Phoenicians, and was probably used by the Romans later on. Involvement with Europeans didn't really begin until the Portuguese arrived on the scene, in 1508. By then, an important religious and cultural centre had already been in place since its foundation in the 12th century by the Almohads. The Portuguese built a fortress, using Essaouira as their base, but despite its monumental proportions (as with all Portuguese military installations), they didn't stay at Safi long, abandoning it in 1541.

This event didn't herald the end of European contact. In the late 17th century the French established a consulate at the port and were responsible for signing trading treaties

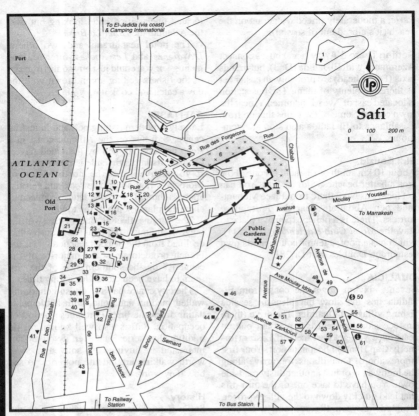

Safi

0   100   200 m

with the indigenous rulers. By the 19th century, however, the port had faded into insignificance. Its revival came in the 20th century, with the expansion of the sardine fishing fleet and the construction of a huge industrial complex for the manufacture fertilisers and sulphuric and phosphoric acids using local pyrites and phosphate ores.

Orientation

The bus and train stations are a few km to the south of the town centre – a long walk or a bus or taxi ride. The post office and the bulk of the cheaper hotels, restaurants and banks are on or near Place de l'Indépendance and just inside the medina walls. More expensive hotels, cafés, the main post office and the syndicat d'initiative are up the hill in the area around Place Mohammed V.

Information

Tourist Office The syndicat d'initiative (☎ 464553) is on a lane a little way off Place Mohammed V. Rachid, the man who staffs it, is friendly and keen to help out, although he can't offer you anything very concrete in terms of maps and the like. The office is open from 9 am to noon and 3 to 6.30 pm.

PLACES TO STAY		25	Restaurant Gegene	18	Great Mosque
		26	Café/Bar de la Poste	20	Chapelle Portugaise
11	Hôtel Sabah	27	Restaurant de Safi	21	Qasr al-Bahr
13	Hôtel & Café L'Avenir	35	Café Restaurant El	23	Post Office
14	Hôtel de Paris		Bahira	24	Local Buses (No 4
15	Hôtel Majestic	38	Cheap Café		to Sidi Bouzid)
16	Hôtel Essaouira	40	Cheap Café	28	BMCE Bank
17	Nameless Hotel	41	Café Safina	29	BMCI Bank
34	Hôtel Sevillana	53	Café Triomphe	30	Zanzi Bar
39	Hôtel L'Océan	54	Glacier Jour et Nuit	31	Shell Service
42	Hôtel Novelty	55	Café La Cascade		Station
43	Hôtel Anis	57	Café al-Marjan	32	Bank al-Maghrib
44	Hôtel Atlantide	58	Café Oukaïmeden	33	Place de
46	Hôtel Safir	59	Café Samif		l'Indépendance
56	Hôtel Assif			36	Crédit du Maroc
		OTHER		37	Cinema
PLACES TO EAT				45	Cinéma Atlantide
		2	Arches of Bab	47	Préfecture (Police)
1	Café La Chope		Khouas	48	Hôtel de Ville
3	Restaurant Les	4	Pottery Souq	49	Place Mohammed V
	Potiers	5	Bab Chabah	50	Banque Populaire
10	Juice Stand	6	Cemetery	51	Souna Mosque
12	Café	7	Kechla	52	Post Office (PTT)
19	Cheap Fish	8	Musée National de	60	Studio Samif
	Restaurants		Céramique		(Kodak)
22	Café/Pâtisserie	9	Mobil Service	61	Syndicat d'Initiative
	M'Zoughen		Station		

Money The BMCE and BMCI have branches on Place de l'Indépendance. The Banque Populaire is on Place Mohammed V.

Post & Telecommunications The phone section of the main post office (PTT), near Place Mohammed V, is open seven days a week from 8 am to 9.45 pm.

Film & Photography There is a Kodak processing shop called Studio Samif, on Ave Zerktouni.

Qasr al-Bahr

Overlooking the Atlantic and in impressively good shape is the main fortress erected by the Portuguese to enforce their short-lived control here. Built not only to protect the port but also to house the town governor, the 'Castle on the Sea' was restored in 1963.

There are good views from the south-west bastion, as well as a number of old Spanish and Dutch cannons dating from the early 17th century. Notably, two of the cannons were manufactured in Rotterdam in 1619 and two in the Hague in 1621.

Just to the right of the entrance is the prison tower. The prisoners went to the bottom, but you can climb to the top for some pretty views across the medina. Visiting hours are 8.30 am to noon and 2.30 to 6 pm and entry costs Dr 10. You can ask for a guide if you want.

Medina

Across the street from the Qasr al-Bahr lies the walled medina. Dominating the medina at its eastern end is the **Kechla**, a massive defensive structure with ramps, gunnery platforms and living quarters. It houses the **Musée National de Céramique**, a moderately interesting display of Safi pottery (although to be honest, a good walk around the potteries themselves is more interesting). The views over the medina and the Qasr al-Bahr, however, make a visit worthwhile.

Inside the medina are the remains of the so-called **Chapelle Portugaise**, which would have become Safi's cathedral had the Portuguese remained; as it turned out, they stayed only long enough to complete the choir. To get to it, head up Rue du Souq (the main thoroughfare through the medina) from Blvd Front de la Mer and turn right just after the **Great Mosque**. It's about 100 metres down the alley. Long used as a hammam, it's not in great condition. Shortly before Rue du Souq leads out of the medina, you'll notice, off to your left, a colourful **pottery souq**. The shopkeepers in here are pretty low-key, and little inclined to bargain. If you are intent on buying a few pieces, take the time to look at the different shops and establish some prices – then head on out to the potteries themselves and see if you can't strike a better deal. If not, you can always come back down to the market.

Potteries

Rue du Souq passes out of the medina by Bab Chabah. Outside this gate and to the left, you'll see an enormous series of arches; they look as though they were an aqueduct at one time but in fact were probably associated with the defensive walls of the medina. Straight ahead, on the hill opposite Bab Chabah, are Safi's famous potteries.

Opinions vary wildly on the quality of the ceramics produced here. Some of the many cooperatives devote themselves to the rather mundane production of tiles (the green variety you see on many important buildings throughout the country), but many manufacture a wide range of jars, vases, decorative plates, candlesticks and other objects. It is well worth taking a walk around and getting a look inside the workshops. Apart from the kilns, you can see potters moulding the clay for tiles and utensils, enamelling and glazing. If you're collared by a guide (possibly an asset here for the uninitiated), buying a small item or two from 'his' cooperative will save you forking out the usual guide's tip (not that there's anything to stop you paying a tip as well).

Places to Stay – bottom end

Camping About three km north of town, just into the coast road to El-Jadida, is the *Camping International*. It's a reasonable site, and much cooler than the town below in the hot summer months. They charge Dr 10 per person, Dr 9 per car, Dr 7 to pitch a tent, Dr 10 for a hot shower and Dr 20 to use the pool. You'll need to get a petit taxi up here from the centre or the bus station.

Hotels There's a fair choice of budget hotels in Safi, most of them clustered around the port end of Rue du Souq and along Rue de R'bat.

Inside the medina itself, the *Hôtel Essaouira* (☎ 464809) has comparatively small and gloomy rooms for Dr 30/50/60. Hot showers are Dr 5. It's adequate. Much the same is the *Hôtel de Paris*, where rooms with big saggy beds cost Dr 30 to Dr 70. Hot showers are Dr 5. A little farther in is a hotel with no name. It's cramped, but quite clean, and costs Dr 30/50, including cold showers. At the same price (but a desperate choice) is the *Hôtel Sabah*, a grim place with no shower at all.

Best value is the *Hôtel Majestic*, right next to the medina wall, at the junction of Ave Moulay Youssef and Place de l'Indépendance. It offers very clean, pleasant rooms with washbasin and bidet for Dr 30/60/90; shared showers with hot water are Dr 5 extra. The best rooms look out onto the Qasr al-Bahr and the ocean. The staff are friendly, and one of the managers speaks French, Spanish and some English.

Another good place is the *Hôtel L'Avenir*, which charges the same as the Majestic. The rooms have toilets and some have cold showers. The drawback is the café and small eatery inside, which can make it a bit noisy. There are good views from the roof.

On the south side of Place de l'Indépendance you can get yourself a tiny room for Dr 30/60 in the *Hôtel Sevillana*, Impasse Ben Hassan. The old guy who runs it claims there are hot showers for Dr 7. This place is not an attractive option.

Considerably better, but not up to the

Majestic's standard, is the *Hôtel L'Océan* (☎ 464207). The rooms are quite OK, and there is a shower (Dr 5 for a hot one) on each floor. Rooms again cost Dr 30/60. The *Hôtel Novelty* (☎ 422999) is unused to foreign guests. Its rooms (Dr 30/50) seem a little grim, but they are kept clean and the beds are fine. There are no showers, but there is a hammam nearby.

Places to Stay – middle

The only mid-range hotel down in the centre is the two-star *Hôtel Anis* (☎ 463078), Rue de R'bat, where you can get a comfortable room with private shower and toilet for Dr 118/141. They have a restaurant and café, too, and limited parking.

The other mid-range hotels are higher up in the city, around Place Mohammed V. Rooms at the *Hôtel Assif* (☎ 622311; fax 621862), Ave de la Liberté, are well decked-out, with heating, telephone and en suite bathrooms (Dr 157/187). The *Hôtel Les Mimosas* (☎ 463208), Rue Ibn Zeidoun, can be a little confusing to find; follow Ave de la Liberté off the map and the hotel is on the second block down a small street off to the right (coming from Place Mohammed V). It charges the same as the Assif, for rooms that are a little the worse for wear. The hotel has its own restaurant and bar, and across the road is the *Golden Fish* nightclub.

Places to Stay – top end

There are two four-star hotels in Safi, the cheaper of the two being the *Hôtel Atlantide* (☎ 462160/1), Rue Chaouki, at Dr 226/273 for singles/doubles. It has a little more character than its more expensive cousin up the road, the *Hôtel Safir* (☎ 464299), Ave Zerktouni. This one charges Dr 362/420 plus taxes.

Places to Eat

There are several cafés (and a good juice stand) along Rue du Souq, and at the port end a few snack stalls are generally set up at night, but the real treat in Safi is sampling the pokey little fish eateries. Several of them are clustered behind the Great Mosque, and it's worth making the effort to find them. A meal of superbly fresh fish with chips, salads and soft drinks will cost about Dr 20 per person.

Near the main port installations at the northern end of town is a bunch of similar places, run by somewhat more aggressive people. Driving through here, you'll probably encounter fishers rushing out in front of you waving half-cooked fish.

The *Café Restaurant El Bahia*, which

Rue du Souq, Safi

takes up the whole top side of Place de l'Indépendance, is a tourist trap. You get the same unexceptional food in the sit-down part as at the takeaway bar downstairs, and pay a lot more for the pleasure. The *Restaurant de Safi* and the *Restaurant Gegene*, on the same square, are much the same story. The *Restaurant Les Potiers*, outside Bab Chabah, looks promising from a distance but is little more than an unappetising café.

The only real alternative to these places are the restaurants in the bigger hotels.

There is an extremely pleasant fish restaurant a few km north of Safi on the coast road to Sidi Bouzid, *Le Refuge* (☎ 464354). It's closed on Mondays and is a little pricey, but is possibly *the* choice restaurant in the area. You'll need your own car or a petit taxi to get there.

There is no shortage of cafés along Place de l'Indépendance and Rue de R'bat. Up around Place Mohammed V, there is a wide selection of slightly fancier places, the most interesting being the cavernous *Al-Marjan*. You can pick up an ice cream at the *Glacier Jour et Nuit*.

Entertainment

You can get a soothing ale is the *Café/Bar de la Poste*, on Place de l'Indépendance, and a couple of the other cafés here may well serve alcohol inside. Otherwise, you're obliged to try the bars in the bigger hotels.

Getting There & Away

Bus Most of the CTM buses stopping in Safi originate elsewhere, so it might be a good idea to book in advance. Generally, though, you shouldn't have much trouble on the main runs. CTM has six buses a day to Casablanca, starting from 4.30 am. Its Marrakesh departure is at 8 pm and costs Dr 28.50. A bus to El-Jadida leaves at 8.30 am (Dr 37; 1st class) and another at 2.30 pm (Dr 24.50; 2nd class).

SATAS, the biggest bus company operating in southern Morocco, has a 7 am departure for Tan Tan, calling at Essaouira, Agadir and Tiznit on the way. It also has connections for Taroudannt and Tafraoute.

The Transit bus company has a bus to

Essaouira at 9 pm (Dr 32.50), and another for Agadir and Tiznit at 10 am.

To the right of the CTM window is a booth advertising five runs a day to Essaouira and two early morning buses to El-Jadida.

Transport Chekkouri has nine buses a day to the main bus station in Casablanca. The same company offers six runs a day to Marrakesh and four to Agadir.

Train There are two trains daily from Safi. The first, at 6 am, can get you to Oujda via Casablanca or Marrakesh – for either destination, you must change at Benguerir. The second goes to Rabat via Casablanca at 5 pm. Again, you must change at Benguerir.

Getting Around

Both the bus terminal (Ave Président Kennedy) and the railway station (Rue de R'bat) are quite some way from the centre of town, so it would be a good idea to either take a bus (No 7 from the bus station) or share a taxi from these places to the centre (Place de l'Indépendance). A bypass (Blvd Hassan II) circles the main part of town, so buses don't go through the centre.

AROUND SAFI
Beaches

The beaches in the immediate vicinity of Safi are not much chop, so you need to go a little farther afield. To the north you have the choice of **Lalla Fatna** (nine km) and **Cap Beddouza** (20 km). In summer there are local buses to both from Place de l'Indépendance. Otherwise, you'll have to rent a grand taxi if you don't have your own transport. The coast road along the first 40 km or so north of Safi is particularly breathtaking in parts.

About 30 km to the south is **Souira Kedima**. This place is not special, whatever anyone in Safi may tell you; however, shortly before it, after you've cleared the Maroc Phosphore plant, there are a couple of wild and woolly Atlantic beaches that beg to be stopped at – if the wind dies down.

Essaouira

Essaouira is the most popular of the coastal towns with independent travellers, and only rarely do you see package tourists here. The town has a magnificent beach that curves for miles to the south, and its atmosphere is in complete contrast to that of the souq cities of Marrakesh, Fès, Meknès and Tangier. It can be summed up in one word: relaxation. It is also Morocco's best-known windsurfing centre, and increasingly promotes itself as 'Wind City, Afrika'. Indeed, the Atlantic winds can be powerful, which is good news for windsurfers, but for much of the year bad news for sunbathers!

The fortifications of the old city are a mixture of Portuguese, French and Berber military architecture, and their massiveness lends a powerful mystique to the town. Inside them it's all light and charm. You'll find narrow lanes, whitewashed houses with blue painted doors, tranquil squares, artisans in tiny workshops beavering away at fragrant thuya wood, friendly cafés, and barely a hustler in sight. Here, for a refreshing change, you aren't made to feel like a walking wallet.

The bad news is that Essaouira's reputation is spreading, and its tranquillity can be stretched to breaking point in summer. Rooms can be difficult to find even outside the summer months.

History
As far back as the 7th century BC, Phoenician sailors had discovered this part of the Moroccan coast, and it is believed the Romans followed in their footsteps. The main evidence for this comes from the little offshore islands, which were celebrated in ancient times for being the site of manufacture of purple dyes (much used by the Romans). It is from this activity that the islets derived their name: the Purple Isles (Îles Purpuraires).

It was the Portuguese who established a commercial and military bridgehead here towards the end of the 15th century, which they named Mogador. They lost it in 1541, however, and the coastal town fell into decline.

Most of what stands today is the result of a curious experiment. In 1765, Sultan Sidi Mohammed bin Abdallah hired a French architect, Théodore Cornut, to design a city suitable for foreign traders. Known from then on as Essaouira, it became an open commercial link with Europe until the French protectorate was established, in 1912, at which time it was rebaptised Mogador and lost much of its importance. With independence, in 1956, it again became Essaouira.

Orientation
Essaouira is a pretty compact place. Most of the cheaper hotels, restaurants, cafés, banks and shops are concentrated in or near the western third of the old town. The bus station and grands taxis are about one km to the north-east of the walled town, in a particularly depressing part of Essaouira's small-scale version of urban sprawl.

Information
Despite the signs, there is no functioning tourist office. There are three banks around Place Prince Moulay Hassan. All are good for exchange, and the BMCE should do credit-card cash advances.

The post office is a 10-minute walk from Place Prince Moulay Hassan. The phone office, two doors down on the left, is open Monday to Saturday but only during normal working hours. An alternative for making phone calls and sending faxes is Jack's Kiosk, on Place Prince Moulay Hassan.

Ramparts
You can walk along most of the ramparts on the seaward part of town and visit the two main forts (skalas) during daylight hours. The **Skala du Port** (closed at lunchtimes) has an entry charge of Dr 10. This bastion was designed to protect the town's sea trade, and today affords picturesque views over the busy fishing port and of the Île de Mogador.

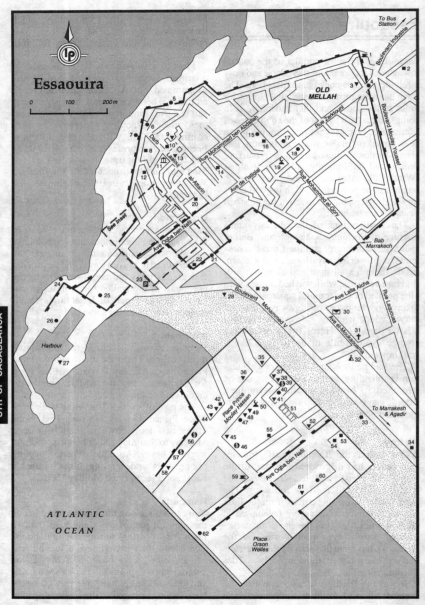

STH OF CASABLANCA

PLACES TO STAY

2	Hôtel Argana
8	Hôtel Smara
10	Hôtel Majestic
12	Hôtel des Remparts
14	Hôtel Chakib
16	Hôtel des Amis
20	Hôtel Tafraout
22	Hôtel du Tourisme
29	Hôtel des Iles
32	Camping International
34	Hôtel Tafoukt
42	Hôtel Beau Rivage
53	Hôtel Mechouar
54	Hôtel Sahara
55	Hôtel Villa Maroc

PLACES TO EAT

3	Cheap Eats
9	Restaurant Riad
13	Restaurant El Khaima
27	Chez Sam Restaurant
28	Restaurant Chalet de la Plage
35	Sam's Fast Food
36	Café/Pâtisserie L'Opéra
37	Café de la Place
38	Driss Pâtisserie
41	Chez Toufik
43	Café de France
44	Café Marrakech
45	Restaurant Essalam
48	Snack Stand
49	Jack's Kiosk
52	Restaurant l'Horloge
58	Restaurant Bab Laachour
61	Restaurant El Minzah

OTHER

1	Café
4	Bab Doukkala
5	Bab al-Bahr
6	Entry to Ramparts
7	Skala de la Ville
11	Museum
15	Spice, Herbs & Cures Shop
17	Souqs
18	Souqs
19	Mosque
21	Bab es-Sebaa
23	Car Parking
24	Skala du Port
25	Customs & Fish Market
26	Shipyards
30	Post Office (PTT)
31	Church
33	Fanatic Fun Center & Café
39	BMCE Bank
40	Carpet & Curio Shops
46	Crédit du Maroc
47	Afalkai Art
50	Mosque
51	Carpet & Curio Shops
56	Banque Populaire
57	Banque Commerciale du Maroc
59	Café
60	Galerie d'Art
62	Bab al-Minzah

Orson Welles spent some time here, too, again working on his film *Othello*. A rather dreary little square was named in his honour in 1992.

The **Skala de la Ville** is more impressive still, with its collection of 18th and 19th-century brass cannon from various European countries, particularly Spain and Holland. There's no entry charge to this part.

Just off the coast to the south-west is the Île de Mogador, on which there's another massive fortification. It's actually two islands and several tiny islets, the famed Purple Isles of antiquity. There is a disused prison on the biggest of the islands. These days, the islands are a sanctuary for Eleanore's falcon – a rare breed – and other birds. Visits are normally prohibited.

Museum

The museum, on Darb Laalouj al-Attarin, has displays of jewellery, costumes and weapons. Given the history of this town, it could be better. It has, in any case, been closed for refurbishment since 1992. Maybe it'll look better if and when it reopens. If you're determined to get in, you may be able to convince someone to open it up. There is nothing to distinguish the museum from the surrounding buildings, so you'll have to ask one of the local shopkeepers to show you which one it is.

Art Expositions

Essaouira plays host to a number of European artists, some of whom have bought houses and apartments in the old town. One of them is Frederic Damgaard, who runs a Galerie d'Art on Ave Oqba ben Nafii, where he and some of the others sometimes display their work.

Beach & Watersports

The beach stretches some 10 km down the

coast to the sand dunes of Cap Sim. On the way you'll pass the ruins of an old fortress and pavilion partially covered in sand, as well as the wreck of a ship. As Essaouira gains in popularity, it is becoming one of the classic windsurfing destinations. Along the beach, shortly before the Hôtel Tafoukt, you'll find at least two places renting windsurfing equipment. Fanatic Fun Centre, a German-run place, charges Dr 100 per hour for full gear. Next door is a more recently established Moroccan equivalent which, when it gets properly up and running, should have competitive prices. Both organise horse-riding excursions along the beach towards Cap Sim (not cheap, and usually only possible in summer). Fanatic Fun Centre can organise more ambitious horse riding excursions farther into the interior, lasting up to a couple of weeks. Out of season, contact Ludmilla de Wendau (☎ 1-42.51.81.59), 6 Rue Garreau, 75018 Paris.

Places to Stay – bottom end

Camping The best camp site is the one near Diabat (see the Diabat section).

Camping International, along Blvd Mohammed V in Essaouira, is nothing but a patch of dirt with no shade whatsoever. You'd have to be hard-up to stay here. In case you are, it costs Dr 7 per person, Dr 8 per car, Dr 10 for electricity and up to Dr 20 to pitch a tent. Hot showers are available.

Hotels The three places traditionally most popular with travellers continue to lead the way among the budget hotels. If you arrive later in the day, don't be surprised to find them full. The first (and probably the most attractive, because of the sea views) is the *Smara Hôtel* (☎ 472655), Rue de la Skala, which is quiet, clean and friendly and offers singles/doubles/triples for Dr 42/65/80. The rooms with sea views are much sought after, so you may have to wait a day or so before you can get one. The same views can be had from the roof – which is not a bad place to catch some sun protected from the wind. Showers cost an extra Dr 2, and breakfast is available for Dr 15.

The second place is the *Hôtel Beau Rivage* (☎ 472925), overlooking Place Prince Moulay Hassan. It is decent value, clean and friendly. Hot water is available most of the time, but it has to be said that the prices are beginning to outstrip the quality of the place. Rooms with two beds and no shower cost Dr 70. The same with private shower is Dr 120. The manager is friendly enough, and sells films and other odds and ends at his reception desk. A good pâtisserie and café next door mean that one of the best spots on the square for breakfast is just outside the front door.

The third place is the *Hôtel des Remparts*, a big building on three floors with a vast roof terrace. Unfortunately, few of the rooms have sea views, and some of them could do with a bit of sea air. Singles/doubles cost Dr 60/90, including use of a shared shower (hot water), and some rooms are equipped with a bath (cold water only). It's clearly not as good as the Smara, especially at the prices, but it's quite acceptable.

A decent place, though not as popular (perhaps because it's a few more minutes from the main square), the *Hôtel du Tourisme*, Rue Mohammed ben Massaoud, offers clean, quiet singles/doubles for Dr 36/47. Hot showers are available for Dr 5. They also have bigger rooms that sleep up to four, and some rooms with views towards the port and beach.

The *Hôtel des Amis* (☎ 473188) is a huge, sprawling place, but pretty poor. The rooms are uninviting, to say the least, the showers are cold and the sheets are decidedly unclean.

The *Hôtel Majestic*, 40 Darb Laalouj al-Attarin, is old and just as basic. Rooms cost Dr 50/80 – well over the top for what's on offer. The only shower (cold) is right by reception.

Farther afield is the fairly modern *Hôtel Chakib*, which charges Dr 35/70/80 for singles/doubles/triples with shared bathroom (cold water only). It's ordinary but acceptable.

Another fairly modern-looking place is the *Hôtel Argana*. Rooms here are OK for Dr 41/55/85, but the awful, dusty, shantytown location makes it a last choice for the desperate.

Going up in price, the one-star *Hôtel Tafraout* (☎ 472120), 7 Rue de Marrakech (off Rue Mohammed ben Abdallah), is clean, comfortable and friendly. Singles/doubles without private bathroom cost Dr 60/80, while those with bathroom cost Dr 70/100. There's hot water in the showers. The 'double' rooms contain a double and a single bed.

Places to Stay – middle

The two-star *Hôtel Sahara* (☎ 472292), Ave Oqba ben Nafii, has a mixed bag of rooms, so if you can get a look at a few before deciding, so much the better. Singles/doubles without shower or toilet cost Dr 105/133 plus tax. Those with shower and toilet are Dr 123/155 plus taxes. There is hot water in the evenings.

Next door is the *Hôtel Mechouar* (☎ 472018), something of a strange place at which few people seem to stay (which is good news if everything else is full). It looks rather like a London Tube tunnel, at the end of which is a noisy bar. As for the rooms, you have the choice of singles/doubles without shower (Dr 74/95) or rooms with cold shower (Dr 95/110). The only hot water is in a shared shower and is unreliable.

Going up in price, there's the three-star *Hôtel Tafoukt* (☎ 784504/5; fax 784416) at 98 Blvd Mohammed V, which has 40 self-contained singles/doubles for Dr 232/285. For the price, the rooms are hardly special, although they're clean, comfortable and have phones. There is a restaurant and bar, and the hotel is virtually on the beach, although a bit of a walk from where things are happening.

Places to Stay – top end

The four-star *Hôtel des Îles* (☎ 472329; fax 472472), Blvd Mohammed V, is closer to the old town than the Tafoukt, but although equipped with pool, bar, nightclub and the conveniences you would expect from such a hotel, it is hardly exciting. Its 70 rooms start at Dr 398/506 for basic singles/doubles and

rise to Dr 2000 for the main suite. All prices are exclusive of taxes.

The *Villa Maroc* (☎ 473147; fax 472806), located just inside the city walls, at 10 Rue Abdallah ben Yassin, is one of those rare top-grade establishments well worth paying for. Consisting of two renovated 18th-century houses, the villa contains only a dozen or so rooms, so booking well ahead is essential – they can be full up for months. Singles/doubles cost Dr 415/515 plus taxes. Guests (only) can eat in the restaurant or in one of the several salons – a meal costs Dr 130.

Places to Eat

Breakfast About the most popular and relaxing place for a slow breakfast is Place Prince Moulay Hassan. The *Driss Pâtisserie* has a good range of croissants and other pastries to get the day going. Equally good is the *Café/Patisserie L'Opéra*, which spills out in front of the Hôtel Beau Rivage. The *Café de France* is popular with locals right through the day, as is the *Café Marrakech*. The *Café de la Place* is not hot on pastries but is a decent spot for coffee. The food is otherwise mediocre (about Dr 30 for a main course and an outrageous Dr 10 to Dr 15 for soups). Some people spend the better part of a day on the square, slowly shifting from café to café with the moving sunlight.

Restaurants For simple snacks and cheap hole-in-the-wall-type food, there are a few little places along Rue Mohammed ben Abdallah, Rue Zerktouni and in the old mellah just inside Bab Doukkala.

On Place Prince Moulay Hassan, you'll find two great snack stands for excellent baguettes stuffed with meat, salad and just about anything else you want. These cost Dr 10 to Dr 15. There's a reasonable food stall next to the Hôtel Chakib too.

The *Restaurant L'Horloge*, tucked away on a shady little square close to the inner walls of the old town, is a popular place with travellers, either for a mint tea or a moderately priced Moroccan meal (the cheapest menu features an omelette as its main dish and costs Dr 25). Just near here is the *Restaurant Chez Toufik*, which has been done up as a traditional Berber salon. It's more expensive, and open only in the evenings – you come more for the setting than the food, which is nothing amazing.

Deservedly popular is the *Restaurant Essalam*, on Place Prince Moulay Hassan, where you can pick up an excellent meal for around Dr 35. The tajine is exceptionally good. The restaurant is generally packed with foreigners, with good reason. They take credit cards here.

A good little place to hunt out for seafood can be the *Restaurant Riad*, at the end of an alley off Rue Mohammed ben Abdallah. If they hit you with stories about bad fishing conditions, they'll only have the usual couscous (Dr 49) and tajine (Dr 60) fixed menus, which are unexciting at best.

Another place with a slight twist is the *Restaurant Dar Baba*, which attempts to do a small range of Italian dishes. It's just by the Hôtel Tafraout.

The *Restaurant El Minzah*, Ave Oqba ben Nafii, has set menus for about Dr 60, and is a perfectly adequate if uninspiring choice.

A step up in the price scale, with a more formal atmosphere, the *Restaurant El Khaima* is set back on a small square off Darb Laalouj al-Attarin. You can eat on the patio or upstairs and inside. Main courses generally cost about Dr 60, and they offer two fixed menus: a cheapie at Dr 70, and a seafood splashout at Dr 160.

A long-standing institution famous throughout Morocco is *Chez Sam Restaurant*, at the far end of the port area, past the boat builders. It looks like it's been transported from some windswept cove on the coast of Cornwall or Brittany, and has a delightfully eccentric atmosphere. Chez Sam specialises in seafood. The cuisine is excellent. You can either eat à la carte (reckon on about Dr 100 a head, including wine) or take one of the two set menus (Dr 60 or Dr 140). Ask for recommendations on the best fish of the day. The restaurant is licensed (beer and wine), takes most major credit cards and is open daily for lunch and dinner. Don't leave Essaouira without having a meal here.

Back on Place Prince Moulay Hassan, the licensed *Restaurant Bab Laachour* also

Breadmaker at work

specialises in seafood. It's probably as good as Chez Sam and the salads are excellent. You're looking at Dr 70 for a full meal.

The *Restaurant Chalet de la Plage* is right on the beach, just outside the city walls. It offers four-course meals for Dr 80 (extra for cheese, tea and coffee). Main courses á la carte range from Dr 40 to Dr 70, and wine is possibly more expensive here than in any of the other restaurants. It's open for dinner only.

Entertainment
Apart from drinking in the licensed restaurants, Essaouira doesn't have many night-time alternatives. Local drinkers gather in the bar under the Hôtel Mechouar. More up-market tipplers can head to the bar at the Hôtel des Îles – which also has a nightclub.

Things to Buy
Essaouira is the main centre for thuya carving, and the quality of the work is superb. Many of the carvers have workshops under the Skala de la Ville, and they're very accommodating, so you can walk around and look at what they are doing without any pressure to buy (but because there's no hard sell, don't expect to be able to reduce their stated prices by much).

A quality store where you can inspect a whole range of thuya wood products, from tables to bizarre life-size statues, is Afalkai, on Place Prince Moulay Hassan. Not the cheapest place around, it will nevertheless give you a good feel for prices and for what's available.

There are also quite a few craft shops in the immediate vicinity, with an equally impressive range of goods. Interesting chess pieces are the only thing you won't find here; although they are made in Essaouira, most are very plain indeed.

Carpet and rug shops, as well as bric-a-brac, jewellery and brassware shops, are clustered together in the narrow street, and on the small square between Place Prince Moulay Hassan and the ramparts that flank the Ave Oqba ben Nafii.

Thuya wood statue, Essaouira

Getting There & Away
Bus The bus station is about one km to the north-east of the old town centre. It's not signposted and is in a pretty awful area.

CTM is at window No 7. There is a bus at 10 am to Safi for Dr 21.50. Another at the same time goes to Casablanca (Dr 56; 6½ hours) via El-Jadida (Dr 40.50). The fast midnight bus to Casa costs Dr 85.50 (five hours). The 12.30 pm bus to Agadir costs Dr 37 (about three hours).

SATAS has a more extensive network in the south than CTM. It, too, runs a 10 am bus to Casablanca via El-Jadida, for about the same price. Buses to Agadir and on to Tiznit leave at 5.30, 9 and 11.30 am and 9.30 pm. There is a 9.30 am departure to Tan Tan, and two buses to Safi, at 1 and 6 pm. The daily bus to Marrakesh leaves at 7 pm.

You can also get tickets on smaller lines to Safi (window No 3; up to 10 services a day) and Marrakesh (window No 9; up to seven runs a day). The Marrakesh bus costs Dr 29 and takes about 3½ hours.

Several other private-line buses also do the run to Casablanca, for about Dr 60. Other destinations include Rabat, Taroudannt and Tafraoute.

Train Supratours, which has an office in the Hôtel des Îles, runs buses to connect with trains. The Supratours bus to Marrakesh train station leaves at 6.30 pm and takes 2½ hours; it's more expensive than a normal bus. You can buy a through ticket from here to any destination served by train.

Taxi The grand taxi lot is next to the bus station. The fare to Agadir (or nearby Inezgane) is Dr 50.

Getting Around
The blue petits taxis are a good idea for getting to and from the bus station. You can also take a ride around town in one of the horse-drawn calèches that gather just outside Bab Doukkala.

AROUND ESSAOUIRA
Diabat
Close to Cap Sim and inland about a km through sand dunes and scrub is the Berber village of Diabat, which became a legend among hippies in the 1960s after a visit by Jimi Hendrix. It subsequently became a freak colony similar to those on the beaches of Goa (in India), but was cleared by the police in the mid-1970s following the murder of several freaks by local junkies. These days it has returned to its own tranquil self, but there seems little reason to visit.

Less than one km farther up the rocky track from Diabat is the long-established *Auberge Tangaro* (☎ 785735). Once a rather basic and cheap place to stay, it has been done up by its Italian owner and costs Dr 450 a double with half-board. Driving from Essaouira, take the coast road for Agadir, and turn up the track just after the bridge about five km out of town. The track is lousy. You

can camp next door – this a better place to do so than at the camping ground in Essaouira.

Sidi Kaouki
About eight km farther south is another windsurfing spot that is fast growing in popularity. About the only way to get here is with your own car, which you'd need anyway to carry all the windsurfing gear.

Agadir

Agadir was destroyed by an earthquake in 1960. Although since rebuilt, it can no longer be described as a typical Moroccan city. Most of the activity centres on catering for the short-stay package tourists from Europe, who arrive daily by the planeload in search of sun, sand and a sanitised version of the mysteries of the Barbary Coast. Agadir's high tourist profile often leads people to forget its growing importance as a commercial and fishing port – a big chunk of Morocco's sardine catch now comes through Agadir, and the driver arriving in Agadir from the north can hardly fail to notice the ugly, sprawling port facilities.

The reek of Ambre Soleil and the rustle of *Paris Match*, *Der Spiegel* and the airmail *Sunday Times* fill the air. Not that it's unpleasant – it's just that it could be any resort town on the northern Mediterranean coast. Modern Agadir, not the most attractive of towns (cheap North African architectural 'styles' predominate), is also one of the more expensive cities in Morocco. However, it is a take-off point for visits east and farther south, so you'll probably find yourself staying here at least overnight.

History
Little is known of Agadir's distant past, but in 1505 an enterprising Portuguese mariner decided to build himself a fort, Santa Cruz de Cap de Gué, a few km north of the modern city. Sold to the Portuguese government eight years later, it became a busy centre of commerce, visited by Portuguese, Genoese

and French merchants. Retaken by the Moroccans in 1541 and subsequently used as the main outlet for products (especially sugar cane) from the Souss region, it slowly began to decline, and was finally eclipsed by the rise of Essaouira in the late 18th century. A century later, only a dozen houses were left standing.

It was here that the Germans took gunboat diplomacy to the limit with France in 1911, sending the warship *Panther* to make noises off the Agadir coast. They managed to avoid going to war on this occasion, but only for three years.

The earthquake that struck on 29 February 1960 flattened the town and killed 15,000 people. Agadir has since been completely rebuilt, and continues to grow as Morocco's top beach resort.

Orientation

Agadir's bus station and most of the budget hotels are in a small area in the north-east of the town. From here it's about a 20-minute walk down to the beach, lined with cafés, restaurants and expensive hotels. Most of the banks and the main post office are located between the beach and Ave du Prince Moulay Abdallah.

Information

Tourist Office The Délégation du Tourisme (☎ 822894, 841367) is in the central market area, just off Ave Prince Héritier Sidi Mohammed (Immeuble A). It's open standard weekday office hours, and has the usual brochures but not a lot else.

More useful is the syndicat d'initiative (☎ 840307) on Blvd Mohammed V at the junction with Ave du Général Kettani. Here, you can buy a small *Guide d'Agadir*, which contains some useful information (such as lists of doctors and the like) for Dr 10. They also have a notice board with bus timetables and details of market days in surrounding towns. It's open from 9 am to noon and 3 to 4.30 pm Monday to Saturday, and on Sunday mornings.

Money Most banks have branches in Agadir.

The BMCE and BMCI, both at the beach end of Ave du Général Kettani, have ATMs, and the BMCE has a bureau de change. If you need money on the weekend and the ATMs fail you, about your only chance will be the big hotels, such as the Beach Club – they change only cash and cheques.

The American Express representative is Voyages Schwartz (☎ 841082; fax 841066), 87 Place du Marché Municipal, Ave Hassan II. They are in the Mopatours office.

Post & Telecommunications The main post office, on Ave du Prince Moulay Abdallah near the Hôtel de Ville (town hall), is open daily from 8.30 am to 6.45 pm. There is another post office (La Poste), on Rue du 29 Février, in the budget hotel area.

The phone office is in the central post office. It's open seven days a week from 8 am to 9 pm. There are also a couple of *Téléboutiques*, one of them about 50 metres up from the *Hôtel Talborjt*. They generally stay open until 10 pm.

Foreign Consulates Foreign consulates in Agadir include:

Belgium
    Consulate: Impasse d'Amman (☎ 842573)
    Visas: Immeuble Rachdi, Ave Hassan II (☎ 844080)
France
    Blvd Mohammed Saadi (☎ 840826)
Italy
    Rue du Souvenir (☎ 823013)
Netherlands
    Visa office for Moroccan citizens only (see under Belgium)
Norway
    c\- Institution al-Hanane, Cité Anouar Souss (☎ 821987)
Spain
    49 Rue Ibn Batouta, Secteur Mixte (☎ 845681; fax 845843)
Sweden
    Rue de l'Entraide (☎ 823048)
U K
    Hôtel Sud Bahia, Rue des Administrations Publiques (☎ 823741)

Language Schools The American Language Center (☎ 821589) has a branch at 6

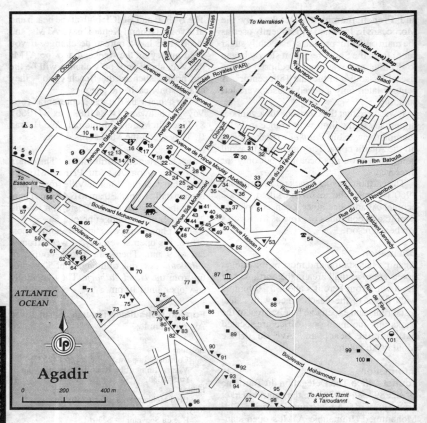

Agadir

ATLANTIC
OCEAN

0   200   400 m

Impasse de Baghdad. The Moroccan Insti-
tute of Management (☎ 823356), on Ave
Hassan II, operates as a representative for the
International Language Centre.

Newsstands There are several decent newsstands with a fair selection of European and
international press (usually a day or two
late). The one on the corner of Ave Hassan II
and Ave des FAR is as good as any.

Laundry There is a coin-operated laundry
(the only one in Morocco?) at the Hôtel
al-Madina Palace.

Film & Photography You can buy film and
have it developed in several places around
town. New Labcolor, on Ave du Prince
Moulay Hassan, is one of the nearest to the
budget hotel area.

Medical Services & Emergencies The
Clinique Al-Massira, on Ave du Prince
Moulay Abdallah, is as good as any. The
Guide d'Agadir contains lists of doctors,
dentists, clinics and pharmacies. The main
tourist office also posts a list of doctors. An
all-night chemist (☎ 820349) is located near
the Hôtel de Ville.

PLACES TO STAY

3 Camping Ground
7 Résidence Tilila
10 Hôtel Petite Suède
14 Hôtel Sud Bahia
29 Hôtel Talborjt
31 Hôtel Itrane
32 Hôtel Ayour
38 Atlantic Hôtel
41 Hôtel Kamal
44 Hôtel Les Palmi-
ers
45 Résidence Sacha
46 Hôtel Aladin
49 Résidence
Yasmina
66 Sheraton
68 Hôtel Ali Baba
69 Hôtel Anezi
70 Hôtel Europa Safir
71 Hôtel Tafoukt
76 Hôtel Al Medina
Palace
77 Hôtel Salam
85 Hôtel Tagadirt
86 Hôtel
Transatlantique
89 Hôtel Adrar
92 Hôtel Mabrouk
94 Résidence Club
La Kasbah
97 Agadir Hôtel
99 Hôtel Solman
100 Hôtel Les Cinq
Parties du Monde

PLACES TO EAT

6 Restaurant
Marine Heim (bei
Hilde)
12 Restaurant
Darkoum
13 Restaurant La
Tour de Paris
19 Cafés
23 Restaurant La
Dolce Vita
24 Restaurant Le
Dôme
25 Restaurant Via
Veneto
36 Restaurant
Chahoua
40 Restaurant
Scampi

44 Restaurante Les
Palmiers
47 Restaurant La
Tonkinoise
48 Steak House
53 Café Tafarnout
58 Restaurant Le
Côte d'Or
59 Restaurant Don
Vito
60 Café Le Kermesse
61 Restaurant Le Nil
Bleu
62 Restaurant Le
Vendôme
63 Hollywood Fast
Food
64 The Palace
Bar/Café
72 Restaurant La
Perla del Mare
73 Restaurants
74 Restaurant
Golden Gate
75 Pizzeria & Gelato
78 Café Le Central &
Disco
79 Restaurant Imin
80 Restaurant Jockey
81 Restaurant Pizza
Pino
82 Restaurant Le
Petit Dôme
83 Restaurant La
Mamma
90 Restaurant El
Marrakchi
91 Restaurant Grill
du Soleil
93 Restaurant Jazz
97 Restaurant
Complex
98 Kim Hoa Vietnam-
ese Restaurant

OTHER

1 American
Language Center
2 Jardin de Olhâo
4 Budget
5 Hertz
8 BMCE Bank
(ATM & Bureau
de Change)
9 BMCI Bank (ATM)
11 Royal Air Maroc

15 Tour Agents
16 Banque Populaire
17 Newsstand
18 Supratours
20 Cinéma Rialto
21 Bar Crystal
22 Voyages
Schwartz (Ameri-
can
Express)
26 Uniprix
27 Central Market
28 Tourist Office
30 Téléboutique
(Phones)
33 Clinique Al
Massira
34 Post Office
35 Hôtel de Ville
37 Liquor Store
39 Car/Motorbike
Hire
42 Place de
l'Espérance
43 Air France
50 Travel Agents
(Local
Excursions &
Charter Flights)
51 New Labcolor
(Kodak)
52 Royal Tennis Club
of Agadir
54 Téléboutique
(Phones)
55 Vallée des
Oiseaux (Zoo)
56 Syndicat
d'Initiative
57 Public Swimming
Pool
65 Banque Populaire
& Clinic
67 Vallée des
Oiseaux
73 Shopping Mall
84 Newsstand
87 Musée Municipal
88 Stadium
95 Cabaret Al
Hambra
96 Newsstand
101 Place Taxis et
Bus (Local
Buses &
Taghezout
Grands Taxis)

STH OF CASABLANCA

The Moroccan Red Cross (☎ 821472) might be a useful emergency contact.

Musée Municipal

This modest museum contains displays of southern Moroccan folk art provided by Dutch art lecturer and long-time resident of Marrakesh Bert Flint (he has opened up the Maison Tiskiwin in Marrakesh with further displays). It's open Monday to Saturday from 9.30 am to 1 pm and 2.30 to 6 pm.

Vallée des Oiseaux

This tiny 'zoo', for want of a better word, runs along a narrow strip between Ave Hassan II and under Blvd Mohammed V, with an entrance on both sides. It costs Dr 5 to get in (Dr 3 for children). The zoo is closed in the middle of the day.

Kasbah

A good hour's walk to the north-east of the town is what's left of the old kasbah. A Dutch inscription from 1746 still adorns the gateway, exhorting visitors to 'fear God and honour your king'. The fort was originally built in 1540, overlooking the former Portuguese emplacement, and was restored and regarrisoned in 1752, lest Portugal decide to make a comeback. The ramparts were partially restored after the 1960 earthquake, but nothing remains within. Thousands of people lie where they died when the quake hit.

Jardim de Olhão

These rather odd-looking gardens mark the twinning of Agadir with the Portuguese town of Olhão, and commemorate the 'historical ties' that have so often had Morocco and Portugal at loggerheads. The gardens are open from 2.30 to 6.30 pm only.

Beach & Watersports

The main reason for being in Agadir is to go to the beach. When the Atlantic winds are blustering elsewhere along the coast, ...'s beach usually remains unruffled. In ... the main beach hotels, you are sup- ... a fee for use of the beach,

deckchairs, umbrellas and the like. In practice you can generally plonk your towel down somewhere without any hassle.

In the area down in front of the Hôtel Beach Club, you can rent various implements to enhance your enjoyment of the water, including pedalos, jetskis, surfboards and surfskis (surf is not one of Agadir's strengths). It ain't cheap – an hour on a surfski (which usually means paddling around) costs Dr 150. A surfboard will set you back Dr 100 an hour, and a wetsuit will be another Dr 30 an hour.

Farther south down the beach you'll find people with horses, camels and dune trikes for hire. Prices, again, are high.

Most of the larger hotels organise all sorts of activities for their guests. Those interested in fishing may want to enquire about the possibilities. Otherwise, try Sports Évasion Maroc (☎ 846122), next to the Hôtel Sud Bahia, which claims to organise ocean fishing trips, including shark fishing. They also offer horse riding.

Organised Tours

Agadir is a thriving centre for locally organised tours, most aimed at charter flight tourists who are in Morocco for a week or two and are anxious to do more than lounge around on the sand. There is any number of agents, many of them branch offices of European package-tour companies. You'll find a bunch of them clustered around the intersection of Ave Hassan II and Ave des FAR. There are more around Ave Sidi Mohammed.

Principal destinations include Marrakesh, Taroudannt, Tafraoute and Immouzzer des Ida Outanane. Of these, only the latter can be a little difficult (but hardly impossible) to do under your own steam – which is by far the better way to approach them, especially as none of the organised trips is cheap. They range from Dr 200 for a day at Immouzzer to Dr 1400 for a day trundling about in a Land Rover.

Places to Stay – bottom end

Camping Agadir's camp site (☎ 846683) is not the worst of Moroccan camping grounds,

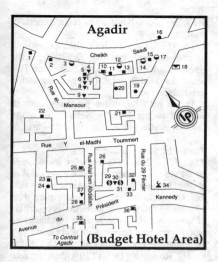

Agadir

(Budget Hotel Area)

To Central Agadir

PLACES TO STAY

1 Hôtel Excelsior
2 Hôtel Aït Laayoune
5 Hôtel Sindibad
11 Hôtel Massa
13 Hôtel Canaria
15 Hôtel Amenou
21 Hôtel El Bahia
22 Hôtel Moderne
23 Hôtel Select
26 Hôtel Diaf
28 Hôtel de la Baie
32 Hôtel La Tour Eiffel
33 Hôtel de Paris

PLACES TO EAT

4 Ice-Cream Place
6 Restaurant Ibtissam
7 Café Restaurant Coq d'Or
8 Restaurant Chahab
9 Restaurant Mille et Une Nuits
27 Restaurant Select
30 Restaurant Tamouate

OTHER

3 CTM (Buses)
10 Café Fairouz
12 SATAS (Buses)
14 Bus Company
16 Ensemble Artisanal
17 Bus Company
18 Post Office
19 American Language Center
20 Cinema Sahara
24 Douche Select
25 Café/Pâtisserie Oufella
29 BMCE Bank
31 Banque Populaire
35 Café Les Arcades
36 Café La Terrasse

but the ground is pretty stony and camper-vans predominate. It costs Dr 10 per person, Dr 10 for a car, Dr 10 to Dr 15 to pitch a tent (depending on its size), Dr 12 for electricity and Dr 7.50 for a hot shower. All this plus 14% tax. There's also a general grocery store.

Hotels Most of the budget hotels and a few of the mid-range hotels are concentrated in a small area around the bus terminal and Rue Allal ben Abdallah. In the high seasons, you must get into Agadir early in the day if you want to be sure of a room. If you arrive late, you may have to sleep out, or pay through the nose at an expensive hotel. Disappointed backpackers wandering around with no-where to stay are a common sight by 8 pm. By standards elsewhere in the country, you pay more for less in Agadir.

The two cheapest places here are also among the worst. The *Hôtel Canaria* (☎ 822291) costs Dr 30/40/62 for basic rooms, with a cold shower. You'll be lucky to get a room here anyway, as it's mainly in the brothel business. Whether or not the same can be said of the *Hôtel Massa* is hard to say, but it's a rather unfriendly

place. The basic but clean rooms cost Dr 30/40/60, and there's a cold shower.

With a little more money, the choices widen somewhat. Although the rooms are little better (and the locks are a joke), the *Hôtel Select*, down a lane off Rue Allal ben Abdallah, is a quieter, more pleasant place to stay than the above two. Rooms cost Dr 45/60. The hotel has no shower, but runs a public shower next door (Dr 4.50), which is guaranteed to be hot.

A trio of hotels charge Dr 70/90 for singles/doubles and are a definite improvement on the above: the *Hôtel La Tour Eiffel* (☎ 823712), *Hôtel Amenou* (☎ 823026) and *Hôtel Aït Laayoune* (☎ 824375). Despite the toilets, the Amenou is marginally better than the Tour Eiffel, and hot water seems a surer thing here. It's right by the bus offices (a mixed blessing) on Rue Yacoub el-Mansour. The pick of them, however, is the Aït Laayoune. Problem is, it's often full.

Just across the road, and another place that is often full, the *Hôtel Excelsior* (☎ 821028) has rooms without shower for Dr 66/90 (a hot shared shower costs Dr 5), and with shower for Dr 100/130. It's quite OK, without being spectacular.

The *Hôtel de la Baie* (☎ 823014), on the corner of Rue Allal ben Abdallah and Ave du Président Kennedy, is a mixed bag. The rooms without shower for Dr 49/66 (a hot, shared shower is Dr 5) are adequate, but certainly no better than those at the previous two hotels. The rooms with shower (Dr 75/96) are not too bad, although for a dollar or two more you could dramatically improve your quality of life elsewhere.

The *Hôtel Moderne* (☎ 823373), Rue Mehdi ibn Toummert, is in a quieter spot and offers parking space. Singles/doubles without shower are overpriced (Dr 90/110), but those with shower are quite acceptable (Dr 100/130). The receptionist is one of the grumpiest people in Agadir.

You need a little money for two of the best places in this area, both of which, you may as well know, act as brothels as well. The activity is usually pretty discreet, though, and shouldn't deter you from staying at them.

The better of the two is the *Hôtel de Paris* (☎ 822694), on Ave du Président Kennedy. It has clean and very comfortable little rooms (with washbasin and wardrobe) for Dr 80/100 without private bathroom, or Dr 136/166 with. The rooms are gathered around a peaceful courtyard dominated by a majestic old tree. You can sit up on the roof,

too. The shared hot shower is generally steaming.

The *Hôtel Diaf* is a little cheaper, and the rooms are fine. You pay Dr 100/150 for singles/doubles with private bathroom. Hot water is available only in the evening and is unreliable.

Those with hot-water problems can, in addition to the Douche Select, go to the Douche Étoile, behind the Hôtel de Paris.

Places to Stay – middle

The *Hôtel Les Cinq Parties du Monde* (☎ 845481) is a good, modern hotel on Ave Hassan II, near the local bus and grand taxi lots. Under normal circumstances there'd be no reason to stay in this particularly ugly part of town, but if you're having trouble elsewhere, or arrive here late at night and can't be bothered going farther afield, it's OK for a night. Rooms are Dr 70/120 without private bathroom, Dr 129/170 with bathroom.

If you want to get out of the budget hotel area, there is a fairly tranquil little place just off Ave du Général Kettani, the *Hôtel Petite Suède* (☎ 840779). Don't let them talk you into taking rooms with breakfast (you can get the same breakfast a lot cheaper in any café), but for Dr 140/173, the comfortable rooms with en suite bathroom are not a bad deal at all.

There are three hotels on Rue de l'Entraide, just on the beach side of Ave du Président Kennedy. The cheapest is the *Hôtel Itrane* (☎ 821407), which charges Dr 99/117 for reasonable singles/doubles but is often full.

The two-star *Hôtel Ayour* (☎ 824976), at No 4, is a modern establishment that even boasts a solarium. It has decent-sized rooms with private bathroom for Dr 164/194.

More expensive still, but very good, the *Hôtel Talborjt* (☎ 841832) offers pleasant, carpeted rooms, some overlooking lush gardens. They cost Dr 215/264 in the low season, Dr 222/275 in the high season, plus taxes.

Back up in the heart of the budget hotel area and near the buses are two slightly fancier hotels than the surrounding ones. The

Hôtel Sindibad (☎ 823477; fax 842474) has pleasant rooms with own phone. They also have a restaurant, and *glacier* for ice creams. Yes, the odd lady of the night has her base here, too (obviously a thriving business in Agadir).

Another comfortable place, and one of the better hotels in this range, is the *Hôtel el Bahia* (☎ 822724; fax 824515). Again, rooms have a phone, and in winter are centrally heated. The cheapest rooms cost Dr 98/130 (a hot shared shower is Dr 6). Rooms with shower only cost Dr 134/158, while those with full bathroom are Dr 170/200. The staff are helpful.

One often overlooked is the *Hôtel/Restaurant Les Palmiers* (☎ 843719), on Ave Sidi Mohammed. This friendly place is reasonably well located, near several restaurants and not too far from the beach. It has decent rooms priced at Dr 164/194.

A little more expensive but a fine two-star place to stay is the *Atlantic Hôtel* (☎ 843661/2), on Ave Hassan II. It's clean and comfortable, and has boiling hot water 24 hours a day. Rooms cost Dr 202/257. Breakfast is available in the pleasant, leafy courtyard. Better still, and with its own small pool, is the *Hôtel Aladin* (☎ 843228; fax 846071), Rue de la Jeunesse. They charge a trifle more than the Atlantic in the low season (Dr 215/264 plus taxes) and Dr 223/275 plus taxes in the high season.

From here on, prices start to climb well beyond the reach of many pockets. The *Hôtel Kamal* (☎ 842817; fax 843940), Ave Hassan II, is a perfectly acceptable place to stay, but breakfast is obligatory, so rooms cost Dr 272/357.

Places to Stay – top end

You will find no shortage of expensive hotels in Agadir. The bulk of them are inhabited by block-booked charter groups, which generally get a considerable discount on the normal individual prices.

At the lower end of the scale, and not in the most appealing position compared to some of its beachside counterparts, the *Hôtel Sud Bahia* (☎ 840782; fax 840863), off Ave du Général Kettani, charges Dr 365/493, including breakfast. The rooms are modern and in reasonable shape, with bathroom and phone, and there are 246 of them, so the place is unlikely to be full. There's a heated swimming pool out the back.

You'd be much better off, however, if you want this kind of hotel, hunting around the beachside places and seeing what kind of deal you can come up with. One of the newer, swankier hotels is the *Transatlantique* (☎ 842110; fax 842076). Their low-season rates start at Dr 362/460, plus taxes, and it's a much better place to stay than the Sud Bahia.

Places like the *Résidence Club La Kasbah* (☎ 823636) cost more like Dr 850/1360.

There are numerous such places up and down Agadir's beachfront, particularly along Blvd Mohammed V and Blvd du 20 Août and on the beach itself (you can get a full list from the tourist offices and in the *Guide d'Agadir*). They usually have swimming pools, restaurants, bars and other amenities. La Kasbah even has tennis courts.

Places to Eat

Agadir is crawling with restaurants and cafés – many, but by no means all, are a little on the expensive side. In addition to the following, a few more are marked on the map – the best idea, especially if you do have a bit of money to throw around, is to wander about and see what takes your fancy. The *Guide d'Agadir* also has a list of the more pricey places. Don't leave it too late – Moroccan foodies are no night owls, so a lot of places close their doors by 10 pm.

Breakfast There are plenty of cafés where you can ease into the day with breakfast. A particularly good one with fairly decent pastries is the *Café/Patisserie Oufella*, just across the road from the Hôtel Diaf, on Rue Allal ben Abdallah.

Another pleasant place for breakfast or a beer is the café by the municipal swimming pool, on the beachfront. A little farther south there is a string of cafés and restaurants up to a large open square.

Budget Restaurants A number of cheap restaurants and sandwich bars are on the same street as the bus terminals, and they're reasonable value, serving almost anything from seafood to kebab sandwiches.

Just at the back of the bus terminal street is a small plaza, four restaurants next to each other are very popular with travellers and night strollers from the tourist district in search of a change. They are the *Restaurant Chabab*, the *Restaurant Mille et Une Nuits*, the *Café Restaurant Coq d'Or* and the *Restaurant Ibtissam* (the latter means 'smile'). They might look expensive but they're not, and the food is very good. All offer you a choice of sitting inside or at tables in the open air. Typical prices are: couscous or tajine (about Dr 20), omelette (about Dr 10) and salads (up to Dr 10).

The *Restaurant Select*, just by the hotel of the same name, does a solid range of old favourites, and you can eat well for about Dr 20. Do *not* order the crêpes – they are awful. Similar in style but a few dirham more expensive is the *Restaurant Tamouate*, next to the BMCE branch on Ave du Président Kennedy.

Getting a little flasher, and commensurately more expensive, *Restaurant Les Palmiers* is under the hotel of the same name. It does similar food to the others, with little appreciable difference in quality. Main courses cost Dr 20 to Dr 40.

Just where Ave Sidi Mohammed runs into Blvd Mohammed V, you'll find a Vietnamese restaurant, *La Tonkinoise* and the incredibly tacky *Steak House*. The latter seems to attract a lot of people, but surely it can't be because of the Julio Iglesias-style duo playing in the gardens!

For a bizarre experience, try the *Restaurant Chahoua*, down a small street behind the post office. There's a liquor store across the road from this Korean restaurant, which seems purpose-built for the small community of Korean workers here. The place is simple and the food very authentic, and for a while you'll forget you're in Morocco as all the family and friends gather about the main table and dig in. The staff speak Korean and English, and maybe a little French. If it's been a while since you last read a Korean pulp novel or magazine, this is the place to come (videos too)! It's not really a budget traveller's haven – you could easily spend close to Dr 100 for a full meal – but it's worth it, and better value than the rather bland standard Vietnamese alternatives.

Expensive Restaurants The *Restaurant La Tour de Paris* is a luxury restaurant at the Ave du Général Kettani end of Ave Hassan II. The mainly French menu is tempting and the food of a reasonably high standard, but it costs a minimum of Dr 150 per person.

No Moroccan tourist city would be complete without at least one 'Moroccan experience'-style restaurant, where you can eat in lavish Moorish surroundings, be entertained with traditional music and be served by waiters in impeccably white robes and red fezzes. In Agadir, the *Restaurant Darkoum* is that place. It's on Ave du Général Kettani, near the Hôtel Sud Bahia, and it will set you back about Dr 150. If you're travelling through Morocco and want to do this sort of thing, wait for Fès, where most of the restaurants of this ilk are at least set in genuine old nobles' palaces.

One place that seems rather popular with Finns and locals is the *Restaurant Scampi*, Ave Hassan II, opposite the Hôtel Atlantic. They have an excellent range of dishes and the food is good. It isn't cheap, at around Dr 250 for two people (including wine), but at least it doesn't involve a long walk from the budget hotel zone.

Set right on the beach, near the Hôtel Tafoukt, is the classy *La Perla del Mare* (☎ 840065). It's not only classy, it's pricey.

Along Blvd du 20 Août, in among some of the swish hotels and tourist boutiques, is any number of expensive restaurants to choose from. *Restaurant Pizza Pino* and *La Mamma*, predictably enough, do Italian food. The *Jazz* and *El Marrakchi* are pricey Moroccan joints – expect to pay in excess of Dr 150 each for a full meal.

The Agador Hôtel complex contains several restaurants, including *Le Cap*, *Pub*

L'Oasis and the *Asmas Restaurant*. The latter puts on evening performances of Moroccan music during meals.

For Vietnamese food (about Dr 70 for a main meal), try the *Restaurant Kim Hoa*. It's a bit of a hike, down past La Kasbah hotel.

Entertainment

Bars & Nightclubs A lively little bar that's popular with the locals is located just by the southern entrance to the Vallée des Oiseaux. You can also get a beer at quite a lot of the beachfront restaurants and cafés, including the one by the swimming pool. Otherwise, there are many bars to choose from in the bigger hotels, if you want to rub shoulders with hordes of short-term visitors from every conceivable part of Europe.

For takeaways, you could try the liquor store opposite the Restaurant Chahoua, the Uniprix supermarket on Ave Hassan II or one of a couple of similar markets dotted about Agadir. Between them, there's a good choice of local and imported beers, wines and spirits.

Most of the bigger hotels have nightclubs. For a comprehensive list, consult the *Guide d'Agadir*. Remember that entry usually costs from Dr 50 up (a drink included), and subsequent drinks can cost as much again. The average backpacker doesn't drag around the kind of glad rags required to be allowed into most these places. If you like cabarets, maybe the *Alhambra Cabaret*, near the Hôtel Sahara on Blvd du 20 Août, is for you.

Theatre & Cinema The Alliance Franco-Marocaine (☎ 841313), 5 Rue Yahchech, puts on films, theatre and lectures. You can usually pick up their program in the syndicat d'initiative. Most of the performances are in French.

There are also a few cinemas scattered about town.

Things to Buy

Agadir is not a great place to pick up souvenirs. Most of what's on offer is trucked in from other parts of the country, and the steady stream of package tourists unaware of what's on offer elsewhere in the country keep prices up on low-quality goods. If you still want to look around, the Central Market is full of kitsch souvenir shops.

Getting There & Away

Air The new Al-Massira airport lies 28 km south of Agadir. Take the Tafraoute road if you're driving out there. The airport bank (cash and travellers' cheques only) is not always open, but there are restaurants and a tourist information counter. The bulk of the traffic through here consists of European charter flights.

RAM (☎ 840145) has an office on Ave du Général Kettani. Most of its flights, internal and abroad, go via Casablanca. There are several flights a day to Casa (Dr 585 one way; 50 minutes) and a few each week to Marrakesh (35 minutes). In addition, there are flights to Laayoune on Monday (via Tan Tan) and Tuesday (Dr 735 one way; 1½ hours direct). Two flights a week connect Agadir with Dakhla, too. RAM has a few direct international flights, including to Las Palmas (Canary Islands) for Dr 2575 one way.

Bus Although a good number of buses and grands taxis serve Agadir (and they should be adequate for the purposes of leaving), there is a huge bus and taxi station in the nearby town of Inezgane. It is quite possible that you'll be dropped here when you arrive. There are grands taxis and local buses between Agadir and Inezgane (see the following Taxi section and Getting There & Away under Inezgane).

In Agadir, all the bus companies have their terminals along Rue Yacoub el-Mansour, in the budget hotel area.

CTM has buses to Casablanca at 7.30 am and 9.30, 10 and 10.30 pm (Dr 117.50; 10 hours). The 10.30 pm bus goes on to Rabat (Dr 139) and Tangier (Dr 205.50; 14 hours). A bus for Essaouira (Dr 36.50) leaves at 7.30 pm, and goes on to Safi and El-Jadida. There are buses for Tiznit at 6.30 am (Dr 16) and 3.30 pm (Dr 24 mumtaz). At 8.30 pm there's a service to Laayoune (Dr 194.50), going on to Smara. The Dakhla bus leaves at 8 pm, and a bus for Taroudannt at 5.30 am (Dr 18.50).

You can also get on to buses bound for France and Belgium here. You need to book a week in advance. See the Getting There & Away chapter for more details.

SATAS is the other main company operating out of Agadir. It has several buses to Essaouira (Dr 38), Marrakesh (Dr 55; four hours), Casablanca (Dr 115 via Marrakesh, Dr 95 via Essaouira), Tiznit (Dr 18), Taroudannt, Tafraoute (one a day, at 1.30 pm), Goulimime and Tan Tan (at 6 am and 2 pm), Safi and El-Jadida.

About 10 other smaller companies have buses to most of these destinations as well.

Train Supratours (☎ 841207), which runs buses in connection with the train network, has an office at 10 Rue des Orangiers. Services to Marrakesh (about four hours) leave at 4.45 and 9.30 am and 1.45 pm, and you are dropped at the train station.

You can get a through ticket from Agadir to any rail destination.

Taxi Grands taxis to Tiznit (Dr 17.50) leave from a lot about one km south-east of the centre of town. Grands taxis also go to Inezgane (Dr 2.50) from here.

Grands taxis for Taghazout (Dr 8) leave from near the local bus station at Place Taxis et Bus.

Car There are at least 40 car rental outlets to choose from in Agadir, many of them on Ave Hassan II, so it is worth shopping around before settling on a deal. Some of the main agencies are:

Avis
    Ave Hassan II (☎ 841755)
    Airport (☎ 840345)
Budget
    Bungalow Marhaba, Blvd Mohammed V (☎ 844600)
    Airport (☎ 839071)
Europcar
    Bungalow Marhaba, Blvd Mohammed V (☎ 840203)
    Airport (☎ 839066)
Hertz
    Bungalow Marhaba, Blvd Mohammed V (☎ 840939)

Motorbike A walk around the big hotels will soon reveal a series of booths that rent out motorbikes and scooters. Again, it is important to hunt around. Dr 80 a day or Dr 350 a week seems to be an average charge for a scooter.

Of greater interest could be some of the 4WD and camel excursions into the desert, but again, they aren't cheap.

Getting Around

To/From the Airport Airport transport is just a little complicated. Local bus No 22 runs from the airport car park to Inezgane every 40 minutes or so (Dr 3) until about 9 pm. From Inezgane you can change to bus Nos 5 and 6 for Agadir, or take a grand taxi (Dr 2.50).

Petits taxis between the airport and Agadir should not cost more than Dr 100.

Otherwise, plenty of travellers have stories of simply walking onto tour and hotel buses with other passengers, since most of them are generally in package tours and it's unlikely any questions will be asked. Don't *ask* for a lift on one of these buses – they may give you one but they'll also charge you the earth.

Bus The main local bus station is a block in from Ave Hassan II, at Place Taxis et Bus, in the southern end of town. Bus Nos 5 and 6 go to Inezgane. The green-and-white No 12 goes to Taghazout.

Taxi Unless you have to get to the airport in a hurry, you're unlikely to use the orange petits taxis.

Bicycle There are several stands set up around the big hotels near the beach renting out bicycles for Dr 20 an hour.

AROUND AGADIR

Immouzzer des Ida Outanane

A pleasant little side excursion, but one that could mean an overnight stay if you rely on public transport and have no luck hitching, takes you about 60 km north of Agadir to the village of Immouzzer des Ida Outanane. The village itself is nothing special, but the trip up is pretty. The waterfalls (cascades) for which the village is known can be a disappointment – often little more than a dribble.

One local bus a day leaves for Inezgane from near the Agadir bus terminals. Ask around the day before, as its departure times (about 4 am at the time of writing) seem to change. You may have to wait until the fol-

lowing day for the bus back, although hitching isn't too difficult. Otherwise, there's a pleasant but fairly expensive hotel at Immouzzer. The best time to get up there would be Thursday, which is market day.

Northern Beaches

If you're looking for less-crowded beaches than those at Agadir, and for fellow independent travellers (most with their own transport), then head north of Agadir. There are beautiful sandy coves every few km.

Most of the beaches closer to Agadir have been colonised by Europeans who have built their winter villas here. Farther north, this gives way to a sea of campervans, but by the time you are 20 to 25 km north of Agadir, you might find something resembling space and even peace and quiet.

The first village of any size you pass is Tamrhakht, about 14 km north of Agadir, and six km farther on is Taghazout. The latter hosts a large and fairly ugly camping ground at the southern end of the town. It's usually crammed with campervans. There are a couple of eateries and cafés, too, but it's really not a very appealing place. The beaches are OK but the ambience is hardly the best. Europeans have built villas along parts of the coast between Taghazout and Agadir, and the stream of foreigners has attracted banana sellers onto the roadsides – you could buy a lot of bananas on your way north from Agadir.

For peaceful and largely unspoilt beaches, you need to go still farther north. Those around Aghrod, 27 km north of Agadir, are more like it. You can find a few other attractive spots just south and north of Cap Rhir (easily identified by its shipwreck), before the road turns inland again to Tamri.

There are local buses from Agadir (Place Taxis et Bus) to Taghazout, but beyond that you'll have to rely on your thumb.

Inezgane

Inezgane is a completely uninteresting and very noisy town 13 km south of Agadir. It also happens to be one of the biggest transport hubs for the whole region, and you could

STH OF CASABLANCA

easily end up here, although, if you're lucky, no longer than it takes to change buses or get a taxi. Should you get stuck, there is no shortage of cheap hotels in the bus station area. A big market is held in the town on Tuesdays.

Getting There & Away There are plenty of buses to most major destinations from here, if you have no luck in Agadir. The bus station (gare routière) is just off the Agadir-Tiznit road. Even at 6 pm, you'll find touts trying to fill places on buses to Marrakesh, Casablanca, Essaouira and other cities. There are also loads of grands taxis to Essaouira (Dr 50), Tiznit (Dr 16) and Taroudannt (Dr 15). Less regular taxis leave for Goulimime (Dr 40) and Tan Tan (Dr 70). Local buses to Agadir and the airport also leave from around here.

Sidi R'bat

About 80 km south of Agadir, off a side track from the main P30 highway, is a tiny little coastal village called Sidi R'bat. There's nothing much here, but two interesting claims are attached to the village. According to one story, this is where the biblical Jonah is supposed to have been spewed up by the whale. And Uqba bin Nafi, the first Arab commander to penetrate Morocco, in the 7th century, supposedly rode his horse triumphantly into the sea here. Believe it or not.

Taroudannt

Just 85 km inland from Agadir, Taroudannt, with its magnificent and well-preserved red mud walls, stands out as a Moroccan city more Moroccan than the rest. The French never tacked on a ville nouvelle here, and although there is not an awful lot to see, it gives the impression of not having changed much in the past hundred or so years. A fairly easy day trip from Agadir (the squadrons of tour buses are proof of that), it is well worth spending a couple of days here. Taroudannt

also makes a good intermediate stop between Agadir and Marrakesh.

Busloads of day-trippers pour into Taroudannt from Agadir, and have given rise to a small-scale irritant in the form of touts. If you hang about for a day or two, they'll soon leave you alone. The central souq, where most of the souvenirs are sold, is so small that guides are completely superfluous. The tout problems overcome, Taroudannt is a relaxed and pleasant place to stay, with a strongly southern Moroccan feel to it.

History

As far back as 1056, Taroudannt was overrun by the Almoravids at the beginning of their conquest of Morocco. It played only a peripheral role in the following years until, in the 16th century, the newly emerging Saadians made it their capital for about 20 years. This dynasty was responsible for the construction of the old part of town and the kasbah; most of the rest dates from the 18th century.

The Saadians eventually moved on to Marrakesh, but not before the fertile Souss valley in which the city stands had been developed into the country's most important producer of sugar cane, cotton, rice and indigo – valuable items of trade along the trans-Saharan caravan routes.

The city narrowly escaped destruction in 1687 at the hands of Moulay Ismail, after it became the centre of a rebellion opposing his rule. Instead, Moulay Ismail contented himself with a massacre of its inhabitants. It regained some of its former prominence when one of Moulay Abdallah's sons was proclaimed sultan here at the end of the following century, but his reign during this, one of the more turbulent periods in Moroccan history, was brief.

Taroudannt was to remain a centre of intrigue and sedition against the central government well into the 20th century, and indeed played host to the Idrissid El-Hiba, a southern chief who attempted to rebel after the Treaty of Fès (introducing French protectorate rule) was signed in 1912.

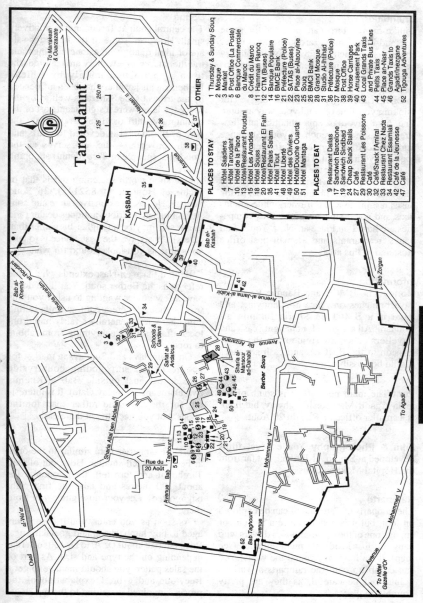

Taroudannt

0 125 250 m

To Marrakesh & Ouarzazate

KASBAH

Bab el-Kasbah

Bab al-Khemis

Bab Zorgan

Berber Souq

Schools & Gardens

Sahat al-Andalous

To Agadir

To Hôtel Gazelle d'Or

Rue du 20 Août

Bab Taghount

Avenue Bab Taghount

Avenue Mohammed V

PLACES TO STAY
- 4   Hôtel Saadiens
- 7   Hôtel Taroudant
- 10 Hôtel de la Place
- 13 Hôtel Restaurant Roudani
- 18 Hôtel Arcades
- 18 Hôtel Souss
- 20 Hôtel/Restaurant El Fath
- 35 Hôtel Palais Salam
- 41 Hôtel Tiout
- 48 Hôtel Liberté
- 49 Hôtel des Oliviers
- 50 Hôtel/Douche Ouarda
- 51 Hôtel Mantaga

PLACES TO EAT
- 9   Restaurant Dallas
- 17 Sandwich Barcelone
- 19 Sandwich Sindibad
- 24 Cheap Snack Stalls
- 27 Café
- 29 Restaurant Les Poissons
- 30 Café/Snack l'Amiral
- 33 Restaurant Chez Nada
- 34 Restaurant Essamiali
- 42 Café de la Jeunesse
- 47 Café

OTHER
- 1   Thursday & Sunday Souq
- 2   Mosque
- 3   Market
- 5   Post Office (La Poste)
- 6   Banque Commerciale du Maroc
- 8   Crédit du Maroc
- 11 Hammam Ranoq
- 12 CTM (Buses)
- 14 Banque Posj
- 16 BMCE Bank
- 21 Banque Populaire
- 22 Préfecture (Police)
- 23 Place al-Alaouyine
- 25 Souq
- 26 BMCI Bank
- 28 Grand Mosque
- 31 Studio Al-Intihad
- 36 Préfecture (Police)
- 37 Mosque
- 38 Post Office
- 39 Horse Carriages
- 40 Amusement Park
- 43 Local Grands Taxis and Private Bus Lines
- 44 Petits Taxis
- 45 Grands Taxis to Nusr
- 46 Grands Taxis to Agadir/Inezgane
- 52 Tigouga Adventures

STH OF CASABLANCA

Orientation

Unlike many Moroccan towns of the same size and importance, Taroudannt was never chosen as a French administrative or military centre. Consequently, there is no 'European' quarter of wide boulevards and modern buildings.

On first arriving, you could be forgiven for thinking you'll never find your way around. The road layout seems chaotic, and few street signs are in French, so you just plunge into the heart of the medina. In fact, you'll soon sort yourself out. The cheaper hotels are all located on or near the two central squares: Place al-Alaouyine (formerly Assarag) and Place an-Nasr (ex-Talmoqlate). Most of the buses terminate at the former, while grands taxis and some smaller private bus companies are based on Place an-Nasr. You'll find banks, restaurants and a small post office clustered in this area.

Information

Money The BMCE and Banque Populaire have branches on Place al-Alaouyine, and there is a BMCI on Sharia Ibrahim ar-Roudani. All are good for changing cash and travellers' cheques (remember the commission in the BMCE), and cash advances should be possible, too.

Post The main post office is south of the main Agadir-Marrakesh highway, but there is a smaller office on Rue du 20 Août.

Film & Photography You can get films developed at Studio Al-Ihtihad, not far from the Hôpital Mokhtar Soussi.

Ramparts

The ramparts of Taroudannt can be explored on foot, but it is better to hire a bicycle, or engage one of the horse-and-cart drivers who hang out just inside the main entrance (see map). It's a long way round the walls! You can climb up onto the ramparts at various points, but be careful, as they are pretty crumbly in places.

Souqs

The central souq at Taroudannt is relatively small. However, some of the items for sale are of high quality; limestone carvings and traditional Berber jewellery are featured (the town is populated mainly by Chleuh Berbers). This jewellery has been influenced by the tribes of the Sahara as well as by the Jews; the latter were a significant part of the community until the late 1960s. Only the core of the market is devoted to crafts and kitsch souvenirs – the rest serves as the Roudanis' (people of Taroudannt) shopping centre.

One shop worth searching out is that of Lichir el Houcine (☎ 852145), 36 Souq Semata. He has an extensive range and considers himself a serious antiques dealer (and as a result may be a tougher bargainer than others). As always, the best advice is to take your time as you look around for what you want.

Behind Place an-Nasr extends what some refer to as the Berber souq. You'll no doubt have a few guides wanting to usher you this way. Although there are a few stalls selling crafts here, it is generally a fairly humdrum local affair, selling everything from rabbits to rope.

On Thursdays and Sundays, a market for people in the surrounding countryside spreads out just outside Bab al-Khemis (which means Thursday Gate). It is interesting for the spectacle rather than for the goods, but you need to get there early.

Tanneries

There are tanneries here similar to the ones at Fès, but much smaller. Head out of Bab Targhount and turn left, then continue for about 100 metres and take the first right (signposted). Let your nose guide you from there.

As soon as you enter, you'll be encouraged to buy lamb, sheep and goatskin rugs. Prices start at about Dr 70 to Dr 100 for a rug, depending on the type and size. As part of the sales patter, you should manage to get a free tour and a brief explanation of the process involved in getting to the rug stage, which is interesting, and less likely to happen in Fès.

Also interesting is a small room on the right as you enter, where various animal skins are hung up. The locals don't fall over themselves to show you these, perhaps aware of Western sensitivities on the subject of wildlife extermination.

Kasbah

The walls around the kasbah date mainly from the time of Saadian rule in Taroudannt, and the area is worth a little stroll, though there are no sights as such inside its walls. Walled off as it is from the rest of the city (you can't get to the Hôtel Palais Salam this way either), it seems almost like a separate little town.

Swimming

It can get mighty hot in Taroudannt during the summer. You can use the pool at the Hôtel Palais Salam for Dr 30 a day, if the hotel is not full of guests.

Organised Tours

Tigouga Adventures (☎ 853122) specialises in trekking expeditions in the Western High Atlas . Run by Tali Abd al-Aziz, the agency is located just inside Bab Targhount and deals mainly with English speakers. Tali can organise short local walks, multiday treks or ski treks on the Tichka Plateau, as well as excursions farther afield, such as to Jebel Sirwa. For more information, write to BP 132, Taroudannt Ville, Morocco.

Places to Stay – bottom end

Most travellers like to stay as close to the centre of activity as possible, and in Taroudannt you can do this without paying a lot of money. There are many hotels around or close to Place al-Alaouyine, and there's not a huge difference in quality or price.

There are four budget places right on the square. One of the cheapest is the *Hôtel de la Place*, which is pleasant enough and has a variety of rooms. Tiny cell-like singles cost Dr 30, and something more roomy with views over the square can be had for Dr 40.

Doubles are Dr 50. The shared shower is bracingly cold.

On the other side of the lane is the *Hôtel/ Restaurant Roudani*. There are good views from the upper terrace but, unlike the rooms on the lower floor, the rooms up here don't have private showers. This hotel is clean and the staff friendly. Singles/doubles, regardless of whether they have a private shower, cost Dr 30/60. Hot water is available in the evenings, but the tank is small, so don't leave it too late. The *Hôtel Les Arcades*, virtually next door, costs the same and is on a par with the Hôtel de la Place.

The *Hôtel Riad* is somewhat sloppier than the others, and should be left until last when looking for a room. Those dying for a hot shower or bath can try the *Hammam Ranoq*, just behind the square.

Just off the square, heading towards Place an-Nasr, you'll find the *Hôtel Souss*. It's dirt cheap (Dr 20 a bed) but not terribly inviting.

Closer to Place an-Nasr is the *Hôtel des Oliviers* (☎ 852021). It's not bad, with clean beds for Dr 40/60. The showers are cold. A pretty reasonable deal for the money is the *Hôtel Mantaga*, which has clean rooms with big beds for Dr 25/50. It's on a little lane off Place an-Nasr. On the square itself, the *Hôtel Liberté* is a little grottier than the Mantaga (there's not a lot in it, though) and has beds for the same prices. On the same lane as the Mantaga is another similarly priced hotel, the *Hôtel Ouarda*. There's a public (read 'hot') douche (shower) in the same building.

There are two alternatives for people on tightish budgets seeking a little more comfort. The *Hôtel Tiout* (☎ 850341), on Ave al-Jama' al-Kabir, is a modern sort of place with decent, clean rooms and comfortable beds. Ask for the upstairs rooms with balcony. All rooms, which cost Dr 80/120, have private bathroom.

While perfectly acceptable, the Tiout has none of the charm of one of this city's institutions – the *Hôtel Taroudant* (☎ 852416). Although fading, this French-run hotel has a unique flavour to it, from the tree-filled courtyard around which the rooms are located to the creaky old dining room, where you can get simple but homely French cooking. Singles/doubles/triples cost Dr 50/ 68/105 without bathroom, Dr 74/95/132 with private shower, and Dr 95/110/147 with shower and toilet. The water is boiling hot, the hotel has one of the few bars in town and the food in the restaurant is good and moderately priced. This is easily the best deal in Taroudannt.

Places to Stay – middle

The only mid-range hotel in Taroudannt is the two-star *Hôtel Saadiens* (☎ 852589; fax 852118), Borj Oumansour, which offers B&B for Dr 155/199. Used by some adventure travel groups, the hotel is clean, comfortable and functional, but unremarkable. They have a rooftop restaurant (no alcohol), a swimming pool and access to locked parking, but overall, it's nothing great.

Places to Stay – top end

The four-star *Hôtel Palais Salam* (☎ 852 312) is right inside the ramparts, by the town's main roundabout and Agadir-Marrakesh road. One of the best of the Salam chain, the building started life as a pasha's residence in the 19th century. Set in luxuriant gardens, with swimming pool, tennis courts, bar and restaurant and guarded parking, it offers singles/doubles/triples for Dr 430/ 585/740.

Quite possibly the snootiest, most conceited establishment in all Africa is the *Hôtel La Gazelle d'Or* (☎ 852039; fax 852537). Built in 1961 by a French baron, it has 40 bungalows set in extensive gardens, with all the amenities you would expect of a five-star hotel, including a swimming pool, tennis courts and even horse riding. Advance booking is compulsory (anyone simply turning up at the gate will be turned away by a rather silly-looking security chap in a red fez) and the bungalows cost a fortune. The hotel is a couple of km out of town, but well signposted.

Places to Eat

There are quite a few small cheap eateries along Sharia Wali al-'Ahd Sidi Mohammed, near the Hôtel Souss, where you can get traditional food like tajine, salads and soups. Some offer quite good fish for very little money at all.

Also good are the restaurants on the ground floors of the hotels on Place al-Alaouyine. The one at the *Hôtel Roudani* is particularly good, with generous helpings of brochettes, chips and salad for Dr 29. Tour groups very often commandeer this place for some lunch-time tea. No matter, the others are about as good.

At *Sandwich Sindibad*, you can buy yourself a very good, fat baguette stuffed with kefta, chips and salad for Dr 17.

The *Restaurant Les Poissons* is exactly what its name suggests: a fish restaurant. It's a pokey little place, but don't let that deter you – you can get a filling plate of the stuff for about Dr 20. It's on Sahat al-Andalous, a little square off Sharia Ibrahim ar-Roudani.

If you want a break from the centre of town, two popular places with locals, and just a little nattier than your run-of-the-mill hole in the wall, are the *Restaurant Essamlali* and *Restaurant Chez Nada*, both on the main street that leads towards Bab al-Kasbah.

In the evening, head for the restaurant and bar at the *Hôtel Taroudant*. The menu here includes the old Moroccan stalwarts, but people looking for a change may want to opt for one of the various French dishes – they don't do a bad steak. Most main courses cost about Dr 40 to Dr 50, and a beer Dr 13 to Dr 15. They also have two set menus (Dr 60 and Dr 70).

There is no end to the cafés scattered throughout Taroudannt's winding streets. A good one with an upstairs terrace can be found on Place an-Nasr, if you're sick of people-watching in the cafés on Place al-Alaouyine and would like to do some elsewhere.

Getting There & Away

Bus The main bus companies have terminals on Place al-Alaouyine. CTM, next door to the Hôtel Les Arcades, has a 9 pm bus to Casablanca (Dr 136.50) via Agadir (Dr

18.50). This bus supposedly goes via Marrakesh (Dr 79) as well, avoiding the Tizi n'Test. Another bus goes to Ouarzazate (Dr 68) en route from Agadir, passing through at about noon.

Across the square is the SATAS station, more useful in this part of Morocco. There are two early morning buses to Marrakesh: one at 4.30 pm via the Tizi n'Test (Dr 55.50, seven hours) and the other at 5 am via Agadir (Dr 70, five hours).

There are three other departures for Agadir, at 5.30 and 11 am and 2.30 pm. A bus to Igherm and Tata (Dr 40.50) leaves at 8 am.

Several other small companies operate buses from the same square and Place an-Nasr, the main destination being Agadir.

Taxi The grands taxis gather at Place an-Nasr. Apart from small towns in the area around Taroudannt, the main regular destination is Inezgane (for Agadir), and some times Agadir itself. Either way, the fare is Dr 15.

Getting Around
It's highly unlikely that you'll need one of the brown petits taxis, but if you do, they gather at Place an-Nasr.

You can hire bicycles (Dr 5 an hour or Dr 35 a day) from a workshop on Place al-Alaouyine.

You could also tour around town in a *calèche* (horse-drawn carriage). They gather just inside Bab al-Kasbah, near the small amusement park.

AROUND TAROUDANNT
Tioute
Some 37 km to the south-east of Taroudannt lie the impressive ruins of the kasbah of Tioute. Part of the kasbah has been turned into an expensive restaurant, but there's nothing to stop you simply enjoying the views over the palmeraies and village below. Scenes for *Ali Baba & The Forty Thieves*, starring Yul Brynner, were shot here in 1952.

Without your own transport, you'll have to organise a taxi to take you out there from Taroudannt. If driving, take the P32 towards Marrakesh for about eight km, turn right and cross the oued just before the village and ruined kasbah of **Freija**. From here it's another 15 km down the S7025 towards Igherm before you hit a turn-off to the right. After five km, this reverts to a two-km stretch of piste. At the point where the bitumen ends, you're bound to be befriended by someone wanting to guide you up to the kasbah and restaurant.

South Coast & Anti-Atlas

From Agadir, the main route south heads inland, maintaining a respectful distance from the coast until it hits Tan Tan Plage, 240 km to the south-west. The terrain rapidly becomes harsher, and by the time you leave Goulimime – the last town on anything approaching the 'tourist circuit' – the stony desert takes over. Few travellers get beyond this point, and it has to be said that there is not an awful lot to see or do down here. It *is* refreshing to get away from the tourist buses, however, and the journey is potentially useful now that convoys are getting through from Dakhla (in Western Sahara) to Mauritania.

The jewel of the area, however, lies 107 km inland from the 19th-century fortress town of Tiznit, in the heart of the Anti-Atlas range. The village of Tafraoute, which lies within this area, is not particularly stunning, but the surrounding mountains, valleys and Berber villages together make up one of the prettiest and most relaxing pieces of walking country in Morocco.

TIZNIT
In an arid corner of the Souss Valley at the very end of the Anti-Atlas range, Tiznit has the appearance of an old town, with six km of encircling red mud walls. In fact, the town is a fairly recent creation, but still worth a short stay if you've come this far south. It's

STH OF CASABLANCA

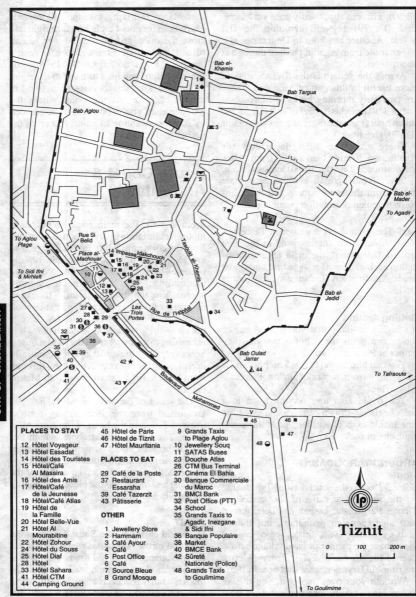

Tiznit

0   100   200 m

PLACES TO STAY
12 Hôtel Voyageur
13 Hôtel Essadat
14 Hôtel des Touristes
15 Hôtel/Café Al Massira
16 Hôtel des Amis
17 Hôtel/Café de la Jeunesse
18 Hôtel/Café Atlas
19 Hôtel de la Famille
20 Hôtel Belle-Vue
21 Hôtel Al Mourabitine
22 Hôtel Zohour
24 Hôtel du Souss
25 Hôtel Diaf
28 Hôtel
33 Hôtel Sahara
41 Hôtel CTM
44 Camping Ground
45 Hôtel de Paris
46 Hôtel de Tiznit
47 Hôtel Mauritania

PLACES TO EAT
29 Café de la Poste
37 Restaurant Essaraha
39 Café Tazerzit
43 Pâtisserie

OTHER
1 Jewellery Store
2 Hammam
3 Café Ayour
4 Café
5 Post Office
6 Café
7 Source Bleue
8 Grand Mosque
9 Grands Taxis to Plage Aglou
10 Jewellery Souq
11 SATAS Buses
23 Douche Atlas
26 CTM Bus Terminal
27 Cinéma El Bahia
30 Banque Commerciale du Maroc
31 BMCI Bank
32 Post Office (PTT)
34 School
35 Grands Taxis to Agadir, Inezgane & Sidi Ifni
36 Banque Populaire
38 Market
40 BMCE Bank
42 Sûreté Nationale (Police)
48 Grands Taxis to Goulimime

Tamdaght kasbah (DS)

Top Left: View from the Bab er-Rih area of Taza (DS)
Top Right: Puerta de Santiago, Melilla la Vieja (DS)
Bottom: Aït Benhaddou (DS)

also not a bad staging point for a couple of other destinations – the quirky former Spanish town of Sidi Ifni, on the coast, and Tafraoute, to the east.

The best time to be in Tiznit is when the package-tour buses from Agadir have left (mid to late afternoon). It then reverts to normality and is a pleasant place to hang around and explore. This is also the best time to have a look at the silver jewellery, reputedly some of the best in the south – indeed, in all Morocco.

History
Although there was a settlement of sorts here previously, the town dates substantially from 1881. In that year it was chosen by Sultan Moulay al-Hassan as a base from which to assert his authority over the semiautonomous and rebellious Berber tribes of the Souss and Anti-Atlas. He was only partly successful in this quest; it wasn't until the 1930s – 20 years after Spain and France had divided Morocco between themselves – that the tribes were finally 'pacified'.

In the first decade of the 20th century, Tiznit became a focal point of the resistance against the 1912 treaty that turned Morocco into a French and Spanish protectorate. The resistance was led by El-Hiba, an Idrissid chief from Mauritania who was regarded as a saint and credited with performing miracles. In 1912 he had himself proclaimed sultan at the mosque in Tiznit, and he succeeded in uniting the tribes of the Anti-Atlas and the Tuareg in what proved to be a vain effort to dislodge the French. Ejected from Tiznit and at one point forced to move to Taroudannt, he pursued the campaign of resistance until his death, in 1919.

Orientation
The main drag, Blvd Mohammed V, runs just outside the south-west wall of the city. At the main set of gates, known as Les Trois Portes (Three Gates), a road leads away from Blvd Mohammed V to the main grand taxi lot. The post office, a couple of banks, restaurants and a food market are on this street. Entering the town through the gates, you end up on

Place al-Machouar, a square on or near which you'll find the jewellery souq and most of the buses and cheap hotels.

Information
The banks in Tiznit include the BMCE, BMCI and Banque Populaire. The post office is open during normal office hours only.

Things to See & Do
Apart from wandering around the sleepy interior of the town or hunting for bargains in the just-as-sleepy **jewellery souq**, there's little to see. Of note is the minaret at the **Grand Mosque**. Souls of the dearly departed supposedly rest on the perches sticking out of its mud walls – not a standard element of orthodox Islam!

Nearby is a pretty mucky spring – a popular bathing spot with local kids. Known as the **Source Bleue**, legend has it that a certain Lalla Zninia, a woman of ill repute, turned up at this spot, repented her wicked ways and gave her name to the village that preceded Moulay al-Hassan's 19th-century fortress town.

It's possible to climb onto sections of the city walls, at Bab Targua for instance. Things liven up a little on Thursday, which is market day.

Places to Stay – bottom end
Camping You'll find a fairly uninspiring camp site about halfway between the main roundabout and Bab Oulad Jarrar. Devoid of shade, it's really only of use to people with campervans. It costs Dr 5 per person and the same per car (Dr 10 per caravan). Water costs Dr 2 and electricity Dr 15.

Hotels Travellers prefer to stay at the hotels right on Place al-Machouar, the main square within the city walls. Many have rooftop terraces where you can escape the tourist hordes during the middle of the day. They're all much the same price and offer similar facilities, so where you stay will largely depend on what you take a fancy to and which hotel has a room.

One of the best is off the square, on Impasse Idakchouch. The *Hôtel Belle-Vue* (☎ 862109) is a cheerfully done-up place with clean rooms. Singles/doubles cost Dr 35/60 and a hot shower is Dr 5. That this place has a shower at all distinguishes it from a lot of the competition.

Many travellers stay at the *Hôtel Atlas*, which has a lively restaurant. Singles/doubles cost Dr 30/50, but frankly it's no better than the others. Some of the front rooms have good views of the square, but that's about it. There are cold communal showers. Similar are the *Hôtel des Amis*, *Hôtel de la Jeunesse*, *Hôtel/Café Al Massira*, *Hôtel des Touristes* and *Hôtel Voyageur*. The latter costs Dr 30/50 for singles/doubles with shared bathroom (cold water only), but for some reason is often full. There's a tiny place just behind it, down an alley: the *Hôtel Essadat*.

In addition to the Belle-Vue, there are half a dozen or so other cheapies along Impasse Idakchouch. *Hôtel Al Mourabitine*, at the end of the street, is not bad. Smaller rooms cost Dr 30/50, but they have a bigger and more pleasant room at the front for Dr 50/70 (single/double occupation). The hotel is up on the first floor with a little café. There is no shower.

Opposite the Belle-Vue is the *Hôtel Zohour*. It's Dr 25 for a bed, they have no sheets and it's basically a dump.

A bit closer to the square, the *Hôtel de la Famille* has acceptable rooms for Dr 25/40. Again, they have no showers. Across the road are two more hotels. Rooms in the *Hôtel du Souss* cost Dr 25/30. The rooms are basic, but some are quite big, and the doubles are about as cheap as you'll find anywhere in Morocco. There's no shower and the loos stink to high heaven. Next door, the *Hôtel Diaf* offers OK rooms for Dr 25 per person.

A little farther away from Place al-Machouar is the dark and gloomy *Hôtel Sahara* (☎ 862498), which charges Dr 20 per person. The rooms have clean double beds and little else.

All those with shower problems in this area can head for the *Douche Atlas*, down a side alley off Impasse Idakchouch. It costs Dr 4.50 and there are separate showers for men and women. Another men's and women's hammam is located just inside Bab el-Khemis.

There's a cheapie near the grand taxi lot, the *Hôtel CTM* (☎ 862211) – CTM used to have its office here. Cells cost Dr 30/50, but they're clean enough. Hot showers are Dr 5 extra. There's also a little hotel with no name, next to the Cinéma El Bahia, on Blvd Mohammed V.

Going up in price, the one-star *Hôtel Mauritania* (☎ 863632), which is on the road to Goulimime, has singles/doubles with private shower and toilet for Dr 110/127. A big room with a kind of alcove at the front of the hotel can sleep three (Dr 150). The hotel, which has its own bar and restaurant, is a very clean and friendly place – a good deal.

Places to Stay – middle

The only mid-range hotel in town is the two-star *Hôtel de Paris* (☎ 862863), on Ave Hassan II, by the big roundabout. Rooms here are comfortable and clean. Singles/doubles/triples with showers and toilets cost Dr 138/165/215. There is hot water and the hotel has its own restaurant.

Places to Stay – top end

Tiznit's top-range hotel is the three-star *Hôtel de Tiznit* (☎ 862411/21), Rue Bir Inzaran, also close to the main roundabout. Self-contained singles/doubles with hot water cost Dr 244/301. The hotel has its own bar, restaurant, swimming pool and guarded parking.

Places to Eat

One of the best restaurants in Tiznit is the *Restaurant Essaraha*, on the corner just across Blvd Mohammed V from Les Trois Portes. Dr 20 will get you a 'petit tajine', which is quite enough for most appetites. The food is good and the service quick. There are a couple of other café/restaurants around here where you can get a bite to eat.

In the evening, a decent place is the restaurant at the *Hôtel Atlas*. Mind you, most of the hotels on the square have cafés offering food, and the difference in quality is not marked.

Those wanting to put together their own meals should go to the covered market, just over Blvd Mohammed V from Les Trois Portes, which offers an excellent selection of meat, vegetables, fruit (fresh and dried) and many other foodstuffs.

There are quite a few cafés dotted about the town, some of them marked on the map. Those with a sweet tooth will find a good pâtisserie in a street off Blvd Mohammed V, just around from the Sûreté Nationale.

Getting There & Away
Bus CTM has two daily buses from its terminal on Place al-Machouar. At 5.30 am there is one to Casablanca (Dr 98.50) via Agadir (Dr 15.50), Essaouira (Dr 43), Safi (Dr 64.50) and El-Jadida (Dr 83.50). At 9 am a *mumtaz* bus leaves for Tangier (Dr 228.50, 16 hours) via Agadir (Dr 24.50; 1¼ hours), Marrakesh (Dr 85, 5¾ hours), Casablanca (Dr 140.50, nine hours) and Rabat (Dr 162, 10½ hours). You may be able to get on a southbound bus to Goulimime and beyond, but these buses come from Agadir (or farther north), so they often leave already full or don't stop in Tiznit at all.

SATAS, whose office is on the same square has buses to Casablanca (8 am), Marrakesh (9.45 pm) and Agadir (9.30 and 9.45 am, noon and 7.30 pm). A bus to Tafraoute leaves at 3.45 pm (Dr 20), and three go to Goulimime (Dr 23), at 8 and 11 am and 4 pm. A bus to Akka and Tata departs at 9.30 am.

Several small companies run a few services from here, too. There is at least one bus to Sidi Ifni, at about 4 pm.

Taxi Grands taxis to Sidi Ifni (Dr 16, about two hours) and Inezgane (for Agadir – Dr 16) leave from the main grand taxi lot. Some taxis go right into Agadir (Dr 17.50). The occasional taxi goes to Tafraoute (Dr 28), but this depends on demand. For Goulimime, there are grands taxis from a rank opposite the Hôtel Mauritania (Dr 25 per person). You

may be able to get one through to Tan Tan, too. Taxis to Aglou Plage leave from another rank, on Blvd Mohammed V by the city walls. They cost Dr 5 a head.

AROUND TIZNIT
Aglou Plage
About 15 km from Tiznit lies Aglou Plage, which has a reasonable beach and good surf, though you'll come across the occasional glass and plastic bottle as well as other rubbish. Most of the time it's deserted and, when Atlantic winds start blustering, it's a wild and woolly sort of place.

Places to Stay There's a walled camp site at the entrance to the village, but it's stony and has no shade whatsoever. Camping at the site (open only in summer) costs next to nothing.

You may well be met there by someone trying to drum up some business. A rocky track off to the left just before the camp site leads up to his house, and to what he has established as a very basic hotel out the back. A bare room with a bed costs Dr 30 and there's a cold shower. You're so far away from everything here that you'll need to cook your own food (no facilities), unless you get lucky with the family.

Forget it and just head down to the beach to the *Motel Aglou*, which has 15 basic cabins (Dr 45) with a sea view. Bathrooms (cold showers) are shared. There's a restaurant – they cook up good meals for Dr 30. It would be 100% better if someone did some work on it, but who cares? – you're only going to sleep there and the beach is all yours. Sherif, the manager, is an obliging guy.

Getting There & Away Grands taxis run to Tiznit fairly regularly during the day (Dr 5 per person).

TAFRAOUTE
Nestled in behind the enchanting Ameln Valley is the village of Tafraoute, itself unspectacular but extremely relaxed – the

Berber Houses

Traditional building methods throughout the Atlas mountain villages had, until recently, changed little over the centuries. Prosperous mountain Berbers now use more modern techniques, but many subsistence farmers and their families continue to employ age-old methods.

The typical house is flat-roofed and made of *pisé*, a French term referring to the combination of clay, stone and sun or kiln-dried brick. A decent house has three or four floors, and argan-wood beams and palm fronds are typically used for the ceilings between each floor. The bottom floor is basically for the animals. Cows and the like are kept in a dark area, to reduce the number of flies. Scraps are dropped through a hole in the ceiling, from the kitchen above – a natural form of waste disposal. Farming tools are also kept on this floor, along with utensils for making flour and for grinding coffee and argan nuts for oil. If there is a toilet, it's down here.

A better house has a stairway or ladder up to the next floor, both inside and out. Visitors thus have no reason to see the bottom floor. The kitchen might occupy the main floorspace on this level. Gathered around it are what amount to corridors. One (the biggest) is the family dining room, while the rest serve as bedrooms. Occasionally, these rooms host women on festive occasions (there is traditionally, although not always, strict segregation of the sexes if men from outside the immediate family are visiting, whatever the reason).

A ramp leads up to the next floor, most of which is occupied by the most sumptuous room in the house, where the men usually eat with guests or take tea. Here you take your shoes off before walking on the mats, and all the silver teaware is brought out. On the same floor or above it would be the inevitable open terrace – especially important in the summer, when it can be far too hot to sleep inside.

The models vary (sometimes the second and top floors are reversed), but the basic formula remains pretty much the same.

Some of these houses have been standing for hundreds of years, but only in a very loose sense. Habitation of villages has historically been cyclic. Berber villages were, until early this century, regularly exposed to epidemics and subject to raids by enemy tribes, and as a result were often abandoned, sometimes for generations. Where the population was severely reduced, the excess houses stood empty and slowly began to crumble. In better days, these same old houses would be reoccupied, the top floors rebuilt and so the cycle begun again. ∎

perfect base for days of hiking in the hills and Berber villages around it. The more ambitious might consider scaling Jebel al-Kest or taking on guides to follow palm-filled gorges leading towards the bald expanses of the southern Anti-Atlas. Stay here a few days, go on some hikes around the countryside and you'll find it hard to leave.

The village can be reached on roads from Tiznit (107 km) or Agadir (198 km); ideally, a circuit taking in both would be the most satisfying way of doing the trip. It is one where you'd definitely appreciate having your own transport.

From Tiznit, the road starts off in an ordinary enough fashion across gentle farming country, until it reaches Oued Assaka. From here it winds up into the mountains, which in the late afternoon light take on every hue imaginable – greens, reds and golden browns. Sprinkled about the hills are precari-

ous Berber pisé (mud brick) villages (most of the Berbers in this region are Souss Chleuh), surrounded by the cultivated terraces that are worked all through the day – mostly by the women. At 1100 metres you cross the stunning Col de Kerdous (there is a four-star hotel up here), and from here you hardly lose altitude for the remainder of the run into Tafraoute.

The route to Agadir is just as fascinating. Leaving Tafraoute, the road passes through the eastern half of the Ameln Valley and over the Tizi Mlil pass before doubling back on itself for the trip north-west to Agadir. The land is generally much gentler and more heavily cultivated on this run, but the road passes through plenty of villages – often little agglomerations of houses bunched together, sometimes in the most unlikely places. The most remarkable along the way is **Ida-ou-Gnidif**, perched on a solitary hilltop back from the highway, about 40 km south of Aït Baha. From Aït Baha the road flattens out, and the final stretch up to Agadir is of no interest.

Tourism is on the increase in Tafraoute, which may well be good news for many locals. The region has a long history of emigration. Apart from almond, argan and palm trees (it is said that, where there's a palmeraie there's a natural spring and where there are almond or argan trees is a mere well), along with limited wheat and barley cultivation, there's not much to the local economy. For centuries, this strikingly beautiful area has allowed its inhabitants to eke out only the barest of livings.

The down side is the Agadir tour buses that inevitably make an appearance in the late morning. Still, they're all gone by the afternoon and, so far at least, have had no noticeable effect on the townspeople.

Information
There are two banks in Tafraoute, the BMCE and the Banque Populaire. The post office (PTT) is on the main square, Sahat Mohammed al-Khamis.

The Painted Rocks & Napoleon's Hat
Tafraoute is famous for its painted rocks – the work of Belgian artist Jean Veran. (He has done similarly bizarre things in places like the Sinai in Egypt.) In this case he had a collection of the smooth, rounded boulders peculiar to this patch of the mountains spray-painted in living colour, predominantly blue, in 1984. It could be argued that this was a silly thing to do, but no great harm was done by it either.

To get to the rocks, take the road heading north-east to the village of Agard-Oudad (the opposite way to the Agadir exit). It's about three km out. On the way you'll notice a distinctive rock formation on the right, known as **Le Chapeau de Napoléon** (Napoleon's Hat). At the sign indicating a fork (about two km), take the right branch and go through the village to the square, where there's a mosque. From here, turn right and then left to get around the mosque,

and head out into the countryside for a farther two to three km. You'll come to some pale-blue rocks on the left-hand side, but keep going and follow the track bearing left to another set, which includes a large blue boulder with a purple rock on top. Go around this and to your right and you'll come to the best display of painted rocks. The walk is worthwhile even without the painted rocks.

If you're driving, head past Oulad Argad and follow the signs to a turn-off about five km beyond the village. Follow the couple of km of piste and leave the car where the track peters out. About 100 metres on you arrive at a good viewpoint over the rocks. You can climb down to get a closer look.

The Carved Gazelle
To get to this beautiful and supposedly very old carving, take the road for Tazka past the Hôtel Les Amandiers and head for the village on your right. The road climbs up a hill from here; you need to get in behind this hill and leave it to your left. You'll see a crude drawing of an animal on a rock on the hill. Walk up to it. The carving is on the top side of a fallen rock right in front of this one. The walk from Tafraoute should take about 20 minutes.

Organised Tours
A couple of local people are setting themselves up as guides to the region around Tafraoute. A friendly and reliable guy seems to be Mohammed Sahnoun Ouhammou. He lives in the village of Tiouadou in the Afella-Ighir oasis south of Tafraoute, and can be contacted through the Hôtel Reddouane or on ☎ 800180. He speaks English and French and specialises in hikes and mountain bike trips through the valleys and oases around his village. When you have fixed a price, he will generally put you up in his home, where you can dump your heavier luggage before setting off.

Places to Stay – bottom end
Camping *Camping Les Trois Palmiers* is set in a small stony compound – all the palm trees are outside the walls – but it's still not

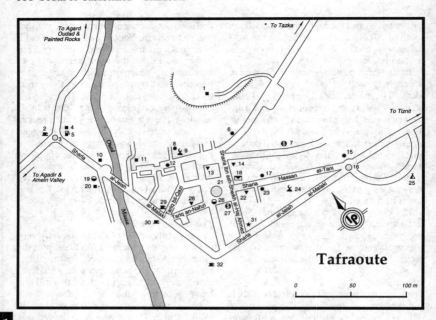

Tafraoute

0   50   100 m

a bad little place. It costs Dr 6 per person, the same to pitch a tent, Dr 7.50 for a car and Dr 7 for a hot shower. The people running it are very laid-back.

Hotels The two cheapest places in Tafraoute are just opposite each other towards the Agadir exit end of town. Of these, the *Hôtel Tanger* (☎ 800033) is the most basic, offering singles/doubles for Dr 20/40 – and a possibly hot shared shower (Dr 7), but don't bank on it. Better is the *Hôtel Reddouane* (☎ 800066), where rooms cost Dr 35/55 and a potentially hot shower is included. There is a sun terrace, and the restaurant downstairs is a popular hang-out.

Should you need one, there is a hammam by the old mosque, near the craft shops.

With a little more money you could make a quantum leap to the *Hôtel Tafraout* (☎ 800061, 800121), Place Moulay Rachid. The guy in the fez is the manager, Ibrahim Arkarkour, and he's an affable chap. The rooms are simple but modern and clean (Dr 60/100). Some of them overlook the square below and all are comfortable. The shared showers are included in the price and are steaming hot.

Places to Stay – middle
The *Hôtel Salam* is on the rebound after 'blowing up' years ago. It is due to reopen as a mid-range 60-room hotel in mid-1995, so by the time you read this, it may be open. They plan to have a sun terrace and a tea room.

Places to Stay – top end
The only remaining choice in Tafraoute is the four-star *Hôtel Les Amandiers* (☎ 800033), an amateur architect's travesty of a kasbah, which sits on the crest of the hill overlooking the town. Self-contained singles/doubles cost Dr 315/393 plus taxes. The hotel has its own bar, restaurant, swimming pool and

PLACES TO STAY		28	Restaurant Marrakech	16	Sahat (Place) Wali al-'Ahad
1	Hôtel Les Amandiers			17	School
4	Hôtel Tafraout		**OTHER**	18	Post Office (PTT)
10	Hôtel Reddouane			19	Satas Buses
11	Hôtel Salam	2	Café La Valleé des Amelenes	21	Sahat (Place) Mohammed al-Khamis
20	Hôtel Tanger	3	Sahata (Place) al-Massira		
25	Camp Site	5	Petrol Station	23	Town Hall
		6	La Maison Tuareg (Craft Stores)	24	Mosque
PLACES TO EAT				26	Taxis
		7	BMCE Bank (ATM)	27	Banque Populaire
13	Crémerie (Ice Cream)	8	Hammam	29	Cafés
14	Restaurant L'Étoile d'Agadir	9	Mosque	30	Cafés
		12	Souq (Craft Shops)	31	Gendarmerie Royale (Police)
22	Restaurant l'Étoile du Sud	15	Army Barracks	32	Café des Sports

guarded parking. They also put on the occasional folkloric dancing and singing show.

For those with a car and a yen for four-star hotels, there is an infinitely better choice 47 km west of Tafraoute on the road to Tiznit. The *Hôtel Kerdous* (☎ 862053; fax 862835), open since 1992, is perched in a former kasbah right on the pass of the same name. There are extraordinary views on all sides, but especially towards Tiznit. The hotel has 39 rooms, two restaurants, a bar and a swimming pool (not heated). Rooms cost Dr 312/377 plus taxes. It's worth stopping here for a drink en route to or from Tafraoute, just for the outlook.

Places to Eat

Both the cheap hotels have their own reasonably priced restaurants, and it's really a toss-up between the two. You can eat your fill for about Dr 25. Another option along similar lines is the *Restaurant Marrakech*, off the main square.

The *Restaurant L'Étoile d'Agadir*, just up from the post office, has undergone several name changes. They do a filling breakfast of orange juice, bread, butter, cheese and jam, finished off with tea or coffee. It's a little expensive though, at Dr 20.

The best restaurant, if you have a bit of money to spare, is the *Restaurant L'Étoile du*

Sud, opposite the post office on Sharia Hassan at-Tani. The Dr 70 menu, although not offering much of a choice of main courses, is tasty. The interior is done up as a traditional Moroccan salon, and the atmosphere is laid back. You can also eat under the tent outside.

For an ice cream you could try the crémerie near the Restaurant L'Étoile d'Agadir.

Getting There & Away

Bus SATAS has a daily bus from Agadir to Tafraoute at 1.30 pm daily, and one from Tiznit at 3.45 pm (Dr 20). Going the other way, the SATAS Tiznit bus leaves at 6.30 am from near the Hôtel Tanger, and goes on to Casablanca. The Agadir run seemed in doubt at the time of writing. There are up to five other buses (with other companies) from various spots along Sharia al-Jeish al-Malaki. They all seem to go to Tiznit.

Taxi The occasional grand taxi goes to Tiznit in the morning (Dr 28). Otherwise, Land Rover taxis do the rounds of various villages in the area around Tafraoute. There is no rhyme or reason to their movements, except demand – which mostly means doing business on market days. If there are any to be had, they hang around Sahat Mohammed al-Khamis or on Sharia al-Jeish al-Malaki.

AROUND TAFRAOUTE
Ameln Valley
Tafraoute lies in a basin, largely surrounded by craggy rocks and cliffs. To the north-west lies one such ridge, on the other side of which runs the Ameln Valley (Ameln is the name given to the local tribe of Chleuh Berbers). North again of this valley is a mountain range dominated by Jebel al-Kest.

The Agadir road takes you to the valley, which is lined by a string of picturesque Berber villages, some of them only partly inhabited. Four km out of Tafraoute, the road forks, the right branch turning off to take you eastwards out of the valley and on to Agadir. The other proceeds ahead, west down the valley. You could take either way and then head off down a track to any of the villages. It is possible to hike for days, going directly from village to village through barley fields or following narrow goat tracks and irrigation channels.

One of the most visited of the villages is **Oumesnat**, a few km farther down the Agadir road after the fork and off to the left along a short piste. The main attraction here is the **Maison Traditionelle**. Si Abdessalam decided to open up his three-storey house to visitors years ago as a way of drumming up a bit of income. Blinded as a young man in Tangier, he is a gentle host and gives you a tour of every nook and cranny of his place, followed by a glass of tea. He expects a small consideration for his efforts, and is worth every dirham. If you go unguided, just ask about for him and the house – it's poorly signposted and you need to follow a string of water channels into the heart of Oumesnat to find the house. A guide may well be useful, as Si Abdessalam speaks only Arabic and French.

Another village popular with foreigners is **Anameur**, although the only thing that sets it apart from the others is a natural spring. It's about 10 km west of Oumesnat.

Taghdichte, between Oumesnat and Anameur, is used by several adventure-travel groups (mainly English and German) as a base for ascents of Jebel al-Kest (which locals maintain is no easy undertaking). You can hire taxis to get you to some of these villages.

Afella-Ighir
The Tafraoute area offers plenty of hiking possibilities for people who want to hang around for a while. Among these are a couple of routes taking you south to the oasis of Afella-Ighir. You could cover most of it in a 4WD, but it's preferable to drive part of the way, then leave the car and do a circuit on foot or mountain bike. The road south of Agard-Oudad takes you some 15 km over a mountain pass (sometimes snowed over in winter) to Tlata Tasrite. From here it is possible to take several pistes that drop into lush palm-filled valleys, and do a loop of about 30 to 40 km through to the Afella-Ighir oasis and back up to Tlata Tasrite. A new road is being built to Souq al-Had, in Afella-Ighir, which will ease things for ordinary cars but detract from the charms of a long hike. About nine km south of Souq al-Had is Oussaka, where there are ancient animal carvings. More can be seen eight km farther on at Tasselbte. It would be best to talk to a guide (see Organised Tours under Tafraoute) about the latter part of this hike. Land Rover taxis will sometimes do the run to various villages of this area on market days (Wednesday in Tafraoute itself).

SIDI IFNI
Known to some simply as Ifni, Sidi Ifni is the town at the heart of the former Spanish enclave of Ifni. Shrouded for much of the year in an Atlantic mist, this haunting and short-lived coastal outpost of Spanish imperial ambitions has a neglected but somehow fascinating air. The town dates largely from the 1930s and features an eclectic mix of Spanish Art Deco and traditional Moroccan styles. The church just off the main plaza and the building (in the form of a ship) on the edge of the cliff next to the Hotel Suerte Loca shouldn't be missed. The old balustraded esplanade is crumbling, the

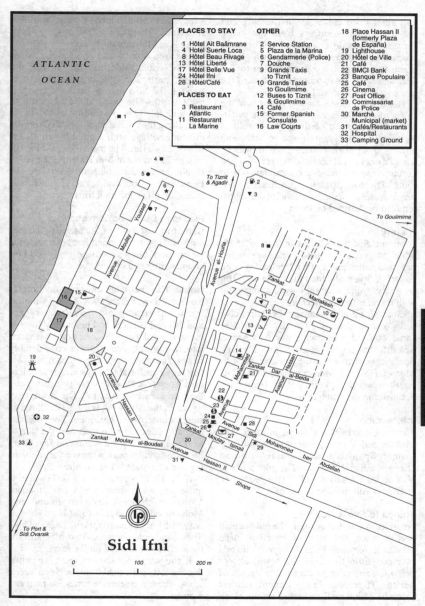

PLACES TO STAY
1 Hôtel Ait Baâmrane
4 Hôtel Suerte Loca
8 Hôtel Beau Rivage
13 Hôtel Liberté
17 Hôtel Belle Vue
24 Hôtel Ifni
28 Hôtel/Café

PLACES TO EAT
3 Restaurant Atlantic
11 Restaurant La Marine

OTHER
2 Service Station
5 Plaza de la Marina
6 Gendarmerie (Police)
7 Douche
9 Grands Taxis to Tiznit
10 Grands Taxis to Goulimime
12 Buses to Tiznit & Goulimime
14 Café
15 Former Spanish Consulate
16 Law Courts
18 Place Hassan II (formerly Plaza de España)
19 Lighthouse
20 Hôtel de Ville
21 Café
22 BMCI Bank
23 Banque Populaire
25 Café
26 Cinema
27 Post Office
29 Commissariat de Police
30 Marchè Municipal (market)
31 Cafés/Restaurants
32 Hospital
33 Camping Ground

ATLANTIC OCEAN

To Tiznit & Agadir

To Goulimime

Avenue el-Houria

Avenue Moulay Youssef

Zankat Marrakesh

Zankat Mohammed

Zankat Dar al-Beida

Avenue Hassan I

Avenue Hassan II

Zankat Moulay al-Boudali

Avenue Moulay Ismail

Avenue Sidi Mohammed ben Abdallah

Shops

To Port & Sidi Ovarsik

Sidi Ifni

0   100   200 m

STH OF CASABLANCA

still-unrenamed calles are half-empty and the town clearly suffers from not being served by a main coastal road. This may change, as there are plans to build a highway down the coast from Agadir and on to Tan Tan, and hotel-chain scouts have looked the place over for potential.

But that all seems far away now, and the town of 15,000 lives mainly from small-scale fishing; most of the catch is sold in Agadir. It is a curious place to visit, and attracts a surprising number of travellers. There's not a great deal to do or see, and you certainly won't have any problems with touts. The town beaches are deserted but unfortunately not the best, as a lot of rubbish tends to be dumped on them.

History

After the Spanish-Moroccan war of 1859, which Morocco lost (just 14 years after being defeated at the hands of a French army from Algeria), Spain obtained the enclave of Ifni by treaty. Quite what they were going to do with it seems to have been a question in a lot of Spanish minds, because they didn't take full possession until 1934. By the 1950s, some 60% of the town's population was Spanish, but under pressure from the UN, Spain agreed to cede the enclave back to Morocco in 1969. Morocco had sealed off its land borders three years before. Only three Spanish families now remain.

Information

There are two banks on the main street, Ave Mohammed V (away from the heart of the former Spanish town), where you can change cash and cheques. The post office is also on Ave Mohammed V (the letter box outside is still marked 'Correos').

Things to See & Do

Apart from wandering round the old Spanish part of town, the heart of which is Place Hassan II (formerly Plaza de España), there's precious little to do in the town, except perhaps search for an acceptable stretch of beach. There's a fairly decent market (Marché Municipal) that takes up the block

where Ave Mohammed V runs into Ave Hassan II. There are a few grocery shops along Ave Mohammed V too.

The area is not a bad one for excursions into the countryside, too (the drive from Tiznit, particularly where the road runs through the hills just in from the coast, is itself worthwhile, as is the 58-km run to Goulimime). One possibility would be to hike along the coastal piste to **Sidi Ouarsik**, a fishing village with a good beach 18 km south of Sidi Ifni. The trip to Mesti, a Berber village 25 km out of Sidi Ifni, off the road to Goulimime, is also a pleasant diversion. The Hotel Suerte Loca can organise guides and mountain bikes for such trips.

Places to Stay – bottom end

Camping Just south of the hospital, a cheap but basic patch of ground has been set aside for campers, but it's really only any good for people with campervans.

Hotels The justifiably most popular hotel is the *Hotel Suerte Loca* (☎ 875350), which is run by a friendly old man (who speaks Spanish and French) and his family (two of the sons speak English). The hotel is divided into two wings, one of them considerably newer than the other. The older rooms are perfectly comfortable, and some have balconies. They cost Dr 45/75 (hot showers along the corridor are Dr 5 extra). The clean, cosy rooms in the new wing (Dr 85/125) have en suite bathrooms and balconies. The hotel has a small collection of novels and the like to lend to guests, a good restaurant (excellent breakfast and crêpes), a terrace for sunbathing and mountain bikes for hire.

If the Hotel Suerte Loca is full (which is quite possible), there are a few standard Moroccan cheapies scattered around Ave Mohammed V. The *Hôtel Ifni* is as good as any, with very basic rooms for Dr 20 a head. They have cold showers. Two others in the same class are marked on the map.

If you want a hot shower, there is a public douche just up the road from the Hotel Suerte Loca. There are separate times for men and women.

The *Hôtel Beau Rivage* is shut (so ignore the signs).

Places to Stay – middle

There are two one-star places in Sidi Ifni, but they are no better than the new wing of the Suerte Loca. They are the *Hôtel Belle Vue* (☎ 875072), 9 Place Hassan II, and the *Hôtel Ait Baâmrane* (☎ 875267), on the beach. Rooms at both have private shower (hot water promised in both cases) and cost Dr 110/127. Those in the Belle Vue are more comfortable; some have sea views while others look onto the plaza. The hotel has a restaurant and bar, and the terrace overlooking the square is a good place for a tea. The slow-moving staff understand more Spanish than anything else.

Rooms in the Ait Baâmrane are tattier but some look right onto the ocean. There is a restaurant and bar, and the English-speaking staff offer a discount if you stay for more than one night.

Places to Eat

Apart from a few small café/restaurants on Ave Hassan II and dotted about the town, the only choices are really the hotel restaurants. The one at the *Hotel Suerte Loca* is particularly good value. Another possibility is the *Restaurant Atlantic*, down by the petrol station at the main town exit.

Getting There & Away

Bus There are one or two buses between Sidi Ifni and both Tiznit and Goulimime. Virtually all the buses leave Sidi Ifni from along Ave Mohammed V, early in the morning.

Taxi By far the easiest way to get to and from Sidi Ifni is by grand taxi. Taxis leave from a couple of dirt lots around the corner from the northern end of Ave Hassan I and cost Dr 16 a head to either Tiznit (about 1½ hours) or Goulimime (one hour).

GOULIMIME

Several things are striking about Goulimime, the dusty little town that proclaims itself the Gateway to the Sahara. The first is the bold crimson colour of almost all the buildings. The second is the disproportionate number of touts – enough people are still drawn here for the legendary Saturday camel market to have created a pool of aggressive and nasty little hustlers. Be careful what stories you believe – the one about the Berber market in the oasis of Aït Bekkou (today only!), and 'could you possibly give me a lift there' (this to people with their own transport) is a good one.

Once upon a time, 'blue men' came in from the desert every week to buy and sell camels at a souq just outside town. In the evenings, the women would perform the

STH OF CASABLANCA

Goulimime

0   50   100 m
Approximate Scale

PLACES TO STAY

9   Hôtel Salam
15   Hôtel Oued Dahab
16   Hôtel Bir Anazarane
20   Hôtel La Jeunesse
23   Hôtel L'Ere Nouvelle

PLACES TO EAT

6   Café de la Poste
11   Café Le Diamant Bleu
17   Rotisserie Al-Jawda
19   Rotisserie El Menara

OTHER

1   Buses & Grands Taxis
2   BMCI Bank
3   Studio Color (Film)
4   CTM Office & Café
5   Café
7   Crédit du Maroc
8   Café
10   Petrom Service Station
12   Post Office (PTT)
13   Hammam
14   Mosque
18   Banque Populaire
21   BMCE Bank
22   Banque Commerciale du Maroc
24   Grands Taxis to Asrir
25   Café Ali Baba
26   Café Paloma

mesmerising *guedra* dance to the beat of drums of the same name. This is what the flocks of package tourists pile into Goulimime for on Friday night and Saturday, but they must leave sorely disappointed. The market is now more of a butchers' convention for goat meat, with busloads of foreigners in search of the one or two camels dragged in here specially for them. Forget the tourist literature; about the only good thing to come out of Goulimime are the roads to Tiznit and Sidi Ifni. The former offers a couple of pretty stretches, particularly about halfway along, when crossing the **Tizi Mighert** pass.

Information
The tourist office (☎ 872545) is at 3 Résidence Sahara, Blvd d'Agadir. Should you find yourself stuck here for any reason, four banks have branches in Goulimime, so changing money should be no problem. The

post office is near the mosque between the two main roundabouts.

Camel Souq
If you feel you must contribute to the myth of the camel market, it takes place a couple of km outside town along the Route de Tan Tan (take a taxi) on Saturday mornings. Unless you get there just after sunrise, you won't be able to see the camels for the tourists.

Places to Stay – bottom end
Camping There is a camp site at Fort Bou Jerif, 40 km from Goulimime. It is an oasis of civilisation in the desert, meals are available and getting there is well worth the effort.

STH OF CASABLANCA

Take the Plage Blanche turn-off just out of Goulimime on the road to Sidi Ifni. Be aware that some of the road is piste.

You could also try *Camping Abainou*, at a village of the same name about 12 km out of Goulimime (take the Sidi Ifni road, turn right after four km and follow the signs). The *Auberge Abainou* also advertises 'free caravanning', which presumably means you can park your campervan there and just pay for use of facilities.

Hotels There are four cheap hotels from which to choose, but none of them is all that enticing. In the centre, the *Hôtel Bir Anzarane* is one of the cheapest, at Dr 20/30 for singles/doubles. The rooms are little cell-style arrangements, and the hotel has no shower at all. Worse still is the *Hôtel Oued Dahab*, on the other side of the roundabout, which is very primitive. They do have a cold shower, and rooms cost the same as at the Bir Anzarane.

Farther down Ave Hassan II, away from the centre, are the other places, across the road from each other and near the BMCE bank. Of these, the *Hôtel L'Ere Nouvelle* is marginally better than the *Hôtel La Jeunesse*, and distinguishes itself from all the others by promising a hot shower (Dr 5).

Places to Stay – middle
The only hotel in this range is the two-star *Hôtel Salam* (☎ 872057), which has its own bar and restaurant and costs 136/165 for rooms with private shower and toilet, plus taxes. They also have cheaper rooms without toilet. It is advisable to book ahead here if you want to turn up for the camel charade.

Places to Eat
There are a couple of good little rotisseries near the Hôtel Bir Anzarane – it's a toss-up between *Al-Jawda* and *El Menara*. You can get a filling meal of chicken, chips and salad for around Dr 20.

Something more like a restaurant, with the usual Moroccan fare, is the *Café de la Poste*, on the BMCI bank end of the Route de Tan Tan. A full meal here will cost about Dr 40.

Similar food is on offer at the *Café Le Diamant Bleu*, and occasionally at the café near the CTM office on the Agadir road. About the only other option is the bar and restaurant at the *Hôtel Salam*.

The most pleasant cafés are the *Café Ali Baba* and the *Café Paloma*, about half a km south of the main roundabout, opposite the Asrir grand taxi lot.

Getting There & Away
Bus The main bus and grand taxi terminals are about one km north of the town centre, although CTM also has a small office on the Agadir road. CTM has buses to Agadir (Dr 48) via Tiznit, leaving at 3.30 and 4 am (!) and one to Casablanca via both, at 8 pm. Buses to Marrakesh leave at 9 pm, midnight and 12.30 am. Others head for Laayoune (Dr 141), at 12.30 am and 2 and 6.30 pm. The first of these goes on to Dakhla, and you can change in Laayoune for Smara. At 6.30 am, a bus leaves for Tan Tan (Dr 26).

SATAS also operates out of this station, along with several smaller local companies, so you have a reasonable choice.

Taxi If bus departure times look inconvenient, you're probably better off with a grand taxi. They leave from behind the bus station. You can get a taxi to Sidi Ifni (Dr 16), Tiznit (Dr 25), Tan Tan (Dr 28), Inezgane (for Agadir; Dr 40) and Laayoune (Dr 100).

AROUND GOULIMIME
Plage Blanche
About 65 km out of Goulimime (take the Sidi Ifni exit and turn left at the signposted road), the Plage Blanche is, as yet, a little visited and unspoilt stretch of Atlantic beach. The road turns to piste after about 20 km, so you want a solid vehicle to get out here. Apart from the beach, there is virtually nothing around, but that is bound to change if schemes to construct a coastal highway south from Agadir ever take off.

Aït Bekkou
About 17 km south-east of Goulimime, Aït Bekkou is a pleasant oasis village – you'll

probably see more camels here than in Goulimime on a Saturday, but don't fall for the old 'Berber market, today only' story. You can get grands taxis as far as Asrir, but you may well have to hitch the remaining seven km of piste to Aït Bekkou. Alternatively, hire a taxi for the day.

TAN TAN

Taking the road south from Goulimime, you soon get the feeling you're heading well into the unknown – few travellers bother to go this far. The 125 km of desert highway is impressive in parts, but is harsh hammada (stony desert) rather than the soft, sandy dune variety. Breaking up the monotony, the road also crosses several oueds, including the Oued Drâa, which is usually dry this far away from its sources. Something else that creates mild interest are the police roadblocks, which become more frequent as you head south; you may or may not have to hang about at these while bored gendarmes check your passport and ask idiotic questions.

You could drive through the main street of Tan Tan (population 50,000) and not realise you had missed most of the town, which spreads south of the highway (known as Ave

Hassan II within the town boundaries). If you're on a bus or grand taxi, however, there's no danger of this. Tan Tan is situated in what was once part of Spanish-occupied Morocco, an area known under the Spaniards as Tarfaya which stretched south to the border with the so-called Spanish Sahara, a colony Spain abandoned only in 1975. The Tarfaya zone was handed over in 1958, two years after independence.

There's nothing much to do in Tan Tan, although it has quite a busy air about it. If you are heading south, it makes a more interesting overnight stop than Tarfaya (to the south).

PLACES TO STAY

1	Hôtel Bir Anzarane
4	Hôtel Aoubour
5	Hôtel Royal
18	Hôtel/Restaurant du Sud
19	Hôtel/Café Chahrazad
20	Hôtel/Café Sahara
21	Hôtel/Café Essaada
22	Hôtel/Café Dakar
25	Hôtel Atlas
26	Hôtel El Ansar
27	Hôtel Rahma

PLACES TO EAT

| 16 | Snack Stand |

OTHER

2	Shell Service Station
3	BMCE Bank
6	Petrol Station
7	Cinema
8	Banque Populaire
9	Grands Taxis to Tarfaya & Laayoune
10	Café
11	Market
12	Mosque
13	Kodak Shop
14	Salon La Jeunesse
15	Telephone Office
17	Petits Taxis
23	Grands Taxis to Goulimime, Tiznit & Agadir
24	Bus Station (Gare Routière)

Tan Tan

Information

BMCE has a branch next to the Shell station where Ave Mohammed V runs into Ave Hassan II. There is a Banque Populaire on the first square heading down Ave Mohammed V away from Ave Hassan II. There's a telephone office on the main square.

Places to Stay & Eat

Tan Tan is crawling with cheap hotels, so you'll have no trouble finding a bed. The best hotel around the bus station square is the *Hôtel Dakar*, although it's hardly great. Rooms with a double bed cost Dr 60 or Dr 80 with private shower (there's a gas heater, so you might even get hot water). The others here and the multitude in side lanes heading north along Ave Mohammed V are generally basic places costing about Dr 30 to Dr 40 per person. Most offer cold showers at best, but can direct you to a hammam (there's one near the bus station).

There are several more such hotels on the main square. Here you can try the *Hôtel/Restaurant du Sud*, *Hôtel/Café Chahrazad*, *Hôtel Sahara* or *Hôtel Essaada*. They all have cafés or restaurants downstairs. The *Hôtel Aoubour*, on Ave Hassan II, is more convenient for people with their own transport, but it's no great shakes.

The best hotel by far, but a bit of a hike from the bus station, is the *Hôtel Bir Anzarane* (☎ 877834). It costs Dr 50 per person in clean, carpeted rooms. The shared showers are clean, and have hot water in the evenings.

Getting There & Away

Bus All the buses leave from the bus station (gare routière), about one km south of the main central square. CTM and SATAS are the best companies operating buses from here, although a lot of the services are through runs from other towns.

Taxi Grands taxis to Laayoune (Dr 70) and, occasionally, Tarfaya leave from a small square off Blvd el-Amir Moulay Abdallah. Others, for Goulimime (Dr 28), Tiznit and Inezgane (for Agadir – Dr 70), leave from a lot by the bus station.

Car Much cheaper petrol is available in the Western Sahara, which begins just south of Tarfaya. The first of the Atlas Sahara petrol stations is just outside Tarfaya and about 240 km south of Tan Tan – try to get there with a tank as close to empty as possible!

Around Tan Tan

Tan Tan Plage About 27 km west of Tan Tan is the beach of the same name. It's a rather uninspiring little spot, with a few cafés in among the scruffy housing and public buildings. With the main business being fish exports, the port area does nothing to improve the atmosphere on the beach.

The High Atlas

The ochre-coloured city of Marrakesh is possibly Morocco's biggest drawcard. Founded almost 1000 years ago, it basks in a clear African light that gives it an entirely different feel from the cities farther north. From the ad hoc, fairground atmosphere of the Djemaa el-Fna to the busy hum of the souqs, there is more than enough to keep the newcomer's senses fully occupied.

If the big city becomes too much, there are several escape routes into the majestic High Atlas mountain range that hovers snowcapped in the background. You can trek with the crowds on some of the more well-trodden routes, or, if you're fit and experienced, embark on more ambitious wanderings that could easily last weeks and take you into territory penetrated by only a handful of outsiders.

Valleys cut through the range and spill out south and east towards the Sahara. Dotted with kasbahs and palm groves, the spectacular natural settings are endowed with largely mediocre towns. These valleys and passes truly exemplify the bastardised maxim that 'it is better to travel than to arrive'.

Marrakesh

There can be few people who have not heard of Marrakesh. During the 1960s and '70s it was a magnet for travellers, along with Istanbul, Kabul and Kathmandu – and rightly so! The hippies have since been replaced by hordes of package tourists with more money

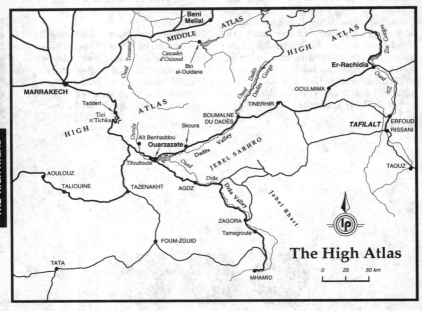

The High Atlas

0   25   50 km

and considerably less time than their more laid-back predecessors. The unfortunate side-effect of this onslaught has been the rise and rise of the unpleasant phenomenon of hustlers. However, although an undoubted irritant, it would take a lot more to detract from the fascination of this place.

Marrakesh is Morocco's second-largest city, with a population of about 1,400,000, although to walk around the centre it would not seem so. The red walls of the old city contain a busy, humming core, but you rarely get the sense of being suffocated by over-population. Perhaps the extensive gardens that spread out around the old city contribute to this – in any event they provide a welcome and tranquil refuge from the bustle of the souqs. Red, by the way, is supposedly the city's 'official' colour, just as it is blue for Fès, green for Meknès and white for Rabat.

Sitting against the backdrop of Morocco's highest mountains, which are snowcapped for much of the year, the city has a scenic setting that is hard to surpass.

History

Once one of the most important artistic and cultural centres in the Islamic world, Marrakesh was founded in 1062 AD by the Almoravid sultan Youssef bin Tachfin. It experienced its heyday under Youssef's son, Ali, who was born to a Christian slave mother. It was Ali who had the extensive underground irrigation canals (khettara) built that still supply the city's gardens with water.

As the Almoravids proceeded with their conquest of Spain, much of the wealth that flowed to the kingdom was lavished on extending and beautifying the city. When Youssef bin Tachfin died in 1106, he could do so content in the knowledge that he had not only consolidated his dynasty's control of Morocco and Spain (in 1085 he had defeated the Christians after they had seized the city of Toledo), but he had also bequeathed an urban jewel to his successors. Inside the city's red stone and earthen ramparts, characteristic of Berber defensive architecture, artisans from Muslim Spain

erected the first of the refined, Andalusian-style buildings that were to grace the city.

These buildings were largely razed to the ground by the Almohads in 1147, although the walls and the gateway to Ali's huge palace were spared. The city was rebuilt shortly afterwards, and, again, it was artisans from Andalusia who were responsible for the greater part of its construction. Marrakesh remained the capital of the Almohad empire until its collapse in 1269, when the Merenids moved the capital north to Fès, which then became the focus of Moroccan brilliance in the arts.

With the rise to power of the Saadians in the 16th century, Marrakesh again became the capital, following a brief period when the city of Taroudannt enjoyed that particular honour. The city had experienced hard times prior to the Saadian takeover. Even the Portuguese had tried to capture Marrakesh in 1515, and in the following years famines had crippled activity in the city and surrounding countryside.

Saadian control brought prosperity once again. During their reign the Portuguese were forced to abandon the bulk of their coastal enclaves. The mellah, the huge Mouassine Mosque and the Ali ben Youssef Medersa were built in these times. The Saadians also set up a customs house for the Christian colony that had been established in Marrakesh. Ahmed al-Mansour was one of the more outstanding of the Saadian sultans, and was known as 'the Golden One' because of his riches, largely accumulated in his 'conquest' of Timbuktu. His legacy included the exquisite Andalusian El-Badi Palace and the long-hidden necropolis of his dynasty, now known simply as the Saadian tombs.

As so often in Morocco's turbulent history, the golden days were soon followed by chaos and decadence. The Saadians' successors, the Alawites, moved the capital to Meknès.

Marrakesh could not be ignored, however. Although Moulay Ismail was responsible for tearing apart the El-Badi Palace for its building materials, his successor, Sidi Mohammed bin Abdallah, poured resources

See Marrakesh Ville Nouvelle Map

PLACES TO STAY

5 Youth Hostel
6 Camping Ground
7 Hôtel de la Ménara
23 Hôtel Islane
27 Hôtel La Mamounia

OTHER

1 Hospital
2 Tourist Office
3 Post Office (PTT)
4 Train Station
8 Bab Larissa
9 Bab Doukkala
10 Bus Station
11 Zawiyya of Sidi ben Slimane
12 Zawiyya of Sidi Bel Abbes
13 Bab el-Khemis
14 Bab Kechich
15 Bab Debbagh
16 Tanneries

17 Ali ben Youssef Medersa
18 Ali ben Youssef Mosque
19 Bab Doukkala Mosque
20 Hôtel de Ville
21 Ensemble Artisanal
22 Public Swimming Pool
24 Koutoubia
25 French Consulate
26 Bab el-Jedid
28 Dar Si Said (Museum
   of Moroccan Arts)
29 Palais de la Bahia
30 Bab Ailen
31 Bab Ghemat
32 Place des Ferblantiers
33 Palais el-Badi
34 Saadian Tombs
35 Kasbah Mosque
36 Bab Agnaou
37 Bab er-Rob
38 Bab Ksiba
39 Royal Palace
40 Mechouar
41 Bab al-Ahmar

THE HIGH ATLAS

Marrakesh

0   250   500 m

To Ouarzazate,
Meknès & Fès

Route Principale No 24

Rue Assouel

Rue de Bab Khemis

Route des Remparts

Rue de Bab Tahtzout

Rue el-Gza

11

12

13

14

15

See Marrakesh
Medina Map

18 17

16

Rue de Bab Debbagh

Rue de Bab Doukkala

19

Rue Dar el-Glaoui

Rue Fatima Zohra

Rue Sidi el-Yamani

Rue Mouassine

Rue Souq as-Smarine

Rue Azbezt

Rue Issebtyine

Rue de Bab Ailen

30

Rue el-Koutoubia

Rue Dabach

Rue Graoul

Rue Ba Ahmad

20

21

Sebti

Rue Abbes

23

Avenue Mohammed V

22

Place Djemaa
el-Fna

See Marrakesh
(Budget Hotel Area)

Rue

28

To Ouarzazate

24

Avenue
el-Mouahidine

25

Rue Riad Zitoun el-Jedid

Rue Zitoun el-Qdem

29

31

Ave Houmane el-Fetouaki

26

27

Rue de Bab Agnaou

Rue Sidi Mimoun

Ave Houmane
el-Fetouaki

32

Mellah

Boulevard el-Yarmouk

37 36

35 34

Rue de la Kasbah

33

41

39

THE HIGH ATLAS

To Airport

To Asni &
Taroudannt

38

Kasbah

40

Jardin
Agdal

into rebuilding or restoring the walls, kasbah, palaces, mosques and mechouars of the city, as well as creating new gardens (such as the Jardin Ménara).

By the 19th century, Marrakesh was again on the decline, although it did regain some of its former prestige when Moulay al-Hassan I was crowned there in 1873. Its most recent return to good fortune is largely the result of French activities during the protectorate period, when the ville nouvelle was built, the medina was revitalised and resettled, and the Place de Foucauld was created below the Djemaa el-Fna. Increasing tourism in Marrakesh since then has ensured its continued prosperity. The importance attached to the city by Morocco itself was symbolised in April 1994, when it was chosen as the location for the final signing of the international GATT agreements on world trade.

Orientation
As in Fès and Meknès, the old city and the ville nouvelle of Marrakesh are about the same size. It's about a half-hour walk from the centre of activity in the ville nouvelle to the Djemaa el-Fna, the main square in the heart of the old city, so you'll find it convenient to use public transport to get from one to the other. The two main areas of the ville nouvelle are Gueliz and Hivernage. The latter contains little more of interest than some middle and top-range hotels, and it borders on the Ménara Gardens.

Gueliz forms the working centre of the ville nouvelle, and the bulk of the city's offices, restaurants, cafés and shops and a collection of hotels are all clustered on or near the city's main thoroughfare, Ave Mohammed V, mostly west of Place du 16 Novembre. The railway station lies southwest of Ave Mohammed V along Ave Hassan II, which joins the former at Place du 16 Novembre. The main bus station is near Bab Doukkala, about a 10-minute walk northeast of the same square, and about 20 minutes on foot from the Djemaa el-Fna.

The walls around the medina enclose a far more open area than that found behind the walls of Fès and Meknès. It is not until you have penetrated to the heart of the old city, the Djemaa el-Fna, that you reach the familiar maze of souqs and twisting alleys.

The Djemaa el-Fna itself is a large, irregularly shaped square dominated from a distance by the city's most prominent landmark, the Koutoubia Mosque. The area is in many ways rather nondescript. There are no grand monuments overlooking the jumble of people, food stalls, tourists, hustlers and snake charmers who lend it its life, but you will soon be beguiled by its atmosphere. For centuries, traders, farmers, thieves, slaves and just about every other possible species have milled around here.

Most of the budget hotels are clustered in the narrow streets branching off the eastern and south-eastern sides of the square. The souqs and principal religious buildings lie to the north of the Djemaa el-Fna, and the palaces are to the south.

Information
Tourist Office The ONMT office (☎ 448 889; fax 448906) is on Place Abdel Moumen ben Ali, at the junction of Ave Mohammed V and Rue de Yougoslavie (or Ave du Président Kennedy, depending on which map you believe). It has the usual range of glossy leaflets and a list (without prices) of the classified hotels in Marrakesh, but precious little else. If you're lucky, it will have a couple of copies of the free booklet *Welcome to Marrakesh*. It may be able to put you in touch with guides in Asni for treks in the High Atlas, but then so can some of the hotels. The office is open Monday to Friday from 8.30 am to noon and again from 3.30 to 6.30 pm.

Money You should have no trouble changing money. As usual, your best bet is the BMCE. The branch across from the tourist office in Gueliz has an ATM as well as a change office, open daily from 10 am to 2 pm and 4 to 8 pm. You can change cash or travellers' cheques or get a cash advance on Visa or MasterCard. The BMCE branch on Rue de Moulay Ismail, just south of the Djemaa el-Fna, offers the same services. The Bank al-Maghrib (Banque du Maroc) on the Djemaa el-Fna will change cash and travellers' cheques.

American Express is represented by Voyages Schwartz (☎ 436600/3), Immeuble Moutaouakil, 1 Rue Mauritania. Although it's a little hard to believe, the operators claim to have someone manning the office from 6 am to 11 pm, Monday to Friday.

Post & Telecommunications The main post office is on Place du 16 Novembre in the ville nouvelle. There is a branch office on the Djemaa el-Fna. The main office is open from 8.30 am to 6.45 pm from Monday to Friday, and on Saturday morning. Poste restante is at Window 6. The rather small phone office is to the left of the main entrance and is open seven days a week from 8.30 am to 9 pm. If you want to send a package, there is a separate office around the corner from the PTT on Ave Hassan II. Your parcel can be wrapped for a small fee after customs inspection.

Foreign Consulates Foreign consulates in Marrakesh include:

France
  Rue Ibn Khaldoun (or Dar Moulay Ali, just by the Koutoubia) (☎ 444006)
Sweden
  Immeuble As-Saada, angle Rue Moulay Ali et Rue de Yougoslavie (☎ 449660)

Cultural Centres The Centre Culturel Français (☎ 443196) is quite a small affair just off the Djemaa el-Fna on Rue de Moulay Ismail. Apart from French classes, it organises a range of films, lectures and the like that might provide an interesting diversion for Francophiles.

The American Language Center (ALC; ☎ 447259) has a branch in Gueliz at 3 Impasse du Moulin. The ALC's main activity is its English classes for Marrakshis – and if you're looking for work you might want to drop by on the off chance that there is a vacancy. Otherwise, they put on the occasional film and lecture.

The International Language Centre is represented by Radi Ahmed (☎ 309237).

Guides You can arrange an official guide for Dr 30 to Dr 50 for a half-day at the tourist office or in the bigger hotels. The benefits of a guide, especially if you don't have a lot of time, are twofold: they can save you from taking wrong turns, and they immediately stop you being pestered by other would-be guides, which considerably reduces your blood pressure.

Travel Agencies The bulk of the travel agents (including RAM's office – see Getting There & Away) are located around Ave Mohammed V, west of Place du 16 Novembre. They include Wagons-Lits and Menara Tours (☎ 446654; fax 446107). The latter, at 41 Rue de Yougoslavie, represents GB Airways, which has a couple of flights a week linking the UK to Marrakesh via Gibraltar. Some of these agencies can organise trips into the High Atlas and also tours down the Drâa Valley. However, they are generally quite expensive and you'd be better off going it alone.

Bookshops For books in English, head straight for the ALC bookshop. It has a range of English literature and quite a few titles on Morocco, but it is open from 3 to 7 pm only.

Otherwise, there are a couple of reasonable bookshops for readers of French and Arabic along Ave Mohammed V, west of Place du 16 Novembre.

Medical Services & Emergency There is an all-night chemist (☎ 430415) on Rue Khalid ben el-Oualid. Private ambulances can be reached on ☎ 443724.

Film & Photography There are several places along Ave Mohammed V where you can buy film and get rolls developed. One reasonable place is Photo Magic.

Ensemble Artisanal As in most of the major Moroccan cities, the Ensemble Artisanal is a sensible first stop to get an idea of *maximum* prices to offer for souvenirs once you are rummaging around in the souqs. It's better for sampling the quality of merchandise than for purchasing.

An awful lot of shops have notices posted in their windows inviting you to call one of several numbers if you feel you've been unfairly treated in a purchase, either on price or quality of the goods. What exactly can be done and what would constitute a rip-off in these circumstances is difficult to imagine. However, if you want to have a chat with the head of the Price Control Service, call ☎ 308430 (ext 360).

Djemaa el-Fna

The focal point of Marrakesh is the Djemaa el-Fna, a huge square in the old part of town where many of the budget hotels are located. According to Paul Bowles, without it, Marrakesh would become just another Moroccan city. Other than the souqs, this is where everything happens; visitors are destined to spend a lot of time here.

Although it's a lively place at any time of day, it comes into its own in the evening, as the curtain goes up on one of the world's most fascinating spectacles. Rows and rows of open-air food stalls are set up and mouth-watering aromas fill the square. Jugglers, storytellers, snake charmers, magicians, acrobats and benign lunatics take over the rest of the space, each surrounded by an audience of jostling spectators who listen and watch intently, or fall about laughing and move on to another act starting up nearby. Before they can get away, assistants hassle them for contributions.

If you are feeling poorly, you might want to try some herbal cures, which the Marrakshis swear by. No matter what your ailment, the vendors of herbs and potions can prescribe something for the common cold or something a little stronger to administer to your worst enemy! In between the groups of spectators, diners, shoppers and tourists weave hustlers, thieves, knick-knack sellers and the occasional glue-sniffing kid. On the outer edges, kerosene lanterns ablaze, are the fruit and juice stalls.

It is a scene that, to one extent or another, was previously played out in the great squares of many Moroccan cities. Unfortunately, TV has killed much of it off. It is often claimed that the activity in the Djemaa el-Fna survives mostly because of the tourists. In the case of the water sellers and snake charmers this may well be the case, but how do you explain the crowds around the storytellers? Precious few outsiders know what marvels or lunacies they are recounting to the obvious delight of the locals.

Around the edge of the square you can take a balcony seat in one of a number of rooftop cafés and restaurants and take in the whole spectacle at a respectful and more relaxing distance. Down below, the medieval pageant presents its nightly cornucopia of delights; Bruegel would have had a field day here!

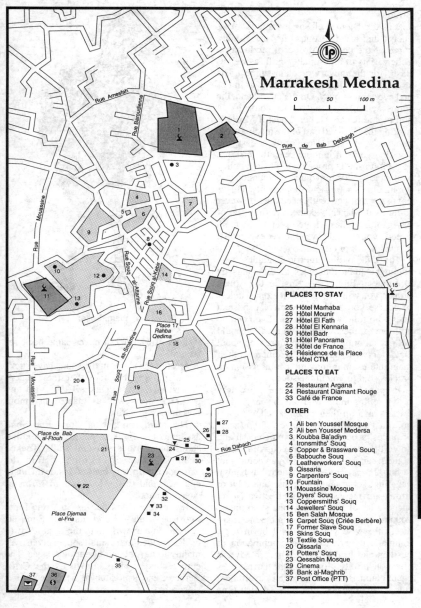

Marrakesh Medina

0   50   100 m

PLACES TO STAY

25 Hôtel Marhaba
26 Hôtel Mounir
27 Hôtel El Fath
28 Hôtel El Kennaria
30 Hôtel Badr
31 Hôtel Panorama
32 Hôtel de France
34 Résidence de la Place
35 Hôtel CTM

PLACES TO EAT

22 Restaurant Argana
24 Restaurant Diamant Rouge
33 Café de France

OTHER

1   Ali ben Youssef Mosque
2   Ali ben Youssef Medersa
3   Koubba Ba'adiyn
4   Ironsmiths' Souq
5   Copper & Brassware Souq
6   Babouche Souq
7   Leatherworkers' Souq
8   Qissaria
9   Carpenters' Souq
10 Fountain
11 Mouassine Mosque
12 Dyers' Souq
13 Coppersmiths' Souq
14 Jewellers' Souq
15 Ben Salah Mosque
16 Carpet Souq (Criée Berbère)
17 Former Slave Souq
18 Skins Souq
19 Textile Souq
20 Qissaria
21 Potters' Souq
23 Qessabin Mosque
29 Cinema
36 Bank al-Maghrib
37 Post Office (PTT)

Rue Amesfah
Rue Baroudienne
Rue de Bab Debbagh
Rue Mouassine
Rue Mouassine
Rue Mouassine
Rue Souq al-Kebir
Rue Souq al-Attarine
Rue Souq es-Smarine
Place Rahba Qedima
Place de Bab al-Ftouh
Place Djemaa el-Fna
Rue Dabach

THE HIGH ATLAS

Souqs

Just as the Djemaa el-Fna is famous for its energy and life, the souqs of Marrakesh are some of the best in Morocco, producing a wide variety of high-quality crafts as well as trash (for the unwary or plain stupid). The streets here are just as labyrinthine as in Fès and every bit as busy. On the other hand, the shops selling arts and crafts come to an abrupt end at the Ali ben Youssef Mosque, making the hard-sell part of the medina comparatively compact. Head north or east, and you find yourself in more peaceful territory.

As in Fès, it is probably a sensible policy to engage a guide for your first excursion into the medina's souqs and monuments. This is not to say that you really need one. However tortuous the lanes become, the first rule of navigation applies – if you keep to the main streets, you will always emerge, eventually, at a landmark or city gate.

The bulk of the unofficial guides hang about the main entrances to the souqs on Djemaa el-Fna. Once inside the souqs proper, you will largely be left alone – unless of course you strike some more persistent ones who follow you right in. If you end up with one of these people (you really should not pay an unofficial guide more than about Dr 20 for two or three hours), remember their main interest is in making a commission on articles sold to you in the souqs.

Prepare yourself for some extremely heavy selling in the Marrakesh souqs. Shop owners size up their potential clients early on, and it is claimed they have a sliding scale of prices, according to how much cash and how little sense they credit you with. Some of them can get quite nasty if you don't want to buy. Forget endlessly patient but benign haggling; some feel that abuse and a bit of strong-arm tactics are just as effective. Never spend a lot of time in any one shop unless you are seriously interested in the merchandise, otherwise you may well be in for a traumatic experience. The combination of hustlers and heavy sell has had an adverse effect on the city's tourism. One harried merchant claimed that a Moroccan government study had revealed that 94% of first-time

Water Seller

visitors to Marrakesh never came back for seconds!

Most of the shops in the souqs have stickers displaying the fact that they accept American Express, Diners Club, Visa and MasterCard, as well as many other more obscure credit cards.

The main entrance is along Rue Souq as-Smarrine, flanked mainly by **textiles** shops and various souvenir stalls. Tucked inside a group of buildings before the entrance is a **pottery** market. Inside the main entrance, and to the left, is a *qissaria*, or covered market.

Just before Rue Souq as-Smarrine forks into Rue Souq al-Kebir and Rue Souq al-Attarine, a narrow lane to the right leads to the Rahba Qedima, a small square given over mainly to **carpet** and **sheepskin** sales. The carpet souq is also known as the Criée Berbère, and it is situated near the former slave souq.

Back on the Rue Souq as-Smarrine, you could take either fork. Both more or less lead to the Ali ben Youssef mosque and medersa. If you take the left fork and veer off to the west, you will find yourself among **dyers**, **carpenters** and **coppersmiths**. Much of their work is not really aimed at tourists, and the atmosphere is a little more relaxed. Closer to the mosque all gives way to the clamour of the iron forges that dominate here. With a little luck, you'll emerge at either the mosque or the Koubba Ba'adiyn. Along the right fork, you'll encounter **jewellers**, whose stores then give way to **leatherwork** and **babouche** shops.

Mosques & Medersas

Like their counterparts elsewhere in Morocco, the mosques and working medersas in Marrakesh are generally closed to non-Muslims, and those inside the medina are so hemmed in by other buildings that little can be seen from the outside.

Koutoubia The only mosque with a perspective you can really appreciate, and the one you are most likely to encounter first, is the Koutoubia, across the other side of Place de Foucauld, south-west of the Djemaa el-Fna. It is also the tallest (70 metres) and most famous landmark in Marrakesh, visible for miles in any direction.

Constructed by the Almohads in the late 12th century, it features the oldest and best preserved of their three most famous minarets – the other two being the Tour Hassan in Rabat and the Giralda in Seville (Spain). The name (from *koutoub* or *kutub*, Arabic for books) comes from a booksellers' market that once existed around the mosque.

The Koutoubia minaret is a classic of Moroccan-Andalusian architecture; its features are mirrored in many other minarets throughout the country, but nowhere else has its sheer size been attempted.

When first built, the Koutoubia was covered with painted plaster and brilliantly coloured *zellij* tiles, but this decoration has all disappeared. What can still be seen, however, are the decorative panels, which

are different on each face and practically constitute a textbook of contemporary design. The views from the summit would be incredible, if non-Muslims were allowed to climb up there. Unfortunately, at the time of writing, the minaret was to some extent hidden by a thick web of sky-blue scaffolding.

Koubba Ba'adiyn After a stroll up through the souqs, the first monument open to non-Muslims that you'll probably come across is the most modest Marrakesh has to offer, and (restoration aside) about the oldest. Most of Almoravid Marrakesh was destroyed by the zealous Almohads who succeeded them, but the Koubba is a rare exception. Built in the early 12th century, it is a small but elegant display of Muslim decorative invention. Signposted on a small square in front of the Ali ben Youssef Mosque, entrance is Dr 10 and the guardian will want to show you around. He'll probably dig up a friend to 'guide' you to the Ali ben Youssef Medersa too, although it's just around the corner.

Ali ben Youssef Mosque The largest of the mosques inside the medina is the Ali ben Youssef Mosque, first built in the second half of the 12th century by the Almoravid sultan of the same name. It's the oldest surviving mosque in Marrakesh. However, the building itself is of fairly recent date, as it was almost completely rebuilt in the 19th century in the Merenid style in response to popular demand. When first constructed it was about twice its present size but it was severely damaged when the Almoravids were overthrown by the Almohads. It was later restored by both the Almohads and the Saadians. The mosque is closed to non-Muslims.

Ali ben Youssef Medersa Next to the Ali ben Youssef Mosque is the medersa of the same name. It is the largest theological college in the Maghreb, and was built by the Saadians in 1565 (and much restored in the 1960s). Heading east from the Koubba, simply follow the mosque walls around to the left, and you'll come to the entrance of the medersa on your right.

Although all Moroccan medersas at least loosely follow a similar ground plan (see Architecture in the Arts section of the Facts about the Country chapter), the Ali ben Youssef is not only bigger but also quite a bit different in layout.

You walk down a corridor and turn right onto the central courtyard, entering which you find yourself facing the *masjid*. Like virtually every other great medersa on view to non-Muslims, this was built under the Merenids, and it betrays the taste of those times for intricate stucco decoration combined with a zellij tile base and crowned by carved cedar.

Go back to the corridor and take the entrance opposite the courtyard. Two sets of stairs lead up to students' cells. As usual, they are small and bare. It's hard to imagine how, as is claimed, they crammed as many as 900 people into these rooms! The big difference between their arrangement here and that in other medersas is that many of them are clustered around seven small 'mini-courtyards'. Moreover, a few look out on to the street – somewhat of an exception to the general rule of Moroccan and Andalusian architecture.

Believe it or not, it is worth giving the lavatories a look. This is where they have always been, and it seems that little has changed. Not the most inviting place to relieve yourself.

Mouassine Mosque The other large mosque in the medina is the Mouassine Mosque, built in the 16th century by the Saadians on land formerly occupied by the Jewish community. Its most notable features are the three huge doorways and the intricately carved cedar ceilings. The fountain attached to this mosque still survives and is quite elaborate, with three sections – two for animals and one for humans. The mosque is closed to non-Muslims.

Ben Salah Mosque Of the other mosques in the medina, the Ben Salah Mosque (also known as the Ben Salah Zawiyya) is the most prominent; its brilliant green-tiled minaret can be seen from many places. It was built by the Merenid sultan Abu Said Uthman between 1318 and 1321. Again, it's closed to non-Muslims.

Zawiyyas In the north-western zone of the medina are two zawiyyas dedicated to two of the seven saints claimed by Marrakesh (pilgrimage to the tombs of all seven is, in the popular mind at any rate, the equivalent of a pilgrimage to Mecca – a considerably more arduous undertaking for Moroccans). North of the Sidi ben Slimane Zawiyya is that of Sidi Bel Abbes, the most important of the seven saints. Entry to the sanctuaries is forbidden to non-Muslims.

Palaces & Environs

Palais el-Badi The most famous of the palaces of Marrakesh was the El-Badi Palace, built by Ahmed al-Mansour between 1578 and 1602. At the time of its construction it was reputed to be one of the most beautiful in the world (and was known as 'the Incomparable'); it included marble from Italy and other precious building materials from as far away as India. The enormous cost of building the palace was met largely from the ransom the Portuguese were forced to pay out following their disastrous defeat at the hands of the Saadians in 1578 in the Battle of the Three Kings. Unfortunately, the palace is now largely a ruin, having been torn apart by Moulay Ismail in 1696 for its building materials, which were used to build his new capital at Meknès.

What remains is essentially a huge square surrounded by devastated walls enclosing a sunken orange grove and a number of modern concrete pools. When you're inside by the orange grove, you'll notice a large structure to the west. This is the Koubba al-Khamsiniyya, which was used as a great reception hall on state occasions and was named after its 50 marble columns.

Proceed south towards the walls of the Royal Palace (which is closed to visitors) and you'll find yourself in a confusing maze of underground corridors, storerooms and dungeons. Which were which is a little hard to tell. For lovers of dark places, there's a bit of potential exploring to do – bring a torch (flashlight).

The El-Badi is open to the public daily, except on certain religious holidays, between 8.30 am and noon and 2.30 and 6 pm. Entry costs Dr 10. You're free to wander around on your own, although guides will initially hassle you to engage their services. The palace is also the venue for the annual Folklore Festival, usually held in June.

The easiest way to get to the palace is to take Ave Houmane el-Fetouaki down from the Koutoubia to Place des Ferblantiers, where the ramparts begin, and you'll see a large gateway. Go through this and turn to the right. The entrance and ticket booth are ahead of you.

Palais de la Bahia The Palais de la Bahia was built towards the end of the 19th century, over a period of 14 years, as the residence of Si' Ahmed ben Musa (also known as Bou Ahmed), the Grand Vizier of Sultan Moulay al-Hassan I. On Bou Ahmed's death it was ransacked, but much has since been restored.

It's a rambling structure with fountains, living quarters, pleasure gardens and numerous secluded, shady courtyards, but it lacks architectural cohesion. This in no way detracts from the visual pleasure of the place, and, as your guide will no doubt point out, the difference between the peace, quiet and coolness inside the palace and the heat, noise and chaos in the streets outside is noticeable. It exemplifies the privacy-conscious priorities behind Muslim architecture. In fact, and this may not have been so deliberate, you will often find that the multiple doorways linking various parts of the palace are so placed that you often can't see much past the open doorway, creating the impression of a series of separate and unconnected zones within the whole.

You can only visit part of the palace, as some of it is still used by the royal family and to house maintenance staff. You will be taken through a series of rooms, among them the vizier's sleeping quarters (he had separate ones for snoozing during the day and evening) and various courtyards set aside for his wives and concubines. The four wives each had a room arranged around a courtyard. The sleeping quarters for the rather more numerous harem were also gathered around a (separate) courtyard.

The palace is open daily from 8.30 am to 1 pm (11.45 am in winter) and 4 to 7 pm (2.30 to 6 pm in winter). Entry is free, but you must take and pay a guide. To get there (orientation is easiest from the Palais el-Badi), go back to the Place des Ferblantiers, and keep following Ave Houmane el-Fetouaki away from the budget hotel area and around to the left (north). You'll soon come to the entrance, set in a garden, on your right.

Dar Si Said Farther on from the Palais de la Bahia and again off to the right (it's signposted), the Dar Si Said, which now houses the **Museum of Moroccan Arts**, is well worth a visit.

Sidi Said, Bou Ahmed's brother, built what became his town house at about the same time as the grand vizier's palace was constructed. Today, the museum houses one of the finest collections in the country, including jewellery from the High Atlas, the Anti-Atlas and the extreme south; carpets from the Haouz and the High Atlas; oil lamps from Taroudannt; blue pottery from Safi and green pottery from Tamegroute; and leatherwork from Marrakesh.

As you enter, you will see a series of doors typical of the richer High Atlas and Anti-Atlas houses. At the end of this corridor is the oldest exhibit in the museum: an old marble basin dating back to about 1000 AD, brought to Marrakesh from Spain by Ali ben Youssef.

Next up are some delightful medieval precursors of the Ferris wheel for tiny tots.

The central garden and courtyard is flanked by rooms housing displays of heavy, southern jewellery in silver, traditional women's garments, household goods, old muskets and daggers.

On the next floor is a magnificently decorated room, its characteristic stucco and zellij tiles capped by a stunning carved and painted cedar ceiling. From here, the signs lead you upstairs again and then down through various rooms dominated by rug and carpet displays. All the explanations are, unfortunately, in Arabic and French only.

It's open from 9 am to noon and 4 to 7 pm (2.30 to 6 pm in winter); closed Tuesday. On Friday it's closed from 11.30 am to 3 pm. Entry costs Dr 10.

Maison Tiskiwin Virtually next door to the Dar Si Said is the house of Bert Flint, a Dutch art lecturer and long-time resident of Morocco. It has been opened to the public as a small museum, and principally contains carpets and traditional textile work. The Maison Tiskiwin (☎ 443335) is only open in the morning.

Mellah The old Jewish quarter, established in the 16th century, is just south of the Palais de la Bahia. Much neglected and now populated mainly by Muslims, it still has quite a different look to it from the rest of the city. The main entrance is off Place des Ferblantiers, and if you want to visit any of the small synagogues (one is still in use) you'll need a local guide.

Saadian Tombs Next to the Kasbah Mosque is the necropolis, which was initiated by the Saadian sultan Ahmed al-Mansour in the late 1500s. Unlike the Palais el-Badi, another of Al-Mansour's projects, the tombs escaped Moulay Ismail's depredations – possibly because he was superstitious about plundering the dead. Instead he sealed the tombs and, as a result, they still convey some of the opulence and superb artistry that must also have been lavished on the palace. Sixty-six of the Saadians, including Al-Mansour, his successors and their closest family members, lie buried under the two main structures, and there are over a hundred more buried outside the buildings.

Although the mad sultan Moulay Yazid was laid to rest here in 1792, the tombs essentially remained sealed following Moulay Ismail's reign. They were not 'rediscovered' until 1917, when General Lyautey, his curiosity awakened by an aerial survey of the area, ordered the construction of a passageway down. They have since been restored.

To get to the tombs, take Rue de Bab Agnaou to Bab Agnaou itself (the only surviving Almohad gateway in Marrakesh), which is on the left and almost adjacent to Bab er-Rob. Go through Bab Agnaou and walk straight past a row of shops until you come to the Kasbah Mosque. Turn right down Rue de la Kasbah and, when you get to the end of the mosque, you'll see a narrow alleyway on the left. Go down it, and the entrance to the tombs is at the end.

After buying your ticket, you follow a very narrow passage that opens onto the main mausoleum, which is divided into three small halls. Those at either end contain tombs of children. The central one, the Hall of the Twelve Columns, is considered to be one of the finest examples of Moroccan-Andalusian decorative art. Among the columns of Italian marble are the tombs of Ahmed al-Mansour, his son and grandson.

The elegant little mausoleum set farther in amid the gardens of the necropolis houses the tomb of Al-Mansour's mother.

The tombs are open to the public every day, except Friday morning, from 8 am to noon and 2.30 to 7 pm (6 pm in winter). Entry costs Dr 10 and you're allowed to wander around at will. If you prefer, a guardian will accompany you and explain what you are looking at. You will be expected to offer a tip at the end.

Tanneries

If you didn't *do* the tanneries in Fès, or feel you need another dose of them, you can give those at Marrakesh a whirl. They are out by Bab Debbagh, at the north-eastern end of the medina and a reasonably straightforward walk from the Ali ben Youssef Mosque. If you have trouble finding them, just ask for the road to the gate or take up the offer of one of the young lads hanging around the entrance to the medersa to guide you there.

Gardens

A slightly more pleasant olfactory experience is provided by the several beautiful gardens which are laid out around the city.

Jardin Ménara About a four-km walk west of the Koutoubia, the Jardin Ménara is the most easily reached of Marrakesh's green spaces. Although it is quite popular with Marrakshis, it is generally a peaceful place to unload some of the stress and escape the summer heat of the city. The centrepiece of what is basically a more organised continuation of the olive groves immediately to the east is a large, still pool backed by a pavilion built in 1866. What is now open to the public was once the exclusive preserve of sultans and high ministers.

Jardin Agdal Stretching for several km south from the Royal Palace, the vegetation is more varied here than in the Jardin Ménara and there are several pavilions. To get there (a bicycle would be ideal), take the path that runs south from the south-western corner of the mechouar (parade ground) in front of the Royal Palace. It appears the gardens are often closed, so having a bicycle should take some of the sting out of the potential disappointment.

Jardin Majorelle Now owned by Yves Saint-Laurent, these exquisite gardens were laid out by the French painter Jacques Majorelle, who lived here from 1922 to 1962. In amongst the floral smorgasbord is what was Majorelle's deep-blue villa, which now houses a modest museum of Islamic art. The gardens are in the ville nouvelle, north of Ave Yacoub el-Mansour.

Hôtel La Mamounia For the price of a very expensive coffee, you could get in to what in this century has become something of a monument itself. La Mamounia (see Places to Stay) was Winston Churchill's favourite hotel, and it is blessed with lush and sedate gardens that do as much good for the frazzled as any of the public gardens.

Église des Saints-Martyrs

Of mild interest is the Catholic church (built in 1926) in Gueliz, south of Ave Yacoub al-Mrini. It was built in keeping with its environment and is a nice example of the European interpretation of Mauresque architecture. Mass is celebrated every day.

Festivals

If you're in Marrakesh in June (the dates seem rather fluid), enquire about the Festival of Folklore which is held in the Palais el-Badi at that time. It's a folk-dancing and singing extravaganza, performed by some of the best troupes from throughout Morocco. In July there's the famous Fantasia, a charge of Berber horsemen that takes place outside the ramparts. You often see pictures of it in the tourist literature.

It's not quite a festival, but if you enjoy watching a bit of athletics you might want to be around at the end of January for the annual Grand Prix de Hassan II Marathon.

Places to Stay – bottom end

Camping The camp site (☎ 435570) is close to the youth hostel, just off the Ave de France. There's little shade and the ground is stony. Camping costs Dr 10 per person, Dr 11 to put up a big tent, Dr 8 for a car (Dr 7 for motorbikes) and Dr 14 for electricity. It's hardly worth it.

Hostel The *youth hostel* (☎ 447713) is close to the railway station and can be a good first stop on arrival. Indeed, some people prefer to spend their whole stay in Marrakesh here, because it's well hidden from the hustle and bustle of the big city. On the other hand, it is a bit far from where things are going on. It costs Dr 20 for a bed, and Dr 5 extra for a decent hot shower. You need your membership card and it's open from 8 to 9 am, noon to 2 pm and 6 to 10 pm.

Hotels – medina Most of the cheapest accommodation deals can be found in the area immediately south of the Djemaa el-Fna and east of Rue de Bab Agnaou, where there are scores of reasonably priced hotels.

THE HIGH ATLAS

There's not a lot to choose between most of them, other than whether they offer hot showers or not (not important in summer but definitely so in winter) and how clean they are. Some places have no showers at all, in which case you could try one of the hammams.

Most of the cheapies will charge extra for hot showers (Dr 5 to Dr 10) and some even charge for cold showers (Dr 2). Prices in most vary little and start at Dr 30 a single, Dr 50 a double and Dr 70 to Dr 75 a triple. Some of the better ones charge more, and in summer most of them hike up their prices according to demand, so you could end up paying more here than you would for a better room in a classified hotel.

A short way down from the Djemaa el-Fna, between Rue Zitoune el-Qedim and Rue de Bab Agnaou, is the *Hôtel Souria*. It is one of the better ones, and charges Dr 50/70 for singles/doubles (or Dr 80 for two big beds) and a slightly over-the-top Dr 10 for a hot shower. Slightly cheaper (Dr 35 for singles) is the adjacent *Hôtel El Atlal*, which has bright and clean (if small) rooms upstairs. It also charges Dr 10 for a hot shower.

Possibly the biggest joke in all Marrakesh is the *Hôtel Le Minaret*. At Dr 100/150 for a basic single/double with private toilet and shower, it's hard to imagine anyone wanting to stay there. How does it make any money?

Along to the north is the *Hôtel Essaouira* (☎ 443805). Its well-placed terrace and tiny café makes it a cut above some of its neighbours, although most of the rooms are very small. You pay from Dr 30 to Dr 40 each, and a hot shower is Dr 5.

Others that appear marginally better than the rest include the *Panorama* (☎ 445047), *Cecil*, *Afriquia* and *Chellah* (☎ 442977). The Chellah charges Dr 60/90 and Dr 10 for a hot shower, making it a bit borderline.

Be careful not to confuse the *Hôtel de France* (☎ 443067) on Rue Zitoune el-Qedim, which charges Dr 30 per head, with its namesake (attached to the Café de France) on the Djemaa el-Fna. Although the latter (☎ 442319) is nothing special, its rooms, at Dr 40/60/80 for doubles/triple/quadruples, are not the worst you'll find and the rooftop café is a good vantage point overlooking the square.

In the centre of the budget hotel area, the *Hôtel de la Paix* must be one of the cheapest places going, at Dr 25/40/50/60. The rooms are cell-like but clean, but it has no showers (and is not alone in this regard).

The *Hôtel Charaf* (☎ 427089), a bit farther south of the Djemaa el-Fna, charges about Dr 30 a person for OK rooms, but there is little to recommend its location and it has no showers.

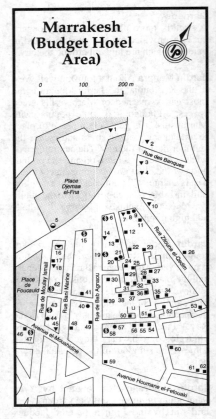

Marrakesh (Budget Hotel Area)

PLACES TO STAY

8	Hôtel CTM
11	Hôtel des Amis
12	Hôtel Cecil
13	Hôtels Jeunesse & Echamal
17	Hôtel Ali
22	Atlas & Menzah Hôtels
23	Hôtel du Sud
24	Hôtel Elazhar
25	Hôtel Nouzha
26	Hôtel de France
27	Hôtel Mauritania
28	Hôtel Provence
29	Hôtel de la Paix
30	Hôtel Central
31	Hôtel Afriquia
32	Hôtel Eddakhla
33	Hôtel Zagora
34	Hôtel Medina
35	Hôtel Essaouira
36	Hôtel Sahara
37	Hôtel Central Annexe
38	Hôtel El Ward
39	Hôtel Mabrouk
41	Hôtel Ichbilia
46	Hôtel de Foucauld
48	Hôtel La Gazelle
49	Hôtel du Tourisme
50	Hôtel El Atlal
51	Hôtel Gallia
52	Hôtel Arabia
53	Hôtel Chellah
54	Hôtel Souria
55	Hôtel Hillal
56	Hôtel El Farak
59	Grand Hôtel du Tazi
60	Hôtel Le Minaret
61	Hôtel El Bouchra
62	Hôtel Kawakib

PLACES TO EAT

1	Café/Restaurant El Fath
2	Restaurant Le Marrakechi
3	Café de France
4	Café de la Place
7	Le Grand Balcon
10	Pâtisserie Toubkal
14	Restaurant Étoile
18	Restaurant Ali
45	Iceberg Restaurant

OTHER

5	Grands Taxis
6	Banque Populaire
9	Old CTM & SATAS Terminals
15	Bank al-Maghrib
16	Post Office (PTT)
19	Crédit du Maroc
20	Women's Hammam
21	Men's Hammam
40	Cinema Mabrouka
42	Wafabank
43	BMCE (ATM)
44	Centre Culturel Français
47	BMCI Bank (ATM)
57	Men's Hammam
58	Banque Populaire

Of the rest, the *Arabia* (☎ 441920), *Sahara*, *Zagora*, *Mauritania*, *El Ward* (☎ 423354), *Hillal* and *El Farak* distinguish themselves mainly by their firm declarations of having only cold showers.

The only other advice that can be given is to wander around a bit for something that suits. All these places are in pretty short walking distance of one another.

Three hotels that are a little more expensive but can be recommended are within a stone's throw of the Djemaa el-Fna, and offer more comfort than the run-of-the-mill cheapies. The *Hôtel Ichbilia* (☎ 434947) is just off Rue Bani Marine, and it has singles/doubles for Dr 60/95. The showers are outside and are hot in the mornings. Try to get a room upstairs, as the street can be noisy. Farther north, the *Hôtel Ali* (☎ 444979) has decent rooms for Dr 70/90/125, or you can sleep on the terrace for about Dr 30 and lock your things up in a storage room. This is a good place to get information on High Atlas trekking possibilities and guides. Back on Rue Bani Marine, the *Hôtel La Gazelle* (☎ 441112) is a good place which offers rooms for Dr 60/100 on the first night and Dr 50/90 on subsequent nights.

On the Djemaa el-Fna itself you could try the *Hôtel CTM* (☎ 442325). The bus company of the same name used to be here and so there is parking space. Singles/doubles with private shower and toilet are Dr 78/103. The rooms are OK, although the beds are on the saggy side. You may be able to get cheaper rooms without shower and toilet, but they don't seem keen to advertise them. With its terrace café, it's the location that really makes the place.

Finally, there are a few cheapies on the north-eastern side of the Djemaa el-Fna which are not so often used by travellers. They are no more exciting than the main group of unclassified hotels, but the position, virtually by the souqs, might appeal to some. They include the *Marhaba*, *Mounir*, *El Fath*, *El Kennaria* and *Badr*.

THE HIGH ATLAS

Hotels – Gueliz There are no unclassified pensions and not too many cheap hotels in the ville nouvelle. You'll find the few there are around Ave Mohammed V, west of Place du 16 Novembre. The cheapest is the one-star *Hôtel Franco-Belge* (☎ 448472), 62 Blvd Mohammed Zerktouni, close to the tourist office. It has a pleasant courtyard and rooms cost Dr 60/80 without shower and Dr 80/104 with shower and toilet.

A few doors down towards Ave Mohammed V is the one-star *Hôtel des Voyageurs* (☎ 431235), at 40 Blvd Mohammed Zerktouni. Singles without a shower or toilet cost Dr 60, while singles and doubles with shower and toilet cost Dr 100/130. The Franco-Belge is preferable.

Another possibility is the *Hôtel Oasis* (☎ 447179), at 50 Ave Mohammed V, which has singles/doubles with private shower and shared toilet for Dr 78/103.

Places to Stay – middle

Medina The two-star *Hôtel Gallia* (☎ 445913 or 444853), 30 Rue de la Recette, is with little doubt about the most pleasant hotel in the medina area. Singles/doubles with toilet cost Dr 82/101 and those with shower as well Dr 123/182. They have hot, steaming showers and central heating in winter. This place is often booked out, especially during holidays and on weekends.

The *Grand Hôtel du Tazi* (☎ 442787; fax 442152), on the corner of Ave El-Mouahidine and Rue de Bab Agnaou, is a much larger and more expensive hotel, at Dr 154/250 for rooms with shower and toilet. The rooms are quite adequate and also have phones, and the hotel boasts a small pool, a bar and a restaurant (20% off meals for people staying in the hotel).

A little farther away, on Ave El-Mouahidine, is the cavernous *Hôtel de Foucauld* (☎ 445499). Although some of the rooms can be noisy and a tad small, they are clean and comfortable, and not bad value at Dr 86/110 with shower or Dr 110/127 with shower and toilet. The hotel has a restaurant and a tiny pool, and the staff can help organise mountain-bike excursions, 4WD trips and cross-country skiing.

Back on the Djemaa el-Fna, another possibility is the *Résidence de la Place* (☎ 445174). The main attraction is, as usual, the terrace café overlooking the square. Singles/doubles cost Dr 100/150, but the rate could come down as the staff seem eager to please. The rooms are OK, especially if you can get one overlooking the Djemaa (although light sleepers may well prefer something on the courtyard out the back).

Along Ave Mohammed V, heading west towards Bab Larissa and the ville nouvelle, is a good two-star place, the *Hôtel Islane* (☎ 440081/3; fax 440085). The rooms are modern and comfortable, and some have balconies with views across to the Koutoubia. This hotel boasts a pleasant rooftop restaurant and café, and the rooms have toilet, shower and phone. Including the obligatory breakfast, singles/doubles go for Dr 177/227. It has parking, and cheerfully accepts credit-card payment – as indeed do most Marrakshi hotels in this class and up.

Gueliz & Hivernage The bulk of the mid-range hotels are located outside the medina, mostly in Gueliz, with a couple closer to the medina boundary in the Hivernage area. There are a lot of them, especially in the three and four-star category.

An older place with a bit of character and reasonable rooms is the *Hôtel des Ambassadeurs* (☎ 447159). It has a restaurant and bar next door, and, as it's in the more lively part of Gueliz, there is a good choice of eateries and cafés nearby. Singles/doubles with shower only cost Dr 129/163, while rooms with full bathroom are Dr 157/187.

Going up in price, and just outside the old city walls, is the somewhat neglected *Hôtel Yasmine* (☎ 446200) on Blvd de Yarmouk. The staff are friendly enough and rooms cost Dr 138/182, including an obligatory breakfast.

For exactly the same rate as the recommended Hôtel Islane, you could end up in the altogether gloomier *Hôtel Al Mouatamid*

Cascades d'Ouzoud (DS)

Top: Tizi n'Test – Marrakesh side of the pass (DS)
Bottom Left: Toubkal massif (DS)
Bottom Right: Dadès Gorge (DS)

(☎ 448094), at 94 Ave Mohammed V, close to the tourist office.

Not far away, on Blvd Mohammed Zerktouni, and edging up the price scale, are the *Hôtel Smara* (☎ 434150 or 434170) and the *Hôtel Al Bustan* (☎ 446810), adjacent at No 68. Both charge Dr 201/252/338 for reasonably spacious rooms with balconies, bathrooms and phone. Somehow they both feel rather characterless and dead. The latter has a little bar downstairs that nonguests can use. Beyond these is the four-star *Hôtel Kenza* (☎ 448330; fax 435386), a newish

place but really getting too far away from the centre. It has a pleasant enough beer garden.

Back on Ave Mohammed V is the three-star *Hôtel Amalay* (☎ 449023; fax 431554) and around the corner past the former Hôtel de la Renaissance is the *Hôtel Tachfine* (☎ 447188; fax 472089), both of which charge Dr 232/285. They both have bars, and the Amalay has a restaurant.

Heading back down Ave Mohammed V towards the medina is the *Hôtel Ibn Batouta* (☎ 434145; fax 434062), which has 40 air-conditioned rooms with full bathroom and

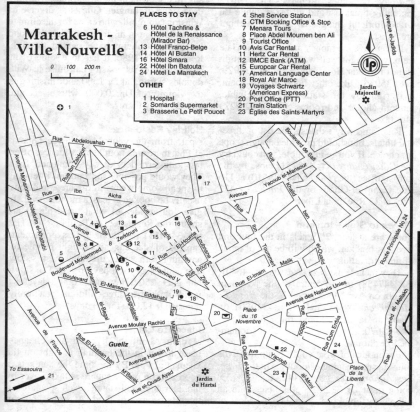

Marrakesh - Ville Nouvelle

0   100   200 m

PLACES TO STAY
6 Hôtel Tachfine &
   Hôtel de la Renaissance
   (Mirador Bar)
13 Hôtel Franco-Belge
14 Hôtel Al Bustan
16 Hôtel Smara
22 Hôtel Ibn Batouta
24 Hôtel Le Marrakech

OTHER
1 Hospital
2 Somardis Supermarket
3 Brasserie Le Petit Poucet
4 Shell Service Station
5 CTM Booking Office & Stop
7 Menara Tours
8 Place Abdel Moumen ben Ali
9 Tourist Office
10 Avis Car Rental
11 Hertz Car Rental
12 BMCE Bank (ATM)
15 Europcar Car Rental
17 American Language Center
18 Royal Air Maroc
19 Voyages Schwartz
   (American Express)
20 Post Office (PTT)
21 Train Station
23 Église des Saints-Martyrs

THE HIGH ATLAS

phone. They cost Dr 226/273/373 plus taxes. Breakfast is Dr 30 per person. It is a good place in its class and also has a number of suites with colour TV thrown in. Virtually parallel to it is the similarly priced *Hôtel Hasna*.

Closer to the medina and in a quiet setting are the *Hôtel de la Ménara* (☎ 436478; fax 436478), Ave des Remparts, and the *Hôtel Le Grand Imilchil* (☎ 447653), Ave Echouhada. They are both good, and have pools, pleasant gardens and rooms with full bathroom, central heating in winter and air-con in summer. The former is probably preferable, as its rooms are generally more spacious and have balconies. It charges Dr 231/312 including breakfast and all taxes, while Le Grand Imilchil charges Dr 252/306 without breakfast.

If you have the money and arrive on a late train, you might well want to spend a night at the three-star *Hôtel Moussafir* (☎ 435929; fax 435936); like other hotels in this chain, it is right by the station. It's a reliable, modern choice and rooms cost Dr 226/273 plus taxes.

This in no way exhausts the list of three-star hotels, but should provide enough scope for choice. If you're in trouble, you could try the *Hôtel Oudaya* (☎ 448751) close by the tourist office, the *Nouzha* (☎ 435510) at 116 Rue Camp el-Ghoul or the *Pacha* (☎ 431 326) at 33 Rue de la Liberté.

Places to Stay – top end

There are at least 26 hotels in the four and five-star bracket, which will be out of range of most travellers.

They include the *Hôtel Nassim* (☎ 446401; fax 447458) in the centre of the action in Gueliz on Ave Mohammed V, the *Hôtel Le Marrakech* (☎ 434351; fax 434980) on Place de la Liberté and the *Hôtel Agdal* (☎ 433670; fax 434980) on Blvd Mohammed Zerktouni.

For an idea of what you'll be up for in the four-star range, singles/doubles in the *Hôtel Les Almoravides* (☎ 445142; fax 443133) come in at Dr 332/415 plus taxes, and an obligatory breakfast costs Dr 44. Most of these places have pools, which are usually closed to outsiders.

Other hotels in the four and five-star categories are on the Ave de France and farther out of town on the road to Casablanca and the Semlalia part of town.

On Ave Houmane el-Fetouaki, just inside Bab el-Jedid, is the jewel in the crown of Marrakesh's hotels – the *La Mamounia* (☎ 448981; fax 444660), although at five-star 'luxe', you'd want to be on an expense account to stay there. The hotel was built between 1925 and 1929 for the (French-controlled) Moroccan railways, and it was the favoured destination of well-heeled Europeans, many of them taking a break from the decadence of Tangier. Guests as diverse as Winston Churchill, who came for the climate and to indulge in his hobby of painting, and Eric von Stroheim have passed through. Renovated in 1986, it has lost some of its charm, but jet-setters still patronise it. With doubles starting at Dr 1500 and finishing in the vicinity of Dr 20,000, who else could afford to stay there?

Holiday Residences

Apart from the Club Med on the Djemaa el-Fna, there are a couple of residences offering long-term lets of self-contained flats. They would possibly suit families intending to spend some weeks in the area, and must usually be booked at least a month ahead. To give you an idea of what these places are about, the Résidence Al Bahja (☎ 448119; fax 346063) in Gueliz offers apartments capable of sleeping up to eight people for anything from a week up. If business is slow, you could stay for a day or two. The single rate is Dr 250 a day, or Dr 600 a day for a family with up to three children; for a family, it costs Dr 12,000 for 30 days.

Places to Eat

Medina About the liveliest and cheapest place to eat in the evening is right on the Djemaa el-Fna. By the time the sun sets, a good portion of the square is taken over by innumerable food stands, each specialising in certain types of food. At some you can pick up kebabs with salad, while at others it's fish and chips Moroccan style. You point to the kind of fish you want, and before you know it, it's in front of you with chips, salad and whatever else might be on offer. At others, you can just sit down to munch on bread rolls stuffed with potato. It is easy to eat your fill for Dr 20 or even less. Wash it down with a Dr 4 orange juice from one of the many juice stands.

If you feel a bit iffy about eating here (the food is cooked quite publicly, so there's little to worry about), try the small restaurants on Rue Bani Marine and Rue de Bab Agnaou. The *Etoile*, for example, offers a filling set menu for Dr 30.

If your purse strings are a little less tight, a place that is deservedly popular with travellers is the self-service restaurant below the *Hôtel Ali*. For Dr 60, you can load up your plate from various pots of typical Moroccan fare, along with a selection of cooked vegetables and/or salad. There's usually a musician to provide that 'authentic' touch. It might sound a little touristy, and it is, but it has a lively atmosphere and the food is good.

Back on the Djemaa itself, most of the rooftop cafés have restaurants attached to them. Some are better than others. The *Argana* (you can't miss the bright neon sign at night) is directly opposite the Bank al-Maghrib. Its set menu is Dr 61. The food is fine, but the crêpes for dessert are better.

The *Restaurant Diamant Rouge* is a pleasant enough place with meals for similar prices, but it's set back a bit off the square.

A short walk south down a narrow lane from the Djemaa, just to the east of the budget hotel area, is the *Restaurant Dar Essalam* (☎ 443520). This belongs to a certain genre of restaurant geared to well-heeled tourists already described in the Fès chapter. For about Dr 200 you get a full traditional meal with music and dance in opulent (if a little kitsch) surroundings. The food is no better than you'll find in cheaper places – you're paying for the 'experience'. If you want this kind of thing, you'd be better off choosing one of the good places in Fès. The show here starts at about 8 pm.

A similar place is to be found farther inside the medina – the *Restaurant Dar Fez* (☎ 310150) at 8 Rue Boussouni.

Both the *Grand Hôtel du Tazi* and *Hôtel de Foucauld* have restaurants (the former on their roof terrace), where a full meal will come to around Dr 80. They're OK, but they lack the visual feast of the terrace restaurants on the Djemaa and the atmosphere of some of the others listed above. On the other hand, you can get a beer at these places. For at least Dr 100 a head, you could eat in the rooftop restaurant at the *Hôtel Islane*, which is very pleasantly located.

Gueliz There are any number of places to eat in the ville nouvelle; a good collection of them are concentrated in or around Ave Mohammed V and Blvd Mohammed Zerktouni.

For bottom-rung local food, you'll find a small group of hole-in-the-wall places on Rue Ibn Aicha, where a solid meal of, say, brochettes, chips and salad will cost about Dr 25.

For a reasonable imitation of a hamburger you could try *Body Food* near the Shell service station, and then top it off with an ice cream from *Boule de Neige* across the road.

Otherwise, meals start getting a little costly, and it'll be hard to find anything for under about Dr 60 a head.

The *Restaurant La Poêle d'Or*, one of a lot of places concentrating on French cuisine, serves up a main meal for about Dr 60 or a set menu for Dr 70, including soft drinks. It's closed on Sunday and service can be slow.

Restaurant al-Fassia (☎ 434060), across Ave Mohammed V from the Hôtel Hasna, is a fairly expensive place specialising in Moroccan cuisine, where a set menu will cost about Dr 120. It's open for lunch from noon to 2.30 pm and for dinner from 7.30 to 11 pm.

Across the road from the Hôtel Tachfine is the *Restaurant La Taverne* (☎ 446126), which offers a mix of Moroccan and French cuisine, mostly the latter. A set menu will relieve you of Dr 75 per person.

The *Restaurant Chez Jack'Line*, across Ave Mohammed V from the Hôtel Al Mouatamid, also does mainly French cuisine, with mains for about Dr 70 and pizzas for about Dr 40. Another in this line, which has had good reports, is the *Restaurant Le Jacaranda*.

If you feel like something Asian, head for the *Dragon d'Or*, a Vietnamese restaurant on Blvd Mohammed Zerktouni. Various other types of foreign cuisine are represented, including Spanish at the *Puerto Banus* (☎ 446534) on Rue Ibn Hanbal and Italian at the *Vivaldi* (☎ 435968) on Rue Al-Mouatamid ben Abbad.

Virtually all the bigger hotels have at least one restaurant. La Mamounia has five rather expensive places. Meals are sometimes accompanied by a show of one sort or another. The *Dar Mounia* (☎ 431241) is a well-established upper-end Moroccan restaurant, for which you must book tables in advance.

Self-Catering The *Somardis* supermarket on Rue Ibn Aicha in the ville nouvelle is a reasonable place to stock up on supplies you might find hard to get elsewhere – like Corn Flakes. It also sells alcohol. There is also a liquor store next to the Hôtel Nassim.

Entertainment

Cafés & Bars As in any Moroccan city, Marrakesh is crawling with cafés and *salons de thé*. The more interesting of them are gathered around the Djemaa el-Fna – but don't be surprised to be charged Dr 5 for coffee or weak tea. Ave Mohammed V in Gueliz is the other part of town that usually attracts a people-watching crowd of tea-sippers.

The *Café Verdi*, on Rue Ibn Aicha in the ville nouvelle, is a bright place for breakfast and there's a mouth-watering chocolate shop across the road. Next to the cinema by the Hôtel Tachfine is the *Café Siroua*, another good place for breakfast.

Possibly the most popular bar in town is at the top of the former Hôtel de la Renaissance, the *Mirador*. The bar on the ground floor of the same building is a great Art Deco relic and a good place for a beer (inside) or coffee (outside).

The *Brasserie Le Petit Poucet* on Ave Mohammed V is a pretty down-to-earth place to get a drink. Even more so is the bar next door to the Restaurant La Taverne. The *Bar L'Escale* is another one you could pop into, although there's nothing special about it. Some of the restaurants in Gueliz also have an alcohol licence.

Discos If you want to party on, many of the hotels in the ville nouvelle have nightclubs. There are several others independent of hotels. As elsewhere in Morocco, the usual entry fee varies between Dr 50 and Dr 100, which includes the first drink. Each drink thereafter costs (usually) at least Dr 50. Most offer the predictable standard fare of Western disco music and cliques who appear to avoid eye contact like the plague, but there are a few exceptions.

One of them is a nightclub in the street at the back of the Hôtel de la Renaissance that caters to Moroccans. It kicks off around 11 pm with two hours of the best folk music you'll hear, after which it's contemporary Moroccan pop music mixed with normal disco music.

As far as regular discos go, two of the most popular are the *Diamant Noir* in the Hôtel Le Marrakech, on Place de la Liberté, and the *Temple de la Musique* in the Hôtel N'Fis, at the junction of Ave de France and Ave de la Ménara. Another is the *Cotton Club*, in the Hôtel Tropicana on the road to Casablanca.

Folkloric Shows As already noted, there are several up-market restaurants, some in the bigger hotels, that put on distractions involving local tribal singing and dancing. Enquire at the tourist office or have a flip through the *Welcome to Marrakesh* booklet.

Getting There & Away

Air RAM (☎ 446444) has an office on Ave Mohammed V. There are at least two flights a day to and from Casablanca and four a week to Agadir and Ouarzazate. The one-way fare to Casablanca is Dr 340, and it's Dr 235 for the 30-minute flight to Ouarzazate. The airport is five km south-west of town.

Bus The main bus station from which all buses (regardless of the company) leave is just outside the city walls by Bab Doukkala. This is a 20-minute walk or a Dr 8 taxi ride from the Djemaa el-Fna.

The main building is a big place with a good many booths covering all sorts of local and long-distance destinations. Window No 10 is the CTM booking desk. CTM has buses to Fès at 6.45 am and 9 pm (Dr 115; nine hours), and buses for Agadir leave at 8 am and 6.30 pm (Dr 43; 3½ hours). CTM also has four daily buses for Casablanca (Dr 57.50; 4½ hours) and Ouarzazate (Dr 49 and Dr 34.50 depending on the service; four hours). There are also buses for Safi, Er-Rachidia, M'Hamid (via Zagora at 7.30 am), Laayoune (7 pm) and Tan Tan (10 pm).

You can get tickets for other bus lines at the other windows. Tickets to Beni Mellal (Dr 34.75) are sold at window No 1, and at window No 2 tickets are sold for nine daily buses to Rabat (Dr 58.50) via Casablanca (Dr 41.80). Note the unusually big difference between this and the CTM Casablanca price. You can buy tickets to Asni (for Jebel Toubkal) at window No 3 (Dr 10.90). Window No 4 is the Safi line, with six daily departures and tickets for Dr 25.60 (normal) and Dr 27.50 (mumtaz). Next door at window No 5 is the El-Jadida line, with 10 buses a day for Dr 35.10. For buses to Ouarzazate, queue at window No 6 (Dr 47). There are also a couple of runs to Agadir and Taroudannt.

For Essaouira, you want window No 7 (Dr 29). These buses go via Chichaoua (Dr 13.50), which is famous for its rugs but has little else of interest. There are two buses a day to Azilal, at 8.30 am and 3.30 pm, and they cost Dr 40.

CTM also has a booking office on Blvd Mohammed Zerktouni, and some of the buses departing from Marrakesh stop outside it on their way out of the city.

Local buses to the villages on the north side of Jebel Toubkal, including Ourika and Asni, leave when full from a dirt patch on the southern side of the medina outside Bab er-Rob. The buses to Asni cost Dr 10.

Train The railway station is on Ave Hassan II and is a long way from the Djemaa el-Fna. Take a taxi or No 8 bus into the centre.

There are direct trains from Marrakesh to Fès via Casablanca, Rabat and Meknès at 7.20 and 9.10 am and 2 pm. They take 8¼ hours. You could take the 5.20 or 6.20 pm trains to Casa-Voyageurs and pick up the 10.17 pm train to Fès, but you wouldn't arrive until 3 am.

Trains to Tangier (via Casablanca and Rabat) depart at 9.10 am (change at Sidi Kacem – a brief wait), 3.30 pm (direct) and 7.45 pm (direct). The 3.30 pm direct train is a bad choice as it arrives in Tangier at about 12.45 am. On the later run the journey takes 10½ hours, and should make it to Tangier in time for the first boat of the day to Algeciras. You can book a couchette on this trip.

To get to Oujda, you have to take the 3.30 pm train to Casablanca and then pick up one of two night trains from there.

All up, there are nine trains to Casablanca and eight on to Rabat. There are four trains to Safi (change at Ben Guerir).

Second-class normal/rapide fares include: Casablanca – Dr 52.50/66.50, Fès – Dr 121.50/153.50, Oujda – Dr 194.50/246, Rabat – Dr 71/90 and Tangier – Dr 134/169.

Supratours The ONCF organises buses through Supratours to take rail passengers from Marrakesh to destinations such as Agadir, Essaouira, Tiznit, Tan Tan, Laayoune, Smara and Dakhla. You might be able to get onto one if you can catch a Supratours representative in the train station café (*buvette*).

Taxi Standard grands taxis to Ourika, Asni (Dr 13; about one hour) and other nearby High Atlas destinations depart from outside Bab er-Rob.

Car There are at least 25 car-rental agencies in Marrakesh (for a more complete list, pick up the free booklet *Welcome to Marrakesh*). One local company to avoid is Sister's Car, which has had bad reports from travellers. The addresses of the main companies are as follows:

Avis
  137 Ave Mohammed V (☎ 433727; fax 449485)
Budget
  583 Ave Mohammed V (☎ 434604)
Europcar
  63 Blvd Mohammed Zerktouni (☎ 431228; fax 432769)
Goldcar
  Hôtel Semiramis Méridien, Route de Casablanca (☎ 431377)
Hertz
  154 Ave Mohammed V (☎ & fax 434680)
Zeit
  Apt 17, 129 Ave Mohammed al-Bakkal (☎ 431888; fax 431701)

Getting Around
To/From the Airport A petit taxi from Marrakesh to the airport should be Dr 50 but you'll rarely get it for that price. Bus No 11 runs irregularly to Djemaa el-Fna.

Bus & Taxi The creamy-beige petits taxis around town cost about Dr 8 per journey, but if you give them a Dr 10 note don't expect any change. From the railway station to the Djemaa el-Fna the official fare is Dr 10 but you'll rarely get away with less than Dr 15.

Local bus No 8 runs from the Djemaa el-Fna area, passing close by the Bab Doukkala bus station and then going on to the main post office and train station. Nos 1 and 20 run right up Ave Mohammed V from near the Djemaa el-Fna into Gueliz. No 11 runs between the airport and the Djemaa el-Fna. The No 3 bus goes to the Bab Doukkala bus station from the Djemaa el-Fna and then on to the main post office.

Horse-Drawn Carriages Horse-drawn carriages *(calèches)* are a feature of Marrakesh you won't find in many other Moroccan cities, and they can be a pleasant way to get around – if you establish the right price. Theoretically, this should present no difficulties. Posted up inside the carriage are the official fares: Dr 9 for a straightforward trip from A to B 'intramuros' (within the medina walls) and Dr 12 for the same 'extramuros' (outside the medina walls). Otherwise, it's Dr 60 an hour for pottering around the sights. This may seem steep – it isn't cheap – but at least you know where you stand. If you're interested, they're based at the south-western side of the Djemaa el-Fna.

Tours It is quite possible to organise tours down the Drâa Valley and to the Atlantic coast through agents in Marrakesh. FRAM Orange tours has one-day excursions (!) to Essaouira for Dr 300 a head and to Ouarzazate for Dr 350.

Adra Aventure (☎ 435663), 43 Rue Mauritanie, organises High Atlas treks in spring, cross-country skiing in winter and 4WD trips.

Marocaquad (☎ 448139), based on Ave Mohammed V, runs trips out of Ouarzazate for up to six days on that odd vehicle, the four-wheeled bike (quad). Six days costs Dr 6250. You could ask at the Hôtel de Foucauld, which also organises mountain bike trips.

For information on High Atlas trekking and the phone numbers of guides in Asni and Imlil, you could do worse than go to the Hôtel Ali, inspect their notice board and make some enquiries.

AROUND MARRAKESH – NORTH
Cascades d'Ouzoud
About 167 km north-east of Marrakesh are the best waterfalls you'll see in Morocco; they're well worth the effort of getting there. If you have a car, it's an easy enough proposition as a day trip; otherwise, you might have to be prepared to stay overnight in the area – not a bad option.

The falls *(ouzoud* is Berber for olives and refers to the cultivation of olive trees in the area) drop about 100 metres into the river below, forming natural pools that are great for a swim. It is possible to walk along the course of the river to the **Gorges of Oued el-Abid**, and indeed the whole area is good hiking territory as it is cool even in summer.

An increasingly popular destination is the so-called **Mexican village** – there's nothing Latin American about the place at all as it's just another Berber village. Plenty of locals and foreign tourists come here, and the souvenir stalls are proof of its popularity, but as yet it is all on a modest scale. The drive between Ouzoud and Afourer, which brings you to the main Marrakesh-Beni Mellal road, is a treat in itself, especially the views of the lake formed by the **Bin el-Ouidane Dam**.

Places to Stay & Eat Around the falls there are several camp sites, all much of a muchness. It is a beautiful place to pitch a tent, and generally you'd be looking at about Dr 7 per person and Dr 5 to pitch a tent. There are a few snack stands in among the souvenir stalls.

In **Azilal**, a nearby town you'll almost have to visit, there is an unclassified hotel, the *Funduq Ouzoud*, which has very basic singles/doubles for Dr 28/50. The sign is in Arabic only and it's close to the buses' departure point. A few km farther on, at the Beni Mellal exit, is the *Hôtel Tanoute* (☎ 488281), next to the Shell service station. It's a pleasant two-star hotel. Singles/doubles with shower cost Dr 121/142, while those with full en suite bathroom are Dr 153/179, plus taxes. The town, by the way, is itself of no interest – it's hard to imagine what its tourist office employees find to tell people.

There are two other accommodation possibilities in this area. About 27 km from Azilal, just north of Bin el-Ouidane, is the *Hôtel du Lac*. It's well signposted and in an idyllic position. You can camp there too. In the town of Afourer, 62 winding km from Azilal, there is the four-star *Hôtel Tazarkount*.

Getting There & Away Coming from Marrakesh, it would be preferable to get transport direct to Azilal. Two buses a day run from the Bab Doukkala bus station (at 8.30 am and 3.30 pm) and cost Dr 40. From Azilal, they leave at 7 am and 2 pm. There are also occasional grands taxis to Marrakesh for Dr 60 per head, so it stands to reason that you

can get them going the other way (try Bab er-Rob).

Some suggest that it's better to go first to Beni Mellal from Marrakesh (Dr 34.75), and get transport to Azilal from there, although with only one bus a day running between Beni Mellal and Azilal, this hardly seems a promising solution. If you do want to head north from Azilal, the Beni Mellal bus leaves at 2 pm and costs Dr 20. There is also a bus south from Azilal to Demnate at 3 pm, from where you may well be able to pick another bus or grand taxi the rest of the way to Marrakesh.

Getting between Azilal and Ouzoud is fairly straightforward, with local grands taxis doing the 38-km run fairly regularly for Dr 10 a head. When you arrive at Ouzoud, follow the dirt track lined with snack and souvenir stalls to get to the waterfalls.

AROUND MARRAKESH – SOUTH

Several roads lead south from Marrakesh. The principal one leads south to Ouarzazate over the **Tizi n'Tichka**, a popular route with tourists exhausted by Marrakesh and eager to taste the oasis valleys of the south. For more on the Marrakesh-Ouarzazate road, see the section on that town.

Two other minor roads wind south of Marrakesh into the High Atlas, one down the **Ourika Valley** to the ski resort of Oukaïmeden, the other over the **Tizi n'Test** towards Taroudannt and on to Agadir. This latter road takes you to Asni, from where the bulk of trekkers take off into the High Atlas, usually with **Jebel Toubkal** as their goal. For more on Asni and trekking, see the High Atlas Trekking section.

Ourika Valley

Skiers and trekkers alike could skip the Asni-Imlil area (see the High Atlas Trekking section) and instead head down the Ourika Valley, to the east of Jebel Toubkal. The main options as bases are the ski resort of Oukaïmeden (which is virtually deserted outside the November-March snow season) or the village of **Setti Fatma** farther south. During spring Oukaïmeden is beautiful, and, in addition to long treks, you can investigate the immediate vicinity in search of rock carvings (see the GTAM book *Gravures Rupestres du Haut Atlas* by Susan Searight & Danièle Hourbette). In winter, if snow cover is decent enough, lift passes cost about Dr 80 a day and equipment hire (there are several outlets in the town) is about Dr 100 a day. Oukaïmeden boasts the highest lift in Africa.

Setti Fatma, 24 km farther south along a poor road, is the site of an important moussem in August and another starting point for treks.

For more details on trekking see the High Atlas Trekking section.

Places to Stay & Eat On the way to Oukaïmeden there are two fairly expensive hotels about 42 km out of Marrakesh. The more expensive of the two is the *Hôtel Ourika* (☎ 117531), with singles/doubles at Dr 262/327. Just beyond it is the more modest *Le Temps de Vivre*.

The only place open to all comers throughout the year in Oukaïmeden is the *Hôtel L'Angour – Chez Ju Ju* (☎ 319005; fax 448378). During the ski season it charges Dr 250 a person for rooms with full board – very nice if you can afford it. Out of season they drop it to half-board if you want (but try to find somewhere else to eat around here!). The CAF refuge here is open exclusively to CAF members. Another hotel open only in winter is the *Hôtel Imlil*.

In Setti Fatma, the best place is the *Hôtel Tafoukt*, with singles/doubles for Dr 90/127. The *Hôtel Azrou* is an unpleasant, unclassified dump with rooms for about Dr 40/60.

Getting There & Away Out of season there is little or no transport to Oukaïmeden from Marrakesh, although you should be able to arrange a grand taxi, for a price. Otherwise you could take a bus or grand taxi as far as Aghbalou and try hitching up the mountain. Buses to Setti Fatma from Bab er-Rob in Marrakesh cost Dr 10 and are not overly fast.

Imilchil

Although it is stretching the idea to describe this remote High Atlas village as 'around Marrakesh', it is from Marrakesh that the bulk of the tours to Imilchil depart. Some 363 km distant, Imilchil has become known for its September moussem, a kind of tribal marriage market where the women do the choosing, and it is in danger of losing all genuineness as more foreigners turn up to gawk.

You can get to Imilchil under your own steam, but it requires some patience. The easy bit is heading north-east by bus or a series of grands taxis to Kasba Tadla. From there you need to get another grand taxi to El-Ksiba. Here you may have to wait to get something for Aghbala. The turn-off for Imilchil is near Tizi n'Isly, before Aghbala. From there 61 km of piste lead south to Imilchil. Around here you will have to rely on souq lorries or the occasional passing private vehicle.

To the Tizi n'Test

Ouirgane Ouirgane is a pretty spot about 15 km south of Asni (see the High Atlas Trekking section), and it makes an attractive place to stop for a night or two if you're in no particular hurry. The cheapest place to stay is the cosy, French-run *Au Sanglier Qui Fume* (☎ 117447). You pay Dr 133 a person for good rooms. It has a swimming pool and the rooms are heated in winter. Camping is possible in the grounds for Dr 20 a person. A little farther back along the road to Marrakesh is the beautiful and expensive *Résidence de la Roseraie* (☎ 432094; fax 432095 – booking numbers in Marrakesh), where you're looking at Dr 500 a person. It has a pool and hammam, and can organise expensive horse rides. The hotel also organises a shuttle to and from Marrakesh for guests.

Tin Mal Mosque Heading south to Tin Mal, along the pretty Oued Nfiss and just past a couple of **kasbahs** (you can't miss the one on the left, perched up on a rocky outcrop), travellers with their own transport should take the time to stop at the only mosque in Morocco which non-Muslims can enter.

Built in 1156 by the Almohads in honour of Mohammed ibn Tumart, the dynasty's 'founding father' and spiritual inspiration, it is now in the process of restoration. Work began in 1991 and is expected to continue until the end of the century. The first of three stages is complete, and the next was due to begin in June 1994 and take two years, which means it may well be closed when you read this. You can still see the outside of it and it's worth the detour in case it is open. The guardian will expect a tip.

Tizi n'Test Over the next 30 km, the road winds its way rapidly up to the pass known as Tizi n'Test – at 2092 metres, one of the highest in the country. The views are breathtaking from numerous points along the way, but if you are driving note that heavy cloud and mist often cuts vision to near zero at the top of the pass and during the descent on the Taroudannt side. In winter it is quite possible that you'll find the road blocked by snow, so be prepared. If you're going the other way, SATAS has a bus from Taroudannt to Marrakesh at 4.30 am that approaches the pass at about daybreak. The road from Taroudannt heads straight on to Agadir on the coast.

High Atlas Trekking

If you have good shoes or boots, plenty of warm clothes and a sleeping bag, trekking to the summit of Jebel (Mt) Toubkal (4165 metres), Morocco's highest mountain, is worth considering. It's a beautiful area and on clear days there are incredible views in all directions, but especially south over the Sahara.

You don't need mountaineering skills to get to the top so long as you're going up the normal route from Imlil, although there are one or two semi-dangerous patches of loose scree along the trail. You can stay at the Toubkal (still commonly known by its old name, Neltner) Hut (*refuge* in French) for the night. This trek can be done in two days – up

to the Toubkal Hut the first day, then up to the summit and back down on the second.

The best time to go is during April and May after most of the snow has melted and before it gets unbearably hot. In October the weather can be very unpredictable, even if there is no snow. You will not get to the summit of Toubkal unless snow has fallen unless you have *full alpine gear*. Of course, unofficial guides will agree to take you, knowing full well that it's impossible (or, at best, extremely dangerous).

Don't take these considerations lightly. Snow, the sudden appearance of dense cloud and fog and high winds can all turn an enjoyable hike into a memorable fright – or worse. An American who was said to be experienced, went up in winter in 1994 with an unofficial guide and never came back. Fearing the damage to Moroccan tourism, a huge hullabaloo went up as official guides and police carried out a 21-day search until they found his body.

The usual starting point for the trek is the village of Imlil, 17 km south of Asni on the Tizi n'Test road from Marrakesh to Agadir. Other possible starting points are the villages of Setti Fatma and Oukaïmeden in the Ourika Valley, but you're looking at a longer trek if you start from these places.

Trekkers intending to go to the summit of Jebel Toubkal should be familiar with the symptoms of altitude sickness (AMS) and hypothermia. Both are dangers at this altitude.

Information
Guides You don't need a guide if you're just doing the normal two-day trek, but if you're going farther afield or for a longer period, then you're going to want to engage one. You may also need a mule to cart your gear – make sure it's a mule you hire and not a donkey – there's a big difference.

All this should be arranged in Imlil. The guide business is gradually being made a little more professional. There is a small and rather empty Bureau des Guides et Accompagnateurs. This is staffed most of the day and they have a list of official guides and

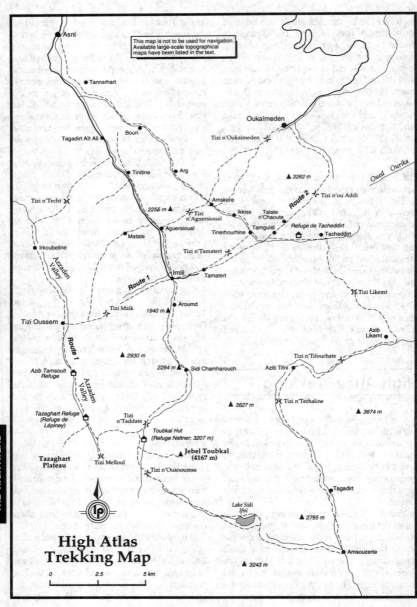

This map is not to be used for navigation.
Available large-scale topographical
maps have been listed in the text.

Asni

Tannsrhart

Oukaïmeden

Tizi n'Oukaïmeden

Bouri

Tagadirt Aït Ali

Arg

▲ 3262 m

Oued Ourika

Tinitine

Amskere

Tizi n'Techt

2255 m ▲

Ikkiss

Route 2

Tizi n'ou Addi

Tizi
n'Aguersioual

Talate
n'Chaoute

Aguersioual

Tinerhourhine

Tamguist

Refuge de Tacheddirt

Tacheddirt

Matate

Irkoubeline

Tizi n'Tamatert

Azzaden Valley

Route 1

Imlil

Tamatert

Tizi Likemt

Tizi Mzik

Aroumd

1940 m ▲

Tizi Oussem

Azib
Likemt

Route 1

▲ 2930 m

2284 m ▲

Sidi Chamharouch

Azib Tifni

Tizi n'Tifourhate

Azib Tamsoult
Refuge

Azzaden
Valley

Tizi n'Terhaline

▲ 3627 m

▲ 3674 m

Tazaghart Refuge
(Refuge de
Lépiney)

Tizi
n'Taddate

Toubkal Hut
(Refuge Neltner; 3207 m)

Tazaghart
Plateau

Tizi Melloul

▲ Jebel Toubkal
(4167 m)

Tizi n'Ouanoumss

Tagadirt

Lake Sidi
Ifni

▲ 2785 m

High Atlas
Trekking Map

Amsouzerte

0   2.5   5 km

▲ 3243 m

even mugshots up on the wall. Depending on whom you strike, you should be able to ask for a little free advice on short local hikes and the basic Toubkal trek without having to fork out money for a guide. It has to be said, though, that even a couple of the official guides feel they should be paid just to take you around the corner.

Some of the official guides specialise in canyoning, climbing or ski-trekking. The latter, known to French trekkers as *ski-mulet*, involves a combination of walking with mules to carry your equipment and then skiing downhill or on cross-country runs.

The French have played a big role in recent years in training these official guides. The Centre Régionale des Enseignements Touristiques (CRET) had a contract until 1993 to lift standards, and a number of guides even did some of their training outside Morocco. In 1992 all the guides joined up to form a national association aimed at laying the groundwork for common rules and keeping standards up to scratch.

It is important, especially in times of uncertain weather, to have an official guide with you rather than any old clown who can probably lead you up the path, but won't have a clue how to deal with any difficult situation, let alone an emergency.

About 50 official guides are based in the Toubkal area. All carry cards to prove their training. Have a good look at the cards, and check any potential guide's credentials with the Bureau des Guides et Accompagnateurs.

Those starting off from the **Ourika Valley** could ask for Lahcen Izahan at the Café Azagya, about two km before the village of Setti Fatma. He knows the Atlas like his pockets and can take you for half-hour walks or treks lasting three to 10 days (or more).

Costs Official guides expect to be paid about Dr 160 a day or more if they are specialists (skiing guides, for example). A mule and muleteer cost around Dr 80 a day, porters from Dr 50 to Dr 70 a day, depending on the season and the difficulty of the terrain. A cook would want Dr 70 a day. Food and drink for all and sundry is extra.

Guidebooks & Maps An extremely useful publication is brought out every year by the Moroccan Tourist Office. It's called *La Grande Traversée des Atlas Marocains (GTAM)*, and is available in several languages. In it you will find a list of guides for various regions in the Atlas, including Toubkal; lists of *gîtes*, huts, refuges and the like and the names of their owners; and a table of official prices for guides, mules, muleteers and porters. Recommended maximum fares on some of the public transport routes also appear. This booklet is not easy to obtain in Imlil or elsewhere in the mountains. Ideally, you should grab a copy in Marrakesh or any main tourist office in Morocco or abroad.

Another useful tool to have, and equally scarce in Imlil, is a decent map. There is a mapping division in Rabat that publishes topographical maps of the whole country on a scale of 1:100,000 and 1:50,000. The Jebel Toubkal area map, on a scale of 1:50,000, is useful and, and another map covering a wider area on a scale of 1:100,000 is also available. They can be purchased in Rabat for Dr 30 a sheet (see the Rabat Information section for more details). The Toubkal map is occasionally available in Imlil shops for Dr 80.

Those intending to do more than the normal two-day trek would be advised to get hold of the guide *La Grande Traversée de l'Atlas Marocain* by Michel Peyron, which is published in English by West Col Productions, UK. Volume one (Moussa Gorges to Aït ben Wgemmez) covers the Toubkal massif. West Col's other guide, *Atlas Mountains* by Robin G Collomb, is nowhere near as useful or detailed, and some of the general comments in the book might leave you wondering how much time the author spent in lowland Morocco as opposed to gazing at snowcapped peaks. Remarks such as 'All Berbers are beggars by nature' and, '...couscous – a sort of Lancashire hot pot cooked in a basin of semolina' stretch the bounds of credibility.

Karl Smith's book, *The Atlas Mountains – A Walker's Guide* (Cicerone Press, 1989), does not have the scope implied by the title, but it's quite sound on the Toubkal region.

Another excellent guide, in French, is *Le Haut Atlas Central* by André Fougerolles (Guide Alpin). This is intended for serious alpinists, not trekkers, and is occasionally available in bookshops on Ave Mohammed V in Marrakesh, as well as in Rabat and Casablanca.

Getting to Asni & Imlil

There are frequent buses to Asni from Marrakesh which leave from the Bab er-Rob when full. They take two hours and cost Dr 10. Alternatively, you can take a shared taxi to Asni from the same place. These cost Dr 13 per person and take about one hour. From Asni there are fairly frequent trucks to Imlil and you can easily get a lift with them for around Dr 15. The journey takes about an hour and the road is fairly rough for much of the way.

There are also taxis from Asni to Imlil but you'll have to negotiate a price, as they could be stuck up there for hours waiting for a return fare.

ASNI

The Grand Hôtel du Toubkal proclaims Asni 'the Chamonix of Morocco'. Obviously the joker who wrote this has never been to Chamonix. Asni is a rather boring little town that vaguely comes alive on Saturdays for a local market. The large numbers of tourists and travellers of all types coming through here over the years have turned it into a minor den of iniquity. Stay overnight if you must, but don't organise anything that even sounds like a trek. It may have been OK once, but there are some very cheeky people ripping serious amounts of money off innocent travellers.

The road to Imlil is lined with professional hitchhikers – you know the ones: in return for your Samaritan deed they feel obliged to invite you to the 'family home' for some tea, and there you are browbeaten into buying some worthless trinket. The hitchhiker, meanwhile, is back on the road looking for a ride the other way...

If you want to stay the night at Asni there is a *youth hostel*, which is decrepit but clean and friendly and costs Dr 20 a night. The only other place to stay is the *Grand Hôtel du Toubkal* (☎ 3 via the operator; or 442222 in Marrakesh), a three-star hotel with singles/doubles/triples for Dr 169/208/282 plus taxes. The hotel has its own bar, restaurant, swimming pool and guarded parking.

Buses and taxis leave here for Bab er-Rob in Marrakesh. You can also pick up the odd bus heading the other way to Ouirgane and Ijoukak.

IMLIL

Most trekkers sensibly give Asni a miss and stay in this fairly relaxed and attractive Berber village for the first night. The area is best known for its walnut trees, but in recent times there has been some diversification, with apples, cherries and other trees being more systematically planted as well.

Places to Stay

A good place to stay is the *CAF (Club Alpin Français) Refuge* on the village square. It offers dormitory-style accommodation for Dr 16 (members), Dr 24 (HI members) and Dr 32 (nonmembers). It also has a common room with an open fireplace, cooking facilities (Dr 5 for use of gas), cutlery and crockery. Bookings for refuges (huts) farther up can no longer be made from here, but instead must go through the CAF (☎ 270090), 1 Rue 6e Henri, BP 6178, Casablanca-Bourgoune, or through CAF, BP 888, Marrakesh. This could be awkward in summer without lots of forward planning, so you might have to be prepared to sleep out. However, guides and local people are often more than willing to put you up for about what you would pay in the refuges. The Toubkal, Tacheddirt and Tazaghart (Lépiney) refuges cost Dr 22 (CAF members), Dr 33 (HI members) and Dr 44 (nonmembers). You need your own bedding. Note that the CAF refuge at Oukaïmeden is open to CAF members only.

Back in Imlil, there are several other accommodation options. The best deal is probably the *Hôtel el Aine*, which charges Dr 25 per person in quite comfortable and bright rooms. It's the first place you pass on your right as you enter the village, and has a pleasant tearoom stacked with coffee-table books about Morocco. Some of the rooms are set back a little around a small garden, and you can sit up on the roof for some private sunbathing. Cold water is the norm.

Next up, also on the right and virtually opposite the CAF is the *Café Aksoual*, which lets out fairly basic rooms for Dr 25. There are no sheets and the showers are cold.

On the little square is the *Café Soleil*. It has fairly simple rooms with three beds for Dr 60, even for lone guests. There's also a family room for Dr 80 that can sleep five. Their claims of being able to provide you with a hot shower should be taken with a pinch of salt. Plans are afoot to expand the place, and it already has a restaurant (the service is mind-bogglingly slow – you could grow the mint for your tea faster than they boil the water).

The 'luxury' place to stay at is the *Hôtel Étoile du Toubkal* (☎ 499767, 434387). You pay Dr 70/100/140/190 for clean singles/doubles/triple/quads with private shower in the low season and Dr 10 more in the high season. If they are not having power problems, hot water comes out of the showers. They can also change money and have a restaurant offering a set menu for Dr 70 and main courses of standard Moroccan fare for Dr 40 to Dr 50.

Some of the guides in Imlil will be happy to put you up in their family homes in the surrounding villages, but set a price for accommodation and food in advance to avoid misunderstandings afterwards.

Places to Eat
Apart from the *Hôtel Étoile du Toubkal* restaurant, about the only choices are *Café Soleil* and *Café Aksoual*, where simple meals will set you back about Dr 30.

There's also a wide range of foodstuffs available in the shops in Imlil, including canned and packaged goods, mineral water, soft drinks, cigarettes, etc, but no beer.

There's also a bakery. Stock up here before starting the trek as there's nothing for sale farther up the mountain.

THE TWO-DAY TREK
On the first day of the trek you walk from Imlil to the Toubkal Hut (3207 metres) via the villages of Aroumd and Sidi Chamharouch. This takes about five hours. Bottled drinks are usually available at both these villages.

The *Toubkal Hut* is a stone cottage built in 1938 and has beds for 29 people in two dormitories, but you have to provide your own sheets and blankets or a sleeping bag. There's also a kitchen with a gas stove and a range of cooking utensils; hot water is available. The charge is Dr 44 per person for non-CAF members, plus an extra charge if you use the cooking facilities or need hot water. The resident warden will let you in. You must bring all your own food with you, as there's none for sale here. The warden may, if you give him plenty of notice, prepare meals for you. Don't turn up at this hut without a booking in the high season or you may find it full.

The ascent from the Toubkal Hut to the summit should take you about four hours and the descent about two hours. It's best to take water with you in summer, but this isn't generally necessary in winter. Any water you take out of the streams on the mountainside should be boiled, otherwise there's a fair chance you'll pick up giardiasis. It can be bitterly cold at the top even in summer, so bring plenty of warm clothing with you.

OTHER TREKS
If you prefer a longer trek (about five hours one way) than that to Tacheddirt from Imlil is recommended. The walk takes you over a pass at 3000 metres above the snow line, then down the other side and up again. There's a good CAF refuge here with panoramic views where you can stay for Dr 44 plus Dr 5 if you want to use the gas for cooking. The warden is helpful and can supply bread and eggs. He may also be willing to cook you a meal in his own home for around Dr 30. It's a beautiful

place and very relaxing. Many other treks are possible from Tacheddirt, including a seven-hour trek at military pace back down to Asni.

There's another CAF refuge at Tazaghart and the key for it can be found at the village of Tizi Oussem to the north. All CAF refuges are open throughout the year.

Those starting out from the Ourika Valley should head first for the village of Setti Fatma (for transport and accommodation details, see the Around Marrakesh section).

An old hand in the High Atlas, Rick Crust, suggests the following treks for those with three to seven days to spare.

Route 1

From Imlil, take mules over the Tizi Mzik to the village of Tizi Oussem. Stay the night at the guesthouse run by Si Mohammed ou Omar. This place is much more relaxed than the CAF refuges at Imlil or Toubkal. Prices are not fixed, but expect to pay about the same as at the CAF refuges. If you're happy with your muleteers keep them; if not, ask Si Mohammed ou Omar if he can provide you with mules for the next stage. The following day, ascend the Azzaden Valley to the Tazaghart Refuge, which is very peaceful. Options for the next day include scrambling on foot up to Tizi Melloul or the Tazaghart Plateau. Be sure to leave early in the day so you can get back to Lépiney before dark. You will need a guide for this.

You could also cross over to Toubkal via the Tizi n'Taddate – this is hard going but worth it. Again, a guide is essential. The track is too steep for mules but they can be sent back the long way round via Imlil and will probably arrive at about the same time.

After the above, you can climb Toubkal itself but it won't be as good as what you've already done. From there you can follow the valleys back down to Imlil via Sidi Cham-harouch and Aroumd.

Route 2

Find transport to Oukaïmeden (see the Around Marrakesh section). There are no mules to be hired here but it should be pos-sible to arrange mules beforehand: ask at the CAF refuge or Hôtel L'Angour-Chez Ju Ju. Better still, plan on a night at the latter and call them a few days in advance from Mar-rakesh to get mules organised for when you arrive. You will need to bring all your own supplies with you from Marrakesh as there are no food shops at Oukaïmeden. Should you have to wait in Oukaïmeden a few days, there's no harm done as plenty of good walking awaits you in the area (see the Around Marrakesh section).

When your mules arrive you have two possibilities: you can descend to Imlil via Tacheddirt (one day), or you can descend the upper Ourika Valley either directly or via Tacheddirt, stopping at Timichchi and ending at Setti Fatma (two to three days).

10-DAY TREK

Local guides suggest several routes that could keep you marching for 10 days or more.

Route 3

One such route would take you in the first two days to the Toubkal summit as per the standard route. On returning to the refuge you then push south-east over Tizi n'Ouanoumss to Lake Sidi Ifni. The third day would see you heading on westwards and a little farther south to the Berber village of Amsouzerte. From there, a two-day hike northwards would get you to the Tacheddirt CAF refuge, spending the intervening night with locals in Azib Likemt.

You have a few options from there, one of them being to pursue a northerly course up to Oukaïmeden. A couple of tracks and passes lead you out of there to the south-west, and on this circuit you would go via the Tizi n'Oukaïmeden (the Oukaïmeden pass) down as far as the village of Amskere. From there you could easily finish off the walk on the eighth day by heading to Imlil either via Ikkiss and the Tizi n'Tamatert or south-west to the main Imlil-Asni road over the Tizi n'Aguersioual.

If you wanted to prolong the walk by a few days, you could either proceed from Aguersioual to Matate and drop south to the

Tizi Mzik and follow Route 1 to Tizi Oussem, or do the same from Imlil. Rather than going south, as in Route 1, you could turn north for Irkoubeline (day nine). The final day could be spent retracing your steps to Imlil, proceeding to Tinitine (Imlil-Asni road) via the Tizi n'Techt and then down to Imlil. You could also add a couple of days to explore the Tazaghart area as described in Route 1.

ORGANISED TREKS

Group treks can be organised for you before you arrive in Morocco by writing (in French) to the brothers Imar and Mohammed Imzilen, Guides de Montagne, Imlil, BP 8, Asni, Région de Marrakech, Morocco, and asking for their leaflet. You can also contact them via the Hôtel Étoile du Toubkal in Imlil. They run a modest ski equipment hire shop in Imlil.

Treks ranging from seven to 14 days from May to October are available on many circuits, including Jebel Toubkal, Jebel M'Goun (to the north-east), Jebel Sarhro (to the east), Jebel Siroua (south-east) and the Plateau de Yagour. The price is approximately Dr 350 per person a day, which includes guides, mules, food and accommodation either in tents, refuges or with local people.

Another guide, Brahim Toudaoui, organises similar treks and 4WD tours, or a combination of both. You can write to him at BP 60,500, Asni, Région de Marrakech, Morocco. He speaks French and English.

The South

If you had to choose one occasion on which to hire a car in Morocco, a visit to the great desert valleys south and south-east of Marrakesh would be the ideal candidate. The towns along the Drâa, Dadès and Ziz valleys are generally drab places, offering the traveller a chance to rest up but little else. The beauty of the region is on the road, and having your own wheels is the best way to experience it.

Marrakesh to Ouarzazate

From Marrakesh, the P31 starts off in gentle enough and unremarkable countryside. After about 50 km (south-east) the road crosses the Oued Zat *(Le Coq Hardi,* a restaurant and hotel of long standing, sits by the bridge).

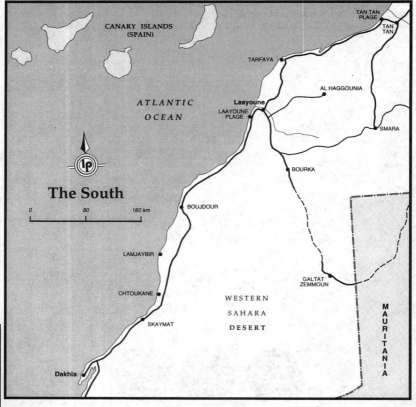

SOUTH MOROCCO

Soon after the road begins to climb towards the village of Taddert. Around here, especially in winter and spring, you could easily think you were in rural France – oaks are the predominant trees. After Taddert, the road quickly climbs and the landscape strips itself of its green mantle. The Tizi n'Tichka pass is higher than the Tizi n'Test (2260 metres) to the west, but perhaps less spectacular. When you get over the last bends, however, a remarkable scene unveils itself: the lunar landscape of the Anti-Atlas and the desert beyond, obliterating memories of the dense woods and green fields behind you.

TELOUET

A recommended turn-off if you have a car is to the village of Telouet (you'll see the turn-off to the left a few km after crossing the pass), 21 km east off the highway. Watch out in winter, as the narrow road can be snowbound. The village is a lively little place and the drive itself is worth the effort. Telouet is dominated by a kasbah that once served as a palatial residence and headquarters of the powerful Glaoui tribe. Until independence in 1956, the Glaouis were virtually given a free hand in southern Morocco by the French, in return for support for the protectorate.

There is a small hotel here. Without your own transport it is a little difficult to get to, as the closest major town is Ouarzazate. Getting a bus or grand taxi to drop you off at the turn-off is easy enough, after which you would have little choice but to stick out your thumb for the last 21 km.

OUARZAZATE

Ouarzazate was created by the French in 1928 as a garrison and regional administrative centre. Before that, all there was around here was the Glaoui kasbah of Taourirt at the eastern end of the modern town on the road to Tinerhir. It's something of a boom town

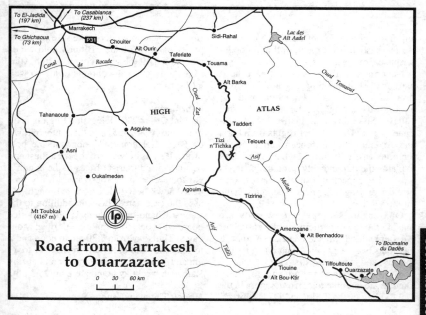

Road from Marrakesh to Ouarzazate

0   30   60 km

The Glaoui Tribe

A minor tribe until the 19th century, the Glaouis (or Glaoua) did not come into their own until 1859, when Si Hammou Glaoui, whose wealth came from salt mine exploitation, was made qaid of Telouet by the sultan. From that time, developments were to move fast. The big promotion came when Al-Maidani, Si Hammou's son and successor, proclaimed his support for Sultan Moulay al-Hassan I in 1893 and in return was put in command of the whole High Atlas region and appointed Qaid of the Tafilalt. After the death of the sultan the following year, it appeared the Glaoui star might fall as quickly as it had risen, as Al-Maidani gradually fell out of favour with Sultan Moulay Abd al-Aziz. The Glaoui clans threw in their lot with Abd al-Aziz's brother, Moulay Abd al-Hafiz, who had himself proclaimed sultan and defeated his brother in 1908. Al-Maidani was then made minister of war, but things started to go sour once again when the sultan dismissed him in 1911.

By this time however, the sultan's power and prestige were all but exhausted, and Al-Maidani could see a new horse to back in the form of the French. When the protectorate was proclaimed in 1912, the Glaouis threw in their lot with Paris. In return for keeping all southern Morocco in order and loyal to the protectorate, France gave the Glaoui clan carte blanche. Paris was not interested in the means, only in the result.

Al-Maidani died in 1918 and was succeeded by his brother, Thami. During his brother's lifetime, Thami had been made pasha of Marrakesh, and was still hanging the heads of tribal enemies on the city gates as late as the 1940s. He continued the family policy of loyalty to the French, and the latter continued to leave him free rein, something he used to become one of the wealthiest men in Morocco by the 1930s.

Things began to go awry after WW II, when he clashed with the future independent king, Mohammed V, over independence. The sultan backed the movement, but Thami, worried that the departure of the French might end the good life, sided solidly with Paris. He was instrumental in having Mohammed V deposed as sultan in 1953, but two years later saw the writing on the wall and begged the sultan's forgiveness. He got it, but didn't live long enough to see any results, dying of cancer in January 1956. With his demise, the Glaoui tribe seemed to disintegrate, and all their great kasbahs now stand abandoned. ■

and has a population of 30,000, but except for the kasbah it's a quiet, dull and nondescript sort of place.

Nevertheless, the Moroccans have been hard at work promoting it as a big destination, or at least as a launching pad for excursions along the Drâa and Dadès valleys. Sparkling new luxury hotels continue to go up, and charter flights from Paris and several other European capitals keep them at least half-full. Maybe all this fuss explains the outlandishly wide main streets – were they expecting an avalanche of crazed hire-car-driving foreigners to descend on the city?

Ouarzazate's biggest drawcards are outside the town, particularly the kasbah of Aït Benhaddou, off the Marrakesh road. It has long been a popular location for filmmakers, and is well worth a visit.

Most travellers spend the night in Ouarzazate en route to or from Zagora in the Drâa Valley or the Todra and Dadès gorges.

If you're here in winter make sure you have plenty of warm clothes. Bitterly cold winds whip down off the snow-covered High Atlas Mountains, and can continue doing so well into spring.

Information

Tourist Office The Délégation Régionale du Tourisme (☎ 882485) is in the centre of town on Blvd Mohammed V, opposite the post office. It's possibly one of the friendliest and best organised tourist offices in the country. Nowhere else in Morocco is a locally produced newssheet-style brochure brought out as is the case here. This is in addition to the standard hand-outs. There is also a notice board with local information. It's open Monday to Thursday from 8.30 am to noon and 2 to 6.30 pm, and on Friday from 8.30 to 11 am and 3 to 6.30 pm. In summer and during Ramadan weekday hours are 8 am to 3 pm.

Money The main Banque Populaire on Blvd

Mohammed V (just west of the post office) is open for changing money Monday to Friday from 8.15 to 11.30 am and 2.30 to 5 pm. On Saturday it's open from 3 to 6 pm and Sunday from 9 am to 1 pm.

For credit-card cash advances, you need to go to the Crédit du Maroc, at the western end of town on Blvd Mohammed V, on the corner of Ave Bir Anzaran. It's open only during standard banking hours.

Post & Telecommunications Both the post and phone offices, on Rue de la Poste, are open normal working hours only. There are a few card phones outside.

Medical Services There is a night pharmacy on Ave Al-Mouahidine. There is also supposed to be one on Blvd Mohammed V (☎ 882708).

Supermarket The Supermarché on Blvd Mohammed V carries an excellent range of goods, including alcoholic drinks (beer and wine) and even nappies (diapers).

Swimming A soothing swim in one of the big hotels' pools will cost from Dr 30 to Dr 50.

Festivals
The moussem of Sidi Daoud is held in Ouarzazate in August.

Kasbah & Around
The only place worth visiting in Ouarzazate itself is the Taourirt Kasbah at the eastern end of town, off Blvd Mohammed V. During the 1930s, in the heyday of the Glaoui chiefs, this was one of the largest kasbahs in the area. It then housed numerous members of the Glaoui dynasty, along with hundreds of their servants and workers. UNESCO is now restoring parts of it, so the general feeling of neglect that the narrow alleyways exude may in future be balanced by this welcome cultural spring-clean.

The 'palace' that the Glaouis occupied consists of courtyards, living quarters, reception rooms and the like, and is open from 8 am to noon and 3 to 6.30 pm seven days a week. Entry costs Dr 10. You can take on a guide for extra if you want to know what each of the now empty rooms was used for. It's worth a visit, but you'll only be shown a part of the complex. There are some good views over the rest of the kasbah and the Oued Ouarzazate, which, like the Oued Dadès, spills into the Al-Mansour ed-Dahabi dam to the immediate south to become the Oued Drâa. The rest of the kasbah can be visited at any time.

Opposite the entrance to the kasbah is another building in the same style, which houses the Ensemble Artisanal. Here you can find stone carvings, pottery and woollen carpets woven by the region's Ouzguita Berbers. It's open Monday to Friday from 8.30 am to noon and 1 to 6 pm, and on Saturday from 8.30 am to noon. There are plenty of other craft shops around here too, but don't expect any bargains – Club Med is virtually next door and there are direct flights to Ouarzazate from Paris!

Places to Stay – bottom end
Camping There's a camping ground (signposted) next to the so-called Tourist Complex off the main road out of town towards Tinerhir, about two km from the bus station. There is some shade, and the camp site is right by Oued Ouarzazate. It also has a grocery store and restaurant. It costs Dr 7 per person, Dr 5 per car, Dr 6 to pitch a tent and Dr 10 for electricity.

Hotels There are effectively only five bottom-end hotels in Ouarzazate (two of them awkwardly placed if you arrive on local transport), so if you arrive late you may have to pay for something more expensive if they're all full (which does happen).

About the best and one of the cheapest places is the *Hôtel Royal* (☎ 882258), 24 Blvd Mohammed V (entrance in the side street). Belkaziz, the owner, has all sorts of rooms for all sorts of prices. Small singles start at Dr 26. Doubles without shower are Dr 63 and those with private shower are Dr 84. A quad made up of two adjoining rooms

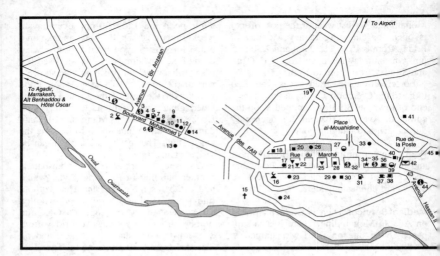

goes for Dr 154. The beds are comfortable, the linen is super clean and the showers have hot water.

Also on Blvd Mohammed V is the *Hôtel Es-Salam* (☎ 882512). It is perfectly good and has reasonable singles/doubles for Dr 52/80. The showers are shared but there is hot water (Dr 5 a go). It can be a bit noisy.

Another decent cheapie is the *Hôtel Atlas* (☎ 882307), 13 Rue du Marché. Clean singles/doubles/triples without shower cost Dr 30/45/65. Doubles and triples with private shower are Dr 55/80. There is hot water in the evening (Dr 5 in the communal shower for those in rooms without shower). It's fine but not as good as the Royal.

About two km out of town on the Zagora road is an excellent deal. The *Hôtel La Vallée* (☎ 882668) is right beside the road and is a friendly, buzzy place. There's a palmeraie just across the way. Pleasant rooms with one big bed and a small bed (no singles) cost Dr 80. There's even a TV in some rooms. The showers are shared and hot water is available. The hotel has its own restaurant.

About 100 metres farther on is the *Hôtel Saghro* on the right, but it's not as good or well located as La Vallée.

If you have a little more money to dispose of, there are two one-star hotels to choose from, too. Of these, the *Hôtel Amlal* (☎ 884030; fax 884600), a block in from Blvd Mohammed V, is newer and streets ahead. The rooms are clean and comfortable, with en suite bathroom (hot water in the evening) and wardrobe, and there is guarded parking out the front. Prices are Dr 108/130/170/210. The *Hôtel Es-Saada* (☎ 883231), 12 Rue de la Poste, also offers singles and doubles for Dr 108/130, but they are gloomy and could do with a paint job.

Places to Stay – middle

Before heading into the higher bracket of hotel options, there are two that cost moderately more than the Amlal. The *Hôtel Résidence Al Warda* (☎ 882349), just by Place du 3 Mars on Blvd Mohammed V, offers a potentially tempting deal. The rooms are basically mini-apartments with up to five beds, bathroom and kitchen. Hot water is promised, as are reductions on longer stays. The asking rates are Dr 124/148 for singles/doubles.

The well-established *Hôtel La Gazelle* (☎ 882151), also on Blvd Mohammed V, is

Ouarzazate

To Tinerhir &
Errachidia

To Hôtel
Le Zat

Avenue Emsbar

Boulevard Mohammed V

Sharia ar-Raha

Taourirt Kasbah

Boulevard Mohammed V

To Zagora &
Hôtel La Vallée

0   250   500 m

Approximate Scale

PLACES TO STAY

4 Hôtel La Gazelle
7 Hôtel Résidence
   Al-Warda
18 Hôtel Amlal
20 Hôtel Atlas
28 Hôtel Royal
30 Hôtel Es-Salam
40 Hôtel Es-Saada
41 Le Berbère Palace
45 Hôtel PLM Azghor
46 Hôtel Karam
49 Hôtels Tichka
   Salam & Riad
   Salam

PLACES TO EAT

19 Restaurant Al
   Waha
21 Restaurant
   Essalam
22 Café de la
   Résistance
25 Chez Dimitri
51 Restaurant
   L'Étoile du Sud

OTHER

1 BMCI Bank
2 Mosque
3 Crédit du Maroc
5 Shell Service
   Station
6 Banque Populaire
   (branch)
8 Budget
9 Palais de la
   Culture et des
   Congrès
10 Place du 3 Mars
   (Car Rental &
   Tour Agencies)
11 Glacier du 3 Mars
12 Europcar
13 Barracks
14 Avis
15 Church
16 Mosque
17 Royal Air Maroc
23 Hertz
24 Barracks
26 Market
27 Bus Station &
   Grand Taxi Lot

29 Supermarché
31 Shell Service
   Station
32 BMCE Bank
33 Water Tower
34 Police
35 Banque Populaire
36 Café du Sud &
   Café des
   Voyageurs
37 Café Mounia
38 Café Errachidia
39 CTM Bus Station
40 Cinema Atlas
42 Post Office (PTT)
43 Place
   Mohammed V
44 Tourist Office
47 Palace
48 Hospital
50 Club Med
52 Café La Kasba
53 Ensemble Artisanal
54 Zoo
55 Tourist Complex
56 Camping Ground

SOUTH MOROCCO

very popular with tour groups, but seems to be living off a worn-out reputation. It has its own swimming pool and rooms surrounding a leafy courtyard, but could do with an overhaul. Singles/doubles with private bathroom cost Dr 127.50/179 – avoid the rooms in the front courtyard. There's hot water only in the morning, which is not much use to tired travellers arriving in the evening. Cars can be parked safely in the hotel's front courtyard.

Places to Stay – top end
The three-star *Hôtel Tichka Salam* (☎ 882206; fax 885680), Blvd Mohammed V, is the cheapest of the top-end hotels. Singles/doubles with private bathroom and hot water are Dr 288/360 plus taxes. There's heating in the rooms and the hotel has its own bar, restaurant, tennis courts and swimming pool.

There are plenty of options in the four and five-star brackets. The two cheapest are the *Hôtel PLM Azghor* (☎ 885555), on Sharia ar-Raha, and the *Motel Zat* (☎ 882558; fax 885394), a couple of km out of the town centre and off the road to Tinerhir. They both cost Dr 314/400 plus taxes. The latter has a modest swimming pool.

The *Hôtel Bélère* (☎ 882303; fax 883145) is one of the best deals at this end of the scale, with rooms costing Dr 385/495. The hotel has a pool.

Heading up the line is the Salam chain's second representative here, the *Hôtel Riad* (☎ 883610; fax 882766), off Blvd Mohammed V. The rooms are modern and the hotel boasts two restaurants (one of them usually the stage for folkloric music performances and the like), a sauna and a tennis court. Singles/doubles/triples cost Dr 600/700/800 plus taxes. In much the same league is the recently opened *Hôtel Oscar*, another Salam member, just outside the town's Marrakesh exit.

Slightly more expensive again is the new *Le Berbère Palace* (☎ 883077; fax 883071), a rather sumptuous place with pool, bars, hammam and boutiques. Singles/doubles are Dr 700/850.

Apart from Club Med, that just leaves Pullman's *Hôtel Karam* (☎ 882225; fax 882319), off Sharia ar-Raha, which offers villas for Dr 1000/1200.

Places to Eat
A lot of travellers eat at the restaurants attached to the hotels *Royal* and *Atlas*. Both have a fair selection of the old favourites, but the *Restaurant Essalam*, between Blvd Mohammed V and Rue du Marché, is better. There are eight set-menu choices, all for Dr 50. You get a salad, generous main meal and dessert (often no more than fruit). It's also popular with travellers. Just as good, and cheaper, is the *Café de la Résistance*, just around the corner on Blvd Mohammed V. A big plate of brochettes, chips and salad cost Dr 28, including a soft drink. You may be able to get something to eat at some of the cafés down near the CTM bus station.

Whatever you are told, do *not* go to the *Restaurant Al Waha*. It's a long walk for absolutely nothing. You too can sit in empty, cavernous surroundings and be served a stingy tajine (a clump of fatty meat decorated with a few prunes) for Dr 40 or a bland couscous for Dr 60. Don't waste your time.

If you *do* want to splash out a little, forget the big hotel restaurants and head for *Chez Dimitri*, between Blvd Mohammed V and Rue du Marché. Founded at the same time as the town, it once served as petrol station, general store, dance hall, telegraph office and just about everything else besides. A good meal from the surprisingly extensive menu of Moroccan and French cuisine will set you back Dr 70 to Dr 100 and be well worth it. It is very popular and is often packed to the hilt with tourists. Try the lemon tart. The restaurant also has one of the best stocked bars in southern Morocco.

The restaurant at the *Hôtel La Gazelle* also has a bar, but the food and service are not a patch on Chez Dimitri.

Getting There & Away
Air RAM has an office (☎ 885102) on Blvd Mohammed V. There are flights to Casablanca (Dr 445; at least five times weekly),

Marrakesh (Dr 235; four times weekly) and possibly Agadir, although at the time of writing it appeared this weekly flight had been suspended. There are direct flights to Paris.

Bus CTM has its own terminal on Blvd Mohammed V, close to the post office. CTM has a bus to Zagora (Dr 35; four hours) and on to M'Hamid (Dr 52.50; seven hours) at 12.30 pm. Another bus for Agadir (Dr 86; seven hours) leaves at noon. There are four departures for Marrakesh. Those at 8.30 am and 9 pm are mumtaz services and cost Dr 49. The others are 1st-class buses; they leave at 11.30 am and 12.30 pm and cost Dr 34.50. The trip takes about four hours. The 9 pm bus to Casablanca is a mumtaz run and costs Dr 106.50. At 10.30 am there's a bus to Er-Rachidia for Dr 65.50. It goes via Boumalne du Dadès (Dr 24.50) and Tinerhir and takes about nine hours.

SATAS and several other smaller bus lines all operate from Place al-Mouahidine. SATAS has at least one departure a day to Marrakesh (Dr 46.50) at 8.30 am, and to Agadir (Dr 80) at 9.30 pm. The latter stops at Taroudannt on the way (Dr 65). A bus leaves for Zagora and M'Hamid at about 6.30 am and another for Er-Rachidia at 8 pm. The other lines between them have several runs to Agadir, Taroudannt and Zagora.

Taxi Grands taxis also leave from Place al-Mouahidine. A place in a taxi to Marrakesh costs Dr 70. To Zagora the fare is Dr 40. The fares to Agdz, Skoura and Boumalne du Dadès are Dr 20, Dr 10 and Dr 25 respectively.

Car Since the Drâa Valley route down to Zagora and beyond to M'Hamid is such a spectacular and interesting journey, it's worth considering car rental before you leave Ouarzazate. With your own vehicle, you'll be able to stop wherever you like to explore the ksour (fortified strongholds) or take photographs. In a bus or shared taxi you'll simply speed through all these places, catch only fleeting glimpses and probably

arrive in Zagora feeling disappointed. It's far better to get a group together and hire a vehicle in Ouarzazate, as there are no car rental places in Zagora. Some of the agencies include:

Avis
    On the corner of Blvd Mohammed V and Rue A Sehraoui (☎ 884870)
Budget
    Résidence Al-Warda, Blvd Mohammed V (☎ 882892)
Europcar
    Bureau 4, Place du 3 Mars (☎ 882035)
Hertz
    33 Blvd Mohammed V (☎ 882084)

Tours The big hotels organise 4WD trips and the like to destinations such as Telouet, Skoura, the Todra Gorge and Zagora. They are not cheap.

AROUND OUARZAZATE
Tifoultoute
About nine km north-west of Ouarzazate is another Glaoui kasbah now converted into a hotel and restaurant, where you can watch evening performances of traditional dance and music. Although the kasbah is quite impressive from a distance, it's a disappointment when you get up close. When you pass the first gateway, you can wander up the first lane on the right through all the litter to have a look at the innards of a kasbah in an advanced state of disrepair. When you then try to pass through the inner gateway, they want to charge you Dr 5! Basically, all you have access to once inside is the restaurant, hotel and roof – the views from the roof are OK, but hardly worth Dr 5. Just tell them you want to go to the restaurant.

The kasbah was first used as a hotel in the 1960s, when the cast of *Lawrence of Arabia* was put up here, and it has since become somewhat kitsch. Package-tour groups are ferried in here regularly for the dinner and show. Rooms cost Dr 140 for a double and are somewhat basic. As for the restaurant, it has set menus for Dr 75 and Dr 110. It would probably be worth it if you had a car to get out there and were not accompanied by busloads of tourists.

The best way to get there is to take the road to Marrakesh and turn off at the sign for Tifoultoute. Without your own car, you'll need to negotiate for a taxi.

Aït Benhaddou

In the same direction, again off the road to Marrakesh, and 32 km from Ouarzazate, is the village of Aït Benhaddou. Here is one of the most exotic and best preserved kasbahs in the whole Atlas region. This is hardly surprising, since it has had money poured into it as a result of being used for scenes in as many as 20 films, notably *Lawrence of Arabia* and *Jesus of Nazareth*. Much of the village was rebuilt for the filming of the latter. Its fame lives on, but the population has dwindled.

When you arrive, walk in off the road past the Auberge Al Baraka and you'll see the kasbah on the other side of the Ounila river-bed. Head down past the souvenir stalls and across the river, which is usually no more than a trickle with a ramp and stepping stones to cross, although it can flow more strongly in early spring. The main entrance to the kasbah complex is a little way upstream (you'll know you've found it when you see more souvenir stalls).

One of the locals may half-heartedly hassle you to engage him as a guide but this is totally unnecessary. There are magnificent views from the upper reaches of the kasbah of the surrounding palmeraie and, beyond, the unforgiving hammada.

You can go on camel treks here, too, if you have a lot of money. The going rate appears to be an absurd Dr 700 for a measly three hours!

Places to Stay & Eat There are three places to stay, and there is a lot to be said for doing so rather than bedding down in Ouarzazate.

The first you'll come across is the least appealing. The roadside *Auberge Al Baraka* (☎ 5 through the operator) has extremely primitive rooms for Dr 100 whether there's one or two of you. Skip it if you can.

The *Auberge El Ouidane* has better (but not spectacular) rooms for Dr 50/100. They only have cold showers. The compensation is that the views across to the kasbah from the adjoining restaurant and some of the rooms are wonderful.

Next door, the *Hôtel Restaurant La Kasbah* (☎ 2 through the operator) offers double rooms for Dr 140 with compulsory half-board. That's not such a bad deal really – where else are you going to eat anyway?

Getting There & Away To get there, take the main road to Marrakesh and turn off after 22 km when you see the signpost for the village; Aït Benhaddou is another nine km down a good bitumen road (stop at the signs for the hotels). Occasionally, local buses travel to Aït Benhaddou from Ouarzazate, but it's a lot easier to get there by sharing a taxi. Otherwise, ask around among tourists in the restaurants or at Hôtel La Gazelle. Hitching is difficult.

Tamdaght

Five km north-east of Aït Benhaddou, the road ends abruptly where it hits the river Ounila. On the other side it continues on for a while before turning into a poor piste leading north to Telouet (an increasingly popular 4WD, mountain-bike and hiking route).

About 1.5 km north-east of where the river cuts the road stands yet another Glaoui kasbah, that of Tamdaght. It is not as spectacular as the Aït Benhaddou complex, but comparatively little visited. You can get sturdy vehicles with a high chassis over the stream, but don't try it if you are unsure. Instead, leave your vehicle at the little café (watch their prices) and wade across. If you're lucky, Larbi Embarak might be hanging around. He's quite a local character and will insist on giving you a piggy-back across to keep your tootsies dry. He will also want to act as your guide and show you a tattered photo of himself as an extra for one of the several films which have been shot here. *The Man Who Would Be King*, with

Sean Connery and Michael Caine, is one of them.

Drâa Valley

From Ouarzazate you have the choice of following two scenic routes. One leads you south through the Drâa Valley, a natural delight that will take you through what can sometimes seem like a tunnel of kasbahs and palmeraies. The other takes you north-east along the Dadès Valley and the Dadès and Todra gorges, also known as the Route des Mille Kasbahs (Road of 1000 Kasbahs). You can then push on to Er-Rachidia and the Ziz Valley or even farther to Erfoud and the oases of the Tafilalt.

If you want to try out both, it makes sense to go down the Drâa Valley first, as, unless you have a 4WD, you have no choice but to come back up the same way when you've reached the end. Heading out along the Dadès Valley, you could proceed all the way to Figuig on the Algerian frontier, or turn up north and either circle slowly back towards

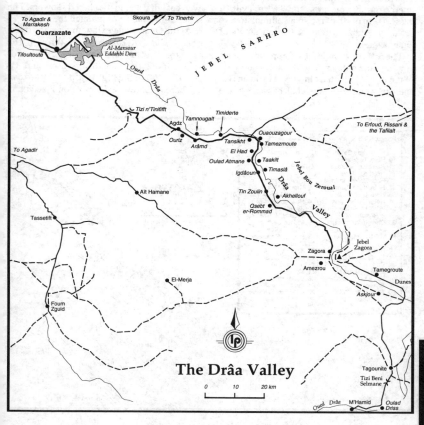

The Drâa Valley

0   10   20 km

Marrakesh via Midelt or keep going north to Fès or Meknès via Azrou.

Although you can get to the main centres by bus, there is no doubt that the freedom of having your own transport is a decided advantage in this part of the country. If you do have a car, beware of the false hitchhiker syndrome. A few less-than-honest Moroccans work the Ouarzazate-Zagora road looking for suckers to take home in 'gratitude' for the lift, only to start the hard carpet sell.

AGDZ

The road south from Ouarzazate only gets interesting as you cross the Tizi n'Tinififft pass, 20 km north of the small administrative town of Agdz, which is 69 km south of Ouarzazate.

There's not much to keep you here, although the palmeraie to the north and west of the town (hidden from view as you arrive) and the weird-looking Jebel Kissane in the background might be enough to justify a brief stop. Ave Mohammed V, the main road, heads straight through the town to a square, Place de la Marche Verte, before heading off to the right and southwards towards Zagora. It is here that the Drâa Valley really begins.

Places to Stay & Eat

The *Camping Kasbah-Palmeraie* (signposted) is located, as the name suggests, near a small kasbah.

There are two cheapies on Place de la Marche Verte. The *Hôtel Restaurant Draa* has big, simple rooms with double beds. Singles/doubles cost Dr 35/70, and you may even get hot water in the shared showers. The *Hôtel des Palmeraies* is much the same.

At the Ouarzazate exit of town is the overpriced *Hôtel Kissane* (☎ 44 through the operator). It offers singles/doubles/triples for Dr 90/160/250 in the low season and Dr 100/180/260 in the high season, plus taxes.

There are a few restaurants on Place de la

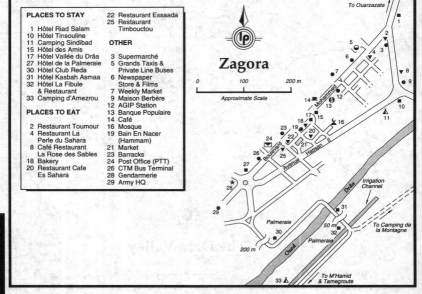

PLACES TO STAY	
1	Hôtel Riad Salam
10	Hôtel Tinsouline
11	Camping Sindibad
15	Hôtel des Amis
17	Hôtel Vallée du Drâa
27	Hôtel de la Palmeraie
30	Hôtel Club Reda
31	Hôtel Kasbah Asmaa
32	Hôtel La Fibule & Restaurant
33	Camping d'Amezrou

PLACES TO EAT	
2	Restaurant Toumour
4	Restaurant La Perle du Sahara
8	Café Restaurant La Rose des Sables
18	Bakery
20	Restaurant Cafe Es Sahara
22	Restaurant Essaada
25	Restaurant Timbouctou

OTHER	
3	Supermarché
5	Grands Taxis & Private Line Buses
6	Newspaper Store & Films
7	Weekly Market
9	Maison Berbère
12	AGIP Station
13	Banque Populaire
14	Café
16	Mosque
19	Bain En Nacer (Hammam)
21	Market
23	Barracks
24	Post Office (PTT)
26	CTM Bus Terminal
28	Gendarmerie
29	Army HQ

Zagora

0   100   200 m

Approximate Scale

To Ouarzazate
To Camping de la Montagne
To M'Hamid & Tamegroute

Irrigation Channel

Palmeraie

Oued

Marche Verte offering the usual old favourites.

Getting There & Away
CTM, SATAS and several other buses stop here en route between Ouarzazate and Zagora. Sometimes you can get on, sometimes you can't. Otherwise, occasional grands taxis go to Ouarzazate and Zagora – Dr 20 either way.

ZAGORA
The road from Agdz to Zagora, featuring 95 km of heavily cultivated oases lining the Drâa and some 50 ksour, is the richest stretch of the Drâa.

Arriving in Zagora, however, can be a bit of a letdown. Like Ouarzazate, it is largely a fairly recent creation, dating from French colonial times, when it was set up as an administrative centre. Nevertheless, the oasis has always been inhabited, and it was from this area that the Saadians began their conquest of Morocco in the 16th century. Moroccan rulers long before them passed through here too, and there are vestiges of an Almoravid fortress atop Jebel Zagora.

There are plenty of interesting places to explore in the vicinity and the town does have its moments, particularly when a dust storm blows up out of the desert in the late afternoon and the lighting becomes totally surreal. Zagora is also where you'll see that somewhat battered sign saying 'Tombuktoo 52 jours' (by camel caravan), against which just about everyone wants to be photographed.

Although little more than an oversized village (population about 15,000), the place has more than its fair share of expensive hotels. Just why the road at the Ouarzazate exit of the town is of runway proportions is a bit of a mystery, too. The steady flow of tourists has given the place a bit of a reputation as a 'little Marrakesh'. Take special care if you start arranging camel treks and the like.

Information
Money The Banque Populaire is open for exchange Monday to Thursday from 8.15 to 11.30 am and 2.15 to 4.30 pm, and Friday from 8.15 to 11.15 am and 2.45 to 4.30 pm.

Market Market days are Wednesday and Sunday. Fruit and vegetables, herbs, hardware, handicrafts, sheep, goats and donkeys are brought in to be bought and sold.

Things to See & Do
The spectacular **Jebel Zagora**, which rises up across the other side of the river, is worth climbing for the views – if you have the stamina and you set off early in the morning. The town is smack in the middle of extensive **palmeraies**, some of them out around the hotels and camp sites at the southern end of town. They are peaceful and beautiful and enough to make you forget the dreary nature of the town centre.

If you are here over the period of Mouloud (check the Islamic calendar in the Facts for the Visitor chapter), you may well coincide with the moussem of Moulay Abdelkader, which brings the town to life.

It is possible to arrange **camel treks** of up to a week or so. You could try calling Yassin Ali on ☎ 847497, or enquire at the two camp sites near the Hôtel La Fibule or at the hotel itself. It should cost about Dr 200 to Dr 250 a day (including an overnight stay in the desert).

Places to Stay – bottom end
Camping Campers have a choice of three sites. About the most popular is *Camping d'Amezrou*, about 200 metres past the Hôtel La Fibule along the dirt track that runs alongside the irrigation channel. It costs Dr 7.50 a person, Dr 5 for a car, Dr 5 to pitch a tent and Dr 7 for electricity. Hot showers are supposedly free. The setting is attractive and close to the restaurants of the hotels La Fibule and Kasbah Asmaa.

Also over this side of town is *Camping de la Montagne*, at the foot of the mountain. You get to it by crossing the bridge over the irrigation channel immediately past La Fibule, and then following the signpost off

SOUTH MOROCCO

to the left. It's about two km down the dirt track from here. There are toilets and plenty of shade. Cold drinks are available, but you're advised to bring your own food. It costs Dr 8 per person and the same for a car. Pitching a tent costs Dr 4.

The third site is *Camping Sindibad*, off Ave Hassan II, where there are toilets, hot showers and a café. It's a perfectly decent camp site surrounded by palm trees, but most travellers choose to stay at the other two. The people here find that a little irksome, but they do their cause little good with the prices they charge. It costs Dr 7 per person, Dr 10 for a car, Dr 10 to pitch a tent, Dr 10 for electricity and Dr 5 for a hot shower.

Hotels There are two unclassified hotels next to each other on the main street, Blvd Mohammed V. The better of the two, if you can get a front room, is the *Hôtel Vallée du Drâa*, or *Oued Drâa* (☎ 847210). Singles/doubles cost Dr 46/65 with shared bathroom, Dr 69/85 with private shower and Dr 77/90 with private bathroom (there's no hot water). It's clean, friendly and has its own restaurant. The *Hôtel des Amis* offers basic but adequate rooms at Dr 30 a person. There are shared, cold showers. Going up in price, there's the popular one-star *Hôtel de la Palmeraie* (☎ 847008), also on Blvd Mohammed V. The place was a bit chaotic at the time of writing, as it was being refurbished, but the rooms, most of which have balconies, are quite reasonable. Singles/doubles/triples cost Dr 66/85/118 with private shower but shared toilet, and Dr 98/131 for doubles/triples with private shower and toilet. There's hot water in the showers. If you have your own bedding they'll also let you sleep on the roof for Dr 15 per person. The hotel has a lively if fly-blown bar full of some very intriguing characters and an excellent restaurant where you can get a three-course meal for about Dr 60. Camel treks can also be arranged here.

If you need a hot shower, go to the *Bain En Nacer* hammam, around the corner from the bakery.

Places to Stay – middle
It can be worth your while booking ahead in the high season for the following places, which are often full. On the other hand, you may well be able to get hefty reductions on room rates in the low season.

If you can afford it, the best value and most relaxing place to stay in Zagora is the two-star *Hôtel La Fibule* (☎ 847318; fax 847271), on the southern side of the Oued Drâa, about one km from the centre. The hotel is set in the palmeraie, with its own shady garden, restaurant, bar and swimming pool, and the rooms have been built and furnished in the traditional Berber style, with the addition of showers (hot water from 7 to 11 am daily) and toilets. Doubles cost Dr 145 with private shower but shared toilet (few of these) and Dr 290 with private shower and toilet. Excellent meals are available in the restaurant. Camel treks can be organised here for about the same price as at the camp sites.

Also pretty decent, and just 50 metres before La Fibule, is the *Hôtel Kasbah Asmaa* (☎ 847599; fax 847527). This is another two-star hotel which has been built to resemble a Berber ksar. In the high season they don't distinguish between the price of single or double occupancy of the rooms, which cost Dr 250. We've had good reports from people who have stayed here. The hotel has its own bar, restaurant and pool, and guarded parking.

Places to Stay – top end
The cheapest place to stay in this category is the *Hôtel Tinsouline* (☎ 847252), which has 90 rooms and its own bar, restaurant and swimming pool. Singles/doubles with private bathroom cost Dr 320/400 plus taxes.

Next up is the brand-new addition to the Salam chain, the *Hôtel Riad* (☎ 847400; fax 847551). It has a swimming pool and a restaurant. It is one of the more luxurious of the Salam chain, and rooms cost Dr 440/495 plus taxes. The location by the Ouarzazate exit leaves a lot to be desired.

Top of the line is the *Hôtel Club Reda* (☎ 847079; fax 847012), set in the palmeraie next to the Oued Drâa. Singles/doubles with private bathroom cost a rather steep Dr 600/700. The hotel has all the amenities you would expect, including bar, restaurant, swimming pool and tennis courts, and has had favourable reports from travellers.

Places to Eat

All the hotels have their own restaurants, and it's probably true to say that they all try hard to produce tasty Moroccan-style dishes – soups, tajine, salad, etc – although the quality does vary from day to day at the cheaper places.

The *Hôtel des Amis* offers cheap meals at Dr 25, but the service can be excruciatingly slow and the tajine is of minimal size. In a similar vein and of uneven quality are the *Restaurant Café Es Sahara* (soup and tajine for Dr 20), *Restaurant Essaada*, *Restaurant Toumour* and *Restaurant La Perle du Sahara*. The *Restaurant Timbouctou* is more reliable and offers dishes at about the standard Dr 25 to Dr 30. Another possibility is the *Café Restaurant La Rose des Sables*, next to the Maison Berbère carpet and souvenir shop.

It's often better to eat at either the *Hôtel Vallée du Drâa* for Dr 40 or the *Hôtel de la Palmeraie* for Dr 60, since the service is quicker and the servings more substantial. The latter stocks beer and wine, but obviously is a little expensive.

Even if you are not staying at *La Fibule* you should try to make it there for a meal. The food is excellent and the surroundings are very relaxing. If you want, the bar will sell you cans of beer over the counter to take away.

Getting There & Away

Buses and shared taxis will give you no chance to stop and take photographs of the many fascinating villages and ksour between Ouarzazate and Zagora, let alone give you time to explore them. So, if there's any chance of you considering car rental and the freedom this will give you, think seriously about it. You will have to do so in Ouarzazate as there are no car rental agencies in Zagora.

Bus The CTM bus terminal is at the south-western end of Blvd Mohammed V, and the main bus and grand taxi lot is at the northern end of Blvd Mohammed V. There's a CTM bus once daily to Ouarzazate at 7 am. This bus starts out at M'Hamid and comes past La Fibule at about 6.30 am so, if you're staying there or at the nearby camp sites, you can flag it down right outside the door. The fare to Ouarzazate is Dr 35, and the bus continues on right through to Marrakesh. The bus coming the other way leaves for M'Hamid at 4.30 pm and also costs Dr 35.

Otherwise, you could try your luck at the bus lot. The best time is in the morning.

Taxi If buses are scarce, a better bet might be a grand taxi. Again the best time to try is the morning. A place costs Dr 40 to Ouarzazate, Dr 20 to Agdz and Dr 22 to M'Hamid.

If you want to try out the direct desert route across to Rissani in the Tafilalt, you may be able to get a ride in a taxi as far as Tazzarine. From there you'll have to arrange further transport, such as a Land Rover taxi as far as Alnif and another taxi from there to Rissani. Be prepared to get stuck overnight on this route. The best time to try is market days.

SOUTH OF ZAGORA
Amezrou

Across the other side of the Oued Drâa, about three km south of Zagora, is the village of Amezrou. It has an interesting old Jewish mellah, which is still a centre for the casting of silver jewellery. Jews lived here for centuries and formerly controlled the silver trade, but they all took off for Israel after 1948, leaving the Berbers to carry on the tradition. If you look like you might buy something, the locals will be willing to show you the whole process. Because the village is so close to Zagora, local children will leap on you offering to be guides, but it's fairly low-key hassle.

Elsewhere in the palmeraie life goes on much as it always has. It's well worth spending a day wandering through the shady groves along the many tracks that dissect it.

The dates grown here are reputed to be the best in Morocco, but times have been getting harder because of a disease that attacks and kills the palms.

Tamegroute

Farther south, about 18 km from Zagora, is Tamegroute. For many centuries, right up until recent times, the town was an important religious and educational centre whose influence was felt throughout the Drâa region and into the desert beyond. Tamegroute consists of a series of interconnected ksour, at the centre of which is the zawiyya and its famous library.

The **library** (signposted on the main road as 'Librairie Coranique') houses a magnificent collection of illustrated religious texts, dictionaries and astrological works, some of them on gazelle hides. The oldest texts date back to around the 13th century. Most of them are kept on shelves behind glass doors but others are displayed in glass cases of the type used in museums. They're beautifully illustrated but perhaps of limited interest to anyone other than an Arabic scholar. Visitors are allowed into the outer sanctuary and the library in the morning and late afternoon (it's generally closed from noon to 3 pm). You'll be expected to leave a donation for the upkeep of the place – Dr 5 to Dr 10 should suffice. There is no shortage of local people willing to act as guides but you don't need one.

Also in Tamegroute is a small potters' souq.

Places to Stay & Eat The town's only hotel and best restaurant is the *Hôtel Riad Nacir*, on the left-hand side as you enter town from Zagora.

Tinfou & the Dunes

About five km south of Tamegroute you can get your first glimpse of the Sahara desert. Off the road to the left are a number of isolated sand dunes. If you've never seen sandy desert and do not intend to head to Merzouga or on into Algeria, these might be

worth a visit. Otherwise, it's hardly worth the effort.

Places to Stay & Eat Tinfou is supposed to be a village, but there's really nothing here but a couple of accommodation options. The first is well worth considering as an alternative to staying in Zagora. The *Auberge Repos du Sable* is a tumbledown kasbah-style building with simple rooms costing Dr 50/70. There is cold water in the shared showers. The atmosphere is relaxed and the food, although it can take a while to arrive, is very good (about Dr 30). It even has a swimming pool, although it's not always in use. The hotel is run by Majid el-Farouj, whose parents, Hassan and Fatima, are artists. Their work (which is for sale) covers the walls of the main courtyard, and the artists themselves occasionally grace the hotel with a visit. You can organise 4WD trips into the desert (Dr 1500 to Dr 2000 a day, up to eight people) and camel treks for a week or so.

A little farther on is a recent and worrying addition to the landscape, the German-run *Bivouac*, where Dr 20 will get you a mattress in a tent inside a soulless compound. This place caters mainly to tour groups from the big Zagora hotels, staging desert soirées where nomads happen to emerge from the sands to indulge in a glass of tea and chat with the guests. It also detracts a little from the peaceful isolation that the Auberge enjoyed until recently.

M'Hamid

Most people who come to Zagora try to make it to the end of the road at M'Hamid, about 95 km to the south. The attraction of this trip is the journey itself. The road south of Tinfou soon crosses the Drâa and leaves it behind to cross a vast tract of implacable hammada desert. After crossing a low pass you hit the village of Tagounite, which has a couple of cafés, including the *Es-Saada* and *Sahara*.

A few more km take you over the dramatic Tizi Beni Selmane pass, from which the oases of the Drâa again come into view. The village and kasbah of Oulad Driss make a

picturesque stop before the final run into M'Hamid.

With a population of about 2000, M'Hamid is nothing special, and the handful of touts can be a pain. There's little to do here except sweat and poke around a few souvenir and craft shops. Alternatively, the hotels can organise donkey and camel treks. Otherwise, they can simply guide you on treks in your own vehicle (which would want to be good and preferably a 4WD) into the dunes and sandy desert that start up 10 km to the south.

Places to Stay & Eat About six km back out along the road is the *Camping des Caravanes*, which was opened in 1993 and is a little better equipped. It costs Dr 10 a person and Dr 5 for a car. There are also claustrophobic rooms for Dr 30 a head. You can have a meal cooked if you ask in advance. Not far away is the *Camping Touareg*.

The *Hôtel Restaurant Sahara* has simple but adequate facilities, and charges Dr 35 per person. There are as yet no showers and the food is overpriced, so it might be an idea to bring some with you. The town is waiting to have electricity put on, and the hotel will install showers if this ever happens. Otherwise you can tramp out about 500 metres to a palmeraie and stay at the *Auberge Al Khaima*. The few rooms, shut in by old, heavy doors with medieval key locks, are primitive and not very clean (Dr 20 a person). You can also pitch a tent here, but there's no water for washing.

Getting There & Away There's a daily CTM bus from Zagora (originating in Marrakesh and passing through Ouarzazate) to M'Hamid around 4.30 pm, and it returns the next day between 4 and 5 am. The fare is Dr 35. If you're lucky, you may be able to get a lift with other tourists or in one of the rare grands taxis.

If you just want to make a day trip from Zagora, it comes down to hiring a taxi. The usual charge is up to Dr 400 for the day, although this is negotiable to a degree. Taxis take up to six people, so it's a good idea to get a group together to share the cost. This is the best way to see the area, as the driver will stop wherever you like.

Dadès Valley & the Gorges

Heading roughly east of Ouarzazate, the Dadès Valley threads its course between the mountains of the High Atlas to the north and the Jebel Sarhro range to the south. If leaving from Ouarzazate, about the first thing you notice is the lake formed by the waters of the Al-Mansour ed-Dahabi dam. Shortly after, you enter the biggest oases on the Dadès route – those preceding the town of Skoura.

SKOURA
Skoura lies about 42 km east of Ouarzazate and makes an easy day excursion if you don't simply want to make a stop before heading farther east. The oases here contain a collection of impressive kasbahs. One of the most

easily accessible is the **Kasbah ben Moro**.
About 150 years old, it's just off the main
road on the right, a couple of km before you
reach the town. The owners, who live next
door, use it mainly for animals and storage
space now, but Mohammed will open it up
for a small fee. There's not an awful lot to
see inside, but from the top there are great
views of the palmeraie and another kasbah,
Amerdihl, which is owned by a wealthy
Casablanca family and cannot be visited.

Places to Stay & Eat

The *Hôtel Nakhil*, in the centre of town, is a
basic place with rooms for Dr 30. Apart from
a few cafés and snack stands, there's not
much in the line of restaurants here.

Getting There & Away

The odd bus passes through from Ouarzazate
and Tinerhir, but an easier bet is a grand taxi
from Ouarzazate (Dr 10). If you want to get
out on the same day, you'll have to be early,
as there's not much happening in terms of
transport from the late afternoon on.

EL-KELAÂ M'GOUNA

Another 50 km north-east up the valley, the
town of El-Kelaâ M'Gouna is really of precious little interest to the traveller. Its main
claim to fame is as a centre of rose-water
production, which is made abundantly clear
long before you reach the town by the hordes
of kids trying to sell you strings of rose petals
on the roadside. There's one cheap hotel and
another four-star job if you feel the urge to
stay.

BOUMALNE DU DADÈS & THE DADÈS GORGE

Another 23 km north-east brings you to a
fork in the road. The left branch takes you up
the stunning Dadès Gorge, while the main
road veers off right over the river to the
hilltop town of Boumalne du Dadès, where
you may end up staying the night if you

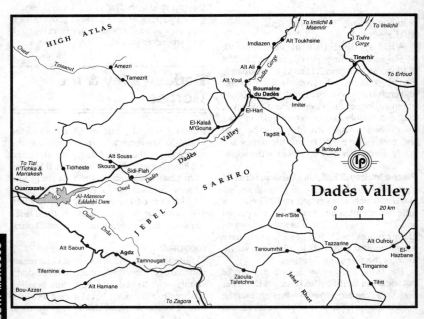

Boumalne du Dadès

PLACES TO STAY
1 Hôtel Madayeq
2 Hôtel Salam
4 Hôtel Adrar
14 Hôtel Vallée des Oiseaux
17 Hôtel Restaurant Chems

PLACES TO EAT
3 Restaurant/Café Bougafer
10 Restaurant Place de la Mosquée
11 Restaurant Dadès
13 Restaurant Vallée des Roses

OTHER
5 CTM Office
6 Café
7 Grands Taxis & Buses
8 Café Ossikis
9 Mosque
12 Covered Market
15 Shell Petrol Station
16 Army Barracks

arrive late in the day. If you have a choice, staying in the gorge is a much more attractive option.

The somewhat potholed road snakes up in a leisurely fashion inside the wide walls of the gorge for about 25 km to Aït Oudinar. On the way you will see plenty of greenery, mostly figs, interspersed with an array of kasbahs and ksour. Some of the rock formations are truly bizarre, resembling globules of molten wax dribbling down the side of a candle. By the time you reach Aït Oudinar, the river Dadès is right next to the road, and, in spring especially, flows strongly. The gorge narrows here quite abruptly, and climbs a couple of km to a cluster of cheap new hotels. Beyond them the bitumen gives way to piste as the trail winds up inside the main canyon in a series of hairpin bends. After a few km of this, the road flattens out as you leave the best of the scenery behind you. You can probably make it as far as Msemrir in an ordinary car, but beyond (say to Imilchil) you will definitely need a 4WD. In any case the driving is very slow, and this is a great place for a puncture. There are some wild and largely untouched stretches of mountain scenery to be enjoyed here, but

be aware that many of the pistes are impassable in winter or after wet weather.

If you decide to stay in the gorge, the natural splendour doesn't stop here. There are some challenging walks up into some of the smaller mountain passes west and east of the Oued Dadès. You can ask at the hotels for advice on where to go, or even take on a guide.

Without your own transport you will have to rely on an uncertain combination of hitching and walking or hire a taxi in Boumalne. Hiring a taxi for a few hours, including photo stops and the like, should cost in the region of Dr 100 to Dr 150. If you're staying at the Hôtel Adrar in the town, the staff will help you negotiate this.

Treks

In addition to the gorges north of Boumalne, Jebel Sarhro stretches out to the south. There is some good trekking to be done in this area, which has been left relatively untouched by tourism. The Hôtel Adrar can organise 4WD and mule treks into the region. The latter would cost between Dr 300 and Dr 400 a day for mule, muleteer, guide and their food.

SOUTH MOROCCO

Places to Stay

In the Gorge The choice of places to stay in the gorge is growing rapidly, and most of what's on offer is good value. At Km 14 is the *Café Mirguirne* and, another km on, the *Hôtel Restaurant Kasba*, which overlooks the fantastic rock formations on the other side of the valley. It's an interesting little place with small balconies, and is constructed in a mixture of modern and traditional styles. The beds are comfortable and hot water is promised. Expect to pay Dr 25 per person. Anywhere else it would be a well-recommended stop, but choices abound farther up.

At Km 25 is the village of Aït Oudinar, where you'll find the *Auberge des Gorges du Dadès* (☎ 830762) perched right over the river. You have a choice of simple rooms for Dr 40/60 (shared hot showers) or classier self-contained rooms for Dr 100/140. Most of the rooms, especially the more expensive ones, overlook the river; breakfast is included in the price. There is also room for camping and you can sleep on couches in the salon for just Dr 10 a head.

There is a group of places even farther up the valley at Km 27. A common phenomenon among these places seems to be the quantum leap in quality from rooms without shower to those with.

The *Hôtel Restaurant Camping du Peuplier*, owned by Mohammed Echaouiche, was the first of what has now become a crowd of hotels. It is one of the more primitive of them and singles/doubles cost Dr 20/25, or Dr 30/40 with private bathroom. Hot water is unlikely. You can also camp right by the stream for Dr 3 a person – you can't get much cheaper than that.

Of the next three hotels, the *Hôtel Tisadrine* is the cheapest and simplest. It costs Dr 30 for a room with two beds. The shared shower is cold (very).

Of the remaining two, the *Hôtel La Kasbah de la Vallée* is probably the best. It is fairly new and has comfortable rooms for Dr 35/60 and better ones with en suite shower and toilet for Dr 60/130. Options include sleeping in the hotel's 'nomad' tent

by the stream for Dr 20, pitching your own for Dr 10 or sleeping on the roof for Dr 15. There is heating in winter, and while you eat your Dr 60 menu dinner the hotel puts on some live fireside music. The hotel management say they can organise **4WD trips** farther north and that **white-water rafting** is possible on a limited scale about 15 km north along the river.

Newer but perhaps not quite as good (though there's little in it) is the *Hôtel La Gazelle du Dadès* next door, which started business in late 1993. It's a little hard to believe the manager's advertised room rates, but if they are accurate, this place automatically becomes deal of the week. Rooms with three comfortable beds cost Dr 30, for however many people. Rooms with three beds and private shower are Dr 50, again for the whole room. They are clean and there is hot water. Sleeping on cushions in the salon or on the roof costs just Dr 5 each.

Five km farther on is one more simple place, the *Hôtel Taghia*.

Boumalne du Dadès If you arrive late or choose not to stay up in the gorge (it's hard to see why you'd make such a choice), there are several accommodation options in Boumalne du Dadès, which lies on the road from Ouarzazate to Er-Rachidia. Most of the hotels in the town are more expensive than those in the gorge.

About the first place you come across in the lower end of the town is also about the best budget deal, the *Hôtel Adrar* (☎ 830355). This is a popular place with travellers (read the comments book if you're unconvinced) and offers singles/doubles for Dr 40/60. The hotel has a good restaurant and can organise treks into Jebel Sarhro. The staff will also help organise share taxis into the gorge.

A long walk up the hill from the bus station is the *Hôtel Salam* (☎ 830762). It's not too bad at Dr 60 for a room (single or double occupancy) and the price includes hot showers. The hotel has its own restaurant and is unlikely to be full if other places are.

Another more or less budget option is a

little farther on still – if you've walked this far, it won't make much difference to you now. It's the *Hôtel Camping Le Soleil Bleu* (☎ 830163). You can pitch a tent for Dr 15 per person, or sleep on the roof for Dr 20. Otherwise, singles/doubles/triples without shower cost Dr 55/75/115, or Dr 75/110/145 with private shower. The rooms without shower also happen to be without sheets and are very small – not good value at all.

Much better but popular and often full is the new *Hôtel Restaurant Chems* (☎ 830 041) on Ave Mohammed V. It has doubles with shower for Dr 110 or slightly less for single occupancy. The hotel has its own restaurant and is in a great position overlooking the valley below.

Not so brilliant is the *Hôtel Vallée des Oiseaux* (☎ 830764). Singles/doubles without shower cost Dr 80/110 or Dr 120/150 with private shower and toilet. The hot water is great, but the beds in some rooms are collapsing and great swathes of paint are peeling off the walls.

The only top-end hotel is the *Hôtel Madayeq* (☎ 830763). It's a weird-looking building – you can see it well before entering the town from the Ouarzazate road. Rooms will set you back Dr 288/360 plus taxes. The restaurant is rather expensive.

Places to Eat
Most of the hotels in the gorges have their own restaurants, and there's nothing to stop you trying the food in a hotel where you're not staying if you want some variety of décor.

The options in Boumalne aren't much wider. The restaurant below the *Hôtel Adrar* serves a filling meal of tajine or brochettes with salad and a drink for Dr 30. Three other little restaurants compete for business nearby. The *Restaurant/Café Bougafer*, just up from the Adrar, is OK but serves less generous meals for about the same price. The other two are next to each other near the mosque: the *Restaurant Place de la Mosquée* and the *Restaurant Dadès*. Up near the Hôtel Vallée des Oiseaux is the somewhat more posh *Restaurant Vallée des Roses*, where a full meal will cost about Dr 60.

Apart from this, there are a couple of cafés, the best of which is the *Café Ossikis* on the square where the grands taxis and buses gather.

Getting There & Away
Bus CTM has a bus to Ouarzazate and on to Marrakesh at 9 am. Going the other way, a bus passes through on its way to Tinerhir and Er-Rachidia at about 12.30 pm. The CTM office on Ave Mohammed V seems to be closed most of the time. A couple of other buses pass through here, including one to Agadir (via Ouarzazate) at 4 pm and another to Rabat (via Ouarzazate) at 7.30 pm.

Taxis As is usual in smaller places like this, grands taxis are probably a better bet. The fare is Dr 25 to Ouarzazate, Dr 12.50 to Tinerhir and about Dr 10 to Aït Oudinar (these last ones up the gorge are not terribly frequent).

More than likely you will have to hire a taxi, especially for the trip up the gorge, and tailor it to your needs. You can hire one by the hour or for a simple one-way trip if you intend to stay there. A straightforward ride to Aït Oudinar should cost no more than Dr 60, but you'll have to employ all your bargaining skills. It will cost more if you want to make photo stops or carry on to the hotels beyond Aït Oudinar.

TINERHIR & THE TODRA GORGE
Some 15 km from Tinerhir (Tineghir on some maps), at the end of a lush valley full of palmeraies and mud-brick villages hemmed in by barren, craggy mountains, is one of Morocco's most magnificent natural sights. This is the Todra Gorge: some 300 metres high but only 10 metres wide at its narrowest point, and with a crystal-clear river running through it. It's at its best in the morning, when the sun penetrates to the bottom of the gorge. In the afternoon it gets very dark and, in winter, bitterly cold.

Although the main gorge can be explored in half a day, those with more time might like

SOUTH MOROCCO

to explore farther up the gorge or walk through the palmeraies on the way to Tinerhir; the people here are very friendly. There are numerous ruined kasbahs flanking the palmeraies and plenty of photographic opportunities.

The more ambitious might consider making their way farther up into the Atlas. A combination of souq lorries, Land Rover taxis and hiking could take you north to Aït Hani, from where you could push on over the Tizi Tirherhouzine towards Imilchil, or do a loop south through the Dadès Gorge that would bring you back to the main highway linking Ouarzazate and Er-Rachidia. A network of difficult pistes links the sporadic villages here in the High and Middle Atlas, many of which are snowbound in winter. You could spend weeks exploring them, but you should bear in mind that you'll be far away from banks, post offices and even basic health services most of the time. Come prepared.

Climbing is also becoming increasingly popular on the vertical rock face of the gorge; it is not uncommon to see tiny human figures clinging to various parts of Todra's sheer stone walls as you wander through.

There's little of interest in Tinerhir itself, although it certainly looks pretty from the hill above town. An enormous amount of building is going on, which has completely smothered the small core of the original town. The highway is known as Ave Mohammed V as it passes through the town on the way to Er-Rachidia. Most of the hotels and restaurants are on or near Ave Hassan II, a block in to the south. Although hardly amazing, the little backstreets and markets behind Ave Hassan II warrant a bit of a wander. Some of the town's cheapest food is to be had in this zone, too. Money is no problem, as there are several banks around the centre of town. The post office is in the centre of town on Ave Hassan II.

Places to Stay

Camping – in the gorge Six km back down along the road from the gorge towards Tinerhir are three good camp sites. They're all next to each other in the palmeraies and are all equipped with showers and toilets. There's a small shop that sells basic supplies across the road from the first of them.

The first you come upon on the way up from Tinerhir is the *Auberge de l'Atlas*. It's very good but marginally more expensive than the other two. It costs Dr 8 per person, Dr 9 for a car, Dr 15 to pitch your tent and Dr 10 for electricity. It has well-overpriced rooms for Dr 80/90. They are for the desperate only. The *Camping Le Lac (Garden of Eden)* and *Camping Auberge* are equally good and a wee bit cheaper. Take your pick.

Camping – Tinerhir About 2.5 km west of the Tinerhir town centre is *Camping Ourfi*. It's awkwardly located and pretty spartan. It costs Dr 8 per person, Dr 5 to pitch a tent, Dr 7 for a car, Dr 5 for a hot shower and Dr 10 for electricity. If the pool is in use, it costs another Dr 10. There are squalid little 'bungalow' rooms for Dr 35 a person. It is difficult to imagine why anyone would want to stay here given the alternatives in the gorge. The same goes for *Camping Almo*, about one km south-east of the town centre. It's a hassle to get to and not worth the effort.

Hotels – in the gorge Just inside the gorge are the two ideal places to stay. The *Hôtel Restaurant Yasmina* (☎ 833013) is the more expensive of them, with good rooms costing Dr 90/160 (less in winter), including breakfast. In summer they'll let you sleep on the roof for about Dr 15 a head.

The *Hôtel Restaurant Les Roches* (☎ 834814) offers rooms with two beds for Dr 60 or a place in a big tent for Dr 20.

You can get reasonable food in both places, which in summer serve meals in big 'Berber' tents out the front by the stream. This is great in summer, but you won't be eating there in winter! Neither of the hotels up here sells alcohol, so bring your own. Often they put on wood fires in winter.

If these two are full, the *Hôtel Le Mansour*, a km or so back downstream (15 km from Tinerhir) and just outside the entrance of the gorge proper, has uninspiring singles/doubles for Dr 50/60. It does have a pleasant café and restaurant.

None of these hotels would have been built in a country where environmental impact studies are required before construction. What is more, while they keep a clean image around their doorsteps, they treat the rest of the upper gorge as their private garbage tip.

Hotels – Tinerhir If you decide not to stay at the gorge itself or need somewhere to stay in Tinerhir, there is a reasonable choice of hotels. Four of the budget ones are virtually in a row on Ave Hassan II.

The *Hôtel Salam*, next to the CTM office, has rooms with one big bed and another small one for Dr 40 and others with two big beds and one small bed for Dr 60. If you have the people to fill these, it's not a bad deal, although the place is basic and a little dreary. The *Hôtel Raha* next door is about the same price but not terribly good. Next up on the same street is the *Hôtel El Fath*, at No 56. It has clean and acceptable rooms with single beds for Dr 35/60. Rooms with a single bed and a double bed cost Dr 75. They promise hot water in the shared shower.

The *Hôtel Al-Qods*, at the end of the block, has bright, simple rooms for Dr 30/60/90.

Another reasonable, if unexciting, option is the *Hôtel L'Oasis* on Ave Mohammed V, the main road through town. It's next to the Total service station and has its own restaurant. The rooms are perfectly clean and comfortable, contain two beds and cost Dr 70 whether one or two people occupy them. There's a shared (hot) shower on the ground floor.

There are two pricier options. The *Hôtel Todra* (☎ 834249), on Ave Hassan II, has plenty of dark-wood panelling and a decayed elegance about it, but the rooms aren't exactly marvellous. The hotel has a restaurant (main meals about Dr 50) and a bar. Rooms without shower cost Dr 84/103 plus taxes. Those with shower go for Dr 103/125 plus taxes.

Back behind Ave Hassan II near the central market area is the popular Spanish-run *Hôtel de l'Avenir* (☎ 834604; fax 834 599). The rooms are good if a little pricey at Dr 85/140, but this includes breakfast. The manager, Roger Mimó, can help organise treks in Jebel Sarhro and mountain-bike trips in the area.

The *Hôtel Bougafer* (☎ 833280; fax 833282) is a three-star hotel on the road to Ouarzazate, opposite the Camping Ourfi. The location is awful, but the rooms are not bad and cost Dr 360/420.

Top of the line is the four-star *Hôtel Sargho* (☎ 834181; fax 834352), which is up on top of the hill overlooking the town. The views are superb and the hotel has an enormous swimming pool as well as a bar and restaurant. However, the rooms are small and tatty, the 'tourist menu' is outrageously expensive and there are always hustlers up here. Singles/doubles cost Dr 320/400 plus taxes. Visa cards are accepted.

Places to Eat

In the gorges you'll probably be eating at your hotel or organising your own food, but in town the best place to look for cheap Moroccan food is in the little market area south of Ave Hassan II. There are loads of simple little stalls here. For meat eaters, they point you to the butchers, where you buy some fresh meat and take it back to the 'restaurant'. If you don't want to play this game, the right gesticulations will get the message across that you'd prefer it if they took care of it for you. There are quite a few busy little cafés around here, too.

Otherwise, there are a few restaurants along Ave Hassan II and Ave Mohammed V. The one at the *Café Centrale* is all right, as is the *Restaurant Essaada*. Better are the *Restaurant La Kasbah* on Ave Mohammed V and the restaurant attached to the *Hôtel L'Oasis*, both of which offer three-course meals for around Dr 60.

At about Dr 50 for a main dish, the *Hôtel Todra* restaurant is overpriced for the bland fare you get. Much better, and a definite change, is the paella available at the *Hôtel de l'Avenir*.

SOUTH MOROCCO

Getting There & Away

Bus CTM has a couple of buses that pass through Tinerhir on their way east and west. Only 10 seats are set aside for passengers boarding at Tinerhir. At noon and 1.30 pm buses go to Er-Rachidia. The first costs Dr 28 and the second Dr 30. At 8 am a mumtaz bus passes through on its way to Marrakesh (Dr 80) via Ouarzazate (Dr 35.50). Another bus leaves for Ouarzazate at 2.30 pm and costs Dr 30.

Otherwise, several private buses also leave from the nearby square, by the park.

Taxi Grands taxis to Ouarzazate (Dr 40) and Er-Rachidia (Dr 20) leave from the eastern end of the same gardens, near the Hôtel Al-Qods. This is also the place to hunt for occasional transport (taxis, lorries or pick-up trucks) up the Todra Gorge and beyond – perhaps as far as Imilchil, although it's unlikely you'd get one vehicle going the whole way.

As a rule, if there is no standard taxi leaving for the gorge (stress that you want to pay for a place in a normal shared taxi), you may need to bargain to hire one specially to take you up.

Ziz Valley & the Tafilalt

ER-RACHIDIA

At the crossroads of important north-south and east-west routes across Morocco, Er-Rachidia (named after the first Alawite leader, Moulay ar-Rashid) was originally built by the French as an administrative centre and was once known as Ksar es-Souq. It is a modern place, laid out in barracks-style grid form, and offers the traveller little to do but rest. Depending on where you are coming from, it can be a very relaxing place to hole up for a day or two just to enjoy being left to your own devices.

The main highlight is outside the town – the **Ziz Gorges** to the north, which link Er-Rachidia to the small town of Rich and on to Fès and Meknès via Midelt. More pre-

cisely, this magnificent route past palm-fringed towns and ksour begins (or ends, depending on which way you are going) with the French-built Tunnel du Légionnaire 20 km south of Rich and stretches to the dam just north of Er-Rachidia. If you take this road, make sure you get a daytime bus or grand taxi.

Information

Tourist Office There is a small local syndicat d'initiative (☎ 572733) in the square opposite the covered market on Ave Moulay

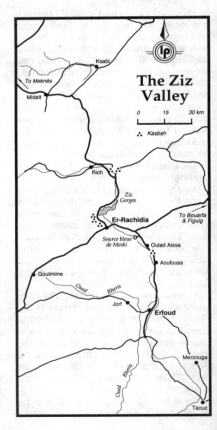

The Ziz Valley

0   15   30 km

To Meknès
Ksabi
Midelt
Kasbah
Rich
Ziz Gorges
Er-Rachidia
To Bouarfa & Figuig
Source bleue de Meski
Oulad Aissa
Aoufouss
Goulmime
Oued Rheris
Jorf
Erfoud
Merzouga
Oued Rheris
Taouz

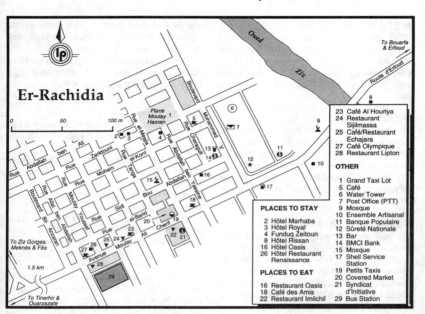

Er-Rachidia

0   50   100 m

To Bouarfa
& Erfoud

Route d'Erfoud

Place
Moulay
Hasran

To Ziz Gorges,
Meknès & Fès

1.5 km

To Tinerhir &
Ouarzazate

23	Café Al Houriya
24	Restaurant Sijilmassa
25	Café/Restaurant Echajara
27	Café Olympique
28	Restaurant Lipton

OTHER

1	Grand Taxi Lot
5	Café
6	Water Tower
7	Post Office (PTT)
9	Mosque
10	Ensemble Artisanal
11	Banque Populaire
12	Sûreté Nationale
13	Bar
14	BMCI Bank
15	Mosque
17	Shell Service Station
19	Petits Taxis
20	Covered Market
21	Syndicat d'Initiative
29	Bus Station

PLACES TO STAY

2	Hôtel Marhaba
3	Hôtel Royal
4	Funduq Zeitoun
8	Hôtel Rissan
16	Hôtel Oasis
26	Hôtel Restaurant Renaissance

PLACES TO EAT

16	Restaurant Oasis
18	Café des Amis
22	Restaurant Imilchil

Ali Cherif, the main road through town. It's rarely open.

Money There are at least two banks: a Banque Populaire and a BMCI branch. The latter is diagonally opposite the post office on Blvd Mohammed V and the former is on the main street heading out to Erfoud.

Post & Telecommunications The phone office is to the left of the main post building (on Blvd Mohammed V), and is open daily from 8.30 am to 9 pm. There are a few card phones outside.

Places to Stay – bottom end
Camping The closest camping ground is *Camping Source Bleue de Meski* (see that section).

Hotels The three cheapest places are all pretty basic and located just off Place Moulay Hassan. At the western end of the

square in a small side street are the *Hôtel Royal* and the *Hôtel Marhaba*. Singles/doubles/triples in both are Dr 30/50/75. There's isn't much to distinguish them, but the Marhaba is perhaps the skuzziest. The woman who runs the Royal speaks only Arabic but you shouldn't have any problems communicating. There are cold communal showers. Perhaps slightly better is the *Funduq Zeitoun* (sign in Arabic only), on Rue Abdallah ben Yassine.

Considerably more comfortable is the *Hôtel Restaurant Renaissance* (☎ 572533), Rue Moulay Youssef, which is where most travellers choose to stay. The showers actually have hot water, but at the time of writing guests were being charged Dr 80 a head for compulsory half-board. The staff speak French and English.

Places to Stay – middle
If you have the money it's worth thinking about staying at the two-star *Hôtel Oasis*

(☎ 572519), Rue Sidi Bou Abdallah, which has 46 attractive warm carpeted rooms, most with private shower and toilet and hot water. It costs Dr 121/142 for singles/doubles without shower and Dr 153/179 for rooms with. The hotel has its own bar and restaurant.

A little cheaper is the *Hôtel Meski* (☎ 572065), Ave Moulay Ali Cherif. It's just far enough towards the road to Fès to be inconvenient for those arriving in the centre of town, but offers reasonable value. Singles/doubles with private shower but shared toilet cost Dr 101/127, or Dr 123/152 with private shower and toilet. The hotel also has a restaurant.

Places to Stay – top end

The only top-end hotel in Er-Rachidia is the four-star *Hôtel Rissani* (☎ 572186; fax 572585), Route d'Erfoud, just across the Ziz bridge. Singles/doubles cost Dr 302/377 plus taxes, and the hotel has all the amenities you would expect, including bar, restaurant and swimming pool.

Places to Eat

One of the most popular places to eat is the *Restaurant Sijilmassa*, on the main street – look out for the sign 'All food is here' in English, French, Spanish and Italian! It has the usual standard Moroccan dishes and a full meal will cost you about Dr 35. Eat inside or at the outdoor tables.

Also good is the *Restaurant Imilchil*, which is opposite the covered market. It, too, has a sign in French, saying 'Look no farther, all food here'.

In much the same league is the *Restaurant Lipton*, more or less across the main road from the Hôtel Restaurant Renaissance. The restaurant part is round the back and can feel a bit cut off from the activity in the street, but they do a decent plate of chicken, chips and salad for Dr 37. The staff almost fall over themselves to be friendly.

For a splurge, try a meal at the licensed *Restaurant Oasis*, which is attached to the hotel of the same name.

Those wishing to put their own meals together should have a look around the covered market, where a wide variety of very reasonably priced food is available.

There is a bar near the BMCI bank on Blvd Mohammed V. It is, predictably enough, a fairly uninspiring watering hole.

Getting There & Away

Bus All buses operate out of the central bus station, which is next to the Restaurant Lipton.

CTM has a daily departure to Marrakesh (Dr 110.50) at 5.45 am via Ouarzazate (Dr 65.50) and Tinerhir. It also has a bus to Meknès (Dr 87) at 10 pm and to Rissani (via Erfoud) at 5 am.

Quite a few other bus companies have services running through Er-Rachidia. There are buses to Fès (via Azrou and Ifrane) at 1 and 9 am and 1 pm (Dr 78.50). Two others run via Sefrou at 2 and 11 am.

There are about seven buses a day to Meknès (Dr 77.50) via Azrou from 6 am to midnight. A bus to Casablanca (Dr 120) runs via Meknès and Rabat at 5.30 pm. Two others go via Azrou and Kasbah Tadla at 8 and 10.30 pm (Dr 113).

There are five daily departures to Rissani via Erfoud and a couple of others to Erfoud via Aoufous or Tinejdad (the long route).

Buses to Ouarzazate (Dr 60) via Tinerhir and Boumalne leave at 11.30 am and 1 pm. There is a bus for Tinerhir only at 6.30 am.

At 3 pm a bus leaves for Bouarfa (Dr 50; five hours), which is unlikely to make it to Bouarfa in time to link up with anything going north or south – very useful.

Taxi Most of the grands taxis leave from Place Moulay Hassan. The fare per person to Erfoud is Dr 20. Heading north, the fare to Azrou is Dr 70, while a seat for Fès or Meknès goes for Dr 100. There are also plenty of taxis heading south for Aoufous, which you could take to get dropped off at the Meski turn-off for the Source Bleue. It may be possible (but don't count on it) to get a taxi east to Bouarfa for Figuig. Try early in the morning.

AROUND ER-RACHIDIA
Source Bleue de Meski

The Source Bleue de Meski, about 23 km south of Er-Rachidia, is a wonderful natural spring and swimming pool that is understandably popular with the locals. On spring and summer weekends heat-plagued Er-Rachidians flock here in droves, but for the rest of the time it's pretty quiet. For the hot and sweaty traveller heading north or south between Er-Rachidia and Erfoud it is a recommended stop.

You can stay at the *Camping Source Bleue de Meski* for Dr 7 a person, Dr 10 for a tent place and Dr 10 per car. The spring is signposted and is about one km west of the main road. Any buses or grands taxis going south to Erfoud or Aoufous from Er-Rachidia will be able to drop you off at the turn-off. When leaving, you should be able to flag down a grand taxi or hitch a ride to Er-Rachidia or even Erfoud from the main road.

ERFOUD

The oasis region of the Tafilalt was one of the last to succumb to French control under the protectorate, its tribes putting up sporadic resistance until 1932. Two years later, Morocco was officially considered 'pacified'. To make sure this state of affairs did not change, Erfoud was built as an administrative and garrison town to keep a watchful eye on the Tafilalt tribes.

With a population of about 7000, Erfoud is a comparatively uninteresting little town, but a useful staging point from which to head farther into the desert. Sunrise excursions to the Erg Chebbi dunes near Merzouga to the south are becoming part of the standard menu for passing travellers. Unfortunately, Erfoud is going the way of Rissani (see that section), and newcomers must expect to be resolutely hassled by hotel touts and the like on arrival. Once ensconced in a hotel, however, and all sales pitches exhausted, the welcome committees seem to vanish as quickly as they materialised.

Hotels, restaurants, the post office and so on are located on the town's main street, Ave Mohammed V, and to a lesser extent on Ave Moulay Ismail, which intersects Ave Mohammed V at the post office and links Erfoud to the Er-Rachidia, Rissani and Tinerhir highways.

Information

The post and phone offices (PTT) are on the corner of Ave Mohammed V and Ave Moulay Ismail. They are open normal office hours only. The Banque Populaire is diagonally across the intersection. You can change money at the Hôtel Salam, too, but watch out for inferior rates and commission charges.

Dunes

Most of the bottom-end hotels will do their best to dig up a clattering old Land Rover taxi to take visitors to the Erg Chebbi (see the Merzouga section). Quite a few cheap hotels have sprung up along the line of the dunes and in the village of Merzouga, about halfway down its length. For many, though, a drive out in time to watch the sunrise is sufficient. The taxi will pick you up at about 4 am and have you back in Erfoud by 10 am. Hire of the taxi costs about Dr 250 to Dr 300 (for up to seven people). Finding other travellers to make up numbers shouldn't be too difficult.

Places to Stay – bottom end

Camping *Camping Erfoud*, located next to the river, is no great shakes. You pay Dr 10 per person whether you choose a patch of dirt to pitch a tent on (another Dr 10 for the place) or one of the little bedless, concrete cells. You pay the same charge for everything else too, including car, electricity and shower – all of which makes it a dubious expense.

Hotels The cheapest and scummiest place to stay is the *Hôtel L'Atlas*, on the road to Rissani. Basic rooms cost Dr 30/60. You should not put too much faith in the boasts about hot water.

The *Hôtel Marzouga* (☎ 576532) on Ave Mohammed V is a better bet, although travellers staying here have denied claims of hot water being available.

In a similar bracket and on the same street

is the *Hôtel des Palmeraies*, which has singles/doubles for Dr 65/86. The *Hôtel Essaada*, Ave Moulay Ismail, is much the same.

Better than all the above and definitely in

possession of a boiler for hot water is the friendly *Hôtel La Gazelle* (☎ 576028), across from the post office. When the water starts flowing though, the plumbing rattles so hard it threatens to come flying off the

PLACES TO STAY		PLACES TO EAT		7	Gendarmerie Royale
1	Hôtel Farah Zouar	6	Restaurant Sijilmassa	8	Post Office (PTT)
2	Hôtel Salam	16	Restaurant des Fleurs	10	Mosque
3	Hôtel Lahmada	18	Restaurant L'Oasis	13	Banque Populaire
4	Hôtel L'Atlas	21	Restaurant de la Jeunesse	15	Hammam (men only)
9	Hôtel La Gazelle	23	Restaurant/Café du Sud	19	Hôtel de Ville
11	Hôtel Essaada			20	CTM Bus Terminal
12	Hôtel Taifilalet	**OTHER**		22	Mosque
14	Hôtel Sable d'Or			26	Non-CTM Bus Terminals
17	Hôtel Marzouga	5	Hospital	28	Law Courts
24	Hôtel des Palmeraies			29	Grands Taxis
25	Hôtel Ziz			30	Sûreté Nationale
27	Camping Erfoud				

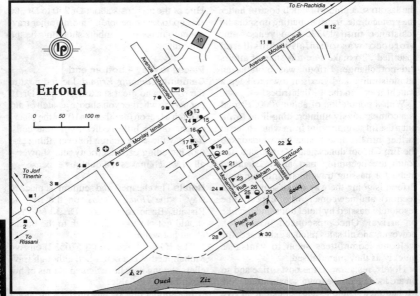

wall. The rooms have private showers and cost Dr 60/95. The hotel has a decent restaurant downstairs.

Places to Stay – middle

The cheapest place in this category is the one-star *Hôtel Sable d'Or* (☎ 576348), Ave Mohammed V. It's clean and comfortable (though the pictures of Jesus seem a little out of place), all the rooms have private shower, toilet, table and chair, and there's hot water 24 hours a day. The management are friendly and there's a rooftop terrace with great views over town. Rooms cost Dr 110/127. The hotel has its own restaurant.

A new spot on the road heading to Rissani is the *Hôtel Lahmada* (☎ 576097). The rooms are spotless and have private bathrooms. At these prices, however , this place is not great value. Singles/doubles/triples cost Dr 150/200/250. The hotel has a restaurant.

Once a gungy cheapie, the *Hôtel Ziz* (☎ 576154; fax 576811), 3 Ave Mohammed V, now has refurbished rooms with en suite bathroom for Dr 150/180/200 plus taxes; however, the air-conditioning doesn't seem to work. The rooms also have phones and the restaurant has one of the few bars in town – it's a better deal than the Lahmada.

For this money, the *Hôtel Farah Zouar* (☎ 576146; fax 576230) is worth considering. It's on the corner of the Rissani and Tinerhir roads. If the prices remain as low as they are, this is possibly the best deal in town. Some of the rooms could do with some replastering, but overall they compare favourably with those of the Ziz and Lahmada, and cost Dr 150/200 (or Dr 250 for a rather comfortable suite). Like most hotels, it comes with its own restaurant.

Places to Stay – top end

The least expensive place to stay in this category is the three-star *Hôtel Tafilalet* (☎ 576535; fax 576036) on Ave Moulay Ismail. The newer rooms on the far side of the swimming pool are superb and feature a large, sunny balcony, a comfortable bedroom and a separate dining area, all floored with local earthen tiles. The old rooms are nowhere near as attractive. Self-contained singles/doubles with hot water cost Dr 233/287. Apart from the swimming pool, the hotel has its own bar and restaurant (breakfast is Dr 30). Visits to Rissani, Taouz and Merzouga by Land Rover, including a night under tents in the desert, can be organised from here, but they're not cheap. The hotel runs a cheap place just south of Merzouga village.

Top of the line is the *Hôtel Salam* (☎ 576665), virtually across the road from the Hôtel Farah Zouar. Rooms here start at Dr 398 and rise to Dr 770 plus taxes. There are two wings, and the rooms in the new one are much better (and more expensive) than the others. The new wing also has a bar, pool and sauna.

Places to Eat

The extremely friendly *Restaurant de la Jeunesse*, Ave Mohammed V, is the place to head for in the evening. The food is excellent and very reasonably priced.

Otherwise, the restaurant at the *Hôtel La Gazelle* has a comfortable Moroccan-style dining room where you can get a three-course evening meal for about Dr 40. There's a visitors' book here containing effusive praise from the four corners of the earth – worth a read.

The *Restaurant L'Oasis* on Ave Mohammed V offers reasonable food for a similar price. Across the road, the *Restaurant des Fleurs* is all right for breakfast, but service can be awesomely slow.

The restaurant at the *Hôtel des Palmeraies* is also rated highly by many travellers, and the restaurant at the *Hôtel Sable d'Or* is worth trying if you have about Dr 60 to spare for a square meal.

The *Restaurant Sijilmassa* on Ave Moulay Ismail is not a bad place and quite popular with locals. The food is nothing special, but it's definitely a pleasant place for tea or coffee at least.

Things to Buy

The main item here is black marble (there are

quarries in the desert), and you can find souvenirs in several shops in Erfoud. Kids will also try to sell you little trinkets of the same substance.

Getting There & Away

Bus All public transport leaves from Place des FAR, except the one CTM bus to Meknès via Er-Rachidia (Dr 21) at 8.30 pm, which leaves from outside the CTM terminal.

There are several other private bus lines, but departure times seem a little uncertain. One bus leaves at about 11 am to go to Er-Rachidia. Other buses to Meknès leave at 2.30 am and 7.30 pm. At noon a bus runs to Tinejdad (Dr 18), from where you can get other transport to Tinerhir. A bus to Rissani (Dr 5) leaves at 4.30 pm. Several minibuses also shuttle between Erfoud and Rissani.

Taxi Grands taxis are, as a rule, a much more reliable bet. They run regularly to Rissani (Dr 6) and Er-Rachidia (Dr 20).

MERZOUGA

About 50 km south of Erfoud, the village of Merzouga, with a population of about 1500, offers virtually nothing of interest to anyone. Nearby, however, is the **Erg Chebbi**, Morocco's only genuine Saharan erg – one of those huge, drifting expanses of sand dunes that typify much of the Algerian Sahara. You can pretty easily arrange a sunrise trip out here (see the Erfoud section), drive down yourself or stay for longer.

The pistes can be rough, but a Renault 4 can make it down, winding across rough, black hammada. Opinions vary on taking your own vehicle. The lousy bitumen road soon gives way to any number of pistes. If you follow the line of telegraph poles you can't really go wrong, but the pistes are hardly smooth and your car will definitely take a bit of a beating in the process.

In spring, a seasonal lake appears to the north-west of Merzouga, attracting flocks of pink flamingos and other bird life. Those

doing the 'sunrise tour' from Erfoud should ask to have this included if the lake hasn't dried out.

Places to Stay

All up, you'll find a good dozen or so basic hotel-cafés dotted along the western side of Erg Chebbi and in the village of Merzouga itself. Most are basic and cost about Dr 30/60. Those along the erg include the *Camping La Vallée*, *Camping Hamada Dunes*, *Auberge Soleil Bleu*, *Café du Sud*, *Auberge Sable d'Or*, *Café Yasmine*, *Auberge Erg Chebbi* and *Café Oasis*. Most of these places allow you to sleep on the roof for about Dr 20 per person – watch your belongings, as theft is a problem. The Café du Sud has been recommended.

Those in the village include the *Café des Dunes*, *Auberge des Amis* and *Camping El Kheima* (in a palmeraie). Just south of the village is the *Auberge Merzouga*, run by the Hôtel Tafilalet in Erfoud. It has basic rooms, but as good as those you'll find at any of the above places and for the same price. There are also cold showers; these are not to be relied on in the others. There is a group of 'Berber tents' out the back, where groups from the hotel in Erfoud often spend a night with food and musical accompaniment. When things are quiet you can sleep there for Dr 25. There is a kitchen, so the guy running the place can cook you up a meal if you ask in advance.

You can arrange camel rides into the erg and around from most of these hotels, but some of the asking prices are absurd – up to Dr 1000 a day!

Getting There & Away

Apart from the 'sunrise tours' from Erfoud, there are Land Rover taxis between Merzouga and Rissani on market days (Sunday, Tuesday and Thursday). There's obviously no timetable as such and demand for them can vary enormously. The fare per person is about Dr 20. If you're driving your own car, you are advised to engage a local guide.

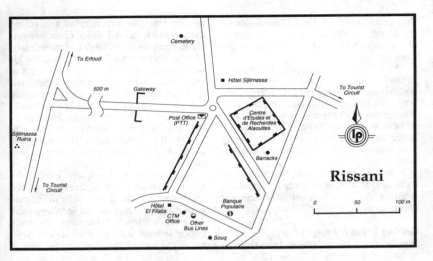

Rissani

To Erfoud
Cemetery
500 m
Gateway
Sijilmassa Ruins
To Tourist Circuit
Post Office (PTT)
Hôtel Sijilmassa
Centre d'Etudes et de Recherdes Alaouites
To Tourist Circuit
Barracks
Hôtel El Filalia
CTM Office
Other Bus Lines
Banque Populaire
Souq
0   50   100 m

RISSANI (ER-RISSANI)

Rissani may once have been a superb place to experience the charm and mystique of a southern Moroccan oasis unsullied by tourism, but these days it's the hustlers that you will remember this hot, dusty place by. They outdo even those in Marrakesh. From the moment you arrive, the hustlers materialise on motorbikes, thrusting cards into your hand inviting you to buy 'Tuareg handicrafts'. Even the one guy in town who claims to be an official guide and pulls out a card to prove it will run rings around you on his moped, haranguing you on the need to have a guide and pulling a very long face indeed if all his efforts remain unrewarded (as they should).

If you still think it's worth coming and want to survive the onslaught, you'll have to contemplate hanging about for more than a day. Arriving on market day (Sunday, Tuesday or Thursday) is inviting problems with hustlers, as it will be assumed you're one of the many package tourists who crowd into Rissani by the busload on market days in search of 'Moroccan experiences', and in so doing help to ruin them.

The town, in the heart of the Tafilalt oases,

sits on the edge of the desert. In a sense, this is the end of the road, where the Ziz Valley peters out into the hot nothingness of stone and sand that stretches out to the south.

Information

The centre of town is quite small. There is a post and phone office open during normal office hours. There is also a Banque Populaire, where you can change cash or travellers' cheques. A branch of the BMCE was being built at the time of writing.

Places to Stay & Eat

The cheapest place to stay is the *Hôtel El Filalia* (☎ 575096), which is basic but adequate. This hotel is where the buses drop off and pick up passengers. It has rooms with two single beds for Dr 60 and others with one double and one single bed for Dr 75. They claim to have hot water and will organise excursions if you want. The owners also claim to be planning a 'tourist village' in a nearby palmeraie – heaven forbid!

Better is the new *Hôtel Sijilmassa* (☎ 575042), on Place al-Massira al-Khadra (Green March), which is clean, comfortable and offers spacious rooms with private

SOUTH MOROCCO

shower and toilet for Dr 120 (there are no single rooms). The management is eager to please and there's a restaurant on the ground floor.

About three km out along the road to Erfoud is the *Hôtel Asmaa* (☎ 575494), which is part of the Kasbah chain. This place is awkward for people without a car and quite incongruous, but the rooms are very comfortable, costing Dr 200/250/300. There is a rather large suite for Dr 500, a swimming pool (not always in operation) and a restaurant.

If you're not staying at the Sijilmassa, there are a number of simple restaurants fronting the market where you can eat cheaply and well.

Getting There & Away

Buses and grands taxis leave from the area in front of the Hôtel El Filalia. CTM has a bus to Meknès via Erfoud and Er-Rachidia at 7.30 pm. Other companies put on three departures to Fès via Erfoud at 6 and 10 am and 10 and 11.30 pm (this last one via Sefrou). A bus also leaves for Casablanca via Erfoud at 8.30 pm. The fare to Erfoud is generally Dr 5, and minibuses make the trip regularly on market days. Grands taxis (Dr 6) are probably the best bet though. Land Rover taxis run between Rissani and Merzouga on market days, and cost about Dr 20 per person. Departures are uncertain and depend on demand.

AROUND RISSANI
Sijilmassa Ruins

Just outside Rissani to the west lie the ruins of the fabled city of Sijilmassa, once the capital of a virtually independent Islamic principality adhering to the Shiite 'heresy' in the early days of the Arab conquest of North Africa. Uncertainty reigns over exactly when it was founded, but by the end of the 8th century it was playing a key role on the trans-Saharan trade routes. Internal feuding led to its collapse some time in the 14th century.

Centuries later, the Filali (from whom the Alawite dynasty is descended) swept north to supplant the Saadians as the ruling dynasty in Morocco. It did not happen overnight, however. The founder of the dynasty, Moulay Ali ash-Sharif, began expanding his power in the early 17th century in a series of small wars with neighbouring tribes. His sons continued a slow campaign of conquest, but only in 1668 was Moulay ar-Rashid recognised as sultan. His brother and successor, Moulay Ismail, would later go on to become the uncontested ruler of Morocco, underlining his power by establishing a new capital at Meknès.

Members of the Filali still inhabit the ksour in this area, but Sijilmassa itself has fallen into ruin and there's little to indicate its past glories except for two decorated gateways and a few other structures. It's really only of interest to archaeologists these days, but you're free to wander around the ruins if the whim so takes you. You will find the ruins off to the right-hand side of the 'Circuit Touristique' (Tourist Circuit) as you enter Rissani from the north.

Circuit Touristique

The so-called Circuit Touristique makes a 21-km loop around the palmeraies south of Rissani, often along appalling stretches of road. It takes you through most of the villages in the palmeraies but is of mild interest only. The exceptions are the beautiful gateway at Oulad Abdelhalim, built by the sultan's elder brother in 1900, and the zawiyya (closed to non-Muslims) of Moulay Ali ash-Sharif, founder of the Alawite dynasty.

The road is extremely dusty (or muddy when wet) and is only really feasible with your own (decent) transport or by hired taxi.

Western Sahara Desert

What the Moroccan tourist brochures refer to as the Saharan provinces largely comprise the still-disputed territory of Western Sahara. Evacuated by Spain in 1975, Morocco and Mauritania both raised claims to the sparsely

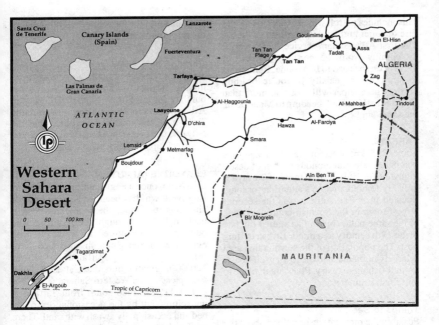

populated desert territory, but the latter soon bailed out, leaving Rabat to fight the rebel group, Polisario, which had contributed to Madrid's decision to abandon the phosphate-rich possessions in the first place. In November 1975, King Hassan II orchestrated the Green March – 350,000 Moroccans, largely unarmed civilians, marched in to stake Morocco's historical claims to the Western Sahara. The border of what had been Spanish Sahara ran just south of Tarfaya. In the following years, as many as 100,000 troops were poured in to stamp out resistance. As Polisario lost Algerian and Libyan backing, and the Moroccans erected a 1600-km-long sand wall to hamper the rebels' movements, it became increasingly clear that Rabat had the upper hand.

The UN organised a ceasefire in 1991, raising the prospect of a referendum to settle the issue of the Western Sahara region's status. The ceasefire has largely held, but the referendum is yet to materialise. In the mean-

time, Morocco has strengthened its hold on the territory, pouring money into infrastructure projects and expanding the city of Laayoune. Work-hungry Moroccans from the north have been enticed to move down by the prospect of employment and tax-free living (hence the cheap petrol). To all intents and purposes, Morocco appears to have succeeded, with the world community too preoccupied by crises elsewhere and foreign diplomats questioning the legitimacy and practicality of Polisario's independence demands.

Apart from the endless police roadblocks and checks, going south to Dakhla is now a routine affair, and it has been possible to cross into Mauritania in convoy (with some exceptions) since the running of the 1994 Paris-Dakar rally.

Information

As part of a drive to attract Moroccans into Western Sahara, many items are tax free.

This includes petrol, which costs Dr 4.72 per litre of super and Dr 2.72 per litre of diesel. The first Atlas Sahara service station you'll hit coming from the north is just out of Tarfaya on the road to Laayoune. Remember to stock up, especially if you're heading north, where super will cost you more than Dr 7 a litre. If you are heading to Mauritania, the same applies.

TARFAYA

Some 235 km west of Tan Tan across a comparatively monotonous stretch of desert highway, the little coastal town of Tarfaya is unlikely to hold anyone's attention for long. Located near Cap Juby, it was the second-largest town in the Spanish-controlled zone of the same name, but in fact started life late in the 19th century as a minor British trading post. The population of the surrounding area is largely nomadic, and the town itself boasts a small fishing industry. Plans are in place to build fish canneries.

Things to See

Possibly the most interesting thing about the town is the unusual building stuck well out from the beach amid the Atlantic breakers. Known as **Casamar** (from 'casa del mar', or house in the sea), it was once a British trading house. Otherwise, there is a monument to the French pilot and writer Antoine de Saint-Exupéry (perhaps best known for his children's story *The Little Prince*), one of several aviators who, in the interwar years, used the town as a stopover on the French airmail service between Toulouse and Dakar.

The **beaches** aren't bad, particularly a few km out of town to the north, where you can also inspect a series of shipwrecks (which are clearly visible from the road). A problem can be the Atlantic winds that whip the coast for much of the year.

Places to Stay & Eat

The *Hôtel Tarfaya* appears to be the only place to stay in Tarfaya, and it was closed at the time of researching. There are a few simple cafés around where you can get a plate of beans or an omelette – no culinary miracles in this town.

Getting There & Away

There are occasional buses and grands taxis linking Tarfaya to Tan Tan and Laayoune, but they are infrequent. Note that there is an Atlas Sahara petrol station just outside Tarfaya on the road to Laayoune (and the only one until you reach that city), where you can stock up on cheap petrol.

LAAYOUNE (AL-'UYUN)

Laayoune, once a neglected Spanish administrative town, has been transformed out of all recognition since the Moroccans took it back in 1975. Although you'll still see the odd street name posted as a 'calle', little evidence of the Spanish presence here remains. With a population of about 120,000, mostly outsiders, it is Rabat's showpiece in the Western Sahara.

The 115-km road south from Tarfaya is unexciting, cut by the occasional dry river-bed and occasionally awash with sand. There are few beaches to speak of, with the desert simply dropping away in sheer cliffs into the ocean below. Sixty-five km north of Laayoune, in the Tah depression (55 metres below sea level), there is a monument commemorating a visit this far south by Sultan Moulay al-Hassan I back in 1885 (probably on an expedition to punish unruly tribes and extract taxes) and Hassan II's 'return' on a visit 100 years later.

There is not an awful lot to see in Laayoune itself, although the atmosphere is odd enough to make a stay of a day or two worthwhile. In any case, whether you're heading north or south, the distances involved are such that you'll almost have no choice but to sleep over for at least a night.

The place is crawling with bored Moroccan soldiers and bright-white UN vehicles. Many of the Moroccans who have come to live and work here hate the place – an ocean wind blows almost without let-up, and the water is bad (basically it's all salty bore water).

Orientation

Although the showpiece town focus is the shiny new Place du Mechouar (where bored Moroccan youths hang about at night drinking lethal home-made hooch), there is no really obvious centre. Most of the practical considerations, such as post and phone offices, banks and some of the hotels, are somewhere along or near Ave Hassan II. There is a collection of budget hotels at the north-west end of town in a lively market area. SATAS buses also gather there, but CTM has its office on Ave de Mecca. Grands taxis north are on a square at the north-west end of Ave Hassan II, but there are several other stations scattered about town.

Information

Tourist Office The Délégation Régionale du Tourisme (☎ 892233/75) is just back from Ave de l'Islam, virtually across the road from the Hôtel Parador. It's open Monday to Friday from 8.30 to 11.30 am and 2 to 6 pm.

Apart from a couple of brochures, they have little to offer, but they are anxious to please and can tell you how to get to bus stations and the like.

Money The BMCE has a branch on Place Hassan II, next to the post office. There is a Banque Populaire and a couple of other banks up from the intersection of Ave Hassan II and Blvd Mohammed V. There is another Banque Populaire on Place Dchira.

Post & Telecommunications The post and phone offices are lumped together at the south-eastern end of Ave Hassan II, and open only from 8.30 am to noon and 2 to 6 pm.

Things to See & Do

Colline aux Oiseaux Set on the hill between the tourist office and Ave de Mecca, this small aviary has a few quite spectacular parrots and other birds. Enter through the Centre Artisanal on Ave de Mecca. It's free.

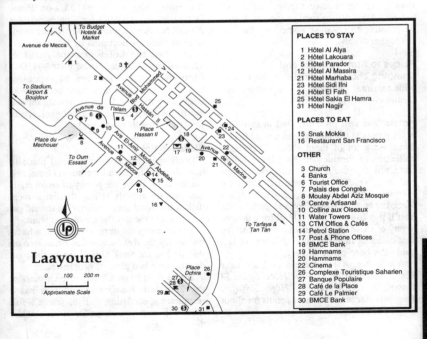

PLACES TO STAY

1 Hôtel Al Alya
2 Hôtel Lakouara
5 Hôtel Parador
12 Hôtel Al Massira
21 Hôtel Marhaba
23 Hôtel Sidi Ifni
24 Hôtel El Fath
25 Hôtel Sakia El Hamra
31 Hôtel Nagjir

PLACES TO EAT

15 Snak Mokka
16 Restaurant San Francisco

OTHER

3 Church
4 Banks
6 Tourist Office
7 Palais des Congrès
8 Moulay Abdel Aziz Mosque
9 Centre Artisanal
10 Colline aux Oiseaux
11 Water Towers
13 CTM Office & Cafés
14 Petrol Station
17 Post & Phone Offices
18 BMCE Bank
19 Hammams
20 Hammams
22 Cinema
26 Complexe Touristique Saharien
27 Banque Populaire
28 Café de la Place
29 Café Le Palmier
30 BMCE Bank

Laayoune

SOUTH MOROCCO

Centre Artisanal The 22 little domed boutiques (the domes are typical of the simpler housing in Laayoune) that constitute the Centre Artisanal on Ave de Mecca are worth a quick look if you're interested in fairly standard Moroccan souvenirs. Pressure to buy is at a minimum.

Laayoune Plage About 25 km out along the road south to Boujdour and Dakhla is a reasonable little beach. There is a simple camp site and Club Med has organised a few rooms here for anglers. Apart from that, a few houses in the village of Foum el-Oued (which is a couple of km inland) and the nearby port, there's nothing else to it. You may need to hire a taxi to get out here, or join the hitchers at the Boujdour exit from Laayoune, near the new stadium.

Dunes Kilometres of dunes spread north and west of Laayoune, and are clearly visible from several vantage points in and around the city. To get in among them, you'd need to take a 4WD off the road to Tarfaya. It may be possible to organise something through the bigger hotels.

Places to Stay – bottom end
Camping There is a simple *camping ground* with minimal facilities at Laayoune Plage (Foum el-Oued).

Hotels You will probably find most of the hotel guests at the budget end are soldiers – there are a lot of them about. There is a collection of cheapies on Ave Maître Salem Bida, out near the market in the north-west end of town. These include the *Hôtel La Victoire*, *Hôtel Atlas*, *Hôtel Tafilalet*, *Hôtel Inezgane* and the *Hôtel Errimal Eddahabia*. You'll pay from Dr 30 to Dr 40 for a double in any of these. They are quite basic and the best cleaning material you can hope for is a cold salty bore-water shower.

A number of similar places back near Place Hassan II include the *Hôtel Sakia El Hamra*, *Hôtel El Fath* and *Hôtel Sidi Ifni*. They all offer primitive little rooms for about Dr 15 per person.

Slightly better and popular with travellers is the *Hôtel Marhaba*, on Ave de la Marine (the continuation of Ave Hassan II). The rooms are clean and have a table, chair and wardrobe, but the mattresses are rather thin. Again the showers are cold and it's bore water only. The bathroom has a habit of flooding. Rooms cost Dr 26/36.

Places to Stay – middle
From the Hôtel Marhaba there is a huge leap in prices. The cheapest and worst is the *Hôtel Al Alya* (☎ 894144), 1 Rue Kadi El Ghalaoui. The rooms are only marginally better than in the Marhaba and they often can't organise hot water. All this costs Dr 174/218.

Much better but block-booked by the UN observer force here is the *Hôtel Lakouara* (☎ 893378), on Ave Hassan II. Rooms cost Dr 200/250.

Places to Stay – top end
The least expensive of the top-end places is the *Hôtel Nagjir* (☎ 894168), on Place Dchira. At Dr 310/393 for singles/doubles it's OK but there are rarely any rooms available, as most are occupied by UN staff.

The two top hotels are the *Hôtel Al Massira* and the *Hôtel Parador* (☎ 894500). Both have all the facilities of expensive hotels but for years now have been block-booked by the UN. Even the restaurant and bar in the Parador are reserved exclusively for guests (ie UN observers).

Places to Eat
The cheapest (and probably best) place to hunt for food is around the budget hotel and market area. There are plenty of small stalls and café-restaurants selling the usual meat dishes and good local fish. Dr 20 should get you a filling meal of whatever you want.

For an adequate impersonation of a hamburger, try the *Restaurant San Francisco* on Ave de Mecca. *Snak Mokka* across the road doesn't do a bad plate of brochettes.

If you want to go a little more up-market, the *Complexe Touristique Saharien* has a restaurant specialising in fish, where a full meal will cost you about Dr 50. It's at the

Place Dchira end of Ave de Mecca, and is hard to miss.

There are numerous cafés scattered about the place, some of which are marked on the map. Getting a real drink may be difficult if the bigger hotels don't let you into their bars – your best bet is the Hôtel Nagjir.

Getting There & Away
Air RAM (☎ 894071) has an office at 7 Place Bir Anzarane. It has daily flights to Casablanca for Dr 1270 one way. Every Thursday there's a flight to Dakhla (Dr 570). You can also fly to Las Palmas (Canary Islands) for Dr 1210 twice a week. The flight takes 50 minutes.

Bus The CTM office and terminal is on Ave de Mecca. A bus leaves for Dakhla at 8 am (Dr 140.50). There are two to Agadir, one direct at 8 pm (Dr 194.50), the other at 6 pm via Smara. The fare as far as Tan Tan is Dr 112. At 3 pm there is a bus to Marrakesh for Dr 250.

SATAS has slightly more runs, and its buses run from a dirt lot in among the budget hotels and market area.

A few other local lines run to Place Dchira.

Train It is possible to book a bus-train ticket to anywhere on the Moroccan rail network. The Supratours/ONCF office is on Place Oum Essaad.

Taxi Grands taxis to Tan Tan (Dr 70), Goulimime (Dr 100) and Inezgane (for Agadir; Dr 150) leave from a lot at the northwestern end of Ave Hassan II. You might even be able to get one right through to Marrakesh. Taxis to Boujdour, Smara and Dakhla leave from another lot (ask for the *station taxis Boujdour*) on the southern periphery of town. A red-and-white petit taxi there will cost you Dr 4.

SMARA (AS-SMARA)
About 240 km east of Laayoune (245 km south of Tan Tan) lies what the ONMT brochure bluntly calls 'A Historic City'. The original town was established here on a Saharan caravan route a century ago. There's really very little left of the old town, except for the mosque.

There are banks and a post office and a few hotels largely full of Moroccan soldiers and UN observers. Buses and taxis run between Smara, Laayoune and Tan Tan.

DAKHLA (AD-DAKHLA)
Established by the Spanish in 1844 and formerly called Villa Cisneros, Dakhla is just north of the Tropic of Cancer on the end of a sandy peninsula stretching out 40 km from the main coastline. It's a long, lonely 542 km drive from Laayoune through endless hammada, and only worth the effort if you are making an attempt to get into Mauritania.

The place is crawling with soldiers, but with the threat posed by Polisario receding, there is little sense of danger.

Dakhla has a bit of a name for ocean fishing, so that may be an added incentive for those travellers who like to catch and cook their own fish. It's not a bad place to take a surfboard either.

Information
The tourist office (☎ 898228) is at 1 Rue Tiris. There is a branch of the BMCE bank on Blvd Mohammed V.

Places to Stay
There are many cheap hotels but these are almost always full of soldiers, so just keep looking. The average price for a double room is around Dr 40. The town's top hotel is the three-star *Hôtel Doums* (☎ 898045/6), Ave al-Waha, but as long as the UN is here you can forget about it.

If you are in a vehicle you are allowed to camp overlooking the sea on the landward side of the peninsula.

Getting There & Away
Air The airport is five km out of town. RAM (☎ 897050), Ave des PTT, has three flights a week to Casablanca, one of them stopping in Laayoune and the other two in Agadir.

SOUTH MOROCCO

Bus, Train & Taxi There's a daily CTM bus to Laayoune for Dr 140.50. SATAS also has buses between Dakhla and Laayoune. There are grands taxis and it is also possible to organise a bus-train ticket from Dakhla with Supratours to any destination on the rail network.

To/From Mauritania Since the beginning of 1994, the border with Mauritania has, as far as Rabat is concerned, been open. There are several exceptions. There are no buses doing this run, so you need to arrange transport (which would have to be good to cope with travelling on the Mauritanian side of the frontier). Once this is done you have to get a permit from the military. It appears this no longer poses a huge problem. Finally, you have to wait until a convoy of at least half a dozen vehicles is assembled. It is then escorted (in case of an attack by Polisario) 363 km to the frontier.

All of this supposes you have been able to get a Mauritanian visa allowing you to enter the country overland. At the time of writing this was not possible in Rabat (see the Information entry under Rabat). You may have more luck at Mauritanian consulates elsewhere; for French citizens it's irrelevant, as they do not require visas to enter Mauritania.

Glossary

This glossary is a list of Arabic (a), Berber (b), French (f) and Spanish (s) terms you will come across in Morocco.

agadir (b) – fortified granary
'aid (a) – feast (also '*eid*)
'ain (a) – water source, spring
aït (b) – 'family (of)', often precedes tribal and town names
akbar (a) – great
Al-Andalus – Muslim Spain and Portugal
Allah (a) – God
Almohads – puritanical Muslim group (1130-1269), originally Berber, which arose in response to the corrupt ruling Almoravid dynasty
Almoravids – fanatical Muslim group (1054-1160) which ruled Spain and the Maghreb
'ashaab – herbal remedies

bab (a) – gate
babouches – traditional leather slippers
bain (f) – see *hammam*
baksheesh (a) – tip
bali (a) – old
baraka (a) – divine blessing or favour
Barbary – European term used to describe the North African coast from the 16th to 19th centuries
basilica – type of Roman administrative building; later used to describe churches
Bedouin (a) – nomadic Arab desert tribe
beni (a) – 'sons of', often precedes tribal name (also *banu*)
Berbers – indigenous inhabitants of North Africa
borj (a) – fort (literally, tower)
brochette (f) – kebab
burnous (a) – traditional full-length cape with a hood, worn by men throughout the Maghreb

caid – see *qaid*
caliph – 'successor of Mohammed'; ruler of the Islamic world, this title was later appropriated by the sultans of Turkey
calle (s) – street
capitol – main temple of Roman town, usually situated in the forum
caravanserai – courtyard inn
cascades (f) – waterfall
chergui – desert wind
corniche (f) – coastal road
couscous – semolina, staple food of North Africa

dar (a) – house
douar (a) – word generally used for village in the High Atlas
douche (f) – public showers (see also *hammam*)

'eid (a) – feast (also '*aid*)
erg (a) – region of sand

Fatimids – Muslim dynasty (909-1171) which defeated the Aghlabid dynasty; descendants of the Prophet's daughter Fatima and her husband, Ali (see *Shiites*)
forum – open space at centre of Roman towns
foum (a) – usually mouth of a river or valley (from Arabic for mouth)
funduq (a) – caravanserai (often used to mean hotel)

gare routière (f) – bus station
ghar (a) – cave
ghurfa (a) – room
gîte (f) – hiker's accommodation
grand taxi (f) – (long-distance) shared taxi
guerba – waterbag made from the skin of a goat or sheep, seen hanging on the side of many Saharan vehicles

hajj (a) – pilgrimage to Mecca; hence *hajji*, one who has made the pilgrimage
hammada – stony desert
hammam (a) – Turkish-style bathhouse with sauna and massage; there's at least one in

virtually every town in the Maghreb. Also known by the French word *bain* (bath) or *bain maure* (Moorish bath).

harira – soup or broth with lentils and other vegetables

hijab (a) – veil and women's head scarf

hôtel de ville (f) – town hall

ibn (a) – son of (also *bin*, *ben*)

Idrissids – Moroccan dynasty (800-1080)

imam (a) – Islamic prayer leader

jamal (a) – camel

jami' (a) – Friday mosque (also *djemaa*, *'jama* or *jemaa*)

jardin (f) – garden

jebel (a) – hill, mountain (sometimes *djebel* in former French possessions)

jedid (a) – new (sometimes spelled *jdid*)

jellaba (a) – flowing men's garment, usually made of cotton

jezira (a) – island

kasbah (a) – fort, citadel; often also the administrative centre (also *qasba*)

khutba – Friday sermon preached by the sheikh of a mosque

koubba (a) – (also *qubba*) sanctuary, *marabout* (literally, cupola)

ksar (a) – (plural: *ksour*) fortified stronghold (also *qasr*)

Maghreb (a) – west (literally, where the sun sets); used to describe the area covered by Morocco, Algeria and Tunisia

marabout – holy man or saint; also often used to describe the mausolea of these men, which are places of worship in themselves

masjid (a) – mosque

mechouar (a) – royal assembly place

medersa (a) – college for teaching theology, law, Arabic literature and grammar; widespread throughout the Maghreb from the 13th century (also *madrassa*)

medina (a) – city; used these days to describe the old Arab part of modern towns and cities

mellah (a) – Jewish quarter of medina

mihrab (a) – prayer niche in the wall of a mosque indicating the direction of Mecca (the *qibla*)

minbar (a) – pulpit in mosque; the *imam* delivers the sermon from one of the lower steps because the Prophet preached from the top step

moulay – ruler

moussem – pilgrimage to *marabout* tomb

muezzin (a) – mosque official who sings the call to prayer from the minaret

mumtaz (a) – top class in buses

musée (f) – museum

navette (f) – shuttle bus/train/boat

oued (a) – riverbed, often dry (sometimes *wad* or *wadi*)

oulad (a) – 'sons (of)' – often precedes tribal or town name

palais de justice (f) – law courts

palmeraie (f) – oasis-like area around a town where date palms, vegetables and fruit are grown

pasha – high official in Ottoman Empire (also *pacha*)

pâtisserie (f) – cake and pastry shop

petit taxi (f) – local taxi

piste (f) – poor unsealed tracks, often requiring 4WD vehicles

pharmacie de garde (f) – late-night pharmacy

plat du jour (f) – daily special (in a restaurant)

place (f) – square, plaza

plage (f) – beach

qaid (a) – local chief, loose equivalent of mayor in some parts of Morocco (also *caid*)

qasba (a) – see *kasbah*

qasr (a) – see *ksar*

qissaria (a) – covered market, sometimes forming commercial centre of a medina

qubba (a) – see *koubba*

Qur'an – sacred book of Islam

Ramadan (a) – ninth month of the Muslim year, a period of fasting

ras (a) – headland

refuge (f) – mountain hut, basic hikers' shelter
reg (b) – stony desert
ribat (a) – combined monastery and fort

Saadians – Moroccan dynasty (1500s)
saha(t) (a) – square (or French *place*)
sebkha (a) – saltpan
shari'a (a) – Islamic law
sharia (a) – street
sheikh (a) – Islamic leader, also religious man
sherif (a) – descendant of the Prophet
Shiites – one of two main Islamic sects, formed by those who believed the true *imams* were descended from Ali
sidi (a) – (also *si*) honorific (like Mr)
souq (a) – market
Sufism – mystical strand of Islam; adherents concentrate on their inner attitude in order to attain communion with God
Sunnis – main Islamic sect, derived from followers of the Umayyad caliphate
syndicat d'initiative (f) – government-run tourist office

tajine – stew, usually with meat as the main ingredient
tariq (a) – road, avenue

tizi (b) – mountain pass (French *col*)
tour (f) – tower
Tuareg – nomadic Berbers of the Sahara. They are among several Berber tribes known as the Blue Men because of their indigo-dyed robes, which gives their skin a bluish tinge

Umayyads – Damascus-based caliphate dynasty (661-750)

ville nouvelle (f) – 'new city' – town built by the French, generally alongside existing towns and cities of the Maghreb
vizier – another term for a provincial governor in the Ottoman Empire, or adviser to the sultan in Morocco

wali – holy man or saint
Wattasids – Moroccan dynasty (1400s)
wilaya (a) – province

zankat (a) – lane, alley (also *zanqat*)
zawiyya (a) – religious fraternity based around a *marabout*; also, location of the fraternity (also *zaouia*)
zeitouna (a) – olive tree or grove
zellij (a) – ceramic tiles used to decorate buildings

Index

TEXT

Map references are in **bold** type

446

Thanks

Eric Antonow (USA), Todd Bailey (USA), Miss F L
Barltrop (UK), Michael Beckerman (D), Rhonda
Bell, J Blase (NL), Pieter Blom (S), Mrs Pina Bonanni
(I), Pam Bowers (UK), Warren K Braucher (USA), P
J Bruyniks (NL), Mark Bukawski (UK), Richard
Bullock (USA), Tyge Busk (DK), Jose Luis Cabo Pan
(E), Denise Cauchi (AUS), Ugo Pica Ciammarra (I),
Michelle Claydon (AUS), Mike Collins (UK), Ronald
Corlette-Theuil (F), Elsa Dalmasso (UK), Martien
Das (NL), Rik De Clercq (B), Maria Demsar, Alice
Dijkman (NL), Jan-Willem Doornenbal (NL),
Gerhilde Egghart (A), David Elliot (UK), Joshua
Emmott (USA), Martin Fiems (B), Nienke Gaastra
(NL), C Garnier (UK), Marios Gavalas (UK),
Annabel Gaywood (UK), Michael Geist (UK), Joseph
Gourneau (USA), Sally Green (UK), Paul Gregory
(UK), Francisco Guix Gros (E), Nils Hack (D), Bob
Hammond (UK), Harry Hansma (NL), Brian Harri-
son (UK), Richard Haverkamp (CDN), Michael
Hawley (USA), Alex Henderson (AUS), Esther
Hommes (NL), Arpad Horvath (CDN), Tony Howard
(UK), Liz Hughes (UK), Attila Ja'ndi (H), Robert
Jeffers, Gregers Jorgensen (DK), Anne Juhl (DK),
Ronald Keijzer (NL), Greg Kennedy (AUS), Shelley
& George Kissil (Isr), John Kitts (UK), Timon
Koulmasis (F), Peter Kuijer (NL), Peter Lawson
(UK), Michael Lee (UK), Russell Leonard (USA), Ian
Lund (NL), Stefan Lundstrom (S), Rachel Manolson
(UK), Mr. Eric Marienfeldt (F), Runar Mathisen (N),
Gillean McCluskey (UK), Richard McHugh (AUS),
Darren McLean (AUS), Francesco Melillo (I), Karla
Milne (UK), Roger Mimo, Chris Murphy (UK), John
Oei (USA), Jacques Paquin (CDN), Frank Patris
(USA), Carlos Pimenta (B), Esther Piulman (NL),
Julie Redgrove (UK), David E Reibscheid (UK), Judy
Reid (UK), Theresa A Richards (USA), Deborah
Roper (USA), Ineke Roverts (NL), Stuart Sanders
(UK), Erik Schober (D), Liliane Schwob (CDN),
Steve Scott (UK), Maria & Eric Searle (UK), T Seiden
(D), Cpt Jeff Sheehan (USA), Jonathon Shellard
(UK), Amy Silverston (UK), Austin Smith (USA),
Robin Smith, Uta Specht (D), Miss A Spignesi,
Rebecca Stancer (UK), B M Stanton (NZ), David
Steinke (D), Donald Stevenson (UK), Syan Tapp
(UK), Thomas Tesch (A), Alsion Thackray (UK),
Laurent Tognazzi (F), Kathleen Torkano (NL),
Yumiko Uehara, Anton Van Niekerk (NL), Bas
Verboom (NL), L Vernon (CDN), Grit Vltavsky (D),
George S Vrontos, Florence Vuillet (F), Adrian
Wainer (UK), Amanda Waite (UK), D Walling
(CDN), Steven Whiffen (UK), Ronald Wijchers (NL),
J P Wilson (UK), Julie Yahiat (AUS)

A – Austria, AUS – Australia, B – Belgium, CDN –
Canada, D – Germany, DK – Denmark, F – France, I
– Italy, N – Norway, NL – Netherlands, NZ – New
Zealand, E – Spain, S – Sweden, UK – United
Kingdom, USA – United States of America

PLANET TALK
Lonely Planet's FREE quarterly newsletter

We love hearing from you and think you'd like to hear from us.

When*...is the right time to see reindeer in Finland?*
Where*...can you hear the best palm-wine music in Ghana?*
How*...do you get from Asunción to Areguá by steam train?*
What*...is the best way to see India?*

For the answer to these and many other questions read PLANET TALK.

Every issue is packed with up-to-date travel news and advice including:

- *a letter from Lonely Planet founders Tony and Maureen Wheeler*
- *travel diary from a Lonely Planet author - find out what it's really like out on the road*
- *feature article on an important and topical travel issue*
- *a selection of recent letters from our readers*
- *the latest travel news from all over the world*
- *details on Lonely Planet's new and forthcoming releases*

To join our mailing list contact any Lonely Planet office (address below).

LONELY PLANET PUBLICATIONS
Australia: PO Box 617, Hawthorn 3122, Victoria (tel: 03-819 1877)
USA: Embarcadero West, 155 Filbert St, Suite 251, Oakland, CA 94607 (tel: 510-893 8555)
TOLL FREE: (800) 275-8555
UK: 10 Barley Mow Passage, Chiswick, London W4 4PH (tel: 0181-742 3161)
France: 71 bis rue du Cardinal Lemoine – 75005 Paris (tel: 1-46 34 00 58)

Also available: Lonely Planet T-shirts. 100% heavyweight cotton (S, M, L, XL)

Guides to Africa

Africa on a shoestring
From Marrakesh to Kampala, Mozambique to Mauritania, Johannesburg to Cairo – this guidebook has all the facts on travelling in Africa. Comprehensive information on more than 50 countries.

Central Africa - a travel survival kit
This guide tells where to go to meet gorillas in the jungle, how to catch a steamer down the Congo...even the best beer to wash down grilled boa constrictor! Covers Cameroun, the Central African Republic, Chad, the Congo, Equatorial Guinea, Gabon, São Tomé & Principe, and Zaïre.

East Africa - a travel survival kit
Detailed information on Kenya, Uganda, Rwanda, Burundi, eastern Zaïre and Tanzania. The latest edition includes a 32-page full-colour Safari Guide.

Egypt & the Sudan - a travel survival kit
This guide takes you into and beyond the spectacular and mysterious pyramids, temples, tombs, monasteries, mosques and bustling main streets of Egypt and the Sudan.

Kenya - a travel survival kit
This superb guide features a 32-page 'Safari Guide' with colour photographs, illustrations and information on East Africa's famous wildlife.

South Africa, Lesotho & Swaziland - a travel survival kit
Travel to southern Africa and you'll be surprised by its cultural diversity and incredible beauty. There's no better place to see Africa's amazing wildlife. All the essential travel details are included in this guide as well as information about wildlife reserves.

Trekking in East Africa
Practical, first-hand information for trekkers for a region renowned for its spectacular national parks and rewarding trekking trails. Covers treks in Kenya, Tanzania, Uganda, Malawi and Zambia.

West Africa - a travel survival kit
All the necessary information for independent travel in Benin, Burkino Faso, Cape Verde, Côte d'Ivoire, The Gambia, Ghana, Guinea, Guinea-Bissau, Liberia, Mali, Mauritania, Niger, Nigeria, Senegal, Sierra Leone and Togo. Includes a comprehensive section on traditional and contemporary music.

Zimbabwe, Botswana & Namibia - a travel survival kit
Exotic wildlife, breathtaking scenery and fascinating people...this comprehensive guide shows a wilder, older side of Africa for the adventurous traveller. Includes a 32-page colour Safari Guide.

Also available:
Swahili phrasebook, *Arabic (Egyptian)* phrasebook & *Arabic (Moroccan)* phrasebook

Lonely Planet Guidebooks

Lonely Planet guidebooks cover every accessible part of Asia as well as Australia, the Pacific, South America, Africa, the Middle East, Europe and parts of North America. There are five series: *travel survival kits*, covering a country for a range of budgets; *shoestring guides* with compact information for low-budget travel in a major region; *walking guides*; *city guides* and *phrasebooks*.